Experiments in Environmental Economics
Volume I

International Library of Environmental Economics and Policy

General Editors: Tom Tietenberg and Wendy Morrison

Titles in the Series

Experiments in Environmental Economics Volume I

Edited by

Jason F. Shogren

University of Wyoming, USA

Routledge
Taylor & Francis Group

LONDON AND NEW YORK

First published 2003 by Ashgate Publishing

Reissued 2018 by Routledge
2 Park Square, Milton Park, Abingdon, Oxon OX14 4RN
711 Third Avenue, New York, NY 10017, USA

Routledge is an imprint of the Taylor & Francis Group, an informa business

A Library of Congress record exists under LC control number: 2003102975

ISBN 13: 978-1-138-71739-8 (hbk)
ISBN 13: 978-1-138-71733-6 (pbk)
ISBN 13: 978-1-315-19635-0 (ebk)

Contents

PART III   ENVIRONMENTAL CONFLICT

Acknowledgements

The editor and publishers wish to thank the following for permission to use copyright material.

American Association for the Advancement of Science for the essay: Amos Tversky and Daniel Kahneman (1981), 'The Framing of Decisions and the Psychology of Choice', *Science*, **211**, pp. 453–8. Copyright © 1981 AAAS.

American Economic Association for the essays: Vernon L. Smith (1982), 'Microeconomic Systems as an Experimental Science', *American Economic Review*, **72**, pp. 923–55; Colin F. Camerer (1997), 'Progress in Behavioral Game Theory', *Journal of Economic Perspectives*, **11**, pp. 167–88; David M. Grether and Charles R. Plott (1979), 'Economic Theory of Choice and the Preference Reversal Phenomenon', *American Economic Review*, **69**, pp. 623–38; Colin F. Camerer (1987), 'Do Biases in Probability Judgment Matter in Markets? Experimental Evidence', *American Economic Review*, **77**, pp. 981–97; Daniel Kahneman, Jack L. Knetsch and Richard H. Thaler (1991), 'The Endowment Effect, Loss Aversion, and Status Quo Bias', *Journal of Economic Perspectives*, **5**, pp. 193–206. Copyright © American Economic Association.

Blackwell Publishers for the essay: James M. Walker and Roy Gardner (1992), 'Probabilistic Destruction of Common-Pool Resources: Experimental Evidence', *Economic Journal*, **102**, pp. 1149–61.

Econometric Society for the essays: Daniel Kahneman and Amos Tversky (1979), 'Prospect Theory: An Analysis of Decision under Risk', *Econometrica*, **47**, pp. 263–91; John D. Hey and Chris Orme (1994), 'Investigating Generalizations of Expected Utility Theory using Experimental Data', *Econometrica*, **62**, pp. 1291–326; Richard D. McKelvey and Thomas R. Palfrey (1992), 'An Experimental Study of the Centipede Game', *Econometrica*, **60**, pp. 803–36.

Elsevier Science for the essay: Jason F. Shogren and Clifford Nowell (1992), 'Economics and Ecology: A Comparison of Experimental Methodologies and Philosophies', *Ecological Economics*, **5**, pp. 101–26. Copyright © 1992 Elsevier Science B.V.

Elsevier Science (USA) for the essays: Steven Hackett, Edella Schlager and James Walker (1994), 'The Role of Communication in Resolving Commons Dilemmas: Experimental Evidence with Heterogeneous Appropriators', *Journal of Environmental Economics and Management*, **27**, pp. 99–126. Copyright © 1994 Elsevier Science (USA); Charles F. Mason and Owen R. Phillips (1997), 'Mitigating the Tragedy of the Commons through Cooperation: An Experimental Evaluation', *Journal of Environmental Economics and Management*, **34**, pp. 148–72. Copyright © 1997 Elsevier Science (USA), reprinted by permission of the publisher.

Series Preface

The *International Library of Environmental Economics and Policy* explores the influence of economics on the development of environmental and natural resource policy. In a series of twenty five volumes, the most significant journal essays in key areas of contemporary environmental and resource policy are collected. Scholars who are recognized for their expertise and contribution to the literature in the various research areas serve as volume editors and write an introductory essay that provides the context for the collection.

Volumes in the series reflect the broad strands of economic research including 1) Natural and Environmental Resources, 2) Policy Instruments and Institutions and 3) Methodology. The editors, in their introduction to each volume, provide a state-of-the-art overview of the topic and explain the influence and relevance of the collected papers on the development of policy. This reference series provides access to the economic literature that has made an enduring contribution to contemporary and natural resource policy.

TOM TIETENBERG
KATHLEEN SEGERSON
General Editors

Introduction

Environmental protection can be messy and complex. People make their consumption and conservation decisions within a confluence of markets, missing markets, no markets, and non-market allocation institutions. As a guide to help policymakers through this muddled confluence, economists offer working rules based on classic rational choice theory. These rules say that people compare gains against losses across time and space to all winners and losers, move resources from low valued uses to high value uses, and equate incremental gains per cost across environmental policies (e.g., Hanley *et al.*, 1997). People who use these rules can make more rational policy decisions that produce more environmental protection at less cost.

The problem, however, is that numerous empirical studies now exist that suggest rational choice theory is a poor guide to understanding the behavioural underpinnings of environmental policy (see e.g., Camerer, 1995; Kahneman and Tversky, 2000; Laibson and Zeckhauser, 1998). Classic examples include inconsistent preferences between risky and safe gambles (Allais, 1953); irrational choices over ambiguous risks (Ellsberg, 1961); inconsistent preferences and valuations for low-probability gambles (Lichtenstein and Slovic, 1971); and a disparity between economic measures of value (Knetsch and Sinden, 1984). Such behavioural anomalies matter because they undercut the internal validity of the economists' rational working rules for environmental protection (see Knetsch, 1997).

Not everyone agrees with this dire conclusion about rational choice. They note that anomalies disappear once people make decisions within markets and institutions in which other people exist to reward rational choices and punish irrational choices (see Becker, 1962; Smith, 1991; Sutton, 2000). Exchange institutions define incentives and articulate knowledge and beliefs about the relevant laws of nature and humans. A person's choice is related to the choices of others and to the consequences these choices produce. People are not always isolated decision makers – they make decisions within and alongside the markets that punish and reward rational decision-making. Institutions like markets matter because this experience can make rational choice more transparent to people (Plott, 1994). One can argue that rational choice theory as a guide to environmental policy makes sense when people make, or act as if they make, consistent and systematic choices towards certain and risky events (Crocker *et al.*, 1998).

But whether rational choice theory is a good or poor guide for environmental policy cannot be decided in the abstract – one needs a relatively inexpensive setting that controls and isolates basic behavioural characteristics to test the predictive power of alternative analytical theories. The laboratory of experimental economics is such a setting. Especially with professors Vernon Smith and Daniel Kahneman winning the 2002 Nobel Prize for their work in the laboratory, most economists today recognized that experimental economics is a cost-effective method to

Jason F. Shogren is Stroock Distinguished Professor of Natural Resource Conservation and Management, Department of Economics and Finance, University of Wyoming, Laramie, WY 82071 USA, jramses@uwyo.edu. Thanks to Todd Cherry, Tom Crocker, and Sally Kane for their helpful comments on related work. Funding provided by the ERS/USDA, NOAA, and EPA. All views remain my own.

isolate and test the robustness of economic behaviour under different institutional mixtures. Economists who run small experiments in the laboratory can address big environmental questions. The lessons from the laboratory can help economists think about how to evaluate policy on clean air, biodiversity, health risks, or climate change. Experimental economics help guide global environmental policy by providing insight into how a proposed change in incentives or benefits might affect behaviour. By supplying information on the behavioural link between incentives, values and choice, experiments might have some influence on how policy is formed and evaluated. Since the laboratory environment differs from the wilds by necessity, experimental data should be viewed as a test of a specific case of a more general phenomenon or theory. Experiments could complement field data to improve our understanding of the underlying assumptions and incentives that drive behavioural responses to policy (Smith, 1982). General introductions into experimental economics include Kagel and Roth (1995) and Davis and Holt (1993). For more on the experimental method applied to environmental issues see Shogren (1993) and Cummings and Taylor (2002).

   This two-set volume showcases forty-seven essays that exemplify how economists use experimental methods to understand the behavioural underpinnings of environmental protection. The volume begins with five essays that address the motives and methods of experimental economics – four archetypal essays lay the general foundation for the use of experiments in economics, and one essay discusses the role of experiments relative to theory in environmental economics. We then group the remaining forty-two essays into five key areas that frame many theoretical and policy debates over environmental protection – risk, conflict, cooperation, control, and valuation. The aim of this introductory essay is to discuss the motives and methods of experimental economics, and to highlight how experimental methods have affected the areas of risk and conflict in environmental economics. We then discuss experiments that examine questions of environmental cooperation, control, and valuation. We consider how experiments can help sharpen the best guesses used to guide environmental policy by providing a deeper understanding of relevant behaviour within the mix of markets and non-market institutions.

I   Motives and Methods

With all the theoretical and empirical tools that already exist in economics, one can ask whether the experimental method is the appropriate approach to test the behavioural question marks about environmental policy. The answer is *yes*, for three reasons: to stress test theory, to look for empirical patterns, and to test-bed new institutions. First, one can use experiments to test a priori expectations about behaviour, rational or otherwise. Researchers use experiments to test the predictive power of a theory, to test the robustness of the axioms underlying the theory, to test the specific boundaries of a general theory, and to measure the gradient of behavioural change (that is, comparative statics). Experiments provide a sterile environment to test theory by controlling for noise and other confounding factors. Given this control, a researcher can assess the ability of a theory and its alternatives to organize observed behaviour. For valuation work, the laboratory is used to test whether stated values are consistent with economic theory (for example, the divergence between willingness to pay and willingness to accept measures of value). Second, people use the laboratory to look for patterns of behaviour. This more pragmatic use of the laboratory allows people to explore how people construct preferences and beliefs, identify and measure breakdowns from rationality, examine how contextual frames affect behaviour, determine reactions to new information, and consider how people coordinate actions voluntarily and under duress. Pattern recognition can provide the motivation for people to develop alternative theories (that is, prospect theory) based on *ex post* explanations of observed behaviour. Raiffa's (1982) work on negotiation is a good example of pattern recognition. He created a classroom 'quasi-laboratory' in which students negotiated over alternative controlled scenarios. They then interpreted their observed behaviour, so as to design modified experiments and resample new subjects. They then collectively discussed whether the heuristic insight gained from observing actual behaviour in the laboratory could translate into real-world applications. For valuation work, pattern recognition involves the direct elicitation of values for goods or services in a laboratory auction or field exchange given alternative incentive mechanisms, endowments, information sets, and with and without the signals set through repeated market experience.

Third, laboratory experiments are used as a test-bed for *economic design* – the construction of new institutions and mechanisms designed for efficient resource allocation, to compare alternative policy options, to explore how friction affects efficiency and the distribution of wealth, and to consider how institutional power can transform patterns of behaviour. The most prominent example is the use of the laboratory to test pilot the efficiency of the proposed FCC spectrum auctions (see for example Plott, 1994). An example of valuation test-bedding is examination of the potential incentive compatibility of alternative value elicitation mechanisms (for example, discrete choice or referenda questions). The ultimate success of test-bedding different mechanisms rests in the open question of external validity – is the behaviour in the laboratory a reliable guide to behaviour in the real world? Experimental economists believe so, albeit within reasonable limits. Laboratory results represent real evidence about how certain people will behave in a given economic environment. Additional real-world complexity can then be added into the laboratory environment in a controlled fashion to identify likely conditions that might cause a mechanism to fail in the wilds.

The essays in the motive and methods collection make the general case for experimental economics. The best defense of the experimental method still rests within the foundations laid down by Vernon Smith and Charles Plott. Their path-breaking work and the ensuing literature has moved economics further towards being considered an experimental science, with its own set of protocols and rules for the laboratory and field. We include in the first volume in Chapter 1 Smith's seminal essay in experimental economics entitled 'Microeconomic Systems as an Experimental Science'. Here Smith lays out in detail his world-view about the underlying analytical and logical foundation upon which all experimental work rests. He provides a detailed description of both the methods and functions of experiments in microeconomics. His message is that laboratory microeconomies are real live economic systems that are in fact richer in behaviour than the systems parametrized in most abstract theories. He argues that economics will be more likely to advance as a science once theorists become less own-literature oriented, take seriously the data and disciplinary function of laboratory experiments, and take seriously their own theories as potential generators of testable hypotheses. Smith also stress that it is equally important that experimentalists take on the task to integrate theory, experimental design, and observation. He stresses the challenge of producing 'a body of knowledge which clarifies the difference between what we have created (theory as hypothesis) and what we have discovered (hypothesis that, to date, is or is not falsified by observation)'.

Smith uses a triad to reflect the three components that underlie any experiment, the initial endowment that defines the human and natural environment, (E); the institution or mechanism of exchange (I); and the actual behaviour of the subjects (A). The environment includes basic economic endowments like preferences, technology, physical constraints, property rights, and information structure. The institution specifies the rules that aggregate and generate information and coordinate actions, and it outlines the rules of exchange and its consequences. Repeated exposure to the institution is common practice in the laboratory so that people have the opportunity to gain experience with the institution, new information, and their own mind to better understand their endowed or personal preferences. Given the environment, people send a message, which could be an auction bid or stated value to the institution. Based on the set of messages received, the institution then allocates resources and costs, given the known rules of exchange. Researchers then observe how people actually make choices in the laboratory or field, and how this behaviour matches up with a specific performance criterion like Pareto efficiency.

Everyone should read something by Charlie Plott. Out of his many experimental essays, the essay included here in Chapter 2 asks the general question of whether economics will ever become an experimental science. Plott outlines the six events that form the foundation for the growth of modern experimental methods. First, Plott points out how economists eventually learned how to pose questions that a laboratory experiment could answer. Second, experimental research made some key discoveries (for example, efficiency could be used to measure market performance), which then created the foundation for laboratory work to evaluate alternative policies before they were actually implemented in the wilds. Third, theory advanced such that now information and strategic gaming behaviour became central to questions of economic behaviour; fourth, the laboratory showed that these theoretical advances were on the right track, for the most part. Fifth, laboratory evidence also started to reveal the limits to rational choice theory, for example, people overbid in common value auctions, we were more altruistic than assumed, and we overreacted to low probability risks. Finally, he argues that 'Say's law of experimental methods' took over – supply created its own demand. Plott concludes the essay by answering the question posed in the title of the essay: 'I do not believe that experimental methods will replace field research. Economies found in the wild can only be understood by studying them in the wild. Field research is absolutely critical to such an understanding. However, the theories and models used in field research necessarily incorporate many judgments about assumptions, parameters and behavioural principles. The simple cases that can be studied in the laboratory can provide the data against which importance of such judgments can be assessed. Economics is one of few sciences that is fortunate to have both the field and the laboratory in which to work.'

And as noted by Plott, questions of method should be answered by experience about what works rather than relying on preconceived notions of methodological principles. Economists who turn to the laboratory to study environmental economic phenomena can appreciate the economists from decades past when pragmatism ruled. Limited capacity, time, and money imposed a discipline to identify and test the most interesting questions. Experimental economics demands the same discipline today. One identifies an interesting phenomenon, designs an experiment, runs the treatments, and explores which restrictions, if any, best organize the patterns of revealed behaviour. Working along with theory and prior empirical information, experiments become habitual; another productive approach to discipline one's thinking about environmental economics.

Other authors also made a significant advance in our thinking about experiments, including Colin Camerer (Chapter 5) and Alvin Roth (Chapter 4). Camerer's essay takes up the challenge of asking whether standard game theory is actually useful for understanding how people do and should make choices within a strategic situation. His advocates the advancement of 'behavioural game theory' – theory that describes actual behaviour driven by empirical observation and that reflects the middle ground between over-rational equilibrium analyses and under-rational adaptive analyses. Camerer offers up a three-step 'recipe' to describing behavioural game theory. First, start with a game or naturally occurring situation in which standard game theory makes a bold prediction based on one or two crucial principles; second, if behaviour differs from the prediction, think of plausible explanations for what is observed; and third, extend formal game theory to incorporate these explanations. His essay also examines three categories of modelling principles and catalogues violations of these principles. First, he focuses on cases in which players, rather than focusing self-interestedly on their own payoff alone, seem to respond to notions of social utility, showing concerns about fairness and the perceived intentions about other players. Second, Camerer focuses on problems of choice and judgment – cases in which players respond to differences in how the game is described, rather than to the outcomes, and in which players systematically overestimate their own capabilities. Finally, he discusses the unaccounted elements that people bring into strategic situations – a common awareness of certain focal points for agreement, a belief that timing of a choice may confer privileged status or change players' thinking, and a natural instinct to look only one or two levels into problems that permit many levels of iterated reasoning. Camerer asks whether traditional game theory is still useful for advising people how to play a game – he concludes that the answer depends on the game and whether deviations are a mistake or not. He argues that game theory should be considered a 'success' when it explains behaviour in early rounds and the processes that produce equilibrium in later rounds.

Shogren and Nowell's essay (1992) (Chapter 3) compares the research methods and philosophies towards the experimental method in economics versus ecology. They first discuss the divergent views of economists and ecologists towards the relative importance of theory versus experimentation. Pragmatic pattern recognition has been the main tool in ecology, whereas logical positivism theory has driven economics. Economics has a hierarchy – theory is the foundation, experimental tests are second. And if the data are consistent with the theory, we have confirmed what we already know; an inconsistency simply implies that something is wrong with the experiment.

Shogren and Nowell use Smith's triad to group environmental economic experiments into two broad classes – *institutional* and *valuation*. Institutional experiments control the environment (E) to explore how alternative market and non-market mechanisms (I) affect the allocation of scarce resources (for example, efficient institutional design given administrative failure, public goods, externalities, asymmetric information, and incomplete markets; see Ledyard, 1995). In contrast, valuation experiments stand the experimental triad on its head (Coursey, 1987). Here the researcher wants to control the institution and actual behaviour through a design that generates predictable patterns of behaviour, and consequently rational statements of value that reflect underlying preferences. Rational valuation can be assessed in the laboratory because the design is under the researcher's control and the decisions subjects make are real, albeit stylized. They conclude by outlining some of the lessons economists and ecologists can learn from each other both from theory and from experimentation.

Based on the work outlined above and research that followed, today when one thinks of the experimental method in economics, one thinks of an actual laboratory in which participants use pen and paper or networked computer terminals to make choices and decisions given different institutions and endowments. Building on the pioneering work of Smith and Plott, experimental economics is now a valid research tool in economics, with its own set of rigorously debated protocols and regulations. The application to environmental protection has to confront the issue that people make decisions in both market and non-market settings, and that this interaction of exchange institutions could well affect how people behave. We now consider the first application – environmental risk.

II Environmental Risk

One goal of environmental protection is to reduce risks to human and environmental health. By risk, we mean the combination of two elements – the *chance* that a bad event might happen, and the *consequences* that are realized if a bad event actually does occur. And although our actions to improve our lives usually are not intended to create risk to others and ourselves, people pollute and accidents happen. Things go wrong – Chernobyl, Bhopal, Love Canal; and some fear our choices have put society on the wrong path – loss of biodiversity, climate change. Tell a regular person, for instance, about a shift in the stream of warm air that keeps much of North America and northern Europe habitable, and he will take climate risks seriously, even if the odds the shift will be realized are low or unknown. This is because, relative to expected utility maximization, people seem to be easily alarmed when dealing with risk, especially these catastrophic scenarios of low-probability/high-severity events that surround climate risk.

When the outcome is potentially very bad, experience tells us little about low-probability risks. And numerous experimental risk perception studies reveal how people commonly overestimate the chance that they will suffer from a risk with low odds and high damage like, say, a nuclear power accident. People confronting low odds of catastrophe often rely on outside sources of information to help them make judgments about the likelihood that a bad event will actually come to pass. And if that outside information stresses severity without giving some notion of the odds, people systematically bias their risk perceptions upwards. Policymakers are not immune to this tendency either.

To understand individual behaviour towards risk, one must address the expected utility model and the observed violations of key assumptions. Expected utility theory says that if people's preferences satisfy certain axioms, their behaviour can be modelled as if the individual is maximizing expected utility. The three basic assumptions of expected utility theory are ordering, continuity, and independence. Ordering implies preferences are complete and transitive. Continuity means that no holes exist in an individual's indifference mapping with respect to gambles. Independence assumes that if a person equally prefers gambles A and B, a gamble composed of a q chance of A (or B) and a $1 - q$ chance of C is also equally preferable.

But people are not always so consistent. They use heuristics, or rules of thumb, to deal with environmental risk, for example, they separate probabilities and consequences, rather than in combination as predicted by expected utility theory, or most generalized utility theories. Experimental methods have long been used to explore how people make decisions under risk. Laboratory experiments exploring choice under uncertainty, rational and otherwise, have a long and powerful track record, going back at least to Bernoulli's classic St Petersburg paradox. Bernoulli asked why a rational person would only pay about $3 to play a gamble with an infinite expected value. The answer was because variance was infinite too. Today economists and psychologists continue to hunt for a descriptive theory of environmental risk by testing whether notions of expected utility or non-expected utility better organize laboratory evidence.

The essays highlighted in Volume I cover a range of topics from the isolated-person psychological experiments in Kahneman and Tversky (1979) (Chapter 8) to the market-driven protection against risk in McClelland *et al.* (1993) (Chapter 14). We focus on general experiments examining risk, and we have obviously excluded numerous other essays. People interested in environmental risk should start here first to understand the general experimental designs and observe behaviour prior to applying the tests to specific questions of environmental risk. Understanding reactions to environmental risk requires that we first understand the nature of the risk, how people perceive and react to the risk, and how collective action can help or hinder private actions. Understanding basic economic behaviour under risk can help make our decisions to control risk more effective – reducing more risk for more people. Knowing how to assess risk accurately, whether people make risky choices with reason or at random, what people are willing to pay to reduce risk, what institutions exist to control risk can only help us make better decisions on how to save lives and reduce injuries.

Becker, DeGroot and Marschak (1964) (Chapter 6) is a classic essay that introduced the so-called BDM incentive compatible mechanism to measure actual utility for a risky event. The BDM mechanism has been implemented countless times over the last four decades by researchers interested in eliciting values for risk. The BDM separates what people say from what they pay, so the weakly dominant strategy is to state one's true value. The BDM mechanism is run as follows. Each buyer and seller is asked to determine independently and privately their maximum willingness to pay or minimum willingness to accept by marking an 'X' on a recording sheet listing a price schedule for some given price range for the good. After collecting all recording sheets from buyers and sellers, one price from the sheet is selected randomly. If a buyer is willing to pay at least the random price, he or she bought the commodity. If a seller is willing to accept less than or equal to the random price, he or she sold the commodity. The random price determines how many buyers and sellers will buy and sell at the random price.

The classic essay by Grether and Plott (1979) (Chapter 7) addresses the question of preference reversals. The preference reversal phenomenon is one of the best documented violations of the assumption of consistent choice required by most rational choice theories (see Lichtenstein and Slovic, 1971). A person is said to reverse his preferences when his choices – a direct reflection of his preferences – between two options is inconsistent with the ranking of his buying/selling prices – an indirect reflection of his preferences. The preference reversal phenomenon contradicts the presumption that elicited preferences should be invariant to the elicitation method. Grether and Plott, doubtful of the earlier work done by psychologists, replicated the tests. Their laboratory evidence has revealed a robust inconsistency in an isolated person's preference orderings and expressed valuations despite inducements like greater rewards, different presentations, training, record keeping, and a hypothetical setting.

The example used to induce preference reversals presents a person with some variation of the following pair of bets who is then asked to choose one bet out of the pair:

Pbet: p chance of $X $bet: q chance of $Y
       1 – p chance of $x   1 – q chance of $y

where $X > x$, $Y > y$, $p > q$, and $Y > X$. Subjects are then asked to value each bet by stating their fair price they were willing to pay to buy or sell the bet. A specific gamble commonly used is: Pbet – 35/36 chances to win \$4 & 1/36 chance to lose \$1; \$bet – a 11/36 chances to win \$16 & 25/36 chances to lose \$1.50. Both gambles have about the same expected value, \$3.86. Expected utility theory requires that the bet selected would also be the bet that was valued the highest. A large number of subjects violated this prediction by choosing the P-bet and assigning a higher value to the \$-bet. Examples like this have caused some observers to conclude that tradition valuation exercises and choice-based surveys are unreliable, and that we need to channel resources to find alternative methods to value environmental resources (see Irwin *et al.*, 1993).

The data developed within the field of psychology that is inconsistent with preference theory would affect the research priorities within economics. Preference reversals suggests that no optimization principles lie behind even the simplest of human choices and that the uniformities in human choice behaviour, which lie behind market behaviour, may result from principles which are of a completely different sort from those generally accepted. This essay reports the results of a series of experiments designed to discredit the psychologists' work as applied to economics. Grether and Plott review the earlier experiments conducted by psychologists and their shortcomings from an economic point of view, which would either make the experiment irrelevant or explain the results by an accepted theory. They then designed and conducted a series of experiments. The format of the experiment was designed to create the most comparable results between the psychologists and these new experiments. The design of the experiments controlled for all the economic–theoretic explanations of the preference reversal phenomenon. The preference reversal phenomenon, which is inconsistent with the traditional statement of preference theory, was still there. Also, several psychological theories about human choice are inconsistent with the observed preference reversal. They conclude that although rational preference theory is subject to exception, it does not mean that they should be discarded. At the time, no alternative theory existed that covered the same broad range of phenomena. They argue that an exception is an important discovery because it provides an answer for those who argue that preference is circular or without empirical content. It also challenges theorists to create a reason to explain this exception without simultaneously making the theory too encompassing such that it explains everything and hence nothing.

Other economists have questioned the robustness of preference reversals in market settings with non-trivial lotteries and arbitrage. Knez and Smith (1987) challenged the robustness of the phenomenon with market trading and repeated responses. They found that in double auction asset trading, market values followed expected utility theory even if individual responses did not. Individual responses even approached rational behaviour with repeated trials. Cox and Epstein (1989) found consistent preference reversals, but observed that by paying subjects for each gamble instead of randomly choosing one, subjects reversed symmetrically. Chu and Chu (1990) showed how arbitrage acts like a money pump to eliminate preference reversals within one or two trials. Cox and Grether (1996) replicated preference reversal phenomenon in second-price and English clock auctions. They observed that with monetary incentives, immediate feedback, and repetition with the market the phenomenon tended to disappear. Also see Bohm (1994) and Bohm and Lind (1993) for three field experiments on preference reversals. Cherry *et al.* (2003) show that the rationality induced in market-like settings can spill over to non-market choices. They find *rationality spillovers* exist – the rationality created in an arbitraged market transfers over to a non-market allocation decision.

Camerer's (1987) essay (Chapter 10) examines a similar theme – he asks whether psychological biases in judgment over the odds of states of the world matter for decisions made within active markets. Psychologists report evidence that people do not behave as a rational Bayesian when it comes to updating beliefs, which is a direct challenge to traditional rational choice theory. These rational probability theories therefore could be poor descriptive models of individual choice in isolation. But in economics, rationality is usually considered a social construct rather than an individual phenomenon. Biases would not matter if people make similar choices within active exchange institutions that punish inconsistent behaviour through arbitrage. People in markets have a reason to be rational because rationality now pays – if not, other people can arbitrage their inconsistent or emotional choices for profit. Camerer tests whether such incomplete descriptions of judgment and choice matter within an active exchange institution like a market. He designs an experimental market to address this issue. In the experimental markets, the traders are paid dividends for holding a one-period asset. The amount of the dividend depends on which of two states is realized. Traders know the prior probabilities of the states, and a sample of likelihood information about which state has occurred. The setting is designed so that prices and allocations reveal whether traders use Bayes' rule to integrate the prior and the sample information, or whether they judge the likelihood of each state by the representativeness of the sample to the state.

We include three essays by Kahneman, Tversky and colleagues. This is the work for which Kahneman was awarded his 2002 Nobel Prize. Based on this seminal research, a substantial literature now exists which supports their original idea that people fear a loss more than they desire the equivalent gain. Loss aversion, alarmist reactions, endowment effects, and the willingness to pay, willingness to accept gap are all manifestations of this asymmetric behavioural reaction to gains and losses. *Loss aversion* type behaviour implies that monetary losses associated with switching to an alternative are given greater weight than corresponding gains (see Tversky and Kahneman, 1981, Chapter 9; Kahneman and Tversky, 1979, Chapter 8). The *endowment effect* exists when people offer to sell a product they possess at a substantially higher rate than they will pay for the identical product they do not possess, which might explain the divergence between willingness to pay and willingness to accept measures of economic value.

The essay by Kahneman, Knetsch and Thaler (1991) (Chapter 13) discusses three behavioural anomalies – the endowment effect, status quo bias, and loss aversion – that have emerged in the laboratory. These persistence anomalies suggest that standard rational choice theory might be too narrow to explain the observed behaviour of people. They focus in on the endowment effect, which is said to exist when people demand more to give up an object than they would be willing to pay to acquire it. Their goal was to test whether the economists' idea that anomalous behaviour disappears once people are exposed to a market environment with chances to learn. Economists argue that the unpredicted discrepancy between buying and selling prices might be generated simply because people understate their true demand and overstate their true opportunity costs, and that this behaviour diminishes with experience in a market setting. They conducted two sets of experiments to determine whether the endowment effect survives when subjects face market discipline and have a chance to learn. The first experiment was repeated several times, with comparable results: median selling prices were about two times median buying prices and volume was less than half of that anticipated. The low volume of trade results that emerged from the second experiment is produced by owners' reluctance to part with their endowment, rather than by buyers' unwillingness to part with their cash. One implication of the endowment effect is that people treat opportunity costs differently from 'out-of pocket' costs. Foregone gains are less painful than perceived loss. Observations like these have produced a rush of new non-expected utility theories to compete with expected utility, including Kahneman and Tversky's (1979) prospect theory, regret theory, and rank dependent utility. Hey and Orme's (1994) essay (Chapter 15) differs from the others in this collection in that it does not run new experiments; rather it uses existing data from other experiments to explore which behavioural model best fits the evidence. They apply econometric methods to experimental data to test which model of decision-making is robust.

The essay by Hogarth and Kunreuther (1989) (Chapter 11) addresses how ambiguity affects decision-making under risk. The vast majority of decisions people make about environmental protection are over ambiguous probabilities. The expected utility model assumes that probability ambiguity does not affect decisions under risk. The model postulates that only the mean of the probability distribution is important. Ellsberg (1961) showed, however, that ambiguity matters in decision-making. He substantiated this theory in the laboratory by giving subjects the choice between choosing a ball from an urn with a known number of coloured balls and an urn with an unknown number of coloured balls in a payoff situation. He found that subjects tended to prefer drawing from the urn with the known distribution. Becker and Brownson (1964) further substantiated the results of Ellsberg by finding that the larger the distribution, the higher the premiums people are willing to pay to avoid the ambiguity.

Hogarth and Kunreuther tested professional actuaries, business executives, and MBA students. The test consisted of two different questionnaire scenarios concerning insurance from the purchaser and insurance company sides. They found universal ambiguity to low probability of loss events. They also found that ambiguity aversion decreases as the probability of loss increases. Consumers showed a preference for ambiguity for high probability of loss events even though firms did not. Firms did, however, show a greater aversion to ambiguity than consumers; they also decreased their aversion as the probability of loss increased.

Finally, Shogren (1990) (Chapter 12) and McClelland *et al.* (1993) (Chapter 14) examine behaviour and stated preferences for alternative risk reduction actions, including self-protection and self-insurance. McClelland *et al.* look at behaviour at insurance auctions, and find that people have a bimodal response to low-probability risks – they either ignore it completely or they overreact and spend too much money relative to expected utility theory. Shogren (1990) explores whether alternative reduction strategies affect a person's reaction to risk. People reduce the expected damages of an environmental risk by using either self-protection or self-insurance, either privately or collectively. Understanding how these risk reduction mechanisms affect behaviour could matter for public policy. Self-protection reduces the probability of the loss, while self-insurance reduces its severity (Ehrlich and Becker, 1972; Shogren and Crocker, 1991). Although a person can access combinations of these risk reduction mechanisms, little is known about how these substitution opportunities affect rational choice under risk. The results suggest that the risk reduction mechanism matters. Shogren (1990) found that the mechanism used to reduce risk mattered; reducing risk by altering the probability or severity of an undesired event through a private or a collective mechanism has been shown to generate significantly different values. He also observed that the addition of repeated bidding after new information is provided induced rapid value formation, and could add insight into preference revelation in a field context. Given repeated market trials, the initial bid is generally a significant predictor of the final bid; the implication is that an initial bid, adjusted for learning, could reflect the value of reduced risk in an experienced market.

III   Environmental Conflict

Environmental conflict is a study in threat points and strategic behaviour. Conflicts arise whenever people threaten to take unilateral strategic (non-cooperative) actions regarding environmental protection and natural resources given ill-defined or weakly enforced property rights (see Schelling, 1960). Examples of environmental conflicts include the Prisoner's Dilemma in harvesting open access commons, environmental law suits filed by citizen groups against polluting firms, these firms' preemptive law suits against noisy citizens complaining about potential or real environmental damage, interlinked games between environmental and free trade policies, and coordination games of environmental policy between states or nations (see, for example, Settle *et al.*, 2002). Environmental conflicts are created when efforts to protect oneself from environmental problems simply transfer the risks to another rather than resolving them (for example, Bird, 1987). In the United States and United Kingdom, the use of tall stacks reduces the citizens' exposure to pollution by transferring it to Canada and to Sweden. North Carolina protects its jobs and its environment by allowing one of its major firms to ship wastes downriver to Tennessee. The pollution from other sources that affect agriculture encourages agricultural land, fertilizer, and pesticide substitutions that produce pollution. Private actions to minimize pollution-induced losses shift pollution to other parties. From a materials balance perspective, most protection actions allow the mass of waste to flow into the environment, only transferring this mass through time and across space. Future generations and other jurisdictions suffer the consequent environmental damages.

The intensity and frequency of environmental conflicts like these seem likely to worsen because of rapid increases in overall population, urban populations, industrial development, and competing land uses. A good example is the environmental conflict created by climate change risk. In 1997, the nations participating in the Kyoto protocol negotiations recognized that since the source of climate change is widespread (for example, use of fossil fuels), responsibility to reduce the risk should be widely shared. The conflict arises here because the more widespread the responsibility, the greater the challenge to create a stable agreement because nations have more incentive to free-ride on the actions of other nations. This challenge is compounded by national differences in income, vulnerability to climate change, and capacities to respond. Nations have a common interest in responding to the risk of climate change, yet many are reluctant to reduce greenhouse gases voluntarily. They are reluctant because climate change is a global public good, and no global police force exists to enforce an international climate agreement. As such, an agreement must be voluntary and self-enforcing – all sovereign parties should have no incentive to deviate unilaterally from the terms of the agreement (for example, Barrett 1994). The problem, however, is that a self-enforcing deal is easiest to reach when either the stakes are small or no other option exists. Such models of environmental conflict rest on the notion that people make rational decisions in their gaming decisions – they make credible threats and form reasonable beliefs about future events such that a rational equilibrium arises within the game. Game theory presumes people are self-interested; they perceive the game clearly and consistently; and they see the relevance in the strategic reasoning principles widely used in game theory (for example, irrelevance of labels and timing, common knowledge, iterated dominance, and backward induction).

Such peppery assumptions about rational gaming behaviour have led researchers quite naturally to the laboratory of experimental economics. Economists want to observe how people actually play in games. Game theory and conflict models provide the perfect theoretical benchmark about how rational people should behave given the predicted equilibrium conditions for any given game structure. The essays selected for this part focus on some of the key ideas studied within gaming experiments. The area, however, is enormous and continues to expand. The reader will have no difficulty finding new essays on numerous facets of gaming behaviour in the top general and field journals.

Some of the earliest laboratory experiments considered the question of the Prisoner's Dilemma. Recall that the Prisoner's Dilemma exists when the best outcome for a pair of arrested bank robbers is to keep silent; but instead they end up at the worst outcome because the incentive for each robber is to give the other up to the police. A similar story can be told for the 'tragedy of the commons'. This unfortunate outcome captures the idea of a Nash equilibrium. Named after Nobel Laureate John Nash, a Nash equilibrium exists when rational players do not have unilateral incentives to change their equilibrium strategies. Neither player can increase his or her payoffs if he or she defects from this strategy. The Nash equilibrium advanced game theory by providing a framework to examine incentives in nearly all social situations of conflicts in individual decision-making, including those of environmental conflict. Most models of environmental conflict use the Nash equilibrium as the organizing principle that points to the likely outcome of the game. While the design seems relatively plain as compared to today's experiments, Lave's (1962) essay (Chapter 16) is included in the first volume to reflect the state of early experimental work designed to explore how people actually did play in a Prisoner's Dilemma game.

We leap three decades forward to consider Walker and Gardner's (1992) conflict game in Chapter 17 on how a group of highly motivated people can exploit the rents of a common resource without losing it. Their experimental design captures the idea that a natural regeneration process exists that creates a range of exploitation in which the probability of destruction is zero. When one goes beyond the 'safe yield', the resource now faces probabilistic destruction. High levels of economic activity would destroy the resource with certainty; low levels would not extract the optimal level of rent. The key is to find the balance between maximizing economic gain and preserving the resources. Walker and Gardner use a game theoretic framework to guide them to frame their laboratory experiments as non-cooperative games with multiple Nash equilibria. They use two treatments in the experiments, depending on whether the safe zone consists of a single point or an interval. They find that when the safe zone was a single point, the resource was rapidly destroyed. If the safe zone was an interval, some groups moved initially towards the socially optimal Nash equilibrium, but in general this equilibrium was unsustainable and the commons were destroyed rather quickly. Their experiments illustrate how alternative institutions can affect common resource survival. The essays by Hackett *et al.* (1994) (Chapter 21) and Mason and Phillips (1997) (Chapter 22) extend this line of research. Hackett *et al.* consider how communication – cheap talk – can reduce commons problems, and they are optimistic about cheap talk, as their results suggest face-to-face communication helps substantially to resolve the tragedy of the commons. Mason and Phillips in Chapter 22 consider laboratory behaviour within an 'infinite' dynamic extraction game in which they vary the number of extractors from the common pool. They also raise the bar on the use of econometric methods to evaluate experimental behaviour of paired decision makers.

When these commons-type conflicts have multiple Nash equilibria they are called *coordination games*. A coordination game differs from the Prisoner's Dilemma (PD) game in that in the PD game the strategies with the best joint payoffs are dominated by another strategy, which contains a Nash equilibrium. The coordination game interests many researchers because it captures the idea that both 'good' and 'bad' equilibria can exist in a micro- or macroeconomic setting, and it is beneficial for a set of non-cooperative players to coordinate their beliefs and actions to select the Pareto-dominant equilibrium (see Ochs, 1995).

Allowing for communication between the players can facilitate coordinating to the best outcome. Cooper *et al.* (1992) (Chapter 18) explore the role of nonbonding cheap talk – preplay communication – in a two-person coordination game. They consider both one-way and two-way cheap talk within two forms of coordination games: a cooperative strategy and a less risky strategy. In cooperative strategy games, one-way cheap talk reduced coordination failure relative to the no communication baseline; but two-way cheap talk did not reduce coordination failure. In the less risky game, they observed the opposite behaviour – two-way cheap talk reduced coordination failure, but one-way cheap talk did not. Kroll *et al.* (1999) also found that two-way cheap talk does not necessarily recapture efficiency losses in an interconnected game (also see Crawford, 1998).

Palfrey and Rosenthal (1994) (Chapter 20) explore whether repeated play induces more coordination than one-shot play in a public good environment with incomplete information. This is a pattern recognition experiment – although non-cooperative players can do better with repetition than without it, nearly every outcome can be supported as equilibrium. The question is whether behaviour in this incomplete information environment differs from similar two-person games with complete information, in which effective coordination emerges relatively quickly. Palfrey and Rosenthal's design varied a number of parameters (for example, group size, the distribution of marginal rates of substitution between the public and private good). They speculated that three patterns of behaviour could emerge: more contributions with repeated play; players separate into either contributors or free-riders, and rotation schemes. Overall, they find that the average person contributes more under the repeated-game treatment than in the one-shot treatment (with greater variance). Their results suggest that while repetition can increase cooperation, the gains depend on unilateral monitoring ability and the parameters.

Parkhurst *et al.* (2002) also examine the problem of coordination games for habitat fragmentation. They use an experiment design to test-bed an incentive mechanism within a coordination game conflict. They examine whether a voluntary incentive mechanism, *the agglomeration bonus*, can voluntarily reunite fragmented habitat across private land. The agglomeration bonus mechanism pays an extra bonus for every acre a landowner retires that borders on any other retired acre. But the downside is that multiple Nash equilibria exist, which can be ranked by the level of habitat fragmentation. Their laboratory results show that a no-bonus mechanism always created fragmented habitat, whereas with the bonus, players found the first–best habitat reserve. Once pre-play cheap talk and random pairings were introduced, players found the first–best outcome in over ninety per cent of play.

So far we have considered games and experiments in which the players select their actions at the same time. But conditions also exist in an environmental conflict when players take their actions at different times – a citizen group first expends effort by complaining to a local official about water quality; the accused firm then follows with its own counter argument (for example, a Stackelberg game). Subgame perfection and backward induction are the key concepts to the sequential-move equilibrium in an endogenous timing contest. Subgame perfection was formulated to restrict players to credible strategies, thereby ruling out incredible threats on- and off-the-equilibrium path. Subgame perfection requires each player to look forward and think about every possible subgame that could be reached in the game tree of the contest, guess what actions players would take in each subgame, and work backwards, using those guesses, to decide what action to take once and for all at the beginning of the contest. The subgame perfect equilibrium is a set of strategies, one for each player, such that in any subgame the strategies form a Nash equilibrium (Selten, 1965; Fudenberg and Tirole, 1991).

While subgame perfection is the most commonly used solution concept for multi-stage games of complete information, the concept has had mixed success as a predictor of observed behaviour in laboratory gaming experiments. Although some researchers have found a correspondence between predicted and observed behaviour, most have not (for example, Camerer *et al.*, 1993; Ochs and Roth, 1989, Chapter 27; Roth, 1995). And even if a person can be trained to use backward induction to think about strategy, looking ahead and reasoning back is unnatural to people who do not see the value in thinking about events that do not seem likely to occur (that is, ruling out off-the-equilibrium path behaviour).

Volume I includes McKelvey and Palfrey's (1992) classic centipede experiments in Chapter 19 to illustrate the capacity of subgame perfection as an organizing principle. They chose an experimental environment in which they expected Nash equilibrium to perform its worst. In the centipede game, two players alternately get a chance to take the larger portion of an increasing stock of money. Once a person *takes*, the game ends and that player earns the larger fraction of the stock. If one views the experiment as a complete information game, game theoretic equilibrium concepts (for example, backward induction or the elimination of dominated strategies) predicts the first mover should take the larger reward in the very first round thus ending the game. Their laboratory results show that such rational gaming behaviour was the exception – most players move beyond the first temptation. McKelvey and Palfrey explain deviations from the standard predictions by combining an asymmetric information game with a parametric specification of the errors people might make in actions and beliefs. They concluded that an incomplete information game that assures the existence of a small proportion of altruists in the population better accounts for many of the salient features of their data.

McKelvey and Palfrey resolve the issue on how to close the gap between theory and observation by creating a richer theoretical behavioural model to explain the behaviour they observed. The essay by Baik *et al.* (1999) (Chapter 23) takes another line of attack – they create an institutional context to reward rational choices over seemingly trivial differences in measurable performance. Rational gaming behaviour presumes a person is purposeful in that it is worthwhile to capture the extra unit of satisfaction, however small. But evidence from the laboratory suggests a person is more likely to misbehave the smaller the gap between optimal and suboptimal payoffs. Baik *et al.* examine whether a gaming tournament with non-linear payoffs (payoffs increase at an increasing rate) might induce more rational behaviour because now even small differences in incremental actions can lead to big differences in final rewards. Their gaming tournament examines how three features affect behaviour – non-linear payoffs, structure to the decision frame, and more time to think about strategy. Their results suggest that within this experimental milieu subgame perfection can be a reasonable predictor of behaviour.

IV Environmental Cooperation

Many observers believe that processes that promote cooperation and collaboration are the future of environmental protection (for example, Crowfoot and Wondolleck, 1990; Sabel *et al.*, 1999; Susskind *et al.*, 2000). People have turned to the collaborative decision-making process more and more to resolve environmental disputes and develop natural resource management plans at the local level. The collaborative decision-making process emphasizes consensus decisions outside the courtroom by seeking solutions based on mutual gain. Allowing voluntary participation of all concerned stakeholders and providing for assistance from facilitators or mediators gives government, business, and citizen groups the opportunity to jointly develop environment and natural resource management strategies.

Such place-based collaboration is promoted at both the federal and state levels. At the federal level, the US Congress enacted the Alternative Dispute Resolution Act of 1990, which moved environmental protection activities away from relying strictly on the federal agencies to a balanced approach that engages local citizen groups. At the local level, collaborative decision-making continues to grow in many rural settings like the western United States, in which collaboration groups number in the hundreds, ranging from informal grassroots gatherings to government-mandated advisory councils. *Enlibra*, the US Western Governors Association's new doctrine for environmental management is a good example of this decentralized, collaborative decision-making. One *Enlibra* principle is 'collaboration, not polarization – use collaborative processes to break down barriers and find solutions'. The western governors believe that community-based collaboration can help produce creative solutions with political momentum. As more attention is given to alternative decision-making processes like *Enlibra*, such as cooperative negotiation and mediation, opportunities increase for local stakeholders to initiate natural resource management plans and resolve environmental disputes.

Most environmental and resource economists are familiar with this idea of more cooperation because of the Coase theorem (see Cooter, 1989). Recall that the Coase theorem says that disputing parties will bargain until they reach an efficient private agreement, regardless of which party is initially assigned to hold the unilateral property rights (Coase, 1960). As long as these legal entitlements can be freely exchanged, government intervention is relegated to designating and enforcing well-defined property rights. But Coase was not championing a zero-transaction costs world; rather he was attacking the Pigovian mindset of many post-war, neo-classical economists. If, as Pigou proposed and followers promoted, a regulator could set an efficient Pigovian tax to remedy a negative externality (for example, pollution, habitat destruction) between two disputing parties, Coase reasoned that it must be only because the transaction costs to collect all the necessary information were either nil or very low. Otherwise, how could the regulator have gathered all the private details on the marginal benefits and marginal costs underlying these citizens' preferences to set the tax accurately? But if transaction costs were so low, Coase argued, the citizens did not need the regulator to intervene with a new tax – rather they could resolve the problem themselves. The regulator could simply assign secure property rights to one party or the other, and the two citizens could then bargain – without cost – until they found an efficient agreement. Coasean bargaining with *secure property rights* and zero transaction costs avoided the need for government interference in the price system. This is the Coase theorem.

Coase was pushing 'the fiction of zero transaction costs reasoning to the limit' (Williamson, 1994). What Coase said was that since a zero-transaction costs world does not exist, what we need to study was the world that does – the one with transaction costs (Coase, 1988). The experimental economics laboratory has proven to be a useful tool to study how and by how much institutional rules matter in generating efficient outcomes in Coasean bargaining. Good environmental policy is only as effective as the coverage and stability of the agreement that unites common purposes across people, states, provinces, or nations. And the laboratory provides one effective tool to test what conditions can undercut or support cooperation and bargaining. While numerous bargaining experiments in psychology since the 1970s have produced a rich literature to build from (see Hoffman and Spitzer, 1982), the economics experiments really emerged when the idea of the *outside option* or *threat point* was introduced in the experimental design. Environmental negotiations are more subtle and complex, and involve more levels and nuances than can be perfectly mimicked in the laboratory. But still experimental tests of environmental cooperation can help us identify elements of weak bargaining protocol that reduce efficiency. Many researchers have documented the inner workings of the collaborative process by exploring how decisions are made and compromises are reached (Raiffa, 1982). See Roth (1995) for a general survey on the large experimental literature on bargaining. Decision makers could benefit from systematic information gleaned from the laboratory that would help them work through selecting an appropriate and cost-effective collaborative process for a particular environmental management dispute (Raiffa, 1995).

Beginning with the experimental work of Prudencio (1982) and Hoffman and Spitzer (1982) (Chapter 24), researchers have investigated the robustness of the key assumptions that underpin the cooperation implied by the Coase theorem:

1. two parties to an externality,
2. perfect information regarding each agent's production or utility functions,
3. competitive markets,
4. no transaction costs,
5. costless court system,
6. profit-maximizing producers and expected utility-maximizing consumers,
7. absence of wealth effects, and
8. parties will arrive at mutually advantageous bargains when no transaction costs are present.

This early work investigating the Coase theorem in the laboratory relaxed certain axioms to better understand the impact on efficiency and distribution of wealth. The first key result, and one seen throughout subsequent Coasean bargaining experiments, is that parties can find a negotiated agreement that is efficient. The second key result differed between the two original Coase bargaining experiments. Bargainers in the Hoffman and Spitzer experiment settled on an equal split of wealth; whereas bargainers in the Prudencio experiment focused more on giving the available gains from trade to the party that did not hold the property right.

The unexpected rationality results triggered the next set of experiments by Harrison and McKee (1985) (Chapter 25). By providing subjects with a complete understanding of the meaning of unilateral property rights, Harrison and McKee generated strong support for both behavioural implications of the Coase Theorem. Hoffman and Spitzer (1985) (Chapter 24) returned to the laboratory and determined that moral authority and allocation mechanisms had no adverse impact on efficiency, but provided more mutually advantageous bargaining agreements. We include the general essay by Rabin (1993) (Chapter 28) for the reader interested in a more thorough discussion of the role that fairness plays in economic theory.

With an experimental design now firmly in place, further investigations probed the boundaries of the Coase Theorem. Generally, these essays suggested that the Coase theorem was robust in its assumptions – efficiency was not dampened by large bargaining groups, asymmetric payoffs, or requiring contractual consent from the other player (for example, Schwab, 1988). Additionally, a Coasean bargaining setting generated efficient solutions to externalities in experimental markets (Harrison *et al.*, 1987, Chapter 26). While the distribution of wealth could be manipulated by relaxing some assumptions, the evidence supported the two key behavioural outcomes implied by the Coase Theorem.

Once these experiments affirmed the importance of the laboratory approach to support the Coase Theorem, experiments are run now to test the robustness of the results once one adds friction, such as uncertain payoff streams, imperfect contract enforcement, and delay costs (Shogren, 1992, 1998). Further, institutional structure played a key role in predicting the distribution of wealth among bargainers. Mutually advantageous distributions became more common with membership on a team directing loyalty and in a tournament setting with non-linearly increasing payoffs (Shogren, 1989, 1997).

Shogren (1998) (Chapter 29) considered how delay costs affected Coasean bargaining. The experiment examined how different specifications of discrete and continuous delay costs impact bargaining efficiency and the distribution of wealth. The results suggest that while Coasean bargaining remained relatively robust to discrete and increasing marginal delay costs, efficiency was significantly reduced with non-increasing marginal delay costs. Bargainers seem to use the heuristic in which they focus on probability and consequences separately rather than in combination as expected utility theory would predict. But bargaining experience improved efficiency.

More research would be useful on how institutional designs with either more experience or more detailed negotiation protocol can recapture efficiency gains lost on bargainers distracted by means over ends. Alternative bargaining rules can further enhance efficiency of the private resolution of environmental conflict by serving as a substitute for bargaining experience (see Rhoads and Shogren, 2003). Such research to test-bed new protocol holds the most immediate promise for Coasean bargaining experiments in shaping dispute resolution in the environmental arena. By providing a source of experience and data about how various rules might work in a collaborative setting, test-bed research offers an initial evaluation of the performance properties of the rules to be examined in this Coasean bargaining setting and becomes necessary to design and refine institutional collaborative frameworks (see Plott and Porter, 1996; Plott, 1997). With a focus on the impact of specific rules on efficiency and distribution in resolving environmental conflicts among private citizens, Coasean bargaining experiments can suggest efficient policy mechanisms in this arena.

V Environmental Control

Despite legal standards on ambient concentration, people have an incentive to shirk on environmental protection. Since private profits derive from market prices that do not reflect social preferences for environmental protection, a person has no economic incentive to supply the level of pollution control society demands. If the market is not sending the correct signal to the producer about the socially optimal level of pollution control, a regulator has three general management tools she can turn to – technological restrictions such as mandated abatement methods, cooperative institutions that share information between regulators, polluters, and victims, and economic incentives that increase the cost of shirking on pollution control (for example, Crocker, 1966).

The series of essays herein explore how the laboratory can be used to test economic incentives used to control environmental protection (also see Bohm, 2003). Economists have long promoted control systems as cost-effective alternatives to technological restrictions and other forms of inflexible command-and-control environmental regulations. Economic incentives both increase the cost of environmental shirking, and provide more flexibility to find the least-cost pollution control strategy. By increasing the cost of shirking, a person has the incentive to supply the socially optimal level of control. In general, economic incentives can be grouped into three broad categories – price rationing, quantity rationing, and liability rules. Price rationing increases the costs of shirking by setting a charge, tax, or subsidy on producer behaviour or products. Emission or effluent charges are the most commonly discussed form of price rationing. Quantity rationing as an economic incentive sets the acceptable level of pollution by allocating marketable permits that provide an incentive to producers with low pollution control costs to reduce pollution and sell their excess permits to producers with high control costs. Liability rules set up a socially acceptable benchmark of behaviour such that if a producer violates this benchmark he suffers some financial consequence. Non-compliance fees, deposit-refund schemes, and performance bonds represent alternative liability rules.

Economists can use laboratory experiments to test-bed for *economic design* – the construction of new institutions and mechanisms designed for efficient resource allocation and cost-effective rules for regulation of markets and firms. A test-bed emission trading system designed in laboratory markets can evaluate the institutional factors that will influence the effectiveness of trading. Experiments can be designed to consider how flexibility in trading, imperfect information, multi-gas trading, links between domestic and international trading, and other factors affect the potential efficiency of trading for example, Bohm and Carlen, 1999; Dinar *et al.*, 2000). Experimental work could prove useful in understanding what elements of emissions trading would reduce the efficiency of say acid rain or climate change policies.

The laboratory can help address how important these questions could be in the design of emission trading (also see Bjornstad *et al.*, 1999). If a proposed trading scheme is worth pursuing in the wilds, the laboratory can be used to address the details. For example, Cason's laboratory work on Acid Rain emission trading has revealed a flaw in the original design of permit auction run by the Environmental Protection Agency (Cason, 1995; Cason and Plott, 1996). Cason examines three hypotheses – winning bids are significantly higher for the experimental treatments with a greater number of bidders; all submitted bids are significantly higher for the experimental treatments with a greater number of bidders; and realized market trading efficiency is significantly lower for the experimental treatments with a greater number of bidders. The laboratory results showed the efficiency of the auction could be improved by changing how permits were allocated.

Originally, buyers and sellers submitted bids and offers for emission permits, and the EPA set the market price discriminatively off the demand curve by first matching the seller with the lowest offer to the buyer with the highest bid. The matching then continued with the second lowest offer to the second highest bid, and so on, until the equilibrium quantity was reached. Rational sellers should see quickly through this auction, and begin capturing rents by understating their true offer so they would be matched with a high bidder. Cason's laboratory results confirmed this intuition – sellers undercut each other to get into the high end of the market. The end result was an inefficient auction. Such lessons can be profitable. But insight like this should be made available before the regulatory tool is already in place, thus avoiding wasting resources due to inefficient design features.

These experimental essays explore the robustness of alternative control mechanisms to realign private incentives with social goals, with a special focus on public good provision (see Ledyard, 1995). Consider the Isaac *et al.* (1994) experiment (Chapter 32) that examined whether the voluntary provision of a public good will increase with larger groups. Traditional theory suggests that voluntary contributions to public goods are inversely related to group size – more people, more free-riding. Their primary objective is to understand whether the results from small-group experiments extend to large-group setting. A second objective is more about experimental methods – who to conduct large-group experiments using 'multi-session' experimental procedures and the use of extra-credit rewards. They conducted experiments that used group-sizes from 4, 10, 40, and 100, in which the dominant strategy for each person is always zero contributions to the public good. Their results contradict the widely held view that a group's ability to provide the optimal level of a pure public good is inversely related to group-size. The treatments with the group-sizes 40 and 100 yield results in which the impact from variations in the magnitude of the marginal per capita return (MPCR) from the public good appears to vanish over the range [0.30, 0.75]. They show that with an MPCR of 0.30, group-size 40 and 100 provide the public good at higher levels of efficiency than group-sizes 4 and 10. There is no significant difference in efficiency due to group size. The existence of an MPCR effect is reconfirmed for larger groups and behaviour is influenced by a subtle interaction between group-size and MPCR rather than the magnitude of either. Isaac and Walker (1998) (Chapter 35) further explore voluntary provision of public goods without an explicit control mechanism.

Plott (1983) (Chapter 30) provided the first experiments to test the efficiency of economic-based incentive systems (for example, taxes, tradeable pollution permits) relative to the more traditional regulatory approach of command-and-control (for example, uniform standard or technology). He examined whether a Pigovian tax could actually correct for negative externalities in a laboratory market (that is, social costs of pollution). Theory predicts that a competitive market with an externality converges to the private optimum that ignores social costs. Given the wedge between the private and social optima, Plott considered three corrective policies: taxes, standards, and tradeable permits. Theory also predicts that the economic price-based incentives (for example, tax and tradeable permits), which make the internal private decisions correspond with the social optimum, is more cost-effective than the command and control standard, which externally restricts output to the social optimum. The regulator has full information to apply the optimal policy.

To test these two predictions, Plott designed a competitive market of buyers and sellers who trade a valuable good. Buyers have a resale value they can sell back to the experimenter. A buyer's profit is the difference between the buying price and the resale value. Similarly, the sellers have a production cost. The difference between the selling price and cost is the seller's profit. As always, this induced valuation requires both the buyer and seller to prefer more money to less. The institutional trading mechanism was a double-oral auction in which buyers make bids that increase in value, and sellers call out offers that decrease in cost. Either the buyer or seller can take one bid or offer per trading period. A minimum of five periods was run; the maximum was twelve periods. No collusion or cooperation was allowed. The externality was constructed by reducing a seller's profits from trades as a function of the total number of trades in the market.

Plott first established that the competitive market with an externality converges to the private optimum. The traders ignored social costs. Next he found that the control mechanisms worked as expected. The results suggest that taxes and tradeable permits could work to equate private incentives with social costs, and they were significantly more efficient than the command and control approach. Efficiency for taxes and permits increased with repeated trading periods and quickly hit 100 per cent efficiency. In contrast, efficiency for the standard did not get much higher than 50 per cent. Plott concluded the standard economic models are 'amazingly accurate' in the simple laboratory setting. Harrison *et al.* (1987) extended Plott's experiment, adding bargaining as another policy, and confirmed his results. The essay by Muller and Mestelman (1994) (Chapter 31) further explores in the laboratory how tradeable permit or quota markets work under alternative trading rules and numbers of players.

The rub, however, is that some incentive mechanisms can be rather complicated such that one wonders whether they would work in practice. Smith (1979) first explored a simplified version of the Groves–Ledyard mechanism in the laboratory. The design allowed subjects to simultaneously reconsider their messages and to repeat the same choices three times to converge on the agreed-upon production of the public good. Once an agreement was reached, they were paid. This mechanism provided more public goods than a voluntary contribution mechanism. Chen and Plott (1996) (Chapter 34) revised the Groves–Ledyard mechanism under different punishment parameters. They examined how differing the magnitude of punishment, if a player's contribution deviated from the mean of other players' contributions, would affect behaviour. Their results suggest that a sufficiently severe punishment parameter caused proposals to converge to efficient levels.

Several essays have examined voluntary contributions given a *provision point* or threshold. The provision point mechanism creates a simple incentive – if group contributions meet or exceed a specific cost, a public good is provided; otherwise, it is not. Although sometimes referred to as an incentive compatible device, the provision point is more of an aggregate target rather than an individual-based mechanism. Rondeau *et al.* (1999) (Chapter 36) explored the properties of a *provision point mechanism* for public good provision. Their design used induced values and an environment designed to mimic field conditions. The one-shot provision point mechanism works as follows: A large group (50+) is pulled together, and each participant is endowed with $6. Each person then enters a bid indicating how much of the $6 he or she will contribute to a group investment fund. If the sum of the bids equals or exceeds a predetermined 'investment cost' (unknown to the bidders), each person receives a randomly assigned private payoff that may differ from other group members' payoffs. Each person's earnings depend on his or her bid and on whether the investment cost for the group was reached. Two possible outcomes could occur: if costs were not met by the group, the full amount of a person's bid was refunded; or if costs were exactly met or exceeded, each person received his or her payoff from the investment. And if the bids exceeded the cost, all of the excess was rebated to the group in direct proportion to one's bid relative to the total bids. The results suggest that the provision point mechanism was 'demand revealing in aggregate' for a large group with heterogeneous preferences. Rondeau *et al.* argue that these results suggest a relatively simple mechanism could be used in the field to elicit preferences leading to the efficient provision of a public good. But the problem is that this mechanism is argued to be incentive compatible at *the group level*. Unfortunately, the economic theory of incentive compatibility is defined at *the individual level* – each person should have incentive to bid sincerely. Incentive compatibility is an individual concept, not a group concept. If the group reaches the provision point because low value bidders overstate WTP and high value bidders understate WTP, this just means that the mechanism might lead to an efficient outcome on average; it does not mean it is incentive compatible. The idea of using this mechanism in field surveys begs the question of whether a mechanism that is 'just right' on average is close enough.

VI Environmental Valuation

Understanding how people value nature remains a key question in environmental economics. The desire for more control and accuracy in revealing non-market values through direct questions about actual goods led researchers towards the experimental methods. The drive to make experimental methods central to non-market valuation with the state of the art assessment of contingent valuations is summarized in Cummings *et al.*, (1986), and the work of Knetsch and Sinden (1984), Coursey and Schulze (1986), and Bennett (1983). Researchers now use experiments, in the laboratory and the field, to explore how people value the environment under different contexts and conditions (see Shogren, 2003 for a more detailed overview).

The essays herein illustrate how economists have used the experimental method to better understand the behavioural underpinnings of environmental valuation. The first key question that relied on the laboratory was the divergence in willingness to pay (WTP) and willingness to accept (WTA) measures of value. Rational choice theory suggests that with small income effects and many available substitutes, WTP should equal the WTA for a good. But evidence suggests that WTA has exceeded WTP by up to tenfold.

Following up on Knetsch and Sinden's (1984) work, Coursey *et al.* (1987) (Chapter 40) asked whether experience with an incentive compatible auction might remove the WTP–WTA gap. They assessed whether the gap would close with experience in bidding. Subjects bid to avoid or accept a bitter-tasting substance, sucrose octa-acetate (SOA), using a modified version of the uniform price Vickrey (1961) auction: a fifth-price auction with a veto rule. The four highest-bidders each bought one unit of a good and paid the fifth highest bid, provided none of the four winners vetoed the exchange. Their results suggest that mean WTP and WTA bids converged with repeated exposure to the Vickrey auction environment, a result weakened significantly by one outlier affecting the average values (see Gregory and Furby, 1987).

Kahneman, Knetsch and Thaler (1990) (Chapter 42) found evidence that supported the idea that an *endowment effect* explained the WTP–WTA gap. The effect exists if people offer to sell a commonly available good in their possession at a substantially higher rate than they will pay for the identical good not in their possession (for example, pens and coffee mugs). They used a Becker–DeGroot–Marschak (1964) mechanism to elicit preferences in the fifth treatment, in which a person's weakly dominant strategy is to state her true WTP or WTA. The results from the Kahneman *et al.* treatments make a case for the existence of a fundamental endowment effect – WTA exceeded WTP in all treatments over all iterations.

Boyce *et al.* (1992) (Chapter 43) designed a laboratory experiment to explore whether it was the precession of non-use values (for example, existence values) for environmental protection that might explain the valuation gap. Their experimental design asked people to value a houseplant (a Norfolk pine) that would be destroyed unless they protected it by buying the plant. People paid more when they were explicitly told that the plant would be killed if they did not buy it.

In contrast, Shogren *et al.* (1994) (Chapter 44) observed no significant divergence between WTP and WTA for similar goods. Their design again tested the notion that with repeated market participation, WTP and WTA will converge for a market good with close substitutes (for example, the candy bar and mugs) but will not converge for the non-market health risk with imperfect substitutes (risky sandwich). They also tested for whether transaction costs could explain the WTP–WTA gap by having a large supply of the market goods right outside the laboratory door that could be purchased by the subjects once the experiment was over. The results showed that WTP and WTA values did converge with repeated trials for candy bars and mugs – goods with many available substitutes; but that the values continued to diverge for the reduced health risks from safer food – one's health has little substitutes. To better understand the issue, Shogren *et al.* (2001) designed a valuation experiment in which the auction was the treatment – the Becker–DeGroot–Marschak mechanism versus Vickery's second-price auction. They observed the auction choice matter to bidding.

Experiments have also been used to directly assess non-market values. The work by Bohm (1972) (Chapter 38) is the classic study of real-world valuation studies of deliverable, non-trivial public goods. Drawn from a random sample in Stockholm, subjects were asked to assign value to a new television programme they could watch if their aggregate WTP were high enough to cover costs. Subjects were divided into six groups, and were told that if their aggregate WTP exceeded the costs, they could watch the programme, prior to which each person would have to pay either the WTP stated; a percentage of the WTP stated; the WTP stated or a percentage of the amount stated or 5 kronor or nothing, all four with equal probability; 5 kronor, the current average price of a cinema ticket, or nothing; taxpayers would foot the bill. Two results emerged – no significant difference existed between the mean WTP in the five groups; but a significant difference existed between the real bids and the hypothetical bids of people in a sixth group.

Although imperfect, the study by Brookshire and Coursey (1987) (Chapter 41) is another classic use of the experiment method for non-market valuation. They compared values obtained from hypothetical elicitation methods to those obtained in a market-like setting. The study consisted of three parts: a hypothetical contingent valuation study, a field study using a Smith auction, and a laboratory experiment with the Smith auction. The Smith auction collects bids, and if aggregate bids exceed costs, each respondent pays a proportional bid.

People vote on whether they agree to the price and quantity of the good vided. Also see the essay in Chapter 39 by Bennett (1987); he uses a modified Smith auction eliminated strategic behaviour in the provision of a hypothetical public good relative to a direct question approach. He found that direct statements of hypothetical values led to over-bidding of induced value, whereas the Smith auction led to under-bidding. He suggested that the most promising avenue to estimate values in real-world cases is to combine the direct statements of value with the laboratory experiments.

Today, researchers around the world use surveys to elicit stated preferences for many environmental questions. But an old concern remains a sticking point for some economists: hypothetical statements of value are not necessarily real (see Bishop and Heberlein, 1979; Seip and Strand, 1992; Frykblom, 1997). Most evidence suggests that people tend to exaggerate their actual willingness to pay across a broad spectrum of goods with vastly different experimental parameters. The ratio of hypothetical-to-actual bidding has been shown to range from 1.0 to 10.0 for many goods including irradiated pork, watercolour paintings, and maps (see Diamond and Hausman, 1994). These results reinforce the notion that people tend to overstate their actual WTP when confronted with hypothetical questions. The essay by Neill *et al.* (1994) in Chapter 45 is an example of this line of hypothetical–real valuation research.

Hypothetical values lead naturally to another question well-suited for the laboratory – can stated values be *calibrated* to reflect what people would actually pay for proposed programmes. The essay by Fox *et al.* (1998) in Chapter 46 proposes an *ex post* method of calibration – the CVM-X method. CVM-X works by surveying hypothetical values, then bringing into the laboratory a sub-sample of respondents to elicit their real bids. One then estimates a calibration function relating the auction market bids of the sub-sample to their hypothetical survey bids, and uses the estimated calibration function to adjust the values of the survey respondents who did not participate in the laboratory auction. People revealed their willingness to pay to upgrade from a less-preferred sandwich to a more preferred sandwich in an open-ended elicitation question. The results suggest that an upward bias in hypothetical bids exists, and that the laboratory can be used to correct for this bias, but the calibration function might be commodity-specific.

The essay by Cummings and Taylor (1999) in Chapter 47 is an alternative *ex ante* approach to calibration. They propose an alternative method to remove the hypothetical bias – a so-called *cheap talk* survey design. Their idea is that one might be able to reduce hypothetical bias before it starts by the choice of wording in the survey. They propose that telling a respondent about the hypothetical bias issue, before he answers the valuation question, might remove the bias. They examine treatments that compare stated values with and without cheap talk to a benchmark treatment that elicited actual contributions to four different public goods (for example, contributions to the Nature Conservancy in Georgia). Their results suggest that the cheap talk design worked to make responses to hypothetical questions indistinguishable to responses involving actual cash payments, and that this effect was robust across changes in script and public good, with one exception.

Concluding Remark

The best way to learn about experiments is to run an experiment. A useful way to think about experiments for environmental problems is to remember that we make our choices both within and outside of market exchange institutions, and that these market and non-market situations are interlinked. Exploring both the market and non-market subdivisions of the experimental literature and the links between the two provides both a challenge and an opportunity. The essays in this two-volume set serve a primary objective toward this end – to help reduce the transaction costs of researchers interested in moving into this area of work. These essays both motivate and justify the use of the experimental method to explore how people make choices under risk, make strategic decisions under conflict, find mutually agreeable outcomes through cooperation, respond to incentives, and assign values in different contexts. The range of essays goes beyond those directly targeted towards environmental problems because a second objective is to illustrate the range and power of the experimental method. Readers interested in specific environmental issues can find insight into both rational economic theory and observed behaviour that apply to questions of environmental risk, conflict, cooperation, control, and valuation. A key point to remember throughout – the power of the experimental method rests in one's ability to create environments that can be replicated or altered by others to test the robustness of any observed finding. Experimental methods applied to environmental problems reveal that economists have tools similar to the natural sciences, allow us to rethink theories and to resample subjects to create new data, and impose a discipline that help one concentrate attention on the key elements behind any issue. The essays in this collection provide excellent examples on how this can be done.

References

Allais, M. (1953), 'Le Comportement de l'Homme Rationnel devant le Risque: Critique des Postulats et Axiomes de l'École Americaine', *Econometrica*, **21**, pp. 503–46.

Baik, K.H., Cherry, T., Kroll, S. and Shogren, J. (1999), 'Endogenous Timing in a Gaming Tournament', *Theory and Decision*, **47**, pp. 1–21.

Barrett, S. (1994), 'Self-Enforcing International Environmental Agreements', *Oxford Economic Papers*, 46 (0) (Supplement), pp. 878–94.

Becker, G. (1962), 'Irrational Behavior and Economic Theory', *Journal of Political Economy*, **70**, pp. 1–13.

Becker, S. and Brownson, F. (1964), 'What Price Ambiguity? On the Role of Ambiguity in Decision-making', *Journal of Political Economy*, **72**, pp. 65–73.

Becker, G., DeGroot, M. and Marschak, J. (1964), 'Measuring Utility by a Single Response Sequential Method', *Behavioral Science*, **9**, pp. 226–36.

Bennett, J. (1983), 'Validating Revealed Preferences', *Economic Analysis and Policy*, **13**, pp. 2–17.

Bennett, J. (1987), 'Strategic Behaviour: Some Experimental Evidence', *Journal of Public Economics*, **32**, pp. 355–68.

Bird, J. (1987), 'The Transferability and Depletability of Externalities', *Journal of Environmental Economics and Management*, **14**, pp. 54–7.

Bishop, R. and Heberlein, T. (1979), 'Measuring Values of Extramarket Goods: Are Indirect Measures Biased?', *American Journal of Agricultural Economics*, **61**, pp. 926–30.

Bjornstad, D., Elliot, S. and Hale, D. (1999), 'Understanding Experimental Economics and Policy Analysis in a Federal Agency: The Case of Marketable Emission Trading', in C. Holt and R.M. Isaac (eds), *Research in Experimental Economics*, volume 7, Greenwich, Connecticut and London, England: JAI Press, pp. 163–80.

Bohm, P. (1972), 'Estimating Demand for Public Goods: An Experiment', *European Economic Review*, **3**, pp. 111–30.

Bohm, P. (1984), 'Revealing Demand for an Actual Public Good', *Journal of Public Economics*, **24**, pp. 135–51.

Bohm, P. (1994), 'Behavior under Uncertainty without Preference Reversal: A Field Experiment', *Empirical Economics* (Special issue, J. Hey, ed.), **19**, pp. 185–200.

Bohm, P. (2003), 'Experimental Evaluations of Policy Instruments', in K.G. Maler and J. Vincent (eds), *Handbook of Environmental Economics*, Amsterdam: North Holland (forthcoming).

Bohm, P. and Carlén, B. (1999), 'Emission Quota Trade among the Few: Laboratory Evidence of Joint Implementation among Committed Countries', *Resource and Energy Economics*, **21** (1), pp. 43–66.

Bohm, P. and Lind, H. (1993), 'Preference Reversal, Real-World Lotteries, and Lottery-Interested Subjects', *Journal of Economic Behavior and Organization*, **22**, pp. 327–48.

Boyce, R., McClelland, G., Brown, T., Peterson, G. and Schulze, W. (1992), 'An Experimental Examination of Intrinsic Values as a Source of the WTA–WTP Disparity', *American Economic Review*, **82**, pp. 1366–73.

Brookshire, D. and Coursey, D. (1987), 'Measuring the Value of a Public Good: An Empirical Comparison of Elicitation Procedures', *American Economic Review*, **77**, pp. 554–66.

Camerer, C. (1987), 'Do Biases in Probability Judgment Matter in Markets? Experimental Evidence', *American Economic Review*, **77** (5), pp. 981–97.

Camerer, C. (1995), 'Individual Decision Making', in J. Kagel and A. Roth (eds), *Handbook of Experimental Economics*, Princeton, NJ: Princeton University Press, pp. 587–703.

Camerer, Colin F. (1997), 'Progress in Behavioral Game Theory', *Journal of Economic Perspectives*, **11** (4) (Fall 1997), pp. 167–88.

Camerer, C., Johnson, E., Rymon, T. and Sen, S. (1993), 'Cognition and Framing in Sequential Bargaining for Gains and Losses', in K. Binmore, A. Kirman and P. Tani (eds), *Contributions to Game Theory*, Cambridge: MIT Press, pp. 27–47.

Cason, T. (1995), 'An Experimental Investigation of the Seller Incentives in the EPA's Emission Trading Auction', *American Economic Review*, **85** (4), pp. 905–22.

Cason, T. and Plott, C. (1996), 'EPA's New Emissions Trading Mechanism: A Laboratory Evaluation', *Journal of Environmental Economics and Management*, **30** (2), pp. 133–60.

Chen, Yan and Plott, Charles R. (1996), 'The Groves–Ledyard Mechanism: An Experimental Study of Institutional Design', *Journal of Public Economics*, **59** (3), March, pp. 335–64.

Cherry, T., Crocker, T. and Shogren, J. (2003), 'Rationality Spillovers', *Journal of Environmental Economics and Management*, **45**, pp. 63–84.

Chu, Y.-P. and Chu, R.-L. (1990), 'The Subsidence of Preference Reversals in Simplified and Marketlike Experimental Settings: A Note', *American Economic Review*, **80**, pp. 902–11.

Coase, R. (1960), 'The Problem of Social Cost', *Journal of Law and Economics*, 3 (1), pp. 1–44.

Coase, R. (1988), *The Firm, the Market and the Law*, Chicago: University of Chicago Press.

Cooper, R.W., DeJong, D.V., Forsythe, R. and Ross, T.W. (1992), 'Communication in Coordination Games', *Quarterly Journal of Economics*, **107**, pp. 739–71.

Cooter, R. (1989), 'The Coase Theorem', in J. Eatwell, M. Milgate and P. Newman (eds), *The New Palgrave: Allocation, Information and Markets*, New York: W.W. Norton & Co. Inc., pp. 64–70.

Coursey, D. (1987), 'Markets and the Measurement of Value', *Public Choice*, **55**, pp. 291–7.

Coursey, D. and Schulze, W. (1986), 'The Application of Laboratory Experimental Economics to the Contingent Valuation of Public Goods', *Public Choice*, **49**, pp. 47–68.

Coursey, D., Hovis, J. and Schulze, W. (1987), 'The Disparity between Willingness to Accept and Willingness to Pay Measures of Value', *Quarterly Journal of Economics*, **102**, pp. 679–90.

Cox, J. and Epstein, S. (1989), 'Preference Reversals without the Independence Axiom', *American Economic Review*, **79**, pp. 408–26.

Cox, J. and Grether, D. (1996), 'The Preference Reversal Phenomena: Response Mode, Markets, and Incentives', *Economic Theory*, 7, pp. 381–405.

Crawford, V. P. (1998), 'A Survey of Experiments on Communication via Cheap Talk', *Journal of Economic Theory*, **78**, pp. 286–98.

Crocker, T. (1966), 'The Structuring of Atmospheric Pollution Control Systems', in H. Wolzin (ed.), *The Economics of Air Pollution*, New York: Norton, pp. 61–86.

Crocker, T., Shogren, J. and Turner, P. (1998), 'Incomplete Beliefs and Nonmarket Valuation', *Resources and Energy Economics*, **20**, pp. 139–62.

Crowfoot, J. and Wondolleck, J. (1990), *Environmental Disputes. Community Involvement in Conflict Resolution*, Washington, DC: Island Press.

Cummings, R. and Taylor, L. (1999), 'Unbiased Value Estimates for Environmental Goods: A Cheap Talk Design for the Contingent Valuation Method', *American Economic Review*, **83**, pp. 649–65.

Cummings, R. and Taylor, L. (2002), 'Experimental Economics in Environmental and Natural Resource Management', in H. Folmer and T. Tietenberg (eds), *International Yearbook of Environmental and Resource Economics*, Cheltenham, UK: Edward Elgar.

Cummings, R., Brookshire, D. and Schulze, W. (1986), *Valuing Environmental Goods: An Assessment of the Contingent Valuation Method*, Totowa, NJ: Rowman & Allanheld.

Davis, D. and Holt, C. (1993), *Experimental Economics*, Princeton, NJ: Princeton University Press.

Diamond, P. and Hausman, J. (1994), 'Contingent Valuation – Is Some Number better than no Number?', *Journal of Economic Perspectives*, **8**, pp. 45–64.

Dinar, A., Howitt, R., Murphy, J., Rassenti, S. and Smith, V.L. (2000), 'The Design of "Smart" Water Market Institutions Using Laboratory Experiments', *Environmental and Resource Economics*, **17**, pp. 375–94.

Ehrlich, I. and Becker, G. (1972), 'Market Insurance, Self-Insurance and Self-Protection', *Journal of Political Economy*, **80**, pp. 623–48.

Ellsberg, D. (1961), 'Risk, Ambiguity, and the Savage Axioms', *Quarterly Journal of Economics*, **75**, pp. 643–69.

Fox, J., Shogren, J., Hayes, D. and Kliebenstein, J. (1998), 'CVM-X: Calibrating Contingent Values with Experimental Auction Markets', *American Journal of Agricultural Economics*, **80**, pp. 455–65.

Frykblom, P. (1997), 'Hypothetical Question Modes and Real Willingness to Pay', *Journal of Environmental Economics and Management*, **34**, pp. 275–87.

Fudenberg, D. and Tirole, J. (1991), *Game Theory*, Cambridge: MIT Press.

Gregory, R. and Furby, L. (1987), 'Auctions, Experiments, and Contingent Valuation', *Public Choice*, **55**, pp. 273–89.

Grether, D. and Plott, C. (1979), 'Economic Theory of Choice and the Preference Reversal Phenomenon', *American Economic Review*, **69**, pp. 623–38.

Hackett, Steven, Schlager, Edella and Walker, James (1994), 'The Role of Communication in Resolving Commons Dilemmas: Experimental Evidence with Heterogeneous Appropriators', *Journal of Environmental Economics and Management*, **27**, pp. 99–126.

Hanley, N., Shogren, J. and White, B. (1997), *Environmental Economics in Theory and Practice*, New York: Oxford University Press.

Harrison, Glenn W. and McKee, Michael (1985), 'Experimental Evaluation of the Coase Theorem', *Journal of Law and Economics*, **28** (3) (October), pp. 653–70.

Harrison, G., Hoffman, E., Rutström, E. and Spitzer, M. (1987), 'Coasian Solutions to the Externality Problem in Experimental Markets', *Economic Journal*, **97**, pp. 388–402.

Hey, J. and Orme, C. (1994), 'Investigating Generalizations of Expected Utility Theory Using Experimental Data', *Econometrica*, **62**, pp. 1291–326.

Hoffman, E. and Spitzer, M. (1982), 'The Coase Theorem: Some Experimental Tests', *Journal of Law and Economics*, **25** (1), pp. 73–98.

Hoffman, E. and Spitzer, M. (1985), 'Entitlements, Rights, and Fairness: An Experimental Examination of Subjects' Concepts of Distributional Justice', *Journal of Legal Studies*, **54** (2), pp. 259–97.

Hogarth, Robin M. and Kunreuther, Howard (1989), 'Risk, Ambiguity, and Insurance', *Journal of Risk and Uncertainty*, **2** (1) (April), pp. 5–35.

Irwin, J., Slovic, P., Lichtenstein, S. and McClelland, G. (1993), 'Preference Reversals and the Measurement of Environmental Values', *Journal of Risk and Uncertainty*, **6**, pp. 5–18.

Isaac, R. Mark and Walker, James M. (1998), 'Nash as an Organizing Principle in the Voluntary Provision of Public Goods: Experimental Evidence', *Experimental Economics*, **1** (3), 191–206.

Isaac, R. Mark, Walker, James M. and Williams, Arlington W. (1994), 'Group Size and the Voluntary Provision of Public Goods: Experimental Evidence Utilizing Large Groups', *Journal of Public Economics*, **54** (1) (May), pp. 1–36.

Kagel, J. and Roth, A. (eds) (1995), *Handbook of Experimental Economics*, Princeton, NJ: Princeton University Press.

Kahneman, Daniel and Tversky, Amos (1979), 'Prospect Theory: An Analysis of Decision under Risk', *Econometrica*, **47** (2) (March), pp. 263–91.

Kahneman, D. and Tversky, A. (eds) (2000), *Choices, Values, and Frames*, Cambridge: Cambridge University Press.

Kahneman, D., Knetsch J. and Thaler, R. (1990), 'Experimental Tests of the Endowment Effect and the Coase Theorem', *Journal of Political Economy*, **98**, pp. 1325–48.

Knetsch, J. (1997), 'Evaluation and Environmental Policies: Recent Behavioural Findings and Further Implications', in A. Dragun and K. Jakobsson (eds), *Sustainability and Global Environmental Policy: New Perspectives*, Cheltenham, UK: Edward Elgar Publishing, pp. 193–212.

Knetsch, J. and Sinden, J.A. (1984), 'Willingness to Pay and Compensation Demanded: Experimental Evidence of an Unexpected Disparity in Measures of Values', *Quarterly Journal of Economics*, **99**, pp. 507–21.

Knez, M. and Smith, V.L. (1987), 'Hypothetical Valuations and Preference Reversals in the Context of Asset Trading', in A. Roth (ed.), *Laboratory Experimentation in Economics: Six Points of View*, New York: Cambridge University Press, pp. 131–54.

Kroll, S., Mason, C. and Shogren, J. (1999), 'Environmental Conflicts and Interconnected Games: An Experimental Note on Institutional Design', in N. Hanley and H. Folmer (eds), *Game Theory and the Global Environment*, Cheltenham, UK: Edward Elgar Publishers.

Laibson, D. and Zeckhauser, R. (1998), 'Amos Tversky and the Ascent of Behavioral Economics', *Journal of Risk and Uncertainty*, **16**, pp. 7–47.

Lave, Lester B. (1962), 'An Empirical Approach to the Prisoner's Dilemma', *Quarterly Journal of Economics*, **76**, pp. 424–36.

Ledyard, J. (1995), 'Public Goods: A Survey of Experimental Research', in J. Kagel and A. Roth (eds), *Handbook of Experimental Economics*, Princeton, NJ: Princeton University Press, pp. 111–94.

Lichtenstein, S. and Slovic, P. (1971), 'Reversals of Preference Between Bids and Choices in Gambling Decisions', *Journal of Experimental Psychology*, **89**, pp. 46–55.

McClelland, Gary H., Schulze, William D. and Coursey, Don L. (1993), 'Insurance for Low-Probability Hazards: A Bimodal Response to Unlikely Events', *Journal of Risk and Uncertainty*, **7**, pp. 95–116.

McKelvey, R. and Palfrey, T. (1992), 'An Experimental Study of the Centipede Game', *Econometrica*, **60**, pp. 803–36.

Mason, Charles F. and Philips, Owen R. (1997), 'Mitigating the Tragedy of the Commons through Cooperation: An Experimental Evaluation', *Journal of Environmental Economics and Management*, **34** (2) (October), pp. 148–72.

Muller, R.A. and Mestelman, S. (1994), 'Emission Trading with Shares and Coupons: A Laboratory Experiment', *Energy Journal*, **15** (2), pp. 185–211.

Neill, H., Cummings, R., Ganderton, P., Harrison, G. and McGuckin, T. (1994), 'Hypothetical Surveys and Real Economic Commitments', *Land Economics*, **70**, pp. 145–54.

Ochs, J. (1995), 'Coordination Problems', in J. Kagel and A. Roth (eds), *The Handbook of Experimental Economics*, Princeton, NJ: Princeton University Press.

Ochs, Jack and Roth, Alvin E. (1989), 'An Experimental Study of Sequential Bargaining', *American Economic Review*, **79** (3) (June), pp. 355–84.

Palfrey, T. R. and Rosenthal, H. (1994), 'Repeated Play, Cooperation, and Coordination: An Experimental Study', *Review of Economic Studies*, **61**, 545–65.

Parkhurst, G., Shogren, J., Bastian, C., Kivi, P., Donner, J. and Smith, R. (2002), 'Agglomeration Bonus: An Incentive Mechanism to Reunite Fragmented Habitat for Biodiversity Conservation', *Ecological Economics*, **41**, pp. 305–28.

Plott, C. (1983), 'Externalities and Corrective Policies in Experimental Markets', *Economic Journal*, **93** (1), pp. 106–27.

Plott, C. (1994), 'Market Architectures, Institutional Landscapes and Testbed Experiments', *Economic Theory*, **4**, pp. 3–10.

Plott, C. (1997), 'Laboratory Experimental Testbeds: Application to the PCS Auction', *Journal of Economics and Management Strategy*, **6** (3), pp. 605–38.

Plott, C. and Porter, D. (1996), 'Market Architectures and Institutional Testbedding: An Experiment with Space Station Pricing Policies', *Journal of Economic Behavior and Organization*, **31**, pp. 237–72.

Prudencio, Y. (1982), 'The Voluntary Approach to Externality Problems: An Experimental Test', *Journal of Environmental Economics and Management*, **9**, pp. 213–28.

Rabin, Matthew (1993), 'Incorporating Fairness into Game Theory and Economics', *American Economic Review*, **83** (December), pp. 1281–302.

Raiffa, H. (1982), *The Art and Science of Negotiation*, Cambridge, MA: Belknap Press of Harvard University Press.

Raiffa, H. (1995), 'Analytical Barriers', in K. Arrow *et al.* (eds), *Barriers to Conflict Resolution*, New York: Norton, pp. 132–48.

Rhoads, T. and Shogren, J. (2003), 'Regulation through Collaboration: Final Authority and Information Symmetry in Environmental Coasean Bargaining', *Journal of Regulatory Economics* (forthcoming).

Rondeau, D., Schulze, W. and Poe, G. (1999), 'Voluntary Revelation of the Demand for Public Goods Using a Provision Point Mechanism', *Journal of Public Economics*, **72**, pp. 455–70.

Roth, A. (1994), 'Let's Keep the Con Out of Experimental Econ.: A Methodological Note', *Empirical Economics* (Special Issue on Experimental Economics), **19**, 279–89.

Roth, A. (1995), 'Bargaining Experiments', in J. Kagel and A. Roth (eds), *Handbook of Experimental Economics*, Princeton, NJ: Princeton University Press, pp. 253–348.

Sabel, C., Fung, A. and Karkkainen, B. (2000), *Beyond Backyard Environmentalism*, Boston, MA: Beacon Press.

Schelling, T. (1960), *The Strategy of Conflict*, London: Oxford University Press.

Schwab, S. (1988), 'A Coasean Experiment on Contract Presumptions', *Journal of Legal Studies*, **17**, pp. 237–68.

Seip, K. and Strand, J. (1992), 'Willingness to Pay for Environmental Goods in Norway: A Contingent Valuation Study with Real Payment', *Environmental and Resource Economics*, **2**, pp. 91–106.

Selten, R. (1965), 'Spieltheoretische Behandlung eines Oligopolmodells mit Nachfrageträgheit', *Zeitschrift für die gesamte Staatswissenschaft*, **12**, pp. 301–24.

Settle, C., Crocker, T.D. and Shogren, J.F. (2002), 'On the Joint Determination of Biological and Economic Systems', *Ecological Economics*, **42**, pp. 301–11.

Shogren, J. (1989), 'Fairness in Bargaining Requires a Context: An Experimental Examination of Loyalty', *Economics Letters*, **31**, pp. 319–23.

Shogren, J. (1990), 'The Impact of Self-Protection and Self-Insurance on Individual Response to Risk', *Journal of Risk and Uncertainty*, **3**, pp. 191–204.

Shogren, J. (1992), 'An Experiment on Coasian Bargaining over Ex Ante Lotteries and Ex Post Rewards', *Journal of Economic Behavior and Organization*, **17** (1), pp. 153–69.

Shogren, J. (1993), 'Experimental Markets and Environmental Policy', *Agricultural and Resource Economic Review*, **22** (2), pp. 117–29.

Shogren, J. (1997), 'Self-Interest and Equity in a Bargaining Tournament with Non-Linear Payoffs', *Journal of Economic Behavior and Organization*, **32** (3), pp. 383–94.

Shogren, J. (1998), 'Coasean Bargaining with Symmetric Delay Costs', *Resources and Energy Economics*, **20** (4), pp. 309–25.

Shogren, J. (2003), 'Experimental Methods and Valuation', in K.G. Maler and J. Vincent (eds), *Handbook of Environmental Economics*, Amsterdam: North Holland (forthcoming).

Shogren, J. and Crocker, T. (1991), 'Risk, Self-Protection, and Ex Ante Economic Value', *Journal of Environmental Economics and Management*, **21**, pp. 1–15.

Shogren, J. and Nowell, C. (1992), 'Economics and Ecology: A Comparison of Experimental Methodologies and Philosophies', *Ecological Economics*, **5**, pp. 101–26.

Shogren, J., Shin, S., Hayes, D. and Kliebenstein, J. (1994), 'Resolving Differences in Willingness to Pay and Willingness to Accept', *American Economic Review*, **84**, pp. 255–70.

Shogren, J., Cho, S., Koo, C., List, J., Park, C., Polo, P. and Wilhelmi, R. (2001), 'Auction Mechanisms and the Measurement of WTP and WTA', *Resource and Energy Economics*, **23**, pp. 97–109.

Smith, V.L. (1979), 'Incentive Compatibility in Experimental Processes for the Provision of Public Goods', in V. Smith (ed.), *Research in Experimental Economics*, **1**, Greenwich, CT: JAI Press.

Smith, V.L. (1982), 'Microeconomic Systems as an Experimental Science', *American Economic Review*, **72**, pp. 923–55.

Smith, V.L. (1991), 'Rational Choice: The Contrast between Economics and Psychology', *Journal of Political Economy*, **99**, pp. 877–97.

Susskind, L., Levy, P. and Thomas-Larmer, J. (2000), *Negotiating Environmental Agreements*, Washington, DC: Island Press.

Sutton, J. (2000), *Marshall's Tendencies: What Can Economists Know?*, Cambridge, MA: MIT Press.

Tversky, A. and Kahneman, D. (1981), 'The Framing of Decisions and the Psychology of Choice', *Science*, **211**, pp. 453–8.

Vickrey, W. (1961), 'Counterspeculation, Auctions, and Competitive Sealed Tenders', *Journal of Finance*, **16**, pp. 8–37.

Walker, James M. and Gardner, Roy (1992), 'Probabilistic Destruction of Common-Pool Resources: Experimental Evidence', *Economic Journal*, **102**, pp. 1149–61.

Williamson, O. (1994), 'Evaluating Coase', *Journal of Economic Perspective*, **8**, 201–4.

Part I
Motives and Methods

[1]

Microeconomic Systems as an Experimental Science

By Vernon L. Smith*

Study nature, not books...
                    Louis Agassiz

After studying economics for six years I have reached the conclusion that there is no difference between discovery and creation...
                    [Graffiti by an unknown student]

The experimental literature contains only a few attempts to articulate a "theory" of laboratory experiments in economics (Charles Plott, 1979; Louis Wilde, 1980; my articles, 1976a, pp. 43–44, 46–47; 1976b; 1980). It is appropriate for this effort to have been modest, since it has been more important for experimentalists to present a rich variety of examples of their work than abstract explanations of why one might perform experiments. Wilde's contribution provides an integration and extension of the earlier papers, and brings a fresh perspective and coherence that invites further examination. This seems to be the time and place to attempt a more complete description of the methodology and function of experiments in microeconomics.

The formal study of information systems in resource allocation theory (Leonid Hurwicz, 1960) and the laboratory experimental study of resource allocation under alternative forms of market organization (Sidney Siegel and Lawrence Fouraker, 1960, Fouraker and Siegel, 1963; my 1962, 1964 articles) had coincident beginnings and, in important respects, have undergone similar, if mostly independent, intellectual developments. The similarity of intellectual development in these two new endeavors is represented by the increasing focus upon the role of institutions in defining the information

and incentive structure within which economic outcomes are determined. While the (new)[2] welfare economics (Stanley Reiter 1977) was articulating a formal structure for the design and evaluation of allocation mechanisms (institutions) as *economic variables* (Hurwicz, 1973), experimentalists were comparing the performance of experimental economies in which the rules of information transfer and of contract appeared as *treatment variables* (Plott and myself, 1978; my 1964, 1976a articles). Since it is not possible to design a laboratory resource allocation experiment without designing an institution in all its detail, it was foreordained by the nature of the questions asked, that the work of experimentalists would parallel that of the (new)[2] welfare economics.[1]

In the sequel, the definition of a microeconomic system will be developed. Then the laboratory market or resource allocation experiment will be developed and discussed as an example of a microeconomic system. This framework will be used to provide a taxonomy for laboratory experimentation which allows the methods, objectives and results of such experiments to be interpreted and perhaps extended.[2] An important message of the paper which has been emphasized before (Plott, 1979, p. 141; my 1976b article, p. 275), but was articulated more satisfactorily by Wilde (1980), is that laboratory microeconomies are real live economic systems, which are certainly richer, behaviorally, than

*University of Arizona. I am grateful to the National Science Foundation for research support, and for many significant encounters over the years which have helped to shape my thinking about experimental microeconomy. Although any list is bound to omit some key sources of inspiration, in addition to the many authors cited in the references, I particularly want to mention Sidney Siegel, Jim Friedman, Charlie Plott, Martin Shubik, and Arlie Williams.

[1] Experimental microeconomics includes the study of individual choice behavior. For an excellent description of the methodology and some of the results from the experimental study of human and animal choice behavior, see the survey by John Kagel and Raymond Battalio (1980).

[2] Nothing in this paper will be very helpful to anyone desiring to learn the important techniques and mechanics of conducting experiments. For explanations of experimental procedures, it will be necessary to consult the references. But learning to run experiments is like learning to play the piano—at some point you have to start practicing. The classic model of good experimental technique is still to be found in Fouraker and Siegel (1963).

the systems parameterized in our theories. Consequently, it is important to economic science for theorists to be less own-literature oriented, to take seriously the data and disciplinary function of laboratory experiments, and even to take seriously their own theories as potential generators of testable hypotheses. Since "the discovery of new facts is open to any blockhead with patience and manual dexterity and acute senses" (attributed to Sir William Hamilton in N. R. Hanson, 1971, p. 23), it is equally important that experimentalists take seriously the collective professional task of integrating theory, experimental design, and observation.

I. Microeconomic System Theory

A. *Defining a Microeconomic System*

In defining a microeconomic system two distinct component elements will be identified: an environment and an institution.

1. *The Environment*

The environment consists of a list of N economic agents $\{1,...,N\}$, a list of $K+1$ commodities (including resources) $\{0,1,...,K\}$, and certain characteristics of each agent i, such as the agent's utility function u^i, technology (knowledge) endowment T^i, and a commodity endowment vector ω^i. Hence, the ith agent is characterized by the vector $e^i = (u^i, T^i, \omega^i)$ whose components are assumed to be defined on the $K+1$ dimensional commodity space R^{K+1}. Hence, a microeconomic *environment* is defined by the collection of characteristics $e = (e^1,...,e^N)$. This specification defines the environment as a set of initial circumstances that cannot be altered by the agents or the institutions within which they interact. The reader should appreciate that by appropriate interpretation this definition does not rule out learning, that is, changes in preferences and/or technology. But if learning is to be part of the economic process, then one must specify agent preferences and technology in terms of learning (or sampling or discovery) activities. In this case the fixed environment would specify the limitations and search opportunities for altering tastes and knowledge in an economy with changeable tastes and resources. It should be noted that, in an experimental environment, e will include some circumstances that cannot be altered by the agents because they are control variables fixed by the experimenter—a matter to which I will return later.

A subtle but important feature of the environment deserves emphasis: the superscript i on the characteristic of each agent i means that the initiating circumstances in an economic environment are *in their nature private*. Tastes, knowledge, and skill endowments are quintessentially private: *I* like, *I* know, *I* work, and *I* make.[3]

2. *The Institution*

The above is no less true in societies with weak than in those with strong private property right systems. Whether private tastes matter little or are sovereign; whether or not an idea can be patented, copyrighted, or trademarked as alienable private property; and to what extent one has a property right in the fruits of one's "own" labor; these are all matters of the institution which is itself public in administration. It is the institution which specifies that soliciting for the purpose of prostitution is punishable by fines and imprisonment; that smoking in the hallway is to be allowed; that forms of indentured labor are prohibited (except in professional sports); that patents expire after seventeen years; that Ohm's law is not patentable; that price discrimination is illegal (except in the Treasury bill auction); that trespassers will be prosecuted; and that no one has the right to obstruct free use of the air by airlines above private land (except that, at one time, alcoholic beverages were not to be served in flights over Kansas).

It is the institution that defines the rules of private property under which agents may communicate and exchange or transform commodities for the purpose of modifying

---

[3] This does *not* mean that an individual's environmental state is autonomous and uninfluenced by others; it means merely that individual skills, knowledge, and willingness to work and buy are not publicly observable —only their consequences are observable.

initial endowments in accordance with private tastes and knowledge. Since all commodity exchange and commodity transformation must be preceded by interagent communication, *property rights in messages are as important as property rights in commodities or ideas.* Thus if stealing can lead to the charge of robbery or burglary, saying "your money or your life" can lead to the charge of attempted robbery. The institution defines the rights of private property which include the right to speak or not speak (you can't say "one hundred" at an auction unless you mean to bid $100), the right to demand payment or delivery, and the right to exclude others from use, that is, to "own." The institution specifies:

a. A *language* $M = (M^1, \ldots, M^N)$ consisting of messages $m = (m^1, \ldots, m^N)$, where m^i is an element of M^i, the set of messages that can be sent by agent i. A message might be a bid, an offer, or an acceptance. The allowable messages M^i for i need not be identical to M^j for j. Thus buyers may tender written bids at an auction, while the seller may have the right to offer or not offer an item for sale, but may not be allowed to bid on his own item or announce a reservation price.

b. A set $H = (h^1(m), \ldots, h^N(m))$ of *allocation rules* for each i. The rule $h^i(m)$ states the final commodity allocation to each i as a function of the messages sent by all agents. Since there may be an exchange of messages which precedes the allocation, m may refer to the final allocation-determining message.

c. A set $C = (c^1(m), \ldots, c^N(m))$ of *cost imputation rules*. The rule $c^i(m)$ states the payment to be made by each agent in numeraire units (money) as a function of the messages sent by all agents. Note that C is redundant in that it could be included in the definition of H, but it will be convenient in many applications (as when there are no income effects) to distinguish between commodity allocations by H and payment imputations by C.

d. A set $G = (g^1(t_0, t, T), \ldots, g^N(t_0, t, T))$ of *adjustment process rules*. In general, these rules consist of a *starting rule* $g^i(t_0, ., .)$ specifying the time or conditions under which the exchange of messages shall

begin, a *transition rule* (or rules) $g^i(., t, .)$ governing the sequencing and exchange of messages, and a *stopping rule* $g^i(., ., T)$ under which the exchange of messages is terminated (and allocations are to begin).[4] For example, an English or progressive auction begins with an announcement by the auctioneer identifying the item to be offered for sale and calling for bids. The starting rule might also allow the seller to specify a reservation price. The transition rule requires any new bid to be higher than the previous standing bid. The stopping rule requires that no new overbid is obtained in response to a call from the auctioneer (for example, three calls for a "final" bid). In an unstructured bilateral negotiation, there is a starting "rule" in that bargaining cannot begin until there is a first bid or offer, and stops with an acceptance. Disputes concerning the negotiation process, and its outcome, are settled under the common law of contracts.

Each agent i's *property rights* in communication and in exchange are defined by $I^i = (M^i, h^i(m), c^i(m), g^i(t_0, t, T))$, which specifies the messages that i has the right to send; the starting, transition, and stopping rules which govern these communication rights; and finally the right to claim commodities or payments in accordance with the outcome rules that apply to messages. A microeconomic *institution* is defined by the collection of all these individual property right characteristics $I = (I^1, \ldots, I^N)$.

It should be noted that none of the above rules of an institution need be formal as in a body of written law. A rule can be simply a tradition as, for example, in the Eskimo polar bear hunting party in which the upper half of the bear's skin, prized for its long mane hairs, was awarded to the individual hunter who (at great personal risk) was the first to fix his spear in the dangerous prey (Peter Freuchen, 1961, p. 53.)

---

[4]Note that the arguments of $g^i(t_0, t, T)$ are public "goods" or characteristics, i.e., the rules governing communication are common to all participating agents. Hence, when comparing the performance of alternative institutions, we are comparing alternative common outcome states.

3. A Microeconomic System

A microeconomic environment together with a microeconomic institution defines a *microeconomic system,* $S = (e, I)$.

B. Agent Behavior

1. Outcome Behavior

A microeconomy is closed by the behavioral actions (choices) of agents in the message set M. In the static description of an economy we are concerned only with the final outcome choices in M. Thus agent i's *outcome behavior* is defined by a function $\beta^i(e^i \mid I)$ which yields the allocation-determining message m^i sent by agent i with characteristic e^i, given the property rights of all agents defined by I. The conditional-on-I notation in β^i is intended to denote that the behavior function β^i depends upon I, that is, is a member of a class indexed by I. The mapping β^i may represent a single message transmission as in a sealed-bid auction, or it may constitute the final result of an exchange of messages in an iterative process such as a negotiation session in the London gold bullion market which stops to yield transactions only when there is agreement (unanimity) (H. G. Jarecki, 1976). Note that the β^i functions generate the message-sending behavior of agents, which need not be based on preference maximization. The latter is a theory (hypothesis) about behavior that could be false.

The branches of the triangle diagram in Figure 1 (compare Stanley Reiter, 1977) illustrate the conceptual process in which, given the institution, the message m^i depends on agent characteristics e^i, and the messages sent by all i in turn determine, via the institution, the outcomes

$$h^i(m) = h^i[\beta^1(e^1 \mid I), \ldots, \beta^N(e^n \mid I)]$$

$$\text{and} \quad c^i(m) = c^i[\beta^1(e^1 \mid I), \ldots, \beta^N(e^N \mid I)].$$

The import of all this is that agents do *not* choose direct commodity allocations. *Agents choose messages, and institutions determine allocations via the rules that carry messages into allocations.* There is a social process that culminates in exchanges. Every country auc-

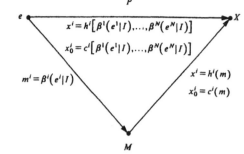

$$e^i = (u^i, \omega^i, T^i), \quad I^i = (M^i, h^i(m), c^i(m), g^i(t_0, t, T))$$

$$e = (e^1, e^2, \ldots, e^N), \quad I = (I^1, I^2, \ldots, I^N)$$

FIGURE 1. A MICROECONOMIC SYSTEM

tion has its own rules and procedures of sale. The New York Stock Exchange specifies the admissible form in which orders to buy or sell shares may be tendered to its broker members by investors—"at the market," limit price, "stop" orders, etc.—and also specifies a detailed list of auction rules governing communication and exchange at each trading post.[5] Within the applicable procedural rules, all markets involve "do-it-yourself" (Robert Clower and Axel Leijonhufvud, 1975) exchange.

2. Response Behavior

In the dynamic or process description of an economy we are concerned with, the exchange of messages in M that precedes the final allocation-determining messages. Agent i's *response behavior* is defined generically by a function f^i in the equation (compare Reiter, 1977)

$$m^i(t) = f^i(m(t-1) \mid e^i, I),$$

---

[5]In retail markets, sellers post offer prices, buyers respond by saying "I'll take it," but the result need not constitute an exchange as when the retailer has a stockout, or the chair is returned to the store after the customer finds that it does not match the living room rug. Institutions vary in the richness and composition of the message space. In stock and commodity markets, the items exchanged are simply defined and well standardized, but the message space is rich in the conditional bid, offer, and acceptance messages that can be sent. In retail markets, commodities are heterogeneous and rich in qualitative dimensions, which may help to explain why a price negotiation institution is not used.

which gives i's message response $m^i(t)$, at sequence point t, to earlier messages $m(t-1)$ by all agents. This response behavior might follow an optimal decision rule, a "rule of thumb," be random, or simply inexplicable. The starting rule triggers the first iteration of f^i, with subsequent messages given by f^i under the transition rules in I. The process stops with $m^i = m^i(T)$ when the stopping rule in I is actuated.

C. *System Performance*

Theorists view the framework we have been describing as one within which alternative resource allocation mechanisms can be evaluated. The traditional performance criterion is Pareto optimality, that is, the relation between outcomes in X (Figure 1) and microeconomic environments "should" be identical to the one provided by the Pareto correspondence criterion (P in Figure 1). Since utility functions and production possibility sets (technologies) are not observable, the evaluation of outcomes in X in terms of the Pareto criterion only has meaning in terms of the Pareto implications of a particular set of *assumptions* about preferences, technology, agent behavior, and institutions. Thus if certain standard conditions on the environment are satisfied, such as continuity and convexity, and if institutions and agent behavior correspond to those of the competitive mechanism, then the classical welfare theorems establish that the Pareto criterion is satisfied. In this literature, a *mechanism* can be defined as a formal theory or model of agent equilibrium behavior within some institution. Thus, in the competitive mechanism, agents maximize utility and profits given prices, and the "institution" (which is unspecified in the sense defined above) is assumed to produce market-clearing prices. An *adjustment mechanism* can be defined as a formal dynamic theory of a trading process for economic agents within some institution as defined above. Examples are the greed process (Hurwicz, 1960) and a stochastic trading process described by Hurwicz, Roy Radner, and Reiter (1975). In the latter, agents choose offers according to a fixed-probability distribution on the set of feasible trades for which utility will not be decreased. These offers are

transmitted to a center where the institutional rules convert those offers which are compatible into binding contracts. The process is then iterated based on the commodity holdings prevailing after this transitional exchange. This process yields probabilistic convergence satisfying the Pareto criterion.

An important concept in the evaluation of a microeconomic system is that of incentive compatibility. In general, an institution's rules are *incentive compatible* if the information and incentive conditions that it provides individual agents are compatible with (i.e., support) the attainment of socially preferred outcomes such as Pareto optimality ($P.O.$). Specifically, in the theoretical literature, an allocation mechanism is incentive compatible if it yields Nash equilibria that are $P.O.$ This means that the *rules* specified in the *institution* in conjunction with the maximizing *behavior* of agents yields a choice of *messages* which constitute a Nash equilibrium whose *outcomes* are $P.O.$

A point which should be emphasized, because it bears on the relationship between laboratory experiments and the model of Figure 1, is the following. The mapping $h^i[\beta^1(e^1 | I), \dots, \beta^N(e^N | I)]$: $e \to m \to x^i$, is generated by any microeconomy, particularly an experimental microeconomy, provided that we have a methodology for systematically varying the elements of E (and also I, if institutions as variables are to be studied) and observing the consequent elements in M and X. This is important because there may *not* exist in all contexts (or in any) a satisfactory theory or hypothesis allowing derivation of the β^i functions. If we can experiment, then we are not bound to study *only theoretical* systems that carry E into X. Experiments permit stable patterns of behavior in relation to institutions to be identified and to motivate more explicit theories.

II. The Microeconomic Experiment

With the above background it is now possible to attempt to say something coherent about the role of the laboratory experiment in the study of microeconomic sysems. Although the concepts in the (new)^2 welfare economics have been used primarily to explicate a class of exercises in normative theory, my particular version of it in the schema of Figure 1 has been developed for the purpose of defining exercises in *measurement, hypothesis testing,* and the *comparative performance of institutions.*

A. *Field Observations and the Possibility of a Microeconomic Science*

1. *What is Observable?*

It will be useful as a starting point to ask which of the elements that compose the schema of Figure 1 are observable (in principle) in the field. Among the observable elements of an economy are (*i*) the list of agents, (*ii*) the list of physical commodities and resources, (*iii*) the physical commodity and resource endowments of individual agents, (*iv*) the language and property right characteristics of institutions, and (*v*) outcomes. What is not observable are (*vi*) preference orderings, (*vii*) technological (knowledge, human capital) endowments, and (*viii*) agent message behavior $\beta^i(e^i \mid I)$, $i = 1, 2, \dots, N$. These last elements are not observable because they are not only private, but to a degree *unrecorded*. Willingness to buy (preferences) and willingness to produce (technology and preferences) can at best only be inferred from agent point actions in the message space. Often we cannot even observe point messages, for example, we may know allocations and prices, but not all bids. In any case, we cannot observe the message behavior *functions* because we cannot observe (and vary) preferences.

As already noted, by making assumptions about preferences, technology, and behavior, we can "test" the logical consistency of such assumptions with the Pareto criterion. The empirical content of the assumptions, such as the monotonicity and convexity of preferences, tend to reflect idealizations, if not caricaturizations, of our *introspective* personal experience as economic agents.[6] But logical completeness laid upon a base of casual introspective "observations" cannot be sufficient to give us an understanding of

the processes we would like to study. There is a vast difference between coherent conjecture (theory) and "true" (i.e., nonfalsified) knowledge of an observed process. If outcomes should turn out to be *P.O.* in the presence of certain institutions, we would like to know if we have predicted this property for the right reasons. If outcomes are not *P.O*, then it would be scientifically irresponsible not to be curious as to which part(s) of our theory is wrong and how to modify it.

2. *What Would We Like to Know?*

In terms of the schema of Figure 1 we would like to know enough about the economic environment, and about agent behavior in the presence of alternative institutions, to be able to classify institutions according to the mapping they provide from environments into outcomes. Are some institutions dependable producers of *P.O.* allocations? If so, how robust are these results with respect to changes in the environment? Do some institutions perform well for only certain classes of environments? If an institution performs well, are all its property right rules essential to this performance or are some redundant? Are some rules redundant for most environments, but become important under contingency conditions that involve unlikely changes in the environment?[7] These are just the tip of the great iceberg of questions that one would like to pose with some prospect of obtaining answers that are replicable, and (ultimately) insightful due to their theoretical coherence.

3. *Learning by "Listening to the Radio Play"*

Econometrics is and has been the mainstay of our attempts to fashion tools that enable us to learn what we would like to know. These tools have been developed primarily on the premises that (*i*) economics is a nonexperimental, or under certain limited cir-

---

[6] In this regard, it has not been clear that being an economic agent has had any advantages in the scientific study of economic behavior.

[7] For example, there are discretionary contingency conditions under which trading in a particular security is suspended for a time on the New York Stock Exchange, while on the Chicago Board of Trade, trading in a commodity is closed for the remainder of the day if price rises or falls from the previous day's close by a specified amount.

VOL. 72 NO. 5 *SMITH: EXPERIMENTAL MICROECONOMIC SYSTEMS* 929

cumstances a field experimental, science, and (*ii*) preferences and technologies are not directly observable or controllable. It follows immediately from the discussion above that these premises prevent us from answering the most elementary scientific questions. What we can do with the tools of econometrics is the following: (*i*) We can specify a model of a market or markets based upon certain observable characteristics of the operant institution, on certain assumptions about preferences and/or technology, for example, Cobb-Douglas, fixed coefficients, *CES*, translog, etc., and upon some assumption about behavior, for example, static maximization of utility and/or profit. (*ii*) Using one of several different estimation procedures with different statistical properties, provided that the model is at least partially "identified," we can estimate, from data on outcomes, all or a subset of the parameters defined by the particular model that was specified. In other words, we can measure certain preference and/or technology parameters (income and substitution coefficients) and the effect of certain institutional rules (Did state law require or not require licensing? Did it prohibit or allow advertising by optometrists, etc.?). Furthermore, within the specifications of the model (the maintained hypothesis), we can test particular hypotheses about elasticities and income effects. Rarely are we able to obtain a test of the model specification. Hence, an econometric model provides a mapping from specifications into conclusions about preferences, technology, and institutions. Insofar as the conclusions are sensitive to the specifications, we are left with scientific propositions that are open-ended with respect to the environment, institutions, and agent behavior. Furthermore, since parameter identifiability and the properties of estimators depend upon model specification, the particular model chosen inevitably must be influenced partly by the technical requirements of the methodology and not only the scientific objectives of the exercise.

But these limitations of conventional econometric methodology have not foreclosed a positive contribution, which has been to allow us to deduce a great deal more information on economic structure from nonexperimental data than would otherwise be possible. Over twenty-five years ago, Guy Orcutt characterized the econometrician as being in the same predicament as that of an electrical engineer who has been charged with the task of deducing the laws of electricity by listening to a radio play. To a limited extent, econometric ingenuity has provided some techniques for conditional solutions to inference problems of this type.

But the econometric methodology is on particularly thin ice when the following scenario applies: Based on introspection, some casual observations of some process, and a contextual interpretation of the self-interest postulate, a model is specified and then "tested" by estimation using the only body of field data that exists. The results turn out to be ambiguous or call for "improvements" (some coefficients—for example, income—have the "wrong" sign or are embarrassingly close to zero), and now one is tempted to modify the model in ways suggested by these results to improve the fit with "reasonable expectations." Any tests of significance within the new model specification now become hopelessly confused if one attempts to apply it to the same data.[8,9]

The controlled field experiment is a recent development designed to relax some of the limitations of econometric methods when applied to the traditional sources of economic data. But the field experiment does not enable us to study the effect of controlled

---

[8]In effect, the whole process becomes an exercise in fitting a particular belief system to field data by manipulating model specification and perhaps estimation methods. There is nothing to prevent exactly the same procedure from being applied to experimental data. The difference is that one can always run another set of experiments. Also, the whole process, including the experiments, are subject to replication by another scholar. The skeptic with a different belief system can seek a set of "crucial" experiments that would enable the opposing hypotheses to be tested.

[9]Within professional econometrics, criticism such as this of naive econometric practice stretches back at least three decades, but recently the critique has grown louder, and constructive formal approaches have been offered in which, for example, the reporting procedures delineate the range of inferences that can be drawn from a given range of model specification (see Edward Leamer and Herman Leonard, 1981).

changes in preferences and/or technology. It does, however, provide important forms of control over institutional rules. Thus in a peak-load pricing experiment it is possible to vary pricing parameters and methods over a much larger range, and to sample scientifically a larger range of income and demographic variables than would occur naturally in ordinary consumer data obtained by "listening to the radio play." It is also possible to experiment with new and innovative pricing institutions. But one is still without control over preferences, and still unable directly to observe preferences and therefore behavior as a mapping from preferences to messages. That is, it is still necessary to interpret the data in terms of (i) assumptions about preferences, and (ii) assumptions about behavior (for example, static or dynamic maximization subject to constraint). Hence, it is *not possible* to evaluate alternative institutions in terms of their ability to produce optimal outcomes. But to the extent that one is interested in observed demand behavior (which may be underrevealing) with improved controls rather than evaluating the performance of institutions under alternative preference configurations, these limitations are not a valid criticism of the field experiment.

B. *Laboratory Experiments with Microeconomic Systems*

The fundamental objective behind a laboratory experiment in economics is to create a manageable "microeconomic environment in the laboratory where adequate control can be maintained and accurate measurement of relevant variables guaranteed" (Wilde, p. 138). "Control" and "measurement" are always matters of degree, but there can be no doubt that control and measurement can be and are much more precise in the laboratory experiment than in the field experiment or in a body of Department of Commerce data.

How laboratory experiments deal operationally with the problems of control, measurement, experimental design, and hypothesis testing is best seen by examining individual experimental studies. Attention

here will be confined to a somewhat more abstract discussion of the principles and underlying precepts of experimental economics. In particular, the concept and objectives of a laboratory experiment will be related to the microeconomic model, consisting of an environment, an institution, and agent behavior, illustrated in Figure 1.

Returning to the question of what we would like to know tells us what we want to be able to accomplish with experiments. First we want to be able to control the elements of $S = (e, I) = (u^i, T^i, \omega^i; M^i, h^i, c^i, g^i)$. To control a variable means that we can fix and maintain it at some constant level, or, alternatively, set it at different levels across different experiments or at different points of time in the same experiment. Secondly, we want to be able to observe and measure the message responses of agents, m^i, and the outcomes h^i and c^i resulting from these messages. We want to measure outcomes because we want to be able to evaluate the performance of the system, S. We want to measure messages because we want to identify the behavioral modes, $\beta^i(e^i | I)$, revealed by the agents and test hypotheses derived from theories about agent behavior.

In order to accomplish these objectives, laboratory experiments must satisfy several conditions, which will be referred to as *precepts* of experimental economics. They are *not* to be regarded as self-evident truths, and therefore are not properly to be considered as axioms.[10] However, with the modifications proposed by Wilde, they do constitute a proposed set of sufficient conditions for a valid controlled microeconomic experiment. Applying (or testing) these conditions in the

---

[10] In reference to the precept parallelism (see subsection 1.f below), this has been misunderstood or misread as follows: "Smith treats this 'parallelism' virtually as an axiom, while Kagel and Battalio go even farther and extend the principle not only beyond the limits of the laboratory but across the boundaries of the human species as well" (John Cross, 1980, p. 403). The word precept rather than axiom was used to guard against any notion that these precepts were self-evident truths, rather than key conditions for experimental validity. The truth of these precepts can only be established empirically. It is hard to find an experimentalist who regards anything as self-evident, including the proposition that people prefer more money to less.

laboratory (and in parallel field studies) requires some skill and thoughtful consideration. The issues that have motivated these precepts are important to have in mind when designing and executing laboratory experiments.

1. Sufficient Conditions for a Microeconomic Experiment

Control over preferences is the most significant element distinguishing laboratory experiments from other methods of economic inquiry. In such experiments, it is of the greatest importance that one be able to state that, as between two experiments, individual values (or derivative concepts such as demand or supply) either do or do not differ in a specified way. This control can be exercised by using a reward structure and a property right system to induce prescribed monetary value on (abstract) outcomes.

a. *Precept 1: Nonsatiation.* The concept of induced valuation (see the examples in subsection c below) depends upon (compare my 1976b article):

Nonsatiation: Given a *costless* choice between two alternatives, identical (i.e., equivalent) except that the first yields more of a reward medium (for example, U.S. currency) than the second, the first will always be chosen (i.e., preferred) over the second, by an *autonomous* individual. Hence utility, $U(V)$, is a monotone increasing function of the monetary reward, $U' > 0$, where V is dollars of currency.

b. *Precept 2: Saliency.* In order that subject rewards in a laboratory experiment have motivational relevance such rewards must be associated indirectly with the message actions of subjects. This is called

Saliency: Individuals are guaranteed the right to claim a reward which is increasing (decreasing) in the goods (bads) outcomes, x^i, of an experiment; individual property rights in messages, and how messages are to be translated into outcomes are defined by the institution of the experiment.

This statement of saliency modifies that of Wilde (1980) which relates rewards to the decisions of subjects. This modification is necessitated by the distinction made here between outcomes and messages. *In both the* *field and the laboratory, value is induced on messages by the institution* whose rules state how messages are to be translated into valuable outcomes. In the field outcomes are valuable because they have "utility" (i.e., agents have preferences). But in the laboratory we also have to induce value on outcomes with a monetary (or other) reward function. Thus in an experiment, in addition to giving a subject certain property rights defined by the institution under study, we must also give the subject a property right to rewards that are related appropriately to the realized experimental outcomes, x^i.[11]

[11] It is sometimes said that the use of currency to induce value on abstract outcomes in a laboratory experiment may be an artificial procedure peculiar to experimental methodology and is not the same thing as having "real preferences." Those who raise this question seem not to realize that all economic systems produce forms of intangible property on which value is induced by specifying the rights of the holder to claim money or goods. All financial instruments, including shares, warrants, and fiat money itself, have value induced upon the instruments by the bundle of rights they convey. Subject rights to claim money in return for their purchase and sale of intangible experimental "goods" are defined by the experimental instructions. This procedure is exactly of the form used by the airlines when, for promotional purposes, they issued travel vouchers to their passengers. These travel vouchers conveyed a legal right to redemption by the bearer as a cash substitute in the purchase of new airline tickets. As a consequence, value was induced on these travel vouchers and they soon commanded an active market price in all busy airports. An airline ticket itself is an abstract claim. It is *not* equivalent to a seat on an airplane. It is a right to *claim* a seat under specified conditions, for example, you can't have a seat if none is available, or if you insist on carrying oversize luggage, or if you want to board with your pet tiger, or if you are carrying a Colt 45, and so on. An important part of the property right rules of any institution is the specification of the conditions under which intangible goods can be redeemed in terms of other intangibles or commodities. Arrangements like these were invented in the context of *field* institutions eons before I or anyone thought of doing laboratory experiments. What we experimentalists have done is to adapt these ingenious institutions to the problem of inducing controlled preferences in experimental microeconomies. Obviously, the reward medium may make a difference, but this is easily studied as a treatment variable by anyone who is haunted by the thought that it is important. But to argue that preferences based on cash-induced value is somehow different than homegrown preferences over commodities is also to argue that preferences among intangible instruments in the field are also somehow different than commodity preferences.

Not all rewards are salient. At the University of Arizona we pay subjects \$3 "up front" for agreeing to participate and arriving at the laboratory in time for the experiment. A second payment equal to a subject's cumulative earnings over the experiment, based on experimental outcomes, is paid when he/she leaves the laboratory. This second payment is a salient reward; the first is not.

c. *Examples and Discussion.* A few examples will be offered to illustrate the application of these precepts, and their role in driving an experimental economy.

Example 1. Suppose each of N subject agents are assigned the values $V_1, V_2, \ldots, V_N$ in dollars representing the currency redemption value of one unit of an abstract commodity to be sold at auction. The instructions to each subject state that the winner of the item at auction, say individual w, will have the unqualified right to claim $V_w - p$ dollars from the experimenter where p is the auction purchase price. Hence each i will have an incentive to pay as little as possible and yet win the item, but in no case pay in excess of V_i. If we assume that agents are numbered so that $V_1 > V_2 > \cdots > V_N$, then this ordered array of values represents the discrete induced (Marshallian) demand for units of the item, the supply of which is inelastic at 1.

Example 2. Consider the problem of inducing specified conditions of demand or supply on individual subjects in an isolated experimental market. Let subject buyers $i = 1, 2, \ldots, n$ each be given reward schedules $V_i(x^i)$ representing the currency redemption value of x^i units of an abstract commodity acquired by subject i in an experimental market. If x^i units are acquired by subject i, he/she has the right to claim $V_i(x^i)$ units of currency less the purchase cost of the x^i units, where $V_i(x^i)$ is increasing and concave in x^i. Demand is defined as the maximum quantity that can be purchased beneficially as a function of a given hypothetical price, p. Hence, if i purchases x^i units at the fixed price p, then i's currency earnings are given by $\pi_i(x^i) = V_i(x^i) - px^i$. If i's utility function for currency is $U_i(\pi_i)$, then from precept 1 subject i will wish to maximize $U_i[V_i(x^i) - px^i]$. An interior maximum results if and

only if $(V_i' - p)U_i' = 0$, or $x^i = V_i'^{(-1)}(p)$, since $U_i' > 0$ and $(V_i' - p)^2 U_i'' + U_i' V_i'' = U_i' V_i'' < 0$.

This reward procedure induces the prespecified demand $V_i'^{(-1)}(p)$ on subject i. Hence, the experimentally controlled market demand is $\sum_{i=1}^{n} V_i'^{(-1)}(p)$ independent of the U_i, that is, we do not have to observe or know the U_i functions. In terms of my previous definition of a microeconomic environment, the market consists of two commodities, money x_0^i and one "good," x^i. In outcome space utility has the no-income-effects form $u^i(x_0^i, x^i) = U_i[x_0^i + V_i(x^i)]$ to be maximized subject to a budget constraint $\omega^i = x_0^i + px^i$ where the endowment $\omega^i = 0$, and $u^i = U_i[-px^i + V_i(x_i)]$.

Similarly on the supply side, let $j = n + 1, \ldots, N$ subject sellers be given increasing convex cost functions $C_j(x^j)$, and, assuming x^j units are sold at price p, let j be allowed to claim cash earnings equal to $\pi_j = px^j - C_j(x^j)$. If utility for money is $U_j(\pi_j)$, then j will want to maximize $U_j[px^j - C_j(x^j)]$ which implies the inverse marginal cost supply function $x^j = C_j'^{(-1)}(p)$. Total supply is then $\sum_{j=n+1}^{N} C_j'^{(-1)}(p)$, and is controlled by the experimenter through the choice of the C_j functions.

The induced total demand $\sum_{i=1}^{n} V_i'^{(-1)}(p)$ and total supply $\sum_{j=n+1}^{N} C_j'^{(-1)}(p)$ become flows per period in experiments conducted over a sequence of periods in which the valuation and cost schedules for each individual are repeated in each period. If p is a competitive equilibrium (*C.E.*) price, then the cash reward per period for each buyer (seller) is the "consumer's" ("producer's") surplus for each buyer (seller). Consequently, each experimental subject has the monetary equivalent of the motivation that we interpret as applying to economic agents in any market outside the laboratory.

Example 3. Let each subject i be given an increasing quasi-concave function (in tabular form) specifying currency receipts, $V^i(x_1^i, x_2^i)$, that can be claimed by i for terminal quantities of two abstract goods (x_1^i, x_2^i). Then i's unknown utility for currency $U_i(\pi_i)$ induces utility $u^i = U_i[V^i(x_1^i, x_2^i)]$ on the Euclidean point (x_1^i, x_2^i). These claim rights induce on subject

i the experimentally controlled indifference map given by the level contours of $V^i(x_1^i, x_2^i)$, independent of i's utility of money. That is, if $U_i' > 0$, i's marginal rate of substitution of x_2^i for x_1^i is given by[12]

$$dx_2^i/dx_1^i = -U_i'V_1^i/U_i'V_2^i = -V_1^i/V_2^i.$$

These examples all apply to classical environments (no externalities), but this should not be misread to mean that the methodology is similarly restricted.[13] Thus in example 3, the induced value function for i might be $V^i(x_1^i, X_2)$ where X_2 is a public good (common outcome) for all individuals (see my 1979 article); or induced value could be $V^i(x_1^i, x_2^i, x_2^j)$ if j's holding of good 2 is an externality to i; or induced value might be $V^i(x_1^i, \Sigma_{k=1}^N x_2^k)$ if the total quantity of good 2 is an externality for i. One's ability to induce any arbitrary pattern of valuation (including "altruistic" interdependence) is limited only by the imagination in inventing the appropriate set of claim conditions.

Three qualifications to the nonsatiation precept have been discussed by myself elsewhere (1980) under the heading of *complexity*. These qualifications arise because the subjects in an experiment are drawn from the population of economic agents and therefore can be expected to have all the characteristics of such agents. Two of these qualifications stem from the adjectives "costless" and "autonomous" in Precept 1, and provide the justification for introducing Precepts 3 and 4 below.

The first qualification, which could sever the link between monetary rewards and control over preferences in a laboratory experiment, is the possibility that economic agents may attach nonmonetary subjective cost (or value) to the process of making and executing individual decisions. The subjective cost of transacting, that is, the cost of thinking, calculating, and acting (compare Jacob Marschak, 1968), need not be inconsequential. In example 1, suppose the values $V_1, V_2, \ldots, V_N$ are drawn from a probability distribution known by the subjects. Suppose subject k receives a value V_k which almost certainly is among the lowest values drawn. This individual is very unlikely to win the item auctioned, and may be poorly motivated to take the auction seriously. If there is a cost to thinking and calculating one's bidding strategy, this effort may not be expended when a "low" value is assigned. Similarly, if it is arduous for an individual to monitor quotations, make counteroffers, and execute transactions in a continuous auction, then willingness to pay may not be measured by the marginal induced value function. Note that this description of the problem suggests that transactional effort is more naturally related to agent messages, m^i, than to institutionally determined outcomes, x^i.

These considerations can be illustrated in terms of the example 2 above. Suppose that subject buyer i who receives a monetary reward π_i must send m^i messages (for example,

[12]As noted in my 1973 paper, this induced-value procedure could be used to study general pure exchange equilibrium between two trading groups with or without a medium of exchange ("stage" money). For example, one could give $N/2$ subjects the endowments $\omega^i = (\omega_1^i, 0)$, $i = 1, 2, \ldots, N/2$, and the remaining $N/2$ subjects the endowments $\omega^j = (0, \omega_2^j)$, $j = (N/2)+1, \ldots, N$, and thus set up "Edgeworth Box" trading between two groups each with homogeneous tastes within the group. To quote from my 1973 paper, "Production and a producers market could be added by introducing production function tables and trading in claims on labor input endowments.... But note that in such a general equilibrium model one would not have to introduce profit tables for producer subjects, as in partial equilibrium oligopoly experiments.... The (payoff) functions of 'consumer' subjects would be the entire driving force of the economy, inducing value, through production, upon artificial labor input endowments" (p. 23).

[13]As, for example, when it is incorrectly claimed that an important assumption by experimentalists is that "individuals are motivated by self-interest" (John Chamberlin, 1979, p. 162), and, consequently, experiments "exclude important parts of 'political reality' in order to achieve internal validity" (p. 164). Nonsatiation requires people to prefer more money to less, whether they want to spend it, burn it, or give it to charity. Given nonsatiation, if we want to study the effect of preferences with the property that A gets positive (negative) satisfaction out of B's consumption, then we simply induce that preference property on A. When great care is used in an experiment to make induced value be the primary source of motivation, it is *not* for the purpose of making sure that subjects have a self-interested motivation; it is for the purpose that we *know* what were the preference patterns of the subjects in the experiment. It is not only fitting, but mandatory, that such preferences be interdependent if that is the purpose of the experiment.

bids) to obtain the reward π_i. The reward is commodious, but messages require discommodious effort. Assume the utility of money-with-effort is $U^i(\pi^i, m^i)$ where U^i is increasing in π_i but decreasing in m^i. Now let the purchase quantity depend on the messages sent according to the institutional rules, so that $x^i = h_i(m^i)$. Individual i now makes a costly choice by choosing m^i to maximize $U^i\{V_i[h_i(m^i)] - ph_i(m^i), m^i\}$. At a maximum we have $(V_i' - p)h_i'U_1^i + U_2^i = 0$, and the expression for induced demand becomes

$$x^i = V_i'^{(-1)}\left(p - U_2^i/U_1^i h_i'\right) < V_i'^{(-1)}(p)$$

if $U_2^i < 0$, $h_i' > 0$. It follows that if there is a disutility associated with messages in the experimental task (i.e., with transacting through the institution to obtain outcomes), the induced demand is lower than in the absence of such a cost.[14]

d. *Precept 3: Dominance.* A condition sufficient to guarantee that we have not lost control over preferences has been suggested by Wilde (1980), namely,

> *Dominance*: The reward structure dominates any subjective costs (or values) associated with participation in the activities of an experiment.

This precept is suggested by the fact that the most common means of rendering nonmonetary task utilities inconsequential is to use payoff levels that are judged to be high for the subject population. The principle here can be seen by letting α be a scale parameter that determines reward level in the induced demand example. Then utility becomes $U^i\{\alpha V_i[h_i(m^i)] - \alpha ph_i(m^i), m^i\}$ and the resulting demand is $x^i = V_i'^{(-1)}\{p - U_2^i/U_1^i h_i' \alpha\}$. As α increases demand ap-

proaches $x^i = V_i'^{(-1)}(p)$ provided that $lim_{\alpha \to \infty} U_2^i/U_1^i h_i'\alpha = 0$. A sufficient condition for the latter is that the marginal rate of substitution U_2^i/U_1^i be nonincreasing in α.[15]

But high payoff levels are not the only means of satisfying the dominance precept. A second procedure is to pay a small "commission," say five or ten cents, for each subject's transaction.[16] For example, in the induced demand illustration if the "commission" is β, utility is $U^i\{V_i[h_i(m^i)] - (p - \beta)h_i(m^i), m^i\}$, and demand is $x^i = V_i'^{(-1)}(p - \beta - U_2^i/U_1^i h_i') \cong V_i'^{(-1)}(p)$ if $-\beta \cong U_2^i/U_1^i h_i'$. Actually β can be thought of as a type of "nonsalient" reward in which the objective is to compensate for transactions cost and thus allow theories which abstract from transactions cost to be tested.[17]

e. *Precept 4: Privacy.* The second qualification to the nonsatiation precept which carries a potential for losing control over

---

[14] This suggests a kind of "principle of indeterminacy" of induced preference," i.e., we know what are the induced preferences in a given experiment only within a margin of error which is determined by the subjective costs of individual choice in the message space. Although experimentalists have devised various ways of finessing this margin of error, one should always have the question of dominance (see below) in mind when designing and running experiments. Since these subjective costs are part of the cost of operating an institution, they should be viewed, not as a nuisance, but as part of the problem of comparative institutional analysis.

[15] An early path-breaking experimental study of the binary choice, or Bernoulli trials, game by Siegel (1961) systematically varied reward level. The results showed an increase in the proportion of reward maximizing choices when the reward level was increased for a constant task complexity. Furthermore, when the task complexity was increased holding reward level constant, this treatment reduced the proportion of reward maximizing choices.

[16] Plott and I (1978, pp. 143–44) report two experiments with identical induced supply and demand conditions but one experiment paid a commission in addition to earned surplus, while the second paid only earned surplus. In the first experiment (#3, p. 143), volume was always below (17–18 units) the competitive equilibrium quantity (20 units) while in the second experiment (#4, p. 144) volume was 19 units in one, and 20 units in seven of eight trading periods. An alternative to commissions has been used by myself and Arlington Williams (1981b) in which the design permits a range of *C.E.* prices to be defined. Within this range, trades with positive gains between all intramarginal buyers and sellers are possible, and each individual reveals his/her supply price of transacting.

[17] A third procedure can be directly inferred from the Siegel (1961) results, namely to design the procedures, displays and computing aids of an experiment so as to make the experimental task as simple and transparent for the subject as is possible without, of course, compromising the essential features of the institution under study. That is, task complexity may be an important part of the *difference* between two institutions in which case such features must be preserved. But if a computing or display aid is used to simplify the subject's task in experiments comparing two institutions, one should use the same aid in both institutional treatments.

VOL. 72 NO. 5   *SMITH: EXPERIMENTAL MICROECONOMIC SYSTEMS*   *935*

preferences is the fact that individuals may not be autonomous own-reward maximizers. Interpersonal utility considerations may upset the achievement of well-defined induced valuations. Thus subject i's utility may depend upon both i and j's reward, or $U^i[\pi_i, \pi_j] = U^i[V_i(x^i) - px^i, V_j(x^j) - px^j]$ in the induced demand example. If this "consumption" externality condition prevails, then i's induced demand will not be independent of j's demand. However, this kind of interdependence is effectively controlled by the experimental condition of "incomplete" information, first defined and studied by Siegel and Fouraker (1960) in experimental studies of bilateral bargaining. Under incomplete information subjects are informed only as to their own payoff contingencies. This leads to a precept that, following Wilde (1980), I call

Privacy: Each subject in an experiment is given information only on his/her own payoff alternatives.

Induced value privacy would be an important experimental condition to reproduce in the laboratory quite apart from the technical requirement of controlling interagent payoff externalities. This is because privacy is a pervasive characteristic, in varying degrees, of virtually all market institutions in the field. Keep in mind that monetary rewards for nonsatiated subjects in the laboratory have the same function that commodity utility indicators (preferences) serve in field microeconomies. In field microeconomies we never observe the preferences of others.[18]

A third qualification to the nonsatiation precept causes no difficulties in inducing value. As with their counterparts in the econ-

omy, experimental subjects may attach "game value" to experimental outcomes (as to messages). Thus winning the item at auction may be joyful quite apart from the satisfaction obtained from possessing or consuming the item. Consequently, in an experiment a make-believe "point" profit $V_i(x^i) - px^i$ may have subjective value $S_i[V_i(x^i) - px^i]$. If S_i is monotone increasing in "points," then such gaming utilities reinforce rather than distort the effect of any explicit reward structure. This qualification would hardly merit mentioning except that it explains why results consistent with maximizing behavior are sometimes obtained in experiments with no monetary rewards. Some evidence indicating that experimental results are less consistent under replication over time, when no rewards or only random rewards are used, is provided in my article (1976b, pp. 277–78).[19]

f. *Precept 5: Parallelism.* Nonsatiation and saliency are sufficient conditions for the existence of an experimental microeconomy, that is, motivated individuals acting within the framework of an institution, but they are not sufficient for a *controlled* microeconomic experiment. For this we also must have dominance and privacy, since individuals may experience important subjective costs (or values) in transacting, and may bring invidious, egalitarian, or altruistic cannons of taste to the laboratory from every day social economy. Precepts 1–4 permit us to study laboratory microeconomic environments in which real economic agents exchange real messages through real property right institutions that yield outcomes redeemable in real money.

Insofar as we are only interested in testing hypotheses derived from theories, we are done, that is, Precepts 1–4 are sufficient to provide rigorous controlled tests of our abil-

---

[18]It might be thought that privacy should not apply where subjects function as firms in a market experiment in which they are assigned cost functions since costs can be observed from corporate published records in the field. But this is not a correct interpretation because assigned (marginal) cost functions in an experiment represent well-defined willingness-to-sell schedules, and subject earnings (exclusive of "commissions") exactly measure realized producer's surplus. Corporate records yield accounting costs and accounting profits which differ for different purposes (stockholder reporting, income taxation, regulatory reporting); the relation between such measures and willingness to sell is obscure if not misleading.

[19]If gaming utilities are associated with messages instead of outcomes, the problem may be more serious and is formally equivalent to the problem of subjective transaction cost discussed above, i.e., messages may yield subjective utility rather than disutility and this may compromise our control over induced valuation. Of course, the same phenomena are evident in nonlaboratory economies when people enjoy their jobs, like trading futures, or prefer Dutch to English auctions because of the "suspense" experience in Dutch auctions.

ity as economists to model elementary behavior. Microeconomic theory abstracts from a rich variety of human activities which are postulated not to be of relevance to human economic behavior. The experimental laboratory, precisely because it uses reward-motivated individuals drawn from the population of economic agents in the socioeconomic system, consists of a far richer and more complex set of circumstances than is parameterized in our theories. Since the abstractions of the laboratory are orders of magnitude smaller than those of economic theory, there can be no question that the laboratory provides ample possibilities for falsifying any theory we might wish to test.

Once replicable results have been documented in laboratory experiments, one's scientific curiosity naturally asks if these results also apply to other environments, particularly those of the field. Since economic theory has been inspired by field environments, we would like to know, if we were lucky enough to have a theory fail to be falsified in the laboratory, whether our good luck will also extend to the field. Even if our theories have been falsified, or if we have no theory of certain well-documented behavioral results in the laboratory, we would like to know if such results are transferable to field environments.

A sufficient condition for this transferability of results can be summarized as a final precept (compare my 1980 article).

Parallelism: Propositions about the behavior of individuals and the performance of institutions that have been tested in laboratory microeconomies apply also to nonlaboratory microeconomies where similar *ceteris paribus* conditions hold.

Harlow Shapley (1964, p. 67) has applied the term "parallelism" to the similarity of evolutionary steps and attained ends in earth animals, but I use the term more comprehensively to generalize the important conjecture that "as far as we can tell, the same physical laws prevail everywhere" (Shapley, p. 43). The data of astronomy and meteorology, like those of economics, fall into the category of "listening to the radio play," but scientific progress in both astronomy and meteorology

has depended on the maintained hypothesis that the physics of mass motion and the thermodynamic properties of gases studied in laboratory experiments have application to the stars and the climate. The abundance of opportunities to make nonexperimental measurements in astronomy and meterology that have not yet contradicted these physical laws means that this maintained hypothesis is yet to be falsified.

In biology, parallelism means that if tobacco smoke, or injected tobacco tars, produce more cancer tumors in treatment group rats than in control group rats, then the likelihood is increased that the greater incidence of lung cancer in human cigarette smokers is due to the cigarette smoke and not to some spurious characteristic of cigarette smokers. Obviously parallelism does not state that all mammals are subject to the same maladies; that hydrogen atoms exhibit the same excitation state in the sun's interior as on the earth's surface; or that Northern Hemisphere storms are indistinguishable from Southern Hemisphere storms. In each of these cases the appropriate proposition requires narrower *ceteris paribus* conditions. Only man, chimpanzees, and monkeys are susceptible to Type 1 polio virus infection; the excitation state of hydrogen atoms depends on temperature; and Northern Hemisphere meteorological conditions differ from those of the Southern Hemisphere. *Which kinds of behavior exhibit parallelism and which do not can only be determined empirically by comparison studies.*

What parallelism hypothesizes in microeconomy is that if institutions make a difference, it is because the rules make a difference, and if the rules make a difference, it is because incentives make a difference. That is, whatever the context of the particular microeconomy—the laboratory (using induced values), the primary market for U.S. Treasury bills, or the auctioning of scarce job interview slots among Chicago Business School graduates whose bids are denominated in "points," and constrained by a fixed endowment of such points—parallelism says that the incentive effects of different bidding rules are qualitatively the same;

if rule A produces lower bids than rule B in one market, it will do so in other markets.[20] Will these incentive effects be the same quantitatively? The answer is likely to be "no" unless the different microeconomies are comparable in terms of the types of bidders, the stakes involved, and so on. The more narrowly defined is the alleged parallelistic phenomena, the more narrowly defined must be the *ceteris paribus* conditions across the different microeconomies. If one is interested in parameter estimation, as in a field experiment with the negative income tax, with the idea of applying the estimates to a population, then the representativeness of the sample is of obvious importance. But if one is testing a theory which assumes only that economic agents are motivated to bid so as to maximize expected utility, any sample of agents not likely to be saturated in money is sufficient to initiate a program of research. If the theory is not falsified in several replications, then one can begin to ask whether the results generalize to different subject pools and to field environments. But what is most

important about any particular experiment is that it be relevant to its purpose. If its purpose is to test a theory, then it is legitimate to ask whether the elements of alleged "unrealism" in the experiment are parameters in the theory. If they are not parameters of the theory, then the criticism of "unrealism" applies equally to the theory and the experiment. If there are field data to support the criticism, then of course it is important to parameterize the theory to include the phenomena in question, and this will affect the design of the relevant experiments.

The appropriate way to falsify parallelism with respect to some particular aspect of behavior is to show that some replicable property of a theory or institution in a laboratory microeconomy is falsified with field data. A few parallel studies have been reported by John Ferejohn, Robert Forsythe, and Roger Noll (1979), Michael Levine and Plott (1977), and myself (1980). In these cases the results are reassuring in the sense that there are several laboratory findings that appear also to characterize nonlaboratory microeconomies. But more such studies are welcome, and are necessary, if answers of substance are to be provided to questions of parallelism.

In terms of the evidential standards and precedents that have been established in this literature, it is not appropriate to list reasons (unencumbered by documentation) why experimental situations might be different from what one imagines might be important about "real world" behavior (Cross, p. 404). Speculation about a list of differences between two microeconomies (laboratory or nonlaboratory) is not the same thing as showing empirically that the microeconomies exhibit different behavior and that this is because of factors appearing in the list. Nor is it likely that experimentalists will be diverted from their work by "an approach to research in economics alternative to experiments... called the phenomenological approach" in which the leading example cited is that of the discredited[21] "Phillips curve a simple empiri-

---

[20]Parallelism has been criticized because it "specifies *ceteris paribus* conditions without naming the variables which are required to be held constant" (Cross, 1980, p. 404). The answer is that the variables to be held constant are those that were constant in the laboratory experiments whose results are alleged to apply to nonlaboratory microeconomies. Such a list is always well defined in advance by the initiating studies and therefore it is ingenuous to conclude that "Given such broad residual powers to restrict the applicability of the principle, counter-examples to the proposition would certainly be hard to defend" (p. 404). Thus, in experiments that compare the incentive effects of discriminative and competitive auctions (Propositions 3 and 14 below), subjects are drawn from the same subject pools, and induced values are drawn from the same distribution under the same information conditions. Clearly, if preferences and/or the population of bidders is different in two nonlaboratory (or any) environments, these differences may swamp any incentive differences due to the different auction rules. But many experiments have established that some behavioral laws are robust with respect to changes in preferences and the type of subjects, in which case this fact would become the (less restrictive) working hypothesis to be tested in nonlaboratory environments. In the context of parallelism, *ceteris paribus* means the same thing that it does in demand theory when we say that the effect of price on the demand quantity may be dominated by the effect of income if the latter is allowed to vary.

[21]See Robert Lucas (1981) for a discussion of the status of the Phillips curve doctrine. The Phillips curve

cal regularity" (Frank Stafford, 1980, p. 408). It is this type of example that motivated some of us long ago to begin exploring experimental methods.

2. An Example of a Microeconomic Experiment: Two Sealed-Bid Auction Institutions

An example of a simple laboratory experiment will be used to illustrate the definition of a microeconomic system developed in Section I. As noted above nonsatiation and saliency are sufficient to allow such an experiment to be defined.

a. *An Experimental Microeconomy with Two Institutional "Treatments."* Consider experiments in which a single unique item is to be sold in a sealed-bid auction organized under the alternative first and second price sealed-bid auction rules (William Vickrey, 1961).

(*i*) Environment: There are $N > 1$ subject agents. The unique item is offered for sale (by the experimenter) at zero cost (i.e., is offered inelastically). Each i knows that the values V_k for all k are independent drawings from the uniform density $(\bar{V})^{-1}$ on $[0, \bar{V}]$. Initially, each i knows his/her own V_i but does not know V_j, for all $j \neq i$. Hence $e^i = (V_i, \bar{V}, N)$.

(*ii*) Agent property rights in message space: The language M consists of bids in dollars for the unique item. One and only

literature is a good example of the incredible life that an economic system of belief can enjoy in the absence of a rigorous methodology of falsification. The methodology of curve fitting with data which do not change much from year to year elevated the Phillips curve to an "empirical regularity" that would still be riding the crest of "fine-tuned" policy were it not for the fact that "nature" (perhaps aided by such policy) finally gave us the "crucial" national experiment in which both inflation and unemployment were so outrageously high that belief in the tradeoff doctrine was no longer sustainable outside of a coterie of devout disciples. For me, the doctrine expired its last gasp in 1971 when in a lecture by a prominent economist it was concluded that the Phillips curve had shifted and that we now had to accept a higher inflation rate to achieve the targeted unemployment rate. At that point it became clear that the whole doctrine was like that of the earth-centered universe which could accommodate any new observation by a Ptolemic juggling of the epicycle via the device of introducing a "movable eccentric" (Arthur Koestler, 1963, p. 67).

one bid is admissible by each individual. Thus $m^i = b_i$ is i's bid in dollars, $0 \leqslant b_i < \infty$, $i = 1, \ldots, N$. Let the bids be numbered so that $b_1 > b_2 \ldots > b_N$ (assuming no ties). Then $m = (b_1, \ldots, b_N)$ is the set of messages sent by N agents.

(*iii*) Agent property rights in outcome space: I identify two distinct institutions.

The first price auction. Define $I_1 = (I_1^1, \ldots, I_1^N)$, where $I_1^1 = [h^1(m) = 1; \ c^1(m) = b_1]$, $I_1^i = [h^i(m) = 0; \ c^i(m) = 0]$, $i > 1$, that is, the item is awarded to the first (highest) bidder and all other i get nothing; the first bidder pays what he/she bid and all other i pay nothing.

The second price auction. Define $I_2 = (I_2^1, \ldots, I_2^N)$, where $I_2^1 = [h^1(m) = 1; \ c^1(m) = b_2]$, $I_2^i[h^i(m) = 0; \ c^i(m) = 0]$, $i > 1$, that is, the item is awarded to the first bidder at a price equal to the amount bid by the second highest bidder. All others receive and pay nothing.

(*iv*) Agent property rights in rewards: If $i = 1$, the experimenter guarantees the payment $V_1 - b_1$ (or b_2) to agent 1. If $i > 1$, the payment is 0 to i.

b. *Agent Behavior.* Agent behavior carries the environment e^i into bids b_i depending upon the institution I_i. If i is assigned value V_i, then $e^i = [V_i, \bar{V}, N]$ and agent behavior *as observed* is

$$b_i = \beta^i[e^i|I] = \begin{cases} \beta_1^i[e^i], & \text{if } I = I_1, \quad \forall i. \\ \beta_2^i[e^i], & \text{if } I = I_2, \quad \forall i. \end{cases}$$

The information state of the environment also allows a Nash equilibrium $(N.E.)$ *theory* of agent behavior to be specified. If i has constant relative risk aversion r_i (unobserved by the experimenter), that is, the utility of money to i is $[V_i - b_i]^{r_i}$, then individual i's $N.E.$ bid is (see Cox, Roberson, and myself, 1982) given by

$$b^i = \beta^i[e^i|I] = \begin{cases} \dfrac{(N-1)V_i}{N-1+r_i}, & \text{if } I = I_1, \quad \forall i. \\ V_i, & \text{if } I = I_2, \quad \forall i. \end{cases}$$

In the first price auction, the $N.E.$ strategy is to bid a constant proportion of one's value depending upon N and r_i. In the second price auction the $N.E.$ strategy (also a dominant strategy equilibrium) is to submit a bid equal to value, that is, to fully reveal demand independent of N and r_i.

c. *System Performance.* Suppose the experimental economy consists of T trials $t = 1,...,T$. One measure of performance might be the percentage of all awards which were to the highest value bidder (the percentage of $P.O.$ awards), T_P/T, where T_P is the number of auctions in which the highest bidder also had the highest value.

Efficiency can be defined as $V_w(t)/V_h(t)$ where $V_w(t)$ is the value drawn by the winning bidder and $V_h(t)$ is the highest value in auction t. A second measure of performance is mean efficiency across T auctions, $\bar{E} = T^{-1}\Sigma_{t=1}^{T}V_w(t)/V_h(t)$.

III. Types of Microeconomic System Experiments

There are many ways of classifying experiments (Abraham Kaplan, 1964, pp. 147–54). I propose to keep things straightforward in this section by considering only two broad classifications—functional and methodological. The functional classification of experiments follows directly from my definition of a microeconomic system. The methodological classification will be limited to only a few very comprehensive categories which can be readily identified in the experimental economics literature.

A. *A Functional Classification of Experiments*

The universe of "interesting" experiments is defined naturally by the set of all possible or feasible elements of a microeconomic system (i.e., if S_e is the set of all environments, and S_I the set of all institutions, this universe is the product of S_e and S_I). Since an experiment yields observations on elements in X and in M, what classes of experiments can we conduct? We can do experiments in which (A) the environment is a variable or (B) the institution is a variable. Within either of these classes, we can compare system performance (outcomes) or individual behavior (messages). For any environment and institution, we can do experiments which (C) com-

pare outcomes (or messages) with a theory or theories. Essentially hypothesis testing directed at theory falsification is a type of comparison in which one or more sets of outcomes (or messages) in the comparison are predicted by theory(ies). Consequently, in all experimental studies we are in some sense making comparisons—comparing observed outcomes arising from different environmental or "institutional treatment" conditions, or comparing observed with theoretical predicted outcomes.

Examples of experimental studies in which the environment is varied include (*i*) the extensive oligopoly studies by Fouraker and Siegel (1963), and James Friedman and Austin Hoggatt (1980) in which the number of participants and the cost or demand conditions are varied, (*ii*) the speculation experiments of Miller, Plott, and myself (1977), and Williams (1979) in which demand is varied in a cyclical "seasonal" pattern, and (*iii*) the committee decision experiments reported by Morris Fiorina and Plott (1978) in which the committee size and induced preferences were varied. Experiments comparing different institutions of contract include (*i*) studies of the effect of discriminative versus uniform pricing (see Section IV.C) on the bids (messages) submitted and the outcomes in sealed-bid auctions (my 1967 article), (*ii*) a comparison of outcomes in Dutch and English auctions (V. Coppinger, myself, and J. Titus, 1980), and (*iii*) studies of the effect of binding or nonbinding price ceilings or floors in continuous double auction trading (see Section IV.B) (R. Mark Isaac and Plott, 1981a; myself and Williams 1981a).

Studies in which both the environment and the institution are varied include (*i*) a comparison of markets with and without speculation under cyclical demand (Williams, 1979), (*ii*) comparisons of discriminative versus uniform price rules under alternative induced demand conditions (Miller and Plott, 1980), and (*iii*) comparisons of first and second price sealed-bid, and Dutch auctions using different numbers of bidders (Cox, Roberson, and myself, 1982).

Experiments comparing observed outcomes with theoretical outcomes or predictions include (*i*) the bilateral bargaining experiments of Fouraker and Siegel (1963) comparing observed outcomes with the Bowley-Nash theory predictions, (*ii*) the public good experiments reported in my 1979 article comparing observed outcomes with the Lindahl and free-rider theories, and (*iii*) the asset market experiments of Plott and Shyam Sunder (1982) comparing experimental outcomes with the predictions of rational expectations theory.

B. *Methodological Classification of Experiments*

Philosophers of science (see, for example, Karl Popper 1959; Hanson 1969, 1971; Kaplan 1964) have written extensively on scientific methodology, particularly experimental methodology. Although most of this work relates to the physical sciences, the main features apply to any experimental effort. An insightful perspective is provided by considering various kinds of microeconomic experiments in terms of their methodological objectives (compare Kaplan, pp. 147–54).

1. *Nomothetic Experiments — Establishing the "Laws" of Behavior*

These are the law-giving experiments that employ replication and rigorous control to reduce error in testing well-defined hypotheses. Nomothetic experiments provide the most compelling and objective means by which each of us, as scientists, comes to see what others see, and by which, together, we become sure of what it is that we think that we know. It is useful to distinguish between nomo-theoretical experiments, concerned with establishing laws of behavior through a process of testing theories, and nomo-empirical experiments designed to test propositions about behavior that are suggested by observed empirical regularities in field data or pilot experiments.

    a. *The Importance of Theory; When does the Priest Wear Robes?* Theory is fundamental to scientific methodology for three reasons:

(*i*) Theory economizes on the statement of behavioral regularities. It is a shorthand way of summarizing more detailed and complex descriptions. Thus Newton's theory (the inverse square law of attraction) provides a much simpler statement than defining an ellipse and explaining that this is the orbit of a planet around the sun, explaining that the distance traversed by a falling body is proportional to the square of the time of descent, and so on. These and many more terrestrial and solar system observations were shown to be deducible from the simple inverse square law.

(*ii*) Theory brings a coherence—an underlying pattern or rationale—that integrates otherwise diverse observations and phenomena into a single whole. Wo(men) experience this result as a liberating understanding (Eureka!) of the whole that is easier to comprehend, to appreciate, to impart to the uninitiated. Thus plate tectonic theory provides an explanation of the worldwide pattern of earthquake activity, and of volcanic activity; explains why the geology of the continents differ from that of the ocean floor; provides one rather than a hierarchy of anecdotal explanations of mountain formation; and also accounts for geophysical data on the earth's interior. In the space of twenty years, this new (general equilibrium?) theory has ignited a renaissance of interest and research in the geological sciences (see, for example, C. L. Drake and J. C. Maxwell, 1981).

(*iii*) Theory can chart the path to new observations based upon predictions of phenomena or events for which there was previously no special motivation or search. Thus the theory that the late Pleistocene wave of large animal extinctions was due to paleo hunter cultures (Paul Martin, 1967) has accelerated the search for evidence that early man may have predated these extinctions in North America. Similarly, a variety of new particles have been predicted by theory, then discovered, in modern physics.

The crowning success of theory in the physical sciences, which is associated so dramatically with Newtonian physics, has elevated theory to the pinnacle of respect, and theorists to an undeclared priesthood in most of the sciences. Yet theory achieves its scientific importance only when closely allied with observation (and, ultimately, vice versa).

VOL. 72 NO. 5   *SMITH: EXPERIMENTAL MICROECONOMIC SYSTEMS*   *941*

Newtonian mechanics created a scientific revolution, not because of the aesthetic beauty of the inverse square law, but because it acccounted for two distinct bodies of observation: Galileo's experimental law of falling bodies, namely that the distance traversed was proportional to the square of the time of fall; and Kepler's three laws of planetary motion distilled from a lifetime of study of the mass of astronomical observations recorded with astonishing accuracy by Tycho Brahe (Koestler, 1963, pp. 496–509). Newton showed that these (and other) empirical laws were derivable from one theoretical gravitational law of attraction—an intellectual triumph which easily established him as the founder of theoretical physics. But it was Galileo who is associated with the necessity of investigating the *how* of things before attempting to explain the *why* of things, and who thereby was enshrined as the founder of modern physics. "The introduction of this point of view really marks the beginning of modern science, and it is to it that the remarkable scientific developments since the sixteenth century have been largely due" (Millikan, Roller and Watson, 1937, p. 3). That this is a metaphorical image of Galileo has been made clear by modern historians of science. However, as noted by Robert Butts, "It also seems to me true that although Galileo did not invent experimentation, he did most importantly modify the epistemological point of doing experiments" (1978, p. 59).

The Galileo-Kepler laws contained the same information as did Newton's law. What was missing in the former was the nifty but insightful interpretation of the latter.

b. *The Necessity for Replicable Empirical Laws—Would You Scale a Mountain Without a Rope?* The priority importance of Galileo's experimental law to the Newtonian system is evidenced by the countless experiments which later confirmed Newton's theory. Indeed, perturbations in the planet Mercury were inconsistent with the Newtonian system so that it was actually the evidence from experimental mechanics that made Newton credible. Only later was the Mercury puzzle explained by Einstein's relativity theory extending the Newtonian mechanics. Ultimately, sophisticated experiments have confirmed that Newton's theory was only an approximation, albeit a good one at "ordinary" velocities small relative to the speed of light. Hence new ropes have made it possible for physics to scale new heights. But, it is the rope that allows the new position to be sustained, lays the basis for a new ascension, and occasionally sparks a totally new transformation (for example, the influence of the Michaelson-Morely experiment on Einstein).

The history of science by no means implies that rigorous observation must precede theoretical speculation. But it is difficult to get off the ground in the absence of a stable pattern of observations and a frank recognition of the ecclesiastical pretense of theory unsupported by measurement. The genius often attributed to Galileo was the revolutionary idea that if you were curious about how a stone falls, then the thing to do was to try it. From the observation that a stone, dropped from the mast tip of a moving ship, shares the ship's forward motion, he inferred that if the earth moved, surface objects would share the earth's momentum, and would not be left behind as claimed by received (ecclesiastical) theory. It is often said that it was the failure to combine controlled systematic observation with rigorous reasoning that accounts for the failure of science to develop more fully in ancient Greece, China and India (Kaplan, 1964, p. 144–45).

In Section IV below is provided a summary, in proposition form, of some of the candidates for the list of nomothetic results from experimental microeconomy. Any such list must of course be subject to further replication or modification by new experimental evidence.

2. *Heuristic Experiments*

Heuristic or exploratory experiments are used to provide empirical probes of new topics of inquiry. Such experiments are less likely to follow a rigorous design pattern than nomothetic experiments because (a) the objectives may not be as sharply defined by theory or by a hypothesized pattern which is thought to characterize previous experimental results, and (b) the procedural mechanics of the experiment may be new and untested. Heuristic experiments may provide nomotheoretical contributions because they may be fortuitously adequate for distinguishing between two or more hypotheses with very distinct, widely separated, outcome implications; but they may be conducted for no better articulated reason than to just "see what will happen." Although there is widespread scientific prejudice against this latter type of "grubbing in the facts," I think this view is much too rigid and purist, and carries the prospect of needlessly discouraging an important source of new discoveries. Science needs the wings of heuristic experiments as much as the foundational support of nomothetic experiments. It is through exploratory probes of new phenomena that attention may be redirected, old belief systems may be reexamined, and new scientific questions may be asked. The early oligopoly (Hoggatt, 1959) and competitive market (my 1962 article) experiments were of this tentative, exploratory character. An excellent recent example is provided by the Plott and Wilde (1982) experiments dealing with products or services requiring seller diagnosis and recommendation (for example, physicians and repairmen) based on uncertain information.

3. Boundary Experiments

Whenever a theory or an empirical regularity has received replicable support from several independent experimental or other empirical studies, and is thereby established as a behavioral law with some claim to generality, it is natural to ask whether one can design experiments that will test for those extreme or boundary conditions under which the law fails. Kaplan (1964, p. 150) refers to such inquiries as boundary experiments. These experiments have an obviously important function in establishing the limits of generality of a theory, and setting the stage for important new extensions in theory.

A few examples of boundary experiments in economics will help to illustrate the concept. The double auction (see Section IV.B below) is a remarkably robust trading institution for yielding outcomes that converge to the $C.E.$ It achieves these results with a small number of agents, under widely different supply and demand conditions, with each individual agent having strict privacy, that is, the agent only knows his/her own value or cost conditions. Several sets of experiments have been conducted to test the boundary of application of these conditions. One set of experiments (my 1981a article; myself and Williams 1981b) used only one or two sellers (Propositions 5 and 8 below). Only in the one-seller experiments is there a failure to arrive consistently at $C.E.$ outcomes, thus establishing "one" as the limiting number of sellers at which competitive price theory fails under double auction trading.

A one-seller experiment can also be viewed as a boundary experiment testing the limits of applicability of cartel theory. A cartel may fail to achieve monopoly outcomes because of incentive failure or "chiseling" incentives by cartel members; because of internal cartel enforcement problems; or because of external demand uncertainty or strategic countervailing behavior by buyers. An experiment using only one seller controls for all the internal circumstances that can cause a breakdown in cartel agreements. Hence single seller behavior provides the extreme boundary of behavior for a cartel. If one individual has difficulty achieving monopoly outcomes when demand is unknown, within a given exchange institution, then one expects a group of cartel conspirators to have even more difficulty in achieving a monopoly result (Propositions 8 and 9 below).

Another type of boundary experiment is represented by the supply and demand schedules shown in Figure 2. This experimental design has been used to test whether the $C.E.$ tendencies of double auction would continue to hold under rent asymmetries so extreme that at the $C.E.$ all the exchange surplus is earned by the buyers. This was a boundary experiment that failed, that is, the design in Figure 2 yields rapid convergence to the $C.E.$ for an excess supply quantity $(Q_s - Q_d)$ of 5 or 8 units (see my 1965; 1976a articles).

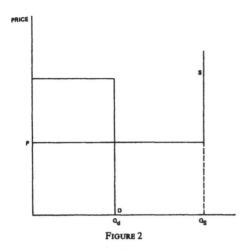

FIGURE 2

IV. Some Institutions and Some Corresponding Experimental "Stylized Facts"

In what follows each of several institutions that have been studied experimentally will be described very briefly, and some of the principal "stylized facts" from these experiments will be summarized in the form of brief empirical propositions. Reference to the original studies will be necessary for readers desiring more comprehensive detail.

There are two basic kinds of auctions—continuous or "oral" auctions, and sealed-bid auctions. In *continuous auctions* an agent may alter his/her bid in response to the bids of others or the failure of a bid to be accepted, that is, an exchange of messages occurs according to specified rules of negotiation prior to each contract. In *sealed-bid auctions* each agent submits one message to a center, which then processes the messages according to publicized rules, and announces aggregate or summary information describing the outcome. The important difference between the two kinds of auctions is the greater information content of the continuous as compared with sealed-bid auctions. Either auction may of course be repeated over time which generates a history of outcome information, but in addition the continuous auction provides a message history between successive contracts. In the experiments reported below the contracting process is repeated sequentially

sometimes for as many as twenty or more consecutive periods.

A. Auctions for a Single Item

From the long history and great variety of auctions (Ralph Cassady, 1967) for the sale of a single item offered by a seller, two continuous auctions, the English and Dutch, and two sealed-bid auctions, the first and second price auction, have been identified for experimental investigation.

English. The process begins with a call for a bid. Once a bid is announced it remains standing until it is displaced by a new bid, which is required to be higher. The process stops with an irrevocable award of the item to the standing bidder when, in the auctioneer's judgment, no new overbid can be elicited. Anonymity is easily preserved by working out a signalling code with the auctioneer (Cassady, 1967, pp. 150–51).

Dutch. The seller's offer price starts at a level judged to be well in excess of what the highest bidder is likely to pay, then lowered in increments by an auctioneer or clock device until one of the buyers accepts the most recent offer to form an irrevocable contract.

First Price. The process begins with a request for bids to be tendered. Privately each bidder submits a bid price. When all the bids have been received by the center, or by the seller, the award is made to the highest bidder at a price equal to the highest bid.

Second Price. This auction is identical to that of the first price, except that the award is made to the highest bidder at a price equal to the second highest bid.

PROPOSITION 1: *Using the subscripts e(English), d(Dutch), 1(First), and 2(Second), and letting E_e, E_d, E_1, and E_2 be measured either by the mean efficiency or the proportion of P.O. awards, then $E_e \cong E_2 > E_1 > E_d$.*[22]

[22] Propositions 1–3 are based on the theoretical analysis and the experimental results (from a total of about 1,000 auctions) reported by Coppinger, myself, and Titus (1980) and Cox, Roberson and myself (1982). Both of these studies were stimulated by the prior theoretical work of Vickrey (1961).

These measures of E vary somewhat depending upon the particular procedure for inducing demand (random from an announced distribution, random from an unannounced distribution, random level of linear demand), but the efficiency ordering appears not to be affected by this procedure.

PROPOSITION 2: *English and second price auctions which are theoretically isomorphic, that is, are subject to the same analysis and which predict identical allocations, appear to be equivalent behaviorally. Dutch and first price auctions which are theoretically isomorphic are not equivalent behaviorally.*

Although English auction prices are higher and the awards slightly more efficient than in the second price auction the difference is not significant. Contract prices in first price auctions are significantly higher, and are more efficient, than in Dutch auctions. This behavioral difference between first price and Dutch auctions can be explained either by a model which postulates a nonmonetary utility for the "suspense of waiting" in the real time Dutch auction or by a model which postulates a systematic underestimate of the Bayes' Rule risk of loss in not stopping the Dutch price decline (Cox, Roberson, and myself, 1982). The second model is consistent with the results of independent experiments testing Bayes' Rule (David Grether, 1980), while the first model is consistent with the reported impression of subjects that they enjoy the "suspense of waiting" in the Dutch auction. Given two theories each predicting prices to be lower in Dutch than in first price auctions, one naturally asks if there is a "crucial"[23] experiment

[23] The quotation marks are used because Hanson shows convincingly that the so-called "crucial" experiment can yield deceptive results. For example, the experiments of Fresnel, Young, and Foucault rejected the hypothesis that the velocity of light in water should be greater than its velocity in air, which was interpreted as implying a rejection of "Hypothesis I," that light consists of particles (rather than waves). As noted by Hanson, the experimental result means either that "light does not consist of high-speed particles, or the assumptions required to give Hypothesis I teeth are (in part or completely) false. One of these assumptions would

that will discriminate between the two theories. In this case a simple such experiment is to replicate an existing set of Dutch and first price auction experiments with all parameters unchanged except that the monetary reward level is doubled. The reported difference between Dutch and first price auction behavior should narrow if the "suspense of waiting" model is correct, while the differences should not narrow if the "Bayes rule underestimation" model is correct.

PROPOSITION 3: *Prices, allocations, and individual bids in the first price auction require the rejection of Nash equilibrium models of bidding behavior based on the assumption that all bidders have the same concave utility function. But the experimental results for $N > 3$ bidders are consistent with a Nash equilibrium model based on the assumption that bidders have power utility functions with different coefficients of constant relative risk aversion.*

All models which achieve tractability by assuming that bidders share the same risk neutral or risk averse utility function flounder on the rocks of predicting that individual bids will be ordered the same as individual values. Consequently, these models predict *P.O.* allocations, whether or not bidders are risk averse, which is not what we observe.

B. *Double Auctions*

The institution most extensively studied by experimentalists has been some version of the double auction (*DA*) rules that characterize trading on the organized security and commodity exchanges. This is because *DA* was one of the first institutions to be studied experimentally, and from the beginning demonstrated "surprising" competitive properties. These properties of *DA* especially recommended its use in testing propositions based on competitive price theory. It is an

be... that light must be either wavelike or corpuscular, but not both.... Every experiment tests, not just an isolated hypothesis, but the whole body of relevant knowledge that is involved by the logic of the problem, the experiment, and the hypothesis" (1969, pp. 253–54).

example of a continuous auction and was probably an outgrowth and generalization of the English auction with origins in Babylon and Rome (Cassady, 1967, pp. 26–29). The following description of *DA* applies to only one of the versions that has been used extensively in experiments. In this description each contract is for a single unit.[24]

Double Auction (Leffler and Farwell, 1963, pp. 186–92). After the market opens an auction for a unit begins with the announcement of a price bid by any buyer or a price offer by any seller. Any subsequent bid (offer) must be at a higher (lower) price to be admissible. Once a bid (offer) has been made public, that is, is "standing", it cannot be withdrawn. A binding contract occurs when any buyer (seller) accepts the offer (bid) of any seller (buyer). The auction ends with a contract. If the standing bid (offer) was not part of the contract (for example, if a buyer other than the one with the standing bid accepted the standing offer), the maker of that bid (offer) is no longer bound to it unless the bid (offer) is now re-entered. Following a contract a new auction begins when a new price bid (offer) is announced. The new bid (offer) may be at any level, and may involve "signalling." This process continues until the market "day" comes to an end.

Although different studies report the use of alternative versions of these *DA* rules, the experimental results do not differ in terms of their equilibrium properties.[25] These propositions are based on the results of perhaps 100 to 150 *DA* experiments reported in the literature.

[24] On the New York Stock Exchange there are also trading post rules governing multiple unit contracts.
[25] The *DA* trading procedure has been programmed for the PLATO computer system (Williams, 1980; myself and Williams, 1982). This program allows subjects in an experiment to negotiate and trade with each other entirely through individual computer terminals. In a comparison of oral with computerized *DA* trading, differences appear to disappear with the use of experienced subjects (Williams, 1980). A comparison of experimental results using four variations on the computerized *DA* rules is reported by myself and Williams (1982). These different rules yield different price dynamics, but do not affect equilibrium or efficiency.

PROPOSITION 4: *Allocations and prices converge to levels near the competitive equilibrium (C.E.) prediction. This convergence is rapid, occurring in three to four trading periods or less when subjects are experienced with the institution (but not the particular induced values).*[26]

Even in the first period of trading, the allocations and price tendencies are generally such as to reject monopoly (monopsony) behavior in favor of the *C.E.* (Isaac and Plott, 1981; my 1962, 1964, 1965, 1976a articles; myself and Williams, 1981a,b; 1982). Repeated "signalling" with high (low) offers (bids) is common, but ineffective.

PROPOSITION 5: *Convergence to C.E. prices and allocations (Proposition 4) occurs with as few as six to eight agents (most experiments have used eight), and as few as two sellers (Smith and Williams, 1981b).*

Many economists express surprise, if not discomfort, when presented with the evidence for Proposition 4 and particularly Proposition 5. The idea that a *C.E.* is an ideal "frictionless" state not likely to be approached in any observable market—and certainly not without a "large" number of agents with its assumed concomitant "price-taking" behavior—is a deeply ingrained belief based on untested theory going back to Cournot. Since Cournot's theory does not specify an institution, it is unclear in what context the theory is supposed to have relevance. As for price-taking behavior, note that every agent in *DA* is as much a price maker (announcing bids or offers) as a price taker (announcing acceptances). Empirically it is now thoroughly documented that this institution exhibits strong *C.E.* tendencies.

PROPOSITION 6: *Complete information on the theoretical supply and demand conditions*

[26] This proposition applies to environments in which supply and demand are stationary over all the periods of an experiment. Work in process suggests that this result may not generalize to environments with period-by-period shifts in demand (Glenn Harrison, Williams, and myself).

946   THE AMERICAN ECONOMIC REVIEW   DECEMBER 1982

of a market (i.e., agent knowledge of the induced values and costs of all agents) is neither necessary nor sufficient for the rapid convergence property in Proposition 4.

That complete information is not necessary is established by the large number of DA experiments that have shown rapid convergence when such information was withheld. That complete information is not sufficient follows from the results of eight experiments, using the "swastika" design of Figure 2. In four of these experiments complete information was withheld; in two, complete information was provided; and in two, the information was incomplete for the first two to three trading periods, and then switched to complete for two additional trading periods. In these experimental comparisons, the incomplete information condition yielded more rapid convergence than the condition of complete information (my 1980 article, p. 357 ff).[27]

PROPOSITION 7: *Price convergence tends to be from above (below) the C.E. price when consumer's surplus is greater (smaller) than producer's surplus (my 1962, 1965, 1976a articles; myself and Williams, 1982).*

PROPOSITION 8: *Experiments with one seller and five buyers do not achieve monopoly outcomes, although some replications achieve the C.E. outcome. Buyers tend to withhold purchases (and repeatedly signal with high bids) giving the seller a reduced profit, especially at the higher prices. This encourages contracts near the C.E. price, but normally at a loss in efficiency due to the withheld demand (my 1981a article).*

---

[27]In this supply and demand design (Figure 2), complete information means that both buyers and sellers are aware of the extreme asymmetry in the gains from exchange at prices near the C.E. Consequently, sellers hold out for higher prices under complete rather than under incomplete information. Similarly, buyers bid higher or accept higher offers, perhaps because of egalitarian motives or because they do not want to risk failing to make a contract if sellers succeed in their effort to maintain prices above unit cost.

This "counterintuitive" result runs roughshod over most belief sysems. But if C.E. theory (as conventionally taught) is questionable, monopoly theory is more seriously questionable: The DA institution yields the C.E. even if the "large" number story is not right, but with DA (also see Propositions 19 and 20 below) monopoly theory goes begging for evidential support.[28]

PROPOSITION 9: *Experiments with four buyers and four sellers in which the sellers (or the buyers) are allowed to "conspire" (i.e., engage in premarket, and between market conversation about pricing strategies) do not converge to the monopoly (or monopsony) outcome; neither do they seem to converge dependably to the C.E. Furthermore, the conspiring group often makes less than the C.E. profit (Isaac and Plott, 1981a; my 1981b article).*

PROPOSITION 10: *Binding price ceilings (floors) yield contract price sequences which converge to the ceiling price from below*

---

[28]Before rejecting the experimental outcomes as "unrealistic," i.e., contrary to your belief system, consider the following points: (A) There is perhaps a tendency to think casually in terms of the perfect information textbook monopoly diagram in which the monopoly outcome seems transparent. But remember that the subject monopolists in Proposition 8 do *not* know their demand curves except as demand is revealed by real subject buyers. (B) Implicit perhaps in monopoly thinking is the assumption of a large number of buyers. Here we have only five buyers, which of course is more than enough to yield the C.E. if there are at least two sellers (Proposition 5). Hence, if you say, "Oh, the result follows because there are only a few buyers," then you have to tell me why a large number is necessary for monopoly but not for a C.E. (C) There is *no* institution in textbook monopoly theory, but there is an implicit assumption that buyers reveal 100 percent of demand, while the seller optimally underreveals supply. Hence, implicit in monopoly theory is an asymmetric processless assumption from which the conclusion is unassailable but trivial.

Proposition 8 is consistent with monopoly theory under random demand, but since this theory predicts either a higher or a lower price than if demand were certain (Leland, 1972, p. 289), this fact is not very satisfying. Also, it is not clear how these "uncertainty" models are related to experiments in which demand is *unknown* by all agents but is stationary. Does the appropriate uncertainty involve randomness in behavior, or sampling theory?

(*above*). If the price ceiling (*floor*) is nonbinding, i.e., if it is above (*below*) the C.E. price, prices converge to the C.E., but along a path which is below (*above*) the price path in a market without a price ceiling (*floor*). If a binding price ceiling (*floor*) is removed, this causes a temporary explosive increase (*decrease*) in contract prices before the C.E. price is approached (Isaac and Plott, 1981a; myself and Williams, 1981a).

The significance of this proposition for price theory is that a binding price control does *not* quickly freeze prices at the control level, and a nonbinding control has demonstrable effects on the dynamics of market price behavior. Neither of these characteristics is part of conventional price theory. My article with Williams (1981a) presents data on the bid and offer distributions, with and without price controls, which show clearly that nonbinding controls affect the bargaining-contracting process, although convergence to the C.E price ultimately occurs. The explosive price changes that Isaac and Plott (1981a) show can follow the removal of a price control is reminiscent of the similar behavior of field observations. However, the latter phenomenon is sometimes explained as due to "pent-up" demand, that is, an accumulation of unsatisfied demand. This cannot be the explanation in the cited experimental markets because all sales are for immediate current period demand. Hence, the observed price dynamics must be due to expectations as they affect current bargaining strategies in the DA institution. Also rejected by the experimental data on nonbinding controls is the hypothesis that the control price will provide a collusive "focal point" for price determination.

PROPOSITION 11: *Asset markets with eight or nine agents converge slowly (eight or more two-period trading cycles) toward the C.E. (rational expectations) price and efficiency determined by the cumulative two-period dividend value of the asset. Convergence is greatly hastened by introducing a first-period "futures" market in second-period holdings, which enables second-period dividend values to be reflected in (or discounted by) period 1*

asset prices more quickly (Forsythe, Palfrey, and Plott, 1982).

PROPOSITION 12: *Asset markets with nine or twelve agents in which the asset yields an uncertain state-contingent dividend, known in advance only by a subset of insiders (3 or 6), converges toward the C.E. (rational expectations) price and efficiency (Plott and Sunder, 1982).*

Propositions 11 and 12 break new experimental ground in studying asset markets under the DA intitution, and demonstrating that the competitive properties of this institution extend to asset markets. The results provide qualified support for the rational expectations theory. In Proposition 11, market replication over time is sufficient to allow private information on divergent induced dividend values across periods to be reflected in asset prices. In Proposition 12, full information on dividend state contingencies by a subset of agents is sufficient to allow asset prices to reflect these dividend values.

Perhaps the most important general feature of the experimental results summarized in all the above DA propositions is the support they provide for what might be termed the Hayek hypothesis: *Markets economize on information in the sense that strict privacy together with the public messages of the market are sufficient to produce efficient C.E. outcomes.* This statement is offered as an interpretation in hypothesis form of what Hayek meant in emphasizing that "the most significant fact about this (price) system is the economy of knowledge with which it operates, or how little the individual participants need to know in order to be able to take the right action..."(Hayek, 1945, p. 35).

C. Sealed-Bid Auctions

There are two types of sealed-bid auctions which apply when there is a single seller offering a specified quantity of a homogeneous commodity in inelastic supply (i.e., without specification of a reservation price).

Discriminative Auction. The process begins with the seller announcing the quantity,

Q, to be offered and requesting that bids be tendered. Each buyer submits a bid (or bids) stating price(s) and corresponding quantity(ies). When the last bid has been received, all bids are arrayed from highest to lowest by price, and the first Q bid units in this ordering are accepted at prices equal to the bid price stated by each successful buyer. A random or proportionality rule is normally used for allocation among tie bids at the lowest accepted price. The process ends with a private communication of the outcome of each individual bid and a public announcement of a truncated summary of the results (as in the auctioning of U.S. Treasury securities); the highest and lowest accepted bid, and the total quantity of bid units that were tendered.

Competitive (or Uniform-Price) Auction. The procedure in this auction is identical to that of the discriminative auction except that the highest Q bid units are all accepted at a *uniform* price equal to the bid price specified by the $Q+1$th (in some versions, the Qth) bid unit.

The discriminative and competitive auctions are multiple-unit generalizations of the first and second price auctions, respectively. A large number of discriminative and competitive auction experiments, conducted under various conditions of induced demand, number of bidders, and quantity offering, have been reported in the literature. These studies form the empirical basis for the following propositions:

PROPOSITION 13: *When all individual values are identical and based on a single draw from a rectangular distribution (made after all bids have been entered) the following results obtain:* [29]

(a) *If $F_C^t(p)$ and $F_D^t(p)$ are the proportions of accepted bids specifying a price of p or higher in auction period t under competitive and discriminative auction rules, respectively,*

then $F_C^t(p) \geqq F_D^t(p)$ *for all t, that is, within the acceptance sets, bids in competitive auctions are at prices at least as high as those in discriminative auctions.*

(b) *Seller revenue in the final ("equilibrium") auction in a sequence is greater in competitive than in discriminative auctions in eight of fourteen paired experiments.* [30]

Proposition 13 is based on thirty-three experiments reported by M. W. Belovicz (1979, p. 314) and myself (1967), with the number of bidders varying from thirteen to thirty-four and each bidder submitting either one, two, or an unspecified number of unit bids.

PROPOSITION 14: *When aggregate induced demand is linear and fixed, but individual private assignments are random (i.e., the assignments are without replacement) and are made prior to the submission of bids, the bids satisfy Proposition 13(a). However, if the slope of the linear induced demand is sufficiently low (i.e., steep) seller revenue is greater in discriminative than in competitive auctions; if the slope of induced demand is increased seller revenue becomes smaller in discriminative than in competitive auctions (Miller and Plott, 1980).* [31]

The ordering property of the bids in Propositions 13 and 14 is consistent with theories showing that when each bidder is a buyer of at most one unit, bidders have an incentive to bid their "true" (or induced) value in competitive auctions but to bid less than this value in discriminative auctions (Vickrey, 1961, 1962). [32]

---

[29] This environment was designed to capture the essential features of the market faced by dealers in U.S. Treasury bills who buy in the primary auction for resale in the secondary market. Dealers buy under bid acceptance uncertainty for resale at an uncertain post-auction price.

[30] Reported incorrectly as 5 in 15 in my 1980 paper, Table 2.

[31] The higher revenue from the discriminative rules when demand is sufficiently steep can be explained as follows: The highest value intramarginal bidders face a high opportunity cost of failing to have their bid accepted. Consequently, they bid more, and the discriminative treatment increases seller rent relative to the case in which demand is less steep and valuations less diverse.

[32] However, it should be noted that in some of the experiments of Proposition 13 and in all of the experiments of Proposition 14, bidders could submit more than a single unit bid.

Since new Treasury security offerings at auction are small relative to the outstanding stock of Treasury securities and the large stock of closely competing private securities, it seems credible to conjecture that the demand for Treasury securities is highly elastic. This suggests the likelihood that the revenue from primary auctions of Treasury securities would be greater in a competitive than in a discriminative auction.

Sealed Bid-Offer (Double) Auctions. Bids are tendered by buyers and offers are tendered by sellers. Experimental markets have examined two different bid-offer rules. (A) $P(Q)$: Each buyer (seller) submits a demand (supply) schedule, that is, specifies a bid (offer) price for each unit demanded (supplied). (B) PQ: Each buyer (seller) submits a single bid (offer) price and corresponding quantity. Under either $P(Q)$ or PQ the bids are then arrayed from highest to lowest by price, and the offers from lowest to highest. A selection algorithm, which incorporates a rule for handling tied bids (offers), determines a single market-clearing price and corresponding quantity. Except for excluded tie bids (offers), bids equal to or greater (offers equal to or less) than this price are accepted. The process ends with a private communication of the outcome resulting from each individual's bid (offer), and a public announcement of the market-clearing price and quantity.

The institution which I call $P(Q)$ above is used on the New York Stock Exchange to obtain the opening price each day in each stock based on the accumulation of buy and sell orders after the previous day's close (J. Hazard and M. Christie, 1964, pp. 177–78). Also it has been proposed that the $P(Q)$ procedure be used in the development of a completely computerized national market for trading all securities (Mendelson, Peake, and Williams, 1979). However, $P(Q)$ has a theoretical "defect," namely it provides an incentive for each agent to underreveal demand (supply), and therefore its outcomes are not *P.O.* The institution which I call PQ corrects this defect. This institution, proposed by Pradeep Dubey and Martin Shubik (1980), has been shown by them to have the property that each *C.E.* is also a Nash equi-

librium and is therefore incentive compatible. Intuitively the all-or-nothing feature of PQ compared with $P(Q)$, enables PQ to neutralize the incentive to strategically "hold back," and is thereby similar to the second price auction (compare Vickrey, 1976, p. 15).

Three institutions, DA with "good" *C.E.* behavioral properties (Propositions 4 and 5); $P(Q)$ with theoretically "poor" incentive properties; and PQ with theoretically "good" incentive properties, have been compared experimentally under conditions in which the environment is held constant while the institutional treatment is varied (my article with Williams, Bratton, and Vannoni, 1982). The results are summarized in the following:

PROPOSITION 15: *Based on the prior empirical performance of DA and theory pertaining to $P(Q)$ and PQ, we expect the efficiency of allocations in these three institutions to be ranked $E[DA] \cong E[PQ] > E[P(Q)]$ and the deviation of prices from the C.E. to be ranked $p[DA] \cong p[PQ] < p[P(Q)]$. The experimental results suggest the contrary observed ordering $E[DA] > E[P(Q)] > E[PQ]$ and $p[DA] < p[P(Q)] < p[PQ]$.*

In terms of the observed experimental outcomes, DA performs (somewhat) better than $P(Q)$, and $P(Q)$ better than PQ. The poor performance of PQ is accounted for by what appears to be a persistent tendency of subject agents to raise their offers (lower their bids) in an attempt to influence price. By comparison with $P(Q)$, this leads to a higher proportion of missed trades because of the block-trading characteristic of PQ. Even with the use of experienced subjects this property of PQ persists, whereas with experience the DA and $P(Q)$ institutions show improved performance.

Sealed Bid-Offer (Double) Auctions: Unanimity Tatonnement. A variation on the $P(Q)$ and PQ institutions called $P(Q)v$ and PQv is the following: After the market-clearing price and quantity has been determined, a *conditional* allocation in the form of accepted bids and offers is made. Each agent, some portion of whose bid (offer) was accepted, is then asked to vote "yes" or "no" as to whether the allocation should be final-ized, that is, only the active traders on a given trial are enfranchised. If all such traders vote yes, the process stops and each individual executes a long-term contract for T times the outcome of that trial. Otherwise the process proceeds to another repeat bid-offer trial with a maximum of T trials.

Unanimity voting in the above sense provides a procedure for operationalizing the concept of tatonnement in which contracts are not binding until a final exchange of messages triggers a market outcome. The London Gold Bullion Exchange appears to be the only ongoing market that uses unanimity voting as a message exchange stopping rule (Jarecki, 1976).

PROPOSITION 16: *Measured in terms of efficiency and deviations from the C.E. price, PQv provides no improvement over PQ. $P(Q)v$ performs better than $P(Q)$ and appears to be the equal of DA (Smith et al. 1982).*

Propositions 15 and 16 (which are based on forty-eight experiments) are important in confirming our expectation that the rules ought to make a difference as to what we observe in a market. These propositions also make clear that not just any institution one might wish to define has $C.E.$ properties as good as DA. Finally, although there are many experimental studies which provide empirical support for the static Nash equilibrium hypothesis (compare Smith et al., 1982, Section III.A), the hypothesis fails to receive support in the context of the sealed bid-offer auction. Something else, perhaps having to do with lumpiness, is driving the results.

D. *Posted Pricing*

Our experience as economic agents does not normally include any of the institutions discussed so far. The ordinary retail markets of daily life use what has been called the posted offer institution (Plott and myself, 1978) in which sellers display take-it-or-leave-it price offers to buyers. With only a few exceptions (such as "big ticket" items like automobiles and houses) the buyer does not bargain with the seller over price. Less well known, but important, is the existence

of markets in which buyers post the bid prices at which they are willing to buy. Thus refiners post bids for crude oil, and canners post bids for produce and other foods.

Posted Offer (Bid) Pricing. The process begins with each seller (buyer) privately selecting a take-it-or-leave-it price offer (bid). These prices are then publicly posted so that they are visible to each buyer and seller. Next a buyer (seller), selected at random, chooses a seller to whom a quantity response or offer is made. The seller (buyer) then responds with an acceptance of all or any part of the buyer's (seller's) quantity offer which forms a binding contract. (However, the seller must accept at least one unit, i.e., the seller may not post an offer price and then refuse to sell any units at that price.) If any part of the quantity offer is not accepted the buyer (seller) may choose a second seller (buyer) and make a quantity response, and so on. When the first buyer (seller) has finished trading, a second, selected at random (without replacement) proceeds to choose a seller (buyer), makes a quantity offer, and so on. This process stops when the last buyer (seller) has completed the exchange cycle. The trading period ends without any further public announcement.[33] Note that under posted offer (bid) pricing, only the sellers (buyers) can "signal" by raising (lowering) their price quotations.

Several experimental studies have investigated the properties of this institution. A few of these properties are summarized below.

PROPOSITION 17: *If $G_o^t(p)$ and $G_b^t(p)$ are the proportions of contract prices at p or higher in trading period t under the posted offer and*

[33] In the PLATO computerized version of "posted offer," seller prices are displayed on each buyer's and seller's terminal screen. Besides a price, each seller also selects the maximum number of units that he/she is willing to deliver, but this information is not public. When a buyer purchases the last unit from a seller, the message "stock out" replaces that seller's price on each buyer's screen. This procedure preserves the privacy of sales and "stockage" for each seller as in the typical retail market. Also, the computerized version has options requiring buyers to pay a fixed fee, corresponding to shopping cost, to obtain a seller's price quotation. Alternatively, the seller may be charged a fee, corresponding to price advertising.

VOL. 72 NO. 5   *SMITH: EXPERIMENTAL MICROECONOMIC SYSTEMS*   951

posted bid institutions, respectively, then $G_o^i(p) \geqq G_b^i(p)$ for all $t > 1$ (*W. Cook and E. Veendorp*, 1975; *Plott and myself*, 1978; *my 1976a article*; *F. Williams*, 1973).

This proposition establishes the empirical characteristic that posted pricing operates to the advantage of the side with the posting initiative. If sellers post offers convergence is from above the *C.E.* price.

PROPOSITION 18: *Experiments with single seller posted-offer pricing, in both increasing and decreasing cost environments, yield convergence to the monopoly price. This convergence appears to be faster with increasing cost (my 1981a article) than with decreasing cost (Don Coursey, Isaac, and myself, 1981). The slow convergence (at least fifteen periods) in three of four replications under decreasing cost appears to be attributable to the fact that buyer withholding of purchases (more likely in earlier periods at the higher posted-price offers) impacts the seller's most profitable units.*

This proposition supports monopoly theory, but only within the institutional context of posted-offer pricing, which from Proposition 17 operates to the advantage of sellers. If single sellers achieve monopoly outcomes under the seller-favored posted-offer institution, how well would they fare under the unfavorable posted-bid institution? If buyers post bids to a single seller will this provide a form of decentralized institutional restraint of monopoly power?

PROPOSITION 19: *In a market with one seller and five buyers using posted-bid pricing, prices tend to converge to the C.E. price, but volume and efficiency are somewhat below the C.E. levels (my 1981a article, pp. 96–99).*

Consequently posted-bid pricing does serve to severely limit monopoly power, but the resulting market falls short of achieving *C.E.* outcomes. However, the average efficiency (three replications) exceeds that which would have prevailed at the monopoly equilibrium.

PROPOSITION 20: *In decreasing cost environments in which demand is insufficient to support more than a single seller, but the* market is "contested" by two sellers with identical costs, there is a strong tendency (six experimental replications, each with fifteen to twenty-five trading periods) for posted-offer prices to decay to the C.E. price range (*Coursey, Isaac, and myself,* 1981).

This proposition provides empirical support for the contested market hypothesis (Elizabeth Bailey and John Panzar, 1980), and for the effect of "bidding to supply a market" in disciplining market power (Harold Demsetz, 1968).

In all of the experimental studies summarized above, it should be noted that institutions are being examined in their *pure* form, without the modifications that might result from attaching supplemental secondary institutions sometimes observed in the field. Thus, if an award fails to be *P.O.* at an organized Dutch auction, there may be an additional "aftermarket" exchange in which the successful Dutch bidder resells the item to the highest value agent. Similarly, "first-cut" inefficiency in posted-offer retail markets may be corrected by the end-of-season "sale" or via the Sears Roebuck special discount catalogue. But studying institutions in their purest form enables one to better understand why some institutions develop secondary correctional procedures and others do not. Also, an institution that makes efficient allocations saves the cost of running secondary markets.

In Section II.B it is stated that one of the scientific objectives of experimental microeconomy is to "measure messages because we want to identify the behavioral modes, $\beta^i(e^i|I)$, revealed by the agents and test hypotheses derived from theories about agent behavior." The reader should note that only Proposition 3 in the above list directly addresses this particular objective. This paucity of experimental results reflects the limited extent to which economic theory has dealt directly with institutional specifications and agent message behavior within these specifications. Bidding and auctioning theory is one of the few exceptions to this generalization. It follows that if future experimental research is to test theories of the message behavior of agents, it is essential that more such theory be developed. In the absence of such theory, experimental research is likely to be directed to comparisons between observed outcomes, and the standard static competitive, monopoly or Nash models of final outcome allocations. This means that all those messages in an experiment, which did not also represent allocations, will be subjected to very limited, if any, analysis, and what analysis is provided will not be guided by explicit theory.

V. Epilogue

At the heart of economics is a scientific mystery: How is it that the pricing system accomplishes the world's work without anyone being in charge? Like language, no one invented it. None of us could have invented it, and its operation depends in no way on anyone's comprehension or understanding of it. Somehow, it is a product of culture; yet in important ways, the pricing system is what makes culture possible. Smash it in the command economy and it rises as a Phoenix with a thousand heads, as the command system becomes shot through with bribery, favors, barter and underground exchange. Indeed, these latter elements may prevent the command system from collapsing. No law and no police force can stop it, for the police may become as large a part of the problem as of the solution. The pricing system—How is order produced from freedom of choice?—is a scientific mystery as deep, fundamental, and inspiring as that of the expanding universe or the forces that bind matter. For to understand it is to understand something about how the human species got from hunting-gathering through the agricultural and industrial revolutions to a state of affluence that allows us to ask questions about the expanding universe, the weak and strong forces that bind particles, and the nature of the pricing system, itself. But what can we as economists say for sure about what we know of the pricing system? It would appear that after 200 years, we know and understand very little. Incredibly, it is only in the last 20 of these 200 years that we have seriously awakened to the hypothesis that property right institutions might be important to the functioning of the pricing system!

Laboratory research in microeconomics over the past two decades has focused on the simplest and most elementary questions—some might say simple-minded questions. This is because the premises of this research are that we possess very little knowledge that can be demonstrated; that the roots of our discipline require a complete reexamination; that we are only just at the beginning. Above all, we need to develop a body of knowledge which clarifies the difference between what we have created (theory as hypothesis) and what we have discovered (hypothesis that, to date, is or is not falsified by observation).

REFERENCES

Bailey, Elizabeth and Panzar, John, "The Contestability of Airline Markets During the Transition to Deregulation," mimeo., May 6, 1980.

Belovicz, M. W., "Sealed-Bid Auctions: Experimental Results and Applications," in Vernon Smith, ed., *Research in Experimental Economics*, Vol. 1, Greenwich: JAI Press, 1979, 279–338.

Butts, Robert E., "Some Tactics in Galileo's Propaganda for the Mathematization of Scientific Experience," in his and J. C. Pitts, eds., *New Perspectives on Galileo*, Dordrecht: Reidel, 1978, 59–85.

Cassady, Ralph, *Auctions and Auctioneering*, Berkeley: University of California Press, 1967.

Chamberlin, John, "Comments on The Application of Laboratory Experimental Methods to Public Choice," in Clifford Russell, ed., *Collective Decision Making*, Washington: Resources for the Future, 1979, 161–66.

Clower, Robert and Leijonhufvud, Axel, "The Coordination of Economic Activities: A Keynesian Perspective," *American Economic Review Proceedings*, May 1975, *65*, 182–88.

Cook, W. D. and Veendorp, E. C. H., "Six Markets in Search of an Auctioneer," *Canadian Journal of Economics*, May 1975, *8*, 238–57.

Coppinger, Vicki, Smith, Vernon and Titus, John, "Incentives and Behavior in English, Dutch and Sealed-Bid Auctions," *Eco-*

nomic Inquiry, January 1980, *18*, 1–22.

Coursey, Don, Isaac, R. Mark and Smith, Vernon, "Natural Monopoly and the Contestable Markets Hypothesis: Some Experimental Results," department of economics discussion paper, University of Arizona, July 1981.

Cox, James, Roberson, Bruce and Smith, Vernon, "Theory and Behavior of Single Object Auctions," in V. Smith, ed., *Research in Experimental Economics* Vol. 2, Greenwich: JAI Press, 1982.

Cross, John, "Some Comments on the Papers by Kagel and Battalio and by Smith," in Jan Kmenta and James Ramsey, eds., *Evaluation of Econometric Models*, New York: New York University Press, 1980, 403–06.

Demsetz, Harold, "Why Regulate Utilities?," *Journal of Law of Economics*, April 1968, *11*, 55–65.

Drake, C. L. and Maxwell, J. C., "Geodynamics —Where Are We and What Lies Ahead?," *Science*, July 3, 1981; *213*, 15–22.

Dubey, Pradeep and Shubik, Martin, "A Strategic Market Game with Price and Quantity Strategies," *Zeitschrift fur Nationalokonomie*, No. 1-2, 1980, *40*, 25–34.

Ferejohn, John, Forsythe, Robert and Noll, Roger, "An Experimental Analysis of Decision Making Procedures for Discrete Public Goods," in Vernon Smith, ed., *Research in Experimental Economics*, Vol. 1, Greenwich: JAI Press, 1979, 1–58.

Fiorina, Morris and Plott, Charles, "Committee Decisions Under Majority Rule: An Experimental Study," *American Political Science Review*, June 1978, 575–98.

Forsythe, R., Palfrey, Thomas and Plott, Charles, "Asset Valuation in an Experimental Market," *Econometrica*, May 1982, *50*, 537–67.

Fouraker, Lawrence and Siegel, Sidney, *Bargaining Behavior*, New York: McGraw-Hill, 1963.

Freuchen, Peter, *Book of the Eskimos*, Cleveland: World Publishing, 1961.

Friedman, James and Hoggatt, Austin, *An Experiment in Noncooperative Oligopoly*, Supplement 1 to Vernon Smith, ed., *Research in Experimental Economics*, Vol. 1, Greenwich: JAI Press, 1980.

Grether, David, "Bayes Rule as a Descriptive Model: The Representativeness Heuristic," *Quarterly Journal of Economics*, November 1980, *95*, 537–57.

Hanson, N. R., *Perception and Discovery*, San Francisco: Freeman, 1969.

_____, *Observation and Explanation*, New York 1971.

Harrison, Glenn, Smith, Vernon and Williams, Arlington, "Learning Behavior in Experimental Auctions Markets," University of California-Los Angeles, November 1981.

Hayek, Friedrich A., "The Use of Knowledge in Society," *American Economic Review*, September 1945, *35*, 519–30.

Hazard, J. and Christie, M., *The Investment Business*, New York 1964.

Hoggatt, Austin, "An Experimental Business Game," *Behavioral Science*, July 1959, *4*, 192–203.

Hurwicz, Leonid, "Optimality and Informational Efficiency in Resource Allocation Processes," in Kenneth Arrow et al., eds., *Mathematical Methods in the Social Sciences*, Stanford: Stanford University, 1960, 27–46.

_____, "The Design of Mechanisms for Resource Allocation," *American Economic Review Proceedings*, May 1973, *63*, 1–30.

_____, Radner, Roy, and Reiter, Stanley, "A Stochastic Decentralized Resource Allocation Process: Part I," *Econometrica*, March 1975, *43*, 187–221; "Part II," May 1975, 363–93.

Isaac, R. Mark and Plott, Charles R., (1981a) "Price Control and the Behavior of Auction Markets: An Experimental Examination," *American Economic Review*, June 1981, *71*, 448–59.

_____ and _____, (1981b) "The Opportunity for Conspiracy in Restraint of Trade: An Experimental Study," *Journal of Economic Behavior and Organization*, March 1981, *2*, 1–30.

Jarecki, Henry G., "Bullion Dealing, Commodity Exchange Trading and the London Gold Fixing: Three Forms of Commodity Auctions," in Y. Amihud, ed., *Bidding and Auctioning for Procurement and Allocation*, New York: New York University 1976, 146–54.

Kagel, John and Battalio, Raymond, "Token

Economy and Animal Models for the Experimental Analysis of Economic Behavior," in Jan Kmenta and James Ramsey, eds., *Evaluation of Econometric Models*, New York: Academic Press, 1980, 379–401.

Kaplan, Abraham, *The Conduct of Inquiry*, New York: Chandler Publishing, 1964.

Ketcham, Jon, Smith, Vernon, and Williams, Arlington, "The Behavior of Posted Offer Pricing Institutions," paper presented at the Southern Economic Association Meeting, November 5–7, 1980.

Koestler, Arthur, *The Sleepwalkers*, New York 1963.

Leamer, Edward and Leonard, Herman, "An Alternative Reporting Style for Econometric Results," discussion paper no. 145, University of California-Los Angeles, June 1981.

Leffler, George and Farwell, C. Loring, *The Stock Market*, New York: Ronald, 1963.

Leland, Hayne, "Theory of the Firm Facing Uncertain Demand," *American Economic Review*, June 1972, *62*, 278–91.

Levine, Michael and Plott, Charles, "Agenda Influence and Its Implications," *Virginia Law Review*, May 1977, *63*, 561–604.

Lucas, Robert E., Jr., "Tobin and Monetarism: A Review Article," *Journal of Economic Literature*, June 1981, *19*, 558–67.

Marschak, Jacob, "Economics of Inquiring, Communicating, Deciding," *American Economic Review Proceedings*, May 1968, *48*, 1–18.

Martin, Paul, "Prehistoric Overkill," in his and H. E. Wright, Jr., eds., *Pleistocene Extinctions*, New Haven: Yale University, 1967.

Mendelson, M., Peake, J. and Williams, R. Jr., "Toward a Modern Exchange: The Peake-Mendelson-Williams Proposal for an Electronically Assisted Auction Market," in E. Blochand and R. Schwartz, eds., *Impending Changes for Securities Markets*, Greenwich: JAI Press, 1979, 53–74.

Miller, Gary and Plott, Charles "Revenue Generating Properties of Sealed-Bid Auctions," Social Science Working Paper No. 234, California Institute of Technology, September 1980.

Miller, Ross, Plott, Charles and Smith, Vernon, "Intertemporal Competitive Equilibrium: An Empirical Study of Speculation," *Quarterly Journal of Economics*, November 1977, *91*, 599–624.

Millikan, R. A., Roller, D. and Watson, E. C., *Mechanics, Molecular Physics, Heat and Sound*, Boston 1937.

Plott, Charles R., "The Application of Laboratory Experimental Methods to Public Choice," in Clifford S. Russell, ed., *Collective Decision Making*, Washington: Resources for the Future, 1979.

_____ and Smith, V. L., "An Experimental Examination of Two Exchange Institutions," *Review of Economic Studies*, February 1978, *45*, 133–53.

_____ and Sunder, Shyam, "Efficiency of Experimental Security Markets with Insider Information," *Journal of Political Economy*, August 1982, *90*, 663–98.

_____ and Wilde, Louis, "Professional Diagnosis vs. Self-Diagnosis: An Experimental Examination of Some Special Features of Markets with Uncertainty," in Vernon Smith, ed., *Research in Experimental Economics*, Vol. 2, Greenwich: JAI Press, 1982.

Popper, Karl R., *The Logic of Scientific Discovery*, London 1959.

Reiter, Stanley, "Information and Performance in the (New)^2 Welfare Economics," *American Economic Review Proceedings*, February 1977, *67*, 226–34.

Shapley, Harlow, *Of Stars and Men*, Boston 1964.

Siegel, Sidney, "Decision Making and Learning Under Varying Conditions of Reinforcement," *Annals of the New York Academy of Science*, 1961, 766–83.

_____ and Fouraker, Laurence, *Bargaining and Group Decision Making*, New York: McGraw-Hill, 1960.

Smith, Vernon L., "An Experimental Study of Competitive Market Behavior," *Journal of Political Economy*, April 1962, *70*, 111–37.

_____, "Effect of Market Organization on Competitive Equilibrium," *Quarterly Journal of Economics*, May 1964, *78*, 181–201.

_____, "Experimental Auction Markets and the Walrasian Hypothesis," *Journal of Political Economy*, August 1965, *73*, 387–93.

_____, "Experimental Studies of Discrimination versus Competition in Sealed-Bid Auction Markets," *Journal of Business*, January 1967, *40*, 58–84.

_____, "Notes on Some Literature in Experimental Economics," Social Science Working Paper no. 21, California Institute of Technology, February 1973.

_____, (1976a) "Bidding and Auctioning Institutions: Experimental Results," in Y. Amihud, ed., *Bidding and Auctioning for Procurement and Allocation*, New York: New York University, 1976, 43–64.

_____, (1976b) "Experimental Economics: Induced Value Theory," *American Economic Review Proceedings*, May 1976, *66*, 274–79.

_____, "Incentive Compatible Experimental Processes for the Provision of Public Goods," in his *Research in Experimental Economics*, Greenwich: JAI Press, 1979, 59–168.

_____, "Relevance of Laboratory Experiments to Testing Resource Allocation Theory," in Jan Kmenta and James B. Ramsey, *Evaluation of Econometric Models*, New York 1980, 345–77.

_____, (1981a) "An Empirical Study of Decentralized Institutions of Monopoly Restraint," G. Horwich and J. Quirk, eds., *Essays in Contemporary Fields of Economics*, W. Lafayette: Purdue University, 1981.

_____, (1981b) "Theory, Experiment and Antitrust Policy," in S. Salop, ed., *Strategy, Predation, and Antitrust Analysis*, Washington: FTC, September 1981.

_____ and Williams, Arlington W., (1981a) "On Nonbinding Price Controls in a Competitive Market," *American Economic Review*, June 1981, *71*, 467–74.

_____ and _____, (1981b) "The Boundaries of Competitive Price Theory: Convergence, Expectations and Transaction Cost," paper presented at the Public Choice Society Meetings, New Orleans, March 13–15, 1981.

_____ and _____, "Effect of Rent Asymmetries in Competitive Markets," *Journal of Economic Behaviour and Organization*, forthcoming.

_____ and _____, "An Experimental Comparison of Alternative Rules for Competitive Market Exchange," in Martin Shubik, ed., *Auctions, Bidding and Contracting: Uses and Theory*, New York: New York University Press, 1982.

Smith, Vernon et al., "Competitive Market Institutions: Double Auctions versus Sealed Bid-Offer Auctions," *American Economic Review*, March 1982, *72*, 58–77.

Stafford, Frank, "Some Comments on the Papers by Kagel and Battalio and by Smith," in Jan Kmenta and James Ramsey, eds., *Evaluation of Econometric Models*, New York: Academic Press, 1980, 407–410.

Vickrey, William, "Counterspeculation, Auctions and Competitive Sealed Tenders," *Journal of Finance*, March 1961, *16*, 8–37.

_____, "Auctions and Bidding Games," in *Recent Advances in Game Theory*, Princeton: Princeton University, 1962, 15–27.

_____, "Auctions, Markets, and Optimal Allocation," in Y. Amihud, ed., *Bidding and Auctioning for Procurement and Allocation*, New York: New York University, 1976, 13–20.

Wilde, Louis, "On the Use of Laboratory Experiments in Economics," in Joseph Pitt, ed., *The Philosophy of Economics*, Dordrecht: Reidel, 1980.

Williams, Arlington, "Intertemporal Competitive Equilibrium: On Further Experimental Results," in Vernon Smith, ed., *Research in Experimental Economics*, Vol.1, Greenwich: JAI Press, 1979, 225–78.

_____, "Computerized Double Auction Markets: Some Initial Experimental Results," *Journal of Business*, July 1980, *53*, 235–58.

Williams, Fred, "Effect of Market Organization on Competitive Equilibrium: The Multiunit Case," *Review of Economic Studies*, January 1973, *40*, 97–113.

[2]

Will Economics Become an Experimental Science?*

CHARLES R. PLOTT
California Institute of Technology
Pasadena, California

The expectations of the audience are rational because the answer I will give to the question posed by the title of this lecture is exactly what they expect. The answer is "yes." No doubt the expectations are also that I will not give a one-word lecture. A justification of such a radical answer is expected. Again, the expectations are rational. The natural way for me to explain my belief is to focus on the events that have facilitated and will continue to facilitate the broad application of laboratory experimental methods. Economics has been a non-laboratory science for several hundred years. Many have used economics as a classical example of a science in which laboratory methods are impossible. What has happened to make experimental methods applicable now and thereby change the way in which one can learn about economics? That question is the focus of this lecture.

The sheer growth of papers, researchers, and laboratories suggests that something has happened. From the early 1970s the number of papers has grown from two or three per year to numbers approximating 100 per year. The number of researchers has grown from a small handful in the early 1970s to hundreds. The number of locations of the research, and the number of laboratories have grown from one or two to the range of 30 or 40. The growth is amazing but these are just trends. Such trends do not show the basic logic that is at work. The logic, the reasons for the activities, provides the proper support for the answer to the question posed in the title. The trends are simply manifestations of the logic and events.

Six Seductive Steps to Sin and Intoxication

I think that the foundations for the revolution that we can now see occurring began to be developed in the early 1970s. These foundations consist of six events. Collectively these events provide the bases for the self-sustaining growth and use of experimental methods in both the basic scientific and in the applied scientific aspects of economics. Now, to me basic science is fun; so much so that it must be sinful. Experimentation is also intoxicating and habituating in the sense that the more one does the more one wants to do. Consequently I will refer to the six events that form the foundation for the growth of modern experimental methods as the "Six Seductive Steps to Sin and Intoxication."

*Presidential Address delivered at the sixtieth annual meeting of the Southern Economic Association, New Orleans, November 20, 1990. The research support of the National Science Foundation and the California Institute of Technology Laboratory for Experimental Economics and Political Science is gratefully acknowledged.

Step 1: We Learned How to Pose a Question

Prior to the early 1970s, the profession did not pose questions that could be answered by the application of experimental methodology. The questions primarily addressed aspects of economies as they are found growing wild in nature. Naturally occurring economies evolve in response to a wide variety of events and historical accidents. The possibility certainly exists that some of such events had nothing at all to do with any economic principles that might be at work. Economies found "in the wild," so to speak, are extremely complicated and the questions posed by the profession had to do with the properties of such creatures. Primarily the questions were about measurement and about the statistical properties of ongoing processes. (What is the elasticity of demand? What is the relationship between concentration and profits? What is the level of employment?) In order to learn about such statistical properties, the economy in question must be studied directly. The laboratory would seem to have nothing to contribute to such effort. The idea of performing replays of the historical evolution of an economy in order to get better observations does not make a lot of sense. Each observation would be very costly, to say the least.

Of course not all questions were about measurement. Many questions were about theory but even the theories tended to be directed to explanations about particular economies and particular situations in those economics. (What was the contribution of monetary policy to the great depression? What was the contribution of debt policies to the inflation of the 1960s? What were the causes of slums and ghettos in New York City? What were the contributions of technological change to the growth of the U.S. economy? What was the relationship between structure and performance in specific industries?) If the analysis is restricted to only questions of this sort, then only the data from these special economies, as they are found naturally evolving during a particular period of history, would seem to be relevant. Clearly, in many parts of economics a body of general theory had developed, but the focus of the profession was not so much on the general behavioral principles of the theory as it was on the application of theory to specific events. Again, in the absence of a capability to inexpensively replay history, a laboratory methodology would appear to have nothing to contribute.

Laboratory methodology involves a shift from a focus on particular economies as they are found in the wild to a focus on general theories, models and principles that govern the behavior of economies. This distinction between the study of an economy and the study of models, theories and principles of economics is subtle so an elaboration might prove useful. The logic is as follows. General theories must apply to simple special cases. The laboratory technology can be used to create simple (but real) economies. These simple economies can then be used to test and evaluate the predictive capability of the general theories when they are applied to the special cases. In this way, a joining of the general theories with data is accomplished.

Before continuing further, an example of a simple, laboratory economy consisting of one market will be given. People are assembled. Some of the people are designated as "buyers" and some are designated "sellers." Buyers are involved with the experimenter through a contract of the following sort. Buyer i is assigned a "redemption value" function, $R^i(X_i)$ which indicates the amount of (real) dollars he or she will receive from the experimenter as a function of X_i, the quantity of the commodity purchased by i. The buyer i keeps as profits the difference between $R^i(X_i)$ and whatever he or she paid to sellers for the units. Similarly, the experimenter's contract with seller j is that j will pay the experimenter an amount of dollars $C^j(X_j)$ depending on the quantity, X_j, sold by j. Seller j keeps as (real dollar) profits the difference between the revenue he or she received from buyers and the cost paid to the experimenter.

If the competitive model is applied to the market, then each buyer can be represented by a demand function that satisfies the equation $(\partial R^i(X_i))/\partial X_i - P = 0$. Each seller can be represented by a supply function that satisfies the equation $P - \partial c^j(X_j)/\partial X_j = 0$. That is, the individual quantity demanded is determined by an equating of price to marginal benefits and the individual quantity supplied is determined by an equating of price to marginal cost. The market demand is derived by a sum of individual demand functions and the market supply is determined by the sum of individual supply functions. The competitive model then predicts that the price will be the one that equates market demand with market supply. Clearly the law of supply and demand is applied very generally and to economies much more complicated than the one just described. It is only natural to expect that if the law works in very complicated cases then one should expect it to work in the simple case as well. If it does not then a substantial reassessment of the theory would be in order. The conclusion of many laboratory experiments is that it does indeed work in the simple cases.

Figure 1-A displays the market demand and supply from a simple laboratory market conducted at Caltech. Figure 1-B shows the time series of trades that took place in the market. The market was organized by a computerized multiple unit double auction. The dots represent contract prices displayed in the order in which contracts occurred. The vertical lines are the end of market periods or "trading days." Each trading day was a replication of the previous day in the sense that the market demand and supply was the same. As can be seen, the time series approaches the prediction of the competitive model. Contract prices approach the competitive equilibrium price and volume approaches the competitive equilibrium volume as the trading periods are replicated.

The demand and supply diagram is useful but it does not reflect the potential variety of laboratory applications that is possible. Almost all economic theories and models have the same form which elsewhere [17] I have called the "fundamental equation" represented in Figure 2. Almost all economic theories and models rest on concepts of preferences, technology, (or feasible sets), and institutions. These concepts form the basic parameters which are supposed to dictate the behavior of the economy. The fundamental equation captures the essence of the relationships. Fix the preferences, the feasible set, and the institution (perhaps along with beliefs) and the models will yield a prediction. It is important to note that it makes no difference where the economy is found. The economy could have been found evolving in nature or it could have been a home-grown, laboratory variety; as long as the parameters are known, the theory will produce a prediction. It is this general property of theory that is important for laboratory experimental work. Figure 2 will help make the point more clearly.

Theories and models can take many competing forms or be based on different principles of behavior and still have the properties of the fundamental equation. Those captured by the box in Figure 2 are examples. Given some fixed "economic environment" of preferences, institution, and feasible sets, the outcomes predicted could be based on any of a number of different cooperative game theoretic models or the prediction could be based on any of a large number of noncooperative models. Consider first the cooperative model options. Cooperative game models can differ according to the choice of dominance relations and can differ depending upon the nature of the characteristic function. Differences in models can also reflect different selections from the set of solution concepts (core, bargaining sets, etc.). Even within the class of cooperative game models the number of models that could be applied to the same environment is large. However, cooperative models do not exhaust the possibilities. The model applied to the same environment might be based on noncooperative theoretic principles. Noncooperative theories can differ according to hypotheses about the information structure generated by the institutional arrangement.

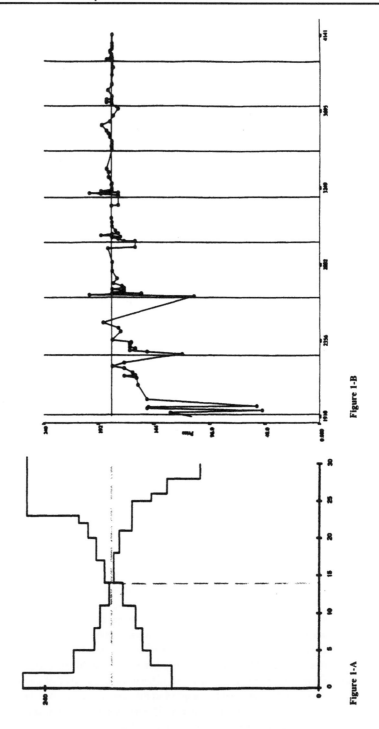

Figure 1-B

Figure 1-A

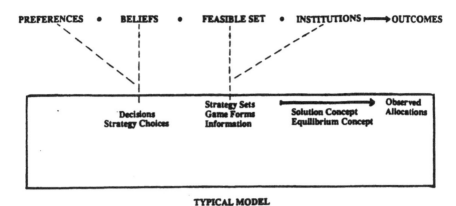

TYPICAL MODEL

Figure 2. Fundamental Equation

The number of possible models is also expanded by the choice of an equilibrium concept (Nash, perfect Nash, etc.). Cooperative games and non-cooperative games do not exhaust the possibilities. The model might be based on principles of nonstrategic behavior and yield outcomes like those predicted by the competitive model. The number of potential models is impressive.

The lessons of Figure 2 are firstly, that models of economies found in the wild tend to have a similar structure and that structure is captured by the fundamental equation. Secondly, such models are general models involving basic principles intended to have applicability independent of time and location except to the extent to which time and location have an effect on the variables of the fundamental equation, (preferences, institutions, information, and feasible sets). Third, we see that a staggeringly large number of theories exist. One purpose of the laboratory is to reduce the number by determining which do not work in the simple cases. The purpose is also to improve the models by exploring how a model might be changed to make it work better in the simple cases. General models, such as those applied to the very complicated economies found in the wild, must apply to simple special cases. Models that do not apply to the simple special cases are not general and thus cannot be viewed as such. The trick is to notice that economies created in the laboratories might be very simple relative to those found in nature, but they are just as real. Real people motivated by real money make real decisions, real mistakes and suffer real frustrations and delights because of their real talents and real limitations. Simplicity should not be confused with reality. Since the laboratory economies are real, the general principles and models that exist in the literature should be expected to apply with the same force to these laboratory economies as to those economies found in the field. The laboratories are simple but the simplicity is an advantage because it allows the reasons for a model's failure to be isolated and sometimes even measured.

The process of learning is roundabout. The questions posed by experimentalists address the points of accuracy and the points of failure of general models and principles of economic behavior. Theories that predict relatively poorly in the laboratory are either rejected or refined. Models and principles that survive the laboratory can then be used to address questions about the field. Why something happened or what might happen in some naturally occurring economy are questions addressed by models that have been refined by laboratory testing. It is the understanding of the nature of those models, some of their points of accuracy and failures, that can be gleaned from laboratory studies. Presumably this understanding helps with field applications. The labora-

906   *Charles R. Plott*

tory is not a source of direct simulation of what might happen in the field. The use of theory is an intervening stage. The learning process is roundabout.

A recognition of this roundabout means of learning removed two intellectual constraints which together had made laboratory methods useless. The first was a belief that the only relevant economies to study are those in the wild. This belief suggested that the only effective way to create an experiment would be to mirror in every detail, to simulate, so to speak, some ongoing natural process. Early experimenters were guilty of yielding to this belief and described experiments as simulations of a market [21] or attempted to include in their experiments much of the rich and complicating detail found in many markets [9]. As a result the experiments tended to be dismissed either because as simulations the experiments were incomplete or because as experiments they were so complicated that tests of models were unconvincing. In other words, the experiment would be dismissed either because it did not mirror some natural process, or because it did. Once models, as opposed to economies, became the focus of research the simplicity of an experiment and perhaps even the absence of features of more complicated economies became an asset. The experiment should be judged by the lessons it teaches about theory and not by its similarity with what nature might happened to have created.

The second constraint to the development of laboratory experiments was a belief about the proper way to test a theory. Typically a theory is viewed as being of the form "if x then y." Following this belief, the proper way to test a theory is to create a circumstance in which all of the assumptions of the theory are satisfied, the x part of the statement, and then conduct the experiment to see if y is the result. If y is not observed then the theory is rejected as being false. The problem with this methodology is not that it is wrong. The problem is that the assumptions of economic theories are seldom stated in operational terms and the theories themselves can be so vague that tests in the sense above are practically impossible. For example, a proposition frequently stated as an "assumption" of the competitive model is that each agent "believes" that his/her actions will have no effect on price. If the theory is stated in that form, then for practical purposes laboratory testing is impossible. In order to test the theory in that form, the experimenter must somehow know what exists in the minds of subjects. Since such data can never be known to the experimenter, the theory cannot be tested in the laboratory, in the field, or in any other way. The "if" part of the conditional cannot be known to be satisfied.

Experimenters learned to sidestep this issue by posing tests as contests among competing models. The question posed by the experimenter evolved from a single question of the form "is this theory true?" to include questions like "which of these models best predicts what is observed in the simple experimental economies?"; or, to include a slight variant of that question "what are the circumstances under which the predictions of this theory/model improve or deteriorate?".[1] This new, broader set of questions is based upon the recognition that simple, special cases of economies are legitimate entities to study and that the predictive capacity of a theory or model might be unrelated to whether or not the assumptions are satisfied.[2] By considering a broader set of questions than historically had been considered, experimentalists began to develop the art of posing questions that a laboratory experiment can answer.

---

1. A clear early statement of this change in perspective to deal with many competing models is in Fiorina and Plott [4].

2. See Goodfellow and Plott [10] for a discussion of this issue. When a sharp differentiation between assumptions and principles is absent in the theory, the classical concept of testing a theory does not work.

Step 2: Some Important Discoveries Were Made

During the very early years of experimentation, three very important discoveries were made. In some sense these establish a foundation for all subsequent work but they were not appreciated at the time. In fact, it is only recently, after many replications, and hundreds of experiments of different types, can we look back and recognize these early events as discoveries.

Chamberlin [1] made major progress toward studying the law of supply and demand, although he really failed to recognize the nature and the importance of his discovery. Hoggatt [11], Sauermann and Selton [19, 20], Fouraker and Siegel [7] all discovered the power of the Nash equilibrium and Fouraker and Siegal were the first to use laboratory methods to study the influence of institutions. Vernon Smith [21] discovered the operation of the law of supply and demand in open outcry markets. Figure 1 is simply one sort of replication of what Smith discovered. The decade following these early discoveries contains several important experiments but I think two discoveries in the early 1970s, both contained in the same paper [18], provide one of the keys to unlocking the door to understanding what happened at Step 2.

The first discovery was that a concept of efficiency can be applied to evaluate and measure the performance of an experimental market. The discovery was simply that a cost/benefit analysis could be applied directly to experimental markets. The area under the demand curve is the amount paid to subjects by the experimenter. The area under the marginal cost curve is what subjects pay to the experimenter. The consumers' surplus plus the producers' surplus is maximum total earnings that subjects can get from participation. The gains from trade in the laboratory market are the subject payment cost of the experiment to the experimenter. If all gains from trade are exhausted, then as a group, subjects have earned the maximum total possible from the experiment. The efficiency with which the market facilitates the acquiring of such gain would be 100% in case the maximum is attained. The efficiency of market operations can then be measured by the actual payments to subjects divided by the maximum possible. In multiple market experiments with production, dollar payments may need to be replaced by other measures found in the welfare economics literature.

This simple technique has very important applications. It can be used to measure the efficiency with which different institutions can operate to solve the same problem. Within a fixed economic environment (preferences and feasible sets), the experimenter can conduct different experiments with different institutions and compare the efficiencies. Thus, the technique provides a way to compare and evaluate the performance of different institutional arrangements. It is especially important to notice that this comparative analysis can take place even though the experimenter may have no reasonable theory of why the institutions affect the markets as they do. Experiments can be useful even in the absence of theory. Experimentalists could proceed in meaningful directions even in cases in which the theory was not worked out at all.

The second discovery was actually a rediscovery that institutions have an effect on market performance. This time, however, the institution and the effect were both clearly identified and the institution was not just any old institution. The institution was posted prices, similar to the rate posing process that have been used by the Department of Transportation and the Interstate Commerce Commission for years. Furthermore, the effect was not just any old effect. Posted prices cause prices to go up and efficiency to go down relative to what would be the case under an open-outcry system. Exactly why this occurs is still an open question although the best model developed so far is the mixed strategy solutions of a Bertrand game representation of the market.

These two discoveries set the stage for the use of laboratory experimental methods in policy analysis. The efficiency measure and related concepts can be used to measure and identify the difference between competing modes of market organization. This comparison can proceed even if no good theoretical representation of processes exists. That is, the empirical work can proceed in the absence of theory although the presence of theory certainly enhances its usefulness. Furthermore, since the posted price was an important variant of market regulatory machinery, the analysis could be focused directly on regulatory issues. Evaluation of the relative performance of market organizations in the laboratory provided a new source of insights about how such institutions might operate when implemented in the field. Laboratory-based policy analysis was made possible [12].

Step 3: Economic Theory Advanced

The stunning changes in theory that took place in the late 1970s and 1980s do not need to be reviewed here. Information became a key variable and, with this variable, scientific interest in noncooperative game theory which, for practical purposes, was a dead subject prior to the late 1970s, began to be stimulated.

The newly developed tools of analysis suggested the existence of very subtle relationships among the actions taken by economic agents and the institutions in which they are operating. The implications of rationality of self and of others began to grow in importance. Efficiency began to expand from simple allocation efficiency to information efficiency and both began to depend critically upon the ability of agents to assimilate information from complex data and the knowledge that others could do the same. Slight changes in institutional form could have dramatic implications in terms of the predictions of the new game theoretic models. Critical features of models used in applications began to be so delicate that any testing in the field would be essentially hopeless. History does not often shape itself to suit the convenience of analysts who might like to test some of the very basic propositions about human actions and market behaviors that modern economic theory suggests might exist.

The matrix game represented in Figure 3 will provide some intuition about the issues for those who are not versed in game theory. In that game the outcome in the lower right hand corner is a Nash equilibrium. If row player chooses B and column player chooses C, neither has an incentive to change given the choice of the other. How might the system get there? Row player can see that column player will not choose B because for column player, B is dominated by both columns A and C. Furthermore, row player understands that column player understands that if column B is not played, then for row player row A is dominated by row B. So, row player is not likely to play A. It follows that column will play C. By such repeated arguments that apply not only rationality of self but also rationality of others, and so forth, a presumption exists that the lower right hand corner will be the outcome.

This role of rationality and public knowledge of rationality is an important feature of models and we will return to this feature of theory later. For now, it is sufficient to note that the choice of concepts of equilibrium used in a model can have an impact on predictions about the ultimate consequences of institutions on allocations. The example is really only illustrative of the issue. Modern theory has produced dozens of interesting new concepts of equilibrium and/or solution concepts, especially in cases in which the economic situation involves asymmetric information. Such theory also suggests the existence of what otherwise might be thought of as strange phenomena such as rational expectations equilibria.

	A	B	C
A	20 10	−3 100	9 7
B	1 12	−1 −10	2 8

Figure 3. Matrix Game with Row Player and Column Player

Even though the solution concepts might have dramatically different consequences for institutional behavior, the data needed to distinguish between them, to determine which of them is the most accurate, can only be revealed at certain critical points of the decision making process. If the data can only come from the field, and from repeated observations of special circumstances found there, then the appropriate tests will probably never be conducted. The only practical source of data that can be obtained within an appropriate time frame and serve as a guide for many of the newly developed theories is the laboratory.

Step 4: Laboratory Data Suggests that Theory Is on the Right Track

It is one thing to say that the laboratory can be used as a source of data. It is very much another thing to say that something exists by way of theory that is worth the effort needed for a test. Experiments conducted in the late 1970s provided strong suggestions that modern theories were not completely hopeless and, indeed, appeared to be on the right track.

Many examples exist. The law of supply and demand was well established by the late 1970s. The importance of the CORE of game representation of committee processes had also been well established by the late 1970s. Rational expectations had received strong support. In addition, the work with nonhuman animals in the early 1970s was extremely important because it leads directly to the hypothesis that a biological bases exists for the preference and optimization behavior that is so fundamental to modern theory.

Perhaps the easiest examples to explain are the experiments with sealed bid auctions. The theory of auctions is one of the most completely developed theories in the social and economic sciences. The theory is well developed in the sense that the basic principles of game theory can be applied to create a model for which many of the definitions and assumptions can be made operational and implemented in an experimental environment.

Consider an economic environment in which one unit of a good is sold by a sealed bid auction process. The values of each of n bidders are drawn independently from a probability density function $f(v)$. Having knowledge of his or her own value v and the knowledge that the value of others are drawn from the same p.d.f., the individual must tender a sealed bid. The item is then sold to the highest bidder at his/her bid.

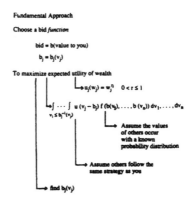

Figure 4. Sealed Bid Auction: Problem of Individual Choice

The value of the object to each individual will, in general, be different. From the point of view of any single individual, the values of the other people are random with some known probability structure. Of course, the individual would like to purchase the object and obtain it at a low price. Specifically, if w is the wealth of the individual, and v is the value of the item to that individual, then the individual's utility given a winning bid at bid price b is $u(w + v - b)$. The utility of the auction outcome if the individual fails to tender the winning bid is simply $u(w)$.

The problem faced by the individual who knows his/her own value v is to choose a bid. Since the bid depends upon the individual's value v, the implicit decision is the choice of a bid function $b = b(v)$ indicating what the individual would do depending upon the circumstances. The individual knows that other individuals face the same task and will develop their own individual bid functions.

The situation lends itself naturally to a game theoretic model. The theory is remarkably complex if $f(v)$ is not uniform and if individuals are not risk neutral. From an individual's point of view, the problem is outlined in Figure 4. Each individual must choose a bid function, a "strategy" in game theoretic terms, from all of the bid functions that might be imagined (the "strategy set"). Each individual's payoff depends upon his/her own choice of strategy and the strategy choices of others. Under suitable conditions on the probability distribution that describes the distribution of values across agents and under suitable conditions on the individual attitudes toward risk, a Nash equilibrium of the implied game exists. These equilibrium bid functions can be computed and compared to the actual bid functions of people participating in auction experiments.

Figure 5 displays three actual decisions of an individual in an auction experiment. Three people were competing.[3] In this environment the values are drawn from 0 to $10. The probability that an individual's value is between 0 and $5 is .8 and the probability that the value is $5 or more is .2. Values within a range are equally likely. The first of the three draws by the individual was $2.45 and the resulting bid was $2.20 as shown on the figure. This was a winning bid so the profit of this individual was $.25. The bids of the other two subjects were $1.24 and $.30. Of course, the amounts of money were real and the individual kept all profits. On the second draw the individual received a value of $1.11 the bid was $1.00. The bids of the other two were

---

3. Space prevents a detailed description of the experimental procedures and environments. For a detailed discussion of procedures see Cox, Roberson and Smith [2]. These data for the use of nonuniform distribution over values are part of a research project of Kay-Yut Chen and Charles Plott.

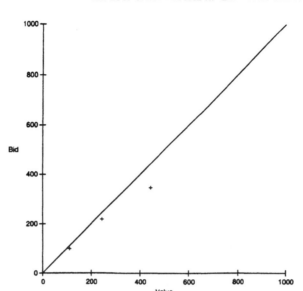

Figure 5. Drawn Values and Bid Choices

$4.01 and $3.06 so the profit of this individual was zero. When the value drawn was $4.44 the individual bid was $3.47. As can be seen, the elements of a bidding function $b(v)$ are beginning to appear in the figure. The question is whether or not the function is one predicted by theory.

Figure 6 contains all of the bids made by this individual. It also contains two different solutions to the game theoretic representation of the auction process. The lowest, most inaccurate bid function is based upon the assumption that this individual and others are risk neutral. As can be seen, the model predicts areas in which nonlinearites might occur but the risk neutral model is certainly inaccurate quantitatively. The bids it predicts are much lower than actual bids.

The second bid function is based upon the assumption that bidders are risk averse (constant relative risk aversion) with a random risk aversion parameter.[4] The simple risk aversion parameter is estimated from the linear portion of the bid function. As is obvious from the figure, the model begins to take the shape of the data. The accuracy of the model when applied to other individuals' data is similar to the one in the figure.

The point of this example is not that game theory has established some sort of iron law of behavior. The point is much more modest. The data from auction experiments, market experiments, committee experiments, etc. all have a common thread. Principles of economics and game theory lead to models that capture much of the essence of behavior. The data strongly suggest the existence of uniformities of behavior in complicated, competitive environments and that theory is on the right track. The data suggest that modern theorizing has been worth the effort. Theory appears to provide windows through which fundamental uniformities of human behavior can be viewed. Even though experimental work suggests that more theory is needed, the message that began to emerge from research in the late 1970s had clear and substantial positive elements. That positive message is an example of Step 4.

4. See Cox, Smith and Walker [3] for the details of such a model. The solutions for the nonuniform distribution case are taken from the Chen and Plott project.

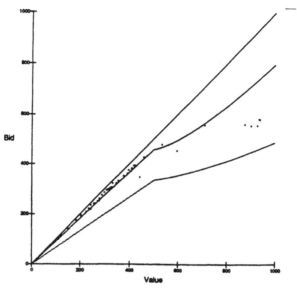

Figure 6. Observe Bid Function and Theoretical Bid Function for One Individual

Step 5: Paradoxes Begin to Appear

When theory appears to be going in the right direction, the natural reaction of the scientist is to explore in those directions as far as possible. Some of the more important directions suggested by modern theory are those provided by principles of game theory. The questions posed by those who explore in such directions are whether or not the theory continues to be accurate when some of its more subtle implications are tested. A second and independent set of research directions is suggested by the procedures and institutions previously explored experimentally. The question posed is whether or not the stylized facts that emerged from the study of very simple environments continue to be observed as the institutions change and take on increasingly complex properties. Such experiments are checks on the robustness of previous results. Failures to obtain positive results in either direction are called "paradoxes" (as opposed to "rejected theories").

Paradoxes began to appear in many contexts. Three of the most fascinating will be considered here. They are, in turn, the winner's curse, the behavior in centipede experiments, and the existence of bubbles in asset markets. These three are interesting because the theory that served well to explain behavior in closely related experiments predicts that the phenomena observed in these experiments cannot exist as a matter of principle. The very existence of the phenomena suggests the need for a reworking of theory at a very fundamental level.

Experiments in which the winner's curse is observed involve only a seemingly, slight alteration in the procedures of the first price auction experiments discussed in the section above. The structure is changed from a private value auction to a common value auction in which the value of the object sold is the same for all bidders. The value of the object is randomly determined. Each agent is then given a clue to the true value. The clue is drawn independently from a probability distribution that depends upon the true value. The agent must then determine a bid based upon the clue.

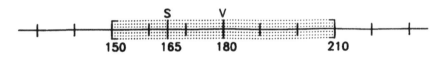

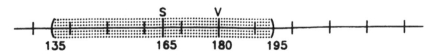

Figure 7. Common Value Auction: Value and Signal Relationship

Our Sample	Range of Possible Values	Our Bid	Winning Bid	Actual Value
100	[70, 130]	90	100	85
136	[106, 166]	126	160	160
158	[128, 188]	148	175	173
182	[152, 212]	162	162	156

Figure 8. Common Value Auction: Example of Information and Bids

The winner's curse phenomena, first observed experimentally by Kagel and Levine [13] is that the winning bid is almost always above the true value of the item. That is, the auction winner almost always loses money. The existence of the phenomena creates a paradox because models constructed from the basic principles of game theory predict that the phenomena cannot exist.

Figure 7 can help with an explanation of the experimental environment. In this experiment, the value of the item v was drawn uniformly from 0 to \$500. Seven bidders tendered bids. The clue for each agent was drawn uniformly from $v \pm \$30$ where v was the actual value of the item. If the winning bid was above v, then the winner lost money. If s_i is the clue received by individual i, the optimal bidding rule for risk neutral agents is $b(s_i) = s_i - \$30$. In the example in the Figure, v is 180 and $s = 165$. The individual sees only 165 and knows that $v \in [135, 195]$.

Figure 8 contains some of the actual data from the point of view of one agent in an experiment conducted by Lind and Plott [15]. The Lind and Plott experiment, conducted in the spirit of distrust, was a replication of the Kagel and Levine experiment. The signal seen by the individual is called "our sample." The bid tendered by the individual is called "our bid." As can be seen, this individual never followed the optimal bidding rule. The bids of this agent and the bids of others were always too high. The table shows that this agent saw losses occurring repeatedly to other agents in auction after auction and in period 4 experienced a loss himself.

The overbidding that contributes to the winner's curse phenomena is exhibited by almost all agents. It continues over repeated trials. When agents who exhibit Nash-type behavior in private value auctions are placed in common value auctions, the winner's curse immediately appears.

914   *Charles R. Plott*

Table 1. Decisions in Centipede Game

| $ Amounts of Money | .40 | .80 | 1.60 | 3.20 | 6.40 | 12.80 | 25.60 |
	.10	.20	.40	.80	1.60	3.20	6.40
Choosing Individual	1	2	1	2	1	2	1
Trials 1–5							
# of People Choosing	145	145	137	112	64	16	4
Number of Terminations	0	8	25	48	48	12	
Probability of Termination	0	.06	.18	.43	.75	.81	
Trials 6–10							
# of People Choosing	136	134	124	93	33	10	1
# of Terminations	2	10	31	60	23	9	
Probability of Termination	.01	.07	.25	.65	.70	.90	

Source: Richard D. McKelvey and Thomas Palfrey [16]

How can individuals who otherwise appear so rational produce such "non-rational" behavior? That is the paradox. The resolution posed by Kagel and Levine was that individuals failed to properly compute an order statistic. If all individuals are rational, then bids increase with the value of the clue. This means that the individual with the largest clue (which will almost certainly be above the value of the item) will win the auction. The bid must then be properly discounted from the clue to reflect the fact that if the bid wins, then the clue was the most extreme above the value of the object. The proposed resolution of the paradox is that individuals may be rational but they fail to anticipate and incorporate the rationality of others into their decisions. They fail to realize that they will win the auction only when they have the highest signal and/or they fail to discount by the appropriate order statistic.

The second example is called the centipede game. In this process, two individuals participate in a finite sequence of moves that involve options of the following sort. The first person has an option of two amounts of money $\{x, y\}$ with the property that $x > 2y$. If the chooser takes one of the amounts of money, the process ends with the choosing agent keeping the amount taken and the other agent receiving the other amount. If the first agent passes, then both amounts of money are doubled and the second player has the choice between $\{2x, 2y\}$ or passing back to player one and allowing both amounts to double. If players continue to pass, then at the kth decision the amounts will be $\{2^k x, 2^k y\}$. The process is known (publicly) to terminate at decision T at which point the choosing agent must choose the higher of $\{2^T x, 2^T y\}$ and does not have an option to pass.

A natural game theoretic representation of the process is a game with perfect information. The Nash equilibrium of such a game is for the first chooser to take the largest amount and terminate the game immediately. This result follows by backward induction from the terminal period, the perfect information, and the "rationality" of both players. The $T - 1$ player should recognize that he or she will get the smaller amount if "pass" is chosen and, therefore, would choose to take the larger amount at $T - 1$ and stop the game. However, the $T - 2$ player anticipates that and so would terminate at $T - 2$. The logic works its way back to $t = 0$. Interest in the game stems directly from the lack of intuitive appeal of the (only) Nash equilibrium.

Experiments with the centipede game conducted by McKelvey and Palfrey [16] started with the amounts {$.40, $.10} and continued for a maximum of seven decisions ending with a maximum of {$25.60, $6.40}. Contrary to the perfect information game theoretic model, agents do not take the cash and terminate the game on the first move. However, as agents have more experience, the terminations occur earlier. The table contains the relevant statistics from the McKelvey and Palfrey study. The data are partitioned into two sets according to subject experience with the game. Each subject participated in 10 trials (each trial could involve up to seven decisions). At the first trial subjects had no previous experience. At the 10th trial subjects had played the game 9 previous times with 9 different people. In the table the results of trials 1–5 are presented separately from trials 6–10.

First notice that the probability of termination at stage 1 is not 100% as predicted by theory. In trials 1–5 no game terminated at the first choice. In trials 6–10 only 2 of 136 people, or 1%, chose to terminate at the first move as theory predicts. However, as can be seen, the probability of having terminated by a given stage in trials 1–6 stochastically dominates the probability of having terminated in that same stage in trials 1–5. Even the *rate* of termination is higher at all stages except the 5th stage.

Such data present an obvious puzzle. Are principles at work which cause behavior to converge with experience toward Nash play? The Nash play captures some of the behavior in the sense that terminations occur substantially prior to the final round. But certainly the Nash equilibrium model does not exactly describe everything that happens. How can the model be modified to account for what is observed? As can be seen, the puzzles and paradoxes begin to emerge as both theory and experiments become more sophisticated.

The final example is the behavior of asset markets. Early experiments with asset markets by Forsythe, Palfrey and Plott [5; 6] gave clear support for rational expectations. The assets studied had two-period lives and the dividends involved no random component. The environment was complicated by Friedman, Harrison and Salman [8] to include a three-period life and random dividends. The results did not differ substantially from those of Forsythe, Palfrey and Plott. Motivated by these early results, Smith, Suchanek and Williams [22] decided to explore assets with long lives and random dividends. Experimentation under generalizations of existing procedures and environments is a natural thing to do.

The asset studied by Smith, Suchanek and Williams had a fifteen-period life. Each period it paid a dividend which was drawn with equal probabilities from the set {$.60, $.28, $.08, 0}. Thus the expected dividend each period was $.24. At period 1 the expected dividend stream was $.24 × 15 = $3.60 and in period 2 the expected value is $.24 less. The middle curve in Figure 9 shows the "fundamental value" of the asset. If the asset paid the maximum possible dividend ($.60) throughout life (a very unlikely event), then the value would be the top curve in the figure.

The dots in the figure are contracts executed through a computerized market. As can be seen, the assets began trading at prices slightly below the expected value and in period 2 prices are near the expected value. However, by period 3 the assets were trading above expected value. Prices increased slowly from period to period even though the expected value was falling. By period 10 the assets were trading at prices equal to the maximum possible yield and by period 11 prices were above the maximum possible yield. Such high prices could not have been due to optimism about fundamental values. In period 14 a violent market crash occurred as prices fall to levels near the expected value. The time series clearly demonstrates the properties of a bubble and a market crash.

A puzzle emerges. How can markets populated with rational agents have such properties? How can the models be changed to account for this phenomena?

The experimental literature and the theoretical literature contain some hints about possible solutions to all three paradoxes, the winner's curse, the centipede and asset market bubbles.

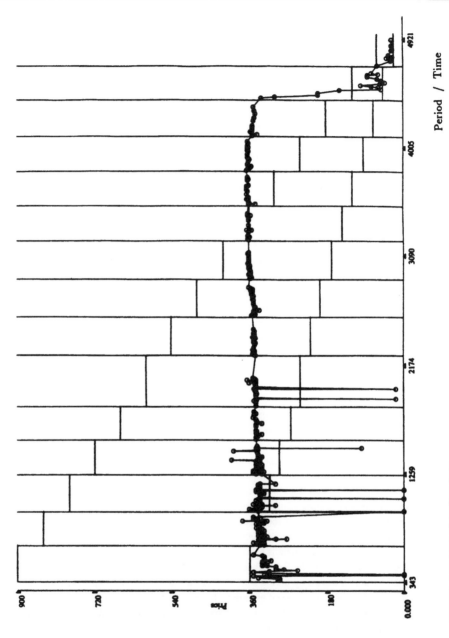

Figure 9. Asset Market Price Time Series

Rationality of agents might not be public information. Each agent might be rational but might also be unsure about the rationality of others. Perhaps the rationality of others is only learned by experience. Recall, in the centipede game, experience seemed to foster more Nash-like behavior. People seemed to learn that other people were prepared to defect. Similarly, the "bigger fool" beliefs could account for asset market bubbles. If an agent believes that he or she can sell the asset to someone else for the same price next period, then the dividend is obtained free. In the bubble experiments experience in asset markets makes the bubble "pop" sooner and after three or four such market experiences, the bubbles almost completely disappear. The fact that "bigger fools" do not exist may become public information with experience in the market. Even the early experiments by Forsythe, Palfrey and Plott exhibited properties that the authors called the "swing back hypothesis"—repeated experiences with final-period behavior become incorporated in the earlier decisions as agents deal repeatedly over the lifetimes of assets.

The suggested solution to the paradoxes is only speculation. However, if it is taken seriously it motivates a host of related questions. Do special market instruments exist (futures markets, options markets) that make public the rationality of individuals? If "irrationality" exists, exactly how might it be integrated into the models? The ideas suggested by Kreps, Milgrom, Roberts and Wilson [14] provide a start. The model developed by McKelvey and Palfrey to explain the centipede game depends heavily on such ideas. However, few people believe that theory should end with the "gang of four" paper and I should emphasize again that this proposed solution is not the only idea that exists.

Step 6: Say's Law of Experimental Methods Takes Over

The famous law of J. B. Say, that supply creates its own demand, seems applicable to the case of experimental research. The application of experimental methods generates research questions that can only be answered by a more intense use of experimental methods. The supply of experimental research creates a demand for even more experimental research. When Say's law of experimental methods takes over, the stage is set for an ever increasing tendency to use experiments. The stage becomes set for economics to slowly but surely become a laboratory experimental science.

The sections above illustrate how it has happened in one case. Experiments suggest that modern theory is on the right track (Step 4). Models based on principles of game theory clearly receive much support in the experimental literature. When applied to simple cases, such models are more accurate than any theory found in any branch of any other science that might be applied to those cases. However, paradoxes exist (Step 5). Phenomena exist that are clearly beyond the explanatory capacities of modern models. But the existence of such phenomena does not mean that theory should stop. Versions of the theory that might readily account for the phenomena by removing the central role of publicness of rationality already exist in the literature. Such theories are not particularly well developed and must be appended by special theories of information and learning. Considerably more experimental work will be necessary to determine if changes in the rationality postulates are the correct way to push theory and to narrow the options from the many different forms that such theory might take. This need for new experiments brings us to Step 6. The supply of experimental research creates a demand for more experimental research.

I'm reminded of the joke about the man who was talking with his physician after having taken a series of tests the week before. The physician first tells the man the good news: "The test report said that you would die in twenty-four hours." Shocked and outraged, the man yells

918   *Charles R. Plott*

"How can you say that? How can that be good news? What could possibly be the bad news?" The physician looks at him sadly. "The bad news is," says the physician, "we got the test results yesterday."

To those who are not enthusiastic about the use of laboratory experimental methods, the prohibitionists so to speak, the good news is that the profession has tasted the devil's brew, the use of experimental methods, and likes it. "If that is the good news, what on earth could be the bad news?", the prohibitionists might ask. The bad news is that all six of the seductive steps to sin and intoxication have occurred in almost every subfield of economics. Those who have not been touched are being tempted. Say's law of experimental methods seems to be operating everywhere. The impact might not be noticeable yet but the process is operating.

Let me be clear about my answer to the question posed by the title of this paper. I do not believe that experimental methods will replace field research. Economies found in the wild can only be understood by studying them in the wild. Field research is absolutely critical to such an understanding. However, the theories and models used in field research necessarily incorporate many judgments about assumptions, parameters and behavioral principles. The simple cases that can be studied in the laboratory can provide the data against which the importance of such judgments can be assessed. Economics is one of the few sciences that is fortunate to have both the field and the laboratory with which to work. The thesis of this paper is that the laboratory methodology, which has historically been absent, will grow and become an important partner in a joint effort to isolate the principles which govern economic behavior.

References

1. Chamberlin, Edward H., "An Experimental Imperfect Market." *Journal of Political Economy* 56 (1948): 95–108.

2. Cox, James C., Bruce Roberson, and Vernon L. Smith. "Theory and Behavior of Single Object Auctions," in *Research in Experimental Economics*, edited by Vernon L. Smith. Greenwich, Conn.: JAI Press, 1982.

3. ———, Vernon L. Smith, and James M. Walker, "Theory and Individual Behavior of First Price Auctions." *Journal of Risk and Uncertainty* 1 (1988): 61–99.

4. Fiorina, Morris P. and Charles R. Plott, "Committee Decisions under Majority Rule." *American Political Science Review*, June 1978, 575–98.

5. Forsythe, R., T. R. Palfrey, and C. R. Plott, "Asset Valuation in an Experimental Market." *Econometrica*, May 1982, 537–67.

6. ———, ———, and ———, "Futures Markets and Informational Efficiency: A Laboratory Examination." *Journal of Finance*, September 1984, 955–81.

7. Fouraker, L. and S. Siegel. *Bargaining and Group Decision Making: Experiments in Bilateral Monopoly.* Reprint of 1960 Edition. Westport, Connecticut: Greenwood Press, 1977.

8. Friedman, Daniel, Glenn W. Harrison, and Jon W. Salman, "The Informational Efficiency of Experimental Asset Markets." *Journal of Political Economy* 92(1984): 349–408.

9. Friedman, James W. and Austin C. Hoggatt. *An Experiment in Noncooperative Oligopoly. Research in Experimental Economics*, Vol. 1, Supplement 1. Greenwich, Conn.: JAI Press, 1980.

10. Goodfellow, Jessica and Charles R. Plott, "An Experimental Examination of the Simultaneous Determination of Input Prices and Output Prices." *Southern Economic Journal*, April 1990, 969–83.

11. Hoggatt, Austin C., "An Experimental Business Game." *Behavioral Science*, July 1959, 192–203.

12. Hong, James T. and Charles R. Plott, "Rate Filing Policies for Inland Water Transportation: An Experimental Approach." *Bell Journal of Economics*, Spring 1982, 1–19.

13. Kagel, John H. and Dan Levin, "The Winner's Curse and Public Information in Common Value Auctions." *American Economic Review*, December 1986, 894–920.

14. Kreps, D., Paul Milgrom, John Roberts, and Robert Wilson, "Rational Cooperation in the Finitely Repeated Prisoner's Dilemma." *Journal of Economic Theory* 23 (1982): 245–52.

15. Lind, Barry and Charles R. Plott, "The Winner's Curse: Experiments with Buyers and Sellers." *American Economic Review* 1991 (forthcoming).

16. McKelvey, Richard D. and Thomas Palfrey. "An Experimental Study of the Centipede Game." Social Science Working Paper No. 732. Pasadena: California Institute of Technology, May 1990.

17. Plott, Charles R. "The Application of Laboratory Experimental Methods to Public Choice," in *Collective Decision Making: Applications from Public Choice Theory*, edited by C. S. Russell. Baltimore: Johns Hopkins Press for Resource for the Future, 1979, pp. 137–60.

18. ——— and Vernon L. Smith, "An Experimental Examination of Two Exchange Institutions." *Review of Economic Studies* February 1978, 133–53.

19. Sauermann, Heinz and Reinhard Selton, "Ein Oligopolexperiment." *Zeitschrift für die Gesamte Staatswissenschaft* 115 (1950): 427–71.

20. ——— and ——— . "An Experiment in Oligopoly," in *General Systems Yearbook of the Society of General Systems Research*, Vol. 5, edited by Ludwig van Bertalanffy and Anatol Rappoport. Ann Arbor, Michigan: Society for General Systems Research, 1960, pp. 85–114.

21. Smith, Vernon L., "An Experimental Study of Competitive Market Behavior." *Journal of Political Economy*, April 1962, 111–37.

22. ——— , Gerry L. Suchanek, and Arlington W. Williams, "Bubbles, Cracks and Endogenous Expectations in Experimental Spot Asset Markets." *Econometrica*, September 1988, 1119–52.

[3]

Economics and ecology: a comparison of experimental methodologies and philosophies *

Jason F. Shogren [a] and Clifford Nowell [b]

[a] *Department of Economics, Iowa State University, Ames, IA 50011, USA*
[b] *Department of Economics, Weber State University, Ogden, UT 84403, USA*

(Accepted 3 December 1990)

ABSTRACT

Shogren, J.F. and Nowell, C., 1992. Economics and ecology: a comparison of experimental methodologies and philosophies. *Ecol. Econ.*, 5: 101–126.

Views of the proper role of experiments in (environmental) economics and ecology have developed quite differently. Economics has devoted the majority of effort to abstract theory, with experimentation coming in a distant second. Kagel quotes a colleague who illustrates a common perception among economists: "I am a 'true believer' in microeconomic theory, and as a result I am perfectly willing to accept mathematical proofs without experimental evidence". In contrast, ecology has focused on observation-based experiments as the primary mechanism of research, almost separate from the development of abstract theoretical ecology. Kareiva notes that "sad truth is that ecological theory exists largely in a world of its own, unnoticed by mainstream ecology". We explore why this divergence has developed and persisted. The main reason is that economists and ecologists differ in their assumptions regarding the objective function of a model. Economists generally assume the objective function is well-defined, ecologists view the function as unknown. We highlight recent research in environmental economics to illustrate the economist's approach to experimentation.

Correspondence to: J.F. Shogren, Department of Economics, Iowa State University, Ames, IA 50011, USA.
* A paper presented at the conference for the International Society for Ecological Economics: *"The Ecological Economics of Sustainability: Making Local and Short-term Goals Consistent with Global and Long-term Goals"*, World Bank, Washington, DC, May 21–23, 1990. We are indebted to Howard Neufeld, Tom Crocker, Marc Evans, Kathy Glenn-Lewin and Matt Rowe for several helpful discussions and comments, and to Charles Plott, Vernon Smith, and Owen Phillips for their encouragement. Three reviewers provided useful suggestions which have improved the paper. This research is partially funded by the US Environmental Protection Agency. All views remain our own.

"Let theory guide your observations."

From Darwin's Notebook
[Gruber and Barrett (1974)]

"...[W]ithout experiments it was impossible to arrive at an understanding of how things worked and that any so called science that did not involve experiment was not a science at all but stamp collecting."

O.V.S. Heath in "In Praise of Experiments" (1976)

1. INTRODUCTION

Ecology has a long, rich tradition of experimental research: from the early pre-"ecology" plant physiological experiments on root pressure by Stephen Hales in the 1700s (Heath, 1976), to the bottle experiments of Carl von Hess and the experimental behavioral ecology of Karl von Frisch in the early 1900s, to the more recent natural variation experiments of Niko Tinbergen. In contrast, controlled experimentation in economics has a much more recent history. Smith (1989) points out that economics is more theory-intensive and less observation-intensive than perhaps any other science. Skeptical economists wonder if any insight can be gained from experiments of well-articulated theory. To illustrate a common perception, Kagel (1987, p. 162) quotes from a colleague's letter, which states "...I am a 'true believer' in microeconomic theory, and as a result I am perfectly willing to accept mathematical proofs without experimental evidence". The work of Vernon Smith and Charles Plott, among others, however, has increased the acceptance of experiments as tools to isolate, control, and test the pure aspects of economic theory. As a result, Kagel notes that the common complaint that economics is not an experimental science is "fast slipping by the wayside".

Along with public choice theorists (e.g., Plott, 1979), leading researchers in environmental economics, such as Peter Bohm and Ralph d'Arge, adopted experimental methods earlier than most economists. Their attempt to more accurately define mechanisms which reveal preferences for nonmarket goods, such as visibility and clear air, led naturally to techniques that were being developed from experimental work. Today, experimental research in environmental economics falls into two broad categories: institutional and valuation. The institutional work — mainly in controlled laboratory settings — examines alternative mechanisms to control pollution efficiently (e.g., tradeable emissions permits, Coasian bargaining). A tradeable emission permits system allows well-defined, tradeable property right permits for environmental resources to be auctioned off to the highest bidder (Crocker, 1966). Coasian bargaining solutions to environmental problems exist when agents bargain with each other to find an efficient solution with no direct government intervention (Coase, 1960). The valuation work has involved primarily field experimentation using survey methods and bidding games. Valuation surveys are now commonly referred to as contingent valuation. The contingent valuation method uses surveys or interviews to construct a hypothetical market where a nonmarket resource can be bought or sold. The market is framed such that features of nonhypothetical markets and institutions are used as mechanisms to reveal preference (see Cummings et al., 1986). However, given the often-noted biases with surveys, attention has turned to the lab to improve the mechanisms used to reveal preferences for environmental goods.

This paper explores the underlying research methodologies and philosophies of experimentation in (environmental) economics and ecology. Our goal is to provide insight into the different methodological approaches to experimentation, creating another bridge of communication. The paper examines general methodologies and philosophies of the disciplines rather than actual techniques of experimental design. As economists, our obvious comparative advantage is in experimental environmental economics. Experiments on valuation — in both field and lab — are highlighted to illustrate the direction of research. Highlighting the economic viewpoint allows economists to see how their approach differs from ecology, and it allows ecologists to point out how their discipline can assist in economic decision making by ensuring that major variables are identified and uncertainties indicated. Doing so satisfies Norgaard's (1989) conditions for conscious methodological pluralism in the conversation between economics and ecology by explicitly making the participants conscious of their own methodologies, conscious of the advantages and disadvantages of the other side's methodologies, and tolerant of the use of different methodologies.

Section 2 considers the divergent views of economists and ecologists toward the relative importance of theory versus experimentation. Section 3 explores why the views diverge: economists and ecologists differ in their assumptions about the objective function of a model. Section 4 examines the role of duality theory and the debated axioms of human behavior. Section 5 describes the experimental approaches in environmental economics for examining the efficiency of alternative institutions to mitigate pollution problems and individual valuation of nonmarketed goods. Section 6 considers the lessons economists and ecologists can learn from each other.

2. THEORY VERSUS EXPERIMENTATION

The methodologies in ecology and economics have developed differently over the years. Until recently, the primary engine of research in ecology has been observation-induced description, while in economics it has been theory-induced propositions. From the perspective of the philosophical literature on methodology, the ecologist's focus on description appears pragmatic while the economist's focus on the axiomatic has evolved from logical positivism. Pragmatism implies that methods and choices result from the workability of common sense rather than formal rules of evidence (see Pomeroy et al., 1988). Johnson (1986, p. 69) notes that "this makes history and case studies more important than data banks" and can often lead to "story telling" rather than rigorous observation. Given the pragmatic approach, Roughgarden (1983) points out that ecology today has a broad methodological base of competing theories without a hierarchy of theoretical axioms, laws, and "truths".

In contrast, the logical positivism that has guided economics rests on two key assumptions: an objective world view and a value-neutral scientist. Under positivism, science can only advance if there is an explicit dichotomy between fact and value; the objective and the subjective. Prediction and control are paramount where one can never affirm a theory, only falsify. McCloskey (1985, p. 25) warns that a positivist (or modernist, McCloskey's term) must "beware of remarks that are nonfalsifiable or nonobservable" (also see Blaug, 1980). It is argued (e.g., McCloskey, 1985; Norgaard, 1989) that positivism has led economics to a definite hierarchy based primarily on one dominant paradigm: neoclassical optimization theory. Often it is argued that the well-defined theoretical structure is inherently correct, thereby eliminating the need for observation.

Pragmatism has shaped ecology into a historical science based on case studies where "theories rarely precede experiments" and "conclusions are sought from accumulated data" (Pomeroy et al., 1988, p. 10). Ecology is "an essentially descriptive compendium of correlations and anecdotes" (Kareiva, 1989). Armed primarily with the first and second laws of thermodynamics and the evolutionary theory of natural selection, ecology emphasizes observation of the natural environment in both bottle experiments and natural variations. From the observations and descriptions, statements are put forth of what normally happens in a particular case given a series of conditional remarks about the situation. Observation led to the discovery of several sensory systems in animals that were theoretically unimaginable: infrared detectors in snakes, ultrasonic sonar in dolphins, infrasonic hearing in birds, and magnetic field sensitivity (Hölldobler, 1985).

Ecologists have developed their broad foundation of competing methodologies where observation and description are accepted, with the more abstract theoretical work coming second. As pointed out by Pomeroy et al. (1988), however, an ecologist's observation of an ecosystem is not the same as an observation of a "stroll through the forest". Observations are an organized, formalized model of structure and functions of a complex system that must exist before more rigorous explorations can move ahead. They argue that given the high level of complexity in ecosystems, ecologists are still far from establishing universal laws. Roughgarden (1983) agrees that "[i]t is difficult to imagine what would ever qualify as a 'law' in ecology. Ecological theory is no more than a collection of tools". Norgaard (1989) points out that ecologists obviously hold different ideas than economists about the possibility and the meaning of science without universal laws. Probabilistic generalizations appear more accepted and useful than universal laws in ecology.

Not all ecologists agree that because of the high complexity and relatively short history of the true ecosystem studies, ecology should abandon the search for universal laws. Loehle (1988, p. 101) argues that "requiring a statement to be precise or exactly predictive before we call it an ecological law is overly restrictive and removes the possibility of laws ever existing in ecology". The possibility of deriving a universal law based on formal logic arguably began with the work of Lotka (1925) and Volterra (1931) on formal mathematical ecological theory, rigorous proposition of behavior. The Lotka–Volterra theory of competition triggered a push toward theory and modeling that shifted attention to biotic interactions (Kareiva, 1989). Although the complexity of ecological systems makes the use of mathematical theory difficult, it is not impossible. By developing propositions which identify the key aspects of the natural system, formal theory can reject earlier anecdotal evidence from direct observation. May (1973) rigorously demonstrated that diversity in ecosystems may not lead to stability, as was earlier suggested. Norgaard (1989) believes such results created antagonism among many ecologists toward theory, and have "pitted the mathematically inclined against the pragmatic and field oriented". As a consequence, Kareiva notes that the "sad truth is that ecological theory exists largely in a world of its own, unnoticed by mainstream ecology". He concludes that a strong dialogue between ecological theorists and empiricists will only develop if theorists make their models accessible and testable, and observationists become more educated in the application of theoretical modeling to answer ecological questions.

While pragmatism led mainstream ecologists to a descriptive-based methodology, logical positivism had the opposite effect on mainstream economists. Although early US economists had a "free-swinging reliance on an amalgam of intuition, observation, erudition and sheer opinionatedness" (Baumol, 1985, p. 11), the methodology today is more systematic. Smith (1982) argues that the methodological paradigm of theory-without-measurement has dominated the economic profession over the past four decades. This observation is borne out by Morgan's (1988) evidence, which indicates that approximately 50% of papers published in the *American Economic Review* and the *Economic Journal* (1972–1986) were mathematical models with no data, and only 1–6% of the papers were based on experiments and simulations. In contrast, of the main papers published in the official journals of physics and chemistry during the 1982–86 period, 12% and 0%, respectively, consisted of mathematical models without any data; 48% and 83% of the main papers were based on experiments and simulations (Morgan, 1988).

Economics has a definite hierarchy, of which theory is considered the foundation, with the implementation of experimental tests coming in a distant second. Smith (1989) illustrates the dominance of the theory-based hierarchy with the following argument. A well-argued theory based on explicit assumptions and devoid of errors in logic will lead to specific correct conclusions; therefore, what is there in a theory to test? If the data are consistent with the theory, we have confirmed what we already know; an inconsistency simply implies that something is wrong with the experiment.

As McClosky (1985) notes, the hold of logical positivism on the sciences has been in decline for decades, but it has left a lasting effect on economics. Economists well-practiced in axiomatic logic and mathematics have often failed to go beyond logic or theory back to observational empirical work. Blaug (1980, p. 259) notes "[a]nalytical elegance, economy of theoretical means, and the widest possible scope obtained by ever more heroic simplifications have been too often prized above predictability and significance for policy questions". Despite the benefits of formal theory in terms of clarifying hypotheses, providing rigorous definitions of assumptions, and reducing hand-waving, the growing uncomfortableness with theory-for-theory's sake has led to the increased use of experimental methods.

Aside from a few exceptions (e.g., Chamberlin, 1948; Mosteller and Nogee, 1951; Flood, 1958), experimentation in economics began in earnest during the early 1960s with the work of Vernon Smith. Smith (1962, 1965, 1967) published a series of papers examining whether market economies produced the competitive equilibrium prices and quantities predicted by the basic model of demand and supply. His goal was to use experimental techniques to advance economics as an observational science. Smith's work throughout the past three decades has emphasized the importance of observation in screening out unpredictive theories from the set of theories policymakers must confront.

Although experimentation is still not totally accepted, it is becoming increasingly recognized that experiments provide a low-cost method to isolate and examine abstract theories of individual behavior. Hoffman and Spitzer (1985) point out five basic reasons why economists are turning to experimental techniques. First, experiments can provide the cleanest possible tests for fundamental theories. By controlling for noise, the experimenter can isolate basic behavioral characteristics. Second, experiments examine the predictive power of a theory. Third, they can provide a test of the predictive power of alternative theories, thereby determining which theory is most descriptive in a relatively sterile environment. Fourth, experiments may chart a path to the creation of a new theory. One of the best-known examples is the work of Allais (1953), who demonstrated that an underlying axiom supporting the traditional model of decision making under uncertainty (von Neumann–Morgenstern expected utility theory) is systematically violated. The observed violation has influenced the theoretical direction of researchers and has generated a flood of work examining the behavioral properties of nonlinear preferences and nonexpected utility theory (see Machina, 1987; Fishburn, 1988). Finally, experiments are relatively inexpensive compared to the cost of collecting new data from the natural world.

In summary, a basic difference in the methodology of ecology and economics is the view towards the proper place of experimentation. Mainstream ecologists accept experimentation, often at the expense of theory; mainstream economists do the opposite. One might overhear the following conversation between the two groups:

Ecolo: What is the big deal about your formal theory? Simply matching your model with my data does not explain anything. It is merely a redescription of reality.

Econo: Well, what is the big deal about your data? Why do you need to test what I have already proven to be internally consistent, and therefore logically correct? If your data are inconsistent with my theory, you must have made an error in your observations.

Ecolo: Look. It's simple. Your theory does not predict anything not shown by the data.

Econo: You are right. It is simple. Your data do not show anything not predicted by the model.

There appears to be a need for a middle ground in both disciplines as there is no universal road to truth or discovery. Kareiva (1989) identifies several areas in which ecology could benefit from insights generated by some of the more modern theoretical results; for example, dynamic and spatial dimensions of coexistence, species interaction with spatial patterns, and stochastic environments. Likewise, economists could benefit from experimental work that has produced convincing evidence for how institutions influence values and choice. As noted by Plott (1987, p. 194),

"...Economists should keep an open mind about experimental methodology and should judge work by the statement of results rather than by methodological principles. Methodological principles should evolve from our experience about what works and what does not work".

3. THE OBJECTIVE FUNCTION: WELL-DEFINED OR UNCERTAIN?

One basic reason for the divergent methodologies is that ecologists and economists have diverse views regarding the objective function of a problem. The objective function describes the cause–effect, or dose–response, relationship between inputs and outputs. Mainstream ecologists appear to be observation-based. Their primary concern is to determine some specific causal relationship in the ecosystem. The ecologists' view is that the objective function is unknown, and the major experimental focus is on trying to describe or define how the function works. A major reason is that little is often understood about the relationship between the cause and effect. The impact of acid deposition on ecosystems is one hotly debated example.

Neufeld et al. (1985) has examined the dose–response relationship between ambient acid deposition and the foliage of native American trees. Neufeld treated four tree species for 11 weeks with acid deposition to determine their adaptive response as measured by photosynthesis, transpiration, and several growth and morphological attributes. The observations of cause and effect suggest that waxy-leaved trees (e.g., tulip poplar) might tolerate acid deposition better and sustain less damage than trees with wettable leaves (e.g., sycamore). In a broader context, Pitelka and Raynal's (1989) review of other literature on acid deposition and forest decline found little evidence of regional impacts. They conclude that at present there is minimal evidence to suggest acidic deposition alone is a major cause of decline. The work on acid deposition appears to typify the observation-based experiments with the objective of explicitly defining a causal relationship, a necessary beginning in the detailed study of an ecosystem.

A second reason for observational dominance is that the overall complexity of the ecosystem does not lend itself well to axiomatic descriptions. Began and Mortimer (1981) describe how the complexity of an ecosystem alters the relationship between a predator and its prey. In a simple ecosystem, a predator can drive the prey to extinction. If complexity increases (e.g., more hiding places), however, both can survive. As the dimensionality of the ecosystem continues to increase, the theoretical tractability of the problem declines leading to an increased reliance on observation to discern the nature of the objective function.

Alternative objective functions have been proposed based on the assumption that a species acts "as if" it optimized the mode of performance of different behaviors and traits; an assumption still much in dispute (see Krebs and Davies, 1981). One proposed objective function of natural selection will be to maximize fitness or total reproductive success — the genetic contribution of an individual plant or animal to future generations (see Bloom, 1986, for example). Another ecological objective function is to maximize assimilated or stored energy — the difference between energy intake and expenditure (see Hannon, 1976; Tschirhart and Crocker, 1987). The species maximizes the difference between the sum of energy inputs and energy outputs, subject to a physiological, functional relationship describing how inputs can be transformed into outputs. A third objective function is the maximum power principle; recently restated more rigorously by Odum (1988) as the principle of self-organization for maximum energy use. This objective function is maximized when a species or relation uses energy that is transformed into a feedback source that reinforces source inputs and improves overall efficiency (Odum, 1988).

The use of an explicit objective function based on an axiomatic definition appears to still be in the minority, however. The ecologist's disposition toward observation can be described by Heath's (1976) definition of science:

> Science consists essentially in an attempt to understand *relations* of selected aspects of things and events in the real world, an attempt which should have both intuitive and logical components, and which must be based on observation and tested by further observation. This definition of course excludes mathematics, which does not have to be based on observation (data) but only on postulates which need not have any relevance to the real world (p. 3).

The economist's perception of the objective function is quite different. Economists generally assume that the objective function, utility or profit, is well-defined, based on fundamental theoretical axioms of preference or production. For behavioral choice theory, the individual is assumed to be able to rank order his preferences conditional on a minimal set of axioms that guarantee that preference can be represented by a utility function. The four axioms which guarantee the existence of utility require the individual to distinguish between more or less preferred bundles of commodities (completeness), that if bundle x is preferred to bundle y and bundle y is preferred to bundle z, then x will be preferred to z (transitivity), each bundle is at least as good as itself (reflexivity), and a mathematical condition requiring the sets of bundles "at least as good as" and "no better than" be closed (i.e., contain their own boundaries).

The economist's view is that since the market embodies all the relevant information of the dose–response relationship, specific attempts to observe relations are not needed. Utility simply requires an ordinal ranking, so measurement of the specific technical relationship is not important; only the ranking of alternative actions is required to derive predictions of behavior. From these axioms, a standard presumption is that increasing wealth increases utility, but at a decreasing rate. This description of the objective function is so well accepted, it has been dubbed the "law of diminishing returns". Other economic laws include Say's Law, Gresham's Law, the law of supply and demand, the law of diminishing marginal productivity, and so on. Although economic laws are often replaced today by "theorems" (e.g., Arrow's Impossibility Theorem), the attempt to rigorously define a law of behavior has promoted internal consistency, precise terminology, suggested critical experiments, clarified assumptions, and identified key concepts, all of which are necessary to advance science (see Blaug, 1980). The assumption of a well-defined objective function in economics has proven to be helpful in advancing our understanding of choice.

4. DUALITY THEORY AND DEBATED AXIOMS OF HUMAN BEHAVIOR

Economists, confident in their knowledge of the objective function, can avoid the direct estimation of a dose–response relation (utility or production) by appealing to duality theory. Duality allows one to obtain information indirectly about the fundamental, primary dose–response relation through observations of actual behavior. Provided the basic axioms are satisfied, the dual approach is simpler but remains valid (see Silberberg, 1978).

The key question then is: are the basic axioms satisfied? For utility theory, there is increasing evidence that the answer is no. Laws and theorems are never really "proved". McCloskey (1985) quotes Kline (1980, p. 315) who states "there is no rigorous definition of rigor. A proof is accepted if it obtains the endorsement of the leading specialists of the time and employs the principles that are fashionable at the moment. But no standard is universally acceptable today". Even the Major General of the neoclassical economists, Nobel Laureate Paul Samuelson, said "if these be [economic] laws Mother nature is a criminal by nature" (Blaug, 1980, p. 161).

Both psychologists and economists are turning up evidence of systematic deviations of individual choice behavior from the predictions of utility theory. Observed behavior often fails to satisfy even the most basic axioms. As evidence points to violations of choice, there is now a recognized need to further understand the cognitive black box of behavior. Economists' confidence in their presumption of a well-defined objective function has been shaken. More and more recognition is given to the argument that we must step back and further explore the workings of the objective function through direct observation, much like the ecologist.

To illustrate our point, consider three systematic deviations in human behavior discovered over the past decades. The first phenomenon we consider is the violation of the independence axiom (i.e., linearity in probabilities condition) in expected utility theory. Formally, the independence axiom requires that if a lottery L^* is preferred to the lottery L, then the combination $\alpha L^* + (1 - \alpha)L^{**}$ will be preferred to the combination $\alpha L + (1 - \alpha)L^{**}$ for all $\alpha > 0$ and L^{**}. Intuitively, the independence axiom requires that the choice between two options depends only on the states in which those options yield different results. Violation of this axiom is especially damaging since it implies nonrecovery of the von Neumann–Morgenstern expected utility function.

Several techniques have been used to construct counterexamples to the independence axiom. The most common method involves obtaining an individual's response to a pair of choices designed to give inconsistent answers. Allais (1953) provided the first counterexample with the following two pairs of choices:

			10% chance of $5m
A:	100% chance of $1m	vs. B:	89% chance of $1m
			1% chance if $0

and

C:	10% chance of $5m	vs. D:	11% chance of $1m
	90% chance of $0		89% chance of $0

If the individual is an expected utility maximizer, then he must either prefer the pair (A, D) or the pair (B, C). Allais and several other experimental studies have found that the modal, and often the majority, of subjects prefer (A, C), however (see Machina, 1982). This suggests that expected utility theory is subject to criticism as a descriptive model of choice under uncertainty.

A criticism of the counterexamples has been that they are hypothetical choices, and choices will probably differ with real, nonhypothetical values and if the individual is experienced with the outcomes. To test this, Battalio et al. (1985) designed a laboratory experiment with nonhypothetical choices repeated over several trials. The subjects were rats. Dominant alternatives were defined in terms of rank ordering uncertain payoffs in the form of actual daily food intake. When the rats were presented with similar counterexamples, their behavior was generally consistent with the Allais-type result.

The evidence of a systematic violation of the independence axiom has led to a rash of new theories of choice under uncertainty. New contenders include nonexpected utility theory, prospect theory, anticipated utility theory, rank-dependent utility theory, prospective reference theory, and probability transformation models. Our goal is not to discuss the relative merits of the contenders, but to point out that Allais' simple observation-based experiment has led to the formulation of new ideas about individual choice behavior.

The second systematic deviation of choice is a violation of the transitivity axiom, commonly referred to as the preference reversal phenomenon. Transitivity implies preferences are well-defined, and that if an individual's preference ordering exists, it is independent of the method used to recover them. Preference reversals upsets this argument. Psychologists Lichtenstein and Slovic (1971) conducted a series of experiments that forced economists to question their belief in the robustness of the transitivity axiom. First, each subject was presented with some variation of the following pair of bets and asked to choose one bet out of the pair:

P-bet: p chance of \$$X$ \$-bet: q chance of \$$Y$
      $1 - p$ chance of \$$x$ $1 - q$ chance of \$$y$

where $X > x$, $Y > y$, $p > q$, and $Y > X$. The subjects were then asked to value each bet by stating the maximum (minimum) they were willing to pay (accept) to buy (sell) the bet. Expected utility theory requires that the bet selected would also be the bet that was valued the highest. Surprisingly, a large number of subjects violated this prediction by selecting the P-bet in direct choice, but assigning a higher value to the \$-bet. This result has been duplicated in numerous settings including with real gamblers in Las Vegas and by skeptical economists doubtful of the earlier work by psychologists (see Grether and Plott, 1979). Economists are now attempting to develop and examine models of nontransitive preferences over bets. Machina (1987) argues that the leading candidate is expected regret theory which explicitly models the impact on choice from the regret of making a bad decision.

The third phenomenon is commonly referred to as framing effects. If a preference ordering exists, then choices between options should be independent of their representation or description. As pointed out by Thaler (1987), this so-called invariance axiom is so basic that it is usually implicitly assumed and is often taken for granted. Again, psychologists have discovered that choice and values are systematically influenced by alternative means of representing or framing an identical problem. Tversky and Kahneman (1981) illustrate the importance of framing effects with the following example. An individual is asked to state his preferences for the following three scenarios:

(1): Which of the following options do you prefer?
   A. A 100% chance to win $30
   B. An 80% chance to win $45
(2): This is a two-stage game. In the first stage, there is a 75% chance the game will end with no prize and a 25% chance to move to the second stage. If you reach the second stage you have a choice between:
   C. A 100% chance to win $30
   D. An 80% chance to win $45
   Your choice must be made before the game starts. Please indicate the option you prefer.
(3): Which of the following options do you prefer?
   E. A 25% chance to win $30
   F. A 20% chance to win $45

Scenarios 2 and 3 are identical in terms of the probabilities and rewards, and therefore should yield identical responses. Tversky and Kahneman (1981) found, however, that subjects treated scenario 2 as equivalent to scenario 1 rather than scenario 3. Nearly 75% of the subjects preferred option C in scenario 2 and option A in scenario 1, while only 42% preferred option E in scenario 3. They dubbed this behavior the "certainty effect", i.e., when the framing of an option suggests certainty, the option appears as attractive as a genuinely certain event. This evidence, along with other examples, makes it difficult to accept on faith that individual choice behavior is unaffected by the framing of an option.

All three of these violations have impacts on ecological economics, especially in the area of environmental risk. A common suggestion for effective regulation of environmental risk is hazard warnings in which the government provides information and the individual then takes private precautionary action. The violation of the independence axiom suggests that individuals will over-estimate the probability of low risk events thereby over-protecting themselves from the risk. The preference reversal phenomenon suggests that values elicited by nonmarket valuation techniques may not actually reflect the actual choices of an individual. The framing effects suggest that how you provide information may be as important as what information you provide (also see Johnson, 1989). Viscusi (1989) argues that what is needed is a "... better understanding to this intervening cognitive black box to assist in designing hazard warning efforts that will remedy the informational shortcomings that have been identified".

The basic point is this: if the individual satisfies the basic axioms of choice such that there is no divergence between choice and predictions, then the objective function is well-defined, duality theory is valid, and the need to directly estimate dose–response relations disappears. If the individual violates the axioms, however, then the nature of the objective function becomes less certain and there is a definite need in economics for the work provided by the observation-based experimentalists, just as in ecology.

5. EXPERIMENTAL METHODS IN ENVIRONMENTAL ECONOMICS

To illustrate the economist's view, consider recent experimental research in environmental economics. Today, experimental research in environmental economics falls into two broad categories: institutional and valuation. Institutional experiments consider the efficacy of alternative mechanisms or "institutions" to reduce the negative impacts of pollution (e.g., a comparison of taxes versus subsidies to control emissions). Valuation experiments examine individual preferences or values for nonmarket environmental goods (e.g., willingness to pay to improve visibility in the Grand Canyon). The institutional experiments have remained primarily in the lab, while the valuation work has generally been conducted in the field through the use of surveys and bidding games.

The key difference between institutional and valuation experiments can be illustrated by using Smith's (1982) triad of experimental methodology. Figure 1 shows the triad consists of (1) the environment within which the economic agents interact (this includes preferences), (2) the institution that

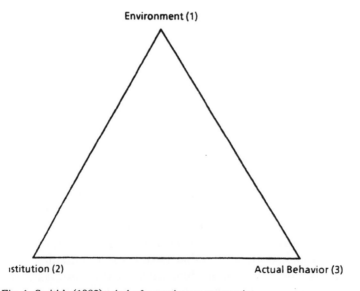

Fig. 1. Smith's (1982) triad of experiment economics.

defines the rules of exchange, and (3) the actual behavior of the agents. Institutional experiments control the environment and institution elements of the triad. The environment is controlled by induced preference theory which relies on the innocuous assumption that individuals prefer more to less money (see Smith, 1982). Valuation experiments, however, attempt to control the institution and actual behavior. By using institutions which accurately reveal preferences, valuation experiments try to control actual behavior, thereby isolating an individual's value for a nonmarket good.

The foundation for institutional experiments on environmental issues is based on the public choice literature. Plott (1979) identifies two arguments responsible for the move toward experimentation in social policy issues. First, it is believed that a major part of social policy analysis is to evaluate the efficiency and choosing between alternative institutions to correct market failure. Market failure exists when the private market fails to allocate resources in a socially efficient manner. Second, it is believed that principles of economics (i.e. fixed preferences) are central to the behavior of social institutions. This implies that social policy now must obtain information on new institutions for which there is little or no data. Experiments offer a natural direction to obtain these data.

Following the general public choice viewpoint, institutional experiments have more or less followed the logical positivism idea of falsification. The laboratory experiments can be used to test the formal theories of alternative mechanisms and bargaining for example. Experimentation on institutions in environmental economics has focused on alternative mechanisms to efficiently control externalities such as pollution (e.g., Plott, 1983; Hahn, 1983), bargaining (Hoffman and Spitzer, 1982; Harrison et al., 1987), the efficiency of auction mechanisms (Brookshire and Coursey, 1987; Smith, 1980, 1982), and mechanisms to eliminate free riding in the provision of public goods (Bohm, 1972).

The experiments which examine the efficiency of economic-based incentive systems (e.g., taxes, tradeable pollution permits) relative to the more traditional regulatory approach of command-and-control (e.g., uniform standard or technology) indicate the economic-based approaches are more cost effective, given an equivalent reduction in pollution. To illustrate, consider Plott's (1983) institutional experiment on negative externalities (i.e., social costs of pollution) and alternative corrective policies. Figure 2 illustrates the general problem the experiment was designed to examine. First, theory predicts that a competitive market with an externality will converge to the private optimum that ignores social costs. Given the wedge between the private and social optima, three corrective policies were considered: taxes, standards, and tradeable permits. Second, theory also predicts that the economic price-based incentives (e.g., tax and tradeable

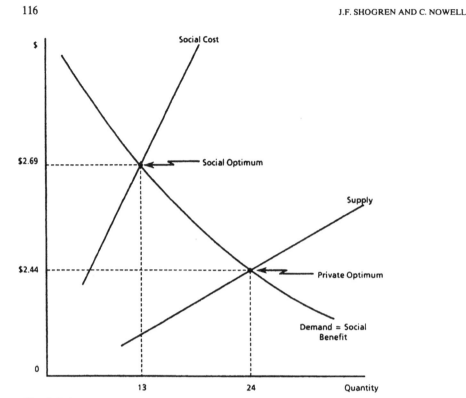

Fig. 2. Private versus social optimum in Plott's (1983) experimental market.

permits) which make the internal private decisions correspond with the social optimum will be more cost efficient than the command-and-control standard which externally restricts output to the social optimum. Note that the regulator is assumed to have full information to apply the optimal policy.

To test these two predictions, Plott designed a competitive market of buyers and sellers who trade a valuable good. In the environment element of Smith's triad, the buyers are given a resale value that they can sell back to the experimenter. The difference between the buying price and the resale value is the buyer's profit. Similarly, the sellers are given a production cost. The difference between the selling price and cost is the seller's profit. The induced preference framework requires both the buyer and seller to prefer more money to less. The institutional trading mechanism was a double-oral auction where the buyers make bids that must increase in value, the sellers call out offers that must decrease in cost. Either the buyer or seller can take one bid or offer per trading period. A minimum of five periods were run; the maximum was 12 periods. No collusion or cooperation was allowed. The externality was constructed by reducing a seller's profits from trades as a function of the total number of trades in the market.

First, Plott established that the competitive market with an externality will converge to the private optimum. Social costs were ignored by the traders. The existence of an externality had no impact on market behavior. Second, the results suggest that taxes and tradeable permits were significantly more efficient than the standards. Efficiency for taxes and permits steadily increased with repeated trading periods quickly approaching 100% efficiency. In contrast, efficiency for the standard did not get much higher than 50%. From these results, Plott concludes that the standard economic models are "amazingly accurate" in the simple lab setting. The corrective policies worked as expected. Note that Harrison et al. (1987) extended Plott's experiment, adding bargaining as another policy, and found similar results.

The second broad area of experimentation has centered on the valuation of nonmarket resources. As Coursey (1987) points out, valuation experiments stand Smith's triad on its head. A valuation experiment elicits preferences (or values) that are part of the environment component of the triad. To control the actual behavior element of the triad, one must incorporate our knowledge of accurate demand-revealing mechanisms which identify individuals' values for the auctioned commodity. Otherwise, the valuation experiments can generate meaningless values.

First in valuation research came field experiments using the so-called contingent valuation method (CV). Based on Davis' (1963) groundwork of iterative bidding games, a CV experiment estimates the economic benefit of a public good through construction of a hypothetical market. The market creates an auction block where the good in question can be bought and sold. The market is constructed to contain features that parallel real-world markets and institutions. By carefully constructing understandable preference-revealing mechanisms, benefits are determined through a survey or interview that elicits a respondent's implicit price for the good; i.e., the maximum willingness to pay for provision or the minimum compensation for removal of the good.

A well-structured CV experiment allows the respondent to solve his or her own trade-off problem, where the trade-off is defined so that each respondent will interpret the problem similarly. CV experiments are flexible, relatively inexpensive, and can construct markets where none presently exist. The market structure and the institutions can be manipulated to conform to the problem at hand. Quantity and quality dimensions such as temporal context, spatial dimensions, property right entitlements, and uncertainty can be varied to reflect specific policy questions.

Although CV use has expanded rapidly over the past two decades, the method has significant drawbacks and detractors. Many economists and public policy analysts question the hypothetical nature of CV. The use of a survey about a hypothetical market violates the logical positivist's or modernist's view that facts are separate from values. McCloskey (1985, p. 181) notes that "one can get an audience of economists to laugh out loud" by suggesting to send out a questionnaire. This tendency to reject surveys for observations of external market behavior has made the CV method controversial in economics. In addition, CV has followed a much more pragmatic road than institutional experiments. Trial and error and observation-based research has dominated CV research. Minimal formal economic theory presently exists to guide researchers in understanding how individuals form values in CV contexts. The pragmatic approach of CV practitioners has somewhat accentuated the hostile reaction, as has the lack of replication and verification of existing CV studies.

The criticism that CV lacks a well-defined theoretical structure as to how individuals form values in a CV context is potentially damaging. In response, both psychologists and economists are now attempting to provide a more rigorous structure to CV. Psychologists Fischhoff and Furby (1988) suggest guidelines to elicit values based on explicitly and carefully defining the three key components of any transaction (the good, the payment mechanism, and the context). Given enough externally provided information, their goal is for each respondent to perceive the nonmarket good identically. Economists approach the problem differently by first recognizing that given prior beliefs it becomes extremely difficult and costly to provide enough information such that each and every individual will perceive the good identically. Instead, Hoehn and Randall (1987) argue that incomplete optimization due to time and decision resource constraints will result in the systematic underestimation of true values in a CV setting. According to Crocker and Shogren (1991), however, CV will overestimate true value given the individual must still form conjectures and accumulate experience about the effect that even a well-specified and clearly communicated good will have on his well-being. The "incomplete optimization" and "preference learning" phenomena suggest the need for more formally defined criteria than "familiarity with the good" as offered by the "reference operating conditions" put forth by Cummings et al. (1986).

Finally, there are also fears of strategic behavior on the part of respondents, and of inaccurate valuations that may result from incentives either in the survey instrument (framing bias) or from the structural design of the survey (procedural bias). See Cummings et al. (1986) for a detailed discussion of the various potential biases and the likely impact on the validity and reliability of CV analysis.

Given the concern over CV biases and the value formation process, economists have turned to laboratory experiments to isolate and control the preference-revelation mechanisms. The accuracy and validity of CV can be increased by engaging in lab work to isolate and control potential CV biases prior to field implementation. Through experimental control, potential biases can be examined in a scientific framework of repetition. CV can also be improved by verification through repeated application and comparison, as well as by extensive pretesting of preference-revealing mechanisms. Ideally, as Coursey and Schulze (1986, p. 48) note, the practitioners of CV will "walk away from the laboratory with a 'best set' of questionnaires", accurately revealing preferences for the environmental asset. Researchers in experimental economics have examined several mechanisms to elicit individual preferences for private and public goods. The oral and sealed bid auctions, and the first and second price auctions, have been examined extensively in the lab (see Smith, 1982). The application to field valuation, however, is still in its infancy (see Brookshire et al., 1987; Dickie et al., 1987).

We illustrate a valuation experiment by examining a study by Brookshire and Coursey (1987). The nonmarket good in this case was the density of trees in a city park in Fort Collins, Colorado. Their objective was to compare and contrast values obtained from hypothetical elicitation methods with values obtained in a market setting. The study consisted of three parts: a CV study, a field study using the Smith auction (which we will define later), and a lab experiment with the Smith auction.

In the CV a series of pictures depicting different tree densities in the park was created by an artist. A door-to-door survey was conducted where interviewers asked citizens of the community how much they would be willing to pay (or accept in compensation) for an increase in the number of trees in the park. Each interviewer carried the artist's renditions of what the park would look like under various different tree densities. Although citizens were not actually required to pay, interviewers tried to bid up the respondents to accurately reveal the maximum they would be willing to pay or the minimum they would accept for increasing (200 to 225 or 250 trees) or decreasing (200 to 175 or 150 trees) the tree density.

Brookshire and Coursey examined an aspect of theory that is often violated in actual CV settings. Theoretically, an individual's willingness to pay (WTP) for provision of a good should be equivalent to his willingness to accept (WTA) for removal of the good given trivial income effects. Results from at least 15 CV studies have found, however, that WTA bids are consistently greater than WTP bids, often on the order of five times as large. Brookshire and Coursey's study also found about a 75-fold difference between WTA and WTP measures (e.g., WTP = $14 and WTA = $855.50).

As Cummings et al. (1986, p. 36) points out there is "little more than intuitive conjecture" as to why this divergence exists in CV studies.

The second part of the Brookshire and Coursey (1987) research on the value of tree density attempted to incorporate a proven lab mechanism, the Smith auction process, into their field experiment. Although the Smith auction was not actually conducted, the questions on willingness to pay or accept attempted to reflect the key elements of the process. The Smith auction (Smith, 1980) has accurately revealed preferences for public goods in the lab and works as follows. The auction involves collecting bids from respondents; if the sum of the bids of all respondents exceeds or equals the cost of providing the public good, then each respondent will pay a proportionally scaled-back amount of their bid. If summed bids do not exceed costs, then the good is not provided. One requirement used in the lab is that the individuals will pay their bids only if agreement is unanimous. The unanimity rule is a crucial part of the Smith auction in the lab. Brookshire and Coursey did not use the unanimity rule in their field test.

The third part of the Brookshire and Coursey study examined valuation in the lab with a repeated market-like structure and nonhypothetical transactions. Five trials of the Smith auction were conducted, where individuals privately submitted willingness-to-pay (WTP) or willingness-to-accept (WTA) bids. If the subjects' bids cover the actual cost of providing additional trees, then they had to actually pay their adjusted bid. The payments were contributed to the Fort Collins recreation department. The divergence between WTA and WTP declined to 5 to 1 in the lab experiments. The divergence is still not consistent with theory, but is considerably smaller than the 75 to 1 difference in the CV study. These results suggest that future valuation experiments need to carefully explore how vigorous lab work can improve the accuracy and validity of measure values for nonmarket goods.

Regarding environmental risk and value formation, Shogren (1990) developed lab experiments with repeated trials and nonhypothetical transactions that examine individual valuation under alternative risk-reduction mechanisms. The findings suggest future avenues for exploration by practitioners of the contingent valuation method. First, the mechanism used to reduce risk matters; reducing risk by altering the probability or severity of an undesired event through a private or a collective mechanism has been shown to generate significantly different values. Generally, the upper bound on value was the private reduction of the probability of an undesired event; the lower bound was the collective reduction of severity. Second, the addition of repeated bidding after new information is provided induced rapid value formation, and could add insight into preference-revelation in a field context. Third, given repeated market trials, the initial bid is generally a significant predictor of the final experienced bid; the implication is that an initial bid, adjusted for learning, could reflect the value of reduced risk in an experienced market. Fourth, the addition of a substitutable pair of risk-reduction mechanisms may add realism to the hypothetical markets constructed under CV experiments. The individual can reveal personal preferences toward the most valued scheme of risk-reduction: private or collective.

At this stage, the nature of the experiments on institutional structure and valuation is quite different. Institutional experiments can and have been verified by replication of design and alternations of assumptions. The valuation experiments, however, have not. Field CV work has proceeded pragmatically, often confirming little or rejecting a lot. Lab valuation work is an attempt to change this. The introduction of more controlled settings where experiments can be replicated under similar conditions or given changes in assumptions can only help to increase the acceptance of the still controversial valuation research.

6. LESSONS FROM THE DESK AND THE LAB

A. What economists can learn from ecologists

In the literature of ecology, a clear distinction is made between a tautology and a theory. A tautology is simply a logical relationship that cannot be disproved. A "theory" should be classified as a tautology if a given set of initial conditions (or assumptions) guarantees a particular outcome. Tautologies cannot make empirically testable predictions — there is no probability for error. Some of ecology's best-known models of behavior have been indicted. Darwin's "theory" of evolution has often been attacked as tautology (Williams, 1970). Peters (1976) argues that "Williams ... has reduced Darwinian evolution to simple deductions based on a series of axioms without empirical meaning". Volterra's model of species competition likewise has been attacked (Peters, 1976) as "strictly mathematical logic". Ecologists do not condemn tautologies as useless, however, if the logical relationships are too complex to be recreated each time they are needed.

Economic tautologies must be separated from economic theories. Resources should not be devoted to testing tautologies. A famous tautology is that presented by Coase's model of bargaining behavior (Coase, 1960). Given a long set of restrictive assumptions, it is expected that bargaining will result in an efficient outcome, or else the subjects misunderstood the rules of the experiment. When this tautology was experimentally examined by Hoffman and Spitzer (1982), every pair of subjects behaved as Coase expected. Hoffman and Spitzer went beyond examining this logical relationship, however, by examining outcomes when Coase's assumptions were relaxed: the Coase model remained robust. See Hoffman and Spitzer (1985), Harrison et al. (1987), and Shogren (1989, 1992) for experimental tests of the Coase theorem under alternative assumptions.

Ecology is still primarily a descriptive science, and ecological experiments are descriptive in nature. Although many ecologists are dismayed by this fact, it is easily substantiated by turning the pages in any of the major ecological journals. Although the descriptive nature may be viewed as a woe to the theoretical ecologists, we suspect most ecologists would be stunned by the lack of behavior-based observation in economics.

Economic experiments are designed primarily to test specific economic theories. Although economic theorists have provided a rich body of material and testable hypotheses, most experiments are based on a few critical behavioral assumptions. Economists need observation-based research to provide more descriptive experiments examining key behavioral assumptions (e.g., preference-reversals).

B. What ecologists can learn from economists

The comparative advantage held by economics over ecology lies in the former's long tradition of theoretical modeling. Experimental ecologists warn that a theory must be given time to develop and mature before testing begins. Loehle (1988) argues that "[i]t is very difficult to conduct a conclusive test of a theory's predictions when the theory is immature, because its predictions may be vague or even contradictory". Loehle (1987), however, recognizes the value of mathematical modeling as an aid in maturation: "Maturation changes a theory from vague and qualitative to precise and predictive.... It is often accompanied by elaboration of experimental, analytical, or mathematical methodologies". Although many field and experimental ecologists are wary of theoretical, mathematical modeling, experimentalists need to recognize that modeling helps theories to mature. Modeling encourages consistent use of terms, checks unstated auxiliary assumptions or boundary conditions, and reduces the derivation of opposite predictions from the same theory. The strong economic tradition of mathematical modeling should be encouraged in the field of ecology. Theory should be critically evaluated to ensure it is falsifiable and usable by experimenters.

Primarily, experimental economists make use of laboratory, or bottle (i.e., controlled environments), experiments. Ecologists make larger use of field experiments. Just as economists must use more field experiments to investigate behavioral assumptions, ecologists must go back to the lab to evaluate specific hypotheses. This idea often is criticized in ecology (Loehle, 1988; Wimsatt, 1979) for its narrow viewpoint. It is argued ecology is a holistic science and bottle experiments are incompatible with a holistic view. The same argument can be made for economics, although it is recognized that individual behavior is important in understanding the workings of the macroeconomy. As Plott (1989) notes, the holistic view is not an argument against experimental methods, but an argument for a specific type of experiment — one where the complexity of the experimental environment is continually increased such that it approaches the environment beyond the laboratory. Researchers can then identify which, if any, complications reduce the applicability of the model.

C. Common ground for economic and ecological experiments

As more researchers agree that integrating economics and ecology is the key to improving our understanding and management of natural resources, the need grows for a common ground in experimentation. While both sides can point methodological fingers, the field of ecological economics allows both the pragmatist and the positivist to converse over the relative merits of integrating their approaches. Relaxing methodological constraints can lead to higher rewards for both groups. Just as Darwin learned from Malthus and Adam Smith, ecological economics today can benefit from methodological pluralism. Costanza and Daly (1987) identify four issues providing a starting point for experiments which combine the insights of ecology and economics: (a) sustainability, (b) inter- and intra-species distribution of wealth, (c) discounting and intergenerational justice, and (d) nonmonetized values, imprecision, and uncertainty. As the theory behind these issues matures, experimentation provides a mechanism for rejecting poor theories, testing competing theories, and examining the robustness of a theory given alternative parameterizations on the relevant variables. Proper identification of those relevant variables is a task for both economists and ecologists.

REFERENCES

Allais, M., 1953. Le comportement de l'homme rationnel devant le risque: critique des postulats et axiomes de 'ecole Americaine. Econometrica, 21: 503–546.
Battalio, R., Kagel, J. and MacDonald, D., 1985. Animals' choices over uncertain outcomes. Am. Econ. Rev., 75: 597–613.
Baumol, W., 1985. On method in U.S. economics a century earlier. Am. Econ. Rev., 75: 53–68.
Begon, M. and Mortimer, M., 1981. Population Ecology. A Unified Study of Animals and Plants. Blackwell Scientific Publications, Oxford.

Blaug, M., 1980. The Methodology of Economics. Cambridge University Press, Cambridge.

Bloom, A., 1986. Plant economics. Tree, 1: 89–91.

Bohm, P., 1972. Estimating the demand for public goods: an experiment. Eur. Econ. Rev., 3: 111–130.

Brookshire, D. and Coursey, D., 1987. Measuring the value of a public good: an empirical comparison of elicitation procedures. Am. Econ. Rev., 77: 554–566.

Brookshire, D., Coursey, D. and Schulze, W., 1987. The external validity of experimental economics techniques. Econ. Inq., 25: 239–250.

Chamberlin, E., 1948. An experimental imperfect market. J. Pol. Econ., 56: 95–108.

Coase, R., 1960. The problem of social cost. J. Law Econ., 3: 1–44.

Costanza, R. and Daly, H., 1987. Toward an ecological economics. Ecol. Mod., 38: 1–7.

Coursey, D., 1987. Markets and the measurement of value. Public Choice, 55: 291–297.

Coursey, D. and Schulze, W., 1986. The application of laboratory experimental economics to the contingent valuation of public goods. Public Choice, 49: 47–68.

Crocker, T., 1966. The structuring of atmospheric pollution control systems. In: H. Wolozing (Editor), The Economics of Air Pollution. Norton, New York, pp. 61–86.

Crocker, T. and Shogren, J., 1991. Preference learning and contingent valuation methods. In: F. Dietz, R. Van der Ploeg and J. van der Straaten (Editors), Environmental Policy and the Economy. North-Holland Publishers, Amsterdam, pp. 77–93.

Cummings, R., Brookshire, D. and Schulze, W., 1986. Valuing Environmental Goods. Rowman and Allenheld, Totowa, NJ.

Davis, R., 1963. Recreation planning as an economic problem. Nat. Res. J., 3: 239–249.

Dickie M., Fisher, A. and Gerking, S., 1987. Market transactions and hypothetical demand data: a comparative study. J. Am. Stat. Assoc., 82: 69–75.

Fischhoff, B. and Furby, L., 1988. Measuring values: a conceptual framework for interpreting transactions with special reference to contingent valuation of visibility. J. Risk Unc., 2: 147–184.

Fishburn, P., 1988. Nonlinear Preference and Utility Theory. Johns Hopkins University Press, Baltimore.

Flood, M., 1958. Some experimental games. Manage. Sci., 5: 5–26.

Grether, D. and Plott, C., 1979. Economic theory of choice and the preference reversal phenomenon. Am. Econ. Rev., 69: 623–638.

Gruber, H. and Barrett, P., 1974. Darwin on Man: A Psychological Study of Scientific Creativity, Together with Darwin's Early and Unpublished Notebooks. Dutton, New York.

Hahn, R., 1983. Buying a better environment: cost effective regulation through permit trading. In: E. Joeres and M. David (Editors), Designing Markets in Transferable Property Rights: A Practitioner's Guide. University of Wisconsin Press, Madison, pp. 83–97.

Hannon, B., 1976. Marginal product pricing in the ecosystem. J. Theor. Biol., 56: 253–267.

Harrison, G., Hoffman, E., Rutstrom, E. and Spitzer, M., 1987. Coasian solutions to the externality problem in experimental markets. Econ. J., 97: 388–402.

Heath, O.V.S., 1976. In Praise of Experiments. Perspectives in Experimental Biology, Vol. 2: Botany [N. Sunderland (Editor)]. Pergamon Press, Oxford, pp. 1–8.

Hoehn, J. and Randall, A., 1987. A satisfactory benefit cost indicator for contingent valuation. J. Environ. Econ. Manage., 14: 226–247.

Hoffman, E. and Spitzer, M., 1982. The Coase Theorem: some experimental tests. J. Law Econ., 25: 73–98.

Hoffman, E. and Spitzer, M., 1985. Experimental law and economics: an introduction. Col. Law Rev., 85: 991–1036.

Hölldobler, B., 1985. Karl von Frisch and the beginning of experimental behavioral ecology. In: B. Hölldobler and M. Lindauer (Editors), Experimental Behavioral Ecology and Sociobiology. Springer-Verlag, Stuttgart, pp. 1–3.

Johnson, G., 1986. Research Methodology for Economists: Philosophy and Practice. MacMillan, New York.

Johnson, R., 1989. Discloser, consent and environmental risk regulation. In: J. Shogren (Editor), The Political Economy of Government Regulation. Kluwer, Norwell, Mass., pp. 191–208.

Kagel, J., 1987. Economics according to the rats (and pigeons, too): what have we learned and what can we hope to learn? In: A. Roth (Editor), Laboratory Experimentation in Economics: Six Points of View. Cambridge University Press, Cambridge, pp. 155–192.

Kareiva, P., 1989. Renewing the dialogue between theory and experiments in population ecology. In: J. Roughgarden, R. May and S. Levin (Editors), Perspectives in Ecological Theory. Princeton University Press, Princeton, pp. 68–88.

Kline, M., 1980. Mathematics: The Loss of Certainty. Oxford University Press, New York.

Krebs, J. and Davies, N., 1981. An Introduction to Behavioral Ecology. Blackwell Scientific Publications, Oxford.

Lichtenstein, S. and Slovic, P., 1971. Reversals of preference between bids and choices in gambling decisions. J. Exp. Psychol., 89: 46–55.

Loehle, C., 1987. Hypothesis testing in ecology: psychological aspects and the importance of theory maturation. Q. Rev. Biol., 62: 397–409.

Loehle, C., 1988. Philosophical tools: potential contributions to ecology. Oikos, 51: 97–104.

Lotka, A., 1925. Elements of Physical Biology. Williams and Wilkins, Baltimore.

Machina, M., 1982. "Expected Utility" analysis without the independence axiom. Econometrica, 50: 277–323.

Machina, M., 1987. Choice under uncertainty: problems solved and unsolved. J. Econ. Perspect., 1: 121–154.

May, R., 1973. Stability and Complexity of Model Ecosystems. Princeton University Press, Princeton.

McCloskey, D., 1985. The Rhetoric of Economics. University of Wisconsin Press, Madison.

Morgan, T., 1988. Theory versus empiricism in academic economics: update and comparisons. J. Econ. Perspect., 2: 159–164.

Mosteller, F. and Nogee, P., 1951. An experimental measurement of utility. J. Pol. Econ., 59: 371–404.

Neufeld, H., Jernstedt, J. and Haines, B., 1985. Direct foliar effects of simulated acid rain, Part I: damage, growth and gas exchange. New Phytol., 99: 389–405.

Norgaard, R., 1989. The case for methodological pluralism. Ecol. Econ., 1: 37–57.

Odum, H., 1988. Self-organization, transformity and information. Science, 242: 1132–1139.

Peters, R., 1976. Tautology in evolution and ecology. Am. Nat., 110: 1–12.

Pitelka, L. and Raynal, D., 1989. Forest decline and acidic deposition. Ecology, 70: 2–10.

Plott, C., 1979. The application of laboratory experimental methods to public choice. In: C. Russell (Editor), Collective Decision Making: Applications from Public Choice Theory. Resources for the Future, Washington, DC, pp. 137–160.

Plott, C., 1983. Externalities and corrective policies in experimental markets. Econ. J., 93: 106–127.

Plott, C., 1987. Dimensions of parallelism: some policy applications of experimental methods. In: A. Roth (Editor), Laboratory Experimentation in Economics: Six Points of View. Cambridge University Press, Cambridge, pp. 193–219.

Plott, C., 1989. An updated review of industrial organization: applications of experimental methods. In: R. Schmalensee and R. Willig (Editors), Handbook of Industrial Organization, Vol. 2. North Holland, Amsterdam, pp. 1111–1176.

Pomeroy, L., Hargrove, E. and Alberts, J., 1988. The ecosystem perspective. In: L. Pomeroy and J. Alberts (Editors), Concepts of Ecosystem Ecology. A Comparative View. Springer-Verlag, New York, pp. 1–17.

Roughgarden, J., 1983. Competition and theory in community ecology. Am. Nat., 122.

Shogren, J., 1989. Fairness in bargaining requires a context: an experimental examination of loyalty. Econ. Lett., 31: 319–323.

Shogren, J., 1990. The impact of self-protection and self-insurance on individual response to risk. J. Risk Unc., 3: 191–204.

Shogren, J., 1992. An experiment of Coasian bargaining over ex ante lotteries and ex post rewards. J. Econ. Beh. Org., 17: 153–169.

Silberberg, E., 1978. The Structure of Economics. McGraw-Hill, New York.

Smith, V.L., 1962. An experimental study of competitive market behavior. J. Pol. Econ., 70: 111–137.

Smith, V.L., 1965. Experimental auction markets and the Walrasian hypothesis. J. Pol. Econ., 73: 387–393.

Smith, V.L., 1967. Experimental studies of discrimination versus competition in sealed-bid auction markets. J. Bus., 40: 56–84.

Smith, V.L., 1980. Experiments with a decentralized mechanism for public good decisions. Am. Econ. Rev., 70: 584–590.

Smith, V.L., 1982. Microeconomic systems as an experimental science. Am. Econ. Rev., 72: 923–955.

Smith, V.L., 1989. Theory, experiment and economics. J. Econ. Perspect., 3: 151–169.

Thaler, R., 1987. The psychology of choice and the assumptions of economics. In: A. Roth (Editor), Laboratory Experimentation in Economics. Six Points of View. Cambridge University Press, Cambridge, pp. 99–130.

Tschirhart, J. and Crocker, T., 1987. Economic valuation of ecosystems. Trans. Am. Fish. Soc., 116: 469–478.

Tversky, A. and Kahneman, D., 1981. The framing of decisions and the psychology of choice. Science, 211: 453–458.

Viscusi, W.K., 1989. The political economy of risk communication policies for food and alcoholic beverages. In: J. Shogren (Editor), The Political Economy of Government Regulation. Kluwer, Norwell, Mass., pp. 83–131.

Volterra, V., 1931. Lecons sur La Theorie Mathematique de la Lutte Pour la Vie. Marcel Brelot, Paris.

Williams, M., 1970. Deducing the consequence of evolution: a mathematical model. J. Theor. Biol., 29: 343–385.

Wimsatt, W., 1979. Reduction and reductionism. In: P. Asquith and H. Kyburg (Editors), Current Research in the Philosophy of Science. Philosophy of Science Foundation, East Lansing, Mich., pp. 352–377.

[4]

Lets Keep the Con out of Experimental Econ.: A Methodological Note

ALVIN E. ROTH

Department of Economics, Faculty of Arts and Sciences, University of Pittsburgh, Pittsburgh PA 15260, USA

JEL-Classification System-Numbers: C90, C91, C92

When Edward Leamer (1983) wrote the well known critique of econometric practice whose title I have adapted and adopted, he was concerned that the credibility and utility of econometric research had suffered because of differences between the way econometric research was conducted and the way it was reported[1]. He wrote (p36–37):

"The econometric art as it is practiced at the computer terminal involves fitting many, perhaps thousands, of statistical models. One or several that the researcher finds pleasing are selected for reporting purposes. This searching for a model is often well intentioned, but there can be no doubt that such a specification search invalidates the traditional theories of inference. The concepts of unbiasedness, consistency, efficiency, maximum-likelihood estimation, in fact, all the concepts of traditional theory, utterly lose their meaning by the time an applied researcher pulls from the bramble of computer output the one thorn of a model he likes best, the one he chooses to portray as a rose. The consuming public is hardly fooled by this chicanery."

Leamer emphasized the contrast between the problems facing an econometrician and those facing an experimenter. He used agricultural experiments as his example of experimental research, and suggested that experimental methods, both in the laboratory and in the field, might prove increasingly useful to economists.

In the intervening years, the rapid growth of laboratory experiments in economics has amply justified this confidence. While we still have much to learn about the uses of experimentation in economics, it is already clear that carefully controlled experiments permit us to draw some kinds of inferences with far more confidence than we could hope to do from any available nonexperimental data.

At the same time, experimental economists, like econometricians, need to be careful not to let the way we report experiments diverge in important dimensions from the way they are sometimes actually conducted. This has become increasingly clear in the last ten years, as there have begun to be enough experi-

---

[1] See also the earlier related critique by Feige [1975], who focused on the incentives for questionable reporting practices inadvertently encouraged by the editorial policies of professional journals, a point to which I shall return in the conclusion. Both Feige and Leamer refrained from citing by name any particularly egregious examples in the literature of the practices they criticized. I will follow their example, in order not to transform into personal criticism what I intend to be remarks of potential relevance to all experimenters.

mental economists so that it is no longer unusual for experimenters with different theoretical predispositions to be investigating the same questions. Some
thought is in order about how to report experiments so as to make these dia-
logues as efficient and informative as possible. In this regard, there are useful
things to be learned from the older experimental traditions in other sciences.
This is so even though, as we gain more experience with economic experiments,
we see that they do not look exactly like experiments in agriculture, or chemistry, or medicine, or even in psychology, but rather that the nascent tradition of
experimental economics has some distinguishing characteristics. And indeed,
some of the issues we need to pay attention to, to make sure that we report
economic experiments in a way that is as informative as possible about the
way we conduct them, arise from these distinctive features of economic
experimentation.

My purpose here is to raise some of these issues, concerning how and in what
detail we report experimental procedures, what data is reported, how it is aggregated for reporting purposes, and how it is analyzed. Some of the potential
pitfalls facing experimenters are similar to those facing econometricians: when
pilot experiments are used to search through alternative experimental procedures and parameters, and to decide which experimental investigations shall
proceed to the reporting stage, then, if this is not fully reported, it is easy to
misinterpret the significance and robustness of the reported results.

Many of these issues can be highlighted by focusing on a deceptively simple
matter, namely the divergent practices among experimental economists about
what unit of data is called "an experiment." While this divergence is sometimes
merely a matter of terminology, it sometimes masks differences in reporting
practices that can lead to ambiguity about what is being reported.

What is "An Experiment?"

I will focus on two approaches to reporting laboratory experiments that have
emerged in the economics literature. They do not exhaust the range of approaches, indeed many reported experiments fall between them. But I think the
difference between these two approaches, and their different strengths and limitations, have not been as widely appreciated as they need to be, and that this
may contribute to some ongoing controversies in experimental economics.

The first approach, which I will call the method of *planned experimental design*, is the approach that has received the most formal attention in other experimental sciences. In it, investigators fill in the cells of an experimental design.
Each *cell* of the experiment consists of *trials* conducted with some fixed set of
experimental conditions, and the experimental design specifies which conditions
will be varied, and what settings will be observed. The whole set of observations

is what is referred to as the "experiment," and these observations are reported and analyzed together. There is a large literature on different kinds of experimental design, i.e. on different ways of identifying the effects of particular variables.

For example, when we speak of an experiment that uses a 3×2 factorial design, we mean one in which there are two experimental variables, one of which is observed at 3 settings and one of which is observed at 2 settings, and in which all 6 combinations of these settings are observed. (It is often impractical to employ factorial designs, which look at all combinations. Many experiments examine only some subset of the possible cells.) Each trial of the experiment consists of an observation at a particular pair of settings (and may be a complicated event involving many transactions by many subjects), and each cell of the experiment consists of independent trials at the same choice of settings. The data of the experiment consist of all the trials in all the cells examined.

Under this approach, once an experiment has been designed and conducted, few if any questions of judgement arise about what data to report. Although the deletion of occasional data points from the analysis may be noted with the explanation that they were outliers, or that some breakdown of the experimental procedures took place in the trial in which they were collected, the presumption is that all the data collected are reported.

This does not mean that there are not ways in which judgement may have played a role that needs to be communicated if the experiment is to be properly understood. While it is obviously a matter of judgement what experiments to conduct, i.e. which conditions to vary and what parameters to set, what is less obvious because it is often unreported is how these decisions might have been influenced by preliminary "pilot" experiments that may have been run. This is where the question of unreported search may arise. I will return to this subject, and why I think there is room for improvement in the way we report these matters, after introducing the second approach to reporting experiments that has become common in the literature.

In what I will call the method of *independent trials*, each trial is itself regarded as an experiment. The inclination to do this in economics experiments arises from the fact that each trial may be a complex event consisting of multiple decisions and observations[2]. But when each trial is regarded as a separate experiment, the potential for problems associated with unreported matters of judgement is magnified, because even the question of what trials to report, or to report together in the same paper, may be taken to be a matter of judgement[3]. This kind of problem is further magnified in an active laboratory which may

---

[2]   For example, allowing subjects to participate in many repetitions of a given market may be desirable, to allow them to gain experience of market parameters and of the behavior of others.

[3]   Some additional confusion is caused by the fact that even some experimenters who conduct and report planned experimental designs have started to follow the practice of calling each trial an experiment. But this confusion can be fixed just by a change in terminology, since these experimenters are simply reporting all the data in their design.

have related investigations proceeding simultaneously, since then the problem of sorting which trials to present as evidence bearing on a particular question may be decided only when the time comes to write a formal report. And the distinction between which trials are pilot experiments and which trials are "actual" experiments may become entirely arbitrary.

The potential for trouble in treating each trial as an independent experiment depends on the kind of conclusions the experimenter seeks to draw from the data. One relatively *un*troublesome use of the method of independent trials in experimental economics is in investigations intended to show that some theory is not a good predictor for every situation to which it might be thought to apply, i.e. investigations intended to find counterexamples.

A good example is the famous "paradox" of Allais (1953). To establish that there are some risky choices for which expected utility theory is not a good predictor, Allais reported two pairs of lotteries for which a substantial percentage of subjects, when faced with the task of choosing one lottery from each pair, made choices inconsistent with expected utility theory. This is a reliable result: you can present a pair of lotteries like Allais' to your class in the confident expectation that many of your students will make the choices that Allais observed. Subsequent experimenters have considerably expanded the kinds of lotteries about which this can be said, and they customarily report these as independent trials. That is, it is customary to report tasks for which subjects consistently violate expected utility theory without reporting the entire set of tasks that the experimenter may have examined.

In this case it is not clear that much information is lost by this practice. Suppose the task reported by some investigator, which shows subjects violating expected utility theory, were the result of a search in which he presented ten different tasks to subjects, and that the responses to the other nine tasks were largely consistent with utility theory. We cannot conclude from this anything about the percentage of cases in which expected utility theory will be unreliable: another experimenter, with less insight, might have had to search through a hundred choice tasks before finding a good counterexample, and yet another investigator might have found the same example on his first try.

A more problematic use of the method of independent trials involves the search for examples that illustrate a theory. Such examples are sometimes thought of as constructive proofs that the theory is not behaviorally vacuous, i.e. as demonstrations that the theory applies at least in some observable situations. Suppose an investigator is interested in finding a game in which a certain kind of equilibrium outcome can be observed, and that, using the method of independent trials he examines ten games, identifies one in which the equilibrium is regularly observed, and reports only that one. (Since he regards each trial as an independent experiment, he regards those trials involving the other nine games as unrelated, failed experiments[4].) Even if the investigator has no

---

[4]   But note that there are circumstances in which even an investigator intending to report a planned experimental design might come to regard the other games as pilot experiments: suppose

intention of implying that this kind of equilibrium will be reached in all games, some information is lost when the nine games in which non-equilibrium outcomes were observed go unreported. In particular, there might be some common process that accounts for the outcomes of all ten games, and which coincides with the equilibrium outcome of the one reported game merely by accident. Including a brief account of the other nine games could give clues to other investigators, while a failure to report them could easily lead astray even investigators seeking to follow up on the reported experiment with new experiments, if they stick too closely to games with the structure of the single reported game. My point is that, while there can be very good reasons to carefully select experimental tasks and conditions through search or other means, the manner in which this selection is carried out is a reportable part of the experiment.

The most troublesome use of the method of independent trials is when the investigator interprets his data as supporting the general predictions of some theory, such as a theory which says that all games will result in a certain kind of equilibrium outcome. If trials in which the theory fails are not reported together with those in which it succeeds, an entirely erroneous impression about the success of the theory can be given[5].

What can we Learn from the Experimental Traditions in Other Sciences?

The first thing that becomes apparent from the experimental traditions of other sciences is that there seems to be no foolproof way to set guidelines for what constitutes "all the relevant data" from an experimental investigation. When the National Academy of Science's Committee on the Conduct of Science at-

---

each game is initially examined with just a few subjects, and only in five of the games are some equilibrium outcomes observed. These five games are then examined with a few more subjects, and only in one of them does the equilibrium outcome occur with really high frequency. Finally that one game is examined with more subjects and reported, with some parametric variations, as part of a small experimental design focused on the one game. The investigator regards the other games as failed pilot experiments, and doesn't report them.

[5]   In this connection I once had the opportunity to hear one experimental economist chide another for having reported that a certain kind of market did not always yield equilibrium behavior. He felt that perhaps a premature negative result had been reported. He went on to say that, in his own research, when he found in an experiment that some economic institution "didn't work," he first tried rewriting the instructions to make sure that they hadn't contributed to the negative result, and if that didn't fix the problem he would try changing the mechanics of the experiment. Often, he said, that fixed the problem. Left unstated was that this search for conditions that would yield the desired result was not reported in the papers that resulted from this activity, which simply presented, as if they were independent experiments, trials that had "worked."

tempted to describe how data should be treated, they noted this difficulty with the following cautiously worded story (1989, pp2–3):

> "One well-known example of this difficulty involves the physicist Robert Millikan, who won the Nobel Prize in 1923 for his work on the charge of the electron. In the 1910s, just as most physicists were coming to accept the existence of the electron, Millikan carried on a protracted and sometimes heated dispute with the Viennese physicist Felix Ehrenhaft over the magnitude of the smallest electrical charge found in nature … Ehrenhaft used all the observations he made, without much discrimination and eventually concluded that there was no lower limit to the size of an electrical charge that could exist in nature. Millikan used only what he regarded as his 'best' data sets to establish the magnitude of the charge and argue against the existence of Ehrenhaft's 'subelectrons.' In other words, Millikan applied methods of data selection to his observations that enabled him to demonstrate the unitary charge of the electron.
>
> "Millikan has been criticized for not disclosing which data he omitted or why he omitted those data. But an examination of his notebooks reveals that Millikan felt he knew just how far he could trust his raw data. He often jotted down in his notebooks what he thought were good reasons for excluding data. However, he glossed over these exclusions in some of his published papers, and by present standards this is not acceptable."

It is of course difficult to judge particular cases, especially in hindsight once the phenomena in question seem well understood. Elsewhere in the same document (p14) the Committee on the Conduct of Science characterize as fraud the deliberate practice of "selecting only those data that support a hypothesis and concealing the rest ('cooking' data)."[6] What is clear is that the larger the role that unreported "methods of data selection" play in determining what data are presented, the harder it is for readers to reliably interpret the data.

Another theme that stands out in the experimental literature is that experimenters must constantly guard against self deception: particularly when an investigator has clear intuitions about what should happen, it is easy to read these into the data[7]. Many of the specialized experimental methods commonly employed in some sciences (e.g. double blind trials) are addressed directly at such problems. And much of the general aim of experimental methodology is to reduce the scope for the subjective expectations of the investigators to play a critical role.

In summary, one method of data selection that is clearly beyond the pale is to select only data that conform to the predictions of the hypothesis being (nominally) tested. But this is not a simple thing to guard against when procedures are used in which experimenters' subjective expectations may play a large role. Many experimental methods, including the use of planned experimental designs, are intended to guard against inadvertently selecting data in this way.

---

[6]   In medical research, where each trial may involve a separate laboratory animal, for example, I have heard the practice of treating each trial as an independent experiment and reporting only those that support the hypothesis referred to as "forgetting about the mouse that died."

[7]   There have even been experiments aimed at elucidating this effect. For example, Rosenthal and Fode [1963] show in a controlled experiment that experimenters who were told that a given rat was experienced or inexperienced at running a maze reported results that reflected their expectations.

The Potential for Mis-Communication due to Different Theoretical Predispositions

A subsequent committee of the National Academy of Sciences, the Panel on Scientific Responsibility and the Conduct of Research, quotes the historian Jan Sapp as follows

"What 'liberties' scientists are allowed in selecting positive data and omitting conflicting or 'messy' data from their reports is not defined by any timeless method. It is a matter of negotiation. It is learned, acquired socially; scientists make judgments about what fellow scientists might expect in order to be convincing. What counts as good evidence may be more or less well-defined after a new discipline or specialty is formed; however, at revolutionary stages in science, when new theories and techniques are being put forward, when standards have yet to be negotiated, scientists are less certain as to what others may require of them to be deemed competent and convincing." (Sapp, 1990, p113 as quoted in NAS, 1992, p39.)

Experimental economics is certainly a relatively new technique in economic research (despite tracing its origins back over sixty years, see Roth, 1993 or Roth, forthcoming), and the rapidly growing acceptance of experimental evidence undoubtedly constitutes something of a revolution, so in light of the above quotation it should not surprise us to find that the views I have outlined here do not meet with complete agreement (recall footnote 5).

The essence of the position I have taken is that negative results, i.e. results contrary to the experimenter's expectations or to received theory, are potentially very informative, and ought to be reported even if the experimenter decides to pursue results more in accord with his expectations or with standard theory. But what one investigator may view as informative results contrary to the predictions of received theory may be seen by another investigator as a failed experiment. For example, I have seen it argued that an experiment to detect a Nash equilibrium is like an experiment to detect a subatomic particle, and that once it has been reliably detected in one experiment, experiments which fail to detect it can be regarded as failures[8].

Now I certainly don't want to discourage scientists who believe that their experimental apparatus is defective from tinkering with it until it works better. (In an economic experiment, this might involve changing the instructions to the subjects, the mechanics of the experiment, some parameters, or even the game or market being investigated.) My point is that there is room for substantial

---

[8]   For the record, I do not agree with the hypothesis that if one game is observed to reach equilibrium it must therefore follow that other games, even similar games, do also, nor do I agree that disequilibrium observations imply an error in the experiment or the analysis. In fact I have reported experiments designed to explore why some games move quickly to their subgame perfect equilibrium while others do not (see Prasnikar and Roth, 1992, Roth, Prasnikar, Okuno-Fujiwara, and Zamir, 1991, and see Roth and Erev, 1993 for a theoretical treatment.) However it is not my intention to discuss the merits of these hypotheses here.

miscommunication if the search for conditions that yield the desired result is not reported in the resulting papers, which instead present as evidence only those trials that "succeeded," and do not mention the nature of the "failures" and the search for conditions which avoided them.

Concluding Remarks

For a variety of reasons, experimental economists have often found that the phenomena they wish to explore, and the hypotheses they wish to test, require experiments in which each trial is a complex event, which may involve many separate transactions. And because of the technology of economics experiments, trials tend to be conducted sequentially rather than (as in agriculture experiments) simultaneously. Perhaps for these reasons, there has been a tendency among some experimental economists to regard each trial as a separate experiment. This practice greatly increases the potential for data selection to play a primary role in the analysis and interpretation of experimental results, and consequently for investigators' subjective expectations to influence the data they report. And when the procedures and parameters for the experimental trials ultimately selected for reporting are influenced by unreported pilot experiments, the process may come to bear more than a passing resemblance to the kind of search about which Leamer (1983) alerted econometricians.

This latter comment can also apply to experiments reported according to a planned experimental design. And under either method, the questions of what experiments to conduct, and which experiments to report together and which separately (and which not at all) are questions of art, as opposed to matters of clearly defined practice. The difference between the two methods, then, has to do with the fact that the method of independent trials, by considering each trial to be an experiment, makes *all* the decisions about data presentation questions of art, while the method of planned design restricts this artistic freedom by requiring the experimenter to first report the design (i.e. all the observations to be made in the experiment), and then to report all of these observations, and to report them together. Insofar as all experimenters need to take care not to let their prior expectations play too great a role in determining which parts of the data they take seriously, experimenters who regard each trial as a separate experiment may want to reconsider whether this is the best approach for the questions they wish to address. And to avoid unnecessary confusion, experimenters who are reporting all the data in their design should probably avoid calling each trial an experiment[9].

---

[9]   It is a simple matter to speak of trials, or experimental "sessions", rather than "experiments" in such a case.

There is room for us all to do a better job reporting what kind of pilot experiments we have conducted, and how they may have influenced the design choices made in the experiments from which the reported data were gathered. It may not always be possible or desirable to conduct pre-planned experimental designs, as the results in an early cell of an experiment may call for a change in plans. But if the process by which the data are collected is reported, the potential for miscommunication can be reduced.

As in econometric research, we may draw different inferences about the robustness of results that result from a search[10]. In this connection, we should also, as editors and referees, give some thought to making sure that we do not create incentives that encourage poor reporting practices. This is not a simple thing, for it means both showing a tolerance for ambiguity of results in well designed experiments, and being prepared to publish replications of various sorts, particularly those aimed at investigating the robustness of conclusions[11],[12] But the experience of other fields suggests that there is a limit to what can be accomplished by exhortation of authors or editors. As a profession, our best defense

---

[10]   To further the analogy with econometrics, the standard error of a (single) regression which is selected from a search understates the ambiguity of the data, and may be a biased estimator. In just such a way, experimental evidence that results from a search through conditions understates the ambiguity of the evidence, and may misrepresent the data, if it omits mention of the search. A related matter is that, because trials are often costly, and because they may involve multiple decisions by subjects who interact with one another in complicated ways, even planned experimental designs for economic experiments often have relatively few cells, few trials per cell, and few truly independent observations per trial. There is room for improved econometric techniques for the analysis of such data. And, here too, replication of results plays a vital role. (Replication in experimental economics means a very different thing than it does in econometrics, where it sometimes refers to the ability of other investigators simply to reproduce the same analyses from the same data – see Dewald, Thursby, and Anderson, 1986. Experimenters seek to replicate a result by generating new data under the same or comparable conditions.)

[11]   Writing about the applied econometrics literature, Feige (1975), in the paper which caused the *Journal of Political Economy* to start accepting papers in the category "Confirmations and Contradictions," wrote:

"... current journal editorial policies have undoubtedly contributed to (1) an incentive to pursue search procedures for statistically significant results which are spurious as often reported, insofar as they take no account of pretest bias; (2) an incentive for less than candid reporting of intermediate results which could highlight the lack of robustness of statistical tests to alternative model specifications and applications of alternative econometric techniques; (3) an underrepresentation of "negative" results which could otherwise signal empirically anomalous results leading to the rejection of currently maintained hypotheses; and (4) an unnoticed proliferation of published Type 1 errors." (pp1292–93).

[12]   Counterproductive incentives about what to report may also exist in areas of economics involving other than econometric or experimental data. I have only an anecdote to offer about economic history, having to do with a forthcoming paper of mine (Roth and Xing, 1994) which contains historical descriptions of the evolution of the timing of transactions in several dozen markets, along with some theoretical models of the observed phenomena. One reviewer suggested that the historical data exhibited an excess variety of behavior compared to that which could be accounted for by the formal theoretical models. Obviously one way to avoid such a criticism would be to report only those historical observations that can be explained by the available theory.

against erroneous conclusions resulting from unreported or incompletely reported search is to encourage experimenters to follow up on one another's work,
with experiments which change elements of the design that might influence the
outcome in ways not accounted for by the theory or theories proposed to account for the results.

Indeed, one of the reasons that experimental economics has been as productive as it has is that reported results have by and large been straightforwardly
replicable: when a carefully conducted experiment is repeated, the likelihood
that the data will be similar seems to be high. But precise replication gives little
information about robustness. What ultimately gives us our best indication of
the robustness of experimental results is replication with some variation of experimental parameters and conditions. And, particularly in the last ten years as
experimental economists have become numerous enough so that investigators
with different theoretical predispositions have started to examine the same questions, we have seen that investigators with different intuitions about a question
can sometimes design experiments that lead them to different conclusions. In
this respect, some of the controversies in the experimental literature focus on
questions of robustness, and will be more productively carried out when methodological issues concerning how much search has been conducted and how
much data selection has been employed are clearly reported.

In conclusion, one of the principal roles of experimental methodology is to
help investigators avoid the danger of too easily accepting their prior hypotheses. The experience of other sciences suggests that this is a problem that will
be always with us: evidence counter to the preferred hypothesis may look like
experimental error ("the subjects didn't understand"), there is a natural tendency to keep trying different parameters when things aren't working out, but
to stick with parameters which do work out, etc. As in econometric research,
experimental results which are the end product of a search for conditions and
parameters that will yield certain kinds of results are difficult to interpret without some understanding of the search process. And all of these problems are
exacerbated when investigators regard each trial as an independent experiment.

But overall, the experimental enterprise contains many elements that promote the identification of robust results. Chief among these is that experimenters don't have to rely on one anothers' data, or even their choices of parameters
and procedures, but can generate their own data from experimental environments well suited to testing their hypotheses precisely. And so *series* of experiments allow the experimental community to build upon and critique one
anothers' work in ways that are not as readily available to economists using
non-experimental methods. There is every reason for optimism about the contribution that series of experiments, particularly when conducted by experimenters with different points of view who take care to address each others'
positions, can make to identifying robust empirical regularities in economics[13].

---

[13] For many fine examples of the success of this approach, see the forthcoming *Handbook of
Experimental Economics* (Kagel and Roth, forthcoming).

The purpose of this note is to help to enhance the efficiency of this kind of dialogue, by raising some of the methodological issues that both producers and consumers of experimental research must consider in interpreting experimental results.

References

Allais M (1953) Le comportement de l'homme rationnel devant le risque: Critique des postulats et axiomes de l'ecole Americane. Econometrica 21:503–546

Dewald WG, Thursby JG, Anderson RG (1986) Replication in empirical economics: The journal of money, credit and banking project. American Economic Review 76:587–603

Feige EL (1975) The consequences of journal editorial policies and a suggestion for revision. Journal of Political Economy 83:1291–1295

Kagel JH, Roth AE (Eds) Handbook of experimental economics. Princeton University Press, forthcoming

Leamer EE (1983) Let's take the con out of econometrics. American Economic Review 73:31–43

National Academy of Sciences (1989) On being a scientist. Committee on the Conduct of Science, Washington, National Academy Press

National Academy of Sciences (1992) Responsible science: Ensuring the integrity of the research process, Volume I. Panel on scientific responsibility and the conduct of research. Washington, National Academy Press.

Prasnikar V, Roth AE (1992) Considerations of fairness and strategy: Experimental data from sequential games. Quarterly Journal of Economics 865–888

Rosenthal R, Fode KL (1963) The effect of experimenter bias on the performance of the albino rat. Behavioral Science 8:183–189

Roth AE (1993) On the early history of experimental economics. Journal of the History of Economic Thought 15:184–209.

Roth AE (1994) Introduction to experimental economics. Chapter 1 of Handbook of experimental economics, Kagel J, Roth AE (Eds) Princeton University Press, forthcoming

Roth AE, Erev I (1993) Learning in extensive-form games: Experimental data and simple dynamic models in the intermediate term. Mimeo, presented at the Nobel Symposium on Game Theory, June 18–20, Bjorkborn, Sweden

Roth AE, Prasnikar V, Okuno-Fujiwara M, Zamir S (1991) Bargaining and market behavior in Jerusalem, Ljubljana, Pittsburgh, and Tokyo: An experimental study. American Economic Review 81:1068–1095

Roth AE, Xing X. Jumping the gun: Imperfections and institutions related to the timing of market transactions. American Economic Review, forthcoming

Sapp J (1990) Where the truth lies: Franz Moewus and the origins of molecular biology. Cambridge, Cambridge University Press

[5]

Progress in Behavioral Game Theory

Colin F. Camerer

I s game theory meant to describe actual choices by people and institutions or
not? It is remarkable how much game theory has been done while largely
ignoring this question. The seminal book by von Neumann and Morgenstern,
The Theory of Games and Economic Behavior, was clearly about how rational players
would play against others they knew were rational. In more recent work, game
theorists are not always explicit about what they aim to describe or advise. At one
extreme, highly mathematical analyses have proposed rationality requirements that
people and firms are probably not smart enough to satisfy in everyday decisions. At
the other extreme, adaptive and evolutionary approaches use very simple models—
mostly developed to describe nonhuman animals—in which players may not realize
they are playing a game at all. When game theory does aim to describe behavior,
it often proceeds with a disturbingly low ratio of careful observation to theorizing.

This paper describes an approach called "behavioral game theory," which aims
to describe actual behavior, is driven by empirical observation (mostly experiments), and charts a middle course between over-rational equilibrium analyses and
under-rational adaptive analyses.

The recipe for behavioral game theory I will describe[1] has three steps: start
with a game or naturally occurring situation in which standard game theory makes
a bold prediction based on one or two crucial principles; if behavior differs from

---

[1] Interested readers familiar with game theory should read Crawford (1997), whose approach is more
eclectic than mine. He concludes (p. 236) that "most strategic behavior can be understood via a synthesis
that combines elements from each of the leading theoretical frameworks [traditional game theory, evolutionary game theory, and adaptive learning] with a modicum of empirical information about
behavior . . ." Behavioral game theory adds psychological interpretations to this synthesis.

■ *Colin F. Camerer is Rea and Lela G. Axline Professor of Business Economics, California
Institute of Technology, Pasadena, California. His e-mail address is ⟨camerer@hss.caltech.edu⟩.*

the prediction, think of plausible explanations for what is observed; and extend formal game theory to incorporate these explanations. This paper considers three categories of modelling principles and catalogues violations of these principles. The first section will focus on cases in which players, rather than focusing self-interestedly on their own payoff alone, seem to respond in terms related to social utility, showing concerns about fairness and the perceived intentions of other players. The next section will focus on problems of choice and judgment: cases in which players respond to differences in how the game is described, rather than to the outcomes, and in which players systematically overestimate their own capabilities. A third section will investigate some elements that people bring to strategic situations that are usually unaccounted for in game theory: a common awareness of certain focal points for agreement, a belief that timing of a choice may confer privileged status or change players' thinking, and a natural instinct to look only one or two levels into problems that permit many levels of iterated reasoning.

Organizing findings in this way is like taking a car engine apart and spreading out the parts, so that each part can be inspected separately and broken ones replaced. The hope is that working parts and necessary replacements can later be reassembled into coherent theory. Just as the rebuilt car engine should run better than before, the eventual goal in behavioral game theory is to be able to take a description of a strategic situation and predict actual behavior at least as well as current theories do. Better descriptive principles should also improve the prescriptive value of game theory, since players who desire to play rationally need to know how others are likely to play.

Simple games are also useful for establishing phenomena that should be incorporated into economics beyond game theory. In experiments, people routinely reject profitable bargains they think are unfair, contribute substantially to public goods and do not take full advantage of others when they can (exhibiting surprisingly little "moral hazard"). Textbook discussions of wage setting, public goods problems and the need for incentive contracts and monitoring to prevent moral hazard paint a different picture, portraying people as more socially isolated, uncooperative and opportunistic than they are in experiments. If the generality of the experimental results is questioned, the generality of the textbook caricature should be, too. Other game experiments show that players will behave "irrationally" when they expect others to behave even more irrationally, which is one common explanation for excessive volatility in financial markets. Establishing and dissecting such effects in games could help inform theorizing about similar behavior in markets.

Games as Social Allocations

Games give payoffs to more than one person. If players care about the financial payoffs of others, the simplifying assumption of pure self-interest, common to so much game theory analysis, must be modified. Most theories sidestep this concern by assuming the individual utilities already take into account the possibility that players care about how much others get, so that players still want to maximize their own individual utilities. But in practice, when payoffs are measured in dollars or other numerical units, predictions depend on the precise form of the "social utility" function that players use to combine their own payoffs and payoffs of others to decide their preferences.

Simple bargaining games have proved to be useful tools for bringing out issues of social utility. For example, in an ultimatum game, a Proposer offers a division of a sum of money X to a Responder who can accept or reject it. If the Responder accepts the offer, then both players receive the amount of money given; if the Responder rejects the offer, then both players receive nothing. The ultimatum game is an instrument for asking Responders, "Is this offer fair?" It forces them to put their money where their mouth is and reject offers they claim are unfair. Dozens of studies with these games establish that people dislike being treated unfairly, and reject offers of less than 20 percent of X about half the time, even though they end up receiving nothing. Proposers seem to anticipate this behavior, and to reduce the risk of rejection, they typically offer 40–50 percent of X. The basic result has been replicated in several countries for stakes of up to two months' wages.

The extent of pure altruism by Proposers can be measured with a "dictator" game, an ultimatum game in which the Proposer dictates the division of the money, because the Responder cannot reject the offer. In the dictator game, Proposers offer substantially less than in ultimatum games, but still generally offer an average of 20–30 percent of the sum to be divided.[2] Recent experiments on "trust" (or "gift exchange") add a stage in which one player can either keep a fixed sum or give a larger sum to a second player, who then allocates it between the two players however she likes, as in a dictator game. The first player can either keep the fixed sum, or trust the second player to give back more. In these games, there is often a surprising amount of trust, and the "return to trust" is slightly positive (Fehr, Kirchsteiger and Reidl, 1993; Berg, Dickhaut and McCabe, 1995; and Bolle, 1995).

The crucial step, of course, is to incorporate findings like these into a theory that is more general but still reasonably parsimonious. A natural alternative is to assume that player 1's utility function incorporates the comparison between 1's payoff and player 2's in some way. For example, the separable form in which the utility of player 1 over the consumption of both players, x_1 and x_2, is given by $u_1(x_1, x_2) = v(x_1) + \alpha v(x_2)$ allows for both sympathy or altruism. Sympathy occurs when $\alpha > 0$, so that player 1 benefits from the consumption of player 2; envy occurs when $\alpha < 0$, so that player 1 suffers from the consumption of player 2. "Sympathy coefficients" were mentioned by Adam Smith, and the linear formulation was discussed by Edgeworth (1881 [1967], pp. 101–102), who wrote: "We must modify the utilitarian integral . . . by multiplying each pleasure, except the pleasure of the

---

[2] For a brief introduction to the literature on ultimatum and dictator games in this journal, see the "Anomalies" column by Camerer and Thaler in the Spring 1995 issue.

Table 1
A Prisoner's Dilemma

	Cooperate	Defect
Cooperate	3, 3	0, 5
Defect	5, 0	1, 1

agent himself, by a fraction—a factor doubtless diminishing with what may be called the social distance between the individual agent and those of whose pleasures he takes account."

But this sort of model looks only at the final allocation between players, and thus does not accommodate the fact that the way in which an unequal allocation came about, and what that implies to one player about the intentions of the other, also affect behavior. For example, Blount (1995) found that players were more willing to accept uneven offers generated by a chance device than the same offer generated by a Proposer who benefits from the unevenness. Exploring the sources of altruism or envy requires a model in which social values are triggered by actions and intentions of others. Rabin (1993) proposed an elegant model that does so. He suggests (roughly speaking) that player 1 has a positive sympathy coefficient $\alpha > 0$ when player 2 "kindly" helps 1; and conversely, $\alpha < 0$ when player 2 behaves "meanly" by choosing an action that hurts 1. Rabin assumes these feelings add to utility from money payoffs, but become relatively less important as money payoffs rise. These assumptions and a few others lead to "fairness equilibrium." The concept of a fairness equilibrium is consistent with observations from three games that are anomalies for most other approaches.

In an ultimatum game, an unfair offer by the Proposer is mean, and hence triggers reciprocated meanness from the Responder (a rejection). An uneven offer generated by chance, however, is not a mean act by the player who benefits from it, so fairness equilibrium predicts correctly that such offers are rejected less often.

In a prisoner's dilemma game, illustrated in Table 1, a rational player recognizes that regardless of whether the other player defects or cooperates, the rational act is to defect. However, when both players follow this logic, they end up worse off than if they could have agreed to cooperate. In experimental games, players seem unexpectedly skillful at avoiding the dilemma and finding their way to cooperation. The concept of fairness equilibrium helps to explain why. At least for small stakes, cooperation in a prisoner's dilemma is a fairness equilibrium. After all, cooperating means sacrificing to help another person, which triggers a reciprocal preference to cooperate. Cooperation is emotionally strategic in this approach, transforming the prisoner's dilemma into a coordination game in which players desire to coordinate their levels of niceness. This jibes with the widely observed fact that players who expect others to cooperate are more likely to cooperate themselves (Sally, 1995).

Table 2
Chicken

| | | Player 2 | |
		Dare (*D*)	Chicken (*C*)
Player 1	Dare (*D*)	$-4x, -4x$	$3x, 0$
	Chicken (*C*)	$0, 3x$	x, x

But intentions matter. Suppose another player is forced to cooperate—perhaps by a game structure in which that person cannot choose to defect. Their forced cooperation does not give the other player an unusually high payoff (it is not "nice," because the forced player did not have the option to defect and treat the other player badly). So fairness equilibrium predicts the free-to-choose player is under no obligation to reciprocate and will be more likely to defect than in the standard dilemma.

The game of chicken, it turns out, is perhaps the ideal game for contrasting fairness and self-interested preferences. Table 2 gives the payoffs in "chicken." In this game, both players would like to Dare (*D*) the other to Chicken out (*C*) (then *D* earns $3x$, and *C* earns 0) but if both Dare they each earn $-4x$. The players move simultaneously. The (pure strategy) Nash equilibria are (*D,C*) and (*C,D*), since a player who expects the other to Dare should Chicken out, and vice versa. However, fairness equilibrium predicts exactly the opposite, at least for small stakes. Start in the upper right (*D,C*) cell. Though the game is actually played simultaneously, suppose the players' reason in their own minds about moves and countermoves, in a kind of mental tatonnement, before deciding what to do. If player 1 moves from this cell, politely choosing *C*, she sacrifices $2x$ (getting x instead of $3x$) to benefit player 2 by the amount x. This nice choice triggers reciprocal niceness in player 2; rather than exploiting player 1's choice of *C* by responding with *D*, player 1 prefers to sacrifice (settling for x instead of $3x$) to "repay" player 1's kindness. Thus, both politely playing Chicken is a fairness equilibrium. By opposite reasoning, (*D,D*) is a mean fairness equilibrium; rather than back down in the face of the other's *D*, both would rather lose more by picking *D*, to hurt their enemy.[3] In a recent study of chicken, 60 percent of the observations in the last half of the experiment were fairness equilibrium choices (*C,C*) and (*D,D*), and only 12 percent were Nash equilibria (*D,C*) and (*C,D*) (McDaniel, Rutström and Williams, 1994).

---

[3] The "mean" fairness equilibrium (*D,D*) illustrates the advantage of chicken over the prisoner's dilemma for studying social values. In the prisoner's dilemma, defection is both a self-interested choice (reflecting neither niceness nor meanness), *and* it is the choice a mean-spirited (or envious) person would make. In chicken, the best response of a self-interested person to an expectation that the other person would play *D* is *C*, but a mean person would pick *D*.

The fairness equilibrium or "reciprocated value" model is a solid new plateau for understanding departures from self-interest in games. The model captures basic facts that the simpler separable and comparative models do not capture, particularly the reciprocal nature of social values and the distinction between uneven outcomes and unfair actions. Its formal specification connects fairness equilibrium closely to standard game theory. Games like chicken allow both nice and mean outcomes to arise in the same game, capturing phenomena like the blissful happiness of a loving couple and their bitter, mutually destructive breakup.

Games Require Choice and Judgment

Rational players will perceive a game and themselves clearly and consistently. However, when "framing effects" are important, players see the game differently according to how it is described. When players are overconfident of their own abilities, they fail in seeing the likely consequences of their actions. This section considers these two phenomena in turn.

Framing Effects

Theories of choice often invoke an axiom of "description invariance," which holds that differences in descriptions that do not alter the actual choices should not alter behavior. A "framing effect" occurs when a difference in description does cause behavior to vary.

For example, give subjects $10 in advance, then ask them whether they would choose a certain loss of $5 (for a net gain of $5) or flip a coin and lose either $10 or 0, depending on the outcome. Those subjects choose to gamble more frequently than subjects who are given nothing and asked to choose between gaining $5 or flipping a coin with $10 and 0 outcomes (Tversky and Kahneman, 1992). Generally, people are more likely to take risks when outcomes are described as losses than when the same outcomes are described as gains. Players in games can exhibit a version of this "reflection effect." Players are more willing to risk disagreement when bargaining over possible losses than when bargaining over possible gains (Neale and Bazerman, 1985; Camerer et al., 1993). In certain coordination games with multiple equilibria, avoidance of losses acts as a "focal principle" that leads players to coordinate their expectations on those equilibria in which nobody loses money (Cachon and Camerer, 1996).

Overconfidence about Relative Skill

The now-standard approach to games of imperfect information pioneered by John Harsanyi presumes that players begin with a "common prior" probability distribution over any chance outcomes. As an example, consider two firms *A* and *B*, who are debating whether to enter a new industry like Internet software. Suppose it is common knowledge that only one firm will survive—the firm with more skilled managers, say—so firms judge the chance that their managers are the more skilled.

The common prior assumption insists both firms cannot think they are each more likely to have the most skill. Put more formally, a game like this can be modelled as a tree where the top node separates the game into two halves—a left half in which *A* is truly more skilled, and a right half in which *B* is truly more skilled. The firms can't play coherently if *A* and *B* believe they are actually on different halves of the tree. In this way, overconfidence about relative skill violates the common prior assumption.

Of course, this requirement of a common prior does not rule out that players may have private information. In the example of the two competing software firms, each could know about its own secret projects or the tastes of its customers, but others must know what that information could possibly be.

Dozens of studies show that people generally overrate the chance of good events, underrate the chance of bad events and are generally overconfident about their relative skill or prospects. For example, 90 percent of American drivers in one study thought they ranked in the top half of their demographic group in driving skill (Svenson, 1981). Feedback does not necessarily dampen overconfidence much (and could make it worse): one study even found overconfidence among drivers surveyed in the hospital after suffering bad car accidents (Preston and Harris, 1965).

But if those involved in game-like interactions are overconfident, the result may matter, dramatically. For example, economic actors behaving in a mutually overconfident way may invest the wrong amount in R&D, prolong strikes or delay agreements inefficiently, opt for high-risk sports or entertainment careers instead of going to college, and so on.

Although overconfidence has been largely ignored in theorizing about games, there are some clear experimental examples of its effects. In the Winter 1997 issue of this journal, Babcock and Loewenstein review several such examples and also describe what they call "self-serving bias."

One possible economic manifestation of overconfidence is the high failure rates of new businesses (around 80 percent fail in their first three years). Of course, high failure rates are not necessarily inconsistent with profit maximization. Maybe new business owners judge their relative skill accurately, but business returns are positively skewed "lottery ticket" payoffs in which the few survivors are extremely profitable. Then a large percentage might fail, even though the expected value of entering is positive. The overconfidence and rational entry explanations are very difficult to distinguish using naturally occurring data. But they can be compared in an experimental paradigm first described in Kahneman (1988) and extended by Rapoport et al. (forthcoming).

In the entry game paradigm, each of *N* subjects can choose to enter a market with capacity *C* or can stay out and earn nothing. The profit for each entrant is the same, but more entrants means that everyone earns a lower level of profit. If *C* or fewer enter, the entrants all earn a positive profit. If more than *C* enter, the entrants all lose money. In pure-strategy Nash equilibria, players should somehow coordinate their choices so that exactly *C* enter and $N - C$ stay out.

Rapoport et al. (forthcoming) found that when subjects played repeatedly with feedback about the number of entrants in each period, about C subjects did enter, even though players could not communicate about which of them would enter and which would stay out.

When all entrants earn the same profit, there is no such thing as a more or less successful entrant, so overconfidence about relative success cannot fuel excessive entry. Dan Lovallo and I (1996) enriched the paradigm to allow that possibility. In one version of the experiment, we informed 14 subjects that they were going to take a trivia quiz and that the six entrants who turned out to be top-ranked in that quiz would share $50 in profits. (The trivia quiz can be considered in economic terms as a difference in product cost or R&D effectiveness that would make certain firms more profitable if they choose to enter.) However, any entrants below the top six would lose $10 each. Notice in this example that if 11 subjects enter, then the total industry profit is zero ($50 divided among the six high scores, and losses of $10 apiece for the other five). Thus, if subjects are risk neutral and think they are equally likely to rank high and low relative to other entrants, about 11 of the 14 players should enter and the rest should stay out. In different versions of the experiment, the number of top-ranked entrants who would receive a share of the positive profits was then systematically varied from six.

We found that in our baseline condition, when the rankings of potential entrants were determined randomly, the number of entrants was typically one or two fewer than the number that would drive industry profits to zero, so the average entrant made a slight profit. However, when the subjects were told that the rankings would be determined by the trivia contest, the number of entrants was typically one or two above the number that would drive industry profits to zero, so the average entrant made losses. The difference in trivia contest entry rates and the random-rank baseline condition was statistically significant. Perhaps even more interesting, when subjects were asked to forecast how many others would enter after the trivia game, they accurately forecast that there would be too many entrants and that the average entrant would lose money—but entrants all thought *they* were above average and would earn money.

The overconfidence bias results from a conflict between wanting to be realistic and wanting to feel good about oneself, and from the psychological "availability" of memories that support the rosy view of oneself. Researchers have documented a number of other systematic biases in probability judgments, including biases resulting from using shortcuts that make difficult judgments easier.

One such shortcut is called "representativeness." People who use this heuristic judge how well a sample represents a statistical process (or a person or category) and use that judgment to estimate the sample's likelihood. This shortcut is sensible, but sometimes conflicts with normative principles of probability. An example from game theory comes from "weak link" coordination games (Van Huyck, Battalio and Beil, 1990). In these games, several players choose numbers from 1 to 7 at the same time. Each player earns a payoff that depends on the minimum number anybody picks—a high minimum is better—and players are penalized for picking a number above the minimum. Because players are penalized for picking too high a number, they would like to match whatever they expect the minimum to be. A little statistical thought suggests that the minimum is likely to be much lower in large groups than it would be in small groups. And it is: in groups of six or more the minimum is usually 1-2, but in groups of two or three the minimum is usually higher. Surprisingly, however, the spread of numbers subjects choose in the first period does not depend on the size of their group. It seem as if players construct a guess about what the "representative" other player will do, then "clone" the representative player several times to represent the group, so they can figure out what the whole group will do. If the representative player's choice is a single number, players who reason this way will not realize intuitively that the minimum number picked by a large group of players will be lower than the minimum from a smaller group. As a result, players in large groups mistakenly pick numbers that are too high and are penalized as a result.

Games as Strategic Situations

Many principles of strategic reasoning that are widely used in game theory have been questioned descriptively. Some of the principles are subtle and took decades for sophisticated theorists to discover and codify, so it seems unlikely that they are applied precisely by average folks. Attention has turned, properly, to the conditions under which principles of strategic reasoning might be learned and what people are thinking before and while they learn. I will focus here on three such principles: irrelevance of labels and timing, iterated dominance and backward induction.

Focal Points and the Irrelevance of Timing

To simplify analyses, game theorists often assume that some features of the game description—like the way strategies are labelled, or the timing of moves— are irrelevant for determining equilibria. But sometimes these features do affect choices.

As one example of how labels can make a difference, Schelling (1960) argued long ago that the labels can create psychologically prominent "focal points" that resolve coordination problems. Schelling gave examples of "matching games" in which players earn a prize if they choose the same strategy as another player, but otherwise get nothing. In matching games, players want to coordinate their choices on some strategy, and they don't care which one it is. Mehta, Starmer and Sugden (1994) report interesting data from matching games. When two strategies are labelled "heads" or "tails," 87 percent of subjects chose "heads," and only 13 percent chose tails. Good coordination can occur even when strategy sets are large. Two-thirds choose "rose" when asked to match a flower name, 59 percent choose "red" from the set of colors, 50 percent choose the boy's name John, and 40 percent choose the number 1 from the (infinite!) set of numbers. Subjects are

Table 3
Battle of the Sexes

		Player Column		Choice Frequencies	
		A	B	Simultaneous	Sequential
Player Row	A	0, 0	2, 6	38%	12%
	B	6, 2	0, 0	62%	88%
Simultaneous		35%	65%		
Sequential		70%	30%		

clearly exhibiting some strategic sophistication, because the frequency of the most common choice is much lower when players are asked only to express preferences, rather than match. For example, when asked to name a favorite day of the year, 88 subjects picked a total of 75 different dates; Christmas was the most popular at 6 percent. But when trying to match with others, 44 percent picked Christmas.

Game theory has a lot to learn from subjects about focal principles, but serious theoretical attention to the topic has been rare. Crawford and Haller (1990) show how focal precedents can emerge over time when games are repeated and players are eager to coordinate. Static theories like Bacharach and Bernasconi (1997) do not explain how focal points come about, but they capture the tradeoff between the chance that people commonly recognize a strategy's distinguishing features and the number of other strategies that share those features. Focal principles have potentially wide economic applications in implicit contracting, evolution of convention, social norms and folk law, and corporate culture (Kreps, 1990).

Timing is another descriptive feature of a game that is often assumed to be irrelevant, but can matter empirically. In laying the foundations of game theory, von Neumann and Morgenstern (1944) deliberately emphasized the central role of information at the expense of timing. They believed that information was more fundamental than timing, because knowing what your opponents did necessarily implies that they moved earlier. Alternatively, if you don't know what your opponents did, you won't care whether they already did it, or are doing it now. Combining these principles implies that information is important but that timing, per se, is not.

But empirical work has found surprising effects of move order in games (holding information constant). Take the battle of the sexes game in Table 3. In this game, one player prefers choice *A* and the other choice *B*, but both players would rather coordinate their choices than end up apart. This game has two pure-strategy multiple equilibria (*A,B*) and (*B,A*) that benefit players differently. There is also a mixed-strategy equilibrium—choosing *B* 75 percent of the time—that yields an expected payoff of 1.5 to both players.[4] Notice that both players prefer either one of the two pure strategy equilibria to mixing, but they each prefer a different one.[5] Cooper et al. (1993) found that when players move simultaneously, they converge roughly to the mixed strategy equilibrium, choosing *B* more than 60 percent of the time, as shown in Table 3. In a sequential condition, say that the Row player moves first, but her move is not known to Column. In this case, Row players choose their preferred equilibrium strategy, *B*, 88 percent of the time, and Column players go along, choosing *A* 70 percent of the time. The mere knowledge that one player moved first, without knowing precisely how she moved, is enough to convey a remarkable first-mover advantage that the second-mover respects. The data suggest a magical "virtual observability," in which simply knowing that others have moved earlier is cognitively similar to having observed what they did (Camerer, Knez and Weber, 1996). After all, if Column figures out that Row probably selected *B*, Column's sensible choice (setting aside mean retaliation) is to go along.

It is not clear how virtual observability works, but it appears that when one player explicitly moves first, other players think about the first-mover's motivations more carefully. If first-movers anticipate this, they can choose the move that is best for themselves, because they know players moving later will figure it out. Psychology experiments have established related ways in which reasoning about events depends curiously on their timing. For example, many people dislike watching taped sports events. Even when they don't know the outcome, simply knowing that the game is over drains it of suspense. People can also generate more explanations for an event that has already happened than for one that has yet to happen.

One experiment investigated the psychology of timing in the game of "matching pennies" (Camerer and Karjalainen, 1992), in which both players independently choose heads (*H*) or tails (*T*). In this game, one player wants to match, but the other player wants to mismatch. If the "mismatching" player moves first, she is more likely to choose either *H* or *T*, trying to outguess what the first mover will later do than to choose a chance device which explicitly randomizes between *H* and *T* for her. But if the "matching" player has already moved, the mismatching player is more likely to choose the chance randomizing device, hedging her bet. Apparently people are more reluctant to bet on their guesses

---

[4] Intuitively, think of the mixed strategy equilibrium in this way. If player 1 knows that player 2 will choose *B* 75 percent of the time, then for player 1, the expected value of choosing *A* will be $.25(0) + 2(.75) = 1.5$, and the expected value of choosing *B* will be $(.25)6 + .75(0) = 1.5$. In other words, the highest payoff for player 1 is 1.5. Of course, the same logic works in reverse; if player 2 knows that player 1 will choose *B* 75 percent of the time, then the highest possible payoff for player 2 is 1.5. Therefore, if both players choose *B* 75 percent of the time, then the best response of both players to that choice will involve a payoff of 1.5.

[5] The outcome (*B,B*) is also a "mean" fairness equilibrium. Suppose that player 1 thinks that player 2 expects them to play *B*, and as a result, player 2 is going to respond meanly by choosing *B* to harm player 1 (and themselves). Then, a mean-spirited player 1 will choose *B* in a sort of preemptive retaliation, so that a mutually destructive (*B,B*) equilibrium results.

about what other players have already done than on guesses about what other players will later do.

Iterated Dominance and "Beauty Contests"

"Iterated dominance" is the strategic principle that means that players first rule out play of dominated strategies by all players, then eliminate strategies that became dominated after the first set was eliminated, and so forth. In many games, this iterative process yields a unique choice after enough steps of iterated dominance are applied.[6]

But do people actually apply many levels of iterated dominance? There are many reasons for doubt. Studies of children show that the concept "beliefs of others" develops slowly. Psycholinguist Herb Clark studies how people infer the meaning of statements with vague references ("Did he do it already?"), which require people to know what others know, what others know they know, and so forth. Clark jokes that the grasp of three or more levels of iterated reasoning "can be obliterated by one glass of decent sherry." Since the process of iteration depends on beliefs about how others will play (and their beliefs . . .), then if even a few people behave irrationally, rational players should be cautious in applying iterated dominance.

Experiments are useful for measuring where the hierarchy of iterated dominance reasoning breaks down. An ideal tool is the "beauty contest game," first studied experimentally by Nagel (1995). A typical beauty contest game has three rules. First, N players choose numbers x_i in [0,100]. Second, an average of the numbers is taken. Third, a target is selected that is equal to the average divided by the highest possible choice. For illustration, say the average number chosen is 70, so the target is 70 percent of the average number. Finally, the player whose number is closest to the target wins a fixed prize. (Ties are broken randomly.) Before proceeding, readers should think of what number they would pick if they were playing against a group of students.

This game is called a "beauty contest" after the famous passage in Keynes's (1936, p. 156) *General Theory of Employment, Interest, and Money* about a newspaper contest in which people guess what faces others will guess are most beautiful. Keynes used this as an analogy to stock market investment. Like people choosing the prettiest picture, players in the beauty contest game must guess what average number others will pick, then pick 70 percent of that average, while knowing that everyone is doing the same.

The beauty contest game can be used to distinguish the number of steps of reasoning people are using. Here's how: suppose a player understands the game and realizes that the rules imply the target will never be above 70. To put it another way, numbers in the range [70,100] violate first-order iterated dominance. Now suppose a subject chooses below 70 and thinks everyone else will as well. Then the

---

[6] These "dominance solvable" games include Cournot duopoly, finitely repeated prisoner's dilemma and some games with strategic complementarities.

Table 4
Beauty Contest Results
(Singapore 7-person groups, p = 7)

Round	Mean	Median	Std. Dev.	Percentage Choosing 0
1	46.07	50	28.04	0.02
2	31.20	28	17.69	0.03
3	25.47	20	20.57	0.00
4	18.79	15	16.23	0.00
5	18.55	10	22.53	0.00
6	15.29	10	18.00	0.05
7	16.31	10	21.53	0.09
8	14.85	8	20.30	0.12
9	15.36	7	22.51	0.11
10	13.89	6	22.53	0.19

subject can infer that the target will be below .7 × 70, or 49, so an optimal choice is in the range [0,49]. Hence, a choice between [49,70] is consistent with a subject being first-order rational, but not being sure others are rational. The next range of choices, [34.3,49], is consistent with second-order rationality but violates third-order rationality. In this way, number choices in the beauty contest game reveal the level of iterated rationality. Infinitely many steps of iterated dominance leads to the unique Nash equilibrium—pick zero.

Table 4 summarizes results from an experimental study with a beauty contest game that involved predicting what 70 percent of the average choice would be (Ho, Camerer and Weigelt, forthcoming). The game was carried on for 10 rounds, with subjects receiving feedback after each round. First-round choices were typically dispersed around 31–40. Few subjects chose the equilibrium of zero in the first round—nor should they have! Some subjects violated dominance by choosing large numbers near 100, but not very many. As the rounds progress, choices are drawn toward zero as subjects learn. Thus, some notion of limited iterated reasoning is essential to understand initial choices and the movement across rounds. Econometric analysis indicates that most players look one or two iterations ahead (Holt, 1993; Stahl and Wilson, 1995).

Since the beauty contest game is easy to conduct, informative and fun, I have collected data from many subject pools playing once for a $20 prize. The mean, median and standard deviation of choices from several groups are shown in Table 5. Some are highly educated professionals—economics Ph.D.'s, portfolio managers and the Caltech Board of Trustees, which includes a subsample of 20 CEOs, corporate presidents and board chairmen. Others are college students from three continents and Los Angeles high school students. The most remarkable fact is that the average choices are very similar for all these groups. Even in the highly educated groups, only 10 percent of the subjects choose 0 (and don't win!). Quadrupling the prize brings numbers only slightly closer to the equilibrium.

Table 5
Beauty Contest Results from Many Subject Pools

	Mean	Median	Std. Dev.	Percentage Choosing 0	Sample Size
Portfolio Managers	24.31	24.35	16.15	0.08	26
Economics Ph.D.'s	27.44	30.00	18.69	0.13	16
Caltech Board of Trustees					
All	42.62	40.00	23.38	0.03	73
CEOs only	37.81	36.50	18.92	0.10	20
College Students					
Caltech	21.88	23.00	10.35	0.07	27
Germany	36.73	33.00	20.21	0.03	67
Singapore	46.07	50.00	28.04	0.02	98
UCLA	42.26	40.50	17.95	0.00	28
Wharton	37.92	35.00	18.84	0.00	35
High school students (U.S.)	32.45	28.00	18.61	0.04	52

Of course, specially trained players might choose closer to the equilibrium,[7] or experts hired to advise institutions might "figure out" that their clients should play zero. But the experts would only be right if other players actually do choose zero. The trick is to be one step of reasoning ahead of the average player, but no further![8]

These results suggest that instead of assuming that players apply iterated rationality through many levels, it is more realistic to assume a limited number of iterations, perhaps with the number of levels depending on the characteristics of the subjects involved. Furthermore, players who use equilibrium analysis alone to guide their choices are making a mistake. Anticipating that other players use limited iterated reasoning, or that strategy labels or timing create focal points that others will realize and act upon, leads players to behave more intelligently.

Backward Induction and Subgame Perfection

A central concept in game theory is "subgame perfection." An equilibrium pattern of behavior is subgame perfect if players think about every possible "subgame" that could be reached later in a game tree, guess what players would do in those subgames, and use the guesses in deciding what to do at the start. Implementing this process requires players to reason about future events and "backward induct" to the present. Subgame perfection is important because games

---

[7] However, keep in mind that Caltech undergraduates are much more analytically capable than average. Last year, the median math SAT score among entering students was 800.

[8] Some research on leadership, reflecting the same principle, suggests the ideal leader should be one standard deviation more intelligent than the group he or she leads, but no smarter than that.

often have several equilibria, and those that are not subgame perfect are considered to be less likely to occur.

As a reasoning principle, however, backward induction is descriptively dubious because studies of how people learn to play chess and write computer programs show that backward reasoning is unnatural and difficult. And backward induction requires players to spend precious time thinking about future events that seem unlikely to occur. Should they bother?

Direct tests of backward induction in games come from work on sequential bargaining (Camerer et al., 1993). In these experiments, player 1 offers a division of a pie. If player 2 accepts the offer, the game ends. But if player 2 rejects the offer, then the pie shrinks in size and player 2 offers a division to player 1. Again, if player 1 accepts the offer then the game ends. Otherwise, the pie shrinks again in size and player 1 again gets to offer a division. If the third-round offer is rejected, the game ends and players get nothing. This is a game of backward induction, where the optimal offer can be reached by working back from the last period. If the third pie is reached, and play is rational, then player 1 will offer only an epsilon slice to player 2, who will accept. Knowing this, player 2 recognizes that when dividing the second pie, she must give player 1 a slice equal to the smallest pie (plus epsilon), and keep the remainder, or else player 1 will reject the offer. Knowing this, player 1 recognizes that when dividing the first pie, offering player 2 a slice equal to the size of the second pie minus the third (plus epsilon), will be an offer that player 2 will accept.

Subjects trained briefly in backward induction reach this result readily enough. But as in many other experiments, first-round offers of untrained subjects lay somewhere between dividing the first pie in half, and the equilibrium offer (pie two minus pie three). More interestingly, the experiment was carried out on computers, so that to discover the exact pie sizes in the three rounds, subjects had to open boxes on a computer screen. Measurements of the cursor's location on the screen indicated the order in which boxes were open and how long they were kept open.[9] By presenting the game to subjects in this way, the subjects are forced to reveal the information they are looking at, giving clues about their mental models and reasoning. Subjects tended to look at the first-round pie first, and longest, before looking ahead, contrary to the "backward induction" looking pattern exhibited by trained subjects. In fact, subjects did not even open the second- and third-round boxes—ignoring the sizes of the second and third pies entirely—on 19 percent and 10 percent of the trials, respectively. These subjects simplify a difficult problem by ignoring future choice nodes that seem unlikely to ever be reached. Their heuristic might be considered sensible, because nearly 90 percent of the trials ended after one round.

---

[9] Psychologists have used similar methods for nearly 100 years, recording movements of eyes as people read, to understand how people comprehend text.

Speculations and New Directions

Systematic violations of game-theoretic principles are not hard to find because all useful modelling principles are simplifications, and hence are sometimes false. Table 6 summarizes the discussion to this point by offering a list of a few principles that are widely used in game theory, along with the systemic violations of those principles and citations for selected experiments documenting those findings. Lists of this sort are a start. The next step is to use the evidence of violations to construct a formal and coherent theory. Substantial progress has already been made in two areas mentioned earlier: measuring social values and extending game theory to include them; and measuring and incorporating differences among players, like players using different steps of iterated reasoning in beauty contests. Behavioral game theory could usefully extend standard theory in three other ways.

Nonexpected utilities. Players do not always choose the strategy with the highest expected utility. They sometimes value losses differently than gains, and can have aversions toward (or preferences for) strategic ambiguity or uncertainty. Several models have been proposed to bring pattern to this behavior. In the prospect theory of Tversky and Kahneman (1992), people value gains and losses from a reference point (rather than final wealth positions) and dislike losses much more than they like equal-sized gains, which can explain why describing payoffs as gains or losses matters in some experiments. Aversion toward ambiguity can be explained by models that use probabilities that are nonadditive.

A less psychologically grounded approach is to allow the possibility of errors in choice or uncertainty over payoffs that imply that while players are more likely to choose the strategy with the highest expected utility, they are not certain to do so. McKelvey and Palfrey (1995) propose what they call a "quantal response" function, which inserts a variable into the choice function to capture the degree of randomness in decisions. A "quantal response equilibrium" exists if players know how much randomness is in the decisions of others and choose accordingly.[10] This approach offers a parsimonious method of explaining several different behavioral phenomena. For example, if some players do not always make the optimal choice, then other players should use only a limited number of iterated rational steps in situations like the beauty contest games. Or in the ultimatum game, a responder may be likely to reject a smaller offer mistakenly, because it is a small mistake, and knowing this, rational proposers are not likely to make very uneven offers. The quantal response approach also seems to explain subtle experimental patterns in contributions to public goods (Anderson, Goeree and Holt, 1996).

Learning. Much recent interest has been focussed on adaptive learning models,

---

[10] A handy quantal response function is the logit form, $P(S_i) = e^{\lambda \pi(S_i)} / \sum_i e^{\lambda \pi(S_i)}$ (where $\pi(S_i)$ is the expected payoff of strategy S_i). The constant λ captures imprecision in choices, and could be interpreted as either sensitivity to dollar payoffs, or existence of nonpecuniary utilities unobserved by the experimenter. If $\lambda = 0$, then players choose equally often among strategies. As λ grows larger, $P(S_i)$ approaches one for the strategy with the highest expected payoff (the best response).

Table 6
Evidence on Game Theory Modelling Principles

Game-Theoretic Modelling Principle	Systematic Violation	Selected Experimental Evidence
Social Utility		
Independence of payoff utilities from . . .		
a. Payoffs of others	Altruism, envy (dictator games)	Berg, Dickhaut and McCabe (1995)
b. "Intentions" of others	Reciprocal fairness, (ultimatum, PD, chicken, trust)	Ledyard (1995); McDaniel, Rutström and Williams (1994)
Choice and Judgment		
a. Invariance to game description (no gain-loss asymmetry)	More disagreements over losses	Neale and Bazerman (1985); Camerer et al. (1993)
b. Mutually-consistent beliefs (common prior)	Overconfidence about outcomes, relative ability	Neale and Bazerman (1983); Camerer and Lovallo (1996)
Strategic Principles		
a. Irrelevance of strategy labels & timing	Focal points, "virtual observability" of earlier moves	Schelling (1960); Cooper et al. (1993)
b. Iterated dominance	Limited steps of iterated dominance (1–3)	Nagel (1995); Ho, Camerer and Weigelt (forthcoming)
c. Backward induction	Limited look-ahead	Camerer et al. (1993)

which come in two basic forms. "Belief-based" models presume that subjects form beliefs about what others will do, based on past observations, and choose the strategy that maximizes utility given these beliefs (the "best response") (Crawford, 1995). "Reinforcement" models ignore beliefs and assume that strategies have different probabilities or propensities of being chosen, which change as successful strategies are "reinforced" by observed successes or failures (Roth and Erev, 1995).[11] Both kinds of models are narrow. Belief learners pay no special attention to their payoff history. Reinforcement learners pay no attention to the outcomes of strategies they didn't choose, and they don't keep track of choices by others. Both learners ignore information about other players' payoffs. Teck Ho and I (1997) recently developed a general model that synthesizes the two approaches, thereby avoiding some of the weaknesses

---

[11] Reinforcement models were popular in cognitive psychology until about 30 years ago, when they were largely replaced by the information processing approach (brains are like computers) and, more recently, by "connectionism" (brains are neural networks). Behaviorism was discredited as a general theory of human learning because it could not easily explain higher-order cognition, like language, and lacked neuroscientific detail. These failures also make it unlikely that reinforcement models can fully explain human learning in strategic situations.

of each. Econometric estimates from five out of six data sets strongly reject the two simpler approaches in favor of the synthetic approach.

"Pregame" theory. Except for the beauty contest game, all the experiments described so far in this paper show the players the game in the form of a matrix or tree. The experiments therefore control for many ways in which subjects might misperceive or simplify a game if it were presented verbally. A useful body of research in this area has been compiled in negotiations research (Neale and Bazerman, 1991). Because those experiments are meant as models of realistic negotiations, not tests of game theory, the subjects usually do not know the precise game associated with the negotiation. These unstructured games are of special use for behavioral game theory, because they allow study of the "mental models" of games people construct. Such experiments are necessary for testing the joint hypothesis that subjects represent the situation correctly (by constructing the proper game theory tree or matrix) and that subjects play according to the axioms of game theory.

As an example, Bazerman and Samuelson (1983) studied a diabolically tricky bidding problem with adverse selection they called "acquire-a-company" (based on Akerlof's (1970) famous "lemons" paper). In this game, the shares of a target firm are worth an amount V uniformly distributed between [$0, $100]. The target knows its own value V, but the bidder does not. Because of improved management or corporate synergy, the shares are worth 50 percent more to the acquiring company. The rules are simple: the acquiring company bids a price P, and the target automatically sells its shares if and only if the true value V is less than P. What is the bid that maximizes expected profits?

The typical subject bids between $50–$75, a result that has been replicated with many subject pools (including business executives and Caltech undergraduates) and over 20 trials with feedback. The logic behind this bid is presumably that the expected value of the company is $50, and that with a 50 percent premium, this would be worth $75 to the acquirer—thus bids ranging from $50–$75. But this analysis leaves out the fact that the target will not accept a bid unless it is higher than the actual value. Once this adverse selection is taken into account, the optimal bid is actually zero.

To follow this logic in practice, consider a typical bid of $60. The target will reject this bid if the true value of the firm exceeds $60. Therefore, by bidding $60, the bidder can only win the company if value under present ownership is between $0 and $60. Given the even probability distribution, this means that a bid of $60 will only be accepted when the expected value is $30. Even with a 50 percent premium for the acquirer, the shares will only be worth $45 after acquisition. Thus, the act of bidding rules out receiving the company if it is worth more than the bid, and this adverse selection always more than offsets the 50 percent value increment.[12] The acquiring company can only lose (in expected value terms) and therefore should not bid.

---

[12] The formal analysis is not hard: a bid of P leads to an expected target value, conditional on acceptance of the bid, of $E(V| V \le P) = P/2$. So the bidder's expected profit is the chance of getting the company times the expected profit if they get it, or $(P/100)[1.5E(V| V \le P)-P] = ((3P/4)-P)P/100$, which is negative for all values of P.

The acquire-a-company problem is amazing because the adverse selection is clear once it is pointed out, but subjects invariably miss it and bid too much. The joint hypothesis that the subjects represent the game correctly and play game theoretically is clearly rejected. A common interpretation (Neale and Bazerman, 1991, p. 73) is that "individuals systematically exclude information from their decision processes that they have the ability to include. . . . Subjects who make this mistake are systematically ignoring the cognitions of the other party."

The first part of this interpretation is surely correct, but the second conclusion is not generally true. In all the experiments reviewed in this paper, for example, subjects exhibit some strategic sophistication, forming a guess about the likely thinking and actions of others: proposers make ultimatum offers that accurately forecast what others will reject; knowing that the other player moved first in a battle-of-the-sexes affects the second move; players in entry games forecast the number of other entrants quite accurately; and most beauty contest players apply one or two steps of iterated dominance.

But if bidders in the acquire-a-company game are not ignoring the cognitions of the target, why do they bid too much? An alternate answer is that subjects simplify the problem; they reduce the uncertainty about the firm's true value by substituting its expected value of $50. Two bits of evidence support this notion. First, consider a version of the game without adverse selection—neither the target nor the acquirer is sure of the true value. Then it is optimal for the bidder to substitute an expected value for the distribution of value, and bid somewhat higher than that, which is precisely what subjects do in experiments. Second, in versions of the game where the target value has only three possible values (like $0, $50 or $100), so that substituting the expected value for all the possible values is not much of a shortcut, nearly half the subjects spontaneously draw a matrix of all possible target values on paper, compute the expected payoffs of bids and deduce the correct answer. Thus, what the acquire-a-company problem really shows is that an oversimplified mental model of a complex game can lead to violations of game theoretic predictions, not because subjects are necessarily incapable of reasoning game theoretically, but because players constructed the wrong model of the game.

Conclusion

Behavioral game theory aims to replace descriptively inaccurate modelling principles with more psychologically reasonable ones, expressed as parsimoniously and formally as possible.

This approach raises the question of whether traditional game theory could still be useful for advising people how to play. The answer depends on the game and whether deviations are a mistake or not. Some patterns observed in experiments can be considered mistakes that could be avoided by doing what game theory prescribes. For example, players who overconfidently enter an industry thinking their prospects are above average should keep in mind that the other entrants think the same, but only some entrants can be right. Players who do not use backward induction can only benefit from doing so (while realizing that others might not be).

In other cases, game theory provides bad advice because underlying assumptions do not describe other players. Knowing how others are likely to deviate will help a player choose more wisely. For example, it is generally dumb to choose the equilibrium of zero in a beauty contest (even playing against CEOs or brilliant Caltech undergraduates). It is smarter to know the number of reasoning steps most people are likely to take and optimize against that number, and to understand the adaptive process that changes others' choices over time. Similarly, players making offers in ultimatum games should know that many players simply regard an offer of 10 percent as unfair and prefer to reject it.

Experiments have supplied tentative answers to some sharply posed questions. Is there a formal way to incorporate reciprocal social values like fairness, altruism, or revenge, which are widely observed in the lab? Yes: Rabin's (1993) fairness equilibrium. Do judgment phenomena like overconfidence about relative skill matter in games? Yes, but we don't yet know how to include these phenomena in formal extensions of game theory. How many steps of iterated dominance do people use? One to three. Do learning and the construction of mental models in unstructured games matter? Yes, but we need much additional data on how they matter. Moving from these sorts of observations to coherent new modelling is the primary challenge for the next wave of research.

A final caveat: The desire to improve descriptive accuracy that guides behavioral game theory does not mean game theory is always wrong. Indeed, it may be only a small exaggeration to conclude that in most games where people gain experience, equilibrium is never reached immediately and always reached eventually. But this is no triumph for game theory until it includes explanations for behavior in early rounds and the processes that produce equilibration in later rounds.

■ *Comments from Linda Babcock, Kong-Pin Chen, Vince Crawford, Bob Gibbons, Teck Ho, Matthew Rabin, JEP editors (Brad De Long, Alan Krueger and Timothy Taylor) and many seminar audiences were helpful. This work resulted from many collaborations and conversations, especially with Gerard Cachon, Teck Ho, Eric Johnson, Risto Karjalainen, Marc Knez, Richard Thaler, Roberto Weber and Keith Weigelt. Support of NSF SBR 9511001 and the Russell Sage Foundation is gratefully appreciated.*

References

Akerlof, George A., "The Market for 'Lemons': Quality Uncertainty and the Market Mechanism," *Quarterly Journal of Economics*, May 1970, *105*, 255–83.

Anderson, Simon P., Jacob K. Goeree, and Charles A. Holt, "A Theoretical Analysis of Altruism and Decision Error in Public Goods Games," working paper, University of Virginia, Department of Economics, 1996.

Babcock, Linda, and George Loewenstein, "Explaining Bargaining Impasse: The Role of Self-Serving Biases," *Journal of Economic Perspectives*, Winter 1997, *11*:1, 109–26.

Bacharach, Michael, and Michele Bernasconi, "The Variable Frame Theory of Focal Points: An Experimental Study," *Games and Economic Behavior*, April 1997, *19*, 1–45.

Bazerman, Max H., and W. F. Samuelson, "I Won the Auction but Don't Want the Prize," *Journal of Conflict Resolution*, December 1983, *27*, 618–34.

Berg, Joyce, John W. Dickhaut, and Kevin A. McCabe, "Trust, Reciprocity, and Social History," *Games and Economic Behavior*, July 1995, *10*, 122–42.

Bolle, Friedel, "Does Trust Pay?" Diskussionpapier 14/95, Europa-Universität Viadrina Frankfurt, Oder, November 1995.

Blount, Sally, "When Social Outcomes aren't Fair: The Effect of Causal Attributions on Preferences," *Organizational Behavior and Human Decision Processes*, August 1995, *63*:2, 131–44.

Cachon, Gérard, and Colin Camerer, "Loss-Avoidance and Forward Induction in Experimental Coordination Games," *Quarterly Journal of Economics*, February 1996, *111*, 165–94.

Camerer, Colin F., and Teck-Hua Ho, "Experience-Weighted Attraction Learning in Games: A Unifying Approach." California Institute of Technology Working Paper No. 1003, 1997.

Camerer, Colin F., and Risto Karjalainen, "Ambiguity-Aversion and Non-Additive Beliefs in Noncooperative Games: Experimental Evidence." In Munier, B., and M. Machina, eds., *Models and Experiments on Risk and Rationality*. Dordrecht: Kluwer Academic Publishers, 1992, pp. 325–58.

Camerer, Colin F., and Daniel Lovallo, "Optimism and Reference-Group Neglect in Experiments on Business Entry." California Institute of Technology Working Paper No. 975, 1996.

Camerer, Colin F., and Richard Thaler, "Anomalies: Ultimatums, Dictators and Manners," *Journal Economic Perspectives*, Spring 1995, *9*:2, 209–19.

Camerer, Colin F., Eric Johnson, Talia Rymon, and Sankar Sen, "Cognition and Framing in Sequential Bargaining for Gains and Losses." In Binmore, K., A. Kirman, and P. Tani, eds., *Contributions to Game Theory*. Cambridge: Massachusetts Institute of Technology Press, 1993, pp. 27–47.

Camerer, Colin F., Marc J. Knez, and Roberto Weber, "Timing and Virtual Observability in Ultimatum Bargaining and 'Weak Link' Coordination Games." California Institute of Technology Working Paper No. 970, 1996.

Cooper, Russell, Douglas DeJong, Robert Forsythe, and Thomas Ross, "Forward Induction in the Battle-of-the-Sexes Games," *American Economic Review*, December 1993, *83*, 1303–16.

Crawford, Vincent P., "Adaptive Dynamics in Coordination Games," *Econometrica*, January 1995, *63*, 103–43.

Crawford, Vincent P., "Theory and Experiment in the Analysis of Strategic Interaction." In Kreps, David M., and Kenneth F. Wallis, eds., *Advances in Economics and Econometrics: Theory and Applications, Seventh World Congress*. Vol. 1, Cambridge: Cambridge University Press, 1997, pp. 206–42.

Crawford, Vincent P., and Hans Haller, "Learning How to Cooperate: Optimal Play in Repeated Coordination Games," *Econometrica*, May 1990, *58*, 571–95.

Edgeworth, Francis Ysidro, *Mathematical Psychics*. 1881. Reprint, New York: Augustus M. Kelley, Publishers, 1967.

Fehr, Ernst, Georg Kirchsteiger, and Arno Riedl, "Does Fairness Prevent Market Clearing? An Experimental Investigation," *Quarterly Journal of Economics*, May 1993, *108*, 437–59.

Ho, Teck, Colin Camerer, and Keith Weigelt, "Iterated Dominance and Learning in Experimental 'P-Beauty Contest' Games," *American Economic Review*, forthcoming.

Holt, Debra J., "An Empirical Model of Strategic Choice with an Application to Coordination Games," working paper, Queen's University, Department of Economics, 1993.

Kahneman, Daniel, "Experimental Economics: A Psychological Perspective." In Tietz, R., W. Albers, and R. Selten, eds., *Bounded Rational Behavior in Experimental Games and Markets*. Berlin: Springer-Verlag, 1988, pp. 11–18.

Keynes, John Maynard, *The General Theory of Interest, Employment, and Money*. London: Macmillan, 1936.

Kreps, David M., "Corporate Culture and Economic Theory." In Alt, J., and K. Shepsle, eds., *Perspectives on Positive Political Economy.* Cambridge: Cambridge University Press, 1990, pp. 90–143.

Ledyard, John, "Public Goods Experiments." In Kagel, J., and A. Roth, eds., *Handbook of Experimental Economics.* Princeton: Princeton University Press, 1995, pp. 111–94.

McDaniel, Tanga, E. Elisabet Rutström, and Melonie Williams, "Incorporating Fairness into Game Theory and Economics: An Experimental Test with Incentive Compatible Belief Elicitation," working paper, University of South Carolina, Department of Economics, March 1994.

McKelvey, Richard, and Thomas Palfrey, "Quantal Response Equilibria for Normal Form Games," *Games and Economic Behavior,* July 1995, *10,* 6–38.

Mehta, Judith, Chris Starmer, and Robert Sugden, "The Nature of Salience: An Experimental Investigation of Pure Coordination Games," *American Economic Review,* June 1994, *84,* 658–73.

Nagel, Rosemarie, "Unraveling in Guessing Games: An Experimental Study," *American Economic Review,* December 1995, *85,* 1313–26.

Neale, Margaret A., and Max H. Bazerman, "The Effects of Framing and Negotiator Overconfidence on Bargaining Behaviors and Outcomes," *Academy of Management Journal,* March 1985, *28,* 34–49.

Neale, Margaret A., and Max H. Bazerman, *Cognition and Rationality in Negotiation.* New York: Free Press, 1991.

Preston, C. E., and S. Harris, "Psychology of Drivers in Traffic Accidents," *Journal of Applied Psychology,* 1965, *49:*4, 284–88.

Rabin, Matthew, "Incorporating Fairness into Game Theory and Economics," *American Economic Review,* December 1993, *83,* 1281–302.

Rapoport, Amnon, Darryle A. Seale, Ido Erev, and James A. Sundali, "Equilibrium Play in Large Group Market Entry Games," *Management Science,* forthcoming.

Roth, Alvin E., and Ido Erev, "Learning in Extensive-Form Games: Experimental Data and Simple Dynamic Models in the Intermediate Term," *Games and Economic Behavior,* January 1995, *8,* 164–212.

Schelling, Thomas, *The Strategy of Conflict.* Cambridge, Mass.: Harvard University Press, 1960.

Sally, David, "Conversation and Cooperation in Social Dilemmas: A Meta-Analysis of Experiments from 1958 to 1992," *Rationality and Society,* January 1994, *7,* 58–92.

Stahl, Dale, and Paul Wilson, "On Players' Models of Other Players: Theory and Experimental Evidence," *Games and Economic Behavior,* July 1995, *10,* 218–54.

Svenson, Ola, "Are We all Less Risky and More Skillful than our Fellow Drivers?," *Acta Psychologica,* February 1981, *47:*2, 143–48.

Tversky, Amos, and Daniel Kahneman, "Advances in Prospect Theory: Cumulative Representations of Uncertainty," *Journal of Risk and Uncertainty,* October 1992, *5,* 297–323.

Van Huyck, John B., Ray B. Battalio, and Richard O. Beil, "Tacit Coordination Games, Strategic Uncertainty, and Coordination Failure," *American Economic Review,* March 1990, *80,* 234–48.

von Neumann, John, and Oskar Morgenstern, *The Theory of Games and Economic Behavior.* Princeton: Princeton University Press, 1944.

Part II
Environmental Risk

[6]

A person deciding on a career, a wife, or a place to live bases his choice on two factors: (1) How much do I like each of the available alternatives? and (2) What are the chances for a successful outcome of each alternative? These two factors comprise the *utility* of each outcome for the person making the choice. This notion of utility is fundamental to most current theories of decision behavior. According to the expected utility hypothesis, if we could know the utility function of a person, we could predict his choice from among any set of actions or objects. But the utility function of a given subject is almost impossible to measure directly. To circumvent this difficulty, stochastic models of choice behavior have been formulated which do not predict the subject's choices but make statements about the probabilities that the subject will choose a given action. This paper reports an experiment to measure utility and to test one stochastic model of choice behavior.

MEASURING UTILITY BY A SINGLE-RESPONSE SEQUENTIAL METHOD

by Gordon M. Becker, Morris H. DeGroot, and Jacob Marschak

TEMPO, Carnegie Institute of Technology, and University of California at Los Angeles

THE purpose of this paper is to describe a sequential experiment that provides, at each stage in the sequence, an estimate of the utility to the subject of some amount of a commodity (e.g., money), and to present a few experimental results obtained with the method. The procedure is based upon the following well-known "expected utility hypothesis." For each person there exist numerical *constants*, called *utilities*, associated with the various possible outcomes of his actions, given the external events not under his control. If, for a given subject, we could know the values of these constants and the ("personal") probabilities he assigns to the various external events we could, according to this model, predict his choice from among any available set of actions. He will choose an action with the highest expected utility; i.e., with the highest average of utilities of outcomes, weighted by the probabilities he assigns to the corresponding events. He will be indifferent between any two actions with equal expected utilities. Note that (by the nature of weighted averages) the comparison between expected utilities does not depend on which two particular outcomes are regarded as having zero-utility and unit-utility.

Other models of choice behavior, called

stochastic models, do not predict the actual choices of a subject from each given set of available actions but rather they make statements about the *probabilities* that the scientist might assign to the various actions being chosen by the subject. It is assumed that these probabilities do not change during the time period under consideration, thus precluding learning or any systematic change of behavior. Relations between these probabilities of choice and the expected utilities described above are postulated.

One such postulate (associated with the name of Fechner) specifies that, for a given subject, action A has a larger expected utility than action B if and only if, when forced to choose between A and B, the probability that he chooses A is larger than the probability that he chooses B. It follows that if a choice between A and B is made many times under identical conditions, the person will choose the action with the larger expected utility more than half of the time. If he is indifferent he will choose each action 50 per cent of the time.

Mosteller and Nogee (1951), in what was perhaps the first laboratory measurement of utility, based their experiment on the Fechner postulate. They offered a subject

226

choices of the following type: either accept a wager $(a,p,-b)$ in which you will win a dollars with probability p and you will win $-b$ dollars (i.e., lose b dollars) with probability $1 - p$, or do not bet at all. They repeated the same offer several times, thereby obtaining the proportion of times that the subject decided to accept the wager. By holding p and b constant and varying a they were able to estimate the amount of money a_o at which this proportion was 50 per cent. Then by assumption the subject was indifferent between accepting the wager $(a_o,\ p,\ -b)$ and not betting at all. Hence, these two actions have equal expected utilities. Therefore, denoting by $u(x)$ the utility of gaining x dollars,

$$u(0) = pu(a_o) + (1 - p)u(-b).$$

As stated above, one can arbitrarily fix $u(0) = 0$ and $u(-b) = -1$. Then

$$u(a_o) = (1 - p)/p.$$

By keeping b constant and using the above technique for seven different values of p, Mosteller and Nogee estimated seven points on the subject's "money-gain utility curve (fuction)," which represents the relation between money gains and their utilities.

The experiment just described depends heavily on the assumption that the subject's probabilities of choice remain constant throughout the many times that he is choosing from the same available set of actions, and also on the assumption that each of the seven values of p used in the experiment is "understood" by the subject: i.e., that his personal probability of winning a dollars in a given wager is in fact p.

The procedure to be presented here differs from that of Mosteller and Nogee in several respects. No choice is repeated, but a check on the subject's consistency, or on his learning process, is provided. This is achieved by letting each set of available actions depend on the subject's previous responses in a manner that leads to repeated estimates of the same points on his utility curve. Some of these checks for consistency would be applicable even if the personal probabilities p of the subject were not known to the experimenter. However, the only odds used in

our experiment were 1:1 and 3:1, and it did not seem unreasonable to assume that the simple probabilities 1/2 and (to a lesser extent) 3/4 were "understood" by the subject.

THE SEQUENTIAL PROCEDURE

Let p be the probability of an event E, and let (y,p,z) be a wager in which one wins the amount y if the event E occurs and one wins the amount z if E does not occur. If a subject is indifferent between accepting the wager (y,p,z) and accepting a certain monetary gain of amount x, we shall call x his cash-equivalent of (y,p,z). Thus, $u(x) = pu(y) + (1 - p)u(z)$.

Let a and b, with $a < b$, be two convenient amounts of money and fix arbitrarily $u(a) = 0$, $u(b) = 1$. In the next section we shall describe a method for determining a subject's cash-equivalent of any given wager. For the moment let us assume that we know how to do this. Then, if x_1 is the cash-equivalent of the wager (a,p,b), we have

$$u(x_1) = pu(a) + (1 - p)u(b) = 1 - p.$$

Similarly, if x_2 is the cash-equivalent of (b,p,a), then

$$u(x_2) = pu(b) + (1 - p)u(a) = p.$$

The amounts x_1, x_2, a, and b can now be used in later stages of a sequential experiment to form ten new wagers, (a,p,x_1), (x_2,p,b), etc., and the cash-equivalents of each of these wagers can also be determined. If we define $u^*(y,p,z) = pu(y) + (1 - p)u(z)$ to be the utility of the wager (y,p,z) then it is easily verified that

$$u^*(x_1,p,a) = u^*(a,p,x_2) = p(1 - p),$$
$$u^*(x_2,p,b) = u^*(b,p,x_1) = 1 - p + p^2,$$
$$u^*(a,p,x_1) = (1 - p)^2,$$
$$u^*(x_1,p,b) = 1 - p^2,$$
$$u^*(x_2,p,a) = p^2,$$
$$u^*(b,p,x_2) = p(2 - p),$$
$$u^*(x_1,p,x_2) = 2p(1 - p),$$
$$u^*(x_2,p,x_1) = 1 - 2p + 2p^2.$$

It is seen from these equations that, regardless of the value of p, the wagers (x_1,p,a) and (a,p,x_2) have the same utility and consequently they also have the same cash-equivalent. Similarly, (x_2,p,b) and (b,p,x_1) have the same cash-equivalent. Thus

228   G. M. BECKER, M. H. DEGROOT, AND J. MARSCHAK

the determination of a subject's cash-equivalents of the wagers (x_1,p,a) and (a,p,x_2), say, provides a check on whether the subject is behaving in a manner consistent with a well-defined utility function as specified by the utility model. If p is known, further checks of this kind can be established, as will be seen later.

The same general procedure can be followed throughout the experiment, using at each stage a different probability p' selected so that some of the wagers formed with p' will have the same utilities as some of the wagers formed with p.

DETERMINING THE CASH-EQUIVALENT OF A WAGER

The following method can be used to determine the cash-equivalent of a wager (y,p,z) for a given subject. The subject is told that he will be rewarded from the wager (y,p,z); i.e., that he will receive the amount y if the event E of probability p occurs and he will receive the amount z otherwise.

The subject is then told that as an alternative to receiving this random reward from the wager he has the privilege of trying to sell the wager for cash. Accordingly, he is asked to state the smallest amount s that he will accept (his *selling price*) in lieu of being rewarded from the wager. The understanding is that if a buyer can be found who is willing to pay an amount $b \geq s$ then the subject will receive b. If no buyer can be found who is willing to pay at least s then the subject retains the wager and receives the random reward, either y or z, as specified by the wager.

Let s be the subject's selling price and let e be his cash-equivalent of the wager. Let b be the maximum amount that any buyer is willing to pay. It is assumed that b does not depend on s, but the method of generating b is otherwise irrelevant. If $b \geq s$, the subject will receive the amount b. If $b < s$, the subject will receive a random reward as specified by the wager.

We claim that it is to the subject's advantage for his selling price to be precisely his cash-equivalent of the wager; that is, to have $s = e$. This can be seen as follows.

From the definition of e, $u(e) = u^*(y,p,z)$

and, hence, receiving the certain cash amount e is equivalent to the subject to receiving a random reward from the wager. Now suppose $s > e$. If $b < e$ or $b \geq s$, the subject's fortune changes just as it would had his selling price been $s = e$. However, if b is such that $e \leq b < s$, the subject does not sell the wager and he receives a random reward whose cash-equivalent is e. Had his selling price been $s = e$, then for the same value of b he would have received the amount $b \geq e$. Thus, for all possible values of b, the expected utility of the subject's reward is at least as large when his selling price is $s = e$ as it is when $s > e$, and for some values of b it is strictly larger.

To complete the argument, suppose $s < e$. If $b < s$ or $b \geq e$, the subject's fortune changes just as it would had his selling price been $s = e$. However, if $s \leq b < e$, the subject receives the amount b whereas had his selling price been $s = e$ he would not sell the wager and would receive a random reward with cash-equivalent $e > b$. Thus, again, for all values of b the expected utility of the reward is at least as much when $s = e$ as it is when $s < e$, and for some values of b it is strictly larger. This demonstrates that the subject's optimal selling price is $s = e$. It brings him the highest expected utility.

EXPERIMENTAL PROCEDURE

At the ith stage $(i = 1, 2, \cdots, 24)$ of the sequential experiment, the subject was presented with a wager from which he would receive the amount A_i if a number X_i selected at random from a rotating bingo basket containing balls with the integers 1 through 100 was less than or equal to C_i, and he would receive the amount B_i if X_i was greater than C_i. (In the notation of the preceding sections, this is the wager $(A_i, C_i/100, B_i)$ if we make the assumption that all integers between 1 and 100 have the same probability of being selected.) After each selection the ball was put back into the basket.

Before X_i was selected, the subject named his selling price s_i for the wager. A random integer Y_i was then selected from the basket. If $Y_i \geq s_i$, the subject received

Measuring Utility by a Single-Response Sequential Method   229

the amount Y_i. In effect, he had sold the wager for the amount Y_i. If $Y_i \leq s_i$, the subject did not sell the wager, X_i was observed, and the subject received either A_i or B_i, according as $X_i \leq C_i$ or $X_i > C_i$.

The amounts A_i, B_i, C_i used at each of the 24 stages of the sequential experiment are shown in Table 1 together with the utilities of the wagers under the arbitrary assignment of the two values $u(0) = 0$ and $u(100) = 1$. It should be noted that several of the 24 wagers have the same utility; e.g., $u(s_3) = u(s_4) = u(s_{13}) = u(s_{22}) = 3/4$,

Moreover, even if the subject does not feel that all integers have the same probability of being selected, it is still true that

$$u(s_8) = u(s_{22}),$$
$$u(s_7) = u(s_{19}),$$
$$u(s_9) = u(s_{21}),$$
$$u(s_{10}) = u(s_{23}).$$

To see why this is so, we will prove, for example, that $u(s_8) = u(s_{22})$.

Let p be the probability that the number selected at random will be at most 25. Then it is seen from Table 1 that $u(s_{22}) = u^*(s_{11}, p, s_8) = pu(s_{11}) + (1 - p)u(s_8)$. But it is also seen from Table 1 that $u(s_{11}) = u^*(0, p, s_3) = (1 - p)u(s_3)$ and $u(s_8) = u^*(100, p, s_3) = p + (1 - p)u(s_3)$. Furthermore, $u(s_3) = u^*(0, p, 100) = 1 - p$. Thus, $u(s_{22}) = p(1 - p)u(s_3) + p(1 - p) + (1 - p)^2 u(s_3) = 1 - p = u(s_8)$.

The selling price s_i at a given stage is sometimes used as one of the rewards in the wagers presented at later stages. It should be noted that the subject can increase the utility of wagers presented at later stages by naming a higher selling price for wagers presented at earlier stages. In order to prevent the subject from recognizing that he had such control, his earlier selling prices were not used until several stages later.

In order to avoid changing the total capital of the subject during the sequence, the subject was not paid on any trial during the experiment and in fact was told that he would be paid on only one of the 24 trials. This trial was determined by drawing a number between 1 and 24 at random at the end of the session.

TABLE 1
EXPERIMENTAL DESIGN

Stage, i	A_i	B_i	C_i	s_i	$u(s_i)$
1	0	100	50	s_1	1/2
2	0	100	75	s_2	1/4
3	0	100	25	s_3	3/4
4	s_1	100	50	s_4	3/4
5	0	s_1	50	s_5	1/4
6	s_2	s_3	75	s_6	3/8
7	s_2	s_3	25	s_7	5/8
8	100	s_3	25	s_8	13/16
9	s_5	100	50	s_9	5/8
10	s_6	s_1	50	s_{10}	3/8
11	0	s_3	25	s_{11}	9/16
12	s_2	100	75	s_{12}	7/16
13	s_4	100	50	s_{13}	7/8
14	s_7	s_8	75	s_{14}	43/64
15	s_5	s_4	50	s_{15}	1/2
16	s_9	100	50	s_{16}	13/16
17	s_6	s_7	75	s_{17}	7/16
18	s_9	s_{13}	50	s_{18}	3/4
19	s_{11}	s_8	75	s_{19}	5/8
20	0	s_{13}	50	s_{20}	7/16
21	s_1	s_4	50	s_{21}	5/8
22	s_{11}	s_8	25	s_{22}	3/4
23	0	s_4	50	s_{23}	3/8
24	s_{11}	100	75	s_{24}	43/64

Instructions

The subjects were instructed as follows:

Stage 1 only. "In this game we will draw a number between 1 and 100. If the number is equal to or less than 50, you will win nothing. If the number is greater than 50 you will win 100 cents. How much are you willing to accept instead of playing the game? After you tell me how much you are willing to take for the game, I will draw a number between 1 and 100. If the number I draw is equal to or greater than the price you asked, I will pay you whatever number I drew and you will not play the game. If the number I draw is less than the price you ask, you will play the game and win nothing if the next number I draw is equal to or less than 50, or you will win 100 cents if that number is greater than 50.

"Do you have any questions?

"What is the lowest amount you are willing to take for the game?"

Stages 2 through 24. "This time you will win the amount A_i if the number is equal

230 G. M. BECKER, M. H. DEGROOT, AND J. MARSCHAK

to or less than C_i or you will win B_i if the number is larger than C_i.

"Do you have any questions?

"What is your lowest price for the game?"

Subjects

Two male students were obtained through the Yale Student Placement Office to serve as subjects in an economic experiment being conducted at the Cowles Foundation for Economic Research, Yale University. Subject 1 was an undergraduate in the Department of Psychology. Subject 2 was a graduate theology student. Each subject was guaranteed $1.25 per session (i.e., for his responses to the full sequence of 24 stages) and each subject participated in three sessions. In addition the subject received a bonus each session consisting of his winnings at one of the stages in the sequence. As already described, the subject was not told which stage would be used to determine his bonus until the end of the session.

RESULTS

Since each subject participated in three sessions the data provide an opportunity for

TABLE 2
SELLING PRICES OF THE WAGERS

Stage	Subject 1			Subject 2		
	Session 1	Session 2	Session 3	Session 1	Session 2	Session 3
1	65 (50)	45 (50)	50 (50)	60 (50)	80 (50)	65 (50)
2	40 (25)	25 (25)	25 (25)	50 (25)	55 (25)	45 (25)
3	80 (75)	80 (75)	75 (75)	80 (75)	90 (75)	75 (75)
4	70 (83)	85 (73)	65 (75)	100 (80)	92 (90)	80 (83)
5	30 (33)	25 (23)	30 (25)	24 (30)	65 (40)	45 (33)
6	40 (50)	25 (39)	50 (38)	65 (58)	75 (64)	79 (53)
7	60 (70)	60 (66)	60 (63)	75 (73)	80 (81)	65 (68)
8	75 (85)	90 (85)	75 (81)	95 (85)	98 (83)	87 (81)
9	45 (65)	40 (63)	45 (65)	75 (62)	80 (83)	75 (73)
10	40 (48)	30 (35)	40 (40)	40 (42)	70 (73)	55 (55)
11	60 (60)	65 (60)	50 (56)	75 (60)	80 (68)	60 (56)
12	50 (55)	40 (44)	50 (44)	80 (63)	75 (66)	70 (59)
13	65 (85)	65 (83)	75 (83)	100 (100)	99 (96)	95 (90)
14	65 (64)	75 (71)	60 (64)	90 (80)	95 (85)	82 (71)
15	40 (50)	40 (45)	50 (48)	60 (62)	78 (79)	70 (63)
16	55 (73)	60 (70)	65 (73)	90 (88)	95 (90)	90 (88)
17	45 (45)	45 (35)	55 (53)	75 (70)	79 (76)	70 (76)
18	50 (55)	55 (53)	60 (60)	95 (88)	98 (90)	93 (85)
19	65 (64)	70 (71)	60 (56)	85 (80)	95 (85)	75 (67)
20	25 (33)	45 (33)	50 (38)	50 (50)	50 (50)	65 (48)
21	65 (68)	55 (55)	60 (58)	75 (80)	89 (86)	78 (73)
22	65 (71)	80 (84)	70 (69)	90 (90)	97 (94)	82 (80)
23	25 (35)	45 (33)	45 (33)	50 (50)	55 (46)	55 (40)
24	65 (70)	65 (74)	60 (63)	90 (81)	98 (85)	80 (70)

Note: The figures given in parentheses are the actuarial values of the wagers.

TABLE 3
DIFFERENCES IN SELLING PRICES OF WAGERS
OF EQUAL UTILITY

	Subject 1			Subject 2		
	Session 1	Session 2	Session 3	Session 1	Session 2	Session 3
$s_{22} - s_3$	−15	0	−5	10	7	7
$s_{19} - s_7$	5	5	0	10	15	10
$s_{21} - s_9$	20	15	15	0	9	3
$s_{22} - s_{10}$	−15	15	5	10	−15	0

the study of the change in the subjects' behavior as they grew familiar with the task.

Their selling prices for the wagers at each stage of each session, and the actuarial value of each wager (i.e., the expected monetary reward $(C_i/100)A_i + (1 - C_i/100)B_i)$ are shown in Table 2. (Note that the selling prices named by Subject 1 were always multiples of 5 cents. Although such rounding violates the assumption of a strictly monotonic utility function, the effects of the violation are negligible here.)

As discussed earlier, $u(s_3) = u(s_{22})$, $u(s_7) = u(s_{19})$, $u(s_9) = u(s_{21})$, and $u(s_{10}) = u(s_{23})$, regardless of the value of p used in computing the utilities of the wagers. Thus, if the subjects' behavior is consistent with the expected utility model their selling prices should be such that $s_3 = s_{22}$, $s_7 = s_{19}$, $s_9 = s_{21}$, and $s_{10} = s_{23}$. The observed differences $s_{22} - s_3$, etc., are shown in Table 3. Since most of these differences are nonzero the data are not consistent with an expected utility model.

It should also be noted, however, that the differences in prices decrease, on the average, from session to session, indicating that behavior does become, in some sense, more consistent with an expected utility model as the subject becomes more familiar with the task. Thus, despite the fact that the model does not precisely fit the behavior of the subjects, there is some indication that it approximates such behavior and that the model becomes more appropriate as the subject becomes more familiar with the experiment.

Now let us again assume that the values ½, ¼, and ¾ are in fact the subjects' personal probabilities of the relevant events (i.e., we assume that, for the subjects, all

MEASURING UTILITY BY A SINGLE-RESPONSE SEQUENTIAL METHOD   231

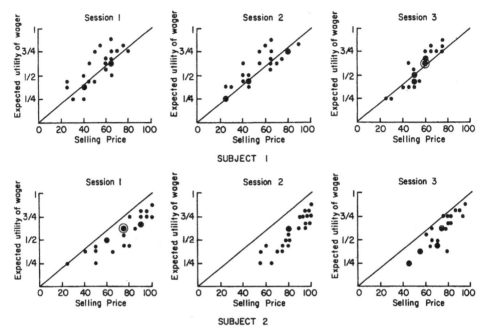

FIG. 1. Scatter Diagram of Subjects' Selling Prices Plotted Against the Utilities of the Wagers. A circled dot indicates two coincident points. A twice-circled dot indicates three coincident points.

integers are equally probable of being selected). The utilities of the wagers used in the experiment are given in Table 1 and, since the optimal selling price of a wager is its cash-equivalent, the selling prices named by a subject provide estimates of the amounts of money having these utilities. Thus, a scatter diagram of the selling prices named by a subject plotted against the utilities of the wagers should provide some suggestion of the subject's utility curve. These diagrams are given in Figure 1.

When viewing these diagrams it should be kept in mind that at each stage the utility of the wager was fixed and the selling price was the observed variable. Hence, the horizontal spread of points with the same utility is indicative of the inconsistency of the subjects' responses. In attempting to fit utility curves to these points, either "by eye" or by some more refined method, the horizontal distances should perhaps be given primary consideration. Nevertheless, this discussion is not intended to minimize the relevance of the vertical spread of the utilities of wagers with the same selling price.

Because of the sequential nature of the experiment there is a dependence among the observations that makes a precise statistical analysis along traditional lines impractical. Accordingly, we content ourselves here with giving just a few general comments.

For both subjects, the horizontal spread of the points obtained in Session 3 at the fixed utility levels is relatively small. Thus, there is a trend toward the adoption of response patterns consistent with a set of constant utilities.

For a given wager, the larger the selling price named by a subject, the more willing he is to take risks. The selling prices named by Subject 1 were, in general, largest in Session 3. The linear (or actuarial) utility curve provides a not unreasonable fit to the observed points for this subject, although he is slightly more willing to take risks with small amounts and less willing with large amounts.

The observed points for Subject 2 in Session 3 lie below the linear utility curve, indicating the subject's willingness to take risks.

232   G. M. Becker, M. H. DeGroot, and J. Marschak

For each subject, it is felt, a reasonable estimate of his utility curve can be sketched.

CONCLUSIONS

An attempt has been made to measure the utility of money. Estimates of the amounts of money having been given, preselected utilities were obtained in a sequential procedure. At each stage of the procedure the subject stated the lowest price he would accept in lieu of a wager in his possession. It was shown that under the utility model this selling price will be the subject's cash-equivalent of the wager.

The inconsistency of the responses of two subjects led to the rejection of the model. However, as the subjects became more familiar with the task their experience appeared to lead to more consistent behavior and less deviation from the results specified by the utility model. Thus, despite the rejection of the model in the strict sense, it is felt that it does, at least, approximate the observed behavior.

It is also our feeling that the procedure used here might provide useful data for the study of specific stochastic models of choice behavior, such as those given by Becker, DeGroot, and Marschak (1963), and that it might be possible to use this procedure, alone or in combination with others, to estimate both personal probabilities and utilities of an experienced subject.

REFERENCES

Becker, G. M., DeGroot, M. H., & Marschak, J. Stochastic models of choice behavior. *Behav. Sci.*, 1963, 8, 41–55.

Mosteller, F., & Nogee, P. An experimental measurement of utility. *J. polit. Econ.*, 1951, 59, 371–404.

(Manuscript received July 1, 1963)

At the very best, we admit, each time you scrutinize a concept of substance, it dissolves into thin air. But conversely, the moment you relax your gaze a bit, it re-forms again. For things *do* have intrinsic natures, whatever may be the quandaries that crowd upon us as soon as we attempt to decide definitively what these intrinsic natures are. If you will, call the category of substance sheer error. Yet it is so fertile a source of error, that only by learning to recognize its nature from within can we hope to detect its many disguises from without.

                                             Kenneth Burke, *A Grammar of Motives*

[7]

Economic Theory of Choice and the Preference Reversal Phenomenon

By David M. Grether and Charles R. Plott*

A body of data and theory has been developing within psychology which should be of interest to economists. Taken at face value the data are simply inconsistent with preference theory and have broad implications about research priorities within economics. The inconsistency is deeper than the mere lack of transitivity or even stochastic transitivity. It suggests that no optimization principles of any sort lie behind even the simplest of human choices and that the uniformities in human choice behavior which lie behind market behavior may result from principles which are of a completely different sort from those generally accepted. This paper reports the results of a series of experiments designed to discredit the psychologists' works as applied to economics.

The phenomenon is characterized by the following stylized example. Individuals under suitable laboratory conditions are asked if they prefer lottery A to lottery B as shown in Figure 1. In lottery A a random dart is thrown to the interior of the circle. If it hits the line, the subject is paid $0 and if it hits anywhere else, the subject is paid $4. Notice that there is a very high probability of winning so this lottery is called the P bet, standing for probability bet. If lottery B is chosen, a random dart is thrown to the interior of the circle and the subject receives either $16 or $0 depending upon where the dart hits. Lottery B is called the $ bet since there is a very high maximum reward. After indicating a preference between the two lotteries, subjects are asked to place a monetary value on each of the lotteries.

*Professors of economics, California Institute of Technology. The financial support supplied by the National Science Foundation and the National Aeronautics and Space Administration is gratefully acknowledged. We wish to express our appreciation to Brian Binger, Elizabeth Hoffman, and Steven Matthews, who served as research assistants.

Psychologists have observed that a large proportion of people will indicate a preference for lottery A, the P bet, but place a higher value on the *other* lottery, the $ bet. The following argument will help us see one way in which this behavior violates preference theory. Let w = initial wealth; $(z,1,0)$ = the state in which A is held and the wealth level is z; $(z,0,1)$ = the state in which B is held and the wealth level is z; $(z,0,0)$ = the state in which neither A nor B are held and the wealth level is z; $\$(A)$ and $\$(B)$ are the respective selling limit prices; $\sim$ and $>$ indicate indifference and preference, respectively.

(1) $(w+\$(A),0,0) \sim (w,1,0)$
$$\text{by definition of } \$(A)$$

(2) $(w+\$(B),0,0) \sim (w,0,1)$
$$\text{by definition of } \$(B)$$

(3) $(w,1,0) > (w\,0,1)$
$$\text{by the statement of preference of } A \text{ over } B$$

(4) $(w+\$(A),0,0) > (w+\$(B),0,0)$
$$\text{by transitivity}$$

(5) $\$(A) > \$(B)$
$$\text{by positive "utility value" of wealth}$$

Though (5) follows from the theory, it is not observed.

Notice this behavior is not simply a violation of some type of expected utility hypothesis. The preference measured one way is the *reverse* of preference measured another and seemingly theoretically compatible way. If indeed preferences exist and if the principle of optimization is applicable, then an individual should place a higher reservation price on the object he prefers. The behavior as observed appears to be simply inconsistent with this basic theoretical proposition.

If the results are accepted uncritically and extended to economics, many questions are raised. If preference theory is subject to systematic exception in these simple cases, how many other cases exist? What type of theory of choice can serve as a basis for market theory and simultaneously account for

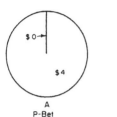 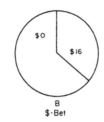

A
P-Bet

B
$-Bet

FIGURE 1

these data? Could such an alternative theory also serve as a basis for welfare economics? Should special extensions of the theory of market choice to other situations such as crime (Gary Becker, 1968), suicide (Daniel Hammermesh and Neal Soss), marriage (Becker, 1973, 1974), extramarital affairs (Ray Fair), politics, etc. be called into question? How are we to regard cost-benefit measures once we have accepted the fact that the sign of the benefit-minus-cost figure can be *reversed* by simply measuring preference in terms of "most preferred" options rather than in terms of a limit selling or purchase price?

There is little doubt that psychologists have uncovered a systematic and interesting aspect of human choice behavior. The key question is, of course, whether this behavior should be of interest to economists. Specifically it seems necessary to answer the following: 1) Does the phenomenon exist in situations where economic theory is generally applied? 2) Can the phenomenon be explained by applying standard economic theory or some immediate variant thereof?

This study was designed to answer these two questions. The experiments prior to those reported here were not designed with economics audiences in mind and thus do not answer either question though they are suggestive. In the first section we review the earlier experiments and their shortcomings from an economics point of view. Our experimental design is covered in the second section, and our results are reviewed in the third section. In the end we will conclude that the answer to the first question is "yes" and the answer to the second appears to be "no." As reflected in our concluding remarks, we remain as

perplexed as the reader who has just been introduced to the problem.

I. Existing Experimental Work

Experimental results of direct relevance are reported in four papers (Sarah Lichtenstein and Paul Slovic, 1971, 1973; Harold Lindman; Slovic). The experiments are listed in Table 1 beside an array of theories, each of which would either render the experiment irrelevant from an economist's point of view or explain the results in terms of accepted theory. Along with the economic-theoretic explanations, we have listed some psychological-theoretic explanations and some theories which seek to explain the results as artifacts of experimental methods.

A. *Economic-Theoretic Hypotheses*

THEORY 1: *Misspecified Incentives*. Almost all economic theory is applied to situations where the agent choosing is seriously concerned or is at least choosing from among options that in some sense matter. No attempt is made to expand the theory to cover choices from options which yield consequences of no importance. Theories about decision-making costs do suggest that unmotivated choice behavior may be very different from highly motivated choice behavior, but the differences remain essentially unexplored. Thus the results of experiments where subjects may be bored, playing games, or otherwise not motivated, present no immediate challenges to theory.

On this basis several experiments can be disregarded as applying to economics even though they may be very enlightening for psychology. In Lichtenstein and Slovic (1971) the first two experiments were made from gambles which involved imaginary money and in the third, the gambles were for points the value of which were not revealed until after the choices were made. All experiments in Lindman involved gambles for "imaginary money." Three of the experiments of Slovic dealt with the choices among fictitious commodity bundles. The only experiments which cannot be criticized on this ground are

TABLE 1—COEXISTING EXPERIMENTAL RESULTS: RELEVANCE AND POSSIBLE EXPLANATIONS

Theoretical Criticism and/or Explanation	Lichtenstein & Slovic (1971) Experiment			Lichtenstein & Slovic (1973)	Lindman (1971)	Slovic (1975) Experiment				This Study Experiment	
	1	2	3			1	2	3	4	1	2
Economic Theory											
1. Misspecified Incentives	I	I	I	N	I	I	I	N	I	N	N
2. Income Effects	N	N	E	?	N	N	N	E	N	N	N
3. Indifference	N	I	I	I	I	I	I	I	I	N	N
Psychological											
4. Strategic Responses	E	E	E	E	E	N	N	N	N	E	N
5. Probabilities	I	I	N	?	N	N	N	N	N	N	N
6. Elimination by Aspect	N	N	N	N							N
7. Lexicographic Semiorder	N	N	N	N							N
8. Information Processing: Decision Costs	E	E	E	?	E	E	E	E	E	N	N
9. Information Processing: Response Mode, Easy Justification	E	E	E	E	E	E	E	E	E	E	E
Experimental Methods											
10. Confusion and Misunderstanding	N	N	N	N	N	N	N	N	N	N	N
11. Frequency Low	N	N	N	N	N	N	N	N	N	N	N
12. Unsophisticated Subjects	?	?	?	N	?	?	?	?	N	N	N
13. Experimenters Were Psychologists	I	I	I	I	I	I	I	I	I	N	N

I = The experiment is irrelevant to economics because of the reason or theory.

N = The experimental results cannot be explained by this reason or theory.

E = The experimental results are consistent with the reason or theory.

? = Data insufficient.

Lichtenstein and Slovic (1973), which was conducted on a Las Vegas casino floor for real and binding cash bets, and experiment 3 of Slovic in which gambles for values of up to $4 cash or nineteen packs of cigarettes were used.

THEORY 2: *Income Effects.* Three different modes of extracting subjects' attitudes have been used in existing experiments. Subjects were asked their preference between pairs[1] of

[1] In Solvic subjects were asked to rank lotteries from sets of different sizes.

lotteries, they were asked the maximum amount they would pay for the right to play various lotteries, and they were asked the minimum amount for which they would sell various lotteries. Clearly the income position of a subject can differ among these situations and this could account for apparent inconsistencies in preference. In three experiments income effects are of potential importance: Lichtenstein and Slovic (1971), experiment 3; Lichtenstein and Slovic (1973); and Slovic, experiment 3.

In Lichtenstein and Slovic (1971), experiment 3, subjects knew that all the gambles would be played at the end of the experiment. First, the subjects indicated their preferences from among a series of pairs of bets, the most preferred of which was to be played. After these choices the subjects were given a series of bets for which selling limit prices were extracted by standard techniques (see Gordon Becker, Morris DeGroot, and Jacob Marschak). After all choices were made, the relevant bets were played. Since all bets had a positive expected value, subjects had an increasing expected income throughout the experiment. Once one has agreed to play several *P* bets and expected income has accordingly increased, it is not so surprising that subsequently one is willing to go for riskier but potentially more rewarding gambles. Standard theories of risk taking suggest that risk aversion decreases with income, so as expected income increases, a tendency toward a higher limit selling price (the certainty equivalent for lotteries) would be expected. Thus the data which show preference reversals are consistent with an "income effect" hypothesis.

In Slovic, experiment 3, subjects first revealed indifference curves in a cigarette-money space. From this exercise they had an expectation of receiving some cigarettes (up to nineteen packs) from lotteries they knew would be played. A preference for a monetary dimension would thus be expected when two or three days later subjects were offered a choice between cigarette-money commodity bundles to which they had previously expressed indifference. Again the "income effect" hypothesis is consistent with the data.

The third case (Lichtenstein and Slovic, 1973) is an experiment conducted on a casino floor. Bets were played as soon as preferences were indicated. The wealth position of the subject at any time depended upon the sequence of wins and losses leading up to that time and these are not reported. Consequently, the relationship between the theory and this experiment cannot be determined.

THEORY 3: *Indifference.* In all experiments except those in Slovic, subjects were required to register a preference among bets. No indications of indifference were allowed. Thus the preference reversals exhibited in all other experiments could have been due to a systematic resolution of indifference on the part of subjects forced to record a preference. Slovic's results are also consistent with this hypothesis.

B. *Psychological-Theoretic Hypotheses*

THEORY 4: *Strategic Responses.* Everyone has engaged in trade and has some awareness of the various distributions of gains which accompany trade. Thus when asked to name a "selling price" an individual's natural strategic response may be to name a price above any true limit price modulated by what an opponent's preferences are conjectured to be. When asked to name a "buying price," one would tend to understate the values. This strategic reaction to the very words "selling price" may be very difficult to overcome even though the subject is selling to a passive lottery in which such strategic posturing may actually be harmful.

This theory predicts the reversals of all experiments except those reported in Slovic where the words buying and selling were not used. Notice that this theory would predict reversals when selling prices are elicited and fewer reversals, or reversals of the opposite sort, when buying prices are asked for. That is, one can argue that there is little ambiguity about the "value" of a *P* bet (for example, with probability of .99 win $4, and lose $1 with probability of .01). However, this is not true for the corresponding $ bets (for example, win $16 with probability one-third and lose $2 with probability two-thirds). Thus any tendency to state selling prices higher than the true reservation prices will primarily affect prices announced for $ bets. This behavior clearly can yield apparent preference reversals of the type reported. The same argument applied to buying prices suggests that there will be a tendency to understate the value of $ bets more than *P* bets.

Experiment 2 of Lichtenstein and Slovic (1971) used buying prices rather than selling prices. Compared with experiment 1 (which involved selling prices), Lichtenstein and Slovic report that for experiment 2 the rate of reversals was significantly lower (significance level at least .01) and the rate of opposite reversals significantly higher (also at least .01). Further, they report that bids for the *P* bets average $.07 below expected value in experiment 1, but $.44 below expected value in experiment 2. Bids for the $ bets were $3.56 higher than expected value in experiment 1, and $.04 below expected value in experiment 2. Thus, the data in these two experiments are quite consistent with this theory.

THEORY 5: *Probabilities.* With the exception of Slovic, experiments 1, 2, and 4, all experiments involved lotteries at some stage. Naturally if subjective probabilities are not well formed, or change during the experiment, consistency among choices is not to be expected. In fact, probabilities in all experiments except Lichtenstein and Slovic (1971), experiments 1 and 2, were operationally defined, and with the exception of Lichtenstein and Slovic (1973), there was no reason to suspect that they may have changed during the experiment.

THEORY 6: *Elimination by Aspect.* (See Amos Tversky, 1972.) Let *A* be a set of "aspects" and let the objects be subsets of *A*. This theory holds that individuals order the elements of *A* and then choose from among objects by a lexicographic application of this underlying order. Specifically, the stochastic version holds that an element *x* of *A* is chosen at random (perhaps with a probability proportional to its importance), and all objects *B*, such that $x \notin B$, are then eliminated. The process continued until only one object remains.

This theory runs counter to traditional economic reasoning on two counts. First the lexicographic application runs directly counter to the principle of substitution (quasi concavity of utility functions). Secondly, the random elimination choice process does not sit well with the idea of maximization or "rational" choice.

One implication of the model is a type of moderate stochastic transitivity.[2] The heart of

[2]If $P(x, y) \geq \frac{1}{2}$ and $P(y, z) \geq \frac{1}{2}$, then $P(x, z) \geq \min [P(x, y), P(y, z)]$.

the preference reversal phenomenon is shown above to be a type of cyclic choice. Such an intransitivity is in violation of the moderate stochastic transitivity property of the model. Thus the preference reversal phenomenon must be added to Tversky's own work (1969) as situations in which the elimination-by-aspects model does not seem to work.

THEORY 7: *Lexicographic Semiorder.* In a classic paper Tversky (1969) demonstrated that binary choices could cycle in a predictable fashion. The argument used was that choices are made on the basic dimensions of objects, but when for two objects the magnitudes along a dimension becomes "close," their magnitudes are treated as being equal. Thus a series of objects *x*, *y*, *z*, and *w* may be ordered as listed when compared in that order because each is close to those adjacent on a given dimension. Yet *w* may be chosen over *x* because the magnitudes on this dimension are far enough apart to be discernible.

It is difficult to see how this argument can be applied to account for the cycles in the reversal phenomenon. No long chains of binary comparisons were involved. No small magnitude differences, such as those used by Tversky, were present. We suspect that whatever ultimately accounts for the preference reversals will also account for the Tversky intransitivities, but we doubt that it will be the lexicographic semiorder model.

THEORY 8: *Information Processing—Decision Costs.* Individuals have preferences over an attribute space, but the location of an object in this attribute space may not be readily discernible. Resolution of choice problems, which involves locating an object in the attribute space, is a costly, disagreeable activity, so in their attempt to avoid decision costs people tend to adopt the following simple rule. An individual first looks at the "most prominent" dimension or aspect of the object. The magnitude of this aspect, called an "anchor," is used as the value of the object and is adjusted upward or downward to account for other features. As an empirical generalization the psychologists note that the adjustments are usually inadequate so the ultimate choice is heavily influenced by the starting point or anchor. Individuals who originally choose the *P* bet have tended to focus upon the probability of winning and inadequately adjust for the low monetary amounts. When asked about selling price or buying price, they naturally focus on dollars first and adjust for the probabilities. Since the adjustments for probabilities are inadequate, the dollar bets tend to be given the higher value. Thus, the "preference reversal" phenomenon is explained.

This theory is consistent with all experiments where no incentives were used. It is also consistent with the choices from among indifferent objects such as those in the Slovic 1975 study. When incentives are used, however, more effort in decision making is warranted and the frequency of reversals should go down. Thus on this theory one might have expected fewer reversals than occurred in the Lichtenstein and Slovic (1973) study, but since no control group (i.e., a group playing the gambles without monetary incentives) existed for this subject pool, the results are inconclusive.

THEORY 9: *Information Processing— Response Mode and Easy Justification.* The anchoring and adjustment mechanism described above may exist but it may be entirely unrelated to the underlying idea of decision-making costs. Indeed Lichtenstein and Slovic argue only that "variations in response mode cause fundamental changes in the way people process information, and thus alter the resulting decisions" (1971, p.16). The view is that of the decision maker "as one who is continually searching for systematic procedures that will produce quick and reasonably satisfactory decisions" (Slovic, p. 280). On occasion, it is argued that the mechanism is "easy to explain and justify to oneself and to others" (Slovic, p. 280). The anchoring process described above is offered as the mechanism that people adopt. The particular dimension used as an anchor is postulated to be a function of the context in which a decision is being made. Such thinking may not necessarily be contrary to preference theory. Rather, it is as though people have "true preferences" but what they *report* as a preference is dependent upon the terms in which the reporting takes place. Certain words or

contexts naturally induce some dimensions as anchors while others induce other dimensions. The theory is consistent with all observations to date. Details can be found in Slovic.

C. *Experimental Methods*

The psychologists whose work we are reporting are careful scientists. Yet a bit of suspicion always accompanies a trip across a disciplinary boundary. In particular, we consider four possible sources of experimental bias.

THEORY 10: *Confusion and Misunderstanding.* In all experiments subjects were trained, rehearsed, and/or tested over procedures and options. In all instances repeated choices were made. In general there is reason to believe there was little confusion or misunderstanding, and in all cases the results hold up even when the responses of potentially confused subjects are removed from the data. However, there is some evidence reported in Lindman that suggests some type of "learning" takes place with experience. All experimenters reported some very "erratic" choices whereby, for example, a subject offered to pay more for a gamble than the maximum that a favorable outcome would yield.

THEORY 11: *Frequency Low.* If the phenomenon only occurs infrequently or with a very few subjects, there may not be a great need for concern or special attention. In fact, however, the behavior is systematic and the rate of reversals is high. Consider, for example, the following results, recalling that a *P* bet is a lottery with a high probability of winning a modest amount while the $ bet has a low probability of winning a relatively large amount of money. The Lichtenstein and Slovic (1971) study found that of 173 subjects indicating a preference for the *P* bet, 127 (73 percent) always placed a higher monetary valuation on the $ bet (they called these predicted reversals). On the other hand, the reverse almost never happens. That is, individuals who state that they prefer the $ bet will announce prices which are consistent with their choices. In this same study, for example, 144 subjects *never* made the other reversal (termed unpredicted reversals).

THEORY 12: *Unsophisticated Subjects.* Psychologists tend to use psychology undergraduates who are required to participate in experiments for a grade. With the exception of Lichtenstein and Slovic (1973) the sources of subjects were not made explicit in the studies. If indeed psychology undergraduates were used, one would be hesitant to generalize from such very special populations.

THEORY 13: *The Experimenters were Psychologists.* In a very real sense this can be a problem. Subjects nearly always speculate about the purposes of experiments and psychologists have the reputation for deceiving subjects. It is also well known that subjects' choices are often influenced by what they perceive to be the purpose of the experiment. In order to give the results additional credibility, we felt that the experimental setting should be removed from psychology.

II. Experimental Design

Our format was designed to facilitate the maximum comparisons of results between experiments. The gambles used for our experiments (see Table 2) were the same ones used in Lichtenstein and Slovic (1971), experiment 3, where actual cash payoffs were made. They used a roulette wheel to play the gambles and, therefore, all probabilities were stated in

thirty-sixths. The random device for our experiments was a bingo cage containing balls numbered 1–36. This eliminates the problem of nonoperational probabilities that was raised by Theory 5. All the gambles were of the form: if the number drawn is less than or equal to n, you lose x, and if the number drawn is greater than n, you win y.

The procedures for both of our experiments were so nearly identical that we shall describe only the first experiment in detail. Only those features of the second experiment that differ from the first will be discussed.

A. *Procedures: Experiment 1*

Student volunteers were recruited from economics and political science classes. They were told that it was an economics experiment, that they would receive a minimum of $5, and that the experiment would take no longer than one hour. As the subjects arrived, they were randomly divided into two groups. The groups were in separate rooms, and there was no communication between them until after the experiment. Once the experiment was started, subjects were not allowed to communicate with each other though they were allowed to ask the experimenters questions.

Table 3 gives the organization of the experiment. At the start of the experiment the subjects received a set of general instructions that described the nature of the gambles they were to consider and explained how they were

TABLE 2—EXPERIMENT 1: PAIRS OF GAMBLES USED IN THE EXPERIMENTS

Pairs	Type	Probability of Winning	Amount if Win	Amount if Lose	Expected Value
1	P	35/36	$ 4.00	−$1.00	3.86
	S	11/36	$16.00	−$1.50	3.85
2	P	29/36	$ 2.00	−$1.00	1.42
	S	7/36	$ 9.00	−$ .50	1.35
3	P	34/36	$ 3.00	−$2.00	2.72
	S	18/36	$ 6.50	−$1.00	2.75
4	P	32/36	$ 4.00	−$ .50	3.50
	S	4/36	$40.00	−$1.00	3.56
5	P	34/36	$ 2.50	−$ .50	2.33
	S	14/36	$ 8.50	−$1.50	2.39
6	P	33/36	$ 2.00	−$2.00	1.67
	S	18/36	$ 5.00	−$1.50	1.75

TABLE 3—EXPERIMENT 1

Parts	Group 1 No Monetary Incentives	Group 2 Monetary Incentives
1	Preferences for Pairs (1), (2), (3)	
2	Selling Prices, All Twelve Gambles	
3	Preferences for Pairs (4), (5), (6)	

to be paid. These are included in the Appendix. Throughout the experiments all instructions and other materials handed out were read aloud. The instructions included a sample gamble (not used in the actual experiment): lose $1 if the number on the ball drawn is less than or equal to 12 and win $8 if the number is greater than 12. The way the gambles worked was demonstrated.

Two different monetary incentive systems were used which together control for Theory 1 and allow Theory 8 to be assessed. In one room (group 1) subjects were told that they would be asked to make a series of decisions concerning various gambles, and that when they were finished they would be paid $7. In the other room (group 2) subjects were told that at the end of the experiments one of their decisions would be chosen at random (using a bingo cage to determine which one) and their payment would depend upon which gamble they chose and upon the outcome of that particular gamble. It was explained that they had a credit of $7 and whatever they won or lost would be added to or substracted from that amount. Finally, it was stated that the most they could lose on any of the gambles was $2 so that $5 was the minimum possible payment.[3]

The use of a randomizing device to pick which decision "counted" was intended to reduce the problem of income effects discussed as Theory 2. Strictly speaking, even this procedure does not completely eliminate the possibility of some income effects, but it should reduce their magnitude substantially. Here there is little opportunity to have a

[3]This was the only difference in the instructions between the two rooms. In the other room also, a decision was to be chosen randomly at the end of the experiment. However, it was stated that this was just for fun as people often wish to know how much they would have won.

growing expectation of rewards over the course of the experiment.

Part 1 of the experiment was distributed (the subjects were allowed to keep the instructions). This part consisted of three pairs of gambles.[4] For each pair subjects were told to indicate which bet they preferred or if they were indifferent. Subjects were told that if one of these three pairs was chosen at the end of the experiment, the two gambles would be played and that individual payments would be made according to which gamble was listed as preferred. Indifference was allowed and the subjects were told, "If you check 'Don't care,' the bet you play will be determined by a coin toss." Indifference was thus allowed and operationally defined in conformance with Theory 3.

After all subjects had completed part 1, the instructions and part 1 were collected and the instructions for part 2 were distributed. For part 2 of the experiments the subjects were asked to give their reservation prices for each of the twelve bets (the order of presentation was randomized). Specifically, subjects were asked "What is the *smallest* price for which you would sell a ticket to the following bet?"[5]

In order to ensure that actual reservation prices were revealed, the method suggested by Becker, DeGroot, and Marschak was employed. If one of the twelve items were chosen to be played at the end of the experiment, an offer price between $0.00 and $9.99 would be randomly generated and the subjects would play the gamble if their announced reservation price exceeded the offer price. Otherwise they would be paid the offer price (in addition to the $7 credit).[6] Thus our procedures

[4]In each pair the bets were referred to as A and B. Assignment of P bets and $ bets to A or B was done randomly. On all materials passed out students were told to write their name, Social Security number, and in the room where payoffs were uncertain, their address.
[5]Announced preferences and those inferred from reservation prices should agree, but as this need not be the case with buying prices, no experiments involving buying prices were considered.
[6]The offer prices were generated by making three draws (with replacement) from a bingo cage containing balls numbered 0–9, these three draws giving the digits of the offer price.

conformed to those used in many other experiments and the problems raised by Theory 1 were avoided.

In order to be sure that all subjects fully understood how payments were to be determined, the instructions to part 2 were rather elaborate. The details, which can be found in the Appendix, include the following: an explanation about why it was in the subjects' best interest to reveal their true reservation prices; a practice gamble; a demonstration of the procedures; and a written test. The correct answers to the test were discussed and subjects' questions were answered. These procedures were designed to anticipate the problems raised by Theory 10. Subjects were allowed to work at part 2 at their own pace and were allowed to determine selling prices in whatever order they pleased.

Part 3 was identical to part 1 except that the remaining three pairs of bets were presented as shown on Table 3. Again, for each pair, subjects were asked to indicate a preference for bet *A*, bet *B*, or indifference. This procedure controls for a possible order effect implicit in the "cost of decision making" arguments of Theory 8. Once the subject has "invested" in a rule which yields a precise dollar value, then he/she would tend to use it repeatedly when the opportunity arises. Thus, we might expect greater consistency between decisions of parts 2 and 3 than between those of parts 1 and 2. After completing this part of the experiment, the subjects were paid as described.

B. *Procedures: Experiment 2*

The purpose of this experiment was to test the strategic behavior theory described as Theory 4. The structure of the experiment was identical to that of experiment 1 with two major exceptions. First, section 2 of the experiment was replaced at points by a section in which "limit prices" were extracted without references to market-type behavior. Second, subjects were not partitioned according to the method of payment. All subjects were paid with the same procedure as group 2 in experiment 1.

The organization of experiment 2 is shown

TABLE 4—EXPERIMENT 2

Parts	Group 1	Group 2
	Monetary Incentives	
1	Preferences for Pairs (1), (2), (3)	
2	Selling Prices,	Dollar Equivalents,
	All Twelve Gambles	All Twelve Gambles
3	Preferences for Pairs (4), (5), (6)	
4	Dollar Equivalents,	Selling Prices,
	All Twelve Gambles	All Twelve Gambles

in Table 4. Subjects were randomly divided into two rooms (the same two as used before) and designated as group 1 and group 2. Each group received identical instructions except the order in which the parts were administered was different as shown in Table 4.

Part 2 for group 1 and part 4 for group 2 were identical to part 2 of experiment 1. Part 4 for group 1 and part 2 for group 2 consisted of a new section. In this new section no words suggestive of market-type activity (for example, selling prices and offer prices) were used. Instead students were asked to give "the exact dollar amount such that you are indifferent between the bet and the amount of money." For the operational details of how this was accomplished the Appendix should be consulted.

III. Results

A. *Experiment 1*

Table 5 summarizes the results for the room in which the subjects' payment was independent of their choices. It is clear that the reversal phenomenon has been replicated: of the 127 choices of *P* bets, 71 (56 percent) were inconsistent with the announced reservation prices. By comparison only 14 (11 percent) of the 130 choices of $ bets were contradicted by the quoted reservation prices. Allowing the subjects to express indifference appears to have had little impact as in only 7 (3 percent) of the 264 choices made, was indifference indicated.

The propensity to reverse was the same for preferences obtained before and after selling prices for both types of bets. Thus, if asking

TABLE 5—FREQUENCIES OF REVERSALS, EXPERIMENT 1 (NO INCENTIVES)

| | Bet | Choices | Reservation Prices | | |
			Consistent	Inconsistent	Equal
Total	P	127	49	71	7
	$	130	111	14	5
Indifferent		7			
Before Giving	P	73	30	39	4
Prices	$	56	48	5	3
After Giving	P	54	19	32	3
Prices	$	74	63	9	2
n = 44					

for selling prices focuses attention on the dollar dimension, it does not stay focused on it. The proportions in which *P* bets and $ bets were chosen before pricing differed significantly from those obtained after the prices (significant at .025 but not at .01). No other statistically significant effects were found.

Table 6 shows the corresponding data for the room in which the decisions were made for real money. Clearly (and unexpectedly) the preference reversal phenomenon is not only replicated, but is even stronger. Seventy percent of the choices of *P* bets were inconsistent with announced selling prices while reversals occurred for just 13 percent of the $ bet choices. Choice patterns and reversal rates appear to be the same for choices made before and after obtaining selling prices. The only significant differences between the performance in the two rooms are a higher proportion of selections of the $ bet in the incentive room (easily significant at .01

levels) and also a greater proportion of reversals on *P* bets (just clears the bar at .05).

We calculated a variety of summary statistics on the prices. The prices for $ bets tend to be higher than the prices for the corresponding *P* bets and were above their expected values. The distributions are apparently different for the two types of bets. In all twelve cases the mean, median, and estimated standard deviations were greater for the $ bet than for the corresponding *P* bet. There does not seem to be any systematic difference between the prices quoted in the two rooms. For each of the twelve bets the hypothesis of equal means was rejected only once (the *P* bet in pair number 2), and the *t*-statistic was just significant at a .05 level. From Table 7 one can see that not only were the preference reversals frequent, but also large. The magnitude of the reversals is generally greater for the predicted reversals than for the unpredicted reversals and also tends to be some-

TABLE 6—FREQUENCIES OF REVERSALS, EXPERIMENT 1 (WITH INCENTIVES)

| | Bet | Choices | Reservation Prices | | |
			Consistent	Inconsistent	Equal
Total	P	99	26	69	4
	$	174	145	22	7
Indifferent		3			
Before Giving	P	49	15	31	3
Prices	$	87	70	12	5
After Giving	P	50	11	38	1
Prices	$	87	75	10	2
n = 46					

TABLE 7—EXPERIMENT 1: MEAN VALUES OF REVERSALS
(In Dollars)

	Predicted		Unpredicted	
Bet	Incentives	No Incentives	Incentives	No Incentives
1	1.71	2.49	.40	.79
2	1.45	2.64	.51	.90
3	1.48	1.29	1.00	.25
4	3.31	5.59	3.00	1.83
5	1.52	1.79	.38	1.29
6	.92	1.18	.33	.31

what smaller for the group with incentives "on." Thirty-four individuals (20 in the incentives room and 14 in the other) reversed every time they chose a P bet and of the 24 individuals who never reversed, 14 of them always chose the $ bet.

B. Experiment 2

Tables 8 and 9 summarize the results of experiment 2. Clearly the preference reversal phenomenon has again been replicated, and the strategic or bargaining behavior explanation shot down. If this explanation had been correct, reversals should have been obtained when using selling prices and not when dollar equivalents were asked for. It is apparent from the tables that this simply is not the

case. Further, this theory would have predicted that selling prices should be higher than the monetary equivalents, but this is not true either. The mean selling price exceeded the mean equivalent in only ten of the twenty-four cases. Again, in every instance the mean price and dollar amount for a $ bet exceeds the respective means for the corresponding P bet. For each bet six t-tests(testing equality of means within and between rooms) were calculated. Of the seventy-two tests calculated the null hypothesis was rejected four times at a significance level of .05 and never at the .01 level. The overall conclusion is that the results obtained using prices and dollar equivalents are essentially the same. In both rooms and by both prices and equivalents approximately one-half the subjects reversed whenever they

TABLE 8—EXPERIMENT 2: SELLING PRICES
GROUP ONE

	Bet	Choices	Consistent	Inconsistent	Equal
				Selling Prices	
Total	P	44	8	30	6
	$	72	54	15	3
Indifferent		4			
Preferences	P	20	5	12	3
before Prices	$	39	24	12	3
Indifferent		1			
Preferences	P	24	3	18	3
after Prices	$	33	30	3	0
Indifferent		3			
				Equivalents	
Total	P	44	4	34	6
	$	72	59	11	2
Indifferent		4			
$n = 20$					

TABLE 9—EXPERIMENT 2: EQUIVALENTS
GROUP TWO

	Bet	Choices	Consistent	Inconsistent	Equal
				Equivalents	
Total	P	44	16	27	1
	S	64	54	9	1
Indifferent		0			
Preferences	P	22	8	14	0
before	S	32	27	4	1
Equivalents					
Preferences	P	22	8	13	1
after	S	32	27	5	0
Equivalents					
				Selling Prices	
Total	P	44	19	22	3
	S	64	51	10	3
$n = 18$					

chose a *P* bet. The number of individuals who chose a *P* bet at least once and never reversed varied between two and four.

IV. Conclusion

Needless to say the results we obtained were not those expected when we initiated this study. Our design controlled for all the economic-theoretic explanations of the phenomenon which we could find. The preference reversal phenomenon which is inconsistent with the traditional statement of preference theory remains. It is rather curious that this inconsistency between the theory and certain human choices should be discovered at a time when the theory is being successfully extended to explain choices of nonhumans (see John H. Kagel and Raymond C. Battalio, 1975, 1976).

As is clear from Table 1 our design not only controlled for the several possible economic explanations of the phenomena, but also for all but one of the psychological theories considered. Note that all the theories for which we exercised control can be rejected as explanations of the phenomena. Thus several psychological theories of human choice are also inconsistent with the observed preference reversals. Theory 8 is rejected since reversals do not go down as rewards go up. Theories 6 and 7 are rejected since the original results of Lichtenstein and Slovic (1971) have been replicated.

The one theory which we cannot reject, 9, is in many ways the least satisfactory of those considered since it allows individual choice to depend upon the context in which the choices are made. For example, if the mode of response or the wording of the question is a primary determinant of choice, then the way to modify accepted theory is not apparent. Even here, however, we have additional insight. If the questions give "cues" which trigger a mode of thinking, such cues do not linger. The reversals occur regardless of the order in which the questions are asked.

The fact that preference theory and related theories of optimization are subject to exception does not mean that they should be discarded. No alternative theory currently available appears to be capable of covering the same extremely broad range of phenomena. In a sense the exception is an important discovery, as it stands as an answer to those who would charge that preference theory is circular and/or without empirical content. It also stands as a challenge to theorists who may attempt to modify the theory to account for this exception without simultaneously making the theory vacuous.

APPENDIX

These instructions are those given to group 1 in experiment 2. From these, with the help of Tables 3 and 4 and the test, the instructions for all experiments can be reproduced. In

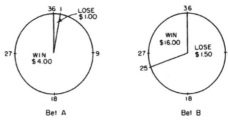

FIGURE 3

order to save space only those portions containing detailed instructions and examples used are shown. For example, part 1 consists of three similar items only one of which is shown.

Instructions

The experimenters are trying to determine how people make decisions. We have designed a simple choice experiment and we shall ask you to make one decision in each of several items. Each decision you shall make will involve one or more *bets*. If a bet is played, then one ball will be drawn from a bingo cage that contains 36 balls numbered 1, 2, ..., 36. Depending upon the nature of the bet, the number drawn will determine whether you lose an amount of money or win an amount of money. Bets will be indicated by Figure 2. For example, if you play the following bet, then you will lose $1 if the number drawn is less than *or equal to* 12, and you will win $8 if the number drawn is greater than 12.

You will be paid in the following fashion. We first give you $7. After you have made a decision on each item, one item will be chosen at random by drawing a ball from a bingo cage. The bet(s) in the chosen item will then be played. You will be paid an amount depending upon your decisions and upon the outcomes of the bets in the chosen item—any amount you win will be added to the $7, and

any amount you lose will be subtracted from the $7. However, the most you can lose on a bet is $2, so you will certainly receive at least $5. All actual payments will occur after the experiment.

PART 1: If an item from this part is chosen at the end of the experiment, you will play the bet you select. If you check "Don't care," the bet you play will be determined by a coin toss.

Item 1: Consider carefully the following two bets shown in Figure 3.

Suppose you have the opportunity to play one of these bets. Make *one* check below to indicate which bet you would prefer to play:

Bet *A*:_____

Bet *B*:_____

Don't care:____

... the instructions continue to items 2 and 3 from Table 2 ...

PART 2: *Instructions*: In each of the items below, you have been presented a ticket that allows you to play a bet. You will then be asked for the *smallest* price at which you would sell the ticket to the bet.

If an item from this part is chosen at the end of the experiment, we will do the following. First, a bingo cage will be filled with 10 balls numbered 0, 1, 2, ..., 9. Then 3 balls will be drawn from this cage, with each ball being replaced before the next is drawn. The numbers on these 3 balls will determine the digits of an offer price between $0.00 and $9.99, with the first number being the penny (right) digit, the second number the dime (middle) digit, and the third number the dollar (left) digit. If this offer price is greater than or equal to the price you state is your

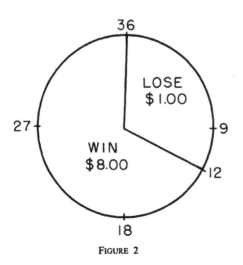

FIGURE 2

minimum selling price for the item's bet, you would receive the offer price. If the offer price is less than your selling price, you would play the bet and be paid according to its outcome.

It is in your best interest to be accurate; that is, the best thing you can do is to be honest. If the price you state is too high or too low, then you are passing up opportunities that you prefer. For example, suppose you would be willing to sell the bet for $4 but instead you say that the lowest price you will sell it for is $6. If the offer price drawn at random is between the two (for example $5) you would be forced to play the bet even though you would rather have sold it for $5. Suppose that you would sell it for $4 but not for less and that you state that you would sell it for $2. If the offer price drawn at random is between the two (for example $3) you would be forced to sell the bet even though at that price you would prefer to play it.

Practice Item: What is the *smallest* price for which you would sell a ticket to the following bet? ———. (The group is then shown the same bet as Figure 2.)

Item 0:[7] What is the *smallest* price for which you would sell the following bet shown in Figure 4?———

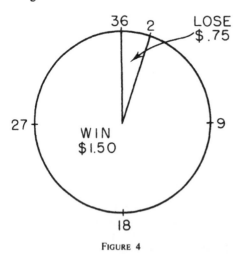

FIGURE 4

[7]Item 0, listed here, and item 00, with $7 with 15/36, lose $1.25 with 21/36, were given as a "test" prior to undertaking part 2.

The offer price is $__. __ __.
The number drawn for the bet was ———.

If this item had actually been played, the amount I would (circle the correct word) gain lose is ———.
. . . (see fn. 7) . . .

Item 4: What is the *smallest* price for which you would sell a ticket to the following bet shown in Figure 5? ———

. . . continue with all items in Table 2 . . .

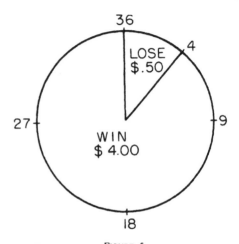

FIGURE 5

PART 3: The items below are like the items of part 1. If one of them is chosen at the end of the experiment, you will play the bet you select. If you check "Don't care," then the bet you play will be determined by a coin toss.

Item 16: Consider carefully the following two bets shown in Figure 6:

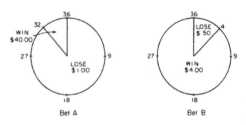

Bet A   Bet B

FIGURE 6

Suppose you have the opportunity to play one of these bets. Make *one* check below to indicate which bet you would prefer to play:

Bet *A*:_____
Bet *B*: _____
Don't care:____

... continue with items 4, 5, and 6, Table 2 ...

PART 4: *Instructions*: Each of the items in this part shows a bet and a monetary scale. As in the example below the dollar amounts increase as you go from the bottom to the top of the scale. (The group is then shown the same bet in Figure 2 plus the scale shown in Figure 7.)

For each item in this part we ask you to do the following. Put your finger at the bottom of the scale and ask yourself which you would prefer to have—the bet shown or the dollar amount. In this case the bet offers 24 chances out of 36 of winning $8 and 12 chances of losing $1. We assume you prefer the bet to giving up $2. Now move your finger up the scale towards the top continuing to ask the same question. At the very top of the scale is an amount of

$10.00
9.00
8.00
7.00
6.00
5.00
4.00
3.00
2.00
1.00
0.00
-1.00
-2.00

FIGURE 7

money greater than that which could be won on the bet. We assume you would prefer the $10 to the bet. All scales in this part will be constructed so that for some of the numbers at the bottom you will prefer to have the bets and for some at the top you will prefer to have the money. What we would like to know is this: what is the exact dollar amount such that you are indifferent between the bet and the amount of money. Mark this amount (with an X) on the scale. Since X's are not always easy to read, and as the scale may not be fine enough for you, we also ask that you write the amount checked in the space provided.

In order to provide you with an incentive to be as accurate as possible, we will do the following. If an item from this part is chosen, we will randomly choose one of the numbers shown on the scale. For example, for this scale a bingo cage would be filled with 10 balls numbered 0, 1, 2, ..., 9. Then 3 balls would be drawn with replacement. The numbers on these 3 balls will determine an amount of money with the first ball drawn being the penny (right) digit, the second number the dime (middle) digit, and the third number the dollar (left) digit. If this number is greater than the amount you check, you will receive the number *drawn*. If the number is less than the amount checked, we will play the bet and you will be paid according to its outcome. If the number drawn is the same as the amount checked, the toss of a fair coin will determine whether you play the bet or get the money. As in this example, we will never generate any negative numbers, but all positive numbers shown on the scale will be equally likely.

Notice that your best interest is served by accurately representing your preference. The best thing you can do is be honest. If the number you mark is too high or too low, then you are passing up opportunities that you prefer. For example, suppose $4 is your point of indifference but you marked $6. If the amount of money drawn at random is anything between the two (for example, $5), you would be forced to play the bet even though you would rather have the drawn amount. Suppose your point of indifference was $4 and you marked $2. If the amount of money drawn at random is between the two (for example, $3) then you would be forced to take the money even though you prefer to play the bet.

Item 0: (The group is shown the bet in Figure 4 and the monetary scale in Figure 7.)

The dollar amount drawn was $__.__ The number drawn for the bet was _____.

If this item had actually been played, the amount I would (circle the correct word) gain lose is _____.
. . . see fn 7 . . .

PART 5:

Item 19: On the scale mark the exact dollar amount such that you are indifferent between the bet and the amount of money. (The group is shown the same bet as Figure 5, and the monetary scale in Figure 7.) . . . continue with Items 1 through 6, Table 2 . . . .

REFERENCES

G. S. Becker, "Crime and Punishment: An Economic Approach," *J. Polit. Econ.*, Mar./Apr. 1968, *76*, 169–217.

_____, "A Theory of Marriage: Part I," *J. Polit. Econ.*, July/Aug. 1973, *81*, 813–46; "Part II," Mar./Apr. 1974, suppl., *82*, 511–26.

G. M. Becker, M. H. DeGroot, and J. Marshak, "Measuring Utility by a Single-Response Sequential Method," *Behav. Sci.*, July 1964, *9*, 226–32.

I. Ehrlich, "The Deterrent Effect of Capital Punishment: A Question of Life and Death," *Amer. Econ. Rev.*, June 1975, *65*, 397–417.

R. C. Fair, "A Theory of Extramarital Affairs," *J. Polit. Econ.*, Feb. 1978, *86*, 45–61.

D. Hammermesh and N. Soss, "An Economic Theory of Suicide," *J. Polit. Econ.*, Jan./Feb. 1974, *82*, 83–98.

J. H. Kagel and R. C. Battalio, "Experimental Studies of Consumer Demand Behavior Using Laboratory Animals," *Econ. Inquiry*, Mar. 1975, *13*, 22–38.

_____ and _____, "Demand Curves for Animal Consumers," mimeo., Washington Univ., St. Louis 1976.

S. Lichtenstein and P. Slovic, "Reversal of Preferences Between Bids and Choices in Gambling Decisions," *J. Exper. Psychol.*, July 1971, *89*, 46–55.

_____ and _____, "Response-Induced Reversals of Preferences in Gambling: An Extended Replication in Las Vegas," *J. Exper. Psychol.*, Nov. 1973, *101*, 16–20.

H. R. Lindman, "Inconsistent Preferences among Gambles," *J. Exper. Psychol.*, Aug. 1971, *89*, 390–97.

P. Slovic, "Choice Between Equally Valued Alternatives," *J. Exper. Psychol.: Hum. Percep. and Perform.*, Aug. 1975, *1*, 280–87.

A. Tversky, "Intransitivity of Preferences," *Psychol. Rev.*, Jan. 1969, *76*, 31–48.

_____, "Elimination by Aspects: A Theory of Choice," *Psychol. Rev.*, July 1972, *79*, 281–99.

[8]

PROSPECT THEORY: AN ANALYSIS OF DECISION UNDER RISK

By Daniel Kahneman and Amos Tversky[1]

This paper presents a critique of expected utility theory as a descriptive model of decision making under risk, and develops an alternative model, called prospect theory. Choices among risky prospects exhibit several pervasive effects that are inconsistent with the basic tenets of utility theory. In particular, people underweight outcomes that are merely probable in comparison with outcomes that are obtained with certainty. This tendency, called the certainty effect, contributes to risk aversion in choices involving sure gains and to risk seeking in choices involving sure losses. In addition, people generally discard components that are shared by all prospects under consideration. This tendency, called the isolation effect, leads to inconsistent preferences when the same choice is presented in different forms. An alternative theory of choice is developed, in which value is assigned to gains and losses rather than to final assets and in which probabilities are replaced by decision weights. The value function is normally concave for gains, commonly convex for losses, and is generally steeper for losses than for gains. Decision weights are generally lower than the corresponding probabilities, except in the range of low probabilities. Overweighting of low probabilities may contribute to the attractiveness of both insurance and gambling.

1. INTRODUCTION

EXPECTED UTILITY THEORY has dominated the analysis of decision making under risk. It has been generally accepted as a normative model of rational choice [24], and widely applied as a descriptive model of economic behavior, e.g. [15, 4]. Thus, it is assumed that all reasonable people would wish to obey the axioms of the theory [47, 36], and that most people actually do, most of the time.

The present paper describes several classes of choice problems in which preferences systematically violate the axioms of expected utility theory. In the light of these observations we argue that utility theory, as it is commonly interpreted and applied, is not an adequate descriptive model and we propose an alternative account of choice under risk.

2. CRITIQUE

Decision making under risk can be viewed as a choice between prospects or gambles. A prospect $(x_1, p_1; \ldots; x_n, p_n)$ is a contract that yields outcome x_i with probability p_i, where $p_1 + p_2 + \ldots + p_n = 1$. To simplify notation, we omit null outcomes and use (x, p) to denote the prospect $(x, p; 0, 1-p)$ that yields x with probability p and 0 with probability $1-p$. The (riskless) prospect that yields x with certainty is denoted by (x). The present discussion is restricted to prospects with so-called objective or standard probabilities.

The application of expected utility theory to choices between prospects is based on the following three tenets.

    (i) Expectation: $U(x_1, p_1; \ldots; x_n, p_n) = p_1 u(x_1) + \ldots + p_n u(x_n)$.

[1] This work was supported in part by grants from the Harry F. Guggenheim Foundation and from the Advanced Research Projects Agency of the Department of Defense and was monitored by Office of Naval Research under Contract N00014-78-C-0100 (ARPA Order No. 3469) under Subcontract 78-072-0722 from Decisions and Designs, Inc. to Perceptronics, Inc. We also thank the Center for Advanced Study in the Behavioral Sciences at Stanford for its support.

That is, the overall utility of a prospect, denoted by U, is the expected utility of its outcomes.

(ii) Asset Integration: $(x_1, p_1; \ldots; x_n, p_n)$ is acceptable at asset position w iff $U(w + x_1, p_1; \ldots; w + x_n, p_n) > u(w)$.

That is, a prospect is acceptable if the utility resulting from integrating the prospect with one's assets exceeds the utility of those assets alone. Thus, the domain of the utility function is final states (which include one's asset position) rather than gains or losses.

Although the domain of the utility function is not limited to any particular class of consequences, most applications of the theory have been concerned with monetary outcomes. Furthermore, most economic applications introduce the following additional assumption.

(iii) Risk Aversion: u is concave ($u'' < 0$).

A person is risk averse if he prefers the certain prospect (x) to any risky prospect with expected value x. In expected utility theory, risk aversion is equivalent to the concavity of the utility function. The prevalence of risk aversion is perhaps the best known generalization regarding risky choices. It led the early decision theorists of the eighteenth century to propose that utility is a concave function of money, and this idea has been retained in modern treatments (Pratt [33], Arrow [4]).

In the following sections we demonstrate several phenomena which violate these tenets of expected utility theory. The demonstrations are based on the responses of students and university faculty to hypothetical choice problems. The respondents were presented with problems of the type illustrated below.

Which of the following would you prefer?

A: 50% chance to win 1,000,   B: 450 for sure.

     50% chance to win nothing;

The outcomes refer to Israeli currency. To appreciate the significance of the amounts involved, note that the median net monthly income for a family is about 3,000 Israeli pounds. The respondents were asked to imagine that they were actually faced with the choice described in the problem, and to indicate the decision they would have made in such a case. The responses were anonymous, and the instructions specified that there was no 'correct' answer to such problems, and that the aim of the study was to find out how people choose among risky prospects. The problems were presented in questionnaire form, with at most a dozen problems per booklet. Several forms of each questionnaire were constructed so that subjects were exposed to the problems in different orders. In addition, two versions of each problem were used in which the left-right position of the prospects was reversed.

The problems described in this paper are selected illustrations of a series of effects. Every effect has been observed in several problems with different outcomes and probabilities. Some of the problems have also been presented to groups of students and faculty at the University of Stockholm and at the

University of Michigan. The pattern of results was essentially identical to the results obtained from Israeli subjects.

The reliance on hypothetical choices raises obvious questions regarding the validity of the method and the generalizability of the results. We are keenly aware of these problems. However, all other methods that have been used to test utility theory also suffer from severe drawbacks. Real choices can be investigated either in the field, by naturalistic or statistical observations of economic behavior, or in the laboratory. Field studies can only provide for rather crude tests of qualitative predictions, because probabilities and utilities cannot be adequately measured in such contexts. Laboratory experiments have been designed to obtain precise measures of utility and probability from actual choices, but these experimental studies typically involve contrived gambles for small stakes, and a large number of repetitions of very similar problems. These features of laboratory gambling complicate the interpretation of the results and restrict their generality.

By default, the method of hypothetical choices emerges as the simplest procedure by which a large number of theoretical questions can be investigated. The use of the method relies on the assumption that people often know how they would behave in actual situations of choice, and on the further assumption that the subjects have no special reason to disguise their true preferences. If people are reasonably accurate in predicting their choices, the presence of common and systematic violations of expected utility theory in hypothetical problems provides presumptive evidence against that theory.

Certainty, Probability, and Possibility

In expected utility theory, the utilities of outcomes are weighted by their probabilities. The present section describes a series of choice problems in which people's preferences systematically violate this principle. We first show that people overweight outcomes that are considered certain, relative to outcomes which are merely probable—a phenomenon which we label the *certainty effect.*

The best known counter-example to expected utility theory which exploits the certainty effect was introduced by the French economist Maurice Allais in 1953 [2]. Allais' example has been discussed from both normative and descriptive standpoints by many authors [28, 38]. The following pair of choice problems is a variation of Allais' example, which differs from the original in that it refers to moderate rather than to extremely large gains. The number of respondents who answered each problem is denoted by *N,* and the percentage who choose each option is given in brackets.

PROBLEM 1: Choose between

	A:	2,500 with probability	.33,	B:	2,400 with certainty.
		2,400 with probability	.66,		
		0 with probability	.01;		

$N = 72$ [18]   [82]*

266   D. KAHNEMAN AND A. TVERSKY

PROBLEM 2: Choose between

C: 2,500 with probability .33,   D: 2,400 with probability .34,

0 with probability   .67;   0 with probability   .66.

$N = 72$ [83]*   [17]

The data show that 82 per cent of the subjects chose B in Problem 1, and 83 per cent of the subjects chose C in Problem 2. Each of these preferences is significant at the .01 level, as denoted by the asterisk. Moreover, the analysis of individual patterns of choice indicates that a majority of respondents (61 per cent) made the modal choice in both problems. This pattern of preferences violates expected utility theory in the manner originally described by Allais. According to that theory, with $u(0) = 0$, the first preference implies

$$u(2,400) > .33u(2,500) + .66u(2,400) \text{ or } .34u(2,400) > .33u(2,500)$$

while the second preference implies the reverse inequality. Note that Problem 2 is obtained from Problem 1 by eliminating a .66 chance of winning 2400 from both prospects under consideration. Evidently, this change produces a greater reduction in desirability when it alters the character of the prospect from a sure gain to a probable one, than when both the original and the reduced prospects are uncertain.

A simpler demonstration of the same phenomenon, involving only two-outcome gambles is given below. This example is also based on Allais [2].

PROBLEM 3:

A: (4,000,.80),   or   B: (3,000).

$N = 95$ [20]   [80]*

PROBLEM 4:

C: (4,000,.20),   or   D: (3,000,.25).

$N = 95$ [65]*   [35]

In this pair of problems as well as in all other problem-pairs in this section, over half the respondents violated expected utility theory. To show that the modal pattern of preferences in Problems 3 and 4 is not compatible with the theory, set $u(0) = 0$, and recall that the choice of B implies $u(3,000)/u(4,000) > 4/5$, whereas the choice of C implies the reverse inequality. Note that the prospect $C = (4,000, .20)$ can be expressed as $(A, .25)$, while the prospect $D = (3,000, .25)$ can be rewritten as $(B,.25)$. The substitution axiom of utility theory asserts that if B is preferred to A, then any (probability) mixture (B, p) must be preferred to the mixture (A, p). Our subjects did not obey this axiom. Apparently, reducing the probability of winning from 1.0 to .25 has a greater effect than the reduction from

.8 to .2. The following pair of choice problems illustrates the certainty effect with non-monetary outcomes.

PROBLEM 5:

A: 50% chance to win a three-week tour of England, France, and Italy;	B: A one-week tour of England, with certainty.
$N = 72$ [22]	[78]*

PROBLEM 6:

C: 5% chance to win a three-week tour of England, France, and Italy;	D: 10% chance to win a one-week tour of England.
$N = 72$ · [67]*	[33]

The certainty effect is not the only type of violation of the substitution axiom. Another situation in which this axiom fails is illustrated by the following problems.

PROBLEM 7:

A: (6,000, .45),   B: (3,000, .90).

$N = 66$ [14]   [86]*

PROBLEM 8:

C: (6,000, .001),   D: (3,000, .002).

$N = 66$ [73]*   [27]

Note that in Problem 7 the probabilities of winning are substantial (.90 and .45), and most people choose the prospect where winning is more probable. In Problem 8, there is a *possibility* of winning, although the probabilities of winning are minuscule (.002 and .001) in both prospects. In this situation where winning is possible but not probable, most people choose the prospect that offers the larger gain. Similar results have been reported by MacCrimmon and Larsson [28].

The above problems illustrate common attitudes toward risk or chance that cannot be captured by the expected utility model. The results suggest the following empirical generalization concerning the manner in which the substitution axiom is violated. If (y, pq) is equivalent to (x, p), then (y, pqr) is preferred to (x, pr), $0 < p, q, r < 1$. This property is incorporated into an alternative theory, developed in the second part of the paper.

268 D. KAHNEMAN AND A. TVERSKY

The Reflection Effect

The previous section discussed preferences between positive prospects, i.e., prospects that involve no losses. What happens when the signs of the outcomes are reversed so that gains are replaced by losses? The left-hand column of Table I displays four of the choice problems that were discussed in the previous section, and the right-hand column displays choice problems in which the signs of the outcomes are reversed. We use $-x$ to denote the loss of x, and $>$ to denote the prevalent preference, i.e., the choice made by the majority of subjects.

TABLE I

PREFERENCES BETWEEN POSITIVE AND NEGATIVE PROSPECTS

Positive prospects			Negative prospects		
Problem 3:	(4,000, .80) <	(3,000).	Problem 3':	(−4,000, .80) >	(−3,000).
N = 95	[20]	[80]*	N = 95	[92]*	[8]
Problem 4:	(4,000, .20) >	(3,000, .25).	Problem 4':	(−4,000, .20) <	(−3,000, .25).
N = 95	[65]*	[35]	N = 95	[42]	[58]
Problem 7:	(3,000, .90) >	(6,000, .45).	Problem 7':	(−3,000, .90) <	(−6,000, .45).
N = 66	[86]*	[14]	N = 66	[8]	[92]*
Problem 8:	(3,000, .002) <	(6,000, .001).	Problem 8':	(−3,000, .002) >	(−6,000, .001).
N = 66	[27]	[73]*	N = 66	[70]*	[30]

In each of the four problems in Table I the preference between negative prospects is the mirror image of the preference between positive prospects. Thus, the reflection of prospects around 0 reverses the preference order. We label this pattern the *reflection effect.*

Let us turn now to the implications of these data. First, note that the reflection effect implies that risk aversion in the positive domain is accompanied by risk seeking in the negative domain. In Problem 3', for example, the majority of subjects were willing to accept a risk of .80 to lose 4,000, in preference to a sure loss of 3,000, although the gamble has a lower expected value. The occurrence of risk seeking in choices between negative prospects was noted early by Markowitz [29]. Williams [48] reported data where a translation of outcomes produces a dramatic shift from risk aversion to risk seeking. For example, his subjects were indifferent between (100, .65; −100, .35) and (0), indicating risk aversion. They were also indifferent between (−200, .80) and (−100), indicating risk seeking. A recent review by Fishburn and Kochenberger [14] documents the prevalence of risk seeking in choices between negative prospects.

Second, recall that the preferences between the positive prospects in Table I are inconsistent with expected utility theory. The preferences between the corresponding negative prospects also violate the expectation principle in the same manner. For example, Problems 3' and 4', like Problems 3 and 4, demonstrate that outcomes which are obtained with certainty are overweighted relative to uncertain outcomes. In the positive domain, the certainty effect contributes to a risk averse preference for a sure gain over a larger gain that is merely probable. In the negative domain, the same effect leads to a risk seeking preference for a loss that is merely probable over a smaller loss that is certain. The same psychological principle—the overweighting of certainty—favors risk aversion in the domain of gains and risk seeking in the domain of losses.

Third, the reflection effect eliminates aversion for uncertainty or variability as an explanation of the certainty effect. Consider, for example, the prevalent preferences for (3,000) over (4,000, .80) and for (4,000, .20) over (3,000, .25). To resolve this apparent inconsistency one could invoke the assumption that people prefer prospects that have high expected value and small variance (see, e.g., Allais [2]; Markowitz [30]; Tobin [41]). Since (3,000) has no variance while (4,000, .80) has large variance, the former prospect could be chosen despite its lower expected value. When the prospects are reduced, however, the difference in variance between (3,000, .25) and (4,000, .20) may be insufficient to overcome the difference in expected value. Because (−3,000) has both higher expected value and lower variance than (−4,000, .80), this account entails that the sure loss should be preferred, contrary to the data. Thus, our data are incompatible with the notion that certainty is generally desirable. Rather, it appears that certainty increases the aversiveness of losses as well as the desirability of gains.

Probabilistic Insurance

The prevalence of the purchase of insurance against both large and small losses has been regarded by many as strong evidence for the concavity of the utility function for money. Why otherwise would people spend so much money to purchase insurance policies at a price that exceeds the expected actuarial cost? However, an examination of the relative attractiveness of various forms of insurance does not support the notion that the utility function for money is concave everywhere. For example, people often prefer insurance programs that offer limited coverage with low or zero deductible over comparable policies that offer higher maximal coverage with higher deductibles—contrary to risk aversion (see, e.g., Fuchs [16]). Another type of insurance problem in which people's responses are inconsistent with the concavity hypothesis may be called probabilistic insurance. To illustrate this concept, consider the following problem, which was presented to 95 Stanford University students.

PROBLEM 9: Suppose you consider the possibility of insuring some property against damage, e.g., fire or theft. After examining the risks and the premium you find that you have no clear preference between the options of purchasing insurance or leaving the property uninsured.

It is then called to your attention that the insurance company offers a new program called *probabilistic insurance*. In this program you pay half of the regular premium. In case of damage, there is a 50 per cent chance that you pay the other half of the premium and the insurance company covers all the losses; and there is a 50 per cent chance that you get back your insurance payment and suffer all the losses. For example, if an accident occurs on an odd day of the month, you pay the other half of the regular premium and your losses are covered; but if the accident occurs on an even day of the month, your insurance payment is refunded and your losses are not covered.

Recall that the premium for full coverage is such that you find this insurance barely worth its cost.

Under these circumstances, would you purchase probabilistic insurance:

	Yes,	No.
$N = 95$	[20]	[80]*

Although Problem 9 may appear contrived, it is worth noting that probabilistic insurance represents many forms of protective action where one pays a certain cost to reduce the probability of an undesirable event—without eliminating it altogether. The installation of a burglar alarm, the replacement of old tires, and the decision to stop smoking can all be viewed as probabilistic insurance.

The responses to Problem 9 and to several other variants of the same question indicate that probabilistic insurance is generally unattractive. Apparently, reducing the probability of a loss from p to $p/2$ is less valuable than reducing the probability of that loss from $p/2$ to 0.

In contrast to these data, expected utility theory (with a concave u) implies that probabilistic insurance is superior to regular insurance. That is, if at asset position w one is just willing to pay a premium y to insure against a probability p of losing x, then one should definitely be willing to pay a smaller premium ry to reduce the probability of losing x from p to $(1-r)p$, $0 < r < 1$. Formally, if one is indifferent between $(w-x, p; w, 1-p)$ and $(w-y)$, then one should prefer probabilistic insurance $(w-x, (1-r)p; w-y, rp; w-ry, 1-p)$ over regular insurance $(w-y)$.

To prove this proposition, we show that

$$pu(w-x)+(1-p)u(w) = u(w-y)$$

implies

$$(1-r)pu(w-x)+rpu(w-y)+(1-p)u(w-ry) > u(w-y).$$

Without loss of generality, we can set $u(w-x)=0$ and $u(w)=1$. Hence, $u(w-y)=1-p$, and we wish to show that

$$rp(1-p)+(1-p)u(w-ry) > 1-p \quad \text{or} \quad u(w-ry) > 1-rp$$

which holds if and only if u is concave.

This is a rather puzzling consequence of the risk aversion hypothesis of utility theory, because probabilistic insurance appears intuitively riskier than regular insurance, which entirely eliminates the element of risk. Evidently, the intuitive notion of risk is not adequately captured by the assumed concavity of the utility function for wealth.

The aversion for probabilistic insurance is particularly intriguing because all insurance is, in a sense, probabilistic. The most avid buyer of insurance remains vulnerable to many financial and other risks which his policies do not cover. There appears to be a significant difference between probabilistic insurance and what may be called contingent insurance, which provides the certainty of coverage for a

PROSPECT THEORY 271

specified type of risk. Compare, for example, probabilistic insurance against all forms of loss or damage to the contents of your home and contingent insurance that eliminates all risk of loss from theft, say, but does not cover other risks, e.g., fire. We conjecture that contingent insurance will be generally more attractive than probabilistic insurance when the probabilities of unprotected loss are equated. Thus, two prospects that are equivalent in probabilities and outcomes could have different values depending on their formulation. Several demonstrations of this general phenomenon are described in the next section.

The Isolation Effect

In order to simplify the choice between alternatives, people often disregard components that the alternatives share, and focus on the components that distinguish them (Tversky [44]). This approach to choice problems may produce inconsistent preferences, because a pair of prospects can be decomposed into common and distinctive components in more than one way, and different decompositions sometimes lead to different preferences. We refer to this phenomenon as the *isolation effect*.

PROBLEM 10: Consider the following two-stage game. In the first stage, there is a probability of .75 to end the game without winning anything, and a probability of .25 to move into the second stage. If you reach the second stage you have a choice between

(4,000, .80)   and   (3,000).

Your choice must be made before the game starts, i.e., before the outcome of the first stage is known.

Note that in this game, one has a choice between .25 × .80 = .20 chance to win 4,000, and a .25 × 1.0 = .25 chance to win 3,000. Thus, in terms of final outcomes and probabilities one faces a choice between (4,000, .20) and (3,000, .25), as in Problem 4 above. However, the dominant preferences are different in the two problems. Of 141 subjects who answered Problem 10, 78 per cent chose the latter prospect, contrary to the modal preference in Problem 4. Evidently, people ignored the first stage of the game, whose outcomes are shared by both prospects, and considered Problem 10 as a choice between (3,000) and (4,000, .80), as in Problem 3 above.

The standard and the sequential formulations of Problem 4 are represented as decision trees in Figures 1 and 2, respectively. Following the usual convention, squares denote decision nodes and circles denote chance nodes. The essential difference between the two representations is in the location of the decision node. In the standard form (Figure 1), the decision maker faces a choice between two risky prospects, whereas in the sequential form (Figure 2) he faces a choice between a risky and a riskless prospect. This is accomplished by introducing a dependency between the prospects without changing either probabilities or

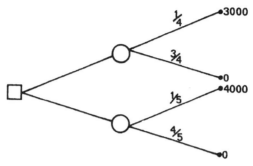

FIGURE 1.—The representation of Problem 4 as a decision tree (standard formulation).

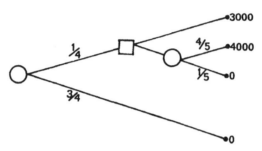

FIGURE 2.—The representation of Problem 10 as a decision tree (sequential formulation).

outcomes. Specifically, the event 'not winning 3,000' is included in the event 'not winning 4,000' in the sequential formulation, while the two events are independent in the standard formulation. Thus, the outcome of winning 3,000 has a certainty advantage in the sequential formulation, which it does not have in the standard formulation.

The reversal of preferences due to the dependency among events is particularly significant because it violates the basic supposition of a decision-theoretical analysis, that choices between prospects are determined solely by the probabilities of final states.

It is easy to think of decision problems that are most naturally represented in one of the forms above rather than in the other. For example, the choice between two different risky ventures is likely to be viewed in the standard form. On the other hand, the following problem is most likely to be represented in the sequential form. One may invest money in a venture with some probability of losing one's capital if the venture fails, and with a choice between a fixed agreed return and a percentage of earnings if it succeeds. The isolation effect implies that the contingent certainty of the fixed return enhances the attractiveness of this option, relative to a risky venture with the same probabilities and outcomes.

The preceding problem illustrated how preferences may be altered by different representations of probabilities. We now show how choices may be altered by varying the representation of outcomes.

Consider the following problems, which were presented to two different groups of subjects.

PROBLEM 11: In addition to whatever you own, you have been given 1,000. You are now asked to choose between

A: (1,000, .50),   and   B: (500).

N = 70 [16]   [84]*

PROBLEM 12: In addition to whatever you own, you have been given 2,000. You are now asked to choose between

C: (−1,000, .50),   and   D: (−500).

N = 68 [69*]   [31]

The majority of subjects chose B in the first problem and C in the second. These preferences conform to the reflection effect observed in Table I, which exhibits risk aversion for positive prospects and risk seeking for negative ones. Note, however, that when viewed in terms of final states, the two choice problems are identical. Specifically,

A = (2,000, .50; 1,000, .50) = C,   and   B = (1,500) = D.

In fact, Problem 12 is obtained from Problem 11 by adding 1,000 to the initial bonus, and subtracting 1,000 from all outcomes. Evidently, the subjects did not integrate the bonus with the prospects. The bonus did not enter into the comparison of prospects because it was common to both options in each problem.

The pattern of results observed in Problems 11 and 12 is clearly inconsistent with utility theory. In that theory, for example, the same utility is assigned to a wealth of $100, 000, regardless of whether it was reached from a prior wealth of $95,000 or $105,000. Consequently, the choice between a total wealth of $100,000 and even chances to own $95,000 or $105,000 should be independent of whether one currently owns the smaller or the larger of these two amounts. With the added assumption of risk aversion, the theory entails that the certainty of owning $100,000 should always be preferred to the gamble. However, the responses to Problem 12 and to several of the previous questions suggest that this pattern will be obtained if the individual owns the smaller amount, but not if he owns the larger amount.

The apparent neglect of a bonus that was common to both options in Problems 11 and 12 implies that the carriers of value or utility are changes of wealth, rather than final asset positions that include current wealth. This conclusion is the cornerstone of an alternative theory of risky choice, which is described in the following sections.

274   D. KAHNEMAN AND A. TVERSKY

3. THEORY

The preceding discussion reviewed several empirical effects which appear to invalidate expected utility theory as a descriptive model. The remainder of the paper presents an alternative account of individual decision making under risk, called prospect theory. The theory is developed for simple prospects with monetary outcomes and stated probabilities, but it can be extended to more involved choices. Prospect theory distinguishes two phases in the choice process: an early phase of editing and a subsequent phase of evaluation. The editing phase consists of a preliminary analysis of the offered prospects, which often yields a simpler representation of these prospects. In the second phase, the edited prospects are evaluated and the prospect of highest value is chosen. We next outline the editing phase, and develop a formal model of the evaluation phase.

The function of the editing phase is to organize and reformulate the options so as to simplify subsequent evaluation and choice. Editing consists of the application of several operations that transform the outcomes and probabilities associated with the offered prospects. The major operations of the editing phase are described below.

Coding. The evidence discussed in the previous section shows that people normally perceive outcomes as gains and losses, rather than as final states of wealth or welfare. Gains and losses, of course, are defined relative to some neutral reference point. The reference point usually corresponds to the current asset position, in which case gains and losses coincide with the actual amounts that are received or paid. However, the location of the reference point, and the consequent coding of outcomes as gains or losses, can be affected by the formulation of the offered prospects, and by the expectations of the decision maker.

Combination. Prospects can sometimes be simplified by combining the probabilities associated with identical outcomes. For example, the prospect (200, .25; 200, .25) will be reduced to (200, .50). and evaluated in this form.

Segregation. Some prospects contain a riskless component that is segregated from the risky component in the editing phase. For example, the prospect (300, .80; 200, .20) is naturally decomposed into a sure gain of 200 and the risky prospect (100, .80). Similarly, the prospect (−400, .40; −100, .60) is readily seen to consist of a sure loss of 100 and of the prospect (−300, .40).

The preceding operations are applied to each prospect separately. The following operation is applied to a set of two or more prospects.

Cancellation. The essence of the isolation effects described earlier is the discarding of components that are shared by the offered prospects. Thus, our respondents apparently ignored the first stage of the sequential game presented in Problem 10, because this stage was common to both options, and they evaluated the prospects with respect to the results of the second stage (see Figure 2). Similarly, they neglected the common bonus that was added to the prospects in Problems 11 and 12. Another type of cancellation involves the discarding of common constituents, i.e., outcome-probability pairs. For example, the choice between (200, .20; 100, .50; −50, .30) and (200, .20; 150, .50; −100, .30) can be reduced by cancellation to a choice between (100, .50; −50, .30) and (150, .50; −100, .30).

Two additional operations that should be mentioned are simplification and the detection of dominance. The first refers to the simplification of prospects by rounding probabilities or outcomes. For example, the prospect (101, .49) is likely to be recoded as an even chance to win 100. A particularly important form of simplification involves the discarding of extremely unlikely outcomes. The second operation involves the scanning of offered prospects to detect dominated alternatives, which are rejected without further evaluation.

Because the editing operations facilitate the task of decision, it is assumed that they are performed whenever possible. However, some editing operations either permit or prevent the application of others. For example, (500, .20; 101, .49) will appear to dominate (500, .15; 99, .51) if the second constituents of both prospects are simplified to (100, .50). The final edited prospects could, therefore, depend on the sequence of editing operations, which is likely to vary with the structure of the offered set and with the format of the display. A detailed study of this problem is beyond the scope of the present treatment. In this paper we discuss choice problems where it is reasonable to assume either that the original formulation of the prospects leaves no room for further editing, or that the edited prospects can be specified without ambiguity.

Many anomalies of preference result from the editing of prospects. For example, the inconsistencies associated with the isolation effect result from the cancellation of common components. Some intransitivities of choice are explained by a simplification that eliminates small differences between prospects (see Tversky [43]). More generally, the preference order between prospects need not be invariant across contexts, because the same offered prospect could be edited in different ways depending on the context in which it appears.

Following the editing phase, the decision maker is assumed to evaluate each of the edited prospects, and to choose the prospect of highest value. The overall value of an edited prospect, denoted V, is expressed in terms of two scales, π and v.

The first scale, π, associates with each probability p a decision weight $\pi(p)$, which reflects the impact of p on the over-all value of the prospect. However, π is not a probability measure, and it will be shown later that $\pi(p) + \pi(1-p)$ is typically less than unity. The second scale, v, assigns to each outcome x a number $v(x)$, which reflects the subjective value of that outcome. Recall that outcomes are defined relative to a reference point, which serves as the zero point of the value scale. Hence, v measures the value of deviations from that reference point, i.e., gains and losses.

The present formulation is concerned with simple prospects of the form $(x, p; y, q)$, which have at most two non-zero outcomes. In such a prospect, one receives x with probability p, y with probability q, and nothing with probability $1-p-q$, where $p+q \leq 1$. An offered prospect is strictly positive if its outcomes are all positive, i.e., if $x, y > 0$ and $p+q = 1$; it is strictly negative if its outcomes

276   D. KAHNEMAN AND A. TVERSKY

are all negative. A prospect is regular if it is neither strictly positive nor strictly negative.

The basic equation of the theory describes the manner in which π and v are combined to determine the over-all value of regular prospects.

If $(x, p; y, q)$ is a regular prospect (i.e., either $p+q<1$, or $x \geq 0 \geq y$, or $x \leq 0 \leq y$), then

(1) $V(x, p; y, q) = \pi(p)v(x) + \pi(q)v(y)$

where $v(0) = 0$, $\pi(0) = 0$, and $\pi(1) = 1$. As in utility theory, V is defined on prospects, while v is defined on outcomes. The two scales coincide for sure prospects, where $V(x, 1.0) = V(x) = v(x)$.

Equation (1) generalizes expected utility theory by relaxing the expectation principle. An axiomatic analysis of this representation is sketched in the Appendix, which describes conditions that ensure the existence of a unique π and a ratio-scale v satisfying equation (1).

The evaluation of strictly positive and strictly negative prospects follows a different rule. In the editing phase such prospects are segregated into two components: (i) the riskless component, i.e., the minimum gain or loss which is certain to be obtained or paid; (ii) the risky component, i.e., the additional gain or loss which is actually at stake. The evaluation of such prospects is described in the next equation.

If $p+q=1$ and either $x>y>0$ or $x<y<0$, then

(2) $V(x, p; y, q) = v(y) + \pi(p)[v(x) - v(y)]$.

That is, the value of a strictly positive or strictly negative prospect equals the value of the riskless component plus the value-difference between the outcomes, multiplied by the weight associated with the more extreme outcome. For example, $V(400, .25; 100, .75) = v(100) + \pi(.25)[v(400) - v(100)]$. The essential feature of equation (2) is that a decision weight is applied to the value-difference $v(x) - v(y)$, which represents the risky component of the prospect, but not to $v(y)$, which represents the riskless component. Note that the right-hand side of equation (2) equals $\pi(p)v(x) + [1 - \pi(p)]v(y)$. Hence, equation (2) reduces to equation (1) if $\pi(p) + \pi(1-p) = 1$. As will be shown later, this condition is not generally satisfied.

Many elements of the evaluation model have appeared in previous attempts to modify expected utility theory. Markowitz [29] was the first to propose that utility be defined on gains and losses rather than on final asset positions, an assumption which has been implicitly accepted in most experimental measurements of utility (see, e.g., [7, 32]). Markowitz also noted the presence of risk seeking in preferences among positive as well as among negative prospects, and he proposed a utility function which has convex and concave regions in both the positive and the negative domains. His treatment, however, retains the expectation principle; hence it cannot account for the many violations of this principle; see, e.g., Table I.

The replacement of probabilities by more general weights was proposed by Edwards [9], and this model was investigated in several empirical studies (e.g.,

[3, 42]). Similar models were developed by Fellner [12], who introduced the concept of decision weight to explain aversion for ambiguity, and by van Dam [46] who attempted to scale decision weights. For other critical analyses of expected utility theory and alternative choice models, see Allais [2], Coombs [6], Fishburn [13], and Hansson [22].

The equations of prospect theory retain the general bilinear form that underlies expected utility theory. However, in order to accomodate the effects described in the first part of the paper, we are compelled to assume that values are attached to changes rather than to final states, and that decision weights do not coincide with stated probabilities. These departures from expected utility theory must lead to normatively unacceptable consequences, such as inconsistencies, intransitivities, and violations of dominance. Such anomalies of preference are normally corrected by the decision maker when he realizes that his preferences are inconsistent, intransitive, or inadmissible. In many situations, however, the decision maker does not have the opportunity to discover that his preferences could violate decision rules that he wishes to obey. In these circumstances the anomalies implied by prospect theory are expected to occur.

The Value Function

An essential feature of the present theory is that the carriers of value are changes in wealth or welfare, rather than final states. This assumption is compatible with basic principles of perception and judgment. Our perceptual apparatus is attuned to the evaluation of changes or differences rather than to the evaluation of absolute magnitudes. When we respond to attributes such as brightness, loudness, or temperature, the past and present context of experience defines an adaptation level, or reference point, and stimuli are perceived in relation to this reference point [23]. Thus, an object at a given temperature may be experienced as hot or cold to the touch depending on the temperature to which one has adapted. The same principle applies to non-sensory attributes such as health, prestige, and wealth. The same level of wealth, for example, may imply abject poverty for one person and great riches for another—depending on their current assets.

The emphasis on changes as the carriers of value should not be taken to imply that the value of a particular change is independent of initial position. Strictly speaking, value should be treated as a function in two arguments: the asset position that serves as reference point, and the magnitude of the change (positive or negative) from that reference point. An individual's attitude to money, say, could be described by a book, where each page presents the value function for changes at a particular asset position. Clearly, the value functions described on different pages are not identical: they are likely to become more linear with increases in assets. However, the preference order of prospects is not greatly altered by small or even moderate variations in asset position. The certainty equivalent of the prospect (1,000, .50), for example, lies between 300 and 400 for most people, in a wide range of asset positions. Consequently, the representation

278   D. KAHNEMAN AND A. TVERSKY

of value as a function in one argument generally provides a satisfactory approximation.

Many sensory and perceptual dimensions share the property that the psychological response is a concave function of the magnitude of physical change. For example, it is easier to discriminate between a change of 3° and a change of 6° in room temperature, than it is to discriminate between a change of 13° and a change of 16°. We propose that this principle applies in particular to the evaluation of monetary changes. Thus, the difference in value between a gain of 100 and a gain of 200 appears to be greater than the difference between a gain of 1,100 and a gain of 1,200. Similarly, the difference between a loss of 100 and a loss of 200 appears greater than the difference between a loss of 1,100 and a loss of 1,200, unless the larger loss is intolerable. Thus, we hypothesize that the value function for changes of wealth is normally concave above the reference point ($v''(x) < 0$, for $x > 0$) and often convex below it ($v''(x) > 0$, for $x < 0$). That is, the marginal value of both gains and losses generally decreases with their magnitude. Some support for this hypothesis has been reported by Galanter and Pliner [17], who scaled the perceived magnitude of monetary and non-monetary gains and losses.

The above hypothesis regarding the shape of the value function was based on responses to gains and losses in a riskless context. We propose that the value function which is derived from risky choices shares the same characteristics, as illustrated in the following problems.

PROBLEM 13:

(6,000, .25),   or   (4,000, .25; 2,000, .25).

$N = 68$ [18]   [82]*

PROBLEM 13':

(−6,000, .25),   or   (−4,000, .25; −2,000, .25).

$N = 64$ [70]*   [30]

Applying equation 1 to the modal preference in these problems yields

$$\pi(.25)v(6,000) < \pi(.25)[v(4,000) + v(2,000)] \quad \text{and}$$
$$\pi(.25)v(-6,000) > \pi(.25)[v(-4,000) + v(-2,000)].$$

Hence, $v(6,000) < v(4,000) + v(2,000)$ and $v(-6,000) > v(-4,000) + v(-2,000)$. These preferences are in accord with the hypothesis that the value function is concave for gains and convex for losses.

Any discussion of the utility function for money must leave room for the effect of special circumstances on preferences. For example, the utility function of an individual who needs $60,000 to purchase a house may reveal an exceptionally steep rise near the critical value. Similarly, an individual's aversion to losses may increase sharply near the loss that would compel him to sell his house and move to a less desirable neighborhood. Hence, the derived value (utility) function of an individual does not always reflect "pure" attitudes to money, since it could be affected by additional consequences associated with specific amounts. Such perturbations can readily produce convex regions in the value function for gains and concave regions in the value function for losses. The latter case may be more common since large losses often necessitate changes in life style.

A salient characteristic of attitudes to changes in welfare is that losses loom larger than gains. The aggravation that one experiences in losing a sum of money appears to be greater than the pleasure associated with gaining the same amount [17]. Indeed, most people find symmetric bets of the form $(x, .50; -x, .50)$ distinctly unattractive. Moreover, the aversiveness of symmetric fair bets generally increases with the size of the stake. That is, if $x > y \geq 0$, then $(y, .50; -y, .50)$ is preferred to $(x, .50; -x, .50)$. According to equation (1), therefore,

$$v(y) + v(-y) > v(x) + v(-x) \qquad \text{and} \qquad v(-y) - v(-x) > v(x) - v(y).$$

Setting $y = 0$ yields $v(x) < -v(-x)$, and letting y approach x yields $v'(x) < v'(-x)$, provided v', the derivative of v, exists. Thus, the value function for losses is steeper than the value function for gains.

In summary, we have proposed that the value function is (i) defined on deviations from the reference point; (ii) generally concave for gains and commonly convex for losses; (iii) steeper for losses than for gains. A value function which satisfies these properties is displayed in Figure 3. Note that the proposed S-shaped value function is steepest at the reference point, in marked contrast to the utility function postulated by Markowitz [29] which is relatively shallow in that region.

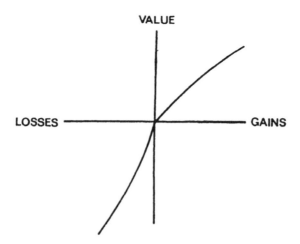

FIGURE 3.—A hypothetical value function.

Although the present theory can be applied to derive the value function from preferences between prospects, the actual scaling is considerably more complicated than in utility theory, because of the introduction of decision weights. For example, decision weights could produce risk aversion and risk seeking even with a linear value function. Nevertheless, it is of interest that the main properties ascribed to the value function have been observed in a detailed analysis of von Neumann–Morgenstern utility functions for changes of wealth (Fishburn and Kochenberger [14]). The functions had been obtained from thirty decision makers in various fields of business, in five independent studies [5, 18, 19, 21, 40]. Most utility functions for gains were concave, most functions for losses were convex, and only three individuals exhibited risk aversion for both gains and losses. With a single exception, utility functions were considerably steeper for losses than for gains.

The Weighting Function

In prospect theory, the value of each outcome is multiplied by a decision weight. Decision weights are inferred from choices between prospects much as subjective probabilities are inferred from preferences in the Ramsey-Savage approach. However, decision weights are not probabilities: they do not obey the probability axioms and they should not be interpreted as measures of degree or belief.

Consider a gamble in which one can win 1,000 or nothing, depending on the toss of a fair coin. For any reasonable person, the probability of winning is .50 in this situation. This can be verified in a variety of ways, e.g., by showing that the subject is indifferent between betting on heads or tails, or by his verbal report that he considers the two events equiprobable. As will be shown below, however, the decision weight $\pi(.50)$ which is derived from choices is likely to be smaller than .50. Decision weights measure the impact of events on the desirability of prospects, and not merely the perceived likelihood of these events. The two scales coincide (i.e., $\pi(p) = p$) if the expectation principle holds, but not otherwise.

The choice problems discussed in the present paper were formulated in terms of explicit numerical probabilities, and our analysis assumes that the respondents adopted the stated values of p. Furthermore, since the events were identified only by their stated probabilities, it is possible in this context to express decision weights as a function of stated probability. In general, however, the decision weight attached to an event could be influenced by other factors, e.g., ambiguity [10, 11].

We turn now to discuss the salient properties of the weighting function π, which relates decision weights to stated probabilities. Naturally, π is an increasing function of p, with $\pi(0) = 0$ and $\pi(1) = 1$. That is, outcomes contingent on an impossible event are ignored, and the scale is normalized so that $\pi(p)$ is the ratio of the weight associated with the probability p to the weight associated with the certain event.

We first discuss some properties of the weighting function for small probabilities. The preferences in Problems 8 and 8' suggest that for small values of p, π

is a subadditive function of p, i.e., $\pi(rp) > r\pi(p)$ for $0 < r < 1$. Recall that in Problem 8, $(6,000, .001)$ is preferred to $(3,000, .002)$. Hence

$$\frac{\pi(.001)}{\pi(.002)} > \frac{v(3,000)}{v(6,000)} > \frac{1}{2} \qquad \text{by the concavity of } v.$$

The reflected preferences in Problem 8' yield the same conclusion. The pattern of preferences in Problems 7 and 7', however, suggests that subadditivity need not hold for large values of p.

Furthermore, we propose that very low probabilities are generally overweighted, that is, $\pi(p) > p$ for small p. Consider the following choice problems.

PROBLEM 14:

$$(5,000, .001), \qquad \text{or} \qquad (5).$$
$$N = 72 \qquad [72]^* \qquad\qquad\qquad [28]$$

PROBLEM 14':

$$(-5,000, .001), \qquad \text{or} \qquad (-5).$$
$$N = 72 \qquad [17] \qquad\qquad\qquad [83]^*$$

Note that in Problem 14, people prefer what is in effect a lottery ticket over the expected value of that ticket. In Problem 14', on the other hand, they prefer a small loss, which can be viewed as the payment of an insurance premium, over a small probability of a large loss. Similar observations have been reported by Markowitz [29]. In the present theory, the preference for the lottery in Problem 14 implies $\pi(.001)v(5,000) > v(5)$, hence $\pi(.001) > v(5)/v(5,000) > .001$, assuming the value function for gains is concave. The readiness to pay for insurance in Problem 14' implies the same conclusion, assuming the value function for losses is convex.

It is important to distinguish overweighting, which refers to a property of decision weights, from the overestimation that is commonly found in the assessment of the probability of rare events. Note that the issue of overestimation does not arise in the present context, where the subject is assumed to adopt the stated value of p. In many real-life situations, overestimation and overweighting may both operate to increase the impact of rare events.

Although $\pi(p) > p$ for low probabilities, there is evidence to suggest that, for all $0 < p < 1$, $\pi(p) + \pi(1-p) < 1$. We label this property subcertainty. It is readily seen that the typical preferences in any version of Allias' example (see, e.g., Problems 1 and 2) imply subcertainty for the relevant value of p. Applying equation (1) to the prevalent preferences in Problems 1 and 2 yields, respectively,

$$v(2,400) > \pi(.66)v(2,400) + \pi(.33)v(2,500), \quad \text{i.e.,}$$

$$[1 - \pi(.66)]v(2,400) > \pi(.33)v(2,500) \quad \text{and}$$

$$\pi(.33)v(2,500) > \pi(.34)v(2,400); \quad \text{hence,}$$

$$1 - \pi(.66) > \pi(.34), \quad \text{or} \quad \pi(.66) + \pi(.34) < 1.$$

Applying the same analysis to Allais' original example yields $\pi(.89) + \pi(.11) < 1$, and some data reported by MacCrimmon and Larsson [28] imply subcertainty for additional values of p.

The slope of π in the interval $(0, 1)$ can be viewed as a measure of the sensitivity of preferences to changes in probability. Subcertainty entails that π is regressive with respect to p, i.e., that preferences are generally less sensitive to variations of probability than the expectation principle would dictate. Thus, subcertainty captures an essential element of people's attitudes to uncertain events, namely that the sum of the weights associated with complementary events is typically less than the weight associated with the certain event.

Recall that the violations of the substitution axiom discussed earlier in this paper conform to the following rule: If (x, p) is equivalent to (y, pq) then (x, pr) is not preferred to (y, pqr), $0 < p, q, r \leqslant 1$. By equation (1),

$$\pi(p)v(x) = \pi(pq)v(y) \quad \text{implies} \quad \pi(pr)v(x) \leqslant \pi(pqr)v(y); \quad \text{hence,}$$

$$\frac{\pi(pq)}{\pi(p)} \leqslant \frac{\pi(pqr)}{\pi(pr)}.$$

Thus, for a fixed ratio of probabilities, the ratio of the corresponding decision weights is closer to unity when the probabilities are low than when they are high. This property of π, called subproportionality, imposes considerable constraints on the shape of π: it holds if and only if log π is a convex function of log p.

It is of interest to note that subproportionality together with the overweighting of small probabilities imply that π is subadditive over that range. Formally, it can be shown that if $\pi(p) > p$ and subproportionality holds, then $\pi(rp) > r\pi(p)$, $0 < r < 1$, provided π is monotone and continuous over $(0, 1)$.

Figure 4 presents a hypothetical weighting function which satisfies overweighting and subadditivity for small values of p, as well as subcertainty and subproportionality. These properties entail that π is relatively shallow in the open interval and changes abruptly near the end-points where $\pi(0) = 0$ and $\pi(1) = 1$. The sharp drops or apparent discontinuities of π at the endpoints are consistent with the notion that there is a limit to how small a decision weight can be attached to an event, if it is given any weight at all. A similar quantum of doubt could impose an upper limit on any decision weight that is less than unity. This quantal effect may reflect the categorical distinction between certainty and uncertainty. On the other hand, the simplification of prospects in the editing phase can lead the individual to discard events of extremely low probability and to treat events of extremely high probability as if they were certain. Because people are limited in

PROSPECT THEORY   283

their ability to comprehend and evaluate extreme probabilities, highly unlikely events are either ignored or overweighted, and the difference between high probability and certainty is either neglected or exaggerated. Consequently, π is not well-behaved near the end-points.

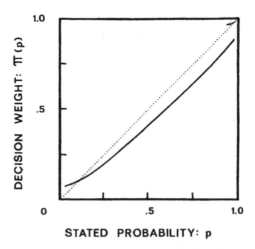

FIGURE 4.—A hypothetical weighting function.

The following example, due to Zeckhauser, illustrates the hypothesized nonlinearity of π. Suppose you are compelled to play Russian roulette, but are given the opportunity to purchase the removal of one bullet from the loaded gun. Would you pay as much to reduce the number of bullets from four to three as you would to reduce the number of bullets from one to zero? Most people feel that they would be willing to pay much more for a reduction of the probability of death from 1/6 to zero than for a reduction from 4/6 to 3/6. Economic considerations would lead one to pay more in the latter case, where the value of money is presumably reduced by the considerable probability that one will not live to enjoy it.

An obvious objection to the assumption that $\pi(p) \neq p$ involves comparisons between prospects of the form $(x, p; x, q)$ and $(x, p'; x, q')$, where $p + q = p' + q' < 1$. Since any individual will surely be indifferent between the two prospects, it could be argued that this observation entails $\pi(p) + \pi(q) = \pi(p') + \pi(q')$, which in turn implies that π is the identity function. This argument is invalid in the present theory, which assumes that the probabilities of identical outcomes are combined in the editing of prospects. A more serious objection to the nonlinearity of π involves potential violations of dominance. Suppose $x > y > 0$, $p > p'$, and $p + q = p' + q' < 1$; hence, $(x, p; y, q)$ dominates $(x, p'; y, q')$. If preference obeys

284   D. KAHNEMAN AND A. TVERSKY

dominance, then

$$\pi(p)v(x)+\pi(q)v(y)>\pi(p')v(x)+\pi(q')v(y),$$

or

$$\frac{\pi(p)-\pi(p')}{\pi(q')-\pi(q)}>\frac{v(y)}{v(x)}.$$

Hence, as y approaches x, $\pi(p)-\pi(p')$ approaches $\pi(q')-\pi(q)$. Since $p-p'=q'-q$, π must be essentially linear, or else dominance must be violated.

Direct violations of dominance are prevented, in the present theory, by the assumption that dominated alternatives are detected and eliminated prior to the evaluation of prospects. However, the theory permits indirect violations of dominance, e.g., triples of prospects so that A is preferred to B, B is preferred to C, and C dominates A. For an example, see Raiffa [34, p. 75].

Finally, it should be noted that the present treatment concerns the simplest decision task in which a person chooses between two available prospects. We have not treated in detail the more complicated production task (e.g., bidding) where the decision maker generates an alternative that is equal in value to a given prospect. The asymmetry between the two options in this situation could introduce systematic biases. Indeed, Lichtenstein and Slovic [27] have constructed pairs of prospects A and B, such that people generally prefer A over B, but bid more for B than for A. This phenomenon has been confirmed in several studies, with both hypothetical and real gambles, e.g., Grether and Plott [20]. Thus, it cannot be generally assumed that the preference order of prospects can be recovered by a bidding procedure.

Because prospect theory has been proposed as a model of choice, the inconsistency of bids and choices implies that the measurement of values and decision weights should be based on choices between specified prospects rather than on bids or other production tasks. This restriction makes the assessment of v and π more difficult because production tasks are more convenient for scaling than pair comparisons.

4. DISCUSSION

In the final section we show how prospect theory accounts for observed attitudes toward risk, discuss alternative representations of choice problems induced by shifts of reference point, and sketch several extensions of the present treatment.

Risk Attitudes

The dominant pattern of preferences observed in Allais' example (Problems 1 and 2) follows from the present theory iff

$$\frac{\pi(.33)}{\pi(.34)}>\frac{v(2,400)}{v(2,500)}>\frac{\pi(.33)}{1-\pi(.66)}.$$

Hence, the violation of the independence axiom is attributed in this case to subcertainty, and more specifically to the inequality $\pi(.34) < 1 - \pi(.66)$. This analysis shows that an Allais-type violation will occur whenever the v-ratio of the two non-zero outcomes is bounded by the corresponding π-ratios.

Problems 3 through 8 share the same structure, hence it suffices to consider one pair, say Problems 7 and 8. The observed choices in these problems are implied by the theory iff

$$\frac{\pi(.001)}{\pi(.002)} > \frac{v(3,000)}{v(6,000)} > \frac{\pi(.45)}{\pi(.90)}.$$

The violation of the substitution axiom is attributed in this case to the subproportionality of π. Expected utility theory is violated in the above manner, therefore, whenever the v-ratio of the two outcomes is bounded by the respective π-ratios. The same analysis applies to other violations of the substitution axiom, both in the positive and in the negative domain.

We next prove that the preference for regular insurance over probabilistic insurance, observed in Problem 9, follows from prospect theory—provided the probability of loss is overweighted. That is, if $(-x, p)$ is indifferent to $(-y)$, then $(-y)$ is preferred to $(-x, p/2; -y, p/2; -y/2, 1-p)$. For simplicity, we define for $x \geq 0$, $f(x) = -v(-x)$. Since the value function for losses is convex, f is a concave function of x. Applying prospect theory, with the natural extension of equation 2, we wish to show that

$$\pi(p)f(x) = f(y) \qquad \text{implies}$$

$$f(y) \leq f(y/2) + \pi(p/2)[f(y) - f(y/2)] + \pi(p/2)[f(x) - f(y/2)]$$

$$= \pi(p/2)f(x) + \pi(p/2)f(y) + [1 - 2\pi(p/2)]f(y/2).$$

Substituting for $f(x)$ and using the concavity of f, it suffices to show that

$$f(y) \leq \frac{\pi(p/2)}{\pi(p)} f(y) + \pi(p/2)f(y) + f(y)/2 - \pi(p/2)f(y)$$

or

$$\pi(p)/2 \leq \pi(p/2), \qquad \text{which follows from the subadditivity of } \pi.$$

According to the present theory, attitudes toward risk are determined jointly by v and π, and not solely by the utility function. It is therefore instructive to examine the conditions under which risk aversion or risk seeking are expected to occur. Consider the choice between the gamble (x, p) and its expected value (px). If $x > 0$, risk seeking is implied whenever $\pi(p) > v(px)/v(x)$, which is greater than p if the value function for gains is concave. Hence, overweighting $(\pi(p) > p)$ is necessary but not sufficient for risk seeking in the domain of gains. Precisely the same condition is necessary but not sufficient for risk aversion when $x < 0$. This analysis restricts risk seeking in the domain of gains and risk aversion in the domain of losses to small probabilities, where overweighting is expected to hold.

286   D. KAHNEMAN AND A. TVERSKY

Indeed these are the typical conditions under which lottery tickets and insurance policies are sold. In prospect theory, the overweighting of small probabilities favors both gambling and insurance, while the *S*-shaped value function tends to inhibit both behaviors.

Although prospect theory predicts both insurance and gambling for small probabilities, we feel that the present analysis falls far short of a fully adequate account of these complex phenomena. Indeed, there is evidence from both experimental studies [37], survey research [26], and observations of economic behavior, e.g., service and medical insurance, that the purchase of insurance often extends to the medium range of probabilities, and that small probabilities of disaster are sometimes entirely ignored. Furthermore, the evidence suggests that minor changes in the formulation of the decision problem can have marked effects on the attractiveness of insurance [37]. A comprehensive theory of insurance behavior should consider, in addition to pure attitudes toward uncertainty and money, such factors as the value of security, social norms of prudence, the aversiveness of a large number of small payments spread over time, information and misinformation regarding probabilities and outcomes, and many others. Some effects of these variables could be described within the present framework, e.g., as changes of reference point, transformations of the value function, or manipulations of probabilities or decision weights. Other effects may require the introduction of variables or concepts which have not been considered in this treatment.

Shifts of Reference

So far in this paper, gains and losses were defined by the amounts of money that are obtained or paid when a prospect is played, and the reference point was taken to be the status quo, or one's current assets. Although this is probably true for most choice problems, there are situations in which gains and losses are coded relative to an expectation or aspiration level that differs from the status quo. For example, an unexpected tax withdrawal from a monthly pay check is experienced as a loss, not as a reduced gain. Similarly, an entrepreneur who is weathering a slump with greater success than his competitors may interpret a small loss as a gain, relative to the larger loss he had reason to expect.

The reference point in the preceding examples corresponded to an asset position that one had expected to attain. A discrepancy between the reference point and the current asset position may also arise because of recent changes in wealth to which one has not yet adapted [29]. Imagine a person who is involved in a business venture, has already lost 2,000 and is now facing a choice between a sure gain of 1,000 and an even chance to win 2,000 or nothing. If he has not yet adapted to his losses, he is likely to code the problem as a choice between (−2,000, .50) and (−1,000) rather than as a choice between (2,000, .50) and (1,000). As we have seen, the former representation induces more adventurous choices than the latter.

A change of reference point alters the preference order for prospects. In particular, the present theory implies that a negative translation of a choice problem, such as arises from incomplete adaptation to recent losses, increases risk seeking in some situations. Specifically, if a risky prospect $(x, p; -y, 1-p)$ is just acceptable, then $(x - z, p; -y - z, 1-p)$ is preferred over $(-z)$ for $x, y, z > 0$, with $x > z$.

To prove this proposition, note that

$$V(x, p; y, 1-p) = 0 \quad \text{iff} \quad \pi(p)v(x) = -\pi(1-p)v(-y).$$

Furthermore,

$$V(x - z, p; -y - z, 1-p)$$

$$= \pi(p)v(x - z) + \pi(1 - p)v(-y - z)$$

$$> \pi(p)v(x) - \pi(p)v(z) + \pi(1 - p)v(-y)$$

$$\quad + \pi(1 - p)v(-z) \quad \text{by the properties of } v,$$

$$= -\pi(1 - p)v(-y) - \pi(p)v(z) + \pi(1 - p)v(-y)$$

$$\quad + \pi(1 - p)v(-z) \quad \text{by substitution,}$$

$$= -\pi(p)v(z) + \pi(1 - p)v(-z)$$

$$> v(-z)[\pi(p) + \pi(1 - p)] \quad \text{since } v(-z) < -v(z),$$

$$> v(-z) \quad \text{by subcertainty.}$$

This analysis suggests that a person who has not made peace with his losses is likely to accept gambles that would be unacceptable to him otherwise. The well known observation [31] that the tendency to bet on long shots increases in the course of the betting day provides some support for the hypothesis that a failure to adapt to losses or to attain an expected gain induces risk seeking. For another example, consider an individual who expects to purchase insurance, perhaps because he has owned it in the past or because his friends do. This individual may code the decision to pay a premium y to protect against a loss x as a choice between $(-x + y, p; y, 1-p)$ and (0) rather than as a choice between $(-x, p)$ and $(-y)$. The preceding argument entails that insurance is likely to be more attractive in the former representation than in the latter.

Another important case of a shift of reference point arises when a person formulates his decision problem in terms of final assets, as advocated in decision analysis, rather than in terms of gains and losses, as people usually do. In this case, the reference point is set to zero on the scale of wealth and the value function is likely to be concave everywhere [39]. According to the present analysis, this formulation essentially eliminates risk seeking, except for gambling with low probabilities. The explicit formulation of decision problems in terms of final assets is perhaps the most effective procedure for eliminating risk seeking in the domain of losses.

Many economic decisions involve transactions in which one pays money in exchange for a desirable prospect. Current decision theories analyze such problems as comparisons between the status quo and an alternative state which includes the acquired prospect minus its cost. For example, the decision whether to pay 10 for the gamble (1,000, .01) is treated as a choice between (990, .01; −10, .99) and (0). In this analysis, readiness to purchase the positive prospect is equated to willingness to accept the corresponding mixed prospect.

The prevalent failure to integrate riskless and risky prospects, dramatized in the isolation effect, suggests that people are unlikely to perform the operation of subtracting the cost from the outcomes in deciding whether to buy a gamble. Instead, we suggest that people usually evaluate the gamble and its cost separately, and decide to purchase the gamble if the combined value is positive. Thus, the gamble (1,000, .01) will be purchased for a price of 10 if π (.01)v(1,000)+v(−10)>0.

If this hypothesis is correct, the decision to pay 10 for (1,000, .01), for example, is no longer equivalent to the decision to accept the gamble (990, .01; −10, .99). Furthermore, prospect theory implies that if one is indifferent between $(x(1-p), p; -px, 1-p)$ and (0) then one will not pay px to purchase the prospect (x, p). Thus, people are expected to exhibit more risk seeking in deciding whether to accept a fair gamble than in deciding whether to purchase a gamble for a fair price. The location of the reference point, and the manner in which choice problems are coded and edited emerge as critical factors in the analysis of decisions.

Extensions

In order to encompass a wider range of decision problems, prospect theory should be extended in several directions. Some generalizations are immediate; others require further development. The extension of equations (1) and (2) to prospects with any number of outcomes is straightforward. When the number of outcomes is large, however, additional editing operations may be invoked to simplify evaluation. The manner in which complex options, e.g. compound prospects, are reduced to simpler ones is yet to be investigated.

Although the present paper has been concerned mainly with monetary outcomes, the theory is readily applicable to choices involving other attributes, e.g., quality of life or the number of lives that could be lost or saved as a consequence of a policy decision. The main properties of the proposed value function for money should apply to other attributes as well. In particular, we expect outcomes to be coded as gains or losses relative to a neutral reference point, and losses to loom larger than gains.

The theory can also be extended to the typical situation of choice, where the probabilities of outcomes are not explicitly given. In such situations, decision weights must be attached to particular events rather than to stated probabilities, but they are expected to exhibit the essential properties that were ascribed to the weighting function. For example, if A and B are complementary events and neither is certain, $\pi(A)+\pi(B)$ should be less than unity—a natural analogue to subcertainty.

PROSPECT THEORY   289

The decision weight associated with an event will depend primarily on the perceived likelihood of that event, which could be subject to major biases [45]. In addition, decision weights may be affected by other considerations, such as ambiguity or vagueness. Indeed, the work of Ellsberg [10] and Fellner [12] implies that vagueness reduces decision weights. Consequently, subcertainty should be more pronounced for vague than for clear probabilities.

The present analysis of preference between risky options has developed two themes. The first theme concerns editing operations that determine how prospects are perceived. The second theme involves the judgmental principles that govern the evaluation of gains and losses and the weighting of uncertain outcomes. Although both themes should be developed further, they appear to provide a useful framework for the descriptive analysis of choice under risk.

The University of British Columbia
    and
Stanford University

Manuscript received November, 1977; final revision received March, 1978.

APPENDIX[2]

In this appendix we sketch an axiomatic analysis of prospect theory. Since a complete self-contained treatment is long and tedious, we merely outline the essential steps and exhibit the key ordinal properties needed to establish the bilinear representation of equation (1). Similar methods could be extended to axiomatize equation (2).

Consider the set of all regular prospects of the form $(x, p; y, q)$ with $p + q < 1$. The extension to regular prospects with $p + q = 1$ is straightforward. Let $\geq$ denote the relation of preference between prospects that is assumed to be connected, symmetric and transitive, and let $\simeq$ denote the associated relation of indifference. Naturally, $(x, p; y, q) \simeq (y, q; x, p)$. We also assume, as is implicit in our notation, that $(x, p; 0, q) \simeq (x, p; 0, r)$, and $(x, p; y, 0) \simeq (x, p; z, 0)$. That is, the null outcome and the impossible event have the property of a multiplicative zero.

Note that the desired representation (equation (1)) is additive in the probability-outcome pairs. Hence, the theory of additive conjoint measurement can be applied to obtain a scale V which preserves the preference order, and interval scales f and g in two arguments such that

$$V(x, p; y, q) = f(x, p) + g(y, q).$$

The key axioms used to derive this representation are:

Independence: $(x, p; y, q) \geq (x, p; y'q')$ iff $(x', p'; y, q) \geq (x', p'; y', q')$.

Cancellation: If $(x, p; y'q') \geq (x', p'; y, q)$ and $(x', p'; y'', q'') \geq (x'', p''; y', q')$, then $(x, p; y'', q'') \geq (x'', p''; y, q)$.

Solvability: If $(x, p; y, q) \geq (z, r) \geq (x, p; y'q')$ for some outcome z and probability r, then there exist y'', q'' such that

$$(x, p; y''q'') \simeq (z, r).$$

It has been shown that these conditions are sufficient to construct the desired additive representation, provided the preference order is Archimedean [8, 25]. Furthermore, since $(x, p; y, q) \simeq (y, q; x, p)$, $f(x, p) + g(y, q) = f(y, q) + g(x, p)$, and letting $q = 0$ yields $f = g$.

Next, consider the set of all prospects of the form (x, p) with a single non-zero outcome. In this case, the bilinear model reduces to $V(x, p) = \pi(p)v(x)$. This is the multiplicative model, investigated in [35] and [25]. To construct the multiplicative representation we assume that the ordering of the probability-outcome pairs satisfies independence, cancellation, solvability, and the Archimedean axiom. In addition, we assume sign dependence [25] to ensure the proper multiplication of signs. It should be noted that the solvability axiom used in [35] and [25] must be weakened because the probability factor permits only bounded solvability.

[2] We are indebted to David H. Krantz for his help in the formulation of this section.

290   D. KAHNEMAN AND A. TVERSKY

Combining the additive and the multiplicative representations yields

$$V(x, p; y, q) = f[\pi(p)v(x)] + f[\pi(q)v(y)].$$

Finally, we impose a new distributivity axiom:

$$(x, p; y, p) \simeq (z, p) \quad \text{iff} \quad (x, q; y, q) \simeq (z, q).$$

Applying this axiom to the above representation, we obtain

$$f[\pi(p)v(x)] + f[\pi(p)v(y)] = f[\pi(p)v(z)]$$

implies

$$f[\pi(q)v(x)] + f[\pi(q)v(y)] = f[\pi(q)v(z)].$$

Assuming, with no loss of generality, that $\pi(q) < \pi(p)$, and letting $\alpha = \pi(p)v(x)$, $\beta = \pi(p)v(y)$, $\gamma = \pi(p)v(z)$, and $\theta = \pi(q)/\pi(p)$, yields $f(\alpha) + f(\beta) = f(\gamma)$ implies $f(\theta\alpha) + f(\theta\beta) = f(\theta\gamma)$ for all $0 < \theta < 1$.

Because f is strictly monotonic we can set $\gamma = f^{-1}[f(\alpha) + f(\beta)]$. Hence, $\theta\gamma = \theta f^{-1}[f(\alpha) + f(\beta)] = f^{-1}[f(\theta\alpha) + f(\theta\beta)]$.

The solution to this functional equation is $f(\alpha) = k\alpha^c$ [1]. Hence, $V(x, p; y, q) = k[\pi(p)v(x)]^c + k[\pi(q)v(y)]^c$, for some k, $c > 0$. The desired bilinear form is obtained by redefining the scales π, v, and V so as to absorb the constants k and c.

REFERENCES

[1] ACZÉL, J.: *Lectures on Functional Equations and Their Applications.* New York: Academic Press, 1966.
[2] ALLAIS, M.: "Le Comportement de l'Homme Rationnel devant le Risque, Critique des Postulats et Axiomes de l'Ecole Americaine," *Econometrica*, 21 (1953), 503–546.
[3] ANDERSON, N. H., AND J. C. SHANTEAU: "Information Integration in Risky Decision Making," *Journal of Experimental Psychology*, 84 (1970), 441–451.
[4] ARROW, K. J.: *Essays in the Theory of Risk-Bearing.* Chicago: Markham, 1971.
[5] BARNES, J. D., AND J. E. REINMUTH: "Comparing Imputed and Actual Utility Functions in a Competitive Bidding Setting," *Decision Sciences*, 7 (1976), 801–812.
[6] COOMBS, C. H.: "Portfolio Theory and the Measurement of Risk," in *Human Judgment and Decision Processes*, ed. by M. F. Kaplan and S. Schwartz. New York: Academic Press, 1975, pp. 63–85.
[7] DAVIDSON, D., P. SUPPES, AND S. SIEGEL: *Decision-making: An Experimental Approach.* Stanford: Stanford University Press, 1957.
[8] DEBREU, G.: "Topological Methods in Cardinal Utility Theory," *Mathematical Methods in the Social Sciences*, ed. by K. J. Arrow, S. Karlin, and P. Suppes. Stanford: Stanford University Press, 1960, pp. 16–26.
[9] EDWARDS, W.: "Subjective Probabilities Inferred from Decisions," *Psychological Review*, 69 (1962), 109–135.
[10] ELLSBERG, D.: "Risk, Ambiguity and the Savage Axioms," *Quarterly Journal of Economics*, 75 (1961), 643–669.
[11] FELLNER, W.: "Distortion of Subjective Probabilities as a Reaction to Uncertainty," *Quarterly Journal of Economics*, 75 (1961), 670–690.
[12] ——: *Probability and Profit—A Study of Economic Behavior Along Bayesian Lines.* Homewood, Illinois: Richard D. Irwin, 1965.
[13] FISHBURN, P. C.: "Mean-Risk Analysis with Risk Associated with Below-Target Returns," *American Economic Review*, 67 (1977), 116–126.
[14] FISHBURN, P. C., AND G. A. KOCHENBERGER: "Two-Piece von Neumann-Morgenstern Utility Functions," forthcoming.
[15] FRIEDMAN, M., AND L. J. SAVAGE: "The Utility Analysis of Choices Involving Risks," *Journal of Political Economy*, 56 (1948), 279–304.
[16] FUCHS, V. R.: "From Bismark to Woodcock: The "Irrational" Pursuit of National Health Insurance," *Journal of Law and Economics*, 19 (1976), 347–359.
[17] GALANTER, E., AND P. PLINER: "Cross-Modality Matching of Money Against Other Continua," in *Sensation and Measurement*, ed. by H. R. Moskowitz et al. Dordrecht, Holland: Reidel, 1974, pp. 65–76.

PROSPECT THEORY 291

[18] GRAYSON, C. J.: *Decisions under Uncertainty: Drilling Decisions by Oil and Gas Operators.* Cambridge, Massachusetts: Graduate School of Business, Harvard University, 1960.
[19] GREEN, P. E.: "Risk Attitudes and Chemical Investment Decisions," *Chemical Engineering Progress*, 59 (1963), 35–40.
[20] GRETHER, D. M., AND C. R. PLOTT: "Economic Theory of Choice and the Preference Reversal Phenomenon," *American Economic Review*, forthcoming.
[21] HALTER, A. N., AND G. W. DEAN: *Decisions under Uncertainty.* Cincinnati: South Western Publishing Co., 1971.
[22] HANSSON, B.: "The Appropriateness of the Expected Utility Model," *Erkenntnis*, 9 (1975), 175–194.
[23] HELSON, H.: *Adaptation-Level Theory.* New York: Harper, 1964.
[24] KEENEY, R. L., AND H. RAIFFA: *Decisions with Multiple Objectives: Preferences and Value Tradeoffs.* New York: Wiley, 1976.
[25] KRANTZ, D. H., D. R. LUCE, P. SUPPES, AND A. TVERSKY: *Foundations of Measurement.* New York: Academic Press, 1971.
[26] KUNREUTHER, H., R. GINSBERG, L. MILLER, P. SAGI, P. SLOVIC, B. BORKAN, AND N. KATZ: *Disaster Insurance Protection: Public Policy Lessons.* New York: Wiley, 1978.
[27] LICHTENSTEIN, S, AND P. SLOVIC: "Reversal of Preference Between Bids and Choices in Gambling Decisions," *Journal of Experimental Psychology*, 89 (1971), 46–55.
[28] MACCRIMMON, K. R., AND S. LARSSON: "Utility Theory: Axioms versus Paradoxes," in *Expected Utility Hypothesis and the Allais Paradox*, ed. by M. Allais and O. Hagen, forthcoming in *Theory and Decision.*
[29] MARKOWITZ, H.: "The Utility of Wealth," *Journal of Political Economy*, 60 (1952), 151–158.
[30] ———: *Portfolio Selection.* New York: Wiley, 1959.
[31] McGLOTHLIN, W. H.: "Stability of Choices among Uncertain Alternatives," *American Journal of Psychology*, 69 (1956), 604–615.
[32] MOSTELLER, F., AND P. NOGEE: "An Experimental Measurement of Utility," *Journal of Political Economy*, 59 (1951), 371–404.
[33] PRATT, J. W.: "Risk Aversion in the Small and in the Large," *Econometrica*, 32 (1964), 122–136.
[34] RAIFFA H.: *Decision Analysis: Introductory Lectures on Choices Under Uncertainty.* Reading, Massachusetts: Addison-Wesley, 1968.
[35] ROSKIES, R.: "A Measurement Axiomatization for an Essentially Multiplicative Representation of Two Factors," *Journal of Mathematical Psychology*, 2 (1965), 266–276.
[36] SAVAGE, L. J.: *The Foundations of Statistics.* New York: Wiley, 1954.
[37] SLOVIC, P., B. FISCHHOFF, S. LICHTENSTEIN, B. CORRIGAN, AND B. COOMBS: "Preference for Insuring Against Probable Small Losses: Insurance Implications," *Journal of Risk and Insurance*, 44 (1977), 237–258.
[38] SLOVIC, P., AND A. TVERSKY: "Who Accepts Savage's Axiom?," *Behavioral Science*, 19 (1974), 368–373.
[39] SPETZLER, C. S.: "The Development of Corporate Risk Policy for Capital Investment Decisions," *IEEE Transactions on Systems Science and Cybernetics*, SSC-4 (1968), 279–300.
[40] SWALM, R. O.: "Utility Theory—Insights into Risk Taking," *Harvard Business Review*, 44 (1966), 123–136.
[41] TOBIN, J.: "Liquidity Preferences as Behavior Towards Risk," *Review of Economic Studies*, 26 (1958), 65–86.
[42] TVERSKY, A.: "Additivity, Utility, and Subjective Probability," *Journal of Mathematical Psychology*, 4 (1967), 175–201.
[43] ———: "Intransitivity of Preferences," *Psychological Review*, 76 (1969), 31–48.
[44] ———: "Elimination by Aspects: A Theory of Choice," *Psychological Review*, 79 (1972), 281–299.
[45] TVERSKY, A., AND D. KAHNEMAN: "Judgment under Uncertainty: Heuristics and Biases," *Science*, 185 (1974), 1124–1131.
[46] VAN DAM, C.: "Another Look at Inconsistency in Financial Decision-Making," presented at the Seminar on Recent Research in Finance and Monetary Economics, Cergy-Pontoise, March, 1975.
[47] VON NEUMANN, J., AND O. MORGENSTERN, *Theory of Games and Economic Behavior,* Princeton: Princeton University Press, 1944.
[48] WILLIAMS, A. C.: "Attitudes toward Speculative Risks as an Indicator of Attitudes toward Pure Risks," *Journal of Risk and Insurance*, 33 (1966), 577–586.

[9]

The Framing of Decisions and the Psychology of Choice

Amos Tversky and Daniel Kahneman

Explanations and predictions of people's choices, in everyday life as well as in the social sciences, are often founded on the assumption of human rationality. The definition of rationality has been much debated, but there is general agreement that rational choices should satisfy some elementary requirements of consistency and coherence. In this article

tional choice requires that the preference between options should not reverse with changes of frame. Because of imperfections of human perception and decision, however, changes of perspective often reverse the relative apparent size of objects and the relative desirability of options.

We have obtained systematic rever-

Summary. The psychological principles that govern the perception of decision problems and the evaluation of probabilities and outcomes produce predictable shifts of preference when the same problem is framed in different ways. Reversals of preference are demonstrated in choices regarding monetary outcomes, both hypothetical and real, and in questions pertaining to the loss of human lives. The effects of frames on preferences are compared to the effects of perspectives on perceptual appearance. The dependence of preferences on the formulation of decision problems is a significant concern for the theory of rational choice.

we describe decision problems in which people systematically violate the requirements of consistency and coherence, and we trace these violations to the psychological principles that govern the perception of decision problems and the evaluation of options.

A decision problem is defined by the acts or options among which one must choose, the possible outcomes or consequences of these acts, and the contingencies or conditional probabilities that relate outcomes to acts. We use the term "decision frame" to refer to the decision-maker's conception of the acts, outcomes, and contingencies associated with a particular choice. The frame that a decision-maker adopts is controlled partly by the formulation of the problem and partly by the norms, habits, and personal characteristics of the decision-maker.

It is often possible to frame a decision problem in more than one way. Alternative frames for a decision problem may be compared to alternative perspectives on a visual scene. Veridical perception requires that the perceived relative height of two neighboring mountains, say, should not reverse with changes of vantage point. Similarly, ra-

sals of preference by variations in the framing of acts, contingencies, or outcomes. These effects have been observed in a variety of problems and in the choices of different groups of respondents. Here we present selected illustrations of preference reversals, with data obtained from students at Stanford University and at the University of British Columbia who answered brief questionnaires in a classroom setting. The total number of respondents for each problem is denoted by N, and the percentage who chose each option is indicated in brackets.

The effect of variations in framing is illustrated in problems 1 and 2.

Problem 1 [$N = 152$]: Imagine that the U.S. is preparing for the outbreak of an unusual Asian disease, which is expected to kill 600 people. Two alternative programs to combat the disease have been proposed. Assume that the exact scientific estimate of the consequences of the programs are as follows:

If Program A is adopted, 200 people will be saved. [72 percent]

If Program B is adopted, there is 1/3 probability that 600 people will be saved, and 2/3 probability that no people will be saved. [28 percent]

Which of the two programs would you favor?

The majority choice in this problem is risk averse: the prospect of certainly saving 200 lives is more attractive than a risky prospect of equal expected value, that is, a one-in-three chance of saving 600 lives.

A second group of respondents was given the cover story of problem 1 with a different formulation of the alternative programs, as follows:

Problem 2 [$N = 155$]:

If Program C is adopted 400 people will die. [22 percent]

If Program D is adopted there is 1/3 probability that nobody will die, and 2/3 probability that 600 people will die. [78 percent]

Which of the two programs would you favor?

The majority choice in problem 2 is risk taking: the certain death of 400 people is less acceptable than the two-in-three chance that 600 will die. The preferences in problems 1 and 2 illustrate a common pattern: choices involving gains are often risk averse and choices involving losses are often risk taking. However, it is easy to see that the two problems are effectively identical. The only difference between them is that the outcomes are described in problem 1 by the number of lives saved and in problem 2 by the number of lives lost. The change is accompanied by a pronounced shift from risk aversion to risk taking. We have observed this reversal in several groups of respondents, including university faculty and physicians. Inconsistent responses to problems 1 and 2 arise from the conjunction of a framing effect with contradictory attitudes toward risks involving gains and losses. We turn now to an analysis of these attitudes.

The Evaluation of Prospects

The major theory of decision-making under risk is the expected utility model. This model is based on a set of axioms, for example, transitivity of preferences, which provide criteria for the rationality of choices. The choices of an individual who conforms to the axioms can be described in terms of the utilities of various outcomes for that individual. The utility of a risky prospect is equal to the expected utility of its outcomes, obtained by weighting the utility of each possible outcome by its probability. When faced with a choice, a rational decision-maker will prefer the prospect that offers the highest expected utility (*1, 2*).

Dr. Tversky is a professor of psychology at Stanford University, Stanford, California 94305, and Dr. Kahneman is a professor of psychology at the University of British Columbia, Vancouver, Canada V6T 1W5.

453

As will be illustrated below, people exhibit patterns of preference which appear incompatible with expected utility theory. We have presented elsewhere (*3*) a descriptive model, called prospect theory, which modifies expected utility theory so as to accommodate these observations. We distinguish two phases in the choice process: an initial phase in which acts, outcomes, and contingencies are framed, and a subsequent phase of evaluation (*4*). For simplicity, we restrict the formal treatment of the theory to choices involving stated numerical probabilities and quantitative outcomes, such as money, time, or number of lives.

Consider a prospect that yields outcome *x* with probability *p*, outcome *y* with probability *q*, and the status quo with probability $1 - p - q$. According to prospect theory, there are values *v*(.) associated with outcomes, and decision weights π(.) associated with probabilities, such that the overall value of the prospect equals $\pi(p)\, v(x) + \pi(q)\, v(y)$. A slightly different equation should be applied if all outcomes of a prospect are on the same side of the zero point (*5*).

In prospect theory, outcomes are expressed as positive or negative deviations (gains or losses) from a neutral reference outcome, which is assigned a value of zero. Although subjective values differ among individuals and attributes, we propose that the value function is commonly S-shaped, concave above the reference point and convex below it, as illustrated in Fig. 1. For example, the difference in subjective value between gains of $10 and $20 is greater than the subjective difference between gains of $110 and $120. The same relation between value differences holds for the corresponding losses. Another property of the value function is that the response to losses is more extreme than the response to gains. The displeasure associated with losing a sum of money is generally greater than the pleasure associated with winning the same amount, as is reflected in people's reluctance to accept fair bets on a toss of a coin. Several studies of decision (*3*, *6*) and judgment (*7*) have confirmed these properties of the value function (*8*).

The second major departure of prospect theory from the expected utility model involves the treatment of probabilities. In expected utility theory the utility of an uncertain outcome is weighted by its probability; in prospect theory the value of an uncertain outcome is multiplied by a decision weight $\pi(p)$, which is a monotonic function of *p* but is not a probability. The weighting function π

454

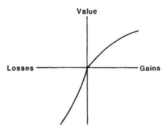

Fig. 1. A hypothetical value function.

has the following properties. First, impossible events are discarded, that is, $\pi(0) = 0$, and the scale is normalized so that $\pi(1) = 1$, but the function is not well behaved near the endpoints. Second, for low probabilities $\pi(p) > p$, but $\pi(p) + \pi(1 - p) \leq 1$. Thus low probabilities are overweighted, moderate and high probabilities are underweighted, and the latter effect is more pronounced than the former. Third, $\pi(pq)/\pi(p) < \pi(pqr)/\pi(pr)$ for all $0 < p, q, r \leq 1$. That is, for any fixed probability ratio *q*, the ratio of decision weights is closer to unity when the probabilities are low than when they are high, for example, $\pi(.1)/\pi(.2) > \pi(.4)/\pi(.8)$. A hypothetical weighting function which satisfies these properties is shown in Fig. 2. The major qualitative properties of decision weights can be extended to cases in which the probabilities of outcomes are subjectively assessed rather than explicitly given. In these situations, however, decision weights may also be affected by other characteristics of an event, such as ambiguity or vagueness (*9*).

Prospect theory, and the scales illustrated in Figs. 1 and 2, should be viewed as an approximate, incomplete, and simplified description of the evaluation of risky prospects. Although the properties of *v* and π summarize a common pattern of choice, they are not universal: the preferences of some individuals are not well described by an S-shaped value function and a consistent set of decision weights. The simultaneous measurement of values and decision weights involves serious experimental and statistical difficulties (*10*).

If π and *v* were linear throughout, the preference order between options would be independent of the framing of acts, outcomes, or contingencies. Because of the characteristic nonlinearities of π and *v*, however, different frames can lead to different choices. The following three sections describe reversals of preference caused by variations in the framing of acts, contingencies, and outcomes.

The Framing of Acts

Problem 3 [*N* = 150]: Imagine that you face the following pair of concurrent decisions. First examine both decisions, then indicate the options you prefer.

Decision (i). Choose between:
A. a sure gain of $240 [84 percent]
B. 25% chance to gain $1000, and
   75% chance to gain nothing [16 percent]

Decision (ii). Choose between:
C. a sure loss of $750 [13 percent]
D. 75% chance to lose $1000, and
   25% chance to lose nothing [87 percent]

The majority choice in decision (i) is risk averse: a riskless prospect is preferred to a risky prospect of equal or greater expected value. In contrast, the majority choice in decision (ii) is risk taking: a risky prospect is preferred to a riskless prospect of equal expected value. This pattern of risk aversion in choices involving gains and risk seeking in choices involving losses is attributable to the properties of *v* and π. Because the value function is S-shaped, the value associated with a gain of $240 is greater than 24 percent of the value associated with a gain of $1000, and the (negative) value associated with a loss of $750 is smaller than 75 percent of the value associated with a loss of $1000. Thus the shape of the value function contributes to risk aversion in decision (i) and to risk seeking in decision (ii). Moreover, the underweighting of moderate and high probabilities contributes to the relative attractiveness of the sure gain in (i) and to the relative aversiveness of the sure loss in (ii). The same analysis applies to problems 1 and 2.

Because (i) and (ii) were presented together, the respondents had in effect to choose one prospect from the set: A and C, B and C, A and D, B and D. The most common pattern (A and D) was chosen by 73 percent of respondents, while the least popular pattern (B and C) was chosen by only 3 percent of respondents. However, the combination of B and C is definitely superior to the combination A and D, as is readily seen in problem 4.

Problem 4 [*N* = 86]. Choose between:
A & D. 25% chance to win $240, and
       75% chance to lose $760. [0 percent]
B & C. 25% chance to win $250, and
       75% chance to lose $750. [100 percent]

When the prospects were combined and the dominance of the second option became obvious, all respondents chose the superior option. The popularity of the inferior option in problem 3 implies that this problem was framed as a pair of separate choices. The respondents apparently failed to entertain the possibility that the conjunction of two seemingly reasonable choices could lead to an untenable result.

The violations of dominance observed in problem 3 do not disappear in the presence of monetary incentives. A different group of respondents who answered a modified version of problem 3, with real payoffs, produced a similar pattern of choices (*11*). Other authors have also reported that violations of the rules of rational choice, originally observed in hypothetical questions, were not eliminated by payoffs (*12*).

We suspect that many concurrent decisions in the real world are framed independently, and that the preference order would often be reversed if the decisions were combined. The respondents in problem 3 failed to combine options, although the integration was relatively simple and was encouraged by instructions (*13*). The complexity of practical problems of concurrent decisions, such as portfolio selection, would prevent people from integrating options without computational aids, even if they were inclined to do so.

The Framing of Contingencies

The following triple of problems illustrates the framing of contingencies. Each problem was presented to a different group of respondents. Each group was told that one participant in ten, preselected at random, would actually be playing for money. Chance events were realized, in the respondents' presence, by drawing a single ball from a bag containing a known proportion of balls of the winning color, and the winners were paid immediately.

Problem 5 [*N* = 77]: Which of the following options do you prefer?
A. a sure win of $30 [78 percent]
B. 80% chance to win $45 [22 percent]

Problem 6 [*N* = 85]: Consider the following two-stage game. In the first stage, there is a 75% chance to end the game without winning anything, and a 25% chance to move into the second stage. If you reach the second stage you have a choice between:
C. a sure win of $30 [74 percent]
D. 80% chance to win $45 [26 percent]
Your choice must be made before the game starts, i.e., before the outcome of the first stage is known. Please indicate the option you prefer.

Problem 7 [*N* = 81]: Which of the following options do you prefer?
E. 25% chance to win $30 [42 percent]
F. 20% chance to win $45 [58 percent]

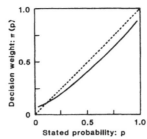

Fig. 2. A hypothetical weighting function.

Let us examine the structure of these problems. First, note that problems 6 and 7 are identical in terms of probabilities and outcomes, because prospect C offers a .25 chance to win $30 and prospect D offers a probability of .25 × .80 = .20 to win $45. Consistency therefore requires that the same choice be made in problems 6 and 7. Second, note that problem 6 differs from problem 5 only by the introduction of a preliminary stage. If the second stage of the game is reached, then problem 6 reduces to problem 5; if the game ends at the first stage, the decision does not affect the outcome. Hence there seems to be no reason to make a different choice in problems 5 and 6. By this logical analysis, problem 6 is equivalent to problem 7 on the one hand and problem 5 on the other. The participants, however, responded similarly to problems 5 and 6 but differently to problem 7. This pattern of responses exhibits two phenomena of choice: the certainty effect and the pseudocertainty effect.

The contrast between problems 5 and 7 illustrates a phenomenon discovered by Allais (*14*), which we have labeled the certainty effect: a reduction of the probability of an outcome by a constant factor has more impact when the outcome was initially certain than when it was merely probable. Prospect theory attributes this effect to the properties of π. It is easy to verify, by applying the equation of prospect theory to problems 5 and 7, that people for whom the value ratio $v(30)/v(45)$ lies between the weight ratios $\pi(.20)/\pi(.25)$ and $\pi(.80)/\pi(1.0)$ will prefer A to B and F to E, contrary to expected utility theory. Prospect theory does not predict a reversal of preference for every individual in problems 5 and 7. It only requires that an individual who has no preference between A and B prefer F to E. For group data, the theory predicts the observed directional shift of preference between the two problems.

The first stage of problem 6 yields the same outcome (no gain) for both acts. Consequently, we propose, people evaluate the options conditionally, as if the second stage had been reached. In this framing, of course, problem 6 reduces to problem 5. More generally, we suggest that a decision problem is evaluated conditionally when (i) there is a state in which all acts yield the same outcome, such as failing to reach the second stage of the game in problem 6, and (ii) the stated probabilities of other outcomes are conditional on the nonoccurrence of this state.

The striking discrepancy between the responses to problems 6 and 7, which are identical in outcomes and probabilities, could be described as a pseudocertainty effect. The prospect yielding $30 is relatively more attractive in problem 6 than in problem 7, as if it had the advantage of certainty. The sense of certainty associated with option C is illusory, however, since the gain is in fact contingent on reaching the second stage of the game (*15*).

We have observed the certainty effect in several sets of problems, with outcomes ranging from vacation trips to the loss of human lives. In the negative domain, certainty exaggerates the aversiveness of losses that are certain relative to losses that are merely probable. In a question dealing with the response to an epidemic, for example, most respondents found "a sure loss of 75 lives" more aversive than "80% chance to lose 100 lives" but preferred "10% chance to lose 75 lives" over "8% chance to lose 100 lives," contrary to expected utility theory.

We also obtained the pseudocertainty effect in several studies where the description of the decision problems favored conditional evaluation. Pseudocertainty can be induced either by a sequential formulation, as in problem 6, or by the introduction of causal contingencies. In another version of the epidemic problem, for instance, respondents were told that risk to life existed only in the event (probability .10) that the disease was carried by a particular virus. Two alternative programs were said to yield "a sure loss of 75 lives" or "80% chance to lose 100 lives" if the critical virus was involved, and no loss of life in the event (probability .90) that the disease was carried by another virus. In effect, the respondents were asked to choose between 10 percent chance of losing 75 lives and 8 percent chance of losing 100 lives, but their preferences were the same as when the choice was between a sure loss of 75 lives and 80 percent chance of losing 100 lives. A conditional framing was evidently adopted in which the contingency of the noncritical virus was eliminated, giving rise to a pseudocertainty effect. The certainty effect reveals attitudes toward risk that are inconsistent with the axioms of rational choice, whereas the pseudocertainty effect violates the more fundamental requirement that preferences should be independent of problem description.

Many significant decisions concern actions that reduce or eliminate the probability of a hazard, at some cost. The shape of π in the range of low probabilities suggests that a protective action which reduces the probability of a harm from 1 percent to zero, say, will be valued more highly than an action that reduces the probability of the same harm from 2 percent to 1 percent. Indeed, probabilistic insurance, which reduces the probability of loss by half, is judged to be worth less than half the price of regular insurance that eliminates the risk altogether (3).

It is often possible to frame protective action in either conditional or unconditional form. For example, an insurance policy that covers fire but not flood could be evaluated either as full protection against the specific risk of fire or as a reduction in the overall probability of property loss. The preceding analysis suggests that insurance should appear more attractive when it is presented as the elimination of risk than when it is described as a reduction of risk. P. Slovic, B. Fischhoff, and S. Lichtenstein, in an unpublished study, found that a hypothetical vaccine which reduces the probability of contracting a disease from .20 to .10 is less attractive if it is described as effective in half the cases than if it is presented as fully effective against one of two (exclusive and equiprobable) virus strains that produce identical symptoms. In accord with the present analysis of pseudocertainty, the respondents valued full protection against an identified virus more than probabilistic protection against the disease.

The preceding discussion highlights the sharp contrast between lay responses to the reduction and the elimination of risk. Because no form of protective action can cover all risks to human welfare, all insurance is essentially probabilistic: it reduces but does not eliminate risk. The probabilistic nature of insurance is commonly masked by formulations that emphasize the completeness of protection against identified harms, but the sense of security that such formulations

provide is an illusion of conditional framing. It appears that insurance is bought as protection against worry, not only against risk, and that worry can be manipulated by the labeling of outcomes and by the framing of contingencies. It is not easy to determine whether people value the elimination of risk too much or the reduction of risk too little. The contrasting attitudes to the two forms of protective action, however, are difficult to justify on normative grounds (16).

The Framing of Outcomes

Outcomes are commonly perceived as positive or negative in relation to a reference outcome that is judged neutral. Variations of the reference point can therefore determine whether a given outcome is evaluated as a gain or as a loss. Because the value function is generally concave for gains, convex for losses, and steeper for losses than for gains, shifts of reference can change the value difference between outcomes and thereby reverse the preference order between options (6). Problems 1 and 2 illustrated a preference reversal induced by a shift of reference that transformed gains into losses.

For another example, consider a person who has spent an afternoon at the race track, has already lost $140, and is considering a $10 bet on a 15 : 1 long shot in the last race. This decision can be framed in two ways, which correspond to two natural reference points. If the status quo is the reference point, the outcomes of the bet are framed as a gain of $140 and a loss of $10. On the other hand, it may be more natural to view the present state as a loss of $140, for the betting day, and accordingly frame the last bet as a chance to return to the reference point or to increase the loss to $150. Prospect theory implies that the latter frame will produce more risk seeking than the former. Hence, people who do not adjust their reference point as they lose are expected to take bets that they would normally find unacceptable. This analysis is supported by the observation that bets on long shots are most popular on the last race of the day (17).

Because the value function is steeper for losses than for gains, a difference between options will loom larger when it is framed as a disadvantage of one option rather than as an advantage of the other option. An interesting example of such an effect in a riskless context has been noted by Thaler (18). In a debate on a proposal to pass to the consumer some of the costs associated with the process-

ing of credit-card purchases, representatives of the credit-card industry requested that the price difference be labeled a cash discount rather than a credit-card surcharge. The two labels induce different reference points by implicitly designating as normal reference the higher or the lower of the two prices. Because losses loom larger than gains, consumers are less willing to accept a surcharge than to forego a discount. A similar effect has been observed in experimental studies of insurance: the proportion of respondents who preferred a sure loss to a larger probable loss was significantly greater when the former was called an insurance premium (19, 20).

These observations highlight the lability of reference outcomes, as well as their role in decision-making. In the examples discussed so far, the neutral reference point was identified by the labeling of outcomes. A diversity of factors determine the reference outcome in everyday life. The reference outcome is usually a state to which one has adapted; it is sometimes set by social norms and expectations; it sometimes corresponds to a level of aspiration, which may or may not be realistic.

We have dealt so far with elementary outcomes, such as gains or losses in a single attribute. In many situations, however, an action gives rise to a compound outcome, which joins a series of changes in a single attribute, such as a sequence of monetary gains and losses, or a set of concurrent changes in several attributes. To describe the framing and evaluation of compound outcomes, we use the notion of a psychological account, defined as an outcome frame which specifies (i) the set of elementary outcomes that are evaluated jointly and the manner in which they are combined and (ii) a reference outcome that is considered neutral or normal. In the account that is set up for the purchase of a car, for example, the cost of the purchase is not treated as a loss nor is the car viewed as a gift. Rather, the transaction as a whole is evaluated as positive, negative, or neutral, depending on such factors as the performance of the car and the price of similar cars in the market. A closely related treatment has been offered by Thaler (18).

We propose that people generally evaluate acts in terms of a minimal account, which includes only the direct consequences of the act. The minimal account associated with the decision to accept a gamble, for example, includes the money won or lost in that gamble and excludes other assets or the outcome of previous gambles. People commonly adopt minimal accounts because this mode of framing (i) simplifies evaluation and reduces cognitive strain, (ii) reflects the intuition that consequences should be causally linked to acts, and (iii) matches the properties of hedonic experience, which is more sensitive to desirable and undesirable changes than to steady states.

There are situations, however, in which the outcomes of an act affect the balance in an account that was previously set up by a related act. In these cases, the decision at hand may be evaluated in terms of a more inclusive account, as in the case of the bettor who views the last race in the context of earlier losses. More generally, a sunk-cost effect arises when a decision is referred to an existing account in which the current balance is negative. Because of the nonlinearities of the evaluation process, the minimal account and a more inclusive one often lead to different choices.

Problems 8 and 9 illustrate another class of situations in which an existing account affects a decision:

Problem 8 [N = 183]: Imagine that you have decided to see a play where admission is $10 per ticket. As you enter the theater you discover that you have lost a $10 bill.
Would you still pay $10 for a ticket for the play?
Yes [88 percent]   No [12 percent]

Problem 9 [N = 200]: Imagine that you have decided to see a play and paid the admission price of $10 per ticket. As you enter the theater you discover that you have lost the ticket. The seat was not marked and the ticket cannot be recovered.
Would you pay $10 for another ticket?
Yes [46 percent]   No [54 percent]

The marked difference between the responses to problems 8 and 9 is an effect of psychological accounting. We propose that the purchase of a new ticket in problem 9 is entered in the account that was set up by the purchase of the original ticket. In terms of this account, the expense required to see the show is $20, a cost which many of our respondents apparently found excessive. In problem 8, on the other hand, the loss of $10 is not linked specifically to the ticket purchase and its effect on the decision is accordingly slight.

The following problem, based on examples by Savage (2, p. 103) and Thaler (18), further illustrates the effect of embedding an option in different accounts. Two versions of this problem were presented to different groups of subjects. One group (N = 93) was given the values that appear in parentheses, and the

other group (N = 88) the values shown in brackets.

Problem 10: Imagine that you are about to purchase a jacket for ($125) [$15], and a calculator for ($15) [$125]. The calculator salesman informs you that the calculator you wish to buy is on sale for ($10) [$120] at the other branch of the store, located 20 minutes drive away. Would you make the trip to the other store?

The response to the two versions of problem 10 were markedly different: 68 percent of the respondents were willing to make an extra trip to save $5 on a $15 calculator; only 29 percent were willing to exert the same effort when the price of the calculator was $125. Evidently the respondents do not frame problem 10 in the minimal account, which involves only a benefit of $5 and a cost of some inconvenience. Instead, they evaluate the potential saving in a more inclusive account, which includes the purchase of the calculator but not of the jacket. By the curvature of v, a discount of $5 has a greater impact when the price of the calculator is low than when it is high.

A closely related observation has been reported by Pratt, Wise, and Zeckhauser (21), who found that the variability of the prices at which a given product is sold by different stores is roughly proportional to the mean price of that product. The same pattern was observed for both frequently and infrequently purchased items. Overall, a ratio of 2 : 1 in the mean price of two products is associated with a ratio of 1.86 : 1 in the standard deviation of the respective quoted prices. If the effort that consumers exert to save each dollar on a purchase, for instance by a phone call, were independent of price, the dispersion of quoted prices should be about the same for all products. In contrast, the data of Pratt *et al.* (21) are consistent with the hypothesis that consumers hardly exert more effort to save $15 on a $150 purchase than to save $5 on a $50 purchase (18). Many readers will recognize the temporary devaluation of money which facilitates extra spending and reduces the significance of small discounts in the context of a large expenditure, such as buying a house or a car. This paradoxical variation in the value of money is incompatible with the standard analysis of consumer behavior.

Discussion

In this article we have presented a series of demonstrations in which seemingly inconsequential changes in the formulation of choice problems caused significant shifts of preference. The in-

consistencies were traced to the interaction of two sets of factors: variations in the framing of acts, contingencies, and outcomes, and the characteristic non-linearities of values and decision weights. The demonstrated effects are large and systematic, although by no means universal. They occur when the outcomes concern the loss of human lives as well as in choices about money; they are not restricted to hypothetical questions and are not eliminated by monetary incentives.

Earlier we compared the dependence of preferences on frames to the dependence of perceptual appearance on perspective. If while traveling in a mountain range you notice that the apparent relative height of mountain peaks varies with your vantage point, you will conclude that some impressions of relative height must be erroneous, even when you have no access to the correct answer. Similarly, one may discover that the relative attractiveness of options varies when the same decision problem is framed in different ways. Such a discovery will normally lead the decision-maker to reconsider the original preferences, even when there is no simple way to resolve the inconsistency. The susceptibility to perspective effects is of special concern in the domain of decision-making because of the absence of objective standards such as the true height of mountains.

The metaphor of changing perspective can be applied to other phenomena of choice, in addition to the framing effects with which we have been concerned here (19). The problem of self-control is naturally construed in these terms. The story of Ulysses' request to be bound to the mast of the ship in anticipation of the irresistible temptation of the Sirens' call is often used as a paradigm case (22). In this example of precommitment, an action taken in the present renders inoperative an anticipated future preference. An unusual feature of the problem of intertemporal conflict is that the agent who views a problem from a particular temporal perspective is also aware of the conflicting views that future perspectives will offer. In most other situations, decision-makers are not normally aware of the potential effects of different decision frames on their preferences.

The perspective metaphor highlights the following aspects of the psychology of choice. Individuals who face a decision problem and have a definite preference (i) might have a different preference in a different framing of the same problem, (ii) are normally unaware of alternative frames and of their potential effects on the relative attractiveness of options,

(iii) would wish their preferences to be independent of frame, but (iv) are often uncertain how to resolve detected inconsistencies (23). In some cases (such as problems 3 and 4 and perhaps problems 8 and 9) the advantage of one frame becomes evident once the competing frames are compared, but in other cases (problems 1 and 2 and problems 6 and 7) it is not obvious which preferences should be abandoned.

These observations do not imply that preference reversals, or other errors of choice or judgment (24), are necessarily irrational. Like other intellectual limitations, discussed by Simon (25) under the heading of "bounded rationality," the practice of acting on the most readily available frame can sometimes be justified by reference to the mental effort required to explore alternative frames and avoid potential inconsistencies. However, we propose that the details of the phenomena described in this article are better explained by prospect theory and by an analysis of framing than by ad hoc appeals to the notion of cost of thinking.

The present work has been concerned primarily with the descriptive question of how decisions are made, but the psychology of choice is also relevant to the normative question of how decisions ought to be made. In order to avoid the difficult problem of justifying values, the modern theory of rational choice has adopted the coherence of specific preferences as the sole criterion of rationality. This approach enjoins the decision-maker to resolve inconsistencies but offers no guidance on how to do so. It implicitly assumes that the decision-maker who carefully answers the question "What do I really want?" will eventually achieve coherent preferences. However, the susceptibility of preferences to variations of framing raises doubt about the feasibility and adequacy of the coherence criterion.

Consistency is only one aspect of the lay notion of rational behavior. As noted by March (26), the common conception of rationality also requires that preferences or utilities for particular outcomes should be predictive of the experiences of satisfaction or displeasure associated with their occurrence. Thus, a man could be judged irrational either because his preferences are contradictory or because his desires and aversions do not reflect his pleasures and pains. The predictive criterion of rationality can be applied to resolve inconsistent preferences and to improve the quality of decisions. A pre-

dictive orientation encourages the decision-maker to focus on future experience and to ask "What will I feel then?" rather than "What do I want now?" The former question, when answered with care, can be the more useful guide in difficult decisions. In particular, predictive considerations may be applied to select the decision frame that best represents the hedonic experience of outcomes.

Further complexities arise in the normative analysis because the framing of an action sometimes affects the actual experience of its outcomes. For example, framing outcomes in terms of the overall wealth or welfare rather than in terms of specific gains and losses may attenuate one's emotional response to an occasional loss. Similarly, the experience of a change for the worse may vary if the change is framed as an uncompensated loss or as a cost incurred to achieve some benefit. The framing of acts and outcomes can also reflect the acceptance or rejection of responsibility for particular consequences, and the deliberate manipulation of framing is commonly used as an instrument of self-control (22). When framing influences the experience of consequences, the adoption of a decision frame is an ethically significant act.

References and Notes

1. J. Von Neumann and O. Morgenstern, *Theory of Games and Economic Behavior* (Princeton Univ. Press, Princeton, N.J., 1947); H. Raiffa, *Decision Analysis: Lectures on Choices Under Uncertainty* (Addison-Wesley, Reading, Mass., 1968); P. Fishburn, *Utility Theory for Decision Making* (Wiley, New York, 1970).
2. L. J. Savage, *The Foundations of Statistics* (Wiley, New York, 1954).
3. D. Kahneman and A. Tversky, *Econometrica* 47, 263 (1979).
4. The framing phase includes various editing operations that are applied to simplify prospects, for example by combining events or outcomes or by discarding negligible components (3).
5. If $p + q = 1$ and either $x > y > 0$ or $x < y < 0$, the equation in the text is replaced by $v(y) + \pi(p) \ [v(x) - v(y)]$, so that decision weights are not applied to sure outcomes.
6. P. Fishburn and G. Kochenberger, *Decision Sci.* 10, 503 (1979); D. J. Laughhunn, J. W. Payne, R. Crum, *Manage. Sci.*, in press; J. W. Payne, D. J. Laughhunn, R. Crum, *ibid.*, in press; S. A. Eraker and H. C. Sox, *Med. Decision Making*, in press. In the last study several hundred clinic patients made hypothetical choices between drug therapies for severe headaches, hypertension, and chest pain. Most patients were risk averse when the outcomes were described as positive (for example, reduced pain or increased life expectancy) and risk taking when the outcomes were described as negative (increased pain or reduced life expectancy). No significant differences were found between patients who actually suffered from the ailments described and patients who did not.
7. E. Galanter and P. Pliner, in *Sensation and Measurement*, H. R. Moskowitz *et al.*, Eds. (Reidel, Dordrecht, 1974), pp. 65-76.
8. The extension of the proposed value function to multiattribute options, with or without risk, deserves careful analysis. In particular, indifference curves between dimensions of loss may be concave upward, even when the value functions for the separate losses are both convex, because of marked subadditivity between dimensions.
9. D. Ellsberg, *Q. J. Econ.* 75, 643 (1961); W. Fellner, *Probability and Profit—A Study of Economic Behavior Along Bayesian Lines* (Irwin, Homewood, Ill., 1965).
10. The scaling of v and π by pair comparisons requires a large number of observations. The procedure of pricing gambles is more convenient for scaling purposes, but it is subject to a severe anchoring bias: the ordering of gambles by their cash equivalents diverges systematically from the preference order observed in direct comparisons (S. Lichtenstein and P. Slovic, *J. Exp. Psychol.* 89, 46 (1971)].
11. A new group of respondents ($N = 126$) was presented with a modified version of problem 3, in which the outcomes were reduced by a factor of 50. The participants were informed that the gambles would actually be played by tossing a pair of fair coins, that one participant in ten would be selected at random to play the gambles of his or her choice. To ensure a positive return for the entire set, a third decision, yielding only positive outcomes, was added. These payoff conditions did not alter the pattern of preferences observed in the hypothetical problem: 67 percent of respondents chose prospect A and 86 percent chose prospect D. The dominated combination of A and D was chosen by 60 percent of respondents, and only 6 percent favored the dominant combination of B and C.
12. S. Lichtenstein and P. Slovic, *J. Exp. Psychol.* 101, 16 (1973); D. M. Grether and C. R. Plott, *Am. Econ. Rev.* 69, 623 (1979); I. Lieblich and A. Lieblich, *Percept. Mot. Skills* 29, 467 (1969); D. M. Grether, *Social Science Working Paper No. 245* (California Institute of Technology, Pasadena, 1979).
13. Other demonstrations of a reluctance to integrate concurrent options have been reported: P. Slovic and S. Lichtenstein, *J. Exp. Psychol.* 78, 646 (1968); J. W. Payne and M. L. Braunstein, *ibid.* 87, 13 (1971).
14. M. Allais, *Econometrica* 21, 503 (1953); K. McCrimmon and S. Larsson, in *Expected Utility Hypotheses and the Allais Paradox*, M. Allais and O. Hagan, Eds. (Reidel, Dordrecht, 1979).
15. Another group of respondents ($N = 205$) was presented with all three problems, in different orders, without monetary payoffs. The joint frequency distribution of choices in problems 5, 6, and 7 was as follows: ACE, 22; ACF, 65; ADE, 4; ADF, 20; BCE, 7; BCF, 18; BDE, 17; BDF, 52. These data confirm in a within-subject design the analysis of conditional evaluation proposed in the text. More than 75 percent of respondents made compatible choices (AC or BD) in problems 5 and 6, and less than half made compatible choices in problems 6 and 7 (CE or DF) or 5 and 7 (AE or BF). The elimination of payoffs in these questions reduced risk aversion but did not substantially alter the effects of certainty and pseudocertainty.
16. For further discussion of rationality in protective action see H. Kunreuther, *Disaster Insurance Protection: Public Policy Lessons* (Wiley, New York, 1978).
17. W. H. McGlothlin, *Am. J. Psychol.* 69, 604 (1956).
18. R. Thaler, *J. Econ. Behav. Organ.* 1, 39 (1980).
19. B. Fischhoff, P. Slovic, S. Lichtenstein, in *Cognitive Processes in Choice and Decision Behavior*, T. Wallsten, Ed. (Erlbaum, Hillsdale, N.J., 1980).
20. J. C. Hershey and P. J. H. Schoemaker, *J. Risk Insur.*, in press.
21. J. Pratt, A. Wise, R. Zeckhauser, *Q. J. Econ.* 93, 189 (1979).
22. R. H. Strotz, *Rev. Econ. Stud.* 23, 165 (1955); G. Ainslie, *Psychol. Bull.* 82, 463 (1975); J. Elster, *Ulysses and the Sirens: Studies in Rationality and Irrationality* (Cambridge Univ. Press, London, 1979); R. Thaler and H. M. Shifrin, *J. Polit. Econ.*, in press.
23. P. Slovic and A. Tversky, *Behav. Sci.* 19, 368 (1974).
24. A. Tversky and D. Kahneman, *Science* 185, 1124 (1974); P. Slovic, B. Fischhoff, S. Lichtenstein, *Annu. Rev. Psychol.* 28, 1 (1977); R. Nisbett and L. Ross, *Human Inference: Strategies and Shortcomings of Social Judgment* (Prentice-Hall, Englewood Cliffs, N.J., 1980); H. Einhorn and R. Hogarth, *Annu. Rev. Psychol.* 32, 53 (1981).
25. H. A. Simon, *Q. J. Econ.* 69, 99 (1955); *Psychol. Rev.* 63, 129 (1956).
26. J. March, *Bell J. Econ.* 9, 587 (1978).
27. This work was supported by the Office of Naval Research under contract N00014-79-C-0077 to Stanford University.

[10]

Do Biases in Probability Judgment Matter in Markets? Experimental Evidence

By Colin F. Camerer*

Microeconomic theory typically concerns exchange between individuals or firms in a market setting. To make predictions precise, individuals are usually assumed to use the laws of probability in structuring and revising beliefs about uncertainties. Recent evidence, mostly gathered by psychologists, suggests probability theories might be inadequate *descriptive* models of *individual* choice. (See the books edited by Daniel Kahneman et al., 1982a, and by Hal Arkes and Kenneth Hammond, 1986.)

Of course, individual violations of normative theories of judgment or choice may be corrected by experience and incentives in markets, thus producing market outcomes which are consistent with the individual-rationality assumption even if that assumption is wrong for most agents. Whether judgment and choice violations matter in markets is a question that begs for empirical analysis.

In this paper I use experimental markets to address this issue (see also Rong Duh and Shyam Sunder, 1986; and Vernon Smith, 1982, for an overview). In these markets, traders are paid dividends for holding a one-period asset. The amount of the dividend depends upon which of two states occurred. Traders know the prior probabilities of the states, and a sample of likelihood information about which state occurred. The

setting is designed so that prices and allocations will reveal whether traders use Bayes' rule to integrate the prior and the sample information, or whether they judge the likelihood of each state by the "representativeness" of the sample to the state (Amos Tversky and Kahneman, 1982b). (Several other non-Bayesian psychological theories can be tested, too.)

Evidence of judgment bias reported by psychologists poses an implicit challenge to economic theory based on rationality. Sometimes that challenge is made explicit, as when Kenneth Arrow suggested that use of the representativeness heuristic "typifies very precisely the excessive reaction to current information which seems to characterize all the securities and futures markets" (1982, p. 5). Others have warned that judgment biases will affect the judgments of well-trained experts who make societal decisions (about the risk of low-probability hazards, for instance, see Paul Slovic, Baruch Fischhoff, and Sarah Lichtenstein, 1976).

Assertions as bold as Arrow's are extremely rare, because the faith that individual irrationality will not affect markets is a strong part of the "oral tradition" in economics. This faith is often defended with Milton Friedman's (1953) famous claim that theories with false assumptions (such as strong assumptions of individual rationality) might still predict market behavior well (see Mark Blaug, 1980, pp. 104–14, for a cogent discussion). Besides that "*F*-twist," there is a standard list of arguments used to defend economic theories from the criticism that people are not rational. (Counterarguments are given in parentheses.)

1) In markets, agents have enough financial incentive, and experience, to avoid mistakes. (Incentives and experience were provided in David Grether's 1980 experiments on the representativeness heuristic. See

*Department of Decision Sciences, The Wharton School, University of Pennsylvania, Philadelphia, PA 19104. I thank Mike Chernew, Marc Knez, Peter Knez, and Lisabeth Miller for research assistance. Helpful comments have been received from three anonymous referees, Greg Fischer, Len Green, David Grether, Dan Kahneman, John Kagel, Peter Knez, George Loewenstein, Charles Plott, Paul Slovic, Shyam Sunder, Richard Thaler, Keith Weigelt, and especially Howard Kunreuther. This research was funded by the Wharton Risk and Decision Processes Center, the Alfred Sloan Foundation grant no. 8551, and the National Science Foundation grant no. SES-8510758.

also Charles Plott and Louis Wilde, 1982, p. 97.)

2) Random mistakes of individuals will cancel out. (The biases found by psychologists are generally *systematic* — most people err in the same direction.)

3) Only a small number of rational agents are needed to make market outcomes rational, if those agents have access to enough capital or factors of production. (Institutional constraints may prevent those agents from making markets rational; see Thomas Russell and Richard Thaler, 1985.)

4) Agents who are less rational may learn *implicitly* from the actions of more rational agents. (This argument requires that "more rational" agents are identifiable, perhaps by their more vigorous trading.)

5) Agents who are less rational may learn *explicitly* from more rational agents by buying advice or information. (Institutional constraints, and the well-known problems of adverse selection and moral hazard, may limit the extent of information markets.)

6) Agents who are less rational may be driven from the market by bankruptcy, either by natural forces or at the hands of more rational competitors. (A new supply of agents who are less rational, or inexperienced, may be constantly entering the market.)

Most of these arguments, though not all of them, are put to the test in the market experiments described below. Subjects trade for up to 7 hours, observing nearly 100 realizations of the state variable, and every trade earns them a (small) dollar profit or loss (argument 1). The representativeness heuristic is systematic in direction (argument 2). Subjects trade with one another in a "double-oral" auction with no constraints on bidding or offering activity (argument 3), so they can learn implicitly from others' trading behavior (argument 4).

Many of the standard arguments are *not* tested in the experiments: There is no explicit market for advice (argument 5); subjects cannot sell short (argument 3); and bankruptcy is unlikely, though conceivable (argument 6). The first two arguments are being tested in further work. Even with these limits, the market experiments provide a greater combination of incentives, experi-

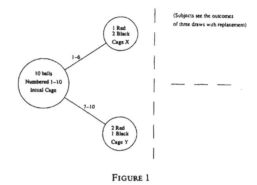

FIGURE 1

ence, and learning opportunity than in previous judgment experiments.

I. Experimental Design

In the experiments, each of 8 or 10 traders is endowed with two assets that live one period and pay a liquidating state-dependent dividend.

A. State Probabilities

The state is represented by which one of two bingo cages (X or Y) is chosen (Figure 1). A third bingo cage containing 10 balls is used to determine whether cage X or cage Y has been chosen. The X cage contains 1 red and 2 black balls. The Y cage contains 2 red balls and 1 black one. The prior probabilities of X and Y are .6 and .4.[1] Figure 1 is shown on a blackboard for all subjects to see, throughout the experiment.

After either X or Y is chosen (but *not* announced), a sample of three balls is drawn from the chosen cage, with replacement, and the sample is announced before trading begins. Since the cages X and Y contain different populations of balls, which are known to traders, they can use Bayes' rule to calculate $P(X/\text{sample})$ from the prior $P(X)$ and

---

[1] Unequal priors were chosen because priors of .5 and .5 might have made it too easy for subjects to intuit the Bayesian posteriors. Experiments with equal priors are a natural direction for future work.

TABLE 1 — BAYESIAN EXPECTED DIVIDEND VALUES

Type	No. of Traders (Experiment No.)	Dividend		Bayesian Posterior $P(X/\text{sample})$ .923 .750 .429 .158 Bayesian Expected Values[a] No. of Reds			
		X	Y	0	1	2	3
I	$5\,(1,3-5,11x-15xh)\,4\,(2,9r,10h)$	500	200	477	425	329	247
II	$5\,(1,3-5,11x-15xh)\,4\,(2,9r,10h)$	350	650	373	425	521	603
I	$5\,(6-7)\,4\,(8,12x)$	525	225	502	450	354	272
II	$5\,(6-7)\,4\,(8,12x)$	180	480	203	255	351	433

Note: All dividends were actually 80 francs higher, for both types of traders and in both states, in experienced subjects experiments $11x$, $13x-15xh$. (Therefore, all Bayesian expected values are 80 francs higher, too.) In all analyses prices are adjusted for this 80-franc difference.

   [a] In francs.

the likelihood functions $P(\text{sample}/X)$ and $P(\text{sample}/Y)$ (which are determined by the cage contents). The top line of Table 1 gives the Bayesian posteriors for all three-ball samples. The possible samples are characterized by the number of reds only, since the order of draws should not matter and the data suggest the order did not matter to subjects. (In some experiments, like John Hey's 1982 experiments on price search, order does seem to matter. Subjects were paid in his 1987 experiments and order still mattered.)

B. Market Procedure

Subjects were undergraduate men, and some women, recruited from quantitative methods and economics classes at the Wharton School. These students have all taken statistics and economics courses. Experiments 1 to 10 used subjects who had not been in any previous market experiments. Five experiments used "experienced" subjects who had been in experiments 1 to 10; these experiments are numbered $11x$ to $15xh$ (the "x" reminds the reader that subjects were experienced). Experiments were conducted in one 3-hour session (experiments 1 and 2, 6, 9 and 10, $11x$ to $15xh$) or two 2-hour sessions held on consecutive evenings (experiments 3 to 5, 7 and 8).

All trading and earnings are in terms of francs, which are converted to dollars at the end of the experiment at a rate of $.001

dollars per franc ($.0015 in experiment 1).[2] Traders are endowed with 10,000 francs and two certificates in each trading period, and 10,000 francs is subtracted from their total francs at the end of each period. In some experiments a known fixed cost (around 5,000 francs) was subtracted from their total earnings at the end of the experiment.

Traders voluntarily exchange assets in a "double-oral auction": Buyers shout out bids at which they will buy, sellers shout out offers at which they will sell. Bids must top outstanding bids and offers must undercut outstanding offers. A matching bid and offer is a trade, which erases all previous bids and offers. All bids, offers, and trades in a period are recorded by the experimenter on a transparency visible to subjects. (No history of previous periods of trading is posted.) Trading periods last 4 minutes in 10-subject experiments, 3 minutes in 8-subject experiments.

At the end of each trading period the state (X or Y) is announced and traders calculate

---

[2] In practice, using francs makes traders more precise in their trading than they would be with dollars, for example. traders routinely haggle over 5-franc differences between bids and offers, which represent half a penny. Francs may also alleviate competition among traders for relative status in dollar earnings, because traders' dollar conversion rates (while identical) are privately known.

their profits. Dollar profits are given by

(1) *PROFITS*

$$= X\left[E_f - R_f + \sum_{i=1}^{x_s} 0_i - \sum_{j=1}^{x_b} B_j + D(S) \right.$$

$$\left. \times (E_c - x_s + x_b) - F \right],$$

where $X =$ dollar-per-franc conversion rate,
    $E_f =$ initial endowment in francs,
    $R_f =$ amount of francs repaid at period-end,
    $E_c =$ initial endowment in certificates,
    $x_s =$ number of certificates sold,
    $0_i =$ selling price of ith certificate sold,
    $x_b =$ number of certificates bought,
    $B_j =$ purchase price of jth certificate bought,
   $D(S) =$ dividends per certificate in state S,
    $F =$ fixed cost per experiment in francs.
Traders may not sell short (that is, $E_c - x_s + x_b$ cannot be negative), and net francs on hand ($E_f + \Sigma 0_i - \Sigma B_j$) cannot be negative.

C. *Market Equilibrium*

Assuming risk neutrality, traders' reservation prices for assets are expected values. (If they are not risk neutral, their reservation prices are certainty equivalents.) Since each trader's endowment of francs is large enough to buy virtually the entire market supply of assets, and the supply is fixed (by the initial endowment, and the short-selling restriction), there is excess demand at any price less than the highest expected value. Thus, in competitive equilibrium, prices should be bid up to the largest expected value of any trader. One irrational trader who pays too much can therefore create a market price that is too high. The empirical question is whether such traders exist, and whether the experience and financial discipline of a market makes them more rational over the course of an experiment.

Of course, the double-oral auction is not Walrasian, so there is no theoretical as-

surance that competitive equilibrium will result. However, simple models of the double-oral auction as a dynamic game with incomplete information are beginning to establish the theoretical tendency of double-oral auctions to converge to competitive equilibrium (Daniel Friedman, 1984; Robert Wilson, 1985; see David Easley and John Ledyard, 1986). The empirical tendency to converge is well-established (for example, Smith, 1982), even in designs meant to inhibit convergence (Smith and Arlington Williams, in press).

D. *Competing Theories*

In each experiment, traders are randomly assigned to either of two "types," which differ in the dividends they receive in the two states X and Y (see Table 1). The dividends are chosen so that competing theories predict different patterns of prices and allocations (see Table 2). Each theory will now be described briefly.

Bayesian. If traders use Bayes' rule to calculate posterior probabilities given the sample data, prices should converge to the Bayesian expected values given in Table 2, assuming risk neutrality. (Tests and controls for risk neutrality are described below.) In the experiments described by the top panel of Table 2, for instance, type I traders should pay up to 477 if the sample is 0 reds, 425 if 1 red, 329 if 2 reds, and 247 if 3 reds. Type II traders should pay up to 373, 425, 521, and 603, respectively. Therefore, if the sample is 0 reds, then type I traders should buy from type II traders at a price of 477. If the sample is 2 or 3 reds, the type II traders should buy all the units, at prices of 521 or 603, respectively. If the sample is 1 red, then type I and type II traders both have a Bayesian expected value of 425 francs, so we expect half the units will be held by each of the two types of traders. (Trades might take place because of uncontrolled differences in risk tastes, but units are still equally as likely to end up in the hands of type I and type II traders.) In experiments 6 to 8 and $12x$, dividends were chosen so that the Bayesian expected values of the type I and type II

TABLE 2—PRICE AND ALLOCATION PREDICTIONS OF COMPETING THEORIES

| | Predictions Expressed as: Price P (Type Holding Assets) Number of Reds in Sample | | | |
Theory	0 Reds	1 Red	2 Reds	3 Reds
Experiments 1–5, 9r–11x, 13x–15xh				
Bayesian	477 (I)	425 (I, II)	521 (II)	603 (II)
Exact Representativeness	477 (I)	P > 425 (I)	P > 521 (II)	603 (II)
Conservatism	P < 477 (I)	P > 425 (II)	P < 521 (II)	P < 603 (II)
Overreaction	P > 477 (I)	P > 425 (I)	P > 521 (II)	P > 603 (II)
Base-Rate Ignorance	467 (I)	450 (II)	550 (II)	617 (II)
Experiments 6–8, 12x				
Bayesian	502 (I)	450 (I)	354 (I)	433 (II)
Exact Representativeness	502 (I)	P > 450 (I)	P > 354 (II)	433 (II)
Conservatism	P < 502 (I)	P < 450 (I)	P > 354 (I)	P < 433 (II)
Overreaction	P > 502 (I)	P > 450 (I)	P > 354 (II)	P > 433 (II)
Base-Rate Ignorance	492 (I)	425 (II)	380 (II)	447 (II)

traders were (nearly) equal when a 2-red sample was drawn.

Exact Representativeness. If subjects take the representativeness of the sample to the cage contents as a psychological index of the cage's likelihood, non-Bayesian expected values might result. Representativeness is a vague notion, but we can distinguish some precise variants of it. For instance, subjects might think $P(X/\text{sample}) = 1$, if the sample resembles the X-cage contents more closely than the Y-cage contents. Or they might think $P(X/\text{sample}) = 1$, if the sample exactly matches the X-cage contents. These extreme hypotheses are clearly ruled out by the data presented below.

More reasonably, subjects may be intuitively Bayesian for most samples, but overestimate a cage's likelihood when a sample resembles the cage *exactly*. This "exact representativeness" theory predicts that subjects will judge $P(X/1 \text{ red})$ to be greater than the Bayesian posterior .75 because a 1-red sample exactly matches the X-cage's contents. Similarly, $P(Y/2 \text{ red})$ will be judged to be greater than .57; other probabilities will be Bayesian. Of course, there are other possible interpretations but since they are either imprecise or clearly incorrect, only exact representativeness will be considered carefully.

Under exact representativeness, prices will be higher than Bayesian in 1- and 2-red periods (as shown in Table 2) and type I

traders will hold units in 1-red periods. (Recall that the Bayesian theory predicts types I and II are equally likely to hold units in 1-red periods.)

Base-Rate Ignorance. If subjects judge $P(\text{state}/\text{sample})$ by the representativeness of samples to states, their judgments may ignore differences in the prior probabilities (or "base rates") of states (Tversky and Kahneman, 1982b). In our setting it is difficult to integrate this aspect of representativeness with other aspects, like the psychological power of exact representativeness, because the two aspects often work in opposite directions. In 1-red samples, for instance, exact representativeness predicts $P(X/1 \text{ red})$ will be overestimated, while ignorance of the higher base rate of X implies $P(X/1 \text{ red})$ will be underestimated. Since predictions of a theory that integrates representativeness with base-rate ignorance are ambiguous, I define base-rate ignorance as using Bayes' rule with erroneous priors $P(X) = P(Y) = .5$. Predictions of this theory are shown in Table 2.

Of course, ignoring base rates completely is rather implausible. For example, in an experiment with a prior probability of .001, it seems unlikely that subjects will act as if the prior is .5. If priors are simply underweighted, but not ignored, the data will show some statistical support for the complete base-rate ignorance theory. The theory should be considered an extreme benchmark that helps us judge whether priors are underweighted at all.

Conservatism. Subjects may be "conservative" in adjusting prior probabilities for sample evidence (for example, Ward Edwards, 1968).

Overreaction. Subjects may adjust prior probabilities *too much*, as if overreacting to sample evidence. The overreaction theory makes the same prediction as representativeness in 1- and 2-red periods, but it predicts bias in 0- and 3-red periods where representativeness does not. Note that the conservatism and overreaction theories make exactly opposite predictions. This implies quite a challenge for the Bayesian theory: Prices must be exactly at the Bayesian prediction, or insignificantly different from it, for both theories to be falsified.

II. Results

Fifteen experiments have been conducted —ten with inexperienced subjects, five with experienced subjects—excluding two inconclusive pilot experiments. For the sake of brevity, many details of the analyses are omitted and can be found in working papers available from the author.

There are two kinds of data which distinguish between theories: prices at which trades occurred, and the number of units of the asset that traders held at the end of trading periods.

A. *Trade Prices*

The mean prices across experiments 1 to 8 are summarized by a time-series of 90 percent confidence intervals, shown in Figure 2.[3] The upper (lower) solid line is the upper

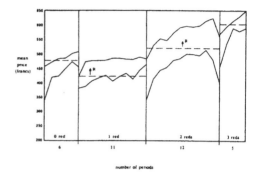

FIGURE 2

(lower) end of the confidence interval. Bayesian expected values are shown by dashed lines, and the direction of the exact representativeness prediction is shown by an arrow marked "*R*." Each of the four panels represents a different sample. From left to right, observations within a panel represent data from the first time that sample was drawn, the second time the same sample was drawn, and so forth.

Prices converge, from below, toward the Bayesian levels. These data clearly rule out many non-Bayesian theories of probability judgment (like the two extreme brands of representativeness mentioned above). However, prices do not converge exactly to the Bayesian expected values. There is some evidence of exact representativeness, because prices drift above the Bayesian expected values in 1- and 2-red periods. However, the confidence intervals are wide, and the degree of bias is rather small. Indeed, since prices should only converge to Bayesian predictions if the hypotheses of risk neutrality,

---

[3]Confidence intervals were constructed by first calculating mean prices in each period of each experiment, then separating the time-series of mean prices for each different sample. Data from experiments 6 to 8 were normalized so that the Bayesian predictions in those experiments were the same as in experiments 1 to 5. This yields groups of data such as 8 mean prices from the first 0-red period in each of the 8 experiments

numbered 1 to 8. The mean of those means, and its standard error (the standard deviation divided by $8^{1/2}$) are used to calculate the 90 percent confidence interval. A second confidence interval was calculated using mean prices from the second 0-red period in each of the 8 experiments, and so on. Not all experiments have the same number of 0-red periods, so the number of observations in each confidence interval gradually decreases. The procedure was stopped just before there was only one experiment left with an Nth observation of a particular sample.

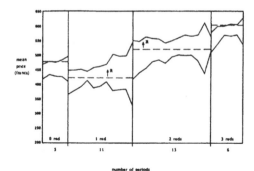

number of periods

FIGURE 3

competitive equilibrium, and Bayesian updating are all true simultaneously, it is rather remarkable that prices converge as closely to the Bayesian predictions as they do.

Figure 3 shows confidence intervals from experiments with experienced subjects. Prices begin closer to the Bayesian expected value, and have less tendency to drift above it in 1- and 2-red periods. The confidence intervals are also wide, because they summarize a small number of experiments.[4]

We can define bias in prices as a deviation from the Bayesian prediction. If the Bayesian theory is true, biases will be around zero. To conduct statistical tests on price biases, the time-series of prices in each experiment must be independent. Since prices are typically autocorrelated, the equilibrium degree of bias is estimated from a simple partial adaptation model (a first-order autoregression),

$$(2) \quad P_t - P_{\text{Bayes}} = a + b\left(P_{t-1} - P_{\text{Bayes}}\right) + e_t,$$

where P_t is the tth observation of price and P_{Bayes} is the Bayesian prediction. This specification implies that the deviation from equilibrium is reduced by a fraction $1 - b$ each trade. If b is close to 1, convergence is very slow; if b is close to 0, convergence is fast. While there is no theoretical rationale

---

[4] Intervals flare out in Figure 3 when the number of different experiments used to construct them drops steeply and standard errors increase dramatically.

for (2), it works well empirically and there is no well-established theory of price convergence which suggests it is wrong.

Call the bias for the tth price B_t; it equals $P_t - P_{\text{Bayes}}$. If we define equilibrium as a bias that does not change each period, we impose $B_t = B_{t-1} = B$ on (2) and get

$$(3) \quad B = a + bB + e_t.$$

Since $E(e_t) = 0$, a little algebra shows that we can estimate the degree of equilibrium bias B consistently by the estimator $B' = a'/(1 - b')$, where a' and b' denote ordinary least squares estimators of a and b in (2). The standard error of B' can be calculated from a Taylor series approximation involving the variances of a' and b' and their covariance.[5]

Regressions were first run separately for each period, effectively allowing a and b to vary each period. The simple specification (2) fit fairly well: The convergence rate b was typically estimated precisely, and residuals were uncorrelated and roughly homoskedastic. An F-test (Jan Kmenta, 1971, p. 373) was used to test whether adjacent periods could be pooled at the 10 percent level. Periods were pooled, starting with the last period, until the F-test was violated.

The estimate B' resulting from the last group of poolable periods in each experiment are shown in Table 3. Also reported is the t-statistic testing the hypothesis that $B = 0$, which is simply B' divided by its (approximated) standard error. Sample sizes are shown in parentheses next to each experiment number. T-statistics marked with asterisks are unreliable because the assumption of normality of residuals was violated at the 1 percent level, by the studentized range

---

[5] I thank Dave Grether for correcting a mistake in earlier estimates of $V(B')$. The Taylor series approximation of $a'/(1 - b')$ around its true value $a/(1 - b)$ is $a/(1 - b) + (a' - a)/(1 - b) + a(b' - b)/(1 - b)^2$, plus some higher-order terms. Using this expression to calculate (approximately) $V(a/(1 - b))$, or $E[(a'/(1 - b') - a/(1 - b))^2]$ yields $V(a')/(1 - b)^2 + a^2V(b')/(1 - b)^4 + 2a\text{COV}(a', b')/(1 - b)^3$. Evaluating this expression at a' and b' gives approximations of $V(B')$.

TABLE 3—ESTIMATES OF BIAS IN EQUILIBRIUM PRICES, AND TESTS OF
THE BAYESIAN HYPOTHESIS AGAINST COMPETING HYPOTHESES

Experiment (n)	Bias B	t-Statistic	0-Red Periods Significance Levels, Bayesian vs. Conservatism	Overreaction	Base-Rate Ignorance
Inexperienced subjects					
1 (24)	−28.31	2.31	.01	.99	.06
2 (46)	19.28	10.95	.999	.000	.000
3 (54)	−11.09	−3.67*	.000	.999	.999
4 (57)	4.97	4.56*	.999	.000	.000
5 (10)	−22.35	−6.57	.000	.000	.999
6 (29)	15.36	5.67*	.999	.000	.999
7 (70)	32.44	.65*	.76	.24	.57
8 (7)	−37.90	−2.20	.99	.01	.12
9r (9)	10.01	8.70	.000	.999	.999
10h (10)	−2.54	−1.16*	.12	.88	.999
mean	−2.95		.49	.51	.57
Experienced subjects					
11x (53)	−44.12	12.15	.000	.999	.999
12x (34)	15.17	1.78	.96	.04	.01
13x (8)	76.50	.49	.69	.31	.51
14x (18)	11.61	3.64	.999	.000	.999
15xh (16)	4.92	1.41	.92	.08	.35
mean		2.14		.71	.29.57

	Bayesian vs.		1-Red Periods Exact Representativeness, Overreaction	Conservatism	Base-Rate Ignorance
1 (13)	5.00	2.63*	.005	.005	.999
2 (40)	56.34	7.94*	.000	.000	.000
3 (40)	1.18	.29*	.46	.46	.999
4 (25)	49.81	18.94	.000	.000	.000
5 (37)	31.19	10.23	.000	.000	.000
6 (28)	51.80	9.10	.000	.999	.999
7 (16)	23.12	4.65	.001	.999	.985
8 (57)	93.83	.18	.43	.57	.51
9r (8)	51.15	6.21	.000	.000	.000
10h (50)	54.63	14.12*	.000	.000	.000
mean	39.92		.09	.30	.45
11x (44)	−2.76	−2.08	.98	.98	.999
12x (7)	32.18	3.82	.001	.999	.999
13x (24)	.96	.49	.31	.31	.999
14x (33)	27.88	1.89*	.03	.03	.21
15xh (8)	29.77	3.49	.005	.005	.001
mean	17.61		.27	.47	.64

(continued)

test. Other diagnostic tests and estimates of b are reported in working papers.

Roughly speaking, biases are distributed around zero in 0-, 2-, and 3-red periods. Biases are positive in 1-red periods of every experiment except 11x, generally with large t-statistics. Biases are also positive in 2-red periods with experienced subjects, but not with inexperienced subjects.

The right-hand columns of Table 3 test the hypothesis that prices are Bayesian against each of the competing theories. The tests of the Bayesian theory against exact representativeness, conservatism, and overreaction are one-tailed t-tests of the null hypothesis $B = 0$ against one-sided alternative hypotheses (which vary depending upon the theory and the sample). Since the base-rate ignorance theory predicts a point estimate of the bias rather than a direction, the significance level of the Bayesian hypothesis against the base-rate ignorance alternative was esti-

TABLE 3—(CONTINUED)

Bayesian vs.		2-Red Periods Exact Representativeness, Overreaction	Conservatism	Base-Rate Ignorance
1 (61)	−27.00	−4.84	.999	.000	.999
2 (24)	60.25	.11	.46	.54	.50
3 (22)	99.00	6.27	.000	.999	.000
4 (83)	77.39	7.74	.000	.999	.000
5 (52)	−53.31	6.55	.76	.24	.64
6 (77)	−1.74	−.02*	.51	.51	.52
7 (16)	98.24	18.16	.000	.000	.000
8 (16)	45.45	3.35	.001	.001	.000
9r (24)	−17.23	−4.55	.999	.000	.999
10h (27)	−7.57	−.95	.67	.33	.999
mean	27.35		.44	.36	.44
11x (18)	49.28	7.55	.000	.999	.000
12x (8)	20.80	12.16*	.000	.000	.000
13x (15)	17.22	14.35	.000	.999	.000
14x (11)	22.62	18.26	.000	.999	.000
15xh (17)	12.47	.80	.21	.79	.62
mean	24.48		.04	.78	.12

Bayesian vs.		3-Red Periods Conservatism	Overreaction	Base-Rate Ignorance
1 (40)	2.47	.40	.65	.35	.04
2 (17)	−209.34	−3.51	.000	.999	.85
3 (41)	41.88	4.12*	.999	.000	.000
4 (48)	11.26	.64*	.74	.26	.41
5 (26)	−10.57	.70	.24	.76	.90
6 (32)	31.55	1.29*	.90	.10	.24
7 (22)	20.04	3.24*	.999	.001	.000
8 (28)	−26.46	−.79	.29	.71	.70
9r (29)	14.01	.29	.61	.39	.48
10h (7)	2.61	.02	.51	.49	.50
mean	−12.23		.59	.41	.41
(2 deleted)		9.64			
11x (37)	−22.51	−6.52	.000	.999	.999
12x (9)	24.98	.49	.69	.31	.39
13x (35)	11.65	.65	.74	.26	.40
14x (28)	114.21	.13	.55	.45	.50
15xh (9)	−38.00	−3.74	.000	.999	.999
mean	4.70		.40	.60	.66

Notes: * denotes studentized range of residuals greater than the 1 percent level for normality, so standard errors are unreliable. Biases are truncated in calculating means when the equilibrium price implied by the bias estimate is greater than the maximum dividend for the type of trader holding a majority of units (for example, 0-red period, experiment 7).

mated from likelihood ratios.[6] Significance levels were estimated by assuming the t-statistics were normally distributed (a reason-

[6] P(data/Bayesian) and P(data/Base-rate Ignorance) were calculated assuming the estimate B' was normally distributed with standard deviation $s(B')$. Assuming one of the two theories is true, and they are equally likely; Bayes' rule can then be used to calculate P(Bayesian/data).

able approximation for most of the sample sizes in Table 3). Levels less than .001 or above .999 are reported as .000 or .999.

The significance levels of tests against most of the alternative theories are roughly 50 percent, suggesting departures from the Bayesian predictions are not systematic. However, the Bayesian theory can be strongly rejected against the alternative of exact representativeness in most 1-red periods and many 2-red periods. Of course, the statistical significance of a bias is simply a measure of whether it could be due to chance. Whether the biases are economically significant is discussed in the conclusion.

Note that the graphs and the statistical tests seem to tell different stories because the confidence intervals are wide while the t-statistics are large. This simply means that biases are not random in each experiment (hence, the extreme significance levels in Table 3), but the degree of bias varies a lot across experiments (hence, the wide confidence intervals).

In most experiments subjects did not make probability calculations during the experiment (though they were given calculators to record profits). However, in experiment 1 two traders *did* write the correct likelihood ratios $P(X/\text{sample})/P(Y/\text{sample})$ on their profit sheets during the experiment; prices were quite close to Bayesian (for example, 1-red prices were only 5 francs too high). A small number of aggressive Bayesians apparently can make the market price Bayesian, but did not do so very often.

B. *Allocations of Assets*

For most samples, competing theories all predict the same type of trader will hold units. When the theories make the same prediction, they are extremely accurate. In 0-red and 3-red periods, for instance, virtually all of the units are held by the traders with the highest expected dividend type in every experiment.

The theories disagree about allocations in 1-red periods of some experiments and 2-red periods of other experiments. In these experiments, the average fraction of traders holding any units at the end of the period and the average fraction of units held were calculated for dividend types I and II. These data are shown in Table 4.

In the 1-red periods, the Bayesian theory predicts type I and type II traders are equally likely to hold units (since their expected values are equal, at 425). Exact representativeness predicts units will be held by type I's.

Across all experiments with inexperienced subjects, type I's hold 78 percent of the units. This fraction is quite stable across experiments, and is about the same in early periods (the first half of the periods) and late periods. With experienced subjects, about 90 percent of the units are held by type I's. Prices biases were apparently not due to simple one or two type I's buying units, because about 80 percent of the type I subjects held any units, compared to roughly 30 percent of the type II subjects. Significance tests using mean data from each experiment strongly reject the Bayesian theory against the alternative of exact representativeness.[7] Such cross-experiment tests are especially reliable because we can be confident that different experiments are genuinely independent because they contain different subjects.

The smaller amount of data from 2-red periods (the bottom panel of Table 4) are not very conclusive. The Bayesian theory predicts type I's will hold, exact representativeness predicts type II's, and holdings are about equal. This corroborates the finding from price data that exact representativeness has little effect in 2-red periods.

The results of Duh and Sunder (1986) are worth summarizing at this point. In their experiments, the two states (called R and W) are two bingo cages containing 16 red and 4 black balls (R) and 4 red and 16 black balls (W). The prior $P(R)$ varied from .65 to .85 across experiments, since their main concern was whether subjects ignored prior probabilities. One ball is drawn from whichever cage (state) is chosen (so there is no possibility of exact representativeness). They find that when an R is drawn, prices are close to Bayesian. When a W was drawn, the Bayesian theory predicted about as well as a base-rate ignorance theory (denoted $NBR2$) in which $P(R)$ and $P(W)$ are judged to be equal, and an extreme version of representativeness in which $P(W)$ is judged to be

---

[7]We can test the hypothesis that the average percentage holding of type I's was 50 percent by assuming the fractions across experiments 1 to 5, 9r and 10h are normally distributed (the t-statistic is 9.28). The more conservative binomial test of successes yields a significance level less than 1 percent. For experienced subjects these statistics are 10.33 and 6 percent.

TABLE 4—HOLDINGS OF UNITS AT PERIOD END, BY TRADER TYPE

Experiment (n = no. of periods)	Type I		Type II	
	1-Red Periods			
Theories predicting Each Type to Hold:	Bayesian, Exact Representativeness, Overreaction		Bayesian, Conservatism, Base-Rate Ignorance	
Inexperienced Subjects	Fraction Holding Any	Fraction Held	Fraction Holding Any	Fraction Held
1 (n = 5)	.76	.85	.24	.15
2 (n = 7)	.76	.82	.50	.18
3 (n = 9)	.94	.75	.42	.25
4 (n = 12)	.67	.73	.38	.27
5 (n = 10)	.76	.64	.56	.36
9r (n = 8)	.91	.85	.30	.15
10h (n = 7)	.69	.85	.37	.15
Means All Periods:	.787	.784	.396	.216
Early Periods:	.82	.73	.53	.27
Late Periods:	.76	.82	.31	.18
Experienced Subjects				
11x	.91	.93	.25	.07
13x	.95	.78	.56	.22
14x	.50	.95	.10	.05
15xh	.91	.97	.09	.03
Means All Periods:	.818	.908	.250	.092
Early Periods:	.88	.87	.29	.13
Late Periods:	.76	.94	.21	.06
	2-Red Periods			
Theories Predicting Each Type to Hold	Bayesian Conservatism		Exact Representativeness, Overreaction, Base-Rate Ignorance	
6 (n = 11)	.53	.36	.75	.64
7 (n = 11)	.57	.60	.45	.40
8 (n = 8)	.71	.49	.83	.51
12x (n = 13)	.76	.40	.88	.60
Means All Periods:	.643	.463	.728	.538
Early Periods:	.64	.42	.77	.58
Late Periods:	.66	.52	.67	.48

one (denoted *NBR*1). They do not estimate the degree of price bias parametrically, but it seems to be smaller in magnitude than the biases observed here. They conclude, "Although the Bayesian model performs best among the four models in its ability to predict transaction prices, the observed market behavior still deviates from the Bayesian prescription." I suspect the Bayesian model predicts better in their experiments than in mine because the exact representativeness in my experiments is a stronger psychological force than the base-rate ignorance in theirs.

C. Further Controls for Risk and Incentives

The analyses of prices and allocations lean heavily on the assumption that traders are risk neutral, so that they trade at expected values. If traders are risk seeking, prices will be above expected values. The higher prices observed in 1-red periods could therefore reflect risk seeking by Bayesian traders rather than judgment bias by risk-neutral traders.

This explanation is unlikely for several reasons. First, the Arrow-Pratt risk premium, which measures the approximate degree to which prices depart from expected values because of risk seeking, depends only on the variance of an asset's value (and possibly its mean) and the shape of traders' utility functions. The mean and variance of the value of units are identical for type I and type II traders in 1-red periods, so their risk premia should be equal (assuming no systematic differences in utility functions). Therefore, the Bayesian prediction that type I and type II traders hold equal amounts of units should be true even if traders are not risk neutral; but the equal holdings prediction is strongly rejected.

Second, most attempts at measuring risk tastes in experimental settings find evidence of risk aversion rather than risk seeking (for example, James Cox, Smith, and James Walker, 1985; Smith, Gerry Suchanek, and Williams, 1987). Third, the allocation data show that about 80 percent of the type I traders are holding units at the high prices in 1-red periods. It seems unlikely that almost every type I trader in every experiment would be risk seeking. Fourth, the data from all four samples can be used to estimate the degree of risk seeking implicit in prices, assuming a specific utility function. Adjusting the apparent price biases in 1-red periods for risk does reduce them by about two-thirds, but not quite to zero.[8]

More direct evidence of whether risk seeking can explain the biases comes from a control experiment (denoted 9r) in which

risk neutrality was induced by design (see Alvin Roth, 1983; Joyce Berg et al., 1986; though, see Cox et al., 1985). Traders accumulated earnings in francs but the francs were not converted into dollars at the end of the experiment. Instead, traders were paid $15 plus a $50 bonus if a uniformly distributed five-digit number between 0 and 50,000 was *below* their amount of earnings. Each franc they earned then raised their probability of winning the $50 prize by 1/50,000; so francs were like units of probability. Since assets are lotteries over possible amounts of francs, and francs are probability units, assets are like compound lotteries. If traders satisfy the reduction of compound lotteries axiom in expected utility theory, they should regard a gamble with an expected franc value of G as identical to a certain payment of G francs, so they should act as if they are risk neutral toward francs. If biases observed in earlier experiments were due to risk seeking, those biases should disappear in experiment 9r.

A second control experiment (denoted 10h) used a "high-stakes" dollar-per-franc conversion rate of $.005 rather than $.001. Subjects in this experiment made about $20 per *hour*. Experiment 15xh used the same level of high stakes with experienced subjects. If apparent price biases are due to insufficient incentive to think carefully about probabilities, biases should be smaller in experiments 10h and 15xh.

Figure 4 shows the mean prices from the risk-control experiment 9r (thick line) and the high-stakes experiment 10h (thin line).[9] Compared to prices from inexperienced subjects shown in Figure 2, prices in these experiments are extremely close to the Bayesian expected values, except in 1-red periods. Price regression results and allocations (in Tables 3 and 4) suggest the exact representativeness bias in 1-red periods is highly significant. Therefore, biases in 1-red periods

---

[8] The value of the risk-seeking constant A was estimated in each experiment, assuming both constant absolute (CARS) and constant relative risk seeking (CRRS). The value of A was chosen to minimize the absolute deviations between observed price bias from Table 3 and the bias predicted by the Arrow-Pratt risk premium with parameter A, summed across the four possible samples. Weighting deviations by the number of trades in each sample minimized risk-adjusted biases better than not weighting them. The CARS and CRRS models fit almost identically. Using CARS, risk-adjusted biases in 1- and 2-red periods averaged 13.8 and -15.6 francs (experiments 1 to 8) and 4.5 and -6 francs (experiments 11x to 15xh). In experiments 9r and 10h risk adjustment actually increased 1-red biases to 55.5 and 56.4 francs. Furthermore, in experiment 9r, the estimated A was about equal in magnitude to A's in other experiments, though it should be zero in theory.

[9] The lines end abruptly because each experiment has a different number of periods of each sample. There are five 0-red periods in 10h, for instance, and only three in 9r. Also, the spike in the second 1-red period of experiment 9r was a short burst of irrational buying at very high prices, which defies explanation.

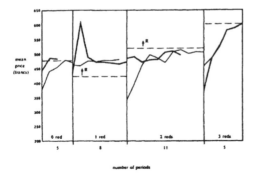

FIGURE 4

in other experiments are probably not due to risk seeking or insufficient motivation. At the same time, the control experiments give evidence *against* the exact representativeness prediction in 2-red periods.

D. Individual Judgments and Market Prices

The point of experiments like these is to compare behavior of individuals with behavior of markets in which individuals participate. So far there has been only an assumption individuals will err in using Bayes' rule, but no direct comparison between individuals and the market. However, we can make such a comparison because subjects did make individual probability judgments before trading began (except in experiments 1 and 2).

Judgments were rewarded with a quadratic scoring rule, with money incentives for accuracy.[10] The scoring rule is incentive compatible assuming risk neutrality (subjects should report their true subjective probabilities), but nonrisk neutrality will cause judgments to deviate from true beliefs. Subjects were given 10 to 20 three-ball samples from the bingo cages, with instant feedback about whether X or Y occurred. After completing the scoring-rule exercise, subjects were informed that they would ranked according to their earnings from the scoring-rule exercise, from 1 to N. They were told to predict their rank, choosing exactly one number between 1 and N, and they were paid $5 if their rank was exactly correct.

We can compare the average scoring-rule judgment with a probability estimate imputed from the equilibrium price bias. For instance, in experiment 3 the estimated bias in 0-red periods was -11.09 francs (see Table 3). Since type I traders are holding in these periods, and their payoffs range from 200 ($P(X) = 0$) to 500 ($P(X) = 1$), the probability scale naturally corresponds to a 300-franc price scale from 200 to 500. A bias of -11.09 francs implies a probability judgment of $P(X/0\text{-red})$ that is $-11.09/300$, or $-.037$, different from the Bayesian posterior of .923. Probabilities were imputed from market prices for each sample and each experiment, using the estimated biases from Table 3.

Average individual probabilities from the scoring rule and probabilities imputed from market prices, averaged across experiments, are shown in Table 5. Both kinds of probabilities are close to Bayesian in 0- and 3-red samples. In 1- and 2-red samples, the individuals' probability estimates are closer to Bayesian than the market prices are,[11] but the gap is smaller with experienced subjects.

It seems that for exactly representative samples, markets are often *more* biased than

[10] Samples of three balls were drawn, exactly as in determining states, and subjects were asked to choose a two-digit "decision number" from 00 to 99. Define that number, divided by 100, as D. If event X occurred, subjects were paid $2D - D^2$ dollars. If event Y occurred, subjects were paid $1 - D^2$ dollars. Subjects were shown a table of the possible numerical payoffs. If a subject's true subjective probability of X occurring was S, and she choose D, her expected payoff was $S(2D - D^2) + (1-S)(1-D^2)$. This payoff has a maximum at $D^* = S$, that is, subjects should truthfully choose their subjective probabilities as their decision numbers, ex-

cept for risk aversion. If subjects are risk averse (risk seeking), their reported probabilities will be biased toward (away from) .5.

[11] The differences between averaged scoring-rule judgments and probabilities implicit in market prices are highly significant by parametric *t*-tests, or by nonparametric matched-pairs or rank-sum tests, except in 2-red periods with inexperienced subjects.

TABLE 5—AVERAGE PROBABILITY JUDGMENTS OF INDIVIDUALS AND PROBABILITIES
IMPLICIT IN MARKET PRICES (EXPRESSED AS DEVIATIONS
FROM THE BAYESIAN POSTERIOR $P(X/\text{SAMPLE})$)

Sample	0-Red	1-Red	2-Red	3-Red
Direction of Deviation Predicted by Exact Representativeness:	0	+	−	0
Inexperienced Subjects (8 Experiments)				
Individual Mean	−.009	−.030	−.031	−.022
(Standard Deviation)	(.044)	(.087)	(.033)	(.076)
Market Prices Mean	−.008	+.141	−.100	−.035
(Standard Deviation)	(.062)	(.081)	(.193)	(.073)
Experienced Subjects (5 Experiments)				
Individual Mean	+.037	−.026	−.043	−.084
(Standard Deviation)	(.022)	(.052)	(.061)	(.069)
Market Prices Mean	+.007	+.059	−.081	−.016
(Standard Deviation)	(.092)	(.049)	(.044)	(.117)

individuals are. One explanation is that market prices are determined by one or two highly biased traders, but almost all traders were holding units at the biased prices. Another possibility is that the market mechanism and the quadratic scoring rule simply elicit different probability judgments.

One consolation is that the biases shrink with experience. A closer look at individual data may suggest why. For market prices to be less biased than individuals, traders who are less biased must exert more influence on the market price. There is no external market to evaluate whether traders are unbiased and allocate more trading capital to them. Therefore, to exert more influence the traders who are less biased must realize they are less biased, and trade more aggressively.

Whether traders realize their relative ability at probability judgment can be measured by whether their predicted ranks in the scoring-rule exercise are correlated with their actual ranks. The two sets of ranks were somewhat correlated—averaging .49 for inexperienced subjects and .30 for experienced subjects[12] —so subjects do have some self-insight. However, predictions about relative ability are not highly correlated with the amount of arbitrage (defined as buying and selling in the same period). Those correlations averaged −.09 for inexperienced subjects, and .23 for experienced subjects. Furthermore, actual ranks and arbitrage were uncorrelated (.05 and −.12) with both inexperienced and experienced subjects. It seems that aggressive trading, as measured by arbitrage, is not something inexperienced subjects do only because they think they are better probability judges than others.

III. Conclusion and Future Research

In many experiments subjects do not follow the laws of probability, particularly Bayes' rule. However, subjects in these experiments are often unpaid and given little practice making judgments. In markets, traders often have incentives and experience, and people who are good at estimating probabilities can often exert more force on prices. Therefore, biases in *individual* judgments need not affect prices and allocations in *markets*.

Whether biases affect market outcomes is tested in a series of simple experimental markets. In the markets, traders exchange units of an asset that pays a state-dependent dividend. A random device yields sample evidence about which state has occurred. Traders' demand for assets depends upon

[12] These are high correlations considering that the range of the predicted rank variable was restricted by subjects' optimism about their ranks. Sixty-two of 74 inexperienced subjects (84 percent) thought they were in the top 50 percent in scoring-rule earnings, compared to 23 of 40 experienced subjects (58 percent). Apparently optimism is nearly erased after one experiment.

their judgments about posterior state probability. If the market functions as if traders are Bayesians, a certain pattern of prices and allocations is predicted to occur. But if traders overestimate P(state/sample), relative to the Bayesian posterior, when the sample exactly matches the contents of a bingo cage that represents the state, then different prices and allocations will occur. This competing theory is called "exact representativeness." It is less useful than the Bayesian theory because it does not predict prices when samples do not exactly match states, but it does have some bite. Other non-Bayesian psychological theories can be defined too.

In eight experiments with inexperienced subjects, prices tend toward the Bayesian predictions, but there is some evidence of exact representativeness bias in prices and allocations. However, the degree of bias is small, and it is even smaller in experiments with experienced subjects. All other non-Bayesian theories can be rejected.[13] Furthermore, the Bayesian theory predicts prices remarkably well when the exact representativeness theory does not apply.

In most experiments, biases are statistically significant for only one of the two samples (the 1-red sample) in which exact representativeness predicts bias. Indeed, if the reader values the only experiment with controls for risk seeking ($9r$), exact representativeness predicts no better than chance: it predicts the significant bias in the 1-red period correctly, but it predicts the wrong sign on the significant bias in the 2-red period.

It is easy to imagine other market settings in which unbiased traders could correct market biases completely.[14] Some of these

settings are the subject of ongoing research. However, if one pretends to not know the results, it is easy to imagine that biases could have been entirely eliminated in these experiments, too.

Whether the exact representativeness biases in 1-red periods are significant depends upon your yardstick of significance. By one overworked yardstick, the statistical test of whether they could be due to chance, the biases in 1-red periods are highly significant. The possibility of excess profits is an important yardstick in economics. There are apparently loss of profits to be earned from exploiting biased subjects, since they overpay by roughly $.20 per trade (a few dollars per experiment) in 1-red periods of the high-stakes experiments $10h$ and $15xh$. Excess profits are a lot smaller, only about $.03 per trade, in the other experiments. On the probability yardstick the biases are errors of about .10, which are large if your purpose is testing students' ability to make exact Bayesian calculations and small if your purpose is comparing these biases with errors found in other studies.[15]

Of course, if the stakes were large enough or (perhaps more importantly) traders had enough experience, the apparent biases might disappear entirely. Therefore, we should hesitate to generalize these results to the New York Stock Exchange (though some have tried[16]), but the results may generalize to settings in which stakes are relatively small and agents have little experience in a repeated situation. For instance, consumers might judge the quality of a new product by how much the product's packaging or advertising resembles that of well-known products. Financial journalists sometimes argue a depression is ahead because a pattern of economic indicators resembles a pattern from

---

[13] If subjects tended to ignore or underweight the unequal prior probabilities of the states, then 2-red biases would be larger than 1-red biases. Exactly the opposite is true. Notice also that overreaction predicts reasonably well in 1- and 2-red samples, when it overlaps with exact representativeness, but it predicts poorly in 0- and 3-red samples.

[14] For instance, if biases caused prices to be lower than expected values, then unbiased traders would pay higher prices than biased traders, effectively setting the market price, so prices might appear unbiased.

[15] For instance, in the well-known blue-green taxi problem (for example, Tversky and Kahneman, 1982b), the Bayesian posterior is around .4 but subjects often answer .80 because they ignore the low base rate of one type of taxi.

[16] Recall Arrow's (1982) suggestion cited above. Werner DeBondt and Richard Thaler (1985) also found empirical support for the representativeness prediction that investors do not expect regression in extreme earnings announcements.

before the Great Depression. (Whether such opinions affect market behavior is debatable.) The belief that the future is likely to be representative of the past could cause a failure to anticipate regression effects (Tversky and Kahneman, 1982b): Forgetting about regression, consumers may avoid all Hyatt hotels or DC-10's after an accident involving one of them; or studios might make movie sequels that are consistently unprofitable. The winner's curse in common-value auctions (see John Kagel and Dan Levin, 1986) might be caused by a heuristiclike representativeness. These conjectures, whether plausible or not, illustrate how representativeness bias akin to that observed in the experiments could affect economic outcomes in natural settings.

There are several directions for future experiments. Institutional extensions of these markets, like short selling or a parallel market for information about probabilities, might eliminate biases entirely. Experiments in which other judgment biases could affect markets might be interesting too (for example, myself, George Loewenstein, and Martin Weber, 1987). A program of empirical work, including both experiments and extending experimental results to natural settings, could establish what kinds of irrationality seem to persist under the incentives and learning opportunities present in natural markets. Such data might lead to economic theory that uses evidence of systematic irrationality to make better predictions.

REFERENCES

Arkes, Hal R. and Hammond, Kenneth R., *Judgment and Decision Making: An Interdisciplinary Reader*, Cambridge: Cambridge University Press, 1986.

Arrow, Kenneth, "Risk Perception in Psychology and Economics," *Economic Inquiry*, January 1982, *20*, 1–9.

Berg, Joyce E., Daley, Lane A., Dickhaut, John W. and O'Brien, John R., "Controlling Preferences for Lotteries on Units of Experimental Exchange," *Quarterly Journal of Economics*, May 1986, *101*, 281–306.

Blaug, Mark, *The Methodology of Economics: or How Economics Explain*, Cambridge:

Cambridge University Press, 1980.

Camerer, Colin, Loewenstein, George and Weber, Martin, "The Curse of Knowledge in Economic Settings: An Experimental Analysis," Wharton Risk and Decision Processes Center, Working Paper No. 87-09-07, 1987.

Cox, James, Smith, Vernon and Walker, James, "Experimental Development of Sealed-bid Auction Theory: Calibrating Controls for Risk Aversion," *American Economic Review*, May 1985, *75*, 160–65.

DeBondt, Werner F. M. and Thaler, Richard, "Does the Stock Market Overreact?," *Journal of Finance*, July 1985, *40*, 793–805.

Duh, Rong Ruey and Sunder, Shyam, "Incentives, Learning and Processing of Information in a Market Environment: An Examination of the Base-Rate Fallacy," in S. Moriarty, ed., *Laboratory Market Research*, Norman, OK: Center for Economic and Management Research, University of Oklahoma, 1986.

Easley, David and Ledyard, John, "Theories of Price Formation and Exchange in Double Oral Auctions," Social Science Working Paper No. 611, California Institute of Technology, 1986.

Edwards, Ward, "Conservatism in Human Information Processing," in B. Kleinmuntz, ed., *Formal Representation of Human Judgment*, New York: Wiley & Sons, 1968.

Friedman, Daniel, "On the Efficiency of Experimental Double Auction Markets," *American Economic Review*, March 1984, *74*, 60–72.

Friedman, Milton, *Essays in Positive Economics*, Chicago: University of Chicago Press, 1953.

Grether, David M., "Bayes' Rule as a Descriptive Model: The Representativeness Heuristic," *Quarterly Journal of Economics*, November 1980, *95*, 537–57.

Hey, John D., "Search for Rules for Search," *Journal of Economic Behavior and Organization*, March 1982, *3*, 65–81.

_____, "Still Searching," *Journal of Economic Behavior and Organization*, March 1987, *8*, 137–44.

Kagel, John H. and Levin, Dan, "The Winner's Curse and Public Information in Common Value Auctions," *American Economic Review*, December 1986, *76*, 894–920.

Kahneman, Daniel, Slovic, Paul and Tversky, Amos, *Judgment Under Uncertainty: Heuristics and Biases*, Cambridge: Cambridge University Press, 1982a.

Kmenta, Jan, *Elements of Econometrics*, New York: Macmillan, 1971.

Plott, Charles R. and Wilde, Louis L., "Professional Diagnosis vs. Self-diagnosis: An Experimental Examination of Some Special Features of Markets with Uncertainty," in V. Smith, ed., *Research in Experimental Economics*, Vol. 2, Greenwich: JAI Press, 1982.

Roth, Alvin, "Toward a Theory of Bargaining: An Experimental Study in Economics," *Science*, May 13, 1983, *220*, 687–91.

Russell, Thomas and Thaler, Richard, "The Relevance of Quasi Rationality in Competitive Markets," *American Economic Review*, December 1985, *75*, 1071–82.

Slovic, Paul, Fischhoff, Baruch and Lichtenstein, Sarah, "Cognitive Processes and Societal Risk Taking," in J. S. Carroll and J. W. Payne, eds., *Cognition and Social Behavior*, Hillsdale, NJ: Erlbaum, 1976.

Smith, Vernon L., "Microeconomic Systems as an Experimental Science," *American Economic Review*, December 1982, *72*, 923–55.

_____ , Suchanek, Gerry and Williams, Arlington, "Bubbles, Crashes, and Endogeneous Expectations in Experimental Asset Markets," Department of Economics Working Paper No. 86-2, University of Arizona, 1987.

_____ and Williams, Arlington, "The Boundaries of Competitive Price Theory: Convergence, Expectations, and Transaction Costs," in L. Green and J. Kagel, eds., *Advances in Behavioral Economics*, Vol. 2, Norwood, NJ: Ablex Publishing, in press.

Tversky, Amos and Kahneman, Daniel, (1982a) "Judgments of and by Representativeness," in D. Kahneman, P. Slovic, and A. Tversky, eds., *Judgment under Uncertainty: Heuristics and Biases*, Cambridge: Cambridge University Press.

_____ and _____, (1982b), "The Evidential Impact of Base Rates," in D. Kahneman, P. Slovic, and A. Tversky, eds., *Judgment Under Uncertainty: Heuristics and Biases*, Cambridge: Cambridge University Press.

Wilson, Robert, "Incentive Efficiency of Double Auctions," *Econometrica*, September 1985, *53*, 1101–115.

[11]

Risk, Ambiguity, and Insurance

ROBIN M. HOGARTH
University of Chicago, Graduate School of Business

HOWARD KUNREUTHER
University of Pennsylvania, The Wharton School

Key words: Ambiguity, expected utility, insurance, risk, subjective probability

Abstract

In a series of experiments, economically sophisticated subjects, including professional actuaries, priced insurance both as consumers and as firms under conditions of ambiguity. Findings support implications of the Einhorn–Hogarth ambiguity model: (1) For low probability-of-loss events, prices of both consumers and firms indicated aversion to ambiguity; (2) As probabilities of losses increased, aversion to ambiguity decreased, with consumers exhibiting ambiguity preference for high probability-of-loss events; and (3) Firms showed greater aversion to ambiguity than consumers. The results are shown to be incompatible with traditional economic analysis of insurance markets and are discussed with respect to the effects of ambiguity on the supply and demand for insurance.

The problem addressed in this article can be illustrated by considering the responses to a series of questions about automobile insurance asked of MBA students and academics: (1) Is your automobile insured against theft? (2) Do you know the cost of this insurance? (3) Do you know the probability that your automobile will be stolen while your insurance contract is in force? The first two questions usually elicit many positive responses. However, this is not the case for the third and indicates that decisions concerning insurance are often made with vague knowledge concerning the probability of losses.

Insurance has been utilized by economists as a paradigmatic example of a pure contingent claim (Arrow, 1963). In theory, it is possible for an individual or firm to purchase protection against the consequences of a given state of nature, paying a premium based on the probability of loss and the amount of insurance coverage in force. The expected utility model has provided the primary theoretical tool by which economists have examined these phenomena (cf. Ehrlich & Becker, 1972). However, recent controlled experiments and field survey data suggest that individuals do not follow the dictates of this model when deciding whether or not to buy insurance (Arrow, 1982). We hypothesize that insurance decisions of both buyers (consumers) and sellers (firms) are partially determined by the precision with which the probabilities of losses can be estimated. More specifically, we con-

6   HOGARTH AND KUNREUTHER

sider how ambiguity regarding probabilities affects the level of premiums and thus the performance of insurance markets.

Whereas the axiomatization of expected utility (von Neumann & Morgenstern, 1947) does not deal explicitly with ambiguity, it is important to note that the presence of ambiguity does not necessarily invalidate this model. Indeed, ambiguity can be modeled within this framework by a distribution over the probability of interest, as in Bayesian analysis. However, the expected utility model implies that it is only the mean of this distribution that should affect action. To illustrate consider the following scenarios.

Defective product scenario: You have little experience regarding the effects of the manufacturing process of a new product and are concerned with the probability that a particular lot may be defective. Your best estimate of this probability is .01, but you experience considerable uncertainty about the precision of this estimate.

Brown River scenario: You are uncertain about the chances of a flood on the Brown River next year. You consult several experts who feel it is equally likely to be anywhere from 0 to .02.

Now imagine purchasing or selling insurance in the above scenarios where the probabilities of losses are ambiguous, and compare each situation to a case where the probability of loss is specified to be .01 with confidence. According to Bayesian expected utility analysis, insurance premiums should be identical in the ambiguous and nonambiguous cases provided that the means of individuals' probability distributions over the losses are the same in both conditions.

This article is organized as follows. The next section develops a simple model for determining the equilibrium values of insurance prices set by firms and coverage bought by consumers under the assumptions that firms maximize expected profits and consumers maximize expected utility. Some anomalies in behavior are discussed that appear to be partially related to ambiguities concerning the probabilities of specific outcomes. Section 2 reviews evidence on how ambiguity affects both judgments of probability and choice. We further show how this evidence is consistent with a psychological model of probabilistic judgments made under conditions of ambiguity developed by Einhorn and Hogarth (1985). Based on this model, several predictions are made regarding consumer and firm behavior under different degrees of ambiguity. Section 3 presents and discusses the results of a series of experiments designed to test these predictions. Finally, section 4 discusses the results further and suggests areas for additional empirical research. We particularly note the importance of developing and testing precise, falsifiable models to complement or challenge implications of the expected utility model, since naturally occurring data frequently lack the power to provide stringent tests of the latter.

1. A simple model of insurance

The following simplified model of firm and consumer behavior is used to investigate the role that ambiguity plays on equilibrium values. Consider a set of individuals who face a known loss, X. The probability, p, of experiencing this loss, however, is highly uncertain in that there are limited data concerning the event itself (e.g., flood) and/or experts disagree about a particular state of nature occurring. Assume further that there is no question of moral hazard in that the individuals can influence neither p nor X by their actions.

Insurance firms are assumed to maximize expected profits $[E(\pi)]$ by setting a constant premium per dollar coverage, r ($0 < r < 1$), that reflects their assessment of the probability of loss. Thus, if each consumer buys I units of coverage, expected profits for each policy sold is given by

$$E(\pi) = [r - M(p)]I, \tag{1}$$

where $M(p)$ denotes the mean of the distribution over the unknown probability of loss, p. Holding the consumer's demand function for insurance constant, an important implication of equation (1) is that whether firms are certain or ambiguous about p, the price charged (r) should not differ provided $M(p)$ is the same in both situations. That is, since expected profits are affected only by $M(p)$ (and not the higher moments of the distribution over p), the degree of uncertainty about p should have no impact on firms' pricing decisions. The actual premium charged by firms will depend on both their knowledge concerning the consumer (e.g., risk attitude and wealth) and the market structure of the industry. In a purely competitive market with risk-neutral firms and no marketing costs, $r = M(p)$ and $E(\pi) = 0$. Loading fees and market imperfections can, however, cause the premium to deviate from $M(p)$.

Consumers with net wealth of W will determine the amount of coverage, I, that maximizes their expected utility, $E[U\{\Phi(I)\}]$. $\Phi(I)$ represents a probability distribution of ex post wealth based on I units of insurance coverage with respect to the premium, r, set by insurance firms. Specifically, if $M^*(p)$ represents the mean of a consumer's probability distribution over the probability of loss, p, and X (the potential loss) is known with certainty, then

$$E[U\{\Phi(I)\}] = M^*(p)U[W - X + (1 - r)I] + [1 - M^*(p)]U(W - rI). \tag{2}$$

Thus consumers' decisions will be affected by (a) attitudes toward risk as expressed in their utility functions and (b) the means of their probability distributions over p.

The theoretical analysis of insurance markets therefore implies that if losses are known, premiums will not be affected by the degree of ambiguity concerning the probability of a loss. Empirical evidence, however, suggests that uncertainty about the probability of losses may impact on both consumers' purchase decisions and firms' pricing decisions.

As to consumers, economists have long puzzled over why people pay excessive rates for insurance in some cases, but then underinsure in others. For example, consider the relatively high premiums paid for flight insurance (Eisner & Strotz, 1961), and yet the lack of interest shown in subsidized flood or earthquake in-

surance (Kunreuther et al., 1978). Both of these events are low-probability oc-
currences about which the general public lacks detailed statistical knowledge.
However, whereas the scenario of an airplane accident can be easily imagined by
inexperienced travelers, it is significant that people tend to buy coverage against
floods or earthquakes only after experiencing a disaster or learning of others who
have suffered severe damage. As we argue below, assessing uncertainty in ambiguous circumstances necessarily depends on imagination and is thus especially
prone to both the availability of particular information and the vividness with
which recent events have been depicted (cf. Nisbett & Ross, 1980).[1]

When probabilities are ambiguous, insurance firms are reluctant to market insurance for a specified amount of coverage. Political risk is a case in point. Few
companies offer protection against the potential losses facing industrial firms investing in developing countries with potentially unstable political systems. The
principal argument voiced by insurers has *not* been the correlation in potential
losses from such a risk but rather the difficulty of estimating the probabilities
associated with losses of different magnitudes (Kunreuther & Kleindorfer, 1983).

Even when data are available, firms may still experience great uncertainty about
probabilities. This is reflected in premiums that are much higher than past loss experience would justify. Consider earthquake insurance. Over the first 60-year
period that this coverage was offered in California (1916–1976), $269 million in
total premiums was collected but only $9 million in losses was experienced. Part of
the rationale for the high premium/loss ratio is the possibility of highly correlated
losses should an earthquake occur. However, companies insure throughout the
state so some diversification in earthquake risks can take place. In the case of
residential insurance where individual losses are not likely to be high, the
premium-to-loss ratio over this time period averaged 30 to 1 (Atkisson & Petak,
1981).[2] Even in a relatively competitive environment such as California (where
there is limited regulation), there is little interest on the part of firms in lowering
their rates.

The above examples of behavior by individuals and firms suggest that ambiguity or uncertainty concerning probabilities plays an important role in insurance decisions. In addition, work on decision making in psychology and
economics over the last 30 years reinforces this possibility.

2. Subjective probabilities, ambiguity, and choice

The concept of ambiguity has been of interest to economists ever since Frank
Knight (1921) made the distinction between risk and uncertainty. Knight defined a
random variable as risky if its probability distribution were known, and uncertain
if its distribution were unknown. The behavioral implications of this distinction
were demonstrated by Daniel Ellsberg (1961) who challenged the notion that subjective probabilities (in the sense of Savage, 1954) could always be inferred from
choices among gambles. In a series of hypothetical choices, Ellsberg showed that

people preferred to choose from urns containing known as opposed to unknown distributions of different colored balls such that probabilities inferred from choices did not conform to the axioms of probability theory. Ellsberg further defined ambiguity as a state between ignorance and knowledge of a probability distribution and argued that this was an important factor when making estimates of uncertainty in decision making.

Subsequently, several investigators have provided experimental evidence indicating a conservative attitude of *ambiguity avoidance* when people are confronted with prospects of gains (see, e.g., Becker & Brownson, 1964; Curley & Yates, 1985; Curley et al., 1986; Gärdenfors & Sahlin, 1982, 1983; Yates & Zukowski, 1976). However, since insurance decision making involves potential losses, from our perspective it is more appropriate to investigate the effects of ambiguity
when people face losses (Hogarth & Kunreuther, 1985; Einhorn & Hogarth, 1986).

Recently, there has been much interest in dealing formally with the implications of Ellsberg's work. Fishburn (1983) and Schmeidler (1984), for example, have axiomatized nonadditive probability models that can account for responses to Ellsberg's paradox. (For an overview, see Fishburn, 1986.) An implication of Luce and Narens' (1985) work on dual bilinear utility provides a further explanation. In addition, Segal (1987) has shown that by relaxing von Neumann and Morgenstern's (1947) axiom involving the reduction of compound lotteries, the anticipated utility theory approach advocated by Quiggin (1982; see also Yaari, 1987), in which the weights associated with utilities of outcomes need not be a linear function of the outcome probabilities, can explain Ellsberg's results. Finally, Bewley (1986) has built on the concepts developed by Knight by dropping the completeness axiom and adding an assumption of inertia (i.e., attraction to the status quo). This approach implies an aversion to uncertainty that, in turn, leads to reluctance to buy or sell insurance when the probability of loss is ambiguous.

All of the above theories rest on formal axiomatic systems and, although motivated by behavioral phenomena, do not provide descriptive accounts of the decision processes of individuals. Moreover, they have not been empirically tested. On the other hand, Einhorn and Hogarth (1985) have recently proposed and tested a model of how people assess probabilities in ambiguous circumstances, and it is this model that will be examined here in the context of insurance decisions.

The Einhorn–Hogarth model is based on three principles. (1) People are first assumed to anchor on an initial estimate of the probability. Let p represent this anchor and note that it may be based on past experience or data, suggested by an analogous situation, or even the figure provided by another party, e.g., an expert. The anchor is then adjusted by imagining or mentally simulating other values that the probability could take. (2) The greater the degree of ambiguity experienced, the more alternative values of the probability are simulated. For example, when experts disagree on a probability estimate, people are assumed to imagine more alternative values compared to situations where the experts agree. (3) The relative weight given in imagination to alternative values of the probability that are greater or smaller than the anchor p depends on the individual's attitude toward ambiguity in the particular situation.

To model this process, let k be the adjustment to the anchor such that the assessment of the ambiguous probability, denoted $S(p)$, is given by

$$S(p) = p + k. \tag{3}$$

Einhorn and Hogarth allow for the effects of ambiguity by decomposing k into two parts that capture forces favoring positive and negative adjustments, respectively. The positive force reflects the weight given to possible values of the probability above the anchor and is taken to be proportional to $(1 - p)$; the negative force reflects the weight given to values below the anchor and is proportional to p. In both cases, the constant of proportionality is a parameter θ that represents the amount of perceived ambiguity ($0 < \theta < 1$). In other words, the effect of possible values of the probability above the anchor are modeled by $\theta(1 - p)$, of those below by θp, and k is the net effect of positive and negative adjustments from the anchor.

To account for the fact that values above and below the anchor may be differentially weighted in imagination, θp is adjusted to the form θp^β where $\beta(\geqslant 0)$ represents the person's attitude toward ambiguity in the circumstances. Hence, $k = \theta(1 - p) - \theta p^\beta$. When $\beta = 1$, equal weight is given to imaginary values above and below the anchor; when $\beta > 1$, more weight is given to larger values, and for $\beta < 1$, more weight is given to smaller values. This leads to the model,

$$S(p) = p + \theta[(1 - p) - p^\beta]. \tag{4}$$

Note that θ (i.e., perceived ambiguity) determines the amount of the adjustment, whereas β in conjunction with the level of p determines the sign. Thus, when p is low, the adjustment will tend to be positive; however, as p increases, the adjustment becomes negative. Moreover, the point at which the adjustment starts to become negative depends on β. When $\beta = 1$, the cross-over point is at $p = .5$; for $\beta < 1$, this occurs when $p < .5$; and for $\beta > 1$, when $p > .5$. This is illustrated in Figure 1, where the solid line illustrates an *ambiguity function* with $\beta < 1$ and the dotted line a case where $\beta > 1$. (θ is the same in both cases.)

An important implication of equation (4) is that it can imply nonadditivity of the probability judgments of complementary events. Specifically, consider the sum of $S(p)$ and $S(1 - p)$. This is

$$S(p) + S(1 - p) = p + \theta[1 - p - p^\beta] + (1 - p) + \theta[1 - (1 - p) - (1 - p)^\beta]$$

$$= 1 + \theta[1 - p^\beta - (1 - p)^\beta]. \tag{5}$$

Equation (5) specifies conditions for additivity and nonadditivity: (i) additivity of the probabilities of complementary events obtains if $\theta = 0$, or $\beta = 1$, or $p = 0$, or

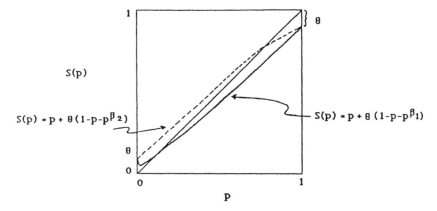

Fig. 1. Two ambiguity functions. Both have the same θ parameter. but different β's. Specifically $\beta_1 < 1$ (solid line) and $\beta_2 > 1$ (dotted line).

$p = 1$: otherwise there is nonadditivity, specifically: (ii) subadditivity if $\beta < 1$; and (iii) superadditivity if $\beta > 1$. Einhorn and Hogarth (1985) provide experimental evidence of nonadditivity in accordance with equation (5).

To summarize. the Einhorn–Hogarth ambiguity model has two parameters, θ and β. θ represents perceived ambiguity and is affected by factors such as the amount of evidence, the unreliability of witnesses, and the lack of causal knowledge of the underlying process generating outcomes. On the other hand, β denotes one's attitude toward ambiguity in the circumstances and reflects the extent to which a person pays more attention in imagination to possible values of p greater or smaller than the initial estimate. Thus, when concerned about the consequences of a potential loss, a cautious person would be expected to exhibit a high value of $\beta (> 1)$. For example, concern about insolvency or bankruptcy would be one reason for a high value of β on the part of an individual or firm. (For further discussion of the model and its parameters, see Einhorn and Hogarth, 1985.)

The ambiguity model has several implications for insurance decision making. As stated in section 2, both insurance companies and consumers can experience varying degrees of ambiguity. Insurance companies, for example, typically have precise knowledge of the probabilities relevant to life insurance and automobile theft. On the other hand, there could be considerable vagueness concerning the probability of successfully launching a satellite from an orbiting space vehicle (cf. Large, 1984).[3] Similarly, a businessman could be vague about the probability of a serious personal accident in a factory, yet estimate precisely the probability of producing defective products with particular equipment.

To consider how ambiguity affects insurance decisions, we first simplify the analysis by dichotomizing the ambiguity variable, i.e., insurance companies (firms) and consumers either are, or are not, ambiguous about the probability of loss. Next, assume that the maximum premium, $C(p)$, that the consumer is prepared to pay to cover a potential loss of $\$X$ when p, the probability of loss, is known with certainty can be determined from the equation

$$U[W - C(p)] = pU(W - X) + (1 - p)U(W). \tag{6}$$

Similarly, when the probability of loss is ambiguous, the maximum premium, $CA(p)$, the consumer is willing to pay can be determined from

$$U[W - CA(p)] = S(p)U(W - X) + S(1 - p)U(W). \tag{7}$$

To assess the effects of ambiguity on the consumer's willingness to pay for insurance, consider the ratio of the left-hand side of equation (7) to that of equation (6). Normalizing the utility of current wealth to zero, i.e., $U(W) = 0$, this ratio becomes

$$R_c = \frac{U[W - CA(p)]}{U[W - C(p)]} = \{p + \theta(1 - p - p^{\beta_c})\}U(W - X)/pU(W - X)$$

$$= \{p + \theta(1 - p - p^{\beta_c})\}/p. \tag{8}$$

where β_c denotes the consumer's β parameter. Assuming that consumers' utility functions are monotonically increasing over wealth states, equation (8) implies the following predictions concerning premiums consumers are prepared to pay in ambiguous as opposed to nonambiguous circumstances. (1) When p is small, the ratio R_c—and thus also $[CA(p)/C(p)]$—will be greater than one. This indicates *ambiguity aversion* (see figure 1). (2) As p increases, the ratio R_c—and thus also $[CA(p)]/C(p)]$—will decrease and eventually become smaller than one, thereby indicating *ambiguity preference*.

Similar predictions can be made for risk-neutral firms. Denote by $F(p)$ the minimum premiums that firms are prepared to charge per dollar coverage when probabilities are precisely known, and the minimum premiums associated with ambiguous probabilities by $FA(p)$. In a competitive environment, $F(p) = p$, since $E\{\pi[F(p)]\} = [F(p) - p]I = 0$. To determine $FA(p)$, firms are assumed to set $E\{\pi[FA(p)]\} = [FA(p) - S(p)]I = 0$. The ratio of $FA(p)$ to $F(p)$ can be written as

$$R_f = S(p)/p = \{p + \theta(1 - p - p^{\beta_f})\}/p, \tag{9}$$

where β_f denotes the β parameter for firms. Equation (9) implies the following predictions for risk-neutral firms (3) When p is small, the ratio R_f will be greater than one thereby indicating ambiguity aversion. (4) As p increases, the ratio R_f will decrease.

3. Experimental evidence

3.1. Subjects

We have collected experimental data on the above issues from many different groups of subjects. These included students, business executives, and professional actuaries.

The student groups consisted of MBA students at the University of Chicago and the Wharton School, undergraduates in Decision Sciences at the Wharton School, and graduate and undergraduate students at the University of Chicago who volunteered to take part in experiments on decision making. The executive groups were comprised of managers attending the University of Chicago's Executive Program as well as some other programs (including a group from life insurance companies). With the exception of the volunteer students at the University of Chicago, each of whom was paid $5 per hour for participating in these and other experiments, data were collected in a classroom setting at the request of the instructor. Subjects were told that there were no "right" answers to the questions, and questionnaires were completed in anonymous fashion. In several cases, the classes were later given feedback on group responses which were discussed in light of subsequent work on decision making.

The data from professional actuaries were obtained by a mail survey of members of the Casualty Actuarial Society residing in North America. Of this population, 489 of 1165 persons (i.e., 42%) provided usable responses. Mean length of experience as actuaries reported by the respondents was 13.8 years (range from 1 to 50 years). Responses were provided anonymously.

It is possible to criticize experiments such as those reported below on several grounds (for a review, see Hogarth & Reder, 1986). One objection is the lack of task-relevant incentives. On the other hand, we believe that readers who entertain such criticisms should predict what effects this would have on results *prior* to seeing the outcomes of our experiments (cf. Grether & Plott, 1979). One possible prediction is carelessness in response. To guard against this possibility, we sought to replicate our results in various ways.

A second objection centers on whether subjects possess sufficient levels of task-relevant expertise and knowledge. However, this criticism does not apply to the actuaries. In addition, it is important to note that most of the student subjects had been exposed to courses in both economics and statistics and thus can be described as sophisticated in terms of the experimental task. Finally, members of the executive groups frequently make decisions concerning insurance in both their private and professional roles. In short, we believe that the subjects were exceptionally well qualified to respond to the questionnaires.

3.2. Stimuli and design

All questionnaires followed the same general format and involved the two scenarios briefly described in the introduction. In one, the *defective product* scenario, the owner of a small business with net assets of $110,000 seeks to insure against a $100,000 loss that could result from claims concerning a defective product. Subjects assigned the role of consumers were told to imagine that they were the owner of the business. Subjects assigned the role of firms were asked to imagine that they headed a department in a large insurance company and were authorized to set premiums for the level of risk involved. The question was worded to indicate a single risk.

Ambiguity was manipulated by factors involving how well the manufacturing process was understood, whether the reliabilities of the machines used in the process were known, and the state of manufacturing records. In both ambiguous and nonambiguous cases a specific probability level was stated (e.g., .01). However, a comment was also added as to whether one could "feel confident" (nonambiguous case) or "experience considerable uncertainty" (ambiguous case) concerning the estimate. Uniformity of perceptions of ambiguity was controlled by describing the situations by the same words in both the consumer and firm versions.

The second scenario, known as the *Brown River* scenario, also involved a small businessman, a loss of $100,000, and a large insurance company. In this case, the potential loss was contingent on the flooding of a warehouse "located on the Penndiana floodplain." In the nonambiguous version subjects were told that the probability of a flood destroying the inventory in the warehouse could be confidently estimated by experts on the basis of considerable hydrological data. In the ambiguous case, subjects were told that limited data existed concerning the flooding of the Brown River. Moreover, hydrologists were "sufficiently uncertain about this event so that this annual probability could range anywhere from zero to 1 in 50 (i.e., .02) depending on climatic conditions." (Copies of the experimental stimuli may be obtained by writing to the authors.)

As emphasized by equations (1) and (2), according to the Bayesian expected utility model, prices for insurance depend only on the means of distributions over the probability of loss. Thus, this model predicts no difference in price between ambiguous and nonambiguous circumstances if the means of the distributions for these two cases are identical. Since it is problematic from a Bayesian viewpoint to constrain the means of the distributions to be the same, two procedures were used. In the defective product scenario, subjects receiving the ambiguous version were told that the stated probability (e.g., .01) was their "best estimate." Although imprecise as to the meaning of "best," this wording was adopted so that subjects would consider that the given probability aptly summarized any distribution they might have over the probability of loss. Moreover, no specification of any range of values around this point was provided. In the Brown River scenario, on the other hand, subjects responding to the ambiguous version were provided both with an anchor value (.01) and a range of possible values (from 0 to .02).

3.3. Experiment 1

Four variables were manipulated in this study using the defective product scenario with a potential loss of $100,000. These were role (consumer or firm), ambiguity (ambiguous or nonambiguous version of the stimulus), probability of loss (p = .01, .35, .65, and .90), and type of respondent (actuaries or MBA students). Subjects were assigned the role of either consumer or firm. Consumers were required to respond by stating the maximum premiums they would be prepared to pay, whereas firms were asked to state the minimum premiums they would be prepared to charge. Each subject responded to both the ambiguous and nonambiguous versions of the stimuli that related to his or her role but at only one probability level (i.e., responses at the different probability levels were made by different subjects). For the actuaries, the two versions (ambiguous and nonambiguous) of the stimulus for this experiment were the first and last questions of several they were asked to answer. Each question appeared on a different page of the questionnaire and the order of the ambiguous and nonambiguous versions was randomized across subjects. For the MBA subjects, the stimuli were included among a series of problems related to decision making, each on a different page of an experimental booklet, in which the ambiguous and nonambiguous versions were also physically separated by several items. Subjects were instructed to work systematically through the booklet at their own pace without looking back at previous responses.

To summarize, the design of this experiment involved four factors: three involved comparisons *between* subjects (i.e., role of consumer or firm, probability level, and type of respondent), and one *within* subjects (i.e., ambiguous vs. nonambiguous scenarios). There were 217 subjects: 101 were actuaries and 116 were MBA students.[4]

Table 1 presents the results of the experiment in the form of the means of the ratios of ambiguous to nonambiguous prices in the different between-subject experimental conditions. This table allows a direct test of the four hypotheses stated above in that each cell entry estimates the mean ambiguous-to-nonambiguous price ratio for subjects in each condition (i.e., $[CA(p)/C(p)]$ and $[FA(p)/F(p)]$ as appropriate. Note, however, that although $R_c \neq [CA(p)/C(p)]$, these ratios are monotonically related; also, by assumption, $R_f = [FA(p)/F(p)]$). All four hypotheses are supported by the data. For consumers: (1) Mean ratios are larger than one for $p = .01$, thereby indicating aversion to ambiguity for low probability-of-loss events; (2) mean ratios decline as p increases and, for high p values (here .90), ambiguity preference is exhibited by mean ratios of less than one. For firms: (3) Mean ratios are larger than one for low probability events; moreover, (4) these ratios decrease as p increases. Note particularly that in all four columns of table 1, the mean ratios of prices decrease in monotonic fashion. A statistical test of the hypotheses was conducted by using an appropriate analysis of variance on the ratios involving three factors (type of subject, probability level, and role) and their possible interactions together with a trend analysis on the probability level factor. The

16 HOGARTH AND KUNREUTHER

Table 1. Experiment 1. Means of ratios of ambiguous to nonambiguous prices

Defective product scenario
Loss = $100,000

Probability of Loss	Consumers		Firms	
	Actuaries	MBA students	Actuaries	MBA students
	$CA(p)/C(p)$	$CA(p)/C(p)$	$FA(p)/F(p)$	$FA(p)/F(p)$
.01	1.69	2.03	2.71	2.92
.35	1.19	0.91	1.33	1.82
.65	1.04	0.81	1.16	1.05
.90	0.78	0.76	1.03	0.88

hypotheses are supported by a significant main effect for probability level ($p < .001$) accompanied by a statistically significant downward trend ($t = -6.99$, $p < .0001$). In addition, the analysis revealed a significant main effect for role ($p < .005$) with consumers showing less concern for ambiguity than firms. However, there was no main effect for type of subject (i.e., actuaries or MBA students), nor any significant interactions between any of the variables (i.e., type of subject, probability level, and role).

Further insight into the data is provided by table 2, which shows the median prices in all experimental conditions. Medians are shown rather than means since several distributions within cells are quite skewed (see also below). Several trends are evident from the data. First, the actuaries' prices are generally higher than those of the students when ambiguity is held constant. (Compare columns 1 vs. 3, 2 vs. 4, 5 vs. 7, and 6 vs. 8.) The reason for this result is unclear, although it is plausible that actuaries would have a greater appreciation of the risks underlying insurance contracts than MBA students and therefore be willing both to pay and charge more.[5] Second, for consumers, the data again reveal aversion to ambiguity for the low probability-of-loss events but ambiguity preference for high probabilities. Firms also show decreasing aversion to ambiguity as the probabilities of losses increase, but firms do not show ambiguity preference. In terms of figure 1, this suggests that the ambiguity curve for firms lies above that of consumers, an issue we shall address further below. Third, there are differences between prices of consumers and firms at the same probability levels.

These observations are supported by statistical tests involving an appropriate analysis of variance model with three between-subject factors (probability level, role, and type of subject), the within-subject factor of ambiguity, and the different possible between- and within-factor interactions. This analysis shows significant main effects for probability level ($p < .0001$), role (i.e., firm or consumer, $p < .0001$), type of subject (i.e., actuary or MBA student, $p < .01$), and ambiguity ($p < .02$). Moreover, there are significant interactions with respect to probability

Table 2. Experiment 1. Median prices ($) of firms and consumers

Defective product scenario
Loss = $100,000

		Consumers' Willingness to Pay					
		Actuaries			MBA students		
		(1) Ambiguous CA(p)	(2) Nonambiguous C(p)		(3) Ambiguous CA(p)	(4) Nonambiguous C(p)	
Probability of Loss	(n)[a]	$	$	(n)	$	$	
.01	(12)	5,000	2,500	(15)	1,500	1,000	
.35	(14)	46,875	40,000	(15)	35,000	35,000	
.65	(13)	75,000	65,000	(15)	50,000	65,000	
.90	(10)	75,000	90,000	(14)	60,000	82,500	

		Firms' Supply Price					
		Actuaries			MBA students		
		(5) Ambiguous FA(p)	(6) Nonambiguous F(p)		(7) Ambiguous FA(p)	(8) Nonambiguous F(p)	
Probability of Loss	(n)	$	$		$	$	
.01	(12)	5,000	1,550	(15)	2,500	1,000	
.35	(10)	50,000	42,674	(14)	52,500	35,500	
.65	(15)	80,250	70,000	(14)	70,000	65,000	
.90	(15)	95,000	90,000	(14)	90,000	90,000	

[a](n) indicates number of subjects in experimental condition.

level $\times$ role ($p < .0005$), ambiguity $\times$ probability level ($p < .0001$), ambiguity $\times$ role ($p < .0001$), and ambiguity $\times$ type of respondent ($p < .001$). In contrast to table 1, where no significant differences between actuaries and MBA students were revealed (based on analyzing ratios of ambiguous to nonambiguous prices), the present analysis suggests that the actuaries are differentially more sensitive to ambiguity than the MBA students.

3.4. Discussion of experiment 1

We now discuss four issues related to this experiment: (1) whether a Bayesian expected utility model could account for the experimental data as well as the Einhorn–Hogarth ambiguity model; (2) the robustness of these particular experimental results; (3) implications of the experimental data for market-level behavior; and (4) differences in responses between consumers and firms.

3.4.1. In a Bayesian model, the mean of an ambiguous distribution could differ from its nonambiguous counterpart. For example, consider the case where subjects are provided with the anchor of $p = .01$. In the nonambiguous case, one can well imagine that a subject's probability distribution over p can be taken to be firmly centered at .01 with little or no variance around this value. In the ambiguous situation, on the other hand, one would expect variance in the distribution and it is not clear that the mean would be at .01.

Whereas a Bayesian interpretation may seem plausible, this model imposes certain coherence or consistency requirements. Specifically, one needs to verify whether the data are consistent with unique utility functions and coherent assessments of probability. Fortunately, these requirements can be verified from the data in table 2, albeit at an aggregate level. To do so, assume that the maximum premium a consumer is prepared to pay against the possibility of a $100,000 loss is such that he or she is indifferent whether or not to buy insurance. From the viewpoint of expected utility theory, this implies

$$M(p)U(W - \$100,000) + [1 - M(p)]U(W) = U(W - C), \tag{10}$$

where $M(p)$ is the mean of the individual's probability distribution over p, the probability of loss; W represents the person's wealth; C is the maximum premium he or she is prepared to pay; and $U(\cdot)$ denotes utility. Consider specifically the data in table 2 concerning MBA students as consumers in the ambiguous condition at the .35 and .65 probability levels (column 3). These data imply

$$M(.35)U(W - \$100,000) + [1 - M(.35)]U(W) = U(W - \$35,000) \tag{11a}$$

and

$$M(.65)U(W - \$100,000) + [1 - M(.65)]U(W) = U(W - \$50,000), \tag{11b}$$

where the notation $M(.35)$ denotes the mean of the probability distribution associated with the .35 anchor value, and so on. As noted above, one might not expect the means of the probability distributions at each level to equal their anchor values. However, it is important to recognize that the means of these distributions are themselves probabilities at the level of the expected utility model. Thus, the values of $M(p)$ must satisfy the coherence requirements of probability theory so that, for example, $M(p) + M(1 - p) = 1$. For example, if $M(.01)$ exceeded .01, $M(.99)$ would have to be correspondingly smaller than .99. Coherence therefore also requires that

$$M(.35) + M(.65) = 1. \tag{12}$$

Given equation (12), note that the sum of equations (11a) and (11b) implies that, for the ambiguous case,

$$U(W - \$100,000) + U(W) = U(W - \$35,000) + U(W - \$50,000). \tag{13}$$

Now consider the consumers' responses for MBA students for the .35 and .65 probability levels in the nonambiguous case (table 2, column 4). Following the same reasoning as above, this leads to the equation

$$U(W - \$100,000) + U(W) = U(W - \$35,000) + U(W - \$65,000). \tag{14}$$

The Bayesian expected utility model must assume that consumers have the same utility function in the ambiguous and nonambiguous cases. However, note that if equation (13) is subtracted from equation (14), this leads to the conclusion that

$$U(W - \$65,000) = U(W - \$50,000), \tag{15}$$

which is inconsistent with the notion that consumers have a unique utility function over wealth.

A similar inconsistency vis-à-vis expected utility theory can also be noted in the prices given by actuaries. In this case (columns 1 and 2 of table 2), the relation corresponding to equation (15) is

$$U(W - \$46,875) + U(W - \$75,000) = U(W - \$40,000) + U(W - \$65,000), \tag{16}$$

which cannot hold since the left-hand side is smaller than the right.

In the case of firms, we have made the assumption of risk neutrality, which seems appropriate for the MBA subjects in the nonambiguous condition (column 8) but not under ambiguity (column 7). For example, consider the cases of $p = .35$ and $p = .65$. In the nonambiguous case, the sum of the median premiums for these two events is close to the risk-neutral prediction of $100,000. The premiums for the analogous ambiguous conditions, however, sum to $122,500. For the actuaries, there is also an important discrepancy between the sums of the nonambiguous and ambiguous premiums at the .35 and .65 levels; these are $112,674 (column 6) and $130,250 (column 5), respectively.

To summarize, the data in table 2 are inconsistent with a Bayesian expected utility model that assumes that consumers have unique utility functions over wealth and that firms are risk-neutral. To be sure, these conclusions have been reached on the basis of aggregate data (median responses). However, note that the Einhorn–Hogarth model specifically predicts violations of Bayesian coherence requirements in the presence of ambiguity (see equation (5)). Moreover, Einhorn and Hogarth (1985) have demonstrated such violations experimentally at both aggregate and individual levels.

3.4.2. How robust are the experimental results? To test this issue, we conducted a number of replications involving both the defective product and Brown River scenarios and different groups of subjects. Subjects responding to the defective product scenario were (a) University of Chicago students ($n = 52$), (b) executives attending a management program at the University of Chicago ($n = 65$), (c) Wharton undergraduates ($n = 318$), (d) University of Chicago MBA students ($n = 158$), and (e) two subsamples from the survey of actuaries ($n = 80$ and 170). In two of the groups (a and b), each subject was assigned the role of consumer or firm and responded to both the ambiguous and nonambiguous versions of the experimental stimulus at one probability level, exactly as in experiment 1. In the three other groups (c, d, and e), however, subjects only saw the ambiguous or nonambiguous version of the stimulus for a particular role (i.e., consumer or firm). That is, ambiguity was manipulated as a between- rather than within-subject variable. The replication of experiment 1 with these five subject groups was partial since all probability levels were not investigated.

The results of these replications are presented graphically in figures 2 and 3.

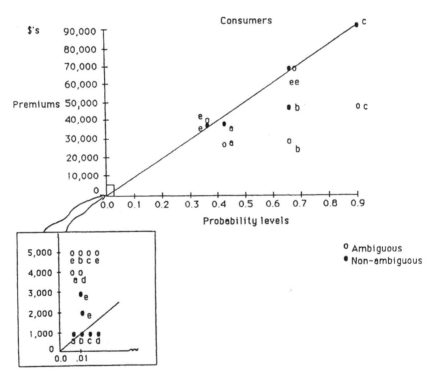

Fig. 2. Median prices of consumers from studies replicating different aspects of experiment 1. Ambiguous prices are represented by O, nonambiguous by ●. Letters refer to different subject populations: (a) University of Chicago students; (b) executives; (c) Wharton undergraduates; (d) University of Chicago MBA students; and (e) actuaries.

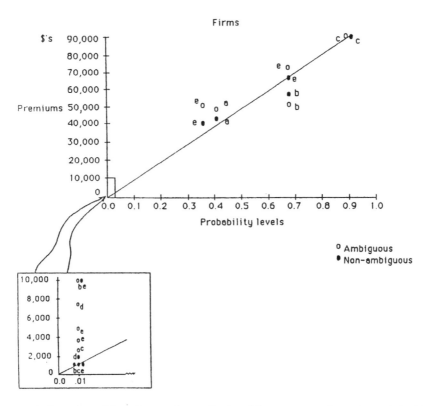

Fig. 3. Median prices of firms from studies replicating different aspects of experiment 1. Ambiguous prices are represented by O. nonambiguous by O. Letters refer to different subject populations: (a) University of Chicago students: (b) executives: (c) Wharton undergraduates: (d) University of Chicago MBA students: and (e) actuaries.

Figure 2 shows median responses from the various studies in respect of consumers. Figure 3 shows the same information for firms. In both figures, median responses to the ambiguous stimuli in the various studies are represented by small circles: median responses to corresponding nonambiguous stimuli are shown in the form of black dots.

The results of the different replications are consistent with the data of experiment 1. Consider consumers (figure 2). Note that at the $p = .01$ level (in the magnified inset at the lower left), all the ambiguous medians lie above the nonambiguous, thereby indicating aversion to ambiguity. Moreover as p increases, the ambiguous medians start to exhibit preference for ambiguity, whereas the nonambiguous medians lie close to the diagonal. Ambiguity preference is not, however, evidenced in all samples of data. In particular, the responses of the actuaries at the .65 probability level are the same in both the ambiguous and nonambiguous cases.

However, as noted in experiment 1, when acting as consumers the actuaries were more averse to ambiguity than the MBA students. Thus, this result is not inconsistent with those data.

Aversion to ambiguity is the predominant response exhibited by firms (figure 3). At the .01 probability level, all but one median in the ambiguous condition lie above their nonambiguous counterparts.[6] Also, consistent with the data from experiment 1, the ratios of ambiguous to nonambiguous prices decrease as p increases with, once again, the sample of actuaries showing greater aversion to ambiguity than the other groups (at $p = .65$).

In addition to these results for groups (a–e), the Brown River scenario was tested with two groups of subjects, namely (f) University of Chicago students ($n = 110$), and (g) Wharton undergraduates ($n = 163$). These tests were only done at one probability level ($p = .01$) and involved between-subject comparisons (i.e., subjects saw only either the ambiguous or nonambiguous version of the stimulus when in the role of a consumer or firm). For both samples, as well as for both consumers and firms, the median response to the ambiguous stimulus was $2,000 (potential loss of $100,000). For the nonambiguous stimulus, median responses for consumers were $1,400 and $1,000 for groups (f) and (g), respectively. For firms, the corresponding figures were $1,030 and $1,000. These results are thus consistent both with the ambiguity model and our other experimental data.

3.4.3. How does ambiguity affect market behavior? Whereas neither the data collected here nor the Einhorn–Hogarth model speak directly to this issue, both have important implications. For example, for low probability-of-loss events where firms are not ambiguous but consumers are, one would expect firms' minimum prices to be much lower than the maximum consumers are prepared to pay. Thus, since consumers would be prepared to incur the transaction costs of acquiring insurance, there would be many opportunities for trade. However, what would happen if either firms were ambiguous or consumers nonambiguous? In the former, firms' supply prices would increase and, in the latter, consumers' willingness to pay premiums and/or incur the costs of locating suppliers would decrease. Both of these situations imply reduced opportunities for trade.[7]

Figures 4a and 4b illustrate how opportunities for trading vary under different conditions of ambiguity with a low probability-of-loss event ($p = .01$). Specifically, aggregating the data from actuaries in experiment 1 and its replications, we have estimated consumer demand curves and firm supply curves under ambiguous and nonambiguous conditions by showing the percentages of consumers and firms prepared to trade at or below given prices. Figure 4a contrasts ambiguous consumers with nonambiguous firms, whereas figure 4b contrasts nonambiguous consumers with ambiguous firms. The figures illustrate how ambiguity interacts with different mechanisms regarding trade in affecting the relative thickness of the market.

First, consider the case where firms announce premiums and the lowest price becomes the market price. For the data presented here, 100% of consumers would

RISK. AMBIGUITY, AND INSURANCE   23

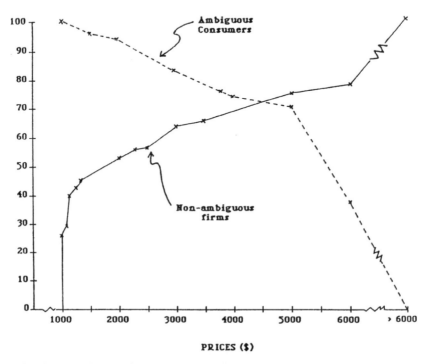

Percentages of
consumers/firms
prepared to trade
at or below prices.

PRICES ($)

Fig. 4a. Supply curve of nonambiguous firms and demand curve of ambiguous consumers estimated from data of actuaries from experiment 1 and its replications for $p = .01$. For any given dollar value on the horizontal axis, the curves indicate the percentages of firms and consumers willing to trade at or below that price.

be willing to pay the minimum price asked by any firm ($1,000 in both figures 4a and 4b). In other words, ambiguity would have had little or no effect on this kind of market.

However, compare this situation to one where firms are only willing to sell a single policy. This results in a much thinner market where the percentage of consumers able to purchase a policy will depend on the number of firms in the market and the process of matching firms with consumers. The maximum number of trades will occur if the firm with the lowest price sells to the consumer with the lowest price that is at or above that firm's asking price, the second lowest price goes to the consumer with the lowest price at or above the second lowest price, and so on. Assuming an equal number of firms and consumers, the maximum percentage of trades taking place under this system can be ascertained from figures 4a and 4b

Percentages of
consumers/firms
prepared to trade
at or below prices.

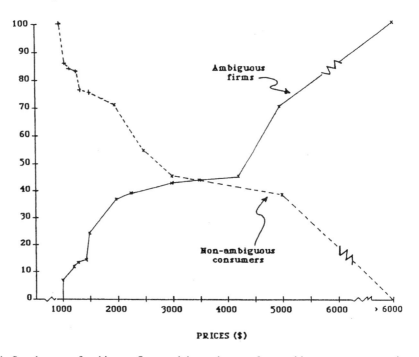

Fig. 4b. Supply curve of ambiguous firms and demand curve of nonambiguous consumers estimated from data of actuaries from experiment 1 and its replications for $p = .01$. For any given dollar value on the horizontal axis, the curves indicate the percentages of firms and consumers willing to trade at or below that price.

by noting where the demand and supply curves intersect. Thus, when consumers are ambiguous but firms are not, the maximum number of trades is 73% at a market price of $4,350 (figure 4a). However, when firms are ambiguous but consumers are not, the maximum drops to 44% at a market price of $3,500 (figure 4b).

Table 3 summarizes the percentages of trades possible under these different trading assumptions for the four possible combinations of ambiguous and nonambiguous firms and consumers. In addition, we have added the number of possible trades that could occur if consumers could only buy at the median of the firms' selling prices. This is an important statistic in that it provides an indication of the likelihood that consumers could locate an insurer with an acceptable price for a specified search rule. (For a discussion of the implications of alternative search rules on behavior, see Hey, 1982). As shown in table 3, whereas 94% of ambiguous consumers have prices at or above the median price asked by nonambiguous

Table 3. Percentages of possible trades[a]

Defective product scenario
Loss = $100.000; $p = .01$

		Maximum Number of Possible Trades		
		At lowest price offered by firms	Single policies: one-to-one basis	At median price offered by firms
Firms	Consumers	%	%	%
Ambiguous	Ambiguous	100	70	70
Ambiguous	Nonambiguous	100	44	39
Nonambiguous	Ambiguous	100	73	94
Nonambiguous	Nonambiguous	100	57	70

[a]The data analyzed here (and in figures 4a and 4b) come from responses by actuaries in experiment I and its replications. Sample sizes were

Ambiguous firms	54
Nonambiguous firms	47
Ambiguous consumers	50
Nonambiguous consumers	44

firms, this percentage drops to 39% for nonambiguous consumers and ambiguous firms.

3.4.4. One striking feature of the data is that the prices of firms exhibit more sensitivity to ambiguity than those of consumers. Specifically, the data from experiment I and the replications allow one to make 20 independent comparisons between the $[CA(p)/C(p)]$ ratios of consumers and the corresponding $[FA(p)/F(p)]$ ratios of firms. In 17 of these 20 comparisons, the firm ratio exceeds that of consumers, i.e., $[FA(p)/F(p)] > [CA(p)/C(p)]$; in two cases, the consumer ratios are larger; and in the remaining case the ratios are equal. (The probability of observing as many as 17 out of 20 ratios in either direction by chance is small, .0004.) Since the ambiguous and nonambiguous versions of the experimental stimuli were specifically written to equate the level of perceived ambiguity between firms and consumers, this tendency implies that the β parameter for firms exceeds that of consumers, i.e., $\beta_f > \beta_c$. (To clarify this implication, examine figure 1, which contrasts two ambiguity functions that have the same θ parameter—perceived ambiguity—but different β parameters. Note that, for $0 < p < 1$, the $S(p)$ values of the function with the larger β parameter must always be greater than the corresponding $S(p)$ values of the other function.[8])

Why does this occur? One explanation, consistent with the Einhorn–Hogarth model, relates to differential attitudes toward ambiguity induced by taking on a risk as opposed to transferring it. Specifically, since a person assuming a risk bears its potential negative consequences, he or she has greater incentive than the person transferring the risk to weight possible values of the probability of loss that are larger than the initial estimate. Thus, according to the mental simulation implicit in the Einhorn–Hogarth model, $\beta_f > \beta_c$. Experimental evidence consistent with this transfer effect has been documented by Hershey, Kunreuther, and Schoemaker (1982) and Thaler (1980).

3.5. Experiment 2

An alternative way of measuring the extent to which ambiguity affects trading in a market setting is to determine the behavior of consumers and firms at prespecified prices. The effects of this response mode were tested in a second experiment using both the defective product and Brown River scenarios. For both scenarios, the loss was $100,000 and one probability level was investigated ($p = .01$). With the exception of a small sample of subjects who responded to the defective product scenario (see below), each subject was allocated at random to one of four conditions created by crossing the two roles (firms and consumers) × two levels of ambiguity (ambiguous and nonambiguous versions of the stimuli). Thus each subject played either the role of a firm or consumer and saw either the ambiguous or nonambiguous version of the stimuli.

Four groups of subjects responded to the defective product scenario: (1) University of Chicago MBA students;[9] (2) executives from life insurance companies attending a residential, professional seminar (life officers); (3) executives from several Chicago area corporations present at a lecture sponsored by the Midwest Planning Association (planners); and (4) actuaries. Because data were only obtained from a small number of planners (24), each planner answered both the ambiguous and nonambiguous versions of the stimulus in a within-subjects design. Subjects responding to the Brown River scenario included both University of Chicago and Wharton MBAs as well as executives attending a University of Chicago management program. Since the results from the different subgroups responding to the Brown River scenario do not differ significantly, they have been aggregated for the purpose of this analysis. However, this is not true of the defective product scenario. Results for this scenario will therefore be presented both in aggregate and by subgroups.

Scenarios were identical to those used in the other studies except that subjects were required to respond by stating whether they would trade ("Yes" or "No") at a given price. Having answered this question, subjects turned a page in their experimental booklets and were asked the same question with respect to a different price. To simulate trading conditions, the second price for consumers was lower than the first, whereas the reverse order was used for firms (i.e., lower prices were stated first). Our previous experiments indicated that the defective product scenario induced more ambiguity than the Brown River scenario. We attempted to allow for this difference by setting the prices for the former at $1,500 and $3,000, and at $1,100 and $2,500 for the latter (expected value = $1,000).

Results concerning the defective product scenario are presented in table 4 which, aggregating across subgroups, shows strong ambiguity effects for both consumers and firms. The main exception is that there is no significant ambiguity effect for consumers at $1,500 (89% vs. 81%). However, the difference at $3,000 as well as the difference at both price levels for the firms are significant ($p < .001$ using χ^2). Note also that the data reveal large differences between consumers and firms in their willingness to trade. For example, even at the $3,000 price, only 38% of firms are prepared to trade in the ambiguous condition compared to the 84% of consumers who would be willing to pay that price.

Results for the Brown River scenario are presented in table 5. This shows no significant effects for ambiguity for consumers at either the $1,100 or $2,500 price levels. Nor is there an ambiguity effect for firms at the higher price ($2,500: 89% vs. 90%). On the other hand, at the lower price of $1,100 the 36% vs. 73% difference is significant ($\chi_i^2 = 14.09, p < .001$).

To summarize, the results of experiment 2 essentially replicate those of experiment 1 at the .01 probability level using a different form of response mode (preparedness to trade at specific prices vs. stating minimum selling/maximum buying prices).[10] The one exception concerns the lack of an ambiguity effect for consumers in the Brown River scenario. A possible reason is that the $2,500 price was too high relative to the ambiguous description used in that scenario. Indeed, this speculation is supported by the fact that there was also no ambiguity effect for firms at this price.[11] On the other hand, the idea that firms should be more sensitive to ambiguity at the lower price ($1,100) is consistent with the model, as are the analogous data concerning the defective-product scenario.

4. Discussion

The experimental results can be characterized by three major conclusions: (1) the pricing decisions of both firms and consumers are sensitive to ambiguity; (2) sensitivity to ambiguity varies as a function of the probability of the potential loss—specifically, aversion to ambiguity decreases (relatively speaking) as probabilities of losses increase and, in the case of consumers, can result in ambiguity preference for high probability-of-loss events; and (3) firms show greater aversion to ambiguity than consumers. These three conclusions are consistent with the underlying process postulated in the Einhorn–Hogarth ambiguity model and raise questions for the analysis of insurance behavior based on more traditional economic models. In particular, the patterns of ambiguity aversion and preference observed in the experimental data were seen to be incompatible with assumptions typically made with respect to the utility functions of both consumers and firms.

Whereas our results emphasize the importance of ambiguity on insurance markets, we recognize the difficulty of separating its effects in naturally occurring situations from other factors affecting choice under uncertainty. Indeed, the presence of such factors is a prime reason for using experimental methods in this

Table 4. Experiment 2. Percentages of subjects prepared to trade at given prices

Loss = $100,000; $p = .01$

Subjects	Ambiguity[b]	Defective Product Scenario					
		$1,500		$3,000		(n)[a]	
		Consumers %	Firms %	Consumers %	Firms %	Consumers	Firms
MBAs	A	87	16	83	36	(23)	(25)
	N-a	77	67	50	87	(22)	(15)
Life officers	A	85	21	85	46	(33)	(28)
	N-a	80	64	67	86	(42)	(36)
Planners	A	93	10	79	30	(14)	(10)
	N-a	85	80	36	100	(14)	(10)
Actuaries	A	100	16	86	32	(22)	(19)
	N-a	81	13	65	25	(21)	(16)
All subjects	A	89	17	84	38	(92)	(82)
	N-a	81	56	53	75	(99)	(77)

[a] (n) indicates number of subjects
[b] A: Ambiguous condition
N-a: Nonambiguous condition

Table 5. Experiment 2. Percentages of subjects prepared to trade at given prices

Loss = $100,000; $p = .01$

Prices:	Brown River Scenario				$(n)^a$	
	$1,100		$2,500			
Condition	Consumers %	Firms %	Consumers %	Firms %	Consumers	Firms
Ambiguous	88	36	47	89	(43)	(45)
Nonambiguous	78	73	48	90	(50)	(48)

[a](n) indicates number of subjects.

work. These include problems such as adverse selection, fear of bankruptcy, and moral hazard as well as possible effects due to framing (cf. Tversky & Kahneman, 1981) and other psychological influences. Thus, specifying how ambiguity interacts with these factors in affecting demand and supply in insurance markets suggests a rich agenda for future research. We now consider some of these issues.

4.1. Ambiguity and demand for insurance

How does ambiguity affect the types of insurance consumers are prepared to buy? For example, the demand for low deductibles in both automobile (Pashigian et al., 1966) and health insurance (Fuchs, 1976) has been particularly puzzling to economists since the premium-to-loss ratio for these types of coverage is extremely high. However, if consumers estimate the probability of an accident as low, but are ambiguous about such estimates, it follows from the ambiguity model that they will be willing to buy this type of protection at prices considerably above actuarial value. Similar reasoning can be applied to protection that is bought against rare but life-threatening events such as various forms of cancer.

Puzzling effects have been noted concerning the role of past experience on demand for insurance. One example is the lack of interest shown in flood or earthquake insurance until a disaster occurs (Kunreuther et al., 1978). People tend to buy this coverage only after experiencing a disaster or learning of others who have suffered severe damage. Since considerable ambiguity exists concerning the chances of these low-probability events, there is a tendency for individuals to focus on salient information such as potential losses. Prior to the disaster occurring, it appears as if they disregard the event by reasoning that "it can't happen to me" and thus do not buy insurance. In other words, there may be a threshold below which individuals effectively assume the probability of an event to be zero due to the mental costs of attending to such an event (Slovic et al., 1978). After an earthquake occurs, however, people do pay attention even if they incurred no damage. One is tempted to explain this behavior by a Bayesian argument whereby the probability of an earthquake increases by being updated on the basis of new information. However, the intriguing fact is that over 40% of the 1,000 respondents in a field survey in earthquake-prone areas of California recognized that once a severe earthquake occurs, it is less likely to occur in the near future (Kunreuther et al., 1978).

We have hypothesized that people who have substantial experience with certain low-probability events have little ambiguity and hence are less likely to purchase insurance or protection against such events. Thus, with respect to flight insurance, this implies that frequent travelers are less likely to purchase coverage than those who fly on an occasional basis. Similarly, consumers who receive so-called free flight insurance when paying for air travel with their credit cards will value this service less to the extent that they are experienced fliers. Indeed, lack of experience regarding certain events may also explain the dread associated with accidents from technological facilities such as nuclear power plants (Slovic et al., 1983). More generally, people may consider events that can only occur once in a lifetime, such as death or a serious illness, as inherently more ambiguous for them personally than events that are repeatable (e.g., a household fire or theft). Firms, on the other hand, have the advantage of treating individual ambiguities as precise statistics at the aggregate level.

The Einhorn–Hogarth model also has some specific implications for marketing insurance when events are inherently ambiguous. For example, the model implies that, as probabilities decrease, consumers are prepared to pay more per dollar of coverage relative to expected loss. This therefore suggests marketing strategies where contracts are framed so that probabilities of loss are perceived to be low. This can be achieved in two ways: (a) reducing the period for which coverage is provided, e.g., from a year to six months; or (b) writing separate contracts for specific risks as opposed to providing more comprehensive policies (cf. Schoemaker & Kunreuther, 1979). In following such prescriptions, however, marketers should take care that probabilities of losses do not become so small that they fall below consumers' thresholds of awareness (cf. Slovic et al., 1978).

4.2. Ambiguity and supply of insurance

The willingness of firms to offer insurance can also be dampened by ambiguity. New and potentially dangerous technologies exemplify this type of risk. Consider, for example, the case of nuclear coverage. Officially, all property liability insurance policies issued in the United States exclude claims for damage to one's dwelling, automobile, boat, and other property by radiation and contamination from a nuclear facility. The insurance industry is opposed to providing this kind of coverage, claiming that the risk is not insurable because of the ambiguity associated wtih potential losses (U.S. Nuclear Regulatory Commission, 1983). It would be interesting to determine what price the industry would be willing to charge for a certain amount of coverage and the demand for this insurance. We hypothesize considerable demand by consumers even with premiums substantially higher than actuarial values because of the great ambiguity associated with the event. However, given the firms' own ambiguities, it is an open question as to whether the premiums they would be prepared to charge would be considered reasonable by consumers.

In our experiments, subjects playing the role of firms were asked to consider insuring one individual against a single ambiguous event. It is thus interesting to speculate how firms might consider situations where many individuals seek insurance against the same ambiguous event. In cases where probabilities are well specified, risk-averse insurance firms attempt to diversify their portfolios (cf. Doherty & Schlesinger, 1983). Thus, we expect that the more ambiguous the risks faced by insurance firms, the less likely it is that they will want to insure a large number of individuals facing a particular loss, even if each risk is independent of the others. This in turn suggests that the market for reinsurance could provide a promising setting to investigate further the effects of ambiguity. Specifically, we hypothesize that reinsurers will exhibit concerns similar to insurers in determining what risks to accept for their portfolios.

Since warranties and service contracts are forms of insurance, one can also investigate these phenomena within the present framework. For example, the warranty experiments of Palfrey and Romer (1984) could be extended to cases in which agents are ambiguous about the probability of a failure. Similarly, experiments could investigate the market for service contracts by varying the probabilities of requiring service, costs, and ambiguity. Indeed, in a recent experiment (Einhorn & Hogarth, 1986), consumers expressed less interest in purchasing a warranty when the probabilities of breakdowns were both high and ambiguous, as opposed to nonambiguous situations where they were known to be high. Reasoning in a manner analogous to our earlier comments on comprehensive insurance, the model predicts greater demand under ambiguity for a series of lower probability-of-loss contracts than for an equivalent comprehensive contract where the probability of requiring at least one of the services is high.

Turning to controlled laboratory experiments, we are interested in extending the results of this study to a market-based situation in the spirit of Plott (1982) and Smith (1982) where buyers and sellers can interact with each other to determine insurance premiums using real monetary stakes. In fact, using an experimental design similar to the 2 × 2 matrix in this study, Camerer and Kunreuther (1988) recently investigated the impact of ambiguity on equilibrium prices in a market setting. These investigators defined *ambiguity* operationally by a uniform (second-order) probability distribution around a given mean and found no significant differences between equilibrium prices in the ambiguous and nonambiguous cases. On the other hand, neither Ellsberg (1961) nor Einhorn and Hogarth (1985) equate ambiguity with specified second-order probability distributions as conceptualized in the Camerer and Kunreuther study. Thus, the nature of *uncertainty about uncertainty* may itself be a variable of significant import requiring further investigation.

In addition, at a theoretical level there is a need to clarify the relations between the Einhorn–Hogarth model and the various axiomatic treatments of ambiguity discussed earlier in order to discriminate their relative ability to predict empirical phenomena.

Finally, it is important to note that insurance markets are characterized by ambiguity concerning the size of losses as well as probabilities. However, in our experimental studies the only ambiguity faced by subjects was on the probability dimension. When the magnitude of the loss is uncertain, expected utility theory suggests that premiums will be higher for risk-averse individuals. This therefore argues for controlled experiments that systematically vary ambiguity of probabilities and losses to determine the individual importance of each component as well as possible interaction effects. One can also investigate how ambiguity is affected by specific design features of risk-sharing mechanisms such as deductibles, coinsurance and upper limits on coverage. Empirical studies of these questions are likely to lead to a fuller understanding of how consumers and firms make decisions when faced with uncertain and ambiguous hazards.

Acknowledgments

This research was supported by NSF Grant #SES 8312123, a contract from the Office of Naval Research, and a grant from the Alfred P. Sloan Foundation. We especially thank Colin Camerer and the late Hillel Einhorn for helpful advice at all stages of this project. In addition, we are grateful to Jay Russo, Paul Schoemaker, and Nancy Pennington for data collection and Gary Becker, Gerald Faulhaber, Bill Goldstein, Jack Hershey, Paul Kleindorfer, Mel Reder, Uzi Segal, Ola Svenson, Georges Szpiro, and Richard Thaler for helpful comments on early drafts. Jay Koehler, Howard Mitzel, Ann McGill, Moon-Gie Kim, and Tae Yoon provided valuable assistance in data collection and analysis.

Notes

1. Robert E. Lucas, Jr. tells the story how several years ago he and some colleagues were shocked when another colleague experienced a severe heart attack. Their immediate reaction was to buy life insurance for themselves.

2. The only year during the 60-year period when losses exceeded premium payments was 1933, when paid claims amounted to $1.1 million and premiums were $.93 million. Note, moreover, that since earthquake coverage comprises a relatively small portion of an insurance company's portfolio, there should have been little if any concern with insolvency, even if losses in specific regions of California were highly correlated with each other.

3. In a *Wall Street Journal* article (June 21, 1984) on the space insurance industry, the effects of ambiguity on premiums charged by firms are clearly recognized. For example, consider the following quote from James Barrett, president of the Washington-based International Technology Underwriters: " ... if you're asking me to risk the capital of my company, then I've got to be comfortable that you're going to succeed. If we're not comfortable, we're not going to insure it, or we'll charge you like hell for it" (Large, 1984).

RISK. AMBIGUITY. AND INSURANCE   33

4. The data concerning the MBA students have previously been reported and discussed in Hogarth and Kunreuther (1985) and Einhorn and Hogarth (1985, 1986).

5. It should also be noted that, to avoid possible confusion, the actuaries were specifically asked to respond by giving "pure premiums" which were defined as "exclusive of all loss adjustment and underwriting expenses." MBA students were simply asked to provide "premiums."

6. The exception is from one small subsample of actuaries ($n = 16$) where the median nonambiguous response is \$10,000. We have no explanation for this result except to note that it is also anomalous relative to other subsamples of actuaries.

7. The number of trades will also be influenced by search costs of consumers as well as the distribution of firms' prices. Our data do not enable us to say anything about search costs. An analysis of the actuaries' estimates of premiums to be charged by firms reveals that there are no significant differences in variances between the ambiguous and nonambiguous cases. Hence, other things being equal, there is no a priori reason for one to expect search behavior by consumers to differ in the two situations.

8. This implication also follows algebraically from considering the ratio of the ratios R_c and R_f. This can be expressed as (see equations (8) and (9))

$$R_c/R_f = \{p + \theta(1 - p - p^{\beta}c)\}/\{p + \theta(1 - p - p^{\beta}f)\}.$$

Thus, for $0 < p < 1$, this ratio is less than one if $\beta_f > \beta_c$. Parenthetically, note that whereas the ratio given above is not the empirically observable ratio of $[CA(p)/C(p)]/[FA(p)/F(p)]$, it is monotonically related to it—see discussion concerning equations (8) and (9).

9. Results of this subsample were originally reported in Hogarth and Kunreuther (1985).

10. Whereas there might appear to be discrepancies between table 2 (experiment 1) and table 4 (experiment 2) concerning the size of effects, these should be interpreted with caution. Data in table 2 are medians from asymmetric distributions, whereas table 4 reports proportions of "Yes" or "No" choices.

11. We followed up on this speculation with an experiment involving 60 executives attending a University of Chicago program and prices of \$1,100 and \$2,000. In this experiment subjects were assigned roles of firms or consumers and ambiguity was manipulated as a within-subjects variable. (Subjects responded to the ambiguous and nonambiguous stimuli with a one-week interval between administrations.) There were significant differences (in the predicted direction) due to ambiguity for both firms ($p = .03$) and consumers ($p = .05$) at the \$2,000 price level.

References

Arrow, Kenneth. (1963). "Uncertainty and the Welfare Economics of Medical Care," *American Economic Review* 53, 941–973.
Arrow, Kenneth. (1982). "Risk Perception in Psychology and Economics," *Economic Inquiry* 20, 1–9.
Atkisson, Arthur, and William Petak. (1981). *Earthquake Insurance: A Public Policy Analysis.* Report prepared for the Federal Insurance Administration, Federal Emergency Management Agency, Washington, DC 20472.
Becker, Selwyn W., and Fred O. Brownson. (1964). "What Price Ambiguity? Or the Role of Ambiguity in Decision Making," *Journal of Political Economy* 72, 62–73.
Bewley, Truman. (1986). Knightian Decision Theory: Part I. Cowles Foundation Discussion Paper No. 807. Yale University.
Camerer, Colin, and Howard Kunreuther. (1988). Experimental Markets for Insurance. Center for Risk and Decision Processes, working paper, Wharton School, University of Pennsylvania.
Curley, Shawn P., and J. Frank Yates. (1985). "The Center and the Range of the Probability Interval as Factors Affecting Ambiguity Preferences," *Organizational Behavior and Human Decision Processes* 36, 273–287.
Curley, Shawn P., J. Frank Yates, and Richard A. Abrams. (1986). "Psychological Sources of Ambiguity Avoidance," *Organizational Behavior and Human Decision Processes* 38, 230–256.

Doherty, Neil A., and Harris Schlesinger. (1983). "Optimal Insurance in Incomplete Markets." *Journal of Political Economy* 91, 1045-1054.

Ehrlich, Isaac, and Gary Becker. (1972). "Market Insurance, Self-Insurance and Self-Protection," *Journal of Political Economy* 80, 623-648.

Einhorn, Hillel J., and Robin M. Hogarth. (1985). "Ambiguity and Uncertainty in Probabilistic Inference," *Psychological Review* 92, 433-461.

Einhorn, Hillel J., and Robin M. Hogarth. (1986). "Decision Making Under Ambiguity," *Journal of Business* 59, (No. 4, part 2), S225-S250.

Eisner, Robert and Robert H. Strotz. (1961). "Flight Insurance and the Theory of Choice," *Journal of Political Economy* 69, 355-368.

Ellsberg, Daniel. (1961). "Risk, Ambiguity, and the Savage Axioms," *Quarterly Journal of Economics* 75, 643-669.

Fishburn, Peter. (1983). "Ellsberg Revisited: A New Look at Comparative Probability," *Annals of Statistics* 11, 1047-1059.

Fishburn, Peter. (1986). "The Axioms of Subjective Probability," *Statistical Science* 1, 335-358.

Fuchs, Victor. (1976). "From Bismarck to Woodcock: The Irrational Pursuit of National Health Insurance," *Journal of Law and Economics* 19, 347-359.

Gärdenfors, Peter, and Nils-Eric Sahlin. (1982). "Unreliable Probabilities, Risk Taking, and Decision Making," *Synthese* 53, 361-386.

Gärdenfors, Peter, and Nils-Eric Sahlin. (1983). "Decision Making with Unreliable Probabilities," *British Journal of Mathematical and Statistical Psychology* 36, 240-251.

Grether, David M., and Charles R. Plott. (1979). "Economic Theory of Choice and the Preference Reversal Phenomenon," *American Economic Review* 69, 623-638.

Hershey, John C., Howard C. Kunreuther, and Paul J. H. Schoemaker. (1982). "Sources of Bias in Assessment Procedures for Utility Functions," *Management Science* 28, 936-954.

Hey, John. (1982). "Search for Rules for Search," *Journal of Economic Behavior and Organizations* 3, 65-81.

Hogarth, Robin M., and Howard C. Kunreuther. (1985). "Ambiguity and Insurance Decisions," *American Economic Review* (*AEA Papers and Proceedings*) 75(2), 386-390.

Hogarth, Robin M., and Melvin W. Reder. (1986). "Editors' Comments: Perspectives from Economics and Psychology," *Journal of Business* 59, (No. 4, part 2), S185-S207.

Knight, Frank H. (1921). *Risk, Uncertainty and Profit*. Boston: Houghton Mifflin.

Kunreuther, Howard C., and Paul R. Kleindorfer. (1983). "Insuring Against Country Risks: Descriptive and Prescriptive Aspects." In R. Herring (ed.), *Managing International Risk*. Cambridge, UK: Cambridge University Press.

Kunreuther, Howard et al. (1978). *Disaster Insurance Protection: Public Policy Lessons*. New York: Wiley.

Large, Arlen J. (1984). "Space Insurance Industry Is Seeking Greater Say In Satellite Technology," *Wall Street Journal*, June 21.

Luce, R. Duncan, and Louis Narens. (1985). "Classification of Concatenation Measurement Structures According to Scale Type," *Journal of Mathematical Psychology* 29, 1-72.

Nisbett, Richard E., and Lee D. Ross. (1980). *Human Inference: Strategies and Shortcomings of Social Judgment*. Englewood Cliffs, NJ: Prentice-Hall.

Palfrey, Thomas R., and Thomas Romer. (1984). An Experimental Study of Warranty Coverage and Dispute Resolution in Competitive Markets. (Working paper #34-83-84). Pittsburgh, PA: Carnegie-Mellon University, Graduate School of Industrial Administration.

Pashigian, Peter, Lawrence Schkade, and George Menefee. (1966). "The Selection of an Optimal Deductible for a Given Insurance Policy," *Journal of Business* 39(1), 35-44.

Plott, Charles R. (1982). "Industrial Organization Theory and Experimental Economics," *Journal of Economic Literature* 20, 1485-1527.

Quiggin, John. (1982). "A Theory of Anticipated Utility," *Journal of Economic and Organizational Behavior* 3, 323-343.

Savage, Leonard J. (1954). *The Foundations of Statistics*. New York: Wiley.

Schmeidler, David. (1984). Subjective Probability and Expected Utility Without Additivity. Preprint 84, Institute for Mathematics and Its Applications, University of Minnesota.

Schoemaker, Paul, and Howard Kunreuther. (1979). "An Experimental Study of Insurance Decisions," *Journal of Risk and Insurance* 46, 603–618.

Segal, Uzi. (1987). "The Ellsberg Paradox and Risk Aversion: An Anticipated Utility Approach," *International Economic Review* 28, 175–202.

Slovic, Paul, Baruch Fischhoff, and Sarah Lichtenstein. (1978). "Accident Probabilities and Seat Belt Usage: A Psychological Perspective," *Accident Analysis and Prevention* 10, 281–285.

Slovic, Paul, Baruch Fischhoff and Sarah Lichtenstein. (1983). "Characterizing Perceived Risks." In R. W. Kates and C. Hohenemser (eds.), *Technological Hazard Management*. Cambridge, MA: Oelgeschlager, Gunn and Hain.

Smith, Vernon L. (1982). "Microeconomic Systems as an Experimental Science," *American Economic Review* 72, 923–955.

Thaler, Richard. (1980). "Toward A Positive Theory of Consumer Choice," *Journal of Economic Behavior and Organization* 1, 39–60.

Tversky, Amos, and Daniel Kahneman. (1981). "The Framing of Decisions and the Psychology of Choice," *Science* 211, 453–458.

U.S. Nuclear Regulatory Commission. (December 1983). *The Price Anderson Act: The Third Decade*. Report to Congress, Washington, DC.

von Neumann, John and Oskar Morgenstern. (1947). *Theory of Games and Economic Behavior* (2nd edition). Princeton, NJ: Princeton University Press.

Yaari, Menahem. (1987). "The Dual Theory of Choice Under Risk," *Econometrica* 55, 95–115.

Yates, J. Frank, and Lisa G. Zukowski. (1976). "Characterization of Ambiguity in Decision Making," *Behavioral Science* 21, 19–25.

[12]

The Impact of Self-Protection and Self-Insurance on Individual Response to Risk

JASON F. SHOGREN*

Department of Economics, Iowa State University, Ames, Iowa 50011

Key words: risk, self-protection, self-insurance

Abstract

We develop four experimental markets to examine how individuals respond to risk: self-protection and self-insurance in both private and collective auctions. First, we find evidence that the mechanism used to reduce risk is important. Results indicate that the upper and lower bounds on value were elicited by the private self-protection and the collective self-insurance markets, respectively. Second, the robustness of these results declined with low-probability lotteries. We find further evidence that individuals overestimate the impact of low-probability events. Overestimation decreased, however, with repeated market exposure. Third, the four markets induced rapid value formation. Usually only one or two additional market trials were necessary before an individual's perception and valuation of reduced risk stabilized.

Two elements define risk: probability and severity. Ehrlich and Becker (1972) recognized that risk can be reduced by decreasing either element, privately or collectively. They define decreased probability as self-protection, and decreased severity as self-insurance. Recent extensions of self-protection and self-insurance models have illustrated their wide applicability and importance to the theory of individual choice under risk (see, for example, Hiebert, 1983; Centner and Wetzstein, 1987; Shogren and Crocker, 1990a).

Although it is now generally recognized that self-protection and self-insurance exist, minimal attention has been given to systematically evaluating their comparative impact on individual response to risk. Given Tversky and Kahneman's (1981) work on choice under alternative decision frames, one might suspect that *how* a risk is reduced may be as important as *what* risk is reduced. The purpose of this article is to examine how individuals respond to risk that is reduced either through private or collective self-protection or self-insurance. We construct an experimental design that incorporates self-protection and

*The financial support of the U.S. Environmental Protection Agency and the John A. Walker College of Business, Appalachian State University is gratefully acknowledged. The comments of Tom Crocker, Don Coursey, Cliff Nowell, and Mark Thayer concerning experimental design have been helpful. Joe Kerkvliet, Fred Wallace, Charles Plott, an anonymous referee, and especially W. Kip Viscusi provided useful advice. Kris Etter, Todd Holt, and Kevin Long provided valuable research assistance. The author accepts sole responsibility for all remaining errors.

self-insurance into four markets with alternative risk-reduction mechanisms. For each market, the experiment elicited individual valuations of four risks in both hypothetical and nonhypothetical lotteries repeated over ten market trials.

The experimental design captures three issues basic to decision-making under risk. First, we examine whether the risk-reduction mechanism matters to valuation. Individuals confronted with risk have an assortment of ex ante reduction mechanisms to decrease the probability or severity of an ex post monetary or nonmonetary loss. For example, an individual exposed to potentially contaminated drinking water can privately reduce the probability of illness by purchasing a water filter, or he can contribute to a collective scheme to filter the water in a centralized location. Alternatively, the individual can privately or collectively reduce the severity of the hazard through preventive medical care, nutrition, or exercise.

Although psychologists have discovered that alternative means of framing equivalent problems lead to systematic differences in choice, economists have previously not addressed whether alternative risk-reduction mechanisms affect valuation. Our results suggest that the mechanism matters. Reducing risk by altering the probability or severity of an undesirable event through a private mechanism induced significantly different value estimates. Private self-protection was preferred to self-insurance. In addition, private mechanisms were valued significantly more greatly than the collective mechanisms for both self-protection and self-insurance. Generally, the upper bound of value is generated by the private provision of self-protection. The lower bound of value is obtained by the collective provision of self-insurance. Consequently, future attempts to value risk should consider all alternative reduction mechanisms to capture a more comprehensive view of economic value.

The second basic issue explored is how individuals value reductions over a range of risks. Both psychologists and economists have uncovered evidence that individuals are oversensitive to changes in the probabilities of low-probability events (see Machina, 1983, for overview). If individuals over-estimate the value of reducing risk associated with low-probability events, then more resources will be devoted to risk reduction that is economically efficient. To determine whether the subjects overestimate low-probability events, a range of risks are examined. Four binary lotteries are constructed, given a fixed loss and gain with probability of a loss being 1%, 10%, 20%, and 40%. To compare across lotteries, we examine the individual's risk-premium payment. We also consider how the risk premiums respond to the alternative reduction mechanisms over repeated market trials.

We find further evidence that individuals overestimate the impacts of low-probability events as evidenced by relatively large initial risk-premium payments. The initial valuations do not conform to the expected utility requirement of linearity in probabilities, as reflected by individual willingness to pay an excessive risk premium for the 1% lottery period. Although this is not encouraging, since many risks are less than 1% per year or per lifetime, risk premiums decrease significantly with repeated market interactions, especially in the self-insurance risk-reduction markets.

Finally, the third issue examined is how value formation for risk reduction is affected by repeated exposure to the market. It is well documented that individuals misperceive risky events in static one-shot environments. The "sharpness" of prior information about the risk has little chance to improve without sequential decisions that involve learning (see Viscusi, 1979). As noted by Hayek (1945), the market provides the opportunity for an individual to update prior misperceptions, since irrelevant information has been forced out. To determine whether repeated exposure to the market significantly influences value formation, the experiment is designed such that each risk is reduced over 12 repeated trials. The first trial is the static one-shot hypothetical reduction often used in nonmarket valuation experiments. The next ten trials are nonhypothetical market auctions for self-protection or self-insurance. The final trial is the "experienced" hypothetical risk reduction.

We find that values form rapidly in all experimental markets. The rapid value formation indicates that learning about risk through the market does occur. The results indicate that the bias associated with the misperception of risk is greatly reduced with only one or two additional market trials. The market for risk reduction induces the process necessary for stable perceptions and values, without additional external information.

The article proceeds as follows. Section 1 describes the experimental design. The experimental results are outlined in Section 2, and the conclusions in Section 3.

1. Experimental design: Self-protection, self-insurance, and the psychology of risk reduction

The experimental design captures three fundamental issues in the theory of choice under risk: how individuals value risk given alternative reduction mechanisms, how individuals value reductions over a range of risks, and how these values are affected by repeated market trials. Consider each issue in more detail. First, we examine whether the risk-reduction mechanisms matter. Psychologists have discovered that choice and values are systematically influenced by alternative means of representing or framing an identical problem (e.g., Tversky and Kahneman, 1981). This evidence makes it increasingly difficult to accept on faith that alternative risk-reduction mechanisms do not influence individual value formation. To test whether alternative mechanisms matter, we construct an experimental market to quantify the framing of reduced risk. The experimental market was framed so that each subject would value reduced risk through one of four mechanisms: private self-protection, private self-insurance, collective self-protection, or collective self-insurance.

Given that one can discriminate between self-protection and self-insurance expenditures, is one reduction scheme preferred to another? Current economic theory yields an ambiguous answer. Boyer and Dionne (1983) argue that a risk-averse consumer will always prefer private self-insurance to self-protection, since the former is more efficient in reducing an equivalent risk. According to Chang and Ehrlich (1985), however, self-insurance will not be preferred to self-protection, since both must be equally desirable in terms of marginal contribution to expected utility. In our experimental design, the individual purchasing self-protection is guaranteed a monetary gain, while the purchaser of self-insurance is not. Self-protection reduces the probability of a loss to zero, implying a 100% chance of receiving the gain. Self-insurance, however, reduces the severity of the probable loss to zero, but does not alter the probability of receiving the monetary gain. Therefore, a risk-averse or risk-neutral individual will value self-protection more highly than self-insurance (see Shogren 1988, for the proof).

In terms of private versus collective risk reduction, if the individual can always produce a given reduction at less cost privately than collectively, he will do so (see Shogren and Crocker, 1990b). The individual's preference for collective or private reduction will depend on the perceived productivity of his payment. The collective reduction may prove more efficient given scale economics, since many private actions are too expensive or complicated to be economically feasible. If the individual perceives excessive free-riding behavior, however, collective action will not be valued as highly as private action. It follows that large collective values exist only when the individual is an inefficient private self-protector, or if he is uninformed about private opportunities.

The second issue in experimental design is how individual value reductions take place over a range of risk. Both psychologists and economists have observed systematic violations of the *linearity in probabilities* property of the independence axiom in expected utility theory (see Machina, 1982, 1983; Covello, 1984). Studies have found individuals to be oversensitive to changes in the probability of low-risk events, and undersensitive to high-risk events (e.g., Fischhoff et al., 1984; Viscusi and Magat, 1987). This violation is particularly damaging, since it implies non-recovery of the von Neumann–Morgenstern expected utility function. To examine this issue, a range of lotteries was constructed to determine if and how behavior in low-risk lotteries differs from behavior in high-risk lotteries. We used a binary lottery to construct the risks $(\pi, -\$L; (1 - \pi), +\$G)$, where $\pi (0 \leq \pi \leq 1)$ is the probability of a monetary loss $\$L$, and $(1 - \pi)$ is the probability of a monetary gain $\$G$. In each experimental market, subjects were asked to report separate bids stating the maximum that they would be willing to pay to reduce four levels of risk (1%, 10%, 20%, and 40%).

The third issue in experimental design is to consider how individual values respond to repeated exposure to self-protection and self-insurance opportunities. Expenditures to reduce risk are rarely in terms of one-shot lifetime contributions. An individual's first market expenditure is often significantly different from his last. The first expenditure is based on prior information, which is often incorrect. From a Bayesian perspective, repeated exposure to the market will allow the individual to update his perception and, therefore, his value of a reduction in risk (see Viscusi, 1979). A market influences individual learning of value due to the learning-feedback environment of a repetitive framework. Therefore, to determine how multiple market exposure to alternative risk-reduction mechanisms affects value formation, we explore the dynamics of repeated market trials compared to a static one-shot response.

The experiment began by eliciting an inexperienced hypothetical bid (UEHB) for each level of risk. The UEHB bid was not binding and did not influence take-home pay, and the lotteries were not resolved. Next, ten nonhypothetical bids were elicited in sequentially repeated trials for each risk (T1–T10). These ten bids were binding and did influence take-home pay, and the lotteries were resolved. Finally, an experienced hypothetical bid (EHB) was obtained. Each subject reported a total of 48 bids.

Table 1 summarizes the experimental design and economic hypotheses. The actual instructions for the private self-protection market are in the appendix. See Shogren (1988) for a detailed description of the experimental design, and the instructions for the other experimental markets.[1]

2. Experimental results

One hundred and twenty subjects participated in the experiment. All subjects were recruited from the undergraduate program at Appalachian State University.[2] Five experiment sessions with six subjects each were run for each of the four asset markets. Table 2 summarizes the results for risk reductions for all four asset markets and levels of risk (lottery periods).[3] The first two columns describe the four experimental asset markets and the four probabilities (risks) of a potential loss in assets. The table reports two measures of central tendency for each bid (inexperienced hypothetical bid, average nonhypothetical bid over ten trials, and experienced hypothetical bid), namely, the estimated mean and median in dollars, and one measure of dispersion, the estimated variance.[4]

2.1. Risk valuation is sensitive to the risk-reduction mechanism

To examine the impact of alternative risk-reduction mechanisms, we first compare the private and collective markets, and then compare the self-protection and self-insurance markets. The private risk-reduction markets were organized as a Vickrey sealed-bid

Table 1. Summary of experimental design

Experimental structure	Economic hypotheses
A. *Alternative risk-reduction mechanisms:* Private self-protection Private self-insurance Collective self-protection Collective self-insurance	Does the risk-reduction mechanism matter? Are individuals indifferent to private versus collective mechanisms? Are individuals indifferent to mechanisms that influence probability versus severity?
B. *Valuation over a range of risks:* $L = [\pi, -\$L; (1 - \pi), +\$G]$ where $\pi = 1\%, 10\%, 20\%,$ or 40% probability of a loss $(-\$L)$	Do individuals overestimate changes in the probability of low-risk events? If so, how does overestimation respond to the alternative risk-reduction mechanisms over repeated trials?
C. *Valuation over repeated market trials:* Inexperienced hypothetical bid (UEHB) Repeated nonhypothetical bids (T1–T10) Experienced hypothetical bid (EHB)	Does repeated exposure to the market induce rapid value formation for risk reductions? Are initial one-shot bids significantly different from final experienced bids?

Table 2. Summary statistic of experimental asset markets for risk reduction

Asset Market[a]	Probability of a loss	Inexperienced hypothetical bid (UEHB)			Average nonhypothetical bid (ANB)			Experienced hypothetical bid (EHB)		
		Mean	Median	Variance	Mean	Median	Variance	Mean	Median	Variance
1. Self-protection	1%	2.73	1.50	11.72	0.78	0.38	0.94	0.81	0.35	2.08
(private)	10%	2.87	3.00	5.42	1.09	2.98	1.42	1.13	1.38	4.19
	20%	3.35	3.08	5.40	2.93	3.36	1.49	3.45	3.50	3.80
	40%	4.62	4.00	7.45	3.93	3.70	2.66	4.37	4.00	4.57
2. Self-insurance	1%	1.85	0.50	10.35	0.09	0.07	0.02	0.07	0.03	2.01
(private)	10%	2.93	2.28	6.23	1.09	0.79	1.10	1.13	0.86	0.92
	20%	3.93	4.00	5.26	2.56	2.16	2.69	2.44	2.25	2.59
	40%	4.91	5.00	5.32	3.35	3.31	1.81	3.33	3.58	1.87
3. Self-protection	1%	2.79	1.00	12.37	0.84	0.06	3.30	0.78	0.06	3.97
(collective)	10%	2.74	2.00	6.57	0.80	0.54	0.60	0.75	0.48	0.89
	20%	2.77	3.00	3.04	1.27	1.02	0.89	1.00	0.90	0.32
	40%	3.04	3.00	2.39	2.13	2.02	1.46	2.09	2.00	1.34
4. Self-insurance	1%	0.97	0.50	2.82	0.77	0.06	7.09	0.78	0.02	0.03
(collective)	10%	1.25	1.00	1.03	0.70	0.50	0.77	0.43	0.38	0.20
	20%	1.81	2.00	0.91	1.26	0.88	2.23	1.11	1.00	1.21
	40%	2.55	2.50	2.22	1.95	1.41	3.19	1.73	1.21	2.14

[a]n = 30 for each asset market: five experiments with six subjects each.

NOTE: We do not accept the null hypothesis that the population mean is zero at the .01 level using a one-tailed test for all UEHB, ANB, and EHB bids across asset markets and lottery periods.

second-price auction (Vickrey, 1961). Each subject competes for the purchase of protection or insurance. The winner is the subject with the highest bid who pays the second highest bid for a 100% reduction in risk. Both the winner and second bid were posted as the only public information for each auction.[5]

The collective risk-reduction markets were organized as modified sealed-bid Smith auctions (Smith, 1980). The Smith auction works as follows. Each subject provides a bid to reduce risk to zero. If the sum of the bids equals or exceeds the costs of providing a 100% reduction in risk, then an adjusted (or average) bid is posted as the reigning price of protection or insurance. Acceptance by the collective of the price occurs only if all members agree. If at least one subject disagrees, then everyone is subject to a controlled draw of the lottery. If the sum of bids does not exceed costs, then a controlled draw of the lottery occurs.[6]

Table 3 shows that the experienced hypothetical bid (EHB) for private risk reductions exceeded the bid for collective reductions (with one exception). Using a Wilcoxon rank-sum test, we did not accept the hypothesis that the mean EHBs for the respective private risk reduction through self-protection or self-insurance were derived from the same parental distribution as the collective reductions.

Table 3 also indicates that for the four risks the mean bids for private self-protection exceeded those for private self-insurance. A Wilcoxon rank-sum test at the 95% confidence level indicates that the experienced hypothetical bids for private self-protection are significantly different from the bids for private self-insurance for all lottery periods.

IMPACT OF SELF-PROTECTION AND SELF-INSURANCE ON INDIVIDUAL RESPONSE 197

Table 3. Wilcoxon rank-sum tests between risk-reduction mechanisms: Experienced hypothetical bid (EHB)

Market	Risk	Test statistic
Private vs. Collective		
Self-protection	1%	1.936[a]
	10%	3.374[a]
	20%	5.073[a]
	40%	4.883[a]
Self-insurance	1%	0.576
	10%	3.882[a]
	20%	4.142[a]
	40%	3.996[a]
Self-protection vs. self-insurance		
Private	1%	3.214[a]
	10%	2.595[a]
	20%	2.837[a]
	40%	1.990[a]
Collective	1%	1.702
	10%	1.289
	20%	0.059
	40%	1.718

[a]Significant at 95% level that bids were not derived from the same parental distribution.

Respondents were willing to pay more for the private mechanism that influenced probability than for the mechanism that influenced severity. This result contradicts Boyer and Dionne's (1983) claim that private self-insurance will be preferred to self-protection. The result supports Shogren's (1988) argument that since self-protection guarantees a monetary gain, it will be preferred to self-insurance, which only guarantees that one will not suffer a loss. Respondents were not willing to pay more, however, for collective mechanisms that influence probability relative to severity. A Wilcoxon rank-sum test indicates that in all probability periods, the differences between experienced hypothetical bids for collective self-protection and those for collective self-insurance are not statistically significant.

In general, the mechanism, whether it is private or collective or whether probability or severity is reduced, is important when eliciting an economic value for a reduction in risk. Our results indicate the upper bound on value was the private, self-protection market. The lower bound on value was the collective, self-insurance market.

The disparity in private and collective values may be due to the free-riding incentive in the collective mechanism. Individuals have an incentive to underreport willingness to pay for nonhypothetical reduced risk.[7] As noted by Bennett (1987), strategic behavior between collective bidders often occurs in Smith auctions even though collective optimality is attained. Smith (1980) found that although optimal aggregate levels of public good were provided, it was often only because the underreported values were balanced by overreported values. This balancing-out phenomenon was also observed in our experimental markets. A larger proportion of subjects bid over, rather than under, the expected consumer surplus. However, this proportion declined over repeated market exposure.

The results have implications for the mechanism used to elicit individual preference for reduced risk. Traditionally, the mechanism is a collective scheme in which an agency exogenously reduces a risk if the sum of individual payments (i.e., higher taxes, group fund) exceeds the costs of reduction (e.g., Weinstein et al., 1980; Smith and Desvousges, 1987). A large number of risks, however, can be reduced privately through self-protection or self-insurance mechanisms. By allowing private risk reduction, our results indicate that traditional use of collective mechanisms may in fact only be a lower bound on the economic value of a reduction in risk.

2.2. Overestimation of low risks declines with repeated market trials

To determine if respondents in the experimental asset markets overemphasize small probabilities and underemphasize large probabilities, we examine the individual's risk preference in terms of a risk premium. A risk premium is the amount above expected consumer surplus that the risk-averse individual is willing to pay ex ante to eliminate the risk of losing L of his or her assets. If the individual overemphasizes small probabilities, then the risk premium for eliminating a 1% probability of a loss should exceed the risk premiums for a 10%, 20%, and 40% probability. Table 4 reports the summary statistic for the four asset markets over the four levels of risk. The individual is risk-averse (-neutral/-loving) if the ratio of bid to expected consumer surplus is greater than (equal to/less than) unity.

Respondents were initially extremely risk-averse, overestimating the 1% probability of a loss in the initial inexperienced nonhypothetical bid. With repeated market exposure through ten nonhypothetical trials, however, the overestimation declined, especially in the self-insurance markets. Although the risk premium for the 1% probability for the self-protection experienced hypothetical bids is still larger than the other levels of risk, oversensitivity declines rapidly with market experience.[8] The result supports Plott and Sunder's (1982) argument that for a well-defined, mature market environment, expected utility is "not universally misleading about the nature of human capabilities and markets" (p. 692).

The observed tendency to overestimate low-probability events has led to safety and health regulation that promote hazard warnings as regulatory alternatives to direct constraints on use or availability (see Viscusi et al., 1986). The evidence indicates that the overall efficacy of hazard warnings is governed not only by the risk level, but also by the information content. Our experiments indicate that the self-insurance markets disseminated information such that consumer valuations were broadly consistent with rational behavior. In both the private and collective self-insurance markets, strict privacy with public information only about the market was sufficient to produce rational behavior. Irrelevant or inefficient information was forced out of the market. As Hayek (1945) notes, ". . . the most significant fact about this (market) system is the economy of knowledge with which it operates, or how little the individual participants need to know in order to take the right action . . ." (p. 35). Consequently, risk information necessary to induce rational risk valuations may well be generated in repeated exposure to risk-reduction markets that

IMPACT OF SELF-PROTECTION AND SELF-INSURANCE ON INDIVIDUAL RESPONSE   199

Table 4. Summary statistic of risk premiums

Risk	Asset market	Inexperienced hypothetical bid Mean/$E[CS]$[a]	Average nonhypothetical bid Mean/$E[CS]$	Experienced hypothetical bid Mean/$E[CS]$
1%	SP[b]	54.60[c]	15.60	16.20
	SI	37.00	1.79	1.41
	CSP	55.80	16.84	15.52
	CSI	19.40	15.40	1.40
10%	SP	5.74	3.48	4.04
	SI	5.80	2.18	2.26
	CSP	5.48	1.60	1.51
	CSI	2.50	1.40	0.86
20%	SP	3.35	2.93	3.45
	SI	3.93	2.56	2.44
	CSP	2.77	1.27	1.00
	CSI	1.81	1.26	1.11
40%	SP	2.31	1.97	2.19
	SI	2.46	1.73	1.67
	CSP	1.52	1.06	1.04
	CSI	1.28	0.98	0.87

[a]$E[CS]$ represents expected consumer surplus $E[CS]$ = $1, $.5, $.05, and $2 for probability = 20%, 10%, 1%, and 40%.
[b]SP: private self-protection; SI: private self-insurance; CSP: collective self-protection; CSI: collective self-insurance
[c]Mean/$E[CS]$ > 1 (= 1/< 1) implies risk aversion (neutrality/lover).

focus on severity. This observation is borne out by Brookshire et al.'s (1985) demonstration that expected utility is a capable predictor of behavior regarding earthquake hazards and self-insurance.

2.3. Repeated market trials induced rapid value formation

Coppinger et al. (1980), Coursey et al. (1987), and others have noted that a *number* of trial iterations are required before the respondent realizes that revealing "true" values is the dominant strategy in a Vickrey or Smith auction. Therefore, it is striking how rapidly respondents adjust their initial inexperienced hypothetical bid (UEHB) in all risk-reduction markets. Learning and adjustment to a dominant strategy occur during the first few nonhypothetical trials. The immediate feedback environment of the experiments induce rapid value formation.[9]

Table 5 illustrates that after the first three trial bids (T1–T3), the remaining trial bids relative to the experienced hypothetical bid (EHB) revealed relatively minor adjustments in value. Using a one-tailed Wilcoxon matched-sample test conducted at the 95% confidence level, we did not accept the hypothesis that the initial inexperienced bid (UEHB) and the EHB were derived from the identical parental distribution in 87.5% of the cases. The majority of initial UEHBs differed significantly from the final EHB. However, this

JASON F. SHOGREN

Table 5. Wilcoxon matched-sampled sign test between the experienced hypothetical bid (EHB) and bids over the repeated market trials

Asset market	Risk (%)	UEHB Z^a	P^b	T1 Z	P	T2 Z	P	T3 Z	P
Private self-protection	1	-3.111^d	.00	-0.015	.99	—	—	—	—
	10	-2.287^d	.02	-1.251	.21	—	—	—	—
	20	-0.900	.37	-2.676^d	.01	-2.490^d	.01	-1.893	.07
	40	-0.659	.51	-2.327^d	.02	-2.798^d	.01	-3.429^d	$.00^c$
Private self-insurance	1	-3.772^d	.00	-1.338	.18	—	—	—	—
	10	-3.945^d	.00	-0.152	.88	—	—	—	—
	20	-3.730^d	.00	-1.764	.08	—	—	—	—
	40	-3.038^d	.00	-2.198^d	.03	-1.686	.09	—	—
Collective self-protection	1	-4.076^d	.00	-1.399	.16	—	—	—	—
	10	-4.444^d	.00	-2.391^d	.02	-2.277^d	.02	-0.744	.46
	20	-4.360^d	.00	-3.495^d	.00	-0.699	.48	—	—
	40	-2.550^d	.01	-1.069	.29	—	—	—	—
Collective self-insurance	1	-4.373^d	.00	-3.736^d	.00	-2.877^d	.00	-1.448	.15
	10	-4.474^d	.00	-2.607^d	.01	-2.184^d	.03	-0.209	.83
	20	-3.712^d	.00	-1.812	.07	—	—	—	—
	40	-3.014^d	.00	-1.457	.15	—	—	—	—

[a] Test statistic.
[b] Observed significance level.
[c] At trial T6, there was no significant difference at the 95% level ($Z = -1.802$ and $P = .07$).
[d] Significant statistical difference at 95% level.

difference decreased substantially with just one or two additional market exposures. In the first nonhypothetical market T1, the number of cases in which T1 differed significantly from the EHB fell to 43.8%. In T2, this declined again to 31.3%. Finally, after only three trials in the market, in only 6.3% of the cases was the T3 bid significantly different from the final EHB. The bids in the remaining trials T4–T10 remained constant with minor fluctuations.

Although we find that the initial UEHB differed significantly from the first trial bid T1, the final EHB did not differ significantly from the first few nonhypothetical trial bids. The results indicate that after the initial UEHB, only one or two nonhypothetical trials were needed to induce rapid value formation. Consequently, misperception of risk may only be a potentially damaging bias if no learning or second-chance bid adjustment is allowed to compensate for incorrect prior information.

Traditional fears of risk misperception have originated from the static framework used in examining individual behavior under risk (see, for example, Lattimore et al., 1988).[10] Our evidence suggests that the static framework does not capture the individual's value formation process, which requires additional trial periods of market feedback or new information. Research on sequential decisions involving learning (e.g., Viscusi, 1979; Viscusi and Magat, 1987) is the more appropriate direction for examining the importance of feedback and value formation in determining accurate measures of value (see also Coursey and Schulze, 1986).

IMPACT OF SELF-PROTECTION AND SELF-INSURANCE ON INDIVIDUAL RESPONSE   201

3. Conclusions

Four alternative risk-reduction mechanisms were considered in experimental markets to determine how individuals respond to and value reduced risk. Our results indicate that private self-protection provides an upper bound on value, while collective self-insurance provides the lower bound. The significant differences in value estimates by the four risk-reduction mechanisms indicate that the current focus on collective self-protection captures only one of four possible values of risk reduction. Future attempts to estimate the value of reduced risk should consider the other three mechanisms to reveal value; by doing so, a more comprehensive view of value will be obtained.

In addition, the four reduction mechanisms with immediate market information feedback induced rapid learning and decreased misperception of risk. Usually, value formation was complete after one or two additional market trials. Note, however, that the robustness of these results declined during the 1% lottery period. The addition of repeated trials, however, still induced value formation to a degree closer to that predicted by expected utility theory, especially in the self-insurance markets that focused on the reduction of severity.

Appendix

[S-P]

Instructions

General

You are about to participate in an experiment about decision making under risk and uncertainty. The purpose of the experiment is to gain insight into certain features of economic processes. If you follow the instructions carefully you can earn money. You will be paid in cash at the end of the experiment.

Specific Instructions

You will be asked to make several decisions. Each decision will involve stating your maximum willingness-to-pay to eliminate a potential risk. *You are not to reveal your bid to any other participant. Note that any communication between bidders during a trial will result in an automatic loss of $4.*

Over the course of the experiment, you will be asked to bid your maximum willingness to pay to prevent a loss of $4 for a series of different probability periods (40%, 20%, 10%, and 1%). For example, given an initial starting income of $10, if there is a 60% chance that you will gain $1, and a 40% chance that you will lose $4, what is the maximum you would be willing to pay to guarantee a 100% chance of winning $1 and a 0% chance of losing $4?

_____ . There will be ten bidding trials in each probability period. Note that for each trial the starting income will always be $10. Your gains or losses do not carry over to the next trial or probability period.

Each participant is competing to purchase the right to protect himself/herself from a certain probability of a $4 loss. The participant with the highest willingness-to-pay bid wins this right of protection and will be guaranteed a 0% chance of a $4 loss and a 100% chance of a $1 gain. The highest bidder *must in all cases* pay the bid of the second highest bidder. All other participants are then subject to a random draw to determine if a loss or gain occurs. Note that in the event that there is a tie for the highest bid, those participants will be asked to rebid.

The actual experiment will proceed as follows:

Step 1: At the beginning of the experiment you will state a separate hypothetical bid for reducing each of the four probabilities of a loss to zero.

Step 2: The experimenter selects a probability period.

Step 3: Ten bidding trials will be run for the selected probability period.

Step 4: At the beginning of each bidding trial for a given probability period, you will state a bid by writing it on the recording card. Note that your initial income remains at $10 for each trial regardless of your winnings or losses in the trial periods before.

Step 5: After the recording card has been collected from each participant, the experimenter will display the winner (the highest bidder) and the price of protection on the blackboard. The winner must pay the displayed price of protection.

Step 6: The experimenter will then draw one chip from the urn. A white chip results in a $1 gain for everyone, a red chip results in a $4 loss for everyone (except the highest bidder).

Step 7: After ten trial periods, a final hypothetical bid will be elicited for the probability period.

Step 8: The process will repeat until all four probability periods have been examined. Your take-home income will consist of your initial income plus or minus your gains, losses, and purchases of protection.

Are there any questions?

Notes

1. The experimental design follows that of Schulze et al. (1986). Schulze et al., however, only consider one of the four markets described in this article, private self-insurance.
2. Bennett (1987) found that there was no statistically significant difference between student responses and those of respondents representative of the general population. This suggests that experimentation may be "satisfactorily performed using student groups" (p. 367).
3. The experimental parameters were consistent across asset markets and lottery periods: initial asset endowment M = $10; monetary loss in assets L = $4; and monetary gain in assets G = $1. The collective costs for self-protection and self-insurance in the same lottery period equaled the sum of expected consumer surplus C = $0.3 (1% risk), $3 (10% risk), $6 (20% risk), and $12 (40% risk). The expected consumer's surplus (ES) equaled the difference between the maximum lottery income ($M + G$) and the expected value of the lottery $EV = P(M - L) + (1 - P)(M + G)$. For example, in the 20% lottery period, ES = (10 + 1) − .2(10 − 4) − .8(10 + 1) = $1.
4. Forsythe et al. (1982) note the frustrating "open problems that are being encountered in almost all experimental work where the costs of conducting experiments places a significant constraint on the number of

IMPACT OF SELF-PROTECTION AND SELF-INSURANCE ON INDIVIDUAL RESPONSE 203

observations" (p. 549). Given the sample size of n = 30 for each asset market, one must heed Forsythe et al.'s (1982) warning that "statistical tests we report should be regarded more as measures than classical hypothesis tests" (p. 549).

5. Since Vickrey's (1961) initial utilization, the second-price auction mechanism has well-known demand-revealing properties. The subject's dominant strategy is to reveal full preferences, since the subject does not pay what he or she bids. Incentives for false bids do not exist. As Coursey (1987) notes, the use of the Vickrey auction allows one to assume "that behavior in situations where *values* are being measured will be well approximated in situations where values are *induced*" (p. 293). As such, the Vickrey auction completes the identification of Smith's (1982) triad of components specific to behavior: the environment (including values), the instrument or institution, and the actual observed behavior.

6. Communications among subjects is forbidden. The experimenter sets the costs of C of 100% risk reduction equal to the sum of expected consumer surplus given the lottery period. Costs were not posted. The Smith auction process was modified in three ways: (1) given a 100% risk reduction, subjects were not asked to provide bids for the quantity of collective good, (2) no rebate rule was used, and (3) there was no stopping rule after unanimous agreement—all 12 auctions were completed.

7. Note that this incentive to understate willingness to pay is due to the nonhypothetical nature of the ten market trials. The subjects' take-home pay was determined by their bids. In hypothetical markets where subjects do not actually pay for protection or insurance, one might find results to support the old notion that individual overstate their bids to bias the results toward certain provision of the public good. Since the individuals do not actually pay anything, they have an incentive to overstate their preferences. Our results indicate that given repeated nonhypothetical market exposure, there was no overstating on the final experienced hypothetical bid (EHB). The EHB behaved similarly to the nonhypothetical bids (T1-T10).

8. Kunreuther et al. (1985) noted the substantial empirical evidence suggesting that individuals are unwilling to insure or protect themselves against low-probability/high-severity events. In light of this finding, our results support a notion of preference reversal in that the willingness to pay a risk premium was the highest for the low-probability lottery. Yet apparently this behavior is reversed in real-world risks, as evidenced by the usage of seat belts and federally subsidized flood insurance (Kunreuther et al., 1985).

9. The speed of convergence could be dependent on the parameters of the experimental market. However, in other experimental contexts, a parameter such as group size has had mixed results in altering the speed of convergence. For example, Smith (1982) notes that allocations and prices converge to predicted competitive equilibrium outcomes within three to four trading periods or less. This result holds with a few as six to eight buyers and as few as two sellers (propositions 4 and 5, p. 945).

10. Lattimore et al. (1988) found that the expected utility model did not fare well in comparison to the probability-transform model of Yaari (1987). However, their experiment was designed as a one-shot decision problem. The subjects did not have an opportunity to learn from repeated action in the market. Consequently, there was no opportunity to update incorrect prior perceptions of risk.

References

Bennett, J. (1987). "Strategic Behavior," *Journal of Public Economics* 32, 355–368.

Boyer, M. and G. Dionne. (1983). "Variations in the Probability and Magnitude of Loss: Their Impacts on Risk," *Canadian Journal of Economics* 16, 409–419.

Brookshire, D., M. Thayer, J. Tschirhart, and W. Schulze. (1985). "A Test of the Expected Utility Model: Evidence from Earthquake Risks," *Journal of Political Economy* 93, 369–389.

Centner, T., and M. Wetzstein. (1987). "Reducing Moral Hazard Associated with Implied Warranties of Animal Health," *American Journal of Agricultural Economics* 69, 143–150.

Change, Y.-M., and I. Ehrlich. (1985). "Insurance, Protection from Risk, and Risk-Bearing," *Canadian Journal of Economics* 18, 574–586.

Coppinger, V., V.L. Smith, and J. Titus. (1980). "Incentives and Behavior in English, Dutch and Sealed-Bid Auctions," *Economic Inquiry* 18, 1–22.

Coursey, D. (1987). "Markets and the Measurement of Value," *Public Choice* 55, 291–297.

Coursey, D., J. Hovis, and W. Schulze. (1987). "The Disparity Between Willingness to Accept and Willingness to Pay Measures of Value," *Quarterly Journal of Economics* 102, 679–690.

Coursey, D., and W. Schulze. (1986). "The Application of Laboratory Experimental Economics to the Contingent Valuation of Public Goods," *Public Choice* 49, 47–68.

Covello, V. (1984). "Actual and Perceived Risk: A Review of the Literature." In P. Ricci, L. Sagen, and C. Whipple (eds.), *Technological Risk Assessment* The Hague: Martinus Nijhoff Publishers, pp. 225–246.

Ehrlich, I. and G. Becker. (1972). "Market Insurance, Self-Protection, and Self-Insurance," *Journal of Political Economy* 80, 623–648.

Fischhoff, B., et al. (1984). *Acceptable Risk*. Cambridge: Cambridge University Press.

Forsythe, R., T. Palfrey, and C. Plott. (1982). "Asset Valuation in an Experimental Market," *Econometrica* 50, 537–567.

Hayek, F. (1945). "The Use of Knowledge in Society," *American Economic Review* 35, 519–530.

Hiebert, L. (1983). "Self-Insurance, Self-Protection, and the Theory of the Competitive Firm," *Southern Economic Journal* 50, 160–168.

Kunreuther, H., W. Sanderson, and R. Vetschera. (1985). "A Behavioral Model of the Adoption of Protective Activities," *Journal of Economic Behavior and Organization* 6, 1–15.

Lattimore, P., A. Whittle, and J. Baker. (1988). "An Empirical Assessment of Alternative Models of Risky Decision Making," NBER (National Bureau of Economic Research) working paper no. 2717.

Machina, M. (1982). " 'Expected Utility' Analysis without the Independence Axiom," *Econometrica* 50, 277–323.

Machina, M. (1983). "The Economic Theory of Individual Behavior Toward Risk: Theory, Evidence, and New Directions," Technical Report No. 433, Stanford University.

Plott, C., and S. Sunder. (1982). "Efficiency of Experimental Securities Markets with Insider Information: An Application of Rational Expectations Models," *Journal of Political Economy* 90, 663–698.

Schulze, W., G. McClelland, and D. Coursey. (1986). "Valuing Risk: A Comparison of Expected Utility with Models from Cognitive Psychology," unpublished manuscript.

Shogren, J. (1988). "Valuing Risk in Experimental Markets: Self-Protection, Self-Insurance, and Collective Action," final draft report, U.S. Environmental Protection Agency.

Shogren, J., and T. Crocker. (1990a). Risk, Self-Protection, and Ex Ante Economic Value, *Journal of Environmental Economics and Management* (forthcoming).

Shogren, J., and T. Crocker. (1990b). "Adaptation and the Option Value of Uncertain Environmental Resources," *Ecological Economics* (forthcoming).

Smith, V.K., and W. Desvousges. (1987). "An Empirical Analysis of the Economic Value of Risk Changes," *Journal of Political Economy* 95, 89–114.

Smith, V.L. (1980). "Experiments with a Decentralized Mechanism for Public Good Decisions," *American Economic Review* 70, 548–590.

Smith, V.L. (1982). "Microeconomic Systems as an Experimental Science," *American Economic Review* 72, 923–955.

Tversky, A., and D. Kahneman. (1981). "The Framing of Decisions and the Psychology of Choice," *Science* 211, 453–458.

Vickrey, W. (1961). "Counterspeculation, Auctions and Competitive Sealed Tenders," *Journal of Finance* 16, 8–37.

Viscusi, W.K. (1979). "Insurance and Individual Incentives in Adaptive Contexts," *Econometrica* 47, 1195–1207.

Viscusi, W.K., W. Magat, and J. Huber. (1986). "Information Regulation of Consumer Health Risks: An Empirical Evaluation of Hazard Warnings," *Rand Journal of Economics* 17, 351–365.

Viscusi, W.K., and W. Magat. (1987). *Learning about Risk: Consumer and Worker Responses to Hazard Information*. Cambridge: Harvard University Press.

Weinstein, M., D. Shepard, and J. Pliskin. (1980). "The Economic Value of Changing Mortality Probabilities: A Decision-Theoretic Approach," *Quarterly Journal of Economics* 94, 373–396.

Yaari, M. (1987). "The Dual Theory of Choice Under Risk," *Econometrica* 55, 95–115.

[13]

The Endowment Effect, Loss Aversion, and Status Quo Bias

Daniel Kahneman, Jack L. Knetsch, and Richard H. Thaler

Economics can be distinguished from other social sciences by the belief that most (all?) behavior can be explained by assuming that agents have stable, well-defined preferences and make rational choices consistent with those preferences in markets that (eventually) clear. An empirical result qualifies as an anomaly if it is difficult to "rationalize," or if implausible assumptions are necessary to explain it within the paradigm. This column presents a series of such anomalies. Readers are invited to suggest topics for future columns by sending a note with some reference to (or better yet copies of) the relevant research. Comments on anomalies printed here are also welcome. The address is: Richard Thaler, c/o Journal of Economic Perspectives, Johnson Graduate School of Management, Malott Hall, Cornell University, Ithaca, NY 14853.

After this issue, the "Anomalies" column will no longer appear in every issue and instead will appear occasionally, when a pressing anomaly crosses Dick Thaler's desk. However, suggestions for new columns and comments on old ones are still welcome. Thaler would like to quash one rumor before it gets started, namely that he is cutting back because he has run out of anomalies. *Au contraire*, it is the dilemma of choosing which juicy anomaly to discuss that takes so much time.

■ *Daniel Kahneman is Professor of Psychology, University of California, Berkeley, California. Jack L. Knetsch is Professor of Economics and Natural Resources Management, Simon Fraser University, Burnaby, British Columbia, Canada. Richard H. Thaler is Henrietta Johnson Louis Professor of Economics, Johnson School of Management, Cornell University, Ithaca, New York.*

Introduction

A wine-loving economist we know purchased some nice Bordeaux wines years ago at low prices. The wines have greatly appreciated in value, so that a bottle that cost only $10 when purchased would now fetch $200 at auction. This economist now drinks some of this wine occasionally, but would neither be willing to sell the wine at the auction price nor buy an additional bottle at that price.

Thaler (1980) called this pattern—the fact that people often demand much more to give up an object than they would be willing to pay to acquire it—the *endowment effect*. The example also illustrates what Samuelson and Zeckhauser (1988) call a *status quo bias*, a preference for the current state that biases the economist against both buying *and* selling his wine. These anomalies are a manifestation of an asymmetry of value that Kahneman and Tversky (1984) call *loss aversion*—the disutility of giving up an object is greater that the utility associated with acquiring it. This column documents the evidence supporting endowment effects and status quo biases, and discusses their relation to loss aversion.

The Endowment Effect

An early laboratory demonstration of the endowment effect was offered by Knetsch and Sinden (1984). The participants in this study were endowed with either a lottery ticket or with $2.00. Some time later, each subject was offered an opportunity to trade the lottery ticket for the money, or vice versa. Very few subjects chose to switch. Those who were given lottery tickets seemed to like them better than those who were given money.

This demonstration and other similar ones (Knetsch, 1989), while striking, did not settle the matter. Some economists felt that the behavior would disappear if subjects were exposed to a market environment with ample learning opportunities. For example, Knez, Smith and Williams (1985) argued that the discrepancy between buying and selling prices might be produced by the thoughtless application of normally sensible bargaining habits, namely understating one's true willingness to pay (WTP) and overstating the minimum acceptable price at which one would sell (willingness to accept or WTA). Coursey, Hovis, and Schultze (1987) reported that the discrepancy between WTP and WTA diminished with experience in a market setting (although it was probably not eliminated, see Knetsch and Sinden, 1987). To clarify the issue, Kahneman, Knetsch, and Thaler (1990) ran a new series of experiments to determine whether the endowment effect survives when subjects face market discipline and have a chance to learn. We will report just two experiments from that series.

Daniel Kahneman, Jack L. Knetsch, and Richard H. Thaler   195

In the first experiment, students in an advanced undergraduate economics class at Cornell University participated in a series of markets. The objects traded in the first three markets were 'induced value tokens.' In such markets all subjects are told how much a token is worth to them, with the amounts varying across subjects. Half the subjects were made owners of tokens, the other half were not. In this way, supply and demand curves for tokens are created. Subjects alternated between the buyer and seller role in the three successive markets, and were assigned a different individual redemption value in each trial. Experimenters collected the forms from all participants after each market period, and immediately calculated and announced the market-clearing price and the number of trades. Three buyers and three sellers were selected at random after each of the induced markets and were paid off according to the preferences stated on their forms and the market clearing price for that period.

These markets contained no grist for the anomaly mill. On each trial, the market clearing price was exactly equal to the intersection of the induced supply and demand curves, and the volume of trade was within one unit of the predicted quantity. These results demonstrate that the subjects understood the task, and that the market mechanism used did not impose high transactions costs.

Immediately after the three induced value markets, subjects on alternating seats were given Cornell coffee mugs, which sell for $6.00 each at the bookstore. The experimenter asked all participants to examine a mug, either their own or their neighbor's. The experimenter then informed the subjects that four markets for mugs would be conducted using the same procedures as the prior induced markets with two exceptions: (1) One of the four market trials would subsequently be selected at random and only the trades made on this trial would be executed. (2) On the binding market trial, *all* trades would be implemented, unlike the subset implemented in the induced value markets. The initial assignment of buyer and seller roles was maintained for all four trading periods. The clearing price and the number of trades were announced after each period. The market that "counted" was indicated after the fourth period, and transactions were executed immediately—all sellers who had indicated that they would give up their mug at the market clearing price exchanged their mugs for cash, and successful buyers paid this same price and received their mug. This design was used to permit learning to take place over successive trials and yet make each trial potentially binding. The same procedure was then followed for four more successive markets using boxed ball-point pens with a visible bookstore price tag of $3.98, which were distributed to the subjects who had been buyers in the mug markets.

What does economic theory predict will happen in these markets for mugs and pens? Since transactions costs have been shown to be insignificant in the induced value markets, and income effects are trivial, a clear prediction is available: When the market clears, the objects will be owned by those subjects who value them most. Call the half of the subjects who like mugs the most "mug lovers" and the half who like mugs least "mug haters." Then, since the mugs were assigned at random, on average half of the mug lovers will be given a mug, and half will not. This implies that in the market, half of the mugs should trade, with mug haters selling to mug lovers.

The 50 percent predicted volume of trade did not materialize. There were 22 mugs and pens distributed so the predicted number of trades was 11. In the four mug markets the number of trades was 4, 1, 2, and 2 respectively. In the pen markets the number of trades was either 4 or 5. In neither market was there any evidence of a trend over the four trials. The reason for the low volume of trade is revealed by the reservation prices of buyers and sellers. For mugs, the median owner was unwilling to sell for less than $5.25, while the median buyer was unwilling to pay more than $2.25-$2.75. The market price varied between $4.25 and $4.75. In the market for pens the ratio of selling to buying prices was also about 2. The experiment was replicated several times, always with similar results: median selling prices are about twice median buying prices and volume is less than half of that expected.

Another experiment from this series allows us to investigate whether the low volume of trading is produced by a reluctance to buy or a reluctance to sell. In this experiment, 77 students at Simon Fraser University were randomly assigned to three conditions. One group, the Sellers, were given SFU coffee mugs and were asked whether they would be willing to sell the mugs at each of a series of prices ranging from $0.25 to $9.25. A second group of Buyers were asked whether they would be willing to buy a mug at the same set of prices. The third group, called Choosers, were not given a mug but were asked to choose, for each of the prices, between receiving a mug or that amount of money.

Notice that the Sellers and the Choosers are in objectively identical situations, deciding at each price between the mug and that amount of money. Nevertheless, the Choosers behaved more like Buyers than like Sellers. The median reservation prices were: Sellers, $7.12; Choosers, $3.12; Buyers, $2.87. This suggests that the low volume of trade is produced mainly by owner's reluctance to part with their endowment, rather than by buyers' unwillingness to part with their cash. This experiment also eliminates the trivial income effect present in the first experiment, since the Sellers and Choosers are in the same economic situation.

One of the first lessons in microeconomics is that two indifference curves can never intersect. This result depends on the implicit assumption that indifference curves are reversible. That is, if an individual owns x and is indifferent between keeping it and trading it for y, then when owning y the individual should be indifferent about trading it for x. If loss aversion is present, however, this reversibility will no longer hold. Knetsch (1990) has demonstrated this point experimentally. One group of subjects received 5 medium priced ball point pens, while another group of subjects received $4.50. They were then made a series of offers which they could accept or reject. The offers were designed to identify an indifference curve. For example, someone

Figure 1
Crossing indifference curves

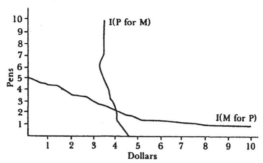

who had been given the pens would be asked if she would give up one of the
pens for a dollar. One of the accepted offers (including the original endowment) was selected at random at the end of the experiment to determine the
subject's payment. By plotting the line between accepted and rejected offers,
Knetsch was able to infer an indifference curve for each subject. Then he
plotted the average indifference curve for each of the two groups (those who
started with pens and those who started with money). These plots are shown in
Figure 1. The curves are quite different: the pens were worth more money to
those subjects who started with pens than to those who started with money. As
a result, the curves intersect.[1]

What produces these "instant endowment effects"? Do subjects who receive
a gift actually value it more than others who do not receive it? A recent study by
Loewenstein and Kahneman (1991) investigated this issue. Half the students in
a class ($N = 63$) were given pens, the others were given a token redeemable for
an unspecified gift. All participants were then asked to rank the attractiveness
of six gifts under consideration as prizes in subsequent experiments. Finally, all
the subjects were then given a choice between a pen and two chocolate bars. As
in previous experiments, there was a pronounced endowment effect. The pen
was preferred by 56 percent of those endowed with it, but only 24 percent of
the other subjects chose a pen. However, when making the attractiveness
ratings, the subjects endowed with pens did not rate them as more attractive.
This suggests that the main effect of endowment is not to enhance the appeal of
the good one owns, only the pain of giving it up.

Status Quo Bias

One implication of loss aversion is that individuals have a strong tendency
to remain at the status quo, because the disadvantages of leaving it loom larger

---

[1]These curves were obtained from different individuals. Because subjects were randomly assigned
to the two endowment groups, however, it is reasonable to attribute crossing indifference curves to
the representative individual.

than advantages. Samuelson and Zeckhauser (1988) have demonstrated this effect, which they term the *status quo bias*. In one experiment, some subjects were given a hypothetical choice task, such as the following, in a 'neutral' version in which no status quo is defined: "You are a serious reader of the financial pages but until recently have had few funds to invest. That is when you inherited a large sum of money from your great-uncle. You are considering different portfolios. Your choices are to invest in: a moderate-risk company, a high risk company, treasury bills, municipal bonds."

Other subjects were presented with the same problem but with one of the options designated as the status quo. In this case, after the same opening sentence the passage continues: "... That is when you inherited a portfolio of cash and securities from your great-uncle. A significant portion of this portfolio is invested in a moderate risk company.... (The tax and broker commission consequences of any change are insignificant.)"

Many different scenarios were investigated, all using the same basic experimental design. Aggregating across all the different questions, Samuelson and Zeckhauser are then able to estimate the probability that an option will be selected when it is the status quo or when it is competing as an alternative to the status quo as a function of how often it is selected in the neutral setting. Their results implied that an alternative became significantly more popular when it was designated as the status quo. Also, the advantage of the status quo increases with the number of alternatives.

A test of status quo bias in a field setting was performed by Hartman, Doane, and Woo (forthcoming) using a survey of California electric power consumers. The consumers were asked about their preferences regarding service reliability and rates. They were told that their answers would help determine company policy in the future. The respondents fell into two groups, one with much more reliable service than the other. Each group was asked to state a preference among six combinations of service reliabilities and rates, with one of the combinations designated as the status quo. The results demonstrated a pronounced status quo bias. In the high reliability group, 60.2 percent selected their status quo as their first choice, while only 5.7 percent expressed a preference for the low reliability option currently being experienced by the other group, though it came with a 30 percent reduction in rates. The low reliability group, however, quite liked their status quo, 58.3 percent of them ranking it first. Only 5.8 percent of this group selected the high reliability option at a proposed 30 percent increase in rates.[2]

---

[2] Differences in income and electricity consumption between the two groups were minor and did not appear to significantly influence the results. Could the results be explained by either learning of habituation? That is, might the low reliability group have learned to cope with frequent outages, or found out that candlelight dinners are romantic? This cannot be ruled out, but it should be stressed that no similar explanation can be used for the mug experiments or the surveys conducted by Samuelson and Zeckhauser, so at least some of the effects observed are attributable to a pure status quo bias.

Daniel Kahneman, Jack L. Knetsch, and Richard H. Thaler   199

A large-scale experiment on status quo bias is now being conducted (inadvertently) by the states of New Jersey and Pennsylvania. Both states now offer a choice between two types of automobile insurance: a cheaper policy that restricts the right to sue, and a more expensive one that maintains the unrestricted right. Motorists in New Jersey are offered the cheaper policy as the default option, with an opportunity to acquire an unrestricted right to sue at a higher price. Since this option was made available in 1988, 83 percent of the drivers have elected the default option. In Pennsylvania's 1990 law, however, the default option is the expensive policy, with an opportunity to opt for the cheaper kind. The potential effect of this legislative framing manipulation was studied by Hershey, Johnson, Meszaros, and Robinson (1990). They asked two groups to choose between alternative policies. One group was presented with the New Jersey plan while the other was presented with the Pennsylvania plan. Of those subjects offered the New Jersey plan, only 23 percent elected to buy the right to sue whereas 53 percent of the subjects offered the Pennsylvania plan retained that right. On the basis of this research, the authors predict that more Pennsylvanians will elect the right to sue than New Jerseyans. Time will tell.

One final example of a presumed status quo bias comes courtesy of the *JEP* staff. Among Carl Shapiro's comments on this column was this gem: "You may be interested to know that when the AEA was considering letting members elect to drop one of the three Association journals and get a credit, prominent economists involved in that decision clearly took the view that fewer members would choose to drop a journal if the default was presented as all three journals (rather than the default being 2 journals with an extra charge for getting all three). We're talking economists here."

Loss Aversion

These observations, and many others, can be explained by a notion of loss aversion. A central conclusion of the study of risky choice has been that such choices are best explained by assuming that the significant carriers of utility are not states of wealth or welfare, but changes relative to a neutral reference point. Another central result is that changes that make things worse (losses) loom larger than improvements or gains. The choice data imply an abrupt change of the slope of the value function at the origin. The existing evidence suggests that the ratio of the slopes of the value function in two domains, for small or moderate gains and losses of money, is about $2:1$ (Tversky and Kahneman, 1991). A schematic value function is shown in Figure 2.

The natural extension of this idea to riskless choice is that the attributes of options in trades and other transactions are also evaluated as gains and losses relative to a neutral reference point. The approach is illustrated in Figure 3. Decision makers have a choice between state *A*, where they have more of good

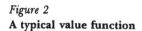

Figure 2
A typical value function

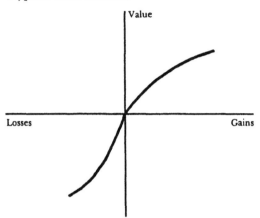

Y and less of good *X*, and state *D*, where they have more of good *X* and less of good *Y*. Four different reference points are indicated in the Figure. The individual faces a positive choice between two gains if the reference point is *C*, a negative choice between two losses if the reference point is *B*, and two different exchanges if the references are *A* or *D*, respectively. For example, if good *Y* is a mug and good *X* is money, the reference points for the sellers and the choosers in the mugs experiment are *A* and *C*. Loss aversion implies that the difference between the states of having a mug and not having one is larger from *A* than from *C*, which explains the different monetary values that subjects attach to the mug in these conditions.[3] For a formal treatment that generalizes consumer theory by introducing the notions of reference and loss aversion, see Tversky and Kahneman (1991).

In general, a given difference between two options will have greater impact if it is viewed as a difference between two disadvantages than if it is viewed as a difference between two advantages. The status quo bias is a natural consequence of this asymmetry: the disadvantages of a change loom larger than its advantages. However, the differential weighting of advantages and disadvantages can be demonstrated even when the retention of the status quo is not an option. For an example, consider the following question (from Tversky and Kahneman, 1991):

> Imagine that as part of your professional training you were assigned to a part-time job. The training is now ending and you must look for employ-

---

[3]Loss aversion does not affect all transactions. In a normal commercial transaction, the seller does not suffer a loss when trading a good. Furthermore, the evidence indicates that buyers do not value the money spent on normal purchases as a loss, so long as the price of the good is not thought to be unusually high. Loss aversion is expected to primarily affect owners of goods that had been bought for use rather than for eventual resale.

Figure 3
**Multiple reference points for the choice between
A and D**

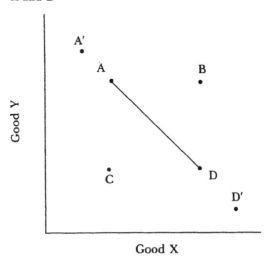

ment. You consider two possibilities. They are like your training job in
most respects except for the amount of social contact and the convenience
of commuting to and from work. To compare the two jobs to each other
and to the present one you have made up the following table:

Job	Contact with others	Commute Time
Present job	isolated for long stretches	10 min.
Job *A*	limited contact with others	20 min.
Job *D*	moderately sociable	60 min.

The options *A* and *D* are evaluated from a reference job which is better on
commute time and worse on personal contact (a point like *A'* in Figure 3).
Another version of the problem presented the same options, but the reference
job involved "much pleasant social interaction and 80 minutes of daily commuting time," which corresponds to the point *D'*. The proportion of subjects
choosing job *A* was 70 percent in the first version, 33 percent in the second.
Subjects are more sensitive to the dimension in which they are losing relative to
their reference point.

Some asymmetries between buying and selling prices are much too large to
be explained by garden-variety loss aversion. For example, Thaler (1980) told
subjects that they had been exposed to a rare fatal disease and that they now
face a .001 chance of painless death within two weeks. They must decide how
much they would be willing to pay for a vaccine, to be purchased immediately.
The same subjects were also asked for the compensation they would demand to

participate in a medical experiment in which they face a .001 chance of a quick and painless death. For most subjects the two prices differed by more than an order of magnitude.

A study by Viscusi, Magat and Huber (1987) documented a similar effect in a more realistic setting. Their respondents were recruited at a shopping mall and hardware store. The respondents were shown a can of fictitious insecticide, and were asked to examine it for their use. The current price of the can was said to be $10. Respondents were informed that all insecticide can cause injuries if misused, including inhalation and skin poisoning (in households with young children, child poisoning replaced skin poisoning). The current risk level was said to be 15 injuries of each type per 10,000 bottles sold. Respondents were asked to state their willingness-to-pay (WTP) to eliminate or reduce the risks. In households without children, the mean WTP to eliminate both risks was $3.78. The respondents were also asked to state the price reduction they would require to accept an increase of 1/10,000 in each of the two risks. The results were dramatic: 77 percent of respondents in this condition said they would refuse to buy the product at any positive price.

The striking difference between WTA and WTP in these studies probably reflects the large difference in the responsibility costs associated with voluntary assumption of additional risk, in contrast to a mere failure to reduce or eliminate existing risk. The asymmetry between omission and commission is familiar in legal doctrine, and its impact on judgments of responsibility has been confirmed by psychological research (Ritov and Baron, forthcoming). The asymmetry affects both blame and regret after a mishap, and the anticipation of blame and regret, in turn, could affect behavior.

A moral attitude is involved in another situation where huge discrepancies between buying and selling prices have been observed, the evaluation of environmental amenities in cost benefit analyses. Suppose some corporation offers to buy the Grand Canyon and make it into a water park complete with the world's largest water slide. How do we know whether the benefits of this idea exceed its costs? As usual there are two ways to ask the question, depending on what is the status quo. If there is no theme park in the status quo, then people can be asked the minimum amount of money they would accept to agree to add one (WTA). Alternatively, if the corporation currently owns the right, people could be asked how much they would be willing to pay to buy it back and prevent the theme park from being built (WTP). Several surveys have been conducted where the researchers asked both types of questions for such things as clean air and well-maintained public parks. Most studies find that the WTA responses greatly exceed the WTP answers (Cummings, Brookshire, and Schulze, 1986). The difference in typical responses actually does not tell the entire story. As two close observers of this literature note (Mitchell and Carson, 1989, p. 34): "Studies using WTA questions have consistently received a large number of protest answers, such as 'I refuse to sell' or 'I want an extremely large or infinite amount of compensation for agreeing to this,' and have frequently experienced protest rates [outright refusals to answer the question] of 50 percent or more." These extreme responses reflect the feelings of outrage often seen when communities are faced with the prospect of accepting a new risk such as a nuclear power plant or waste disposal facility (Kunreuther, Easterling, Desvousges, and Slovic, forthcoming). Offers of compensation to proposed communities often do not help as they are typically perceived as bribes.[4]

Judgments of Fairness and Justice

An implication of the endowment effect is that people treat opportunity costs differently than "out-of-pocket" costs. Foregone gains are less painful than perceived losses. This perception is strongly manifested in people's judgments about fair behavior. Kahneman, Knetsch and Thaler (1986) present survey evidence supporting this proposition. Samples of the residents of Toronto and Vancouver were asked a series of questions over the telephone about whether they thought a particular economic action was "fair." In some cases, alternative versions of the same question were presented to different groups of respondents. For each question, respondents were asked to judge whether the action was completely fair, acceptable, somewhat unfair, or very unfair. In reporting the results the first two categories were combined and called "acceptable" and the last two combined and called "unfair." Perceptions of fairness strongly depended on whether the question was framed as a reduction in a gain or an actual loss. For example:

> Question 1a. A shortage has developed for a popular model of automobile, and customers must now wait two months for delivery. A dealer has been selling these cars at list price. Now the dealer prices this model at $200 above list price.

> $N = 130$ Acceptable 29 percent   Unfair 71 percent

> Question 1b. A shortage has developed for a popular model of automobile, and customers must now wait two months for delivery. A dealer has been selling these cars at a discount of $200 below list price. Now the dealer sells this model only at list price.

> $N = 123$ Acceptable 58 percent   Unfair 42 percent

---

[4]This is a situation in which people loudly say one thing and the theory asserts another. It is of interest that the practitioners of contingent valuation elected to listen to the theory, rather than to the respondents (Cummings, Brookshire and Schulze, 1986). The accepted procedure uses WTP questions to assess value even in a context of compensation, relying on the theoretical argument that WTP and WTA should not be far apart when income effects are small.

Imposing a surcharge (which is likely to be judged a loss) is considered more unfair than eliminating a discount (a reduction of a gain). This distinction explains why firms that charge cash customers one price and credit card customers a higher price always refer to the cash price as a discount rather than to the credit card price as a surcharge (Thaler, 1980).

The different intensity of responses to losses and to foregone gains may help explain why it is easier to cut real wages during inflationary periods:

> Question 2a. A company is making a small profit. It is located in a community experiencing a recession with substantial unemployment but no inflation. The company decides to decrease wages and salaries 7 percent this year.
>
> $N = 125$ Acceptable 37 percent   Unfair 63 percent
>
> Question 2b. A company is making a small profit. It is located in a community experiencing a recession with substantial unemployment and inflation of 12 percent. The company decides to increase salaries only 5 percent this year.
>
> $N = 129$ Acceptable 78 percent   Unfair 22 percent

In this case a 7 percent cut in real wages is judged reasonably fair when it is framed as a nominal wage increase, but quite unfair when it is posed as a nominal wage cut.

The attitudes of the lay public about fairness, which are represented in their answers to these fairness questions, also pervade the decisions made by judges in many fields of the law. Supreme Court Justice Oliver Wendell Holmes (1897) put the principle this way: "It is in the nature of a man's mind. A thing which you enjoyed and used as your own for a long time, whether property or opinion, takes root in your being and cannot be torn away without your resenting the act and trying to defend yourself, however you came by it. The law can ask no better justification than the deepest instincts of man."

Cohen and Knetsch (1990) showed that this principle, embodied in the old expression that "possession is nine tenths of the law," is reflected in many judicial opinions. For example, in tort law judges make the distinction between "loss by way of expenditure and failure to make gain." In one case, several bales fell from the defendant's truck and hit a utility pole, cutting off power to the plaintiff's plant. The plaintiff was able to recover wages paid to employees which were considered "positive outlays" but could not recover lost profits which were merely "negative losses consisting of a mere deprivation of an opportunity to earn an income" (p. 18). A similar distinction is made in contract law. A party that breaches a contract is more likely to be held to the original terms if the action is taken to make an unforeseen gain than if it is taken to avoid a loss.

Commentary

It is in the nature of economic anomalies that they violate standard theory. The next question is what to do about it. In many cases there is no obvious way to amend the theory to fit the facts, either because too little is known, or because the changes would greatly increase the complexity of the theory and reduce its predictive yield. The anomalies that we have described under the labels of the endowment effect, the status quo bias and loss aversion may be an exceptional case, where the needed amendments in the theory are both obvious and tractable.

The amendments are not trivial: the important notion of a stable preference order must be abandoned in favor of a preference order that depends on the current reference level. A revised version of preference theory would assign a special role to the status quo, giving up some standard assumptions of stability, symmetry and reversibility which the data have shown to be false. But the task is manageable. The generalization of preference theory to indifference curves that are indexed to reference level is straightforward (Tversky and Kahneman, 1991). The factors that determine the reference point in the evaluations of outcomes are reasonably well understood: the role of the status quo, and of entitlements and expectations are sufficiently well established to allow these factors to be used in locating the relevant reference levels for particular analyses.

As Samuelson and Zeckhauser noted, rational models that ignore the status quo tend to predict "greater instability than is observed in the world" (p. 47). We have added the claim that models that ignore loss aversion predict more symmetry and reversibility than are observed in the world, ignoring potentially large differences in the magnitude of responses to gains and to losses. Responses to increases and to decreases in price, for example, might not always be mirror images of each other. The possibility of loss aversion effects suggests, more generally, that treatments of responses to *changes* in economic variables should routinely separate the cases of favorable and unfavorable changes. Introducing such distinctions could improve the precision of predictions at a tolerable price in increased complexity.

After more than a decade of research on this topic we have become convinced that the endowment effect, status quo bias, and the aversion to losses are both robust and important. Then again, we admit that the idea is now part of our endowment, and we are naturally keener to retain it than others might be to acquire it.

■ *The authors wish to acknowledge financial support from Fisheries and Oceans Canada, the Ontario Ministry of the Environment, the Russell Sage Foundation, and Concord Capital Management.*

References

Cohen, David, and Jack L. Knetsch "Judicial Choice and Disparities Between Measures of Economic Values," Simon Fraser University Working Paper, 1990.

Coursey, Don L., John L. Hovis, and William D. Schulze, "The Disparity Between Willingness to Accept and Willingness to Pay Measures of Value," *The Quarterly Journal of Economics*, 1987, *102*, 679–90.

Cummings, Ronald G., David S. Brookshire, and William D. Schulze, eds., *Valuing Environmental Goods*. Totowa, NJ: Rowman and Allanheld, 1986.

Hartman, Raymond, Michael J. Doane, and Chi-Keung Woo, "Consumer Rationality and the Status Quo," *Quarterly Journal of Economics*, forthcoming.

Hershey, John, Eric Johnson, Jacqueline Meszaros, and Matthew Robinson, "What Is the Right to Sue Worth?" Wharton School, University of Pennsylvania, June 1990.

Holmes, Oliver Wendell, "The Path of the Law," *Harvard Law Review*, 1897, *10*, 457–478.

Kahneman, Daniel, Jack L. Knetsch, and Richard Thaler, "Fairness As a Constraint on Profit Seeking: Entitlements in the Market," *American Economic Review*, 1986, *76*, 728–41.

Kahneman, Daniel, Jack L. Knetsch, and Richard Thaler, "Experimental Tests of the Endowment Effect and the Coase Theorem," *Journal of Political Economy*, December 1990, *98*, 1325–1348.

Kahneman, Daniel, and Amos Tversky, "Choices, Values and Frames," *American Psychologist*, April 1984, *39*, 341–350.

Knetsch, Jack L., "The Endowment Effect and Evidence of Nonreversible Indifference Curves," *American Economic Review*, 1989, *79*, 1277–1284.

Knetsch, Jack L., "Derived Indifference Curves," working paper, Simon Fraser University, 1990.

Knetsch, Jack L., and J. A. Sinden, "Willingness to Pay and Compensation Demanded: Experimental Evidence of an Unexpected Disparity in Measures of Value," *Quarterly Journal of Economics*, August 1984, *99*, 507–521.

Knetsch, Jack L., and J. A. Sinden, "The Persistence of Evaluation Disparities," *Quarterly Journal of Economics*, 1987, *102*, 691–695.

Knez, Peter, Vernon Smith, and Arlington W. Williams, "Individual Rationality, Market Rationality, and Value Estimation," *American Economic Review*, May 1985, *75*, 397–402.

Kunreuther, Howard, Douglas Easterling, William Desvousges, and Paul Slovic, "Public Attitudes Toward Citing a High Level Nuclear Waste Depository in Nevada," *Risk Analysis*, forthcoming.

Lowenstein, George, and Daniel Kahneman, "Explaining the Endowment Effect," working paper, Department of Social and Decision Sciences, Carnegie Mellon University, 1991.

Mitchell, Robert C., and R. T. Carson, *Using Surveys to Value Public Goods*. Washington, D.C.: Resources for the Future, 1989.

Ritov, Rita, and Jonathan Baron, "Status-quo and Omission Biases," *Journal of Risk and Uncertainty*, forthcoming.

Samuelson, William, and Richard Zeckhauser, "Status Quo Bias in Decision Making," *Journal of Risk and Uncertainty*, 1988, *1*, 7–59.

Thaler, Richard, "Toward a Positive Theory of Consumer Choice," *Journal of Economic Behavior and Organization*, 1980, *1*, 39–60.

Tversky, Amos, and Daniel Kahneman, "Loss Aversion and Riskless Choice: A Reference Dependent Model," *Quarterly Journal of Economics*, 1991.

Viscusi, W. Kip, Wesley A. Magat, and Joel Huber, "An Investigation of the Rationality of Consumer Valuations of Multiple Health Risks," *RAND Journal of Economics*, 1987, *18*, 465–79.

[14]

Insurance for Low-Probability Hazards:
A Bimodal Response to Unlikely Events

GARY H. MCCLELLAND
Department of Psychology, CB 345, University of Colorado, Boulder, CO 80309-0345

WILLIAM D. SCHULZE
Department of Economics, University of Colorado, Boulder, CO 80309

DON L. COURSEY*
Harris School of Public Policy Studies, University of Chicago, 1155 E. 60th Street, Chicago, IL 60637

Abstract

Two insurance experiments using real-money consequences and multiple rounds to provide experience are described. In the first experiment, subjects bid for insurance to prevent a fixed loss of $4 at probabilities ranging from .01 to .9. Mean bids were near expected value except at the lowest probability of .01, for which a very bimodal distribution was observed (some subjects bid zero and others bid much more than expected value). A second experiment explored this bimodality at a probability of .01 with loss increased to $40. A similar bimodal distribution was obtained that persisted over 50 rounds of experience. These laboratory results are consistent with field evidence for low-probability hazards, for which people appear either to dismiss the risks or to worry too much about them.

Key words: low-probability hazards, bimodality, unlikely events, insurance

Given the opportunity to purchase insurance or otherwise protect themselves against low-probability, high-consequence risks, people often behave in ways that are surprising from a decision-making or economic perspective. For example, in the case of hazardous wastes (Smith and Desvouges, 1987; McClelland, Schulze, and Hurd, 1990), many people have inexplicably large values for avoiding low-probability risks. Yet in other cases, such as floods (Kunreuther et al., 1978), many people refuse to purchase insurance against objectively greater risks. We report here two laboratory studies that investigate insurance behavior in both low-probability and high-probability risk situations. It is difficult or impossible to replicate the high-loss nature of significant real-world risks in the

*We would like to thank Alan Carlin, Ann Fisher, Risa Palm, and David Brookshire for their helpful comments on an earlier version of this article, and Rebecca Boyce, Julie Irwin, Glenn Russell, and Joy Smith for research assistance. We also gratefully acknowledge support from the University of Colorado Council on Research and Creative Work for human subject payments and from the U.S. Environmental Protection Agency, Office of Policy, Planning and Evaluation for support for research design and analysis provided as part of Cooperative Agreement #CR812054. All errors, opinions and conclusions are the sole responsibility of the authors.

laboratory, but it is possible to determine whether insurance behavior at relatively low probabilities (e.g., .01) differs from insurance behavior at relatively high probabilities (e.g., .9).

In these studies we use a simple laboratory model or simulation of risky situations and insurance purchase. In this simulation, the risk is represented by drawing a red poker chip from a bag containing both red and white chips. If a red chip is drawn, the subject experiences a specified monetary loss; if a white chip is drawn, each subject receives a small monetary gain (primarily to keep the subjects funded). Before each draw, subjects have the opportunity to purchase insurance that will completely protect them against the risk (i.e., they will lose nothing if a red chip is drawn and they hold an insurance policy). Using this laboratory model, it is easy to explore various aspects of insurance behavior by varying the probability of the hazard (i.e., the proportion of red chips in the bag) and the magnitude of the hazard (the size of the monetary loss).

There are advantages and disadvantages to using a simple laboratory analogue for a complex real-world decision. Obvious advantages are that the laboratory permits much greater control and allows observation of multiple behaviors. It is difficult, for example, to observe purchase decisions about flood insurance over many years and to examine the effect of an unexpected flood on the next purchase decision. However, it is relatively easy in the laboratory to expose individuals to a low-probability risk many times and to observe their behavior immediately after the loss occurs.

One common complaint about laboratory models is that they are not sufficiently realistic to engage fully the attention of the participants. To reduce this problem, we follow the dictates of experimental economics in using real monetary gains and losses. But of necessity these losses are trivial compared to the potential losses of, say, living in a flood plain or next to a hazardous landfill. Nevertheless, anecdotal observations in the laboratory indicate that the small monetary losses are large enough so that everyone clearly prefers that the risk not happen. For example, subjects in these experiments paid close attention to the drawing of the red or white chips and reacted with visible unhappiness whenever a red chip (indicating a loss of $4) was drawn.

An important defense of the laboratory model is that it provides people with a relatively calm setting and repeated experience with a single risk. If individuals do not have the cognitive resources to determine how to deal with low-probability risks in this calm setting, it seems unlikely that they will be cognitively more adept in the more highly charged emotional environment of deciding whether to worry or not about a risk such as a hazardous landfill in their neighborhood. Whatever the advantages and disadvantages of laboratory models, we believe that both field and lab studies provide complementary information that will lead to a fuller understanding of insurance purchase and other protective behaviors for low-probability risks.

Of particular interest here is whether insurance behavior is fundamentally different for low-probability events than high-probability events. Thus, in the first study, we manipulate the probability of loss over a wide range from very high (.9) to very low (.01), while keeping the size of the monetary loss fixed. Expected utility theory (EUT) would predict no fundamental change in insurance behavior as probability changes; that is, individuals should be willing to pay for insurance an amount approximately equal to their expected value for the loss. However, generalized expected utility theory (GEU) in which utility itself is a function of the probabilities (Machina, 1982) can result in over-sensitivity to risks with low probabilities. Similarly, Kahneman and Tversky's (1979) prospect theory (PT) suggests an overweighting of low probabilities. These theories were motivated by experimental results of the sort originally summarized by Edwards (1954) in his early survey article on decision making under uncertainty. Edwards argued that subjective weights used in decision making often differ from objective probabilities and may not follow probability laws at all. Thus, we may find unusual insurance purchase behavior as the probability decreases.

In addition to experimental evidence that suggests that there may be difficulties at low probabilities, there is also some empirical field research that suggests that people have problems dealing with low-probability risks. For example, in a study of the risk beliefs of people living near a landfill that had accepted hazardous materials, McClelland, Schulze, and Hurd (1990) found a very bimodal distribution. That is, many people dismissed the risk and thought there was no hazard, while others thought the risk was comparable to smoking a pack or more of cigarettes per day. Almost no one had risk beliefs between these two extremes, even though the objective risk was almost surely between those two extreme modes. Most importantly, McClelland et al. (1990) demonstrated that these risks beliefs correspond to real behavior: the higher the perceived risk, the less amounts for which people were willing to sell their houses.

1. Theoretical issues

This section develops the implications of expected utility theory for experimental varia-tions in the probability of loss and the size of the loss. These implications are used as a baseline to detect anomalies in the experimental results. The experimental paradigm is as follows: each subject is given the opportunity to make a bid of B dollars in an incentive-compatible, competitive auction for insurance against a possible loss of L dollars that occurs with probability p, with p and L specified. With probability $1-p$, each subject is rewarded with a relatively small gain of G dollars. This gain was used to fund subjects over repeated rounds. If a subject has an initial wealth of Y^0 dollars at the start of a trial and utility is a function $U(Y)$ of wealth, Y, then the expected utility of the situation described above without purchase of insurance is

$$pU(Y^0 - L) + (1 - p)U(Y^0 + G) \tag{1}$$

and the expected utility with purchase of insurance is

$$pU(Y^0 - B) + (1 - p)U(Y^0 + G - B). \tag{2}$$

The most that an individual would be willing to pay for insurance can be obtained by setting equation (2) equal to equation (1) and solving for the bid B. Individuals should be willing to increase the bid only to the point that the expected utility with insurance falls to the level of expected utility without insurance.

Risk aversion is sometimes invoked to explain deviations of behavior from expected value. The coefficient of relative risk aversion, a common measure, is defined as

$$c = \frac{-U''}{U'}Y. \tag{3}$$

Note that risk aversion implies $U'' < 0$, so c is necessarily positive. To incorporate the coefficient of relative risk aversion, we substitute a second-order Taylor series approximation of $U(Y)$ into equations (1) and (2), set the two equations equal to each other, and solve[1] for B/EV (where $EV = pL$) to obtain

$$\frac{B}{EV} = 1 + \frac{c}{Y^0}[.5(1 - p(B/EV)^2)L + (1 - p)(B/EV)G]. \tag{4}$$

Based on field data, Friend and Blume (1975) estimated that c is greater than one but probably not higher than two. Assuming that $c = 2$ and assuming any reasonable value for initial wealth Y^0 implies that if individuals are consistent with the EU model, the contribution from the bracketed term in equation (4) will be negligible, which in turn implies that B/EV should be approximately one. Further note that in laboratory situations, G's are also very small relative to Y^0. Clearly, existing field evidence on risk aversion implies risk neutrality for losses of $4 and $40 used in our experiments. In fact, based on the field evidence, it would be difficult to imagine that risk aversion can play any role in laboratory experimental settings where the usual stakes are employed. This statement, of course, assumes that expected utility theory (EUT) provides an adequate description of behavior. Other models such as generalized expected utility theory (GEU) can readily explain risk-averse behavior in the laboratory by, for example, assuming that utility itself is a function of the probabilities so the marginal rate of substitution between p and Y increases for small p, yielding more sensitivity to risk for small p. In prospect theory (PT), more weight is given to small than large p through a weighting function π (p), which replaces p in a formulation similar to EUT.

2. Experiment 1

The goal of this experiment was to examine insurance purchase decisions over a range of probabilities. We first describe the basic paradigm for the risk and for obtaining incentive-compatible bids in a competitive auction. Then we describe the experimental sequence and the various orders in which the probabilities of the risk were manipulated.

2.1. Method

2.1.1 Subjects. Sixty-four volunteers from undergraduate economics classes participated in the experiment in eight sessions of eight subjects each. Subjects received a guaranteed payment of $5 for participating, in addition to whatever gains they might realize in the experiment.

2.1.2. Risk. Risk was operationalized by drawing a poker chip from a bag containing 100 red and white chips. If a red chip was drawn, those not holding an insurance policy lost $4 while those holding an insurance policy were completely protected and therefore lost nothing. If a white chip was drawn, everyone received $1 regardless of whether they held an insurance policy. Subjects began with a $10 balance. The $1 gain served to keep subjects funded so that they would have adequate funds with which to bid for insurance. The probability of the risk was varied by simply changing the proportion of red chips in the bag. Before being placed in the bag, stacks of red and white chips were shown to the subjects so that they would have a visual impression of the likelihood that a red chip would be drawn.

2.1.3. Auction. On each round of the experiment, there were four insurance policies available for purchase. A competitive Vickrey auction (Vickrey, 1961; Coppinger, Smith, and Titus, 1980) determined which of the eight subjects received an insurance policy. A computer program conducted the auction so that on each round each subject entered a bid for the insurance ("the most you would be willing to pay for insurance against the risk of a red chip") on his or her own computer terminal. After everyone had entered a bid, the computer rank-ordered the eight bids from highest to lowest and displayed the *reigning price*—the fifth highest bid for insurance—on each subject's terminal screen. Only the four subjects with bids above the reigning price received insurance. In the case of ties for the fourth highest bid, remaining insurance policies were randomly allocated among those with tied bids. The key feature of the Vickrey auction is that those receiving insurance paid only the reigning price, which was necessarily less than or equal to their bids. This feature is intended to eliminate incentives for strategic behavior in auctions in which individuals must pay exactly what they bid. That is, if subjects bid the most they are willing to pay, then they should be happy with the outcome of the auction. If the reigning price is higher than their bid, then they should be satisfied at not buying insurance at what they consider too high a price. If the reigning price is below their bid, then they should be satisfied to buy the insurance at the lowest possible bid, at least as low as their actual bid, that would ensure they were among the top four bidders. For each probability level, there was a set of 10 auction rounds; subjects knew that there were to be 10 auction rounds at each probability level.

The computer kept track of all bookkeeping and displayed all information for subjects. Thus, after each auction, the computer displayed on each subject's computer terminal the balance when the round began, the subject's bid, the resulting reigning price, whether or not insurance had been purchased, adjustments to the balance, if any, and the new balance before the chip was drawn. Other than the reigning price, subjects received no information about the bids of other subjects. Terminals were arranged so that subjects could not see each other's terminals, and subjects were not allowed to talk with one another.

Great care was taken to avoid the use of any judgmental words about the auction in the written and oral instructions. This is in contrast to some previous auction experiments that have referred to those who have received insurance as "winners." The use of such words might artificially increase the subjective value of holding insurance above its value as protection against the loss associated with the draw of a red chip.

2.1.4. Hypothetical bids.   There is great interest in knowing whether results about decision behavior from psychology experiments, which often use hypothetical or ''as-if'' responses, are comparable to those from economics experiments, which generally use responses that have real monetary consequences (e.g., Irwin, McClelland, and Schulze, 1992; Smith, 1976; Smith and Walker, 1993). Also, it is important to know whether hypothetical responses collected using the contingent valuation methodology (Cummings, Brookshire, and Schulze, 1986; Mitchell and Carson, 1989) are useful predictors of actual behavior. To address these issues, in addition to the binding bids in the competitive auction we also collected two types of hypothetical bids. First, in hypothetical bids that we refer to as *inexperienced*, after describing the risk but before any auctions, we asked subjects how much they would be willing to pay for insurance for specified numbers of red chips in the bag. These bids were not binding and were not collected in an auction format; instead, they were hypothetical responses to written questionnaire items like those that would appear in a contingent value survey or psychology experiment.

Second, in hypothetical bids that we refer to as *experienced*, we asked subjects the hypothetical question immediately before each set of 10 rounds with a new probability level. That is, immediately before, say, the binding auction rounds for the probability of 0.1, subjects were asked hypothetically how much they would be willing to pay for insurance. These were experienced hypothetical bids because after the first set of rounds, subjects had had experience with both the auction mechanism and the realities of the risky event. In the results section, both inexperienced and experienced hypothetical bids are compared to the actual bids for the competitive auction.

2.1.5. Risk event.   After the auction and the allocation of the four insurance policies, the experimenter reached into the bag of chips, stirred the chips noisily to reinforce beliefs of randomness, and drew a chip from the bag so that all subjects could see its color. Another experimenter entered the color of this chip at a control terminal so that the appropriate adjustments—$1 to all if a white chip was drawn and a $4 loss to those without insurance if a red chip was drawn—could be made to the subjects' balances and displayed on their terminals. To ensure that all subjects received the same probabilistic experience and the same sequence of events so that results could be pooled for statistical analysis, the drawing was controlled (the different colors of the chips were distinguishable by texture as in Phillips and Edwards (1966) and many similar psychology experiments). Although the sequences of red and white chips were determined randomly *before* the experiment, the sequences were indeed random as purported to the subjects. However, subjects were led to believe[2] that the drawing was random at the time they saw it. To ensure that the reputation of the experiment remained intact, subjects were chosen and sessions were arranged so that communication between subjects participating in different sessions outside of the laboratory was unlikely. In fact, the supposedly random draws were never questioned by subjects.

2.1.6. Probability groups.   Financing issues dictated assigning subjects to one of two groups of probabilities. Those subjects in the lower-probability group experienced the risk at probabilities of .01, .1, .2, and .4, while those in the higher-probability group experienced the risk at probabilities of .6 and .9. There were five experimental sessions of eight subjects each for a total of 40 participants for the lower-probability group, and there were three experimental sessions for a total of 24 participants for the higher-probability group. At the beginning of the experiment, each subject in the lower-probability group was given an initial balance of $10 that he or she could either keep or use to purchase insurance. This initial balance was adjusted according to the auction outcome and the risky event. Each subject in the higher-probability group was given an initial balance of $65 so that he or she could afford the expected higher prices for insurance at probabilities of .6 and .9. Subjects were allowed to keep any of the stake remaining and any gains at the end of the experiment. Subjects were assured that even if they lost all their stake, they would receive the $5 payment.

2.1.7. Order. The different components of the experiment were presented in a fixed order. For the lower-probability experimental sessions, the following order was used:

a. Inexperienced Hypothetical Bids at p = .2, .1, .01, and .4.
b. Auction Practice Bids, 4 rounds at p = .2
c. Auction Binding Bids, 10 rounds at p = .2
   Chip sequence: WWRWWWRWWW
d. Experienced Hypothetical Bid at p = .1
e. Auction Binding Bids, 10 rounds at p = .1
   Chip sequence: WWRWWWWWWW
f. Experienced Hypothetical Bid at p = .4
g. Auction Binding Bids, 10 rounds at p = .4.
   Chip sequence: WRRWWWRWWW
h. Experienced Hypothetical Bid at p = .01
i. Auction Binding Bids, 10 rounds at p = .01
   Chip sequence: WWWWWWWWWW

In the higher-probability experimental sessions, the following fixed order was used:

a. Inexperienced Hypothetical Bids at p = .6 and .9
b. Auction Practice Bids, 4 rounds at p = .6
c. Auction Binding Bids, 10 rounds at p = .6
   Chip sequence: RWRRWWRRRR
d. Experienced Hypothetical Bid at p = .9
e. Auction Binding Bids, 10 rounds at p = .9
   Chip sequence: RRRWRRRRRR

The fixed order of probabilities makes it impossible to have experienced hypothetical bids for p = .2 and p = .6 because these were always the first probability levels presented in the sequence of actual auctions. Thus, subjects facing p = .2 and p = .6 had not experienced other loss probabilities before answering the hypothetical question. The

102   GARY H. MCCLELLAND/WILLIAM D. SCHULZE/DON L. COURSEY

nonbinding auction rounds in step (b) of both sequences allowed subjects to practice with the auction mechanism before having to make binding bids in the risky situation.

2.2. Results

Figure 1 presents means of bids pooled across rounds divided by expected value, *B/EV*, as a function of the probability of loss. As noted in section 2, we normalize bids for insurance by dividing by expected values so we can directly compare results at different probability levels with each other and with the predictions of EUT. According to EUT and field evidence on risk aversion, we would expect mean measures of *B/EV* to approximate unity. Note that, at probabilities of loss of .2 and above, mean *B/EV* is close to unity. However, the mean bid rises to about two and one-half times *EV* at a probability of loss of .01. Thus, on average, individuals overbid for insurance at low probabilities, supporting the oversensitivity or overweighting hypothesis.[3] We rule out a number of possible explanations for this result such as rounding error by raising the loss from $4 to $40 in the second experiment, described below.

Aggregate measures such as the means depicted in figure 1 can sometimes hide important differences among the individual bids. To investigate this possibility, figure 2 presents frequency distributions for auction values of *B/EV*, pooled across rounds, for each probability. The variance increases greatly at lower probabilities, so a logarithmic horizontal axis is used to facilitate comparisons across probabilities. The value of *B/EV* for the center of each bin in figure 2 is shown under the bar representing the frequency of bids falling within the bin.[4] If the same relative error is present at the different probabilities, then the frequency distributions across probabilities should be similar.

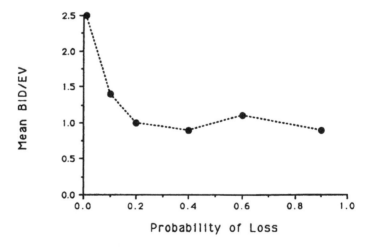

Figure 1. Mean BID/EV for insurance as a function of the probability of loss.

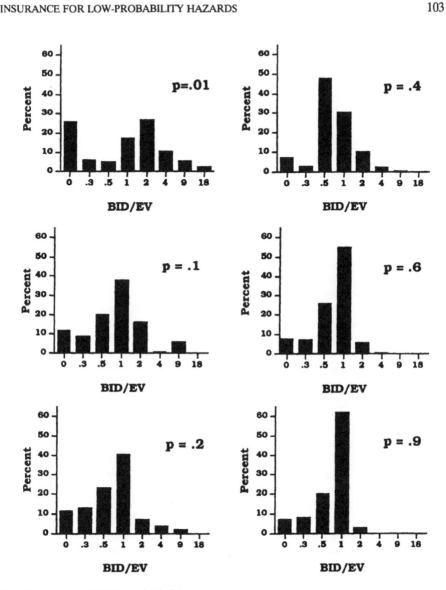

Figure 2. Frequency distributions of *BID/EV*.

A striking feature in figure 2 is the pronounced bimodality of the distribution of bids when the probability of loss equals .01. More than 25% of the bids in the sample are equal to zero, forming a lower mode. The distribution of positive bids on the logarithmic scale is approximately normal, thereby implying a log-normal distribution of the positive bids. The two modes suggest that two different processes may be operating at low probabilities. Zero bids apparently reflect a judgment that the risk is too small to be worth making a bid. In effect, such bids indicate a choice to self-insure. Those bids above *EV* by two or more times are extraordinarily risk averse, showing great sensitivity to the low-probability risk. Note that the log scale used in the top panel of figure 2 greatly compresses the horizontal axis, somewhat disguising the many very large bids obtained in the auction.

As the probability increases, the proportion of zero bids drops dramatically, but never disappears. The decrease in the zero bids effectively eliminates the bimodality so that at the higher probabilities there is a clear center peak at or near expected value. The height of this peak increases with probability until, at $p = .9$, over 60% of the responses are in the bin for *BID/EV* $= 1$. If displayed using an untransformed scale, the frequency distributions for lower probabilities would have a pronounced positive skew; this skew disappears for higher probabilities so that those distributions are approximately normal.

The frequency distributions in figure 2 are distributions of individual bids. Thus, each individual produced 10 different bids in each panel of figure 2. It is therefore interesting to ask whether individuals are consistent (always in the lower or upper mode) or whether they jump from one mode to the other. Neither result would be any more or less consistent with the theoretical issues raised above. That is, individuals may make an initial judgment that a probability of loss of .01 is either worth worrying about or not and stick with that judgment for the whole set of 10 rounds. Or, individuals may decide as a function of experience to switch from one mode to the other. For example, individuals who initially dismiss the risk and bid zero may, over rounds, as the loss does not occur, be influenced by the gambler's fallacy (e.g., McClelland and Hackenberg, 1978) to judge that the risk is becoming more likely; at some point, they would then switch to the upper mode. Conversely, individuals who initially are oversensitive to the low probability may, over rounds, as they experience paying a lot for insurance on which they do not collect, be influenced by the benign experience to judge that the risk is less likely than they thought; at some point, they would switch to the lower mode.

Figure 3 displays the frequency distribution of individuals as a function of the number of times they bid in the upper mode when the probability of loss was .01 (upper mode is defined as those bids greater than or equal to expected value in this case). If everyone were aiming at a target equal to or somewhat above *EV*, but missed from round to round due to random error, then there would be no individual consistency, and the distribution in figure 3 would be approximately normal and centered slightly above five (because figure 2 indicates that, more often than not, bids are in the upper mode). Figure 3 is clearly not a normal distribution and therefore suggests that there are consistent individual differences. For example, 13 individuals were in the upper mode for all but at most 1 of the 10 rounds; these individuals were consistently oversensitive to the low-probability risk. At the other end, 12 individuals were in the lower mode for all but at most 2 of the 10 rounds; these individuals consistently dismissed the risk. Of the 15 between the two extremes, 8 showed the gambler's fallacy pattern of bidding in the lower mode for the early rounds and then suddenly switching to the upper mode for later rounds. The bids of the remaining 6 individuals appeared to be randomly above or below *EV*. In sum, most individuals (88%) were consistent in one of the following ways: always dismissing the

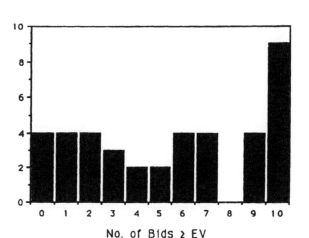

Figure 3. Individual propensity to bid above *EV* across ten rounds for $p = .01$.

risk, always bidding above EV for the risk, or making at most one switch from dismissing to the risk to worrying about it in later rounds for $p = .01$.

As noted in the introduction, psychology experiments of risky decision making have often used hypothetical bids and risks. In contrast, experimental economics traditionally employs actual financial transactions. Similarly, the use of hypothetical values from surveys by economists for benefit–cost analysis (contingent valuation) has become widespread. The obvious question is whether using real monetary consequences differs from using hypothetical amounts. Figure 4 displays the mean hypothetical bids divided by the mean of the binding auction bids, pooled across rounds, as a function of the probability of loss. The inexperienced hypothetical bids collected at the start of the experiment clearly overestimate actual auction bids at low probabilities (i.e., the ratio shown in figure 4 is greater than one) and underestimate actual auction bids at the higher probabilities. In contrast, experienced hypothetical bids, which were collected after actual auction experience at other probabilities, were good predictors of auction bids at probabilities of .2 and above.[5] Both inexperienced and experienced hypothetical bids are about twice actual auction bids at $p = .1$ and .01. This suggests that the overestimation of hypothetical bids that occurs at low probabilities may be due to inexperience. In other words, practice with the auction mechanism and experience with the risk may bring bids closer to *EV*. At the lower probabilities, more practice my be required; both inexperienced and experienced hypothetical bids in this experiment may simply represent the first iteration in the adjustment process.

3. Experiment 2

The results from experiment 1 definitely indicate that there are problems associated with insurance purchase for low-probability risks. In particular, bids for insurance deviated

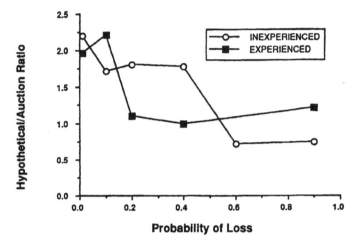

Figure 4. Ratio of mean hypothetical bid to mean auction bid as a function of the probability of loss.

the most from EV for low probabilities, and there were consistent individual differences producing a bimodal distribution of bids at low, but not at higher, probabilities. The purpose of experiment 2 is to explore in more depth the bidding behavior for low-probability risks. A weakness of experiment 1 is that the loss was fixed at $4. This meant that the EV when $p = .01$ was only $0.04 and that many of those who were bidding over EV were only bidding about $0.10. There may simply have been more error in estimating such a low value. So in this experiment, the loss is fixed at $40, making the $EV = $0.40. Furthermore, the results hinted that perhaps bids were moving closer to EV with experience. So in this experiment subjects made bids for 50 rounds, making the total EV of the insurance across rounds equal to $20. Finally, subjects in the first experiment had considerable experience with the auction and the risk before facing the low-probability risk. In this experiment, they begin the actual binding rounds with no prior experience.

3.1. Method

3.1.1. Subjects.   Different volunteers from undergraduate economics classes participated in the experiment in six sessions of eight subjects each. Subjects received a guaranteed payment of $5 for participating, in addition to whatever gains they might realize in the experiment.

3.1.2. Auction and risk.   The auction for four insurance policies was conducted exactly as in the first experiment: The risk was also operationalized as drawing a red chip from a bag containing 100 chips. The probability was always .01, so subjects were shown a stack of 99 white chips and one red chip that were placed in the bag. Unlike in experiment 1, subjects had made no prior hypothetical bids and had no practice rounds before the first binding round. There was a total of 50 binding rounds. Again, the drawing of the red chip was controlled to provide comparability across sessions so that a red chip was drawn only on round 33 of 50 rounds. All subjects began with an initial balance of $50 and each person received $1 each time a white chip was drawn.

3.2. Results

The frequency distribution[6] of B/EV for the $40 loss is shown in figure 5. This frequency distribution looks remarkably similar to the frequency distribution shown for the $4 loss in the top panel of figure 2. Both distributions are strongly bimodal, with one mode at zero and another above EV (EV is shown as $B/EV = 1$ in the figure). Note that the horizontal axes are logarithmic, so the upper modes in both cases appear to have approximately log-normal distributions. Two minor differences are also apparent. First the upper mode for the $40 loss is shifted slightly to the right compared to the $4 loss. Second, in the $40 loss experiment there are fewer zero bids (26% for $4 loss but only 15% for $40 loss). The frequencies in the EV bin and the two intermediate bins between zero and EV do not differ appreciably. This means that fewer people were in the lower mode when the loss was higher; that is, fewer people dismissed the risk of losing $40. However, those who did not dismiss it were no more likely to bid very near EV; instead, those in the upper mode tended to bid even higher above EV (note that the maximum is also larger) when the low-probability loss was $40 rather than $4.

Round dynamics are shown in figure 6, which depicts mean bid divided by EV and the mean reigning price divided by EV across rounds. Early bids for insurance averaged about five times expected value, which, consistent with our above conjecture, suggests that hypothetical bids are similar to inexperienced auction values. Mean bids decreased

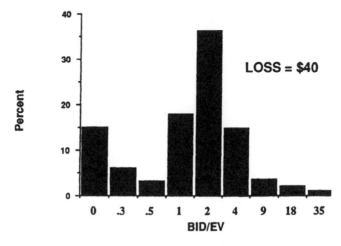

Figure 5. Frequency distribution of *BID/EV* for $p = .01$ and loss = $40.

108   GARY H. MCCLELLAND/WILLIAM D. SCHULZE/DON L. COURSEY

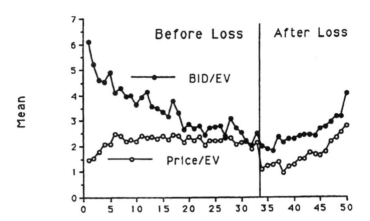

Figure 6. Mean bid/*EV* and mean reigning price/*EV* before and after the $40 loss on round 33.

to about two times expected value just before a red chip was drawn on round 33. Reigning price, after an initial rise, remained constant at about 2.5 times *EV* until, following
the draw of the red chip, a sharp drop in reigning price occurred in round 34. Both mean
bid and reigning price then increased to the conclusion of the experiment at round 50.
We conjecture that bids fell in early rounds because individuals gained experience both
with the auction mechanism and the risk. Benign experience (a succession of white
chips) may reduce the subjective probability of loss. Note that in the first experiment
subjects both had experience in forming values at other probabilities prior to facing odds
of loss of .01 and had actually experienced the loss of $4 on the draw of a red chip. After
the draw of the red chip in the $40 loss, experiment bids rose over following rounds.
Thus, we suspect that, in the absence of the experience of loss, draws of white chips may
convince some that they should dismiss the risk and bid lower or bid zero for insurance.
Experience with loss, however, seems to reverse this process. Convinced by experience
that the loss can occur, some subjects seemingly believe, consistent with the gambler's
fallacy, that successive draws of white increased the need for insurance.

4. Discussion

The results from both experiments demonstrate that insurance behavior in the face of
low-probability risks is different from that for risks of higher probability in two important
respects. First, in contrast to the bids for insurance against higher-probability losses,
which approximate expected value, mean bids for insurance against low-probability risks
are substantially higher than expected value. Second, the mean bids hide important and
consistent individual differences. That is, again contrary to the higher-probability conditions, which have unimodal distributions of bids, the distribution of bids for insurance

against the low-probability risk is strongly bimodal. Individuals appear either to dismiss low-probability risks by bidding zero or near zero or to worry about the risk so much that they bid in a mode substantially above expected value. In this section we consider possible threats to the validity of these results; we then conclude by examining the relationship of the laboratory results to field studies of low-probability risks.

The first threat to the validity concerns whether or not the Vickrey auction actually produces incentive-compatible bids. The second concerns whether risk aversion could produce the pattern of results in our studies, and the third involves possible confounds in the experimental design. We then conclude with a discussion of the suitability of this laboratory simulation as a model of behavior in the face of low-probability risks in the real world.

4.1. Auction mechanism

Although the Vickrey auction is known to be incentive-compatible from a theoretical perspective, research using induced-values has shown that it and similar auctions are not always so empirically. In particular, individuals in such auctions pay only a small penalty for sloppy bidding because payoff functions tend to be quite flat (Harrison, 1989). It is difficult to see how the general problem of imprecise bidding with this auction could have produced the differential results in experiment 1. That is, if the Vickrey is flawed, then why did it produce unimodal distributions approximately centered at expected value for probabilities of $p = .2$ and greater? The anomalous results occurred for $p = .01$; it is not obvious a priori why the Vickrey auction should be any more or less problematical for low probabilities than for high. Note also that the expected value of insurance and the expected penalty for sloppy bidding are the same for the $40 loss with $p = .01$ in experiment 2 and the $4 loss with $p = .1$ in experiment 1. If the anomalous results had been due to the low expected value and flat payoff functions in the Vickrey auction, then the frequency distributions for these two conditions should have been similar. However, it is clear in terms of the mode being shifted above expected value and the relatively high frequency of very high bids that the $40 loss with $p = .01$ is more similar to the $4 loss with $p = .01$, rather than $p = .1$ (see figures 2 and 5). However, zero bids or bids below expected value are consistent with a willingness to self-insure and are not costly to subjects in terms of the expected payoffs. In contrast, bids above expected value are very costly in terms of reducing the expected payoff. Note that shifting the zero bids to be equal to expected value (consistent with self-insurance) would still produce a highly bimodal distribution of bids. On the whole, it seems unlikely that the anomalous results for low probabilities are due to the inexactness associated with the Vickrey auction.

4.2. Risk aversion

Risk aversion is sometimes proffered by economists as an explanation for economically anomalous results obtained in laboratory experiments. It is useful to show that values of the risk-aversion coefficient necessary to explain the present results or indeed most laboratory experiments are unrealistically high. Equation (4), derived from EUT, contains a risk-aversion parameter c. Using data values for B/EV and experimental parameters for p, L, and G, we can solve for c as a function of Y^0. For the \$4 loss at .01 probability, the mean B/EV of 2.5 yields

$$\hat{c} = .34Y^0$$

and for the \$40 loss at .01 probability, the mean B/EV of 3.13 yields

$$\hat{c} = .10Y^0.$$

Any reasonable estimate of an individual's wealth (e.g., studies estimating this coefficient from investment data have often used a discounted net present value of several hundred thousand dollars) yields estimates of relative risk aversion that are many orders of magnitude larger than any field estimates. If we dismiss the possibility that people are inordinately more risk averse in the laboratory studies involving small losses than they are when making major financial decisions, then these large estimates of the risk aversion coefficient imply that either EUT is not a credible model for our data or that people use dramatically smaller estimates of their wealth than economists think they should. Thus, at least for low probabilities, another theory such as GUT or PT must be employed to explain the apparent oversensitivity to small probabilities observed in our experiments.

4.3. Confounds

Our experiments were not complete factorial designs, so there is a possibility of confounds. For example, in experiment 1, the initial stakes (\$10 or \$65) were, because of concerns about expense, confounded with lower (.01, .1, .2, and .4) and higher (.6 and .9) probabilities. For some potential pattern of results, this might have been a problem. For example, had there been a large difference in the bids between $p = .2$ and $p = .9$ conditions, we would not have known whether to attribute that difference to the difference in initial stakes, the difference in the probabilities, or the combination of the two. However, finding no difference (bids in both cases approximated expected value) requires no explanation and raises no problems with confounds.

  The new and important result from these experiments is the bimodal distribution of responses for low-probability risks. What in some contexts might be considered confounds in fact in this context demonstrates the robustness of the bimodality result. For p = .01, there was bimodality (and relatively few bids around EV) for a stake of \$10 and a stake of \$50, for few rounds (10) or for many rounds (50), when subjects were experienced at other probabilities at which they did well and when subjects had no experience, when the loss was only \$4 and when it was \$40, and when subjects encountered the low-probability risk with balances mostly "earned" by their judgments in prior trials and when their balances were entirely "house money" (see Thaler and Johnson (1990) for a discussion of the house money issue). For high probabilities (i.e., greater than or equal to .2), there was no bimodality, and mean and modal bids approximate EV no matter whether initial stakes were \$10 or \$65 or whether subjects were experienced at other probabilities or not (the comparison of .4 versus .6). In sum, we observed bimodality at p = .01 no matter what else we did, and we did not observe bimodality at probabilities greater than that, no matter what we did. The most interesting question would be to see if there is some way to make the bimodality at p = .01 go away. Perhaps, a very different market institution would help. Perhaps, a different kind of prior risk experience would alter bids for insurance at low probabilities. But it seems most unlikely that any particular combinations of things we have already tried (such as 50 rounds with a \$4 loss and a higher stake) would be very helpful.

4.4. Lab-field parallelism

Finally, we consider the degree of parallelism between our laboratory model of insurance purchase and protective behavior against low-probability risks in the real world. There is always some question as to how well responses to laboratory risks generalize to real risks such as those posed by earthquakes, floods, landfills, nuclear power plants, and other natural and technological hazards. Although the precise responses might not generalize, there is a good reason to expect that the cognitive processes underlying the responses will generalize. That is, it seems unlikely that people in emotionally charged situations attempting to deal with real risks will suddenly have access to cognitive processes to aid them in their decisions that they do not have access to in the relative calmness of the laboratory. On the other hand, perhaps emotion could motivate some people to use different cognitive strategies (see Petty and Cacioppo, 1986; Showers and Cantor, 1985) that might lead to better risk judgments. Definitive evidence remains to be collected on this issue. In the meantime, results from the lab can at least serve as suggestions as to what to anticipate in the field.

Parallelism between behavior in the laboratory and behavior in the field is an important issue because the control provided by the laboratory makes hypothesis testing both easier and less expensive than relying on field studies. This experiment was conducted to help understand real-world policy problems associated with low-probability hazards. Hazardous waste sites have received much public attention, and very expensive programs such as Superfund seem by all scientific estimates of risk to do very little to reduce objective risk. Smith and Desvouges (1987) and McClelland, Schulze, and Hurd (1990) have attempted to quantify the subjective damages from such sites. The prediction from our laboratory experiments is that residents living near such sites should show a very bimodal response to the risks of exposure they face. One group should respond by ignoring the risk as too small to be concerned with self-insuring, while the second group, showing great oversensitivity to the risk, should demand immediate action to clean up the site and should be willing to pay for cleanup *or* be willing to move away even if group members can get less for selling their homes now than by waiting for some future cleanup action. Both of the field studies cited above support the pattern of behavior found in our experiments.

The study conducted by Smith and Desvouges (1987) asked a representative sample of households in suburban Boston for contingent values for proposed reductions in risks of exposure from hazardous waste sites. Even though nonzero risk changes were clearly specified in the survey, the frequency distribution of bids contained a substantial mode consisting of zero bids. In fact, the frequency distribution of willingness to pay obtained by Smith and Desvouges looks almost identical to the frequency distributions found in our experiments, supporting the hypothesis of a bimodal value response to low probabilities.

The values obtained in the Smith and Desvouges (1987) study were hypothetical. Although our experiments lend some support to such responses, additional evidence supporting a bimodal response was found by McClelland, Schulze, and Hurd (1990) in the property-value market adjacent to a landfill containing hazardous wastes. These authors obtained data on sale prices of homes and asked local residents what level of risk of death (presented on a ladder showing a hierarchy of increasing example risks) they felt represented the risk of the landfill to them. Figure 7 shows a frequency distribution of the responses to this risk ladder. Note the bimodality of responses obtained. One group in the lower mode felt the risk was similar to drinking saccharin or flying on a commercial airliner, while the second group, in the upper mode, thought the risk was similar to smoking. The risk judgments in figure 7 are not directly comparable to the insurance bids in figures 2 and 5. However, McClelland et al. (1990) make the link between the bimodal risk judgments and protective behavior. They showed that the greater the proportion of residents in a neighborhood whose risk judgments were in the upper mode, the more the houses in that neighborhood sold for a discount, controlling of

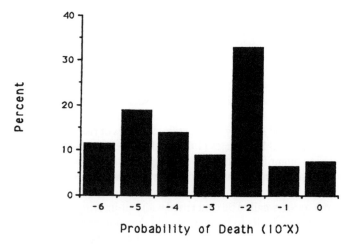

Figure 7. Subjective health risk before landfill closure.

course for other characteristics of the property. They estimated that property losses around the site due to subjective risk judgments were on the order of $40 million. Scientific studies of the risk to neighborhoods surrounding the site, including a careful epidemiological analysis of local health problems, could not find measurable health effects. Even though most residents were unaware of these studies, one explanation for the large subjective damages found in the property value market near the landfill is the oversensitivity to small risks proposed by Machina (1982) and Kahneman and Tversky (1979) and demonstrated by many subjects in our experiments.

However, the site has also been characterized by conflict between residents who fear the site and demand immediate cleanup and those who feel the site poses little threat. This latter group feels that the adverse publicity generated by those who fear the site will lower their property values. The bimodal response to low-probability events shown in our experiments may thus also help explain the intense conflict that often develops in the public arena concerning low-probability, high-loss events.

Bimodality has been found in other field studies of low-probability, high-consequence risks. For example, Kunreuther, Desvousges, and Slovic (1988) found bimodality in a national telephone survey about a proposed high-level nuclear waste repository; the two most frequent responses on a 10-point seriousness-of-risk scale were "1, not at all serious" (16%) and "10, very serious" (21%). Loewenstein and Mather (1990), on the basis of an analysis of aggregate public responses to risks in the media, conclude. "While it is difficult to determine the ideal level of response to a problem, public responses are often sufficiently extreme in one direction or the other to conclude that concern has overshot or undershot the appropriate level." Our results suggest that the aggregate public response may hide an underlying bimodality; if so, whether the public response overshoots or undershoots the appropriate level may simply be due to the proportion of the public in the upper and lower modes. If so, interesting future research should try to determine the factors that predispose individuals to be in one mode or the other and especially the factors that cause an individual to switch from one mode to the other.

Slovic, Fischhoff, and Lichtenstein (1981) have noted, "People often attempt to reduce the anxiety generated in the face of uncertainty by denying the uncertainty, thus making the risk seem so small it can safely be ignored or so large that it clearly should be avoided." That is an appropriate description for the insurance purchase behavior for low-probability risks in our experiment.

Appendix: Instructions

This is an experiment in the economics of decision making. You will have an opportunity to earn a considerable amount of CASH through your participation in this experiment. Please follow these instructions carefully and do not hesitate to raise your hand if you have a question.

You are a member of a group of eight individuals who will participate in an auction. However, you will not be permitted to speak with the other members of the group. The auction has two phases. The first phase involves a group bid-making process. The second phase consists of making final allocations of monetary rewards to the group members. You, as well as each of the group members, will be given an initial credit of $10.00 which is yours to keep or spend as long as you consent to remain active in this experiment. If you withdraw you will receive no money above the $5.00 originally promised to you for showing up. If you do remain in the experiment then your objective is to try to make as much money as you can.

The experiment takes the form of a lottery from which you may receive a monetary gain or loss. Initially, a bag of 80 white poker chips and 20 red poker chips will be placed at the front of the room. A monitor will randomly select a chip from the bag. If a red chip is selected, each participant will lose $4.00. If a white chip is selected, each participant will gain $1.00. Thus, whether you win or lose depends on the random drawing of the chip.

However, each participant will have the option of purchasing one of four insurance policies offered to the group of eight which gives protection to the holder in the event a red chip is drawn. If a red chip is drawn and you are one of the four people who has purchased insurance, you will not have to pay the $4.00 loss. Since only four insurance policies will be available, four of the individuals will be exposed to the risk of drawing a red chip and four individuals will be exempt from it. An auction will be held before each draw in which you will bid along with the other participants for one of the four insurance policies. Thus, you will submit a "dollars and cents" offer by entering your bid on the computer terminal which you feel best represents the amount of money you would be willing to pay to avoid the risk of drawing a red chip and losing $4.00.

Once all eight bids have been collected, they will be ranked from the highest to lowest to determine the "Reigning Bid." The Reigning Bid is determined in the following way. Suppose the ranking of the eight bids representing the group members' willingness to pay to avoid the red chip turns out be (from highest to lowest):

$1.00, $.90, $.80, $.70, $.60, $.50, $.40, $.30.

The Reigning Bid is the fifth highest bid, and in this example is $.60. All bids that are greater than the Reigning Bid will be "Accepted." That is, each group member who bids above the Reigning Bid (those four who bid $1.00, $.90, $.80, $.70) will tentatively have to pay for, and will receive, an insurance policy to avoid the risk of drawing a red chip with a consequent $4.00 loss.

However, each member of the group whose bid is accepted will only have to pay a price for the insurance equal to the Reigning Bid. Thus, in the example above, the individuals who bid $1.00, $.90, $.80, and $.70 will pay only the Reigning Bid, or $.60, for their insurance policy. These people are exempt from the risk of drawing a red chip, and they get to pay less than what they were originally willing to pay for the insurance policy.

Now, on the other hand, all those group members whose bids are equal to or less than the Reigning Bid will be *rejected*. That is, the members in our example who bid $.60, $.50, $.40, and $.30 will not receive an insurance policy and will have no protection from a monetary loss if a red chip is selected. In the event of a tie, the computer will randomly allocate the insurance policies between the participants with equal bids.

After the random selection of a chip, funds will be allocated in accordance with the draw. Your monetary fund will be adjusted to reflect your new cash balance. We now proceed to the next trial where you will again bid for one of four insurance policies for a new independent draw. Note that when you purchase an insurance policy it applies only to that trial which you are in. Follow the same bidding procedures as before in the new trial.

We will begin with four practice trials to familiarize you with the workings of the Auction. In these practice trials the Auction will be carried out as previously described. However, no chip will be drawn from the bag in these trials. Therefore you will neither win nor lose any money and your account balance will be restored to $10 after the four practice trials. In the remaining ten trials of Part II, the results of the auction are binding. That is, there will be an actual draw following each auction and funds will be allocated accordingly.

You must bid anew in each trial period. Each trial is independent, since after a chip is drawn it will be returned to the bag. If your balance becomes zero, or falls below zero, you must still participate in the auction, but you can only bid $0 for an insurance policy. At the end of the experiment, should your final cash balance be negative, you will only receive the $5.00 originally awarded to you for participating in the experiment.

Notes

1. We solve for B/EV because it will be convenient in the analysis to normalize bids by expected value to facilitate comparisons across different probabilities. Note that if there is no risk aversion (i.e., $c = 0$), then $B/EV = 1$.
2. When we have presented this research at meetings, we have been strongly criticized by some psychologists and experimental economists for this deception. Although we thought there were good reasons for doing so at the time this research was conducted, and although we thought the deception was minor because the sequence was indeed random and was not conditioned on the subjects' behavior, we now share concerns about such deception and, thus, we no longer use controlled drawings of the risky event in our research (cf., McClelland and Schulze, 1990).
3. Despite bidding over expected value, no subject approached bankruptcy for several reasons. First, the low-probability risk came late in the sequence after subjects had acquired sizable balances with the other risks due to the $1 gain for a white chip. Second, the Vickrey auction did not usually require subjects to pay the full amount of their bids that exceeded EV by a large amount. Third, the EV for the low-probability risk was so low that paying considerably more than EV did not lead to bankruptcy, because bids were generally below the $1 gain for a white chip. Typical balances at the end of the experiment were approximately $20.
4. Bins were chosen as follows. The largest values of B/EV obtained in the experiment were equal to 50 and occurred at $p = .01$. A logarithmic scale was created by successive halving of this value. Thus, bins were created for values of $B/EV \le 50$ and > 25, ≤ 25 and > 12.5, ≤ 12.5 and > 6.25, ≤ 6.25 and > 3.125, ≤ 3.125 and > 1.5625, ≤ 1.5625 and $> .78125$, $\le .78125$ and $> .390625$, $\le .1953$ and $>$ zero. A separate bin was provided for zero bids. The rounded geometric means of the endpoints of each of the bins are shown along the horizontal axis of figure 2.
5. The experienced hyothetical data point for $p = .2$ was not taken from the experiment described herein but from a pilot study (used to pretest the methodology) where the order of probabilities was different. Thus, an experienced hypothetical value could be obtained for $p = .2$ from this pilot study that, though consistent with this study, is not reported here.
6. These data were included as a comparison condition in a study of the effects of hypothetical versus real consequences by Irwin, McClelland, and Schulze (1992). Additional aspects of these data are reported there.

References

Coppinger, Vicki M., Vernon L. Smith, and Jon A. Titus. (1980). "Incentives and Behavior in English, Dutch, and Sealed-Bid Auctions," *Economics Inquiry* 18, 1–22.

Cummings, Ronald G., David S. Brookshire, and William D. Schulze. (1986). *Valuing Environmental Goods: An Assessment of the Contingent Valuation Method.* Savage, MD: Rowman and Littlefield.

Edwards, Ward (1954). "The Theory of Decision Making." Pslychological Bulletin 41, 380–417

Friend, I. and M.E. Blume. (1975). "The Demand for Risky Assets," *American Economic Review* 65, 900–922.

Harrison, Glenn W. (1989). "Theory and Misbehavior in First-Price Auctions," *American Economic Review* 79, 749–762.

Irwin, Julie R., Gary H. McClelland, and William D. Schulze. (1992). "Hypothetical and Real Consequences in Experimental Auctions for Insurance against Low-probability Risks," *Journal of Behavioral Decision Making* 5, 107–116.

Kahneman, Daniel and Amos Tversky. (1979). "Prospect Theory: An Analysis of Decision Under Risk," *Econometrica* 47, 263–291.

Kunreuther, Howard R., William H. Desvousges, and Paul Slovic. (1988). "Nevada's Predicament: Public Perceptions of Risk from the Proposed Nuclear Waste Repository," *Environment,* 30(8), 16–20, 30–33.

Kunreuther, Howard, R. Ginsberg, L. Miller, P. Sagi, P. Slovic, B. Borkan, and N. Katz. (1978). *Disaster Insurance Protection: Public Policy Lessons.* New York: Wiley.

Loewenstein, George and Jane Mather (1990). "Dynamic Processes in Risk Perception," *Journal of Risk and Uncertainty* 3, 155–175.

Machina, Mark J. (1982). "Expected Utility Analysis without the Independence Axiom," *Econometrica* 50, 227–323.

McClelland, Gary H. and Beverly H. Hackenberg. (1976). "Subjective Probabilities for Sex of Next Child: U.S. College Students and Philippine Villagers," *Journal of Population* 1, 132–147.

McClelland, Gary H., William D. Schulze, and Brian Hurd, (1990). "The Effect of Risk Beliefs on Property Values: A Case Study of a Hazardous Waste Site," *Risk Analysis* 10, 485–497.

Mitchell, Robert C. and Richard T. Carson (1989). *Using Surveys to Value Public Goods: The Contingent Valuation Method.* Washington, DC: Resources for the Future.

Petty, Richard E. and John T. Cacioppo. (1986). "The Motivation to Elaborate in a Relatively Objective Manner." In R.E. Petty and J.T. Cacioppo (eds.), *Communication and Persuasion: Central and Peripheral Routes to Attitude Change.* New York: Springer-Verlag.

Phillips, L.D. and Ward Edwards. (1966). "Conservatism in a Simple Probability Inference Task," *Journal of Experimental Psychology* 72, 346–357.

Showers, Carolin and Nancy Cantor. (1985). "Social Cognition: A Look at Motivated Strategies," *Annual Review of Psychology* 36, 275–305.

Slovic, Paul, Baruch Fischhoff, and Sarah Lichtenstein. (1981). "Informing the Public about the Risks from Ionizing Radiation," *Health Physics* 41, 589–598.

Smith, Vernon L. (1976). "Experimental Economics: Induced Value Theory," *American Economic Review* 66, 274–279.

Smith, Vernon L. and James M. Walker. (1993). "Monetary Rewards and Decision Cost in Experimental Economics," Economic Inquiry 31, 245–261.

Smith, V. Kerry and William H. Desvousges. (1987). "An Empirical Analysis of the Economic Value of Risk Changes," *Journal of Political Economy* 95, 89–114.

Thaler, Richard H. and Eric J. Johnson. (1990). "Gambling with the House Money and Trying to Break Even: The Effects of Prior Outcomes on Risky Choice," *Management Science* 36, 643–660.

Vickrey, W. (1961). "Counterspeculation, Auctions and Competitive Sealed Tenders," *Journal of Finance* 16, 8–37.

[15]

INVESTIGATING GENERALIZATIONS OF EXPECTED UTILITY THEORY USING EXPERIMENTAL DATA

By John D. Hey and Chris Orme[1]

A number of generalizations of the expected utility preference functional are estimated using experimentally generated data involving 100 pairwise choice questions repeated on two separate occasions. Likelihood ratio tests are conducted to investigate the statistical superiority of the various generalizations, and the Akaike information criterion is used to distinguish between them. The economic superiority of the various generalizations is also explored and the paper concludes that, for many subjects, the superiority of several of the generalizations is not established.

Keywords: Expected utility, non-expected utility, risk, preference functionals, pairwise choice, experiments.

1. INTRODUCTION

Experimentally observed violations of expected utility theory (EUT) have stimulated a deluge of generalized preference functionals, almost all containing EUT as a special case. Rather obviously, such generalizations "explain" observed preferences better than EUT, at the expense, equally obviously, of predictive power. This paper reports the outcome of an experimental investigation designed to discover whether (a subset of) these generalizations explain observed data *significantly* better (in a statistical sense) and whether the implied behavior (in an economic sense) is significantly different.

We use experimentally-generated data on preferences to estimate a number of preference functionals. Within the constraints imposed by our data, we tried to estimate as many of the alternative preference functionals as possible. The simplest, of course, is the risk neutral preference functional; an individual with such a functional simply chooses on the basis of *expected value*. The most popular preference functional in use in economics is the expected utility functional; if an individual has such a functional then he or she chooses on the basis of *expected utility*. In this case, estimation of the preference functional is equivalent to estimation of the (Neumann-Morgenstern) utility function. This can be done either without restriction (that is, by estimating the utility associated with each possible outcome) or with some restriction on the functional form (for example, by assuming constant absolute risk aversion). Here we report results using the former approach. Given that our experiment involved just four

[1] We are grateful to the ESRC for financing the experiments reported in this paper and EXEC, the Centre for Experimental Economics at the University of York. Our thanks also to Norman Spivey for writing the software for this experiment and to Michele Bernasconi and Giacomo Pignataro, Research Fellows at the Centre. Our thanks to Graham Loomes for numerous comments, and also to participants at the FUR-VI conference in Paris in June 1992, particularly Colin Camerer, Paul Schoemaker, and Barry Sopher, and to participants at numerous other seminars and conferences, particularly Glenn Harrison. Finally, our grateful thanks to two extremely helpful and constructive referees whose comments improved the paper enormously, as did the comments of a co-editor.

1292 J. D. HEY AND C. ORME

outcomes, this implies that estimation of the expected utility preference functional involves the estimation of four utility values.[2]

The various generalizations of expected utility theory (EUT) estimated in this paper can be classified in a number of ways. For our present purposes the most convenient way is related to the number of *extra* parameters involved in the respective theories: some theories have relatively few extra parameters; some have relatively many—though the numbers may be reduced by the adoption of particular functional forms. The most parsimonious generalizations are disappointment aversion theory (Gul (1991)) and prospective reference theory (Viscusi (1989)); both these involve just *one* extra parameter—irrespective of the number of outcomes and the values of the probabilities. Somewhat less parsimonious is weighted utility theory (Chew (1983)) which requires $(n-2)$ extra parameters—where n is the number of outcomes in the decision problem; these are the *weights* referred to in the theory's name.

The class of models which come under the title of rank dependent expected utility (see, inter alia, Quiggin (1982), Yaari (1987), and Chew, Karni, and Safra (1987)) involve a second function which operates on the cumulative probabilities. The same considerations apply to this function as to the utility function discussed earlier: it can either be estimated without any restrictions or some specific functional form can be assumed. The problem with the first approach is that a relatively large number of parameters have to be estimated. In the context of this experiment, where the cumulative probabilities take the values $i/8$, for $i = 0,\dots,8$, this would involve the estimation of 7 additional parameters.[3] Given the nature of our data we felt that this was too many parameters to estimate. We therefore adopted the following strategy: first, we took two specific functional forms for this probability function—one the power function, and the other a form recommended in Quiggin (1982)—each of these involved just one parameter, so estimation of the rank dependent preference functional under either of these specific functional forms involved just one extra parameter relative to expected utility theory; second, we imposed no functional form on the probability function, but, in order to cut down the number of estimated parameters, we imposed linearity on the utility function; that is, we assumed risk neutrality (in the context of the rank dependent story)—this is Yaari's dual theory (Yaari (1987)). This theory, unlike the other theories which *are* generalizations of expected utility theory, is not such a generalization—though it *is* a generalization of the risk neutral theory.

A preference functional which approaches the pairwise decision problem from a totally different (nonholistic) perspective is that of regret theory. This involves the comparison of each outcome with every other possible outcome, and, in the absence of any restriction on the functional form of these relative "preferences," it involves the estimation of $(n-1)(n/2-1)$ extra parameters relative to expected utility theory. A theory with a rather similar perspective is

[2] Though, because of normalization, one of these can be fixed arbitrarily—see later.
[3] The values for $i = 0$ and $i = 8$ are fixed at 0 and 1 respectively.

that of quadratic utility theory (Chew et al. (1991)); this involves $n(n - 1)/2$ extra parameters.

For each of our subjects, we estimate each of these preference functionals. These estimations enable us to begin to answer the question as to whether (any of) these generalizations is significantly better than EUT (and, indeed, whether EUT and Yaari's dual theory are in turn significantly better than risk neutrality).

The plan of the paper is as follows: Section 2 describes the experimental design and Section 3 the preference functionals under investigation; Section 4 discusses the estimation procedure and Section 5 the results of the estimation; Section 6 then looks at the economic significance of the results, while Section 7 concludes. Appendices contain technical material. The invitation and instructions for the experiment can be obtained from the authors, as well as the computer program and the data generated by the experiment.

2. THE EXPERIMENTAL DATA

The results reported in this paper are part of the findings of a four-part experiment conducted with 80 subjects over a period of a week to 10 days. Each of the 80 subjects performed on separate days (separated by at least one day in every case) a total of four experiments: *Circles* 1, *Dynamics* 1, *Circles* 2, and *Dynamics* 2, in that order. The experiments which concern this paper are the two *Circles* experiments; the two *Dynamics* experiments consisted of a fairly complicated dynamic decision problem under risk. For the analysis of these latter experiments some indication of the subjects' preference functionals was required; this was part of the reason for running the *Circles* experiments, but the analysis of these experiments is self-contained. The average payment made to the 80 subjects over these four experiments was £46.86, with a standard deviation of £15.65; the maximum payment to any one subject was £83.35 and the minimum £7.41. The time taken to complete the experiments varied from subject to subject (we allowed them, and indeed encouraged them, to proceed at their own pace), but the average time was about 45 minutes for each of the *Dynamics* experiments and about 35 minutes for each of the *Circles* experiments. Thus, ignoring any time taken outside the experimental laboratory, the average payment was around £17.50 per hour spent doing the experiments. This is considerably above the marginal wage rate of the subjects performing the experiment, who were all students at the University of York on EXEC's computerized register and who were recruited by mail-shot. Details of the invitation posted to those on the register and the instructions given to those who volunteered are available on request. It was repeatedly emphasized that payment for each experiment was independent of the other experiments, but that no payment would be made until all four experiments had been completed by the subject. Accordingly, we paid subjects for all four experiments after they had performed the final one. Precise details of the payment mechanism are given below.

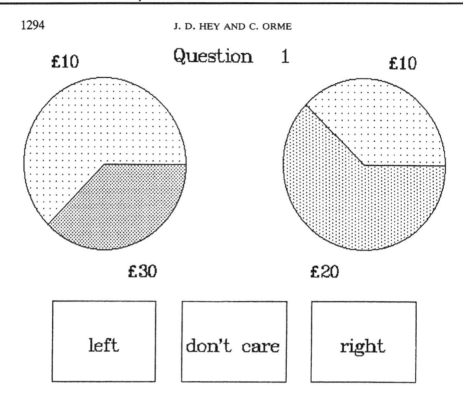

1: left   d: don't care   r: right   enter: confirm choice

FIGURE 1.—A screen dump from the circles experiment.

Each of the *Circles* experiments consisted of 100 pairwise choice questions presented on a computer screen. In each of the 100 questions, subjects were presented with a choice between two risky prospects, portrayed in the form of segmented circles. An example is illustrated in Figure 1; in this, the left-hand circle represents a risky prospect in which there is a five-eighths chance of getting £10 and a three-eighths chance of getting £30; the right-hand circle represents a risky prospect in which there is a three-eighths chance of getting £10 and a five-eighths chance of getting £20. By pressing "*l*" (respectively "*d*" or "*r*") subjects could indicate a preference for the left-hand prospect (respectively indifference or a preference for the right hand prospect). Once they were satisfied with the indicated preference they pressed "Enter" to confirm their choice and moved on to the next question. The incentive mechanism was straightforward: subjects were told that when they had answered all 100 questions, then one of the questions would be chosen at random (using a "roulette wheel" the circumference of which was calibrated from 1 to 100) and their answer to that particular question recalled. Their preferred choice on that particular question was then noted for playing out on completion of all four

EXPECTED UTILITY THEORY

TABLE I

The Twenty-five Pairs of Questions[a]

p_1	p_2	p_3	q_1	q_2	q_3
.625	.000	.375	.375	.625	.000
.375	.625	.000	.500	.250	.250
.000	1.000	.000	.125	.500	.375
.125	.750	.125	.250	.500	.250
.500	.375	.125	.625	.125	.250
.250	.750	.000	.375	.000	.625
.250	.625	.125	.375	.250	.375
.250	.250	.500	.125	.625	.250
.125	.375	.500	.000	1.000	.000
.125	.250	.625	.000	.500	.500
.125	.875	.000	.250	.625	.125
.250	.750	.000	.500	.000	.500
.625	.375	.000	.750	.125	.125
.125	.500	.375	.250	.000	.750
.125	.750	.125	.375	.125	.500
.375	.375	.250	.500	.125	.375
.000	.750	.250	.125	.375	.500
.500	.125	.375	.375	.500	.125
.750	.000	.250	.625	.375	.000
.250	.375	.375	.375	.000	.625
.000	.875	.125	.125	.625	.250
.000	.625	.375	.125	.250	.625
.250	.500	.250	.125	.875	.000
.500	.500	.000	.625	.125	.250
.250	.500	.250	.375	.250	.375

[a] The left-hand gamble takes the values y_1, y_2, and y_3 with respective probabilities p_1, p_2, and p_3 and the right-hand side gamble takes the values y_1, y_2, and y_3 with respective probabilities q_1, q_2, and q_3. The y vector takes the values (£0, £10, £20), (£0, £10, £30), (£0, £20, £30), and (£10, £20, £30).

experiments; if on that question they had indicated indifference, then the experimenter decided which prospect was to be played out.[4] The actual mechanism for "playing out" a particular prospect (at the conclusion of all four experiments) was also straightforward: the prospect had previously been noted on a circular template which was then physically put on top of the "roulette wheel" which the subject then spun themselves. The implication for honest reporting of preferences seemed to be abundantly clear to the subjects.[5] This procedure had been used earlier in a pilot experiment reported in Hey and Di Cagno (1990). In this pilot, subjects were asked just 60 questions and we discovered that 60 was fewer than we could reasonably ask within the attention span of the subjects.

---

[4] The mechanism by which the experimenter would choose was not specified.

[5] We are, of course, aware of the objections raised by Holt (1986) to the effect that, if the subject's preference functional is not EU, then this incentive mechanism may not induce honest reporting of preferences. We are also aware of work by Starmer and Sugden (1991) which suggests that this may not be a problem in practice. Much depends on how subjects reduce multi-stage gambles to single stage gambles, and, in particular, on whether they use the certainty-equivalent mechanism. If they do, then Holt's objection loses much of its force.

The 100 questions were composed of 4 sets of (the same) 25 questions, each set applied to 3 of the 4 amounts £0, £10, £20, and £30. The probabilities were all multiplies of one-eighth—and the subjects were informed of this.[6] Table I gives details of these 25 pairs.[7] The 100 questions were arranged in random order. The same 100 questions were used in *Circles* 1 and *Circles* 2, except insofar as the order was changed randomly and the positions of the two circles in each question reversed (so that if a prospect was on the left in *Circles* 1 it was on the right in *Circles* 2 and *vice versa*). This procedure enabled us to carry out a consistency check on the subjects' answers; this is something which is very rarely done in this type of experiment. The average consistency rate turned out to be around 75%.[8]

3. THE PREFERENCE FUNCTIONALS

First, some notation. Let $x = (x_1, x_2, x_3, x_4)$ denote the four consequences (£0, £10, £20, and £30) used in this experiment; let $p = (p_1, p_2, p_3, p_4)$ denote the respective probabilities in the gamble on the left-hand side of the computer screen and $q = (q_1, q_2, q_3, q_4)$ denote the respective probabilities in the gamble on the right-hand side. All the theories considered imply a valuation of the left-hand gamble relative to the right-hand gamble; and, *except* in the case of regret theory, these valuations are obtained by simply subtracting the valuation of the right-hand gamble from the valuation of the left-hand gamble. Regret theory arrives directly at a relative evaluation. The details are as follows, where $V(p, q)$ denotes the relative evaluation (that is, the subject prefers the left-hand gamble to the right-hand gamble if and only if $V(p, q)$ is greater than zero, and is indifferent between them if $V(p, q)$ is equal to zero). The two letters to the left of the theory's name are the abbreviation that we will be using henceforth to refer to that theory.

RN—R*isk* N*eutrality*:

$$V(p, q) = W(p) - W(q) \qquad \text{where}$$

$$W(r) = k[r_2 x_2 + r_3 x_3 + r_4 x_4].$$

(Recall that $x_1 = 0$.)

Here the parameter to be estimated is k. (See later concerning the normalization of the error variance to unity.)

---

[6] This avoids possible misperceptions of the probabilities. We decided that any finer division of the probabilities—say into tenths—would be too difficult for the subjects; whilst any cruder division —say into sixths—would be too uninformative for us.

[7] Perhaps we should note that there is a design problem in the choice of these 25 pairs, and, more generally, in the choice of the 100 pairs. Some choices will lead to more accurate estimates than other choices. However, the "best" choice depends on the subject's actual preference functional—which we do not know *ex ante*. A useful discussion of these and related issues can be found in Mueller and Ponce de Leon (1992).

[8] Note that this is a check as to whether subjects give the same answer when confronted with essentially the same question, though with left and right reversed and with the question appearing in a different position in the set of questions. They were never given exactly identical questions so we cannot test the consistency rate under identical conditions.

EXPECTED UTILITY THEORY   1297

EU—*Subjective Expected Utility Theory*:

$$V(p,q) = W(p) - W(q) \quad \text{where}$$

$$W(r) = r_2 u(x_2) + r_3 u(x_3) + r_4 u(x_4).$$

Here the parameters to be estimated are $u(x_i)$, $i = 2, 3, 4$. Note that we have normalized[9] so that $u(x_1) = 0$. For expected utility theory, as is well known, the utility function is unique only up to a linear transformation, which usually means that one can set *two* utility values arbitrarily. However, as we shall show later, the second normalization is taken care of by our assumption concerning the nature of the error term. Note that **EU** reduces to **RN** when $u(x) = kx$—implying two restrictions in the context of this experiment.

DA—*Disappointment Aversion Theory*:

This is a model introduced by Gul (1991); it models behavior as incorporating ex post disappointment or elation, depending on whether the actual outcome is worse or better than that expected, with the decision-maker anticipating such feelings ex ante. Here our characterization appears different from that in Gul (1991), but it can be shown (see Appendix 1) that they are identical; ours is more useful for our present purposes.

$$V(p,q) = W(p) - W(q) \quad \text{where}$$

$$W(r) = \min\{W_1, W_2, W_3\} \quad \text{and where}$$

$$W_1 = \frac{[(1+\beta)r_2 u(x_2) + (1+\beta)r_3 u(x_3) + r_4 u(x_4)]}{(1 + \beta r_1 + \beta r_2 + \beta r_3)},$$

$$W_2 = [(1+\beta)r_2 u(x_2) + r_3 u(x_3) + r_4 u(x_4)]/(1 + \beta r_1 + \beta r_2),$$

$$W_3 = [r_2 u(x_2) + r_3 u(x_3) + r_4 u(x_4)]/(1 + \beta r_1).$$

Again, we have normalized so that $u(x_1) = 0$. Here the parameters to be estimated are $u(x_i)$, $i = 2, 3, 4$ and β. The parameter β is Gul's additional parameter; if $\beta = 0$, **DA** reduces to **EU**.

PR—*Prospective Reference Theory*:

This is a model introduced by Viscusi (1989); it models behavior as depending upon a preference functional which is a weighted average of the expected utility functional using the correct probability weights and the expected utility functional using equal probability weights for all the non-null outcomes.

$$V(p,q) = W(p) - W(q) \quad \text{where}$$

$$W(r) = \lambda[r_2 u(x_2) + r_3 u(x_3) + r_4 u(x_4)]$$
$$+ (1-\lambda)[c_2 u(x_2) + c_3 u(x_3) + c_4 u(x_4)]$$

where $c_i = 1/n(r)$ if $r_i > 0$ and 0 otherwise, and where $n(r)$ is the number of nonzero elements in the vector r. Here the normalization is the same as the

---

[9] An alternative interpretation, of course, is that $u(x_i)$ measures the difference between the utility of x_i and the utility of x_1. The difference is inessential.

expected utility normalization: $u(x_1) = 0$. Here the parameters to be estimated are $u(x_i)$, $i = 2, 3, 4$ and λ. Viscusi (1989) refers to λ as the weight of the "relative information content... associated with the stated lottery" and $(1 - \lambda)$ as the weight of the "relative information content... associated with the reference probability." Note that if $\lambda = 1$ then **PR** reduces to **EU**.

QU—Q*uadratic Utility*:

This is a model introduced by Chew, Epstein, and Segal (1991). Its motivation is the weakening of the independence axiom of EUT to an axiom (even weaker than the betweenness axiom) known as mixture symmetry. This requires that if F and G are the cumulative probability functions of two risky prospects about which an individual feels indifferent, then for any mixture $\alpha F + (1 - \alpha)G$ with $0 < \alpha < 0.5$ there is some β ($0.5 < \beta < 1$) such that this mixture is indifferent for this individual to the mixture $\beta F + (1 - \beta)G$. The implied preference functional:

$$V(p, q) = W(p) - W(q) \qquad \text{where}$$

$$W(r) = \sum_{i=1}^{4} \sum_{j=1}^{4} \psi(x_i, x_j) r_i r_j$$

and where $\psi(x_i, x_j) = \psi(x_j, x_i)$. Here we normalize so that $\psi(x_1, x_1) = 0$. Note that **QU** reduces to **EU** if $\psi(x_i, x_j) = [u(x_i) + u(x_j)]/2$ for all i and j, a total of 6 restrictions in the context of this experiment.

RD—R*egret Theory* (*with* D*ependence*):

The regret model was effectively introduced simultaneously by Bell (1982) and by Loomes and Sugden (1982); it was later generalized by Loomes and Sugden (1987). It models behavior as incorporating ex post regret or rejoicing depending upon whether the outcome under the actual choice is worse or better than the outcome that would have resulted from the rejected choice, with the decision-maker anticipating such feelings ex ante. We estimate two versions, this first assuming dependence between the two gambles in the manner described below:

$$V(p, q) = z_1 \psi(x_2, x_1) + z_2 \psi(x_3, x_2) + z_3 \psi(x_4, x_3)$$
$$+ z_4 \psi(x_3, x_1) + z_5 \psi(x_4, x_2) + z_6 \psi(x_4, x_1).$$

Here the $z = (z_1, z_2, z_3, z_4, z_5, z_6)$ is a function (which cannot easily be written in analytical form—see Appendix 1) of p and q. This "dependence" characterization assumes that the subject juxtaposes the two gambles in the orientation in which they appear on the screen. So, for example, in Question 1 as it appears in Figure 1, we have $z_1 = 0.0$ (because £0 and £10 are never juxtaposed), $z_2 = 0.250$ (because £20 appears on the right-hand gamble and £10 appears on the left-hand gamble between southwest and northwest (one-quarter of the time)), $z_3 = -0.375$ (because £30 appears on the left-hand gamble and £20 appears on the right-hand gamble between southwest and east (three-eighths of the time)), and $z_4 = z_5 = z_6 = 0.0$ (because £20 and £0, and £30 and £10, and £30 and £0 are never juxtaposed). Here the parameters to be estimated are the $\psi(x_i, x_j)$ for $j = 1, 2, 3$ and $i > j$, though, given the gambles used in this experiment $\psi(x_4, x_1)$

cannot be estimated since x_4 and x_1 are never juxtaposed. Note that **RD** reduces to **EU** if $\psi(x_i, x_j) = u(x_i) - u(x_j)$ for all x_i and x_j; a total of two restrictions in the context of this experiment.

RI—*Regret Theory (with Independence)*:

This second version of regret theory assumes independence between the two gambles, as described below.

$$V(p,q) = (p_1q_2 - p_2q_1)\psi(x_2, x_1) + (p_2q_3 - p_3q_2)\psi(x_3, x_2)$$
$$+ (p_3q_4 - p_4q_3)\psi(x_4, x_3) + (p_1q_3 - p_3q_1)\psi(x_3, x_1)$$
$$+ (p_2q_4 - p_4q_2)\psi(x_4, x_2) + (p_1q_4 - p_4q_1)\psi(x_4, x_1).$$

This characterization assumes that the subject views the two gambles as being statistically independent. The parameters to be estimated are the same as in the **RD** model. Note that **RI** reduces to **EU** if $\psi(x_i, x_j) = u(x_i) - u(x_j)$ for all x_i and x_j; a total of three restrictions in the context of this experiment.

RP—*Rank Dependence with the Power Weighting Function*:

The rank dependent expected utility model is the outcome of a number of contributions, including Quiggin (1982), Yaari (1987), and Chew, Karni and Safra (1987). It models behavior as ranking the outcomes in order of preference and then distorting the decumulative probabilities (of getting at least a given outcome) through some "probability weighting function." We estimate two versions, this first assuming that the probability weighting function takes the specific functional form of the *power* function.

$$V(p,q) = u(x_2)[W_1(p) - W_1(q)] + u(x_3)[W_2(p) - W_2(q)]$$
$$+ u(x_4)[W_3(p) - W_3(q)] \qquad \text{where}$$
$$W_1(r) = w(r_2 + r_3 + r_4) - w(r_3 + r_4),$$
$$W_2(r) = w(r_3 + r_4) - w(r_4),$$
$$W_3(r) = w(r_4),$$
$$w(r) = r^\gamma.$$

Here the parameters to be estimated are $u(x_i)$, $i = 2, 3, 4$, and γ. Note that **RP** reduces to **EU** if $\gamma = 1$.

RQ—*Rank Dependence with the 'Quiggin' Weighting Function*:

This second version of rank dependent **EU** assumes that the weighting function $w(\cdot)$ takes the specific functional form recommended by Quiggin (1982). It allows the probability function to be S-shaped:

$$w(r) = r^\gamma / [r^\gamma + (1 - r)^\gamma]^{1/\gamma}.$$

Here the parameters to be estimated are $u(x_i)$, $i = 2, 3, 4$, and γ. Note that **RQ** reduces to **EU** if $\gamma = 1$.

WU—*Weighted Utility Theory*:

This model was proposed by Chew (1983) and Dekel (1986) inter alia. It takes as its raison d'etre the relaxation of the strong independence axiom (of EUT) to a form known as the weak independence axiom (see Chew (1983)). This requires that if F and G are the cumulative probability functions of two risky prospects about which the individual feels indifferent, then for any mixture $\alpha F + (1 - \alpha)H$ there is some β for which this mixture is indifferent for this individual to the mixture $\beta G + (1 - \beta)H$ for all H:

$$V(p,q) = W(p) - W(q) \qquad \text{where}$$

$$W(r) = \left[w_2 r_2 u(x_2) + w_3 r_3 u(x_3) + r_4 u(x_4) \right] / \left[r_1 + r_2 w_2 + r_3 w_3 + r_4 \right].$$

Here w_2 and w_3 are the *weights* attached to x_2 and x_3. Once again, the normalization is that $u(x_1)$ is put equal to zero; in addition, we set the weights attached to x_1 and x_4 equal to unity (see Chew (1983)). Here the parameters to be estimated are $u(x_i)$, $i = 2, 3, 4$, and w_2 and w_3. Note that **WU** reduces to **EU** if w_2 and w_3 (the weights attached to x_2 and x_3 respectively) are additionally both equal to unity.

YD—*Yaari's Dual Model*:

As already discussed, this model proposed by Yaari (1987) is a special case of the rank dependent expected utility model where the probability function is left completely general but the utility function is assumed to be linear:

$$V(p,q) = W(p) - W(q) \qquad \text{where}$$

$$W(r) = k \left[(x_2 - x_1)w(r_2 + r_3 + r_4) + (x_3 - x_2) \right.$$

$$\left. \times w(r_3 + r_4) + (x_4 - x_3)w(r_4) \right] \qquad \text{where}$$

$$w(r) = \beta_i \qquad \text{if} \qquad r = 0.125i, \qquad i = 1, \ldots, 7;$$

$$w(0) = 0 \quad \text{and} \quad w(1) = 1.$$

Here the parameters to be estimated are the β_i $(i = 1, \ldots, 7)$ and k. Note that **YD** reduces to **RN** if $\beta_i = 0.125i$ (for $i = 1, \ldots, 7$), a total of 7 restrictions in the context of this experiment.

4. THE ESTIMATION PROCEDURE

We assume that all subjects are different. We therefore fit each of the 11 preference functionals discussed above to the subject's stated preferences for each of the 80 subjects *individually*. For the purposes of estimation, we need to make some assumption about the *stochastic* structure underlying the observations. The theories themselves are of no help in this respect since they are all theories of *deterministic* choice.[10] This, in turn, implies (if none of the preference functionals discussed above fits any subject's stated preferences exactly and if no other preference functional not considered here is in fact the correct functional) that the subject must be stating his or her preferences *with some error*. Such error may arise from a variety of sources: the subjects could misunderstand the nature of the experiment; they could press the wrong key by

---

[10] There *are* theories of stochastic choice, but these are not the concern of this paper, nor indeed of much of the recent debate concerning preference functionals.

accident; they could be in a hurry to complete the experiment; they could be motivated by something other than maximizing their welfare from participating in the experiment. For rather obvious reasons, we confine attention to what we might term "genuine" error—mistakes, carelessness, slips, inattentiveness, etc. —and we make what is possibly the most natural assumption for an economist to make: namely that the effect of such error is to add a white noise, normally distributed, zero-mean error term to the valuations given by the various preference functionals. The Central Limit Theorem could be invoked to support such an assumption.[11] This would suggest that the stated preferences were based on the value of y^*, given by:

$$y^* = V(p,q) + \varepsilon \qquad \text{where } \varepsilon \text{ is } N(0,1).$$

Note that we have put the error variance equal to unity. This is a further normalization. An alternative procedure, say with the expected utility characterization, would be, in addition to $u(x_1) = 0$, to put (say) $u(x_4) = 1$ and then specify the error variance to be σ^2; in this case we would estimate σ in addition to $u(x_2)$ and $u(x_3)$. We choose instead to put the error variance equal to unity and then estimate $u(x_2)$, $u(x_3)$, and $u(x_4)$. The difference is inessential, though we do have to be careful in interpreting the results: other things being equal, under our procedure, a subject who makes relatively small errors will have relatively large values for $u(x_2)$, $u(x_3)$, and $u(x_4)$, while a subject who makes relatively large errors will have relatively small values for $u(x_2)$, $u(x_3)$, and $u(x_4)$. Under the alternative procedure, the relatively careful subject would have a relatively small value for σ.

We need now to distinguish between two types of subject: (1) a subject who *always* expressed a strict preference for either the left-hand gamble or the right-hand gamble; (2) a subject who *sometimes*[12] expressed indifference between the left- and right-hand gambles. We should emphasize that these distinctions must be made separately for each of the two circles experiments, since there were some subjects who always expressed strict preference in *Circles* 1 but sometimes expressed indifference in *Circles* 2, and vice versa.

These two types of subjects need to be treated differently. The first type is straightforward; our assumptions imply that the data generating mechanism is

---

[11] We are, however, exploring other possibilities: for example, that questions vary in their difficulty, and hence that the error variance varies from question to question. In a sense, this simply removes the problem one stage: we now need to specify what determines the difficulty of a question. However, we do have data, for each subject, on how long it took the subject to answer each question; preliminary estimations suggest that the error variance may be proportional to this time, though one needs to correct for a general speeding up of the time to answer as subjects proceeded through the 100 questions. For some other thoughts in this direction see Wilcox (1993).

[12] It is not clear why they might do this, for even if they are genuinely indifferent between the two gambles, there is nothing for them to gain by saying so. Contrariwise, there is no reason for them not to do so. This *might* have serious consequences for our estimation procedures, if, for example, a subject were to always reply "1" when genuinely indifferent, but it is not clear what might be done to identify or rectify such bias.

1302   J. D. HEY AND C. ORME

given by:

left-hand gamble stated as preferred if $y^* > 0$,

right-hand gamble stated as preferred if $y^* \leq 0$.

For the second type, we need to make an additional assumption about the circumstances under which indifference is stated. The natural assumption is that this occurs whenever y^* is close to zero, and that closeness should be defined in a symmetrical manner. This gives as the data generating mechanism:

left-hand gamble stated as preferred if $y^* > \tau$,

right-hand gamble stated as preferred if $y^* \leq -\tau$,

indifference stated if $-\tau < y^* \leq \tau$.

Here we have an additional parameter to estimate: the *threshold* parameter τ. Note that for the first type of subject, our assumptions effectively constrain τ to be equal to zero; if, on the other hand, we tried to use the second data generating mechanism for type (1) subjects, the maximum likelihood estimate of τ for them would also be zero, since by definition such subjects never reported indifference.

Finally, we assume that the errors are independently distributed across questions. This completes the stochastic specification. Maximum likelihood methods were used to derive the parameter estimates. Technical details are given in Appendix 2 and Orme (1995).

5. THE ESTIMATED PREFERENCE FUNCTIONALS

We refer to the data obtained from *Circles* 1 as *Data Set* 1; that obtained from *Circles* 2 as *Data Set* 2; and these two data sets combined as *Data Set* 3. We estimated each of the 11 preference functions described in Section 3 for each of the 80 subjects for each of these three data sets. This gives a total of 2,640 estimated preference functionals, a grand total of 12,960 behavioral parameters[13] and 1,221 threshold parameters.[14] Clearly there is not space to present all estimates here,[15] but we should draw attention to some of the more interesting features of the estimated models.

Possibly of fairly immediate concern is whether the estimated models "make sense" in terms of their coefficients. There are a number of criteria one might use in judging this. The first is whether the coefficients have the right signs, or more generally are in the right ranges. For all the models which involve some kind of utility valuations, we would expect (on the presumption that some money is preferred to none) that all these utility coefficients would be positive; likewise, in the regret models we would expect all the Ψ coefficients to be

---

[13] RN has just 1 parameter; EU has 3; each of **DA, PR, RK**, and **RP** has 4; **RD** and **WU** both have 5; **RI** has 6; **YD** has 8 parameters; and **QU** has 9 parameters.
[14] Of the 240 = (3 times 80) subject/data sets, 111 expressed indifference on at least one of the 100 questions.
[15] We can provide a full set of results, and data, on request.

positive, and in the quadratic utility model likewise. In addition, in prospective reference theory, the parameter λ should lie between 0 and 1 for the theory to "make sense;" in the two versions of rank dependent expected utility theory the parameter γ should be positive; and in weighted utility theory, the weights w_2 and w_3 should both be positive. In disappointment aversion theory the parameter β should be greater than -1. Finally, in Yaari's dual model we would expect the parameter k to be positive and all the β values to lie between 0 and 1 (since they are (distorted) probabilities). Table II gives a summary (across subjects for each data set) of how often such restrictions were met. Clearly risk neutrality does not fare particularly well, since, as we shall see, this functional does not fit the data very well for the majority of the subjects. Most of the other theories however perform fairly well on this criterion, though **YD** understandably falls down rather often—as the criteria are rather strict.

In addition, Figure 2 presents a number of informative histograms: in Figure 2a of the distribution of the β parameter in the disappointment aversion model; in Figure 2b of the λ parameter in the prospective reference model; and in Figures 2c and 2d of the γ parameter in the two versions of the rank dependent model. Additionally, Figure 3a presents a scatter diagram of the w_2 versus the w_3 parameters in the weighted utility model.

There are a number of things to note from these figures. First (from Figure 2a) it can be seen that the β parameter in the disappointment aversion model takes both negative and positive values, which is at odds with the explanation proffered by Gul (1991), where a positive value is suggested. Second (from Figure 2b), the λ parameter in the prospective reference model is occasionally larger than unity—which is disallowed by the theory; this, of course, is reflected in the entries in Table 2.[16] Third (from Figures 2c and 2d) the γ parameter in the two versions of the rank dependent model take values both greater and smaller than unity; this indicates that the weighting function takes a variety of shapes. Fourth (from Figure 3a) it seems to be the case that the estimated w_2 and w_3 values are fairly symmetrically distributed around unity (which is the special case when **WU** reduces to **EU**).

A second possible criterion is whether the estimated coefficients satisfy the implied (strict) *monotonicity* conditions. For example, in the various models which imply some kind of utility valuations, we would expect the coefficients to be increasing in the monetary amounts; that is $u(x_4) > u(x_3) > u(x_2) > 0$. In the regret formulations, the theory requires that $\psi(x_i, x_j)$ be increasing in x_i and decreasing in x_j. In the quadratic utility model, the theory requires that $\psi(x_i, x_j)$ be increasing in x_i and that $\psi(x_i, x_i)$ be larger than $\psi(x_j, x_j)$ if x_i is larger than x_j. Finally, in Yaari's dual model, (strict) monotonicity requires that the coefficients β_i be (strictly) increasing in i, and that β_1 be (strictly) positive and β_7 (strictly) less than 1. Table III summarizes how well the various models

---

[16] We did not constrain any of the parameters to lie in their theoretically-approved ranges in the estimation process. If we had, then in those cases such as those in the prospective reference model where the estimated value of λ is outside the range zero to one, with the imposition of the restriction the model would simply have reduced to expected utility.

TABLE II

SUMMARY OF CORRECT SIGNS ON COEFFICIENTS

		b		
Model	a	Data Set 1	Data Set 2	Data Set 3
RN	80	34	26	30
EU	240	240	240	240
DA	320	320	320	320
PR	320	297	298	302
QU	720	693	678	693
RD	400	387	376	391
RI	480	467	457	471
RP	320	319	320	320
RQ	320	320	320	320
WU	400	398	399	400
YD	640	465	423	459

Key: a—total number of estimated coefficients; b—total number of coefficients with the correct sign.

satisfy these monotonicity requirements. Understandably, those models with more requirements (particularly **QU**, **RD**, **RI**, and **YD**) do rather worse than those with less requirements. Nevertheless, it is instructive to see how well **EU**, **DA**, **PR**, **RP**, **RQ**, and **WU** do on this test.

A third possible criterion concerns the *concavity/convexity* properties of the various models. Table IV summarizes these properties for the various estimated functionals. As far as **EU** and its various near generalizations (**DA, PR, WU, RP,** and **RQ**) are concerned, it is interesting to note that the dominant pattern is either concavity everywhere (indicating risk aversion everywhere) or concavity followed by convexity—indicating risk aversion for small amounts of money and risk loving for larger amounts. We should note that for the two special cases of rank dependence where a specific functional form is chosen for the probability weighting function (**RP** and **RQ**), the table entries refer to the utility function. This is not the case for **YD**—but here no clear pattern emerges (which is hardly surprising).

Figure 3 presents a number of scatter diagrams of certain key parameters. Table III confirms that the regret specifications do not conform particularly well to the convexity property assumed by Loomes and Sugden (1987); this reflects the results of Table IV.

A fourth possible criterion is whether the parameter estimates are stable across data sets. The usual Chow test can be applied in this context: if we denote by LL_i the log-likelihood of a particular model under Data Set i, then under the null hypothesis that the coefficients *are* the same in both Data Set 1 and Data Set 2, the statistic

$$2[(LL_1 + LL_2) - LL_3]$$

will have a chi-square distribution with k degrees of freedom where k is the number of estimated parameters in that particular model. Table V summarizes the results of carrying out this test for each of the 11 preference functionals at

(a) Histogram for the beta variable in the disappointment aversion model (outlying values for subjects 16, 38, 59, and 64 put equal to zero).

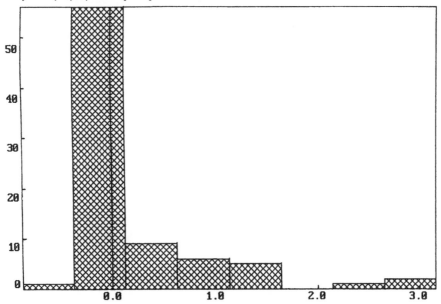

(b) Histogram for lambda parameter in prospective reference model (value of missing estimate for subject 76 put equal to 0.0).

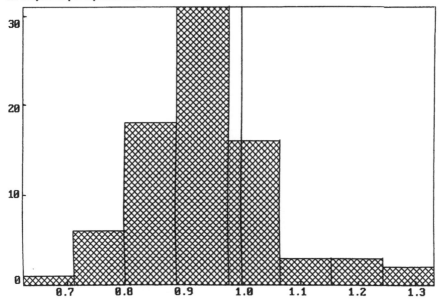

FIGURE 2.—Distributions of certain selected estimated coefficients.

(c) Histogram for gamma parameter in rank dependent model RK.

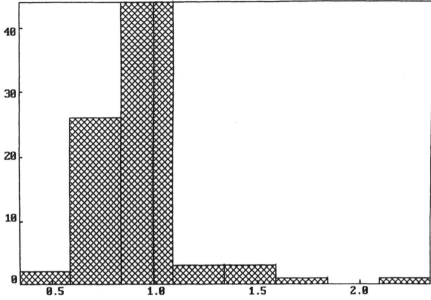

(d) Histogram for gamma parameter in rank dependent model RP (missing and outlying values for subjects 16, 59, and 62 put to 1.0).

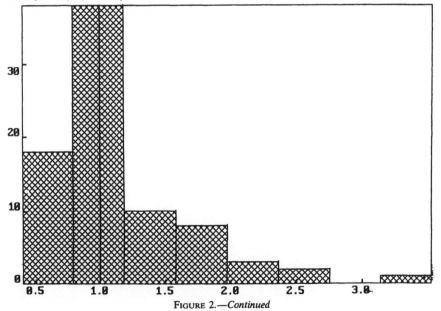

FIGURE 2.—*Continued*

TABLE III

SUMMARY OF SATISFACTION OF MONOTONICITY CONDITIONS
ON COEFFICIENTS

Model	Data Set 1	Data Set 2	Data Set 3
EU	77	75	75
DA	77	70	77
PR	78	74	79
QU	25	35	40
RD	47	34	53
RI	46	44	52
RP	76	77	74
RQ	79	76	79
WU	74	72	77
YD	26	20	26

both the 5% and the 1% significance level. It will be seen that there is considerable instability between the two data sets, with significantly different estimates (at the 5% level) for more than half the subjects. One might legitimately enquire why this is the case. One possible explanation is that between the first and second repetitions of the experiment the subjects thought about the nature of the experiment rather more deeply than they had before the first repetition, to the effect that the second repetition reflects their "true" preferences, whilst the first contains more "noise." It is not clear that the data supports this interpretation; an alternative explanation is that each repetition is just a smallish sample of observations of the true behavior—with randomness *suggesting* different explanations on the two repetitions. Further repetitions would be needed to distinguish between these two alternatives.

We now turn to one of the key issues: do the more general theories fit the data significantly better than the less general theories? Of our 11 preference functionals, we have three "levels" of functional: at the bottom level is **RN**; at the middle level are **EU** and **YD**; and at the top level are the remaining 8

TABLE IV

SUMMARY OF CONVEXITY / CONCAVITY PROPERTIES

Model	Data Set 1				Data Set 2				Data Set 3			
	a	b	c	d	a	b	c	d	a	b	c	d
EU	40	3	33	4	52	3	24	1	49	2	27	2
DA	35	2	39	3	49	1	29	1	45	2	32	1
PR	46	2	30	2	56	2	21	1	55	0	24	1
QU	25	2	*	*	35	1	*	*	36	2	*	*
RD	11	18	*	*	15	12	*	*	12	19	*	*
RI	9	22	*	*	11	19	*	*	8	23	*	*
RP	40	1	36	3	47	1	31	1	48	1	30	1
RQ	42	3	33	2	50	2	27	1	47	0	32	1
WU	35	4	37	4	54	1	23	2	49	1	26	4
YD	0	5	0	0	0	6	0	0	0	9	0	0

Key: a: strictly concave everywhere; b: strictly convex everywhere; c: s-shaped—first concave then convex; d: s-shaped—first convex then concave; *: not tested (see text).

1308   J. D. HEY AND C. ORME

(a) Scatter plot of $w2$ vs. $w3$ for weighted utility model (missing and outlying values for subjects 10, 51, 53, and 80 put at 1.0).

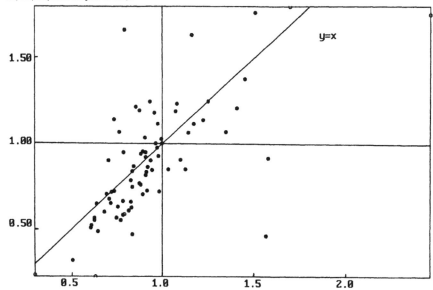

(b) Scatter plot of $\psi(£20, £0)$ vs. $\psi(£20, £10) + \psi(£10, £0)$ for regret RD model.

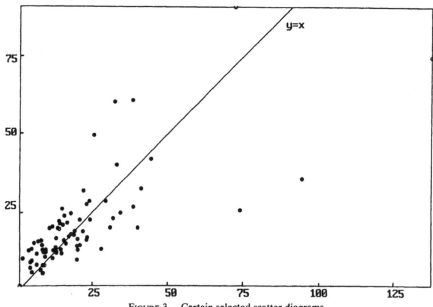

FIGURE 3.—Certain selected scatter diagrams.

(c) Scatter plot of ψ(£30, £10) vs. ψ(£30, £20) + ψ(£20, £10) for regret RD model.

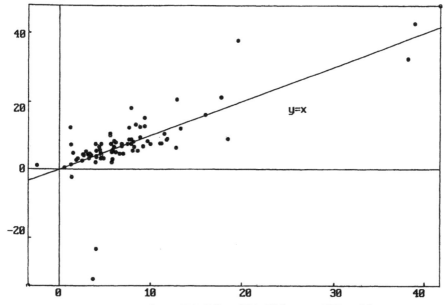

(d) Scatter plot of ψ(£30, £0) vs. ψ(£30, £10) + ψ(£10, £0) for regret RD model.

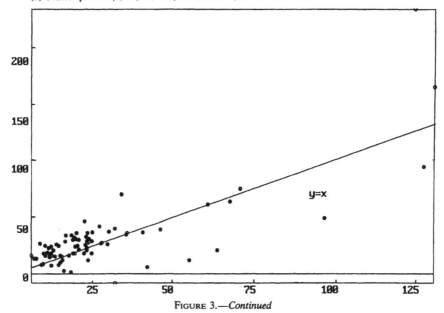

FIGURE 3.—*Continued*

TABLE V

RESULTS OF TESTS OF STABILITY
OF COEFFICIENTS ACROSS THE TWO DATA SETS

Preference Functional	Number of subjects for whom test significant at	
	5%	1%
RN	39	27
EU	48	36
DA	47	35
PR	49	40
QU	50	32
RD	49	35
RI	49	36
RP	50	39
RK	50	39
WU	51	38
YD	34	25

functionals. **EU** and **YD** are generalizations of **RN** in the sense that the latter is a special case of each of the former; and the 8 top-level functionals are all generalizations of **EU** in the sense that the latter is a special case of all 8 of the former. Moving down from the higher levels to the lower levels involves parameter restrictions: in the context of this experiment going from **EU** to **RN** involves 2 parameter restrictions, going from **YD** to **RN** involves 7 parameter restrictions, whilst going from **DA, PR, QU, RD, RI, RP, RQ,** and **WU** to **EU** involves respectively 1, 1, 6, 2, 3, 1, 1, and 2 parameter restrictions (for details see Section 4 above). Accordingly, we can use standard likelihood ratio tests to investigate whether the higher level functionals fit significantly better than the lower level functionals—by which we mean that the parameter restrictions which reduce the higher-level functional to the lower-level functional are rejected at the appropriate significance level.

Formally, if LL_a and LL_b are the estimated log-likelihoods for models a and b respectively, and if model a is obtained from model b by imposing k parameter restrictions, then, under the null hypothesis that these restrictions are satisfied, the test statistic $2(LL_b - LL_a)$ has a chi-squared distribution with k degrees of freedom.[17]

[17] We acknowledge the fact that care should be taken when interpreting the results of a likelihood ratio test for which the null hypothesis constrains one or more of the parameters of the alternative model to lie on the boundary of the parameter space. For example, prospective reference theory reduces to expected utility theory by forcing the "weight," λ, to be unity, a value which is on the boundary of admissible values for λ. Formal maximum likelihood estimation of the former (more general) model should enforce this restriction on λ and this effects the resulting limiting distribution of the likelihood ratio test statistic (it will not be the usual chi-square). However, if "pseudo-maximum likelihood" is adopted then the familiar asymptotic results remain valid (see Godrey (1988, pp. 92–96), for a brief but illuminating discussion). In this study, inequality restrictions were not enforced and we are content to apply usual asymptotic theory to the likelihood ratio test statistic. Finally, we should also comment on the fact that, for some parameter sets, the likelihood function in the **DA** model can have a cusp at the value $\beta = 0$ (the **EU** special case); this means that the likelihood functional is not differentiable at the maximum value—which creates problems for the usual test procedures.

EXPECTED UTILITY THEORY   1311

TABLE VI

LIKELIHOOD RATIO TESTS OF THE SUPERIORITY
OF THE HIGHER LEVEL MODELS

(1) The Top Level Functionals versus Expected Utility

| | Number of subjects for whom test significant at | | | | | |
| | 5% | | | 1% | | |
Preference Functional	Data Set 1	Data Set 2	Data Set 3	Data Set 1	Data Set 2	Data Set 3
DA	18	26	27	11	13	22
PR	30	41	44	24	27	36
QU	31	38	46	20	23	36
RD	16	15	22	8	7	10
RI	36	36	44	21	19	33
RP	24	22	31	12	13	22
RQ	38	42	46	28	34	39
WU	36	35	43	20	23	28

(2) Expected Utility and Yaari Dual Model versus Risk Neutrality

| | Number of subjects for whom test significant at | | | | | |
| | 5% | | | 1% | | |
Preference Functional	Data Set 1	Data Set 2	Data Set 3	Data Set 1	Data Set 2	Data Set 3
EU	72	73	74	69	72	73
YD	61	74	74	54	68	71

Table VI reports the results of carrying out such tests for each of the three Data Sets. The bottom part of the table shows that risk neutrality is rejected in favor of both **EU** and **YD** for the vast majority of the subjects. The top part of the table contains a number of interesting features, perhaps the most notable of which is the rather obvious fact, particularly at the 1% level, that **EU** is rejected (in favor of one of the top-level functionals) for considerably more subjects on the combined data set (Data Set 3) than on each of the two individual data sets. This lends support to the tentative hypothesis suggested above that behavior actually is more complicated than **EU**, but that in small samples (because of the rather weak nature of our data) **EU** is not rejected (because of the lack of significant evidence against).

Table VI also gives some insight into which of the top level functionals might be better explanations than others.[18] Looking first at the two regret formulations, **RD** and **RI**, it can be seen that the data support the latter. This suggests that subjects perceived the two lotteries as being played out independently, rather than juxtaposed in the fashion that they appear on the screen. We must admit that our original supposition was that subjects would assume independence, and that the idea to estimate regret assuming dependence was suggested by one of the referees, but it is nice to estimate the two and see the independence result emerging (rather than being assumed). Generally, regret does well,

---

[18] Though we must emphasize that we believe that individuals are different and that what might be a good theory for one individual might be a bad theory for another.

TABLE VII

AVERAGE RANKINGS (USING THE AKAIKE INFORMATION CRITERION)

	RN	EU	DA	PR	QU	RD	RI	RP	RQ	WU	YD
Data Set 1	10.1	5.2	6.0	4.0	6.3	6.3	5.3	4.8	3.5	4.7	9.6
Data Set 2	10.5	5.4	5.2	4.0	6.2	6.5	5.4	5.4	3.9	4.9	8.7
Data Set 3	10.5	5.9	5.7	3.9	5.2	6.7	5.1	5.4	3.8	4.9	8.9

as does prospective reference theory and the two versions of the rank dependent model (**RP** and **RQ**), but disappointment aversion does rather badly. Quadratic utility does reasonably well.

The eight top level functionals are *not* nested within each other, so one cannot use nested test statistics to test between them. Nor are **EU** and **YD** nested within each other. However, one can use the Akaike information criterion to provide a ranking of the various functionals. In this context, the Akaike information criterion is given by (see Amemiya (1980))

$$\text{AIC} = -2\log L(\hat{\alpha})/T + 2k/T$$

where $L(\hat{\alpha})$ is the maximized log-likelihood for a particular estimated preference functional, k is the number of estimated parameters in that functional, and T is the number of observations. Akaike suggests the ranking of different models on the basis of this: the smaller is AIC the better the model. Since T is constant across all models, this implies ranking the models according to the magnitude of $CLL = \log L(\hat{\alpha}) - k$. (Here we are using CLL to denote the corrected-log-likelihood.)

The table in Appendix Three gives the details of the rankings which emerge from this exercise. In Table VII are average rankings—averaged over all subjects. We doubt if these have much meaning, given our firm belief that different subjects are different, and have different preference functionals. But, for what it is worth, Table VII suggests that the rank dependent model with the Quiggin weighting function emerges as the overall winner on this criterion, with the prospective reference model a reasonably close second (but recall that for a sizeable number of subjects the λ parameter is in the wrong range). **EU** does reasonably well, though both **RN** and **YD** do very badly. However, this does mask a considerable variation across subjects—as Appendix 3 clearly demonstrates. For example, whilst **YD** does very badly when averaged, it is ranked highest for subjects 10 and 65 on Data Set 3.

In Table VIII we bring together the significance tests and the rankings. It is constructed as follows (ignore for the time being the *small* numbers in the table and the material at the foot of the table). For each subject and for each data set we first see if expected utility, Yaari's dual model, or any of the eight top-level functionals are significantly better at the 1% level than risk neutrality; if none are, we put **RN** in Table VIII. If only one (of **EU**, **YD** and the 8 top level functionals) is, we enter it into Table VIII. If **EU** and at least one of the top level functionals are significantly better than **RN** at the 1% level, we then test to

EXPECTED UTILITY THEORY 1313

TABLE VIII

SUMMARY OF OVERALL VIEW AT 1%; ECONOMIC SIGNIFICANCE OF DEPARTURES
FROM EXPECTED UTILITY
(For explanation of the procedures used see the text.)

Subject	Data Set 1	Data Set 2	Data Set 3	Subject	Data Set 1	Data Set 2	Data Set 3
1	EU 23	8RQ 34	EU 27	41	16QU428	16QU423	12WU625
2	5PR231	7RQ 34	6RQ232	42	EU 32	9RI625	4PR 28
3	31RI77	18QU53	23QU72	43	13PR225	13RD 31	11DA433
4	21DA530	5RQ 26	15DA527	44	EU 19	7QU315	5QU416
5	12QU 29	EU 29	6RI528	45	8RD 10	9RI 8	8RI29
6	12WU328	18QU629	14QU529	46	7RI 28	7WU 33	EU 31
7	EU 20	EU 28	EU 20	47	8RP 29	EU 32	6RP229
8	10RP 10	14RP219	12RP214	48	18RD 31	22PR232	13PR 28
9	EU 14	EU 13	EU 11	49	RN	RN	RN
10	19QU320	YD 12	YD 10	50	13RQ421	13RQ418	12RQ620
11	EU 23	11QU 23	EU 23	51	EU 24	EU 24	EU 24
12	9PR232	10PR331	11QU632	52	22PR66	EU 28	12PR311
13	EU 16	RN	EU 10	53	EU 28	EU 26	5QU 26
14	EU 27	EU 26	EU 26	54	22PR56	21PR321	21PR63
15	EU 35	EU 31	EU 33	55	EU 30	11RP331	8RP230
16	EU 20	26RQ726	15RQ419	56	16QU319	18QU219	16QU519
17	8RQ231	10RQ327	8RQ529	57	9WU727	5RQ229	6WU727
18	EU 30	EU 26	EU 28	58	16RI219	17RI531	10RI321
19	EU 29	9WU527	13QU528	59	YD 28	27RQ73	19RQ710
20	EU 26	EU 30	EU 28	60	EU 33	23WU738	15QU736
21	13PR223	EU 32	9PR227	61	RN	RN	8QU 2
22	10RI 29	7RQ227	7RI328	62	RN	YD 41	24PR79
23	EU 27	EU 27	EU 27	63	18PR424	EU 29	9PR226
24	23QU36	EU 17	RN	64	10RQ323	7RQ332	9RQ627
25	15RQ429	8WU227	11RQ528	65	EU 14	YD 23	YD 17
26	7PR 32	EU 36	7PR233	66	12RQ327	EU 31	8RQ228
27	EU 15	EU 17	8WU216	67	5DA 26	EU 21	EU 24
28	10RP 22	14QU226	10QU223	68	21PR521	12PR222	16PR521
29	25RI323	EU 30	11RQ225	69	14RI519	13RI517	13PR518
30	15PR240	EU 25	11PR233	70	EU 24	21PR223	14PR 24
31	EU 37	11RQ424	15RQ330	71	13RQ523	YD 26	12RQ720
32	EU 37	EU 27	EU 31	72	RN	RN	RN
33	22RQ315	7RQ 23	15RQ321	73	12RI644	20QU538	16QU840
34	EU 30	EU 32	EU 30	74	17RI226	16DA 24	13RI325
35	9RQ223	22QU521	14PR522	75	13RQ 20	8WU332	EU 23
36	12RP319	YD 33	21QU723	76	10RQ226	9PR229	9RQ428
37	16QU 17	EU 23	14QU319	77	EU 27	10PR233	EU 30
38	16RQ321	16PR410	16PR715	78	EU 30	EU 32	EU 30
39	EU 31	7RP322	4DA226	79	14RI417	10RD 32	9RI323
40	EU 22	EU 33	EU 27	80	13PR542	9WU525	14RI634

Average percentage differences in prediction

	Data Set 1	Data Set 2	Data Set 3
Using EU rather than "best"	8.2%	7.3%	8.2%
Using RN rather than EU or YD	23.1%	24.6%	22.8%

see if any of the 8 top-level preference functionals are significantly better than EU at the 1% level; if none are, we put either **YD** or **EU** in Table VIII—the choice being determined by which of the two has the highest ranking on the Akaike criterion. If only one is we enter that in Table VIII. If more than one is, we then determine a "winner" using the rankings of the Appendix 3 table based on the Akaike information criterion; so, for example, if **PR, DA,** and **WU** are all significantly better than **EU** at the 1% level, and if **DA** has the highest corrected log-likelihood of **PR, DA, WU** (and **YD** if it is itself significantly better than **RN**), we enter **DA** into Table VIII. Where there are several such top-level functionals significantly better than **EU**, we also enter the *number* of such functionals in Table VIII (in *italics* after the "best" functional). Consider, for example, subject 1: on Data Set 1, **EU** is significantly better than **RN** but none of the top level functionals are significantly better than **EU**; the same is true for this subject for Data Set 3; for Data Set 2, **EU** is significantly better than **RN** *and* only **RQ** is significantly better than **EU**. This is a relatively clear-cut case; others are not so clear cut. Consider, for example, Subject 3: on Data Set 1, **EU** is significantly better than **RN**, and *seven* of the eight top level functionals are significantly better than **EU**—of these **RI** emerges as the best on the Akaike information criterion. So even though we conclude that for this subject and this data set, **RI** is the overall "best," this interpretation should be treated with caution. Indeed, a notable feature of Table VIII is the rather large number of top level functionals significantly better than **EU** when at least one is (an average of 3.60 on Data Set 1, of 3.71 on Data Set 2, and 4.27 on Data Set 3). This indicates *either* that our data are insufficiently informative to distinguish between the top level functionals *or* that the top level functionals are observationally very close. If the latter is the case, then the issue of which is the "best" of them loses much of its urgency; the advice would then be to choose the simplest to implement.

In Table IX is a summary of the "winners at 1%" using this procedure. For Data Set 1 (2), 32 (30) of the subjects seem to be best explained by **EU** or its special case (risk neutrality). For the remaining subjects, the two regret formulations "account" for some 7 to 11 of the subjects (with once again, the independence version emerging as the better of the two), while the two rank dependent formulations "account" for 15 or 16. Prospective reference theory again puts up a creditable performance, and quadratic utility does reasonably well, while disappointment aversion and Yaari's dual model come in very clearly at the back. On Data Set 3, **EU** and **RN** now "account" for just 21 of the subjects—for possible reasons that we have already discussed—with **PR, QU,** and **RQ** emerging as the strongest rival contenders. Table IX also gives a summary of "winners at 5%" using the same procedure. The previously **EU** and **RN** cases seem to be fairly uniformly distributed across the other models.

The inferences that can be drawn from Table IX about the adequacy or otherwise of **EU** are not, however, clear cut—mainly because of the large number of generalizations of **EU** under consideration. As this research has evolved, and as the number of generalizations under consideration has increased, the number of subjects for whom **EU** emerges as "the winner" has

TABLE IX
SUMMARY OF "WINNERS" AT 1% AND "WINNERS" AT 5%

Winners at 1%	Model	Data Set 1	Data Set 2	Data Set 3
	RN	4	4	3
	EU	28	26	18
	DA	2	1	3
	PR	11	8	14
	QU	6	9	14
	RD	2	2	0
	RI	9	4	7
	RP	4	3	3
	RQ	11	12	13
	WU	2	6	3
	YD	1	5	2

Winners at 5%	Model	Data Set 1	Data Set 2	Data Set 3
	RN	3	0	1
	EU	18	15	13
	DA	3	4	4
	PR	12	11	15
	QU	7	10	15
	RD	3	3	0
	RI	11	5	7
	RP	5	5	4
	RQ	14	14	15
	WU	3	7	4
	YD	1	6	2

declined. This is inevitable, though it is not clear how one should judge the rate of decline. With just one generalization (of **EU**) under consideration, one would expect to find it emerge "the winner at 5%" *even if* **EU** *was the true model* for approximately 5% of the subjects—that is, for 4 subjects. With 9 generalizations, totally independent in some appropriate sense, one might expect *one* of them to emerge "the winner at 5%" *even if* **EU** *was the true model* for up to a maximum of 9 times 4 (equals 36) subjects (though the precise number depends on the relationships between the various generalizations). On this argument, **EU** does indeed seem to perform rather well—though Monte Carlo work would be needed to shed more accurate light on such issues.

One rather interesting feature of Table VIII is the pattern that emerges from a comparison of the "best fitting" preference functional on Data Set 1 and that on Data Set 2. Table X gives a summary of the transition matrix. This implies that 17 out of the 32 **EU** and **RN** subjects on Data Set 1 stayed loyal to **EU** (and **RN**) on Data Set 2, 5 out of the 15 rank dependent subjects (**RP** and **RQ**) on Data Set 1 stayed loyal to rank dependency on Data Set 2, and that just 4 of the 11 regret subjects (**RD** and **RI**) stayed loyal to regret on Data Set 2. However, one should be a little careful in interpreting this table, since a particular model could be the winner on one data set and a loser on the other—whilst only having "lost" by a very small margin.

TABLE XI

DETERMINATION / VACILLATION INDEX VALUES
Value of 100 indicates complete determination,
value of 0 complete vacillation.
All index values are averages over 100 questions.
Histogram of above index values over all subjects.

Data Set 1 Range	RN	EU	DA	PR	QU	RD	RI	RP	RQ	WU	YD
0–10	15	0	0	0	0	0	0	0	0	0	0
11–20	18	1	0	0	0	0	0	1	0	0	1
21–30	18	4	4	1	0	3	1	1	1	1	4
31–40	16	9	7	8	5	6	6	9	7	8	15
41–50	8	18	20	16	11	17	12	17	15	14	24
51–60	0	15	15	15	20	19	25	15	20	21	18
61–70	2	12	12	16	16	12	13	14	13	12	10
71–80	3	17	15	19	12	15	11	18	17	15	6
81–90	0	3	6	3	15	7	11	4	6	8	1
91–100	0	1	1	2	1	1	1	1	1	1	1

Data Set 2 Range	RN	EU	DA	PR	QU	RD	RI	RP	RQ	WU	YD
0–10	18	1	0	0	0	1	0	0	0	0	0
11–20	12	1	0	0	0	1	0	0	0	0	0
21–30	14	3	5	0	0	2	0	5	1	0	2
31–40	11	7	5	4	3	6	4	6	4	5	6
41–50	17	12	13	13	8	9	13	8	10	14	19
51–60	3	6	7	11	14	11	12	11	13	9	16
61–70	2	14	10	13	8	9	8	9	9	10	18
71–80	3	22	19	20	17	20	20	21	24	22	12
81–90	0	13	19	16	22	18	17	17	17	16	4
91–100	0	1	2	3	8	3	6	3	2	4	3

Data Set 3 Range	RN	EU	DA	PR	QU	RD	RI	RP	RQ	WU	YD
0–10	20	0	0	0	0	0	0	0	0	0	0
11–20	15	0	0	0	0	0	0	1	0	0	1
21–30	15	6	5	1	1	5	2	4	1	3	4
31–40	15	13	13	10	8	12	11	10	12	10	21
41–50	8	12	12	15	14	11	15	15	14	15	19
51–60	3	10	9	14	12	10	9	8	12	10	11
61–70	2	16	19	16	14	18	18	18	16	18	16
71–80	2	20	18	20	18	18	15	20	21	18	6
81–90	0	1	2	2	11	4	8	2	2	4	1
91–100	0	2	2	2	2	2	2	2	2	2	1

preference for the right-hand gamble a proportion p of the time.[19] If either p or r is unity, then the subject is certain which of the two will be reported as preferred; if $p = r = 1/2$ then the subject is completely uncertain as to which will be reported as preferred. Thus the value of $100|p - r|$ indicates the degree of determination or vacillation in the subject's response: if $100|p - r| = 100$ then the subject is completely determined; if $100|p - r| = 0$ then the subject is completely vacillating. Our index (for a preference subject) is the average value

[19] Note: $r = \text{Prob}(\varepsilon > -\hat{V})$, $p = \text{Prob}(\varepsilon \leqslant -\hat{V})$, and $p + r = 1$.

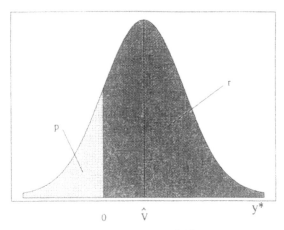

1: A Preference Subject

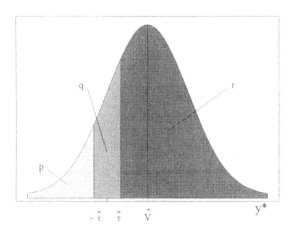

2 An Indifference Subject

FIGURE 4.—Characterization of determination/vacillation index.

of $100|p - r|$ over all 100 questions. For an indifference subject, that is a subject who reports indifference sometimes (in terms of our models when $\hat{V} + \varepsilon$ lies between $-\hat{\tau}$ and $\hat{\tau}$, where $\hat{\tau}$ is the estimated threshold), our index is again calculated as the average value of $100|p - r|$, though here the meaning of p and r are slightly different.[20]

Table XI reflects remarkable differences in subjects' determination. For some subjects, for some data sets, and for some preference functionals the index is as low as 0; figures below 50 occur frequently: such a subject would, on average, choose one of the two gambles 75% of the time and the other 25% of the time.

[20] Note: $r = \text{Prob}(\varepsilon > -\hat{V} + \hat{\tau})$, $p = \text{Prob}(\varepsilon < \hat{V} - \hat{\tau})$, and $p + r < 1$.

This implies sizeable error. Or, of course, it could indicate genuine indifference combined with an infinitesimally small error.

The results of a comparative test are reported in the *small* numbers in Table VIII. Here the *small* number *before* the name of the winning preference functionals represents the average percentage of the time that the best fitting top-level functional comes up with a different prediction from the expected utility functional. (Of course, if there are no top level functionals better than **EU**, then no number is entered.) The argument goes as follows (examine Figure 5): consider first a preference subject. Let $\hat{V}_a$ and $\hat{V}_b$ be the estimated valuation of the difference between the left-hand and right-hand gambles given

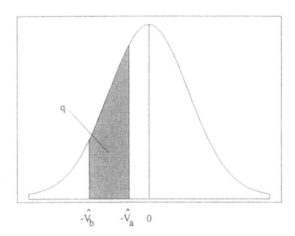

1: A Preference Subject

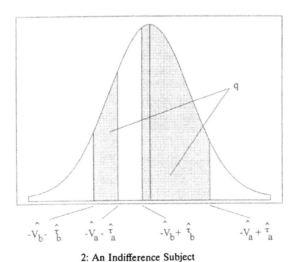

2: An Indifference Subject

FIGURE 5.—Calculation of proportions with different predictions.

by Models a and b respectively. Then left (right) is reported as preferred under Model a if $\varepsilon > (\leqslant) - \hat{V}_a$ and left (right) as preferred under Model b if $\varepsilon > (\leqslant)$ $- \hat{V}_b$. Thus (if $\cdot \hat{V}_a < \hat{V}_b$ as illustrated in Figure 5) different predictions will emerge from the two models if ε lies between $-\hat{V}_b$ and $-\hat{V}_a$ which occurs with probability q. The average value of 100 times this is reported as the (small) number before the name of the functional in Table VIII.

For an indifference subject, the calculation is slightly different, and now involves not only $\hat{V}_a$ and $\hat{V}_b$ but also the estimated thresholds $\hat{\tau}_a$ and $\hat{\tau}_b$ under the two models. In Figure 5 we present a particular configuration. Here different predictions would occur from the two models if

$$-\hat{V}_b - \hat{\tau}_b \leqslant \varepsilon < -\hat{V}_a - \hat{\tau}_a$$

(indifference reported under b and right reported as preferred under a) or if

$$-\hat{V}_b + \hat{\tau}_b \leqslant \varepsilon < -\hat{V}_a + \hat{\tau}_a$$

(left reported as preferred under b and indifference reported under a). So the percentage of the time that different predictions would result from the two models is 100 times the total of the shaded area. We have similar arguments under different configurations. The number before the name of the preference functional in Table VIII reports the average value of these percentage differences.

The *small* number *after* the name of the best-fitting preference functional in Table VIII reports the average percentage of the time that the **EU** (or **YD** if it is the "best-fitting") functional comes up with a different prediction from the risk neutral functional. (Of course, if **RN** is the best-fitting functional then no number is entered.) So, for example, for Subject 2 on Data Set 1, for whom **PR** is the best-fitting functional, the two numbers 5 and 31 indicate that **PR** and **EU** predict different choices on 5 of the 100 questions, while **EU** and **RN** predict different choice on 31 of the 100 questions. Note that this measure is entirely symmetrical—and does not imply anything about "correctness." So, for Subject 2 on Data Set 1, if **PR** were this subject's correct functional, but instead we used the estimated **EU** functional we would make mistakes in prediction 5% of the time; similarly, if **EU** were this subject's correct functional, but instead we used the estimated **PR** functional, then again we would make mistakes in prediction 5% of the time. Note also that, although this measure is symmetrical, the theories are not—in the sense that the top functionals are more complicated and more difficult to apply than **EU**. So, if one were faced with a choice between using **PR** and getting things wrong 5% of the time, or using **EU** and getting things wrong 5% of the time, then the latter would be preferred since **EU** is a simpler theory to apply.[21]

The foot of Table VIII provides a summary. It is abundantly clear from this that using **RN** rather than **EU** (or **YD**) can lead to sizeable errors, whilst the

---

[21] Apropos of this, it is instructive to observe the almost complete lack of applications of the new theories; contrast this to the enormous number of applications of **EU** in all areas of economics. Of course, this statement is one of fact, not of opinion concerning the merit of such applications.

magnitude of the errors in using **EU** rather than the "appropriate" top level functional is considerably smaller. But whether "just over 8%" is within acceptable margins of error we leave to others to judge.

7. CONCLUSIONS

Expected utility theory (and its special case, risk neutrality) emerges from this analysis fairly intact. For possibly 39% of the subjects (on the two individual data sets), **EU** appears to fit no worse than any of the other models (though the situation is not so clear when the two individual data sets are combined). For the other 61% of the subjects, one or more of the eight "top-level" functionals (or, occasionally, **YD**) fits significantly better in statistical terms, though often the economic significance is not all that great. Of the eight "top-level" functionals it would appear that the two rank dependent functionals and the quadratic utility model emerge as strongest contenders (with the Quiggin weighting function having a modest lead over its power weighting function rival). Next comes the two regret formulations combined (with the independence version having a decisive advantage in this context over the dependence version), followed by prospective reference theory. Disappointment aversion theory and Yaari's dual model come a rather poor last.

However, we should emphasize once more that this interpretation of our results needs to be taken with caution—since our sample of 80 subjects was in no sense representative. So there is no guarantee that our results are in any sense representative.[22] Perhaps the next step in this line of research is to work with representative samples?

However, possibly the overriding feature of our analysis is the importance of *error*. Table XI (our determination/vacillation indices) shows very clearly how important such errors are. Until now, most authors have been relatively unconcerned about such errors, except insofar as their implication for the appropriate statistical procedures to use when testing between various competing hypotheses is concerned—though there are exceptions to this general rule, in particular, Starmer and Sugden (1991) and Loomes, Starmer, and Sudgen (1991). Some discussion is also contained in Harless and Camerer (1992). There is also a voluminous, though now rather dated and curiously neglected, literature on *stochastic choice* models (see, for an introduction to the literature and one of the few attempts to relate it to the present debate, the paper by Machina (1985)). But the present debate is almost entirely concerned with deterministic choice models. Our results suggest quite strongly that the truth is *not* going to be found along this deterministic choice route, unless some account is taken of errors. There is clearly a problem of identifying the underlying "true" model because of these errors—indeed it could be argued that the lack of significance for some of the top-level functionals for some of the subjects in our study could

---

[22] Yet, at the same time, there is no reason to believe that our results are necessarily *un*representative of the economic population at large, or more unrepresentative than the results from previous experiments which stimulated the various new models to a large degree.

1322   J. D. HEY AND C. ORME

simply result from this noise, combined with rather uninformative data. (Perhaps we should try to find ways of generating more powerful data?[23])

Nevertheless, we are tempted to conclude by saying that our study indicates that behavior can be reasonably well modelled (to what might be termed a "reasonable approximation") as "EU plus noise." Perhaps we should now spend some time on thinking about the noise, rather than about even more alternatives to EU?

Dept. of Economics and Related Studies, University of York, Heslington, York YO1 5DD, United Kingdom.

Manuscript received March, 1992; final revision received January, 1994.

APPENDIX 1

A. THE DERIVATION OF THE DISAPPOINTMENT AVERSION SPECIFICATION

We provide just an outline of the proof. We restrict attention to a gamble involving at most three outcomes, the utilities of which we denote by u_i with respective probabilities p_i ($i = 1, 2, 3$). From Gul (1991, p. 678) it is clear that we can write (where V is the value of the preference functional for the gamble):

$$V = V_1 \quad \text{if} \quad p_3 \geq (1 + \beta)(u_2 - u_1)/(u_3 - u_2)p_1,$$
$$V = V_2 \quad \text{if} \quad p_3 < (1 + \beta)(u_2 - u_1)/(u_3 - u_2)p_1,$$

where

$$V_1 = [(1 + \beta)p_1 u_1 + (1 + \beta)p_2 u_2 + p_3 u_3]/[1 + \beta p_1 + \beta p_2],$$
$$V_2 = [(1 + \beta)p_1 u_1 + p_2 u_2 + p_3 u_3]/[1 + \beta p_1].$$

Elementary algebra shows that $V_1 \geq V_2$ if and only if $p_3 < (1 + \beta)(u_2 - u_1)/(u_3 - u_2)p_1$, from which it follows that

$$V = \min(V_1, V_2).$$

The formula in Section 3 follows by generalizing this result to four outcomes. A detailed proof is available on request.

B. COMPUTER PROGRAM GENERATING PROBABILITIES FOR RD SPECIFICATION

This program takes as input the vector (p_1, p_2, p_3, p_4) giving the probabilities in the left-hand circle and the vector (q_1, q_2, q_3, q_4) giving the probabilities in the right-hand circle and computes the vector z which is used in the formula for the RD model given in Section 3 above.

```
subroutine regprobs(p,q,z,n)
double precision z(400,50)
integer p(200,4),q(200,4)
dimension ncp(4),ncq(4),npc(6),nop(4,4)
do 100 i = 1,n
ncp(1) = p(i,1)
ncq(1) = q(i,1)
do 100 j = 2,4
jm1 = j - 1
ncp(j) = ncp(jm1) + p(i,j)
ncq(j) = ncq(jm1) + q(i,j)
```

---

[23] See, for a start in this direction, Carbone and Hey (1992). See also Mueller and Ponce de Leon (1992).

```
100     continue
        ip = 1
        iq = 1
        do 200 j = 1,4
        do 200 k = 1,4
        nop(j, k) = 0
200     continue
        do 300 j = 1,1000
210     if (j.le.ncp(ip)) go to 250
        ip = ip + 1
        go to 210
250     if (j.le.ncq(iq)) go to 260
        iq = iq + 1
        go to 250
260     nop(ip,iq) = nop(ip,iq) + 1
300     continue
        npc(1) = nop(2,1)-nop(1,2)
        npc(2) = nop(3,2)-nop(2,3)
        npc(3) = nop(4,3)-nop(3,4)
        npc(4) = nop(3,1)-nop(1,3)
        npc(5) = nop(4,2)-nop(2,4)
        npc(6) = nop(4,1)-nop(1,4)
        do 400 j = 1,6
        z(i,j) = dble(npc(j))/1000
400     continue
1000    continue
        return
        end
```

APPENDIX 2

DETAILS OF THE ESTIMATION SOFTWARE

Although available software, such as *LIMDEP 6.0* (Greene (1991)), can be employed to estimate the standard *probit* and *ordered probit* models encountered here, the standard assumption imposed on the deterministic specification would have to be one of linearity in parameters. This, however, can be at odds with the maintained theory, as in the case of the disappointment aversion model. Also, standard software does not necessarily exploit the global concavity property of the log-likelihoods (in the context of probit and ordered probit models) which guarantees the uniqueness of any obtained maximum (if one exists). For these reasons, and because of the large number of model estimations required, a purpose built program was developed in order to find the appropriate maximum likelihood estimates.

The numerical optimization procedure, which proved to be very efficient computationally, was based on the ideas described in Orme (1995). Orme's work focuses on the calculation of efficient test statistics after maximum likelihood estimation of a model which is specified solely in terms of a "regression" function (which, it is emphasized, need not be linear in parameters) and an ancillary parameter. Such models include the familiar *Tobit* or *censored regression model*, the *truncated regression model*, and, in particular, the *ordered probit model* where the ancillary parameter is the threshold, τ. The iteration routine employed to locate the maximum likelihood estimates is developed from Fisher's method of scoring, whereby

$$\hat{\theta}_{s+1} = \hat{\theta}_s + \lambda_s \hat{A}_s^{-1} \hat{g}_s$$

where $\hat{\theta}_s$ is the value of θ (the unknown parameter vector to be estimated) at the sth iterate, $\hat{A}_s$ is the expected information matrix evaluated at $\hat{\theta}_s$ (which is guaranteed positive definite), $\hat{g}_s$ is the gradient vector, and λ_s is a suitably chosen step length. Using this, a standard first order Taylor series expansion of the log-likelihood about $\hat{\theta}_s$ shows that, for λ_s sufficiently small an improvement in the log-likelihood can always be achieved until the maximum is reached. A search procedure, invoked at each iterate, was used to find the appropriate value for λ.

The above is a fairly well known and standard technique. The computational simplicity and efficiency arises from the observation that the *direction* at the sth iterate, $\hat{d}_s = \hat{A}_s^{-1} \hat{g}_s$, can be constructed as $(W'W)^{-1}W'r$, which is the *ordinary least squares* "slope" estimate obtained from a regression of r on W. Furthermore, one convergence criterion which can be usefully employed is $\hat{d}'_s \hat{A}_s^{-1} \hat{d}_s = r'W(W'W)^{-1}W'r$, the *uncentered explained sum of squares* from the same regression. Finally at the last iterate asymptotic standard errors can be easily estimated using the square-roots of the diagonal elements of $(W'W)^{-1}$, and this is how they were calculated here; alternatively, the standard errors outputted from the OLS regression of r on W (at the final iterate) would be asymptotically valid.

The regressor matrix, W, and the left hand side vector, r, needed for these regressions are in *double-length form* having dimensions $(2n \times k)$ and $(2n \times 1)$, respectively, where n is the sample size and k is the number of unknown parameters to be estimated by maximum likelihood. These variables require some calculation and the interested reader is referred to Orme (1995) for further details.

Apart from affording a certain amount of computational simplicity, not to mention elegance, this procedure proved to be extremely efficient at locating the maximum of the log-likelihood for most models and subjects with the minimum of intervention. This is quite a remarkable feature given the large number of numerical optimizations required. It should also be noted here that standard likelihood inferential procedures should be treated with caution in the case of the *disappointment aversion* model since it is not continuously differentiable in parameters. (For notational details see Orme (1995).)

APPENDIX 3

DETAILED RANKINGS USING THE AKAIKE CRITERION

S	Data Set 1 REDPQRRRRWY NUARUDIPQUD	Data Set 2 REDPQRRRRWY NUARUDIPQUD	Data Set 3 REDPQRRRRWY NUARUDIPQUD
1	B 3 4 2 9 7 8 5 1 6 A	B 6 5 2 9 8 4 7 1 3 A	B 5 3 2 9 8 7 4 1 6 A
2	B 5 6 1 9 8 7 4 2 3 A	B 7 6 2 4 9 5 8 1 3 A	B 5 7 2 8 9 3 6 1 4 A
3	9 A B 6 2 3 1 8 5 4 7	8 A B 5 1 9 3 7 4 2 6	9 A B 6 1 7 2 8 4 3 5
4	B 9 1 8 2 7 5 3 6 4 A	B 5 2 3 9 8 7 4 1 6 A	B 9 1 8 2 7 5 3 6 4 A
5	B 8 6 5 1 7 2 9 4 3 A	B 7 2 8 6 9 3 1 5 4 A	B 9 4 6 3 8 1 7 5 2 A
6	B 5 9 8 2 7 3 4 6 1 A	B 8 9 6 1 7 4 3 2 5 A	B 7 9 6 1 8 3 5 2 4 A
7	A 3 7 2 9 1 5 6 4 8 B	B 3 6 2 9 5 8 7 1 4 A	B 3 5 1 9 6 8 4 2 7 A
8	9 4 8 7 3 A 5 1 6 2 B	A 4 6 3 2 8 9 1 5 7 B	A 3 7 4 2 9 8 1 6 5 B
9	A 1 5 2 9 7 8 4 3 6 B	B 2 5 1 A 9 8 6 3 4 7	B 1 5 4 9 7 8 2 3 6 A
10	A 5 8 7 1 9 2 4 6 3 B	A 6 4 5 B 2 8 3 7 9 1	7 6 A 8 2 B 3 5 9 4 1
11	B 4 5 6 9 7 1 3 8 2 A	B 3 6 7 1 9 4 2 5 8 A	B 3 6 7 2 9 4 1 5 8 A
12	B 6 8 1 2 9 7 4 3 5 A	B 7 8 1 3 9 6 5 2 4 A	B 7 8 2 1 9 6 5 3 4 A
13	A 6 8 4 3 9 1 7 5 2 B	4 2 5 8 6 3 A 1 7 9 B	B 5 8 6 1 9 2 3 7 4 A
14	B 1 5 2 9 6 8 4 3 7 A	B 1 5 3 9 7 8 2 4 6 A	B 2 3 1 9 4 8 6 5 7 A
15	B 2 3 5 6 8 9 1 4 7 A	B 4 1 2 9 7 8 5 3 6 A	B 3 1 2 8 7 9 5 4 6 A
16	B 5 6 8 9 1 2 3 7 4 A	B 9 2 3 7 A 6 5 1 4 8	B 9 3 4 8 A 6 5 1 7 2
17	B 6 8 2 4 9 5 7 1 3 A	B 8 9 7 2 4 3 5 1 6 A	B 8 9 4 2 6 3 7 1 5 A
18	B 1 5 3 9 6 7 4 2 8 A	B 1 5 2 9 7 8 3 4 6 A	B 1 5 2 9 7 6 4 3 8 A
19	B 7 1 4 6 9 8 2 3 5 A	B 8 6 9 4 3 2 5 7 1 A	B 8 4 6 1 9 7 2 5 3 A
20	B 2 8 6 7 1 9 3 4 5 A	B 1 6 3 9 7 8 2 5 4 A	B 2 5 8 9 3 4 7 6 1 A
21	B 4 5 1 9 7 8 3 2 6 A	B 6 1 2 9 4 3 7 8 5 A	B 3 4 1 9 8 7 5 2 6 A
22	B 8 9 5 2 4 1 6 3 7 A	B 3 5 2 9 8 6 7 1 4 A	B 5 9 3 7 4 1 6 2 8 A
23	B 6 5 8 7 3 2 9 1 4 A	B 2 5 3 9 7 8 1 4 6 A	B 9 6 7 2 3 5 8 1 4 A
24	4 5 A 9 1 6 3 7 8 2 B	B 2 3 1 9 6 8 5 4 7 A	8 1 5 3 2 A 9 7 6 4 B
25	B 7 2 4 8 9 5 6 1 3 A	B 7 2 8 5 9 3 4 6 1 A	B 8 3 5 7 9 4 6 1 2 A
26	B 3 5 1 9 7 8 4 2 6 A	B 6 8 1 4 3 2 9 5 7 A	B 3 5 1 9 7 8 6 2 4 A
27	A 8 6 5 3 4 9 2 7 1 B	B 2 6 5 9 8 1 7 4 3 A	B 9 8 7 2 4 3 6 5 1 A
28	A 4 6 7 3 2 9 1 5 8 B	B 8 9 7 1 3 2 6 5 4 A	B 4 8 5 1 3 9 2 6 7 A
29	B 7 A 4 9 3 1 5 2 6 8	B 2 1 5 9 7 8 4 3 6 A	B 6 7 4 9 3 2 8 1 5 A
30	B 6 5 1 9 7 4 8 2 3 A	B 3 4 2 9 5 8 6 1 7 A	B 5 3 1 9 8 6 7 2 4 A
31	A 5 6 1 7 3 9 4 2 8 B	B 8 7 2 5 6 4 9 1 3 A	B 8 9 2 3 4 5 7 1 6 A
32	B 2 4 3 6 9 8 1 5 7 A	B 5 2 8 9 3 4 6 7 1 A	B 4 2 6 9 5 3 8 7 1 A
33	A 7 3 2 B 9 6 8 1 4 5	B 7 2 3 8 9 5 4 1 6 A	B 8 3 2 9 6 4 7 1 5 A
34	B 1 5 2 9 6 8 4 3 7 A	B 3 1 8 9 2 4 7 6 5 A	B 1 2 3 9 4 8 5 6 7 A
35	B 5 9 2 6 7 4 8 1 3 A	B 7 A 4 1 8 2 9 5 3 6	B 7 A 1 4 8 3 9 2 5 6
36	B 9 3 7 2 8 6 1 5 4 A	B 9 5 8 2 A 7 3 4 6 1	B A 3 8 1 9 7 2 6 5 4

APPENDIX 3 (*Continued*)

S	Data Set 1	Data Set 2	Data Set 3
37	B 7 9 5 1 8 3 2 6 4 A	B 6 8 1 3 7 5 2 4 9 A	B 7 9 3 1 8 5 2 4 6 A
38	B 8 3 2 5 6 7 A 1 4 9	B 8 7 1 9 6 4 A 2 5 3	B 9 4 1 7 8 5 A 2 6 3
39	B 5 2 7 8 9 4 6 1 3 A	B 6 4 7 2 8 9 1 3 5 A	B 7 1 9 3 8 6 2 5 4 A
40	B 1 5 3 9 7 8 2 4 6 A	B 1 5 2 9 6 8 3 4 7 A	B 2 9 6 8 1 3 4 5 7 A
41	B 8 5 6 1 9 3 7 4 2 A	B 8 5 6 1 7 4 9 3 2 A	B 9 5 6 2 7 3 8 4 1 A
42	B 2 5 3 9 7 8 1 4 6 A	B 7 5 4 6 2 1 8 9 3 A	B 6 2 1 9 3 4 8 7 5 A
43	B 7 3 1 9 6 5 8 2 4 A	B 4 2 6 9 1 3 8 7 5 A	B 8 1 5 6 2 4 9 7 3 A
44	B 2 5 4 A 8 9 3 1 7 6	B 7 6 A 1 8 9 2 4 5 3	B 8 5 A 1 7 9 6 3 4 2
45	A 3 9 7 8 1 2 6 5 4 B	A 5 6 3 9 2 1 7 4 8 B	B 7 9 6 3 2 1 8 5 4 A
46	B 5 7 3 9 2 1 8 4 6 A	B 5 4 8 6 2 3 7 9 1 A	B 2 4 1 9 6 7 5 3 8 A
47	A 2 5 3 6 7 9 1 4 8 B	B 4 6 8 2 1 5 3 7 9 A	B 3 7 5 2 4 8 1 6 9 A
48	A 2 8 7 9 1 3 4 6 5 B	B 4 6 1 A 8 5 7 2 3 9	B 4 6 1 8 2 9 5 3 7 A
49	1 2 5 4 9 8 A 6 3 7 B	6 5 3 1 A 8 9 4 2 7 B	1 3 2 6 A 5 9 4 7 8 B
50	B 9 8 4 5 7 2 6 1 3 A	B 9 4 2 7 A 6 8 1 5 3	B 8 5 2 6 A 4 9 1 3 7
51	B 2 5 1 9 7 8 4 3 6 A	B 1 2 3 9 6 8 4 5 7 A	B 3 5 1 9 7 8 4 2 6 A
52	8 B 9 1 5 A 6 7 2 4 3	B 3 7 2 9 1 8 5 6 4 A	B 6 7 1 8 A 5 3 2 4 9
53	B 1 6 4 7 8 9 3 2 5 A	B 5 8 2 4 9 1 7 3 6 A	B 7 9 4 1 6 2 8 3 5 A
54	8 A B 1 6 9 7 5 3 2 4	B 8 7 1 6 9 4 A 2 3 5	B 9 A 1 7 8 4 6 2 5 3
55	B 3 4 2 A 8 9 1 5 7 6	B 8 3 9 2 7 5 1 6 4 A	B 4 2 6 3 8 9 1 7 5 A
56	A 6 9 7 1 5 4 2 8 3 B	A 6 9 7 1 3 4 2 8 5 B	A 6 9 7 1 5 3 2 8 4 B
57	B 9 4 8 3 6 2 5 7 1 A	B 5 3 2 9 8 6 7 1 4 A	B 9 3 8 4 7 2 6 5 1 A
58	A 3 6 7 9 2 1 4 5 8 B	B 6 8 5 4 9 1 7 3 2 A	B 7 9 3 4 8 1 6 2 5 A
59	B 9 6 3 7 A 8 5 2 4 1	9 A 8 3 5 B 7 6 1 4 2	B 9 5 3 7 A 8 4 1 6 2
60	B 4 6 2 7 1 9 8 3 5 A	B 8 4 9 3 6 2 5 7 1 A	B 9 4 8 1 3 2 5 6 7 A
61	2 7 8 9 1 B 3 5 6 4 A	2 3 1 6 9 4 A 5 7 B 8	2 8 3 9 1 B 5 4 7 6 A
62	1 2 4 6 B 8 9 3 5 7 A	9 A 7 3 6 B 5 8 2 4 1	9 A 8 1 7 B 5 6 2 4 3
63	B 7 8 1 5 6 3 9 2 4 A	B 3 4 6 9 1 8 2 5 7 A	B 6 5 1 8 9 4 7 2 3 A
64	B 7 3 2 9 8 6 5 1 4 A	B 8 3 2 7 6 5 9 1 4 A	B 9 3 2 6 7 5 8 1 4 A
65	B 6 8 2 A 9 4 5 1 3 7	B 6 8 3 7 A 5 9 4 2 1	B 4 7 5 6 A 3 8 9 2 1
66	B 6 9 2 3 8 7 4 1 5 A	B 4 1 2 9 8 6 5 3 7 A	B 5 9 2 3 8 4 7 1 6 A
67	B 7 1 6 9 4 3 5 8 2 A	B 1 2 3 9 6 8 5 4 7 A	B 5 1 3 9 8 7 2 6 4 A
68	B 7 9 1 5 8 4 6 2 3 A	B 3 8 1 9 5 7 4 2 6 A	B 8 9 1 5 7 4 6 2 3 A
69	B 7 6 3 5 9 1 8 2 4 A	B 8 9 2 7 5 1 6 3 4 A	B 8 9 1 5 7 3 6 2 4 A
70	B 1 5 2 9 6 8 4 3 7 A	B 3 7 1 A 9 8 5 2 6 4	B 3 5 1 9 6 8 4 2 7 A
71	B 8 6 3 2 A 5 7 1 4 9	B 9 4 3 7 A 8 5 2 6 1	B 9 6 4 3 A 8 7 1 5 2
72	3 2 7 1 B 8 9 5 4 6 A	3 4 8 5 2 7 B 9 6 A 1	6 4 8 2 1 9 A 7 3 5 B
73	B 9 5 7 4 3 1 8 6 2 A	B 8 3 7 1 9 6 2 5 4 A	B 9 2 8 1 7 5 4 6 3 A
74	B 3 7 5 9 2 1 8 6 4 A	B 5 1 6 7 9 3 8 4 2 A	B 6 3 9 5 2 1 7 8 4 A
75	B 6 4 2 9 3 5 7 1 8 A	B 6 9 2 5 8 4 7 3 1 A	B 2 7 5 8 1 4 6 3 9 A
76	B 8 2 7 4 9 5 3 1 6 A	B 7 6 1 5 9 3 8 2 4 A	B 6 7 2 4 9 3 8 1 5 A
77	A 3 7 6 9 1 4 2 5 8 B	B 5 8 1 9 6 4 7 2 3 A	B 3 6 1 9 8 7 2 4 5 A
78	B 1 6 3 9 2 8 5 4 7 A	B 4 6 3 1 7 9 2 5 8 A	B 5 7 1 4 2 9 3 6 8 A
79	B 7 9 3 8 5 1 6 2 4 A	B 4 3 6 9 1 2 5 7 8 A	B 6 7 2 9 4 1 8 3 5 A
80	B 8 9 1 2 7 4 6 3 5 A	B 8 7 2 4 5 3 9 6 1 A	B 8 9 3 2 6 1 7 5 4 A

Key: A: 10th; B: 11th; S: Subject Number.

REFERENCES

AMEMIYA, T. (1980): "Selection of Regressors," *International Economic Review*, 2, 331–354.

BELL, D. (1982): "Regret in Decision Making Under Uncertainty," *Operations Research*, 30, 961–981.

CARBONE, E., AND J. D. HEY (1992): "Estimation of Expected Utility and Non-Expected Utility Preference Functionals Using Complete Ranking Data," in *Models and Experiments on Risk and Rationality*, ed. by B. Munier and M. J. Machina. Dordricht: Kluwer Academic Publishers.

CHEW, C. S. (1983): "A Generalization of the Quasilinear Mean with Applications to the Measurement of Income Inequality and Decision Theory Resolving the Allais Paradox," *Econometrica*, 51, 1065–1092.

1326 J. D. HEY AND C. ORME

CHEW, C. S., L. G. EPSTEIN, AND U. SEGAL (1991): "Mixture Symmetry and Quadratic Utility," *Econometrica*, 59, 139–164.

CHEW, C. S., E. KARNI, AND Z. SAFRA (1987): "Empirical Tests of Weighted Utility Theory," *Journal of Mathematical Psychology*, 30, 55–72.

DEKEL, E. (1986): "An Axiomatic Characterization of Preferences Under Uncertainty—Weakening the Independence Axiom," *Journal of Economic Theory*, 40, 304–318.

GODFREY, L. G. (1988): *Misspecification Tests in Econometrics*, Econometric Society Monograph Number 16. Cambridge: Cambridge University Press.

GREENE, W. H. (1991): *LIMDEP 6.0*. Econometric Software Inc.

GUL, F. (1991): "A Theory of Disappointment Aversion," *Econometrica*, 59, 667–686.

HARLESS, D., AND C. D. F. CAMERER (1992): "The Utility of Generalized Expected Utility Theories," paper presented at the FUR-VI conference at GRID, June, 1992.

HEY, J. D., AND D. DI CAGNO (1990): "Circles and Triangles: An Experimental Estimation of Indifference Lines in the Marschak-Machina Triangle," *Journal of Behavioral Decision Making*, 3, 279–306.

HOLT, C. A. (1986): "Preference Reversals and the Independence Axiom," *American Economic Review*, 76, 508–515.

LOOMES, G. C., C. STARMER, AND R. SUGDEN (1991): "Observing Violations of Transitivity by Experimental Methods," *Econometrica*, 59, 425–439.

LOOMES, G. C., AND R. SUGDEN (1982): "Regret Theory: An Alternative Theory of Rational Choice Under Uncertainty," *Economic Journal*, 92, 805–824.

——— (1987): "Some Implications of a More General Form of Regret Theory," *Journal of Economic Theory*, 41, 270–287.

MACHINA, M. J. (1985): "Stochastic Choice Functions Generated from Deterministic Preferences over Lotteries," *Economic Journal*, 95, 575–594.

MUELLER, W. G., AND A. C. PONCE DE LEON (1992): "Optimal Design of an Experiment in Economics," Research Report No. 31, Department of Statistics, University of Economics, Vienna.

ORME, CHRIS (1995): "On the Use of Artificial Regressions in Certain Microeconometric Models," *Econometric Theory*, 11, forthcoming.

QUIGGIN, J. (1982): "A Theory of Anticipated Utility," *Journal of Economic Behavior and Organization*, 3, 323–343.

STARMER, C., AND R. SUGDEN (1991): "Does the Random-Lottery Incentive System Elicit True Preferences?" *American Economic Review*, 81, 971–978.

VISCUSI, W. K. (1989): "Prospective Reference Theory: Toward an Explanation of the Paradoxes," *Journal of Risk and Uncertainty*, 2, 235–264.

WILCOX, N. T. (1993): "Lottery Choice: Incentives, Complexity and Decision Time," *Economic Journal*, 103 (forthcoming).

YAARI, M. E. (1987): "The Dual Theory of Choice Under Risk," *Econometrica*, 55, 95–115.

Part III
Environmental Conflict

[16]

AN EMPIRICAL APPROACH TO THE PRISONERS' DILEMMA GAME *

LESTER B. LAVE

INTRODUCTION

Adam Smith's invisible hand had the important property that, if each individual pursued his profit in optimal fashion, the total profit of the community would be maximized. Game theory has proposed a simple situation reversing this conclusion: two prisoners, arrested for a crime, are questioned separately. Each is informed it cannot be proved they committed the crime but that if (1) A does not confess to the crime and (1') B does not confess, both will receive six months in jail on a minor charge; if (1) A does not confess and (2') B does confess, A will receive ten years in prison while B goes free. On the other hand, if (2) A confesses and (1') B does not confess, A will go free while B goes to prison for ten years; while if (2) A confesses and (2') B confesses also, both will go to jail for eight years.

When this "prisoners' dilemma" is transformed into monetary payoffs, several economic applications are immediate. Cournot's two sellers of mineral water[1] are in a prisoners' dilemma, as indeed is any oligopoly situation where the, even explicit, agreements between firms are not enforceable. Each firm has an immediate advantage in not colluding, but all will lose if collusion fails. International trade under tariffs forms a second illustration. Although the world is better off under free trade, each nation can benefit from an "optimum" tariff; yet, if any nation tries to gain this advantage, it is even more profitable for other nations to follow suit. Finally, if all do impose "optimum" tariffs, in general every nation will be worse off than under free trade.

A variety of treatments have been applied to the prisoners'

* I am indebted to Miss Ruth Westheimer and Mrs. Barbara Isgur for experimental help, to George Hay, Thomas C. Schelling, Gerald Kraft, Bernhardt Lieberman, and Daniel Ellsberg for criticism.

1. Augustin Cournot, *Researches into the Mathematical Principles of the Theory of Wealth*, trans. N. Bacon (New York: Macmillan, 1897).

dilemma, ranging from a purely game theoretical one of Luce and Raiffa,[2] to a psychological one of Scodel *et al.*,[3] and a socio-behavioral one of Morton Deutsch.[4] All three are not equally satisfactory: Luce and Raiffa prove a mathematical theorem from uninteresting axioms (see page 431 below) to conclude "rational" players will not collude; Scodel *et al.* use an experimental procedure which prevents players from colluding even when the game is modified so that the "collude" strategy dominates.

This paper uses a behavioral approach to develop a normative theory. It attempts to answer the question of how a player should behave to maximize his objective function when faced with this game and real opponents. The methodological advantages of this treatment include freedom from axioms of rational behavior for the player. In an iterated game the philosophy and process of reasoning need not be considered; consideration need only be given to the behavior in *response* to a given pattern of moves. But there is also a great disadvantage to the behavioral approach: it is inherently limited in scope. If this approach is to be applied without question, attention must be limited to a single "representative" game from which the theory can be generalized.

A BEHAVIORAL THEORY FOR OPTIMIZING IN THE PRISONERS' DILEMMA

In its general form the prisoners' dilemma is a two-person, nonconstant sum game where, for experimental simplicity, no communication is permitted between players. When the game is iterated, implicit communication may develop. Condition (1) implies strict dominance of strategy 2 (since $\begin{matrix} c > a \\ c' > a' \end{matrix}$ and $\begin{matrix} d > b \\ d' > b' \end{matrix}$) and secondly a loss to both players if each plays his dominant strategy (since $(d, d') < (a, a')$). Condition (2) insures that no mixed strategy has a higher joint payoff than (1,1). This game has a solution prescribed by a naive application of the dominance

2. Duncan Luce and Howard Raiffa, *Games and Decisions* (New York: Wiley, 1957), p. 100.

3. Alvin Scodel, J. Sayer Minas, Philburn Ratoosh, and Milton Lipetz, "Some Descriptive Aspects of Two-Person Non-Zero-Sum Games," *The Journal of Conflict Resolution,* V (June 1959). J. Sayer Minas, Alvin Scodel, David Marlowe and Harve Rawson, "Some Descriptive Aspects of Two-Person Non-Zero-Sum Games II," *The Journal of Conflict Resolution,* VI (June 1960).

4. Morton Deutsch, "Trust and Suspicion," *Journal of Conflict Resolution,* IV (1958); "The Effect of Motivational Orientation Upon Trust and Suspicion," *Human Relations,* XIII (1960).

Player B

	Strategy 1	Strategy 2
Strategy 1	a, a'	b, c'
Strategy 2	c, b'	d, d'

Player A

(1) $c > a > d > b$
$c' > a' > d' > b'$

(2) $a > \dfrac{nc + mb}{n + m}$ $m, n = 1, 2, 3 \ldots$

$a' > \dfrac{nc' + mb'}{n + m}$

FIGURE I

notion of game theory: since strategy 2 dominates for both players, (2,2) is the solution. But the point (1,1) offers a higher payoff to each player.

The basic problems of this game center around the willingness and ability of players to co-operate by choosing strategies (1,1). If a single player decides (1,1) is the only satisfactory point, how can he communicate his wishes to the other player? Under what conditions should a player decide to attempt communication of his wishes to the other player so that they may enjoy the rewards of the dominant point?

The willingness of a player to attempt to get to (1,1) is a function of the number of trials, since the magnitude of his profit or loss varies as the number of trials for a given matrix. His ability to communicate his decision to the other player is also a function of the number of iterations since "learning" must take place and the other player must have an opportunity to react to the first player's attempt at communication. For a given matrix and class of opponents, there is some number of iterations that makes an attempt at communication profitable. Any game with so large a number of trials is qualitatively different from a game with a smaller number of trials.

Perhaps the easiest answer to how large this number is follows from three curves concerning the reaction of a player[5] to (1) an

5. "Experimenter" designates the player being prescribed for; "player" refers to some playing the game who may or may not have knowledge of this theory.

experimenter actively trying to induce co-operation, (2) a passive experimenter, and (3) another player who knows no more about the game. Given these three curves, prescriptions are generated by the experimenter's goals. For this paper the experimenter is assumed to maximize his expected value. In more detail the experimenter should attempt co-operation when a priori knowledge of the other player (i.e., these three curves for the population) permits a calculation showing that, in view of the number of iterations, the expected value of attempting co-operation is greater than the expected value of nonco-operation.

A first curve, of purely descriptive relevance, depicts the number of pairs of players arriving at (1,1) when neither player has knowledge of the theory. The curve is conjectured to be a function of (a) the entries in the matrix, (b) the total number of iterations, and (c) the number of trials already played. Holding the first two constant with the number of iterations infinite, Figure II is derived.

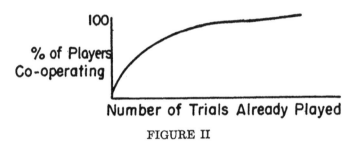

FIGURE II

The curve does not begin at (0,0) since some players see through the game immediately and react immediately. It increases as a function of the trials since, as trials accumulate, players should find their reluctance to act overcome by the relative loss $(a - d)$ they are suffering.

A second curve needed here is one of the number of players who, having decided to co-operate at (1,1), attempt to induce co-operation in their opponent. For this curve, that opponent is a passive experimenter (he has been playing strategy 2) who must be induced to co-operate by reacting to a mixed strategy.

A third curve of relevance indicates the number of players who co-operate after a given number of trials when the experimenter has been using a pattern of strategies to indicate he wants to co-operate. In addition to (a), (b), and (c) this curve will be a function of the method of teaching used. Exact specification of the method of teaching cannot be given until learning theory and more

428   *QUARTERLY JOURNAL OF ECONOMICS*

experiments have established a unique answer; however, a general comment is possible. The experimenter should limit his pattern of strategy choices so that the expected value of co-operation for the other player is greater than that of delaying action.

There are now three curves to be derived experimentally: (1) number of players responding to co-operation by an "active experimenter," (2) co-operation between "two real players," and (3) players deciding to co-operate in spite of a "passive experimenter." The curve of "two players" is seen to lie between the other two

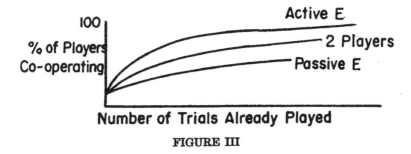

Number of Trials Already Played

FIGURE III

curves since in the "active E" curve the experimenter is acting to produce co-operation efficiently, while in the "passive E" curve one of the players is likely to be acting more positively than the passive experimenter. This lower limit is a tentative one since the passive experimenter will be better at co-operating once the player has begun to "teach" than another player would be. Thus the possibility that one player will decide to act quickly is conjectured to overweigh the difficulty of co-ordinating.

The theory can be summarized: Given the behavioral curves described above, a player merely need go through the mathematics of maximizing expectations to find a uniquely prescribed course of action. One further problem does arise when the number of iterations is known in advance: what to choose on the last few trials. But here again the question is essentially behavioral depending on what choices other players make.

EXPERIMENTS: METHOD

Four sets of experiments have been performed to test the preceding theory and draw two of the three curves. The first two were done at Reed College in the spring of 1960 to determine the middle curve.[6] The second two were done in early spring 1961 at M.I.T.

6. For a more detailed exposition see Lester B. Lave, "Applications of the

to determine, respectively, an additional approximation of the middle curve and the lower one.

The First Series

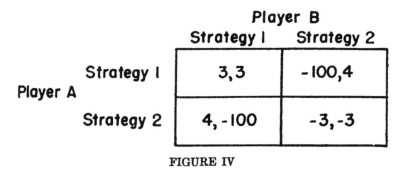

FIGURE IV

The players of the first series, using the matrix above, were juniors and seniors of Reed College who answered a note sent to all registered students (19 pairs were used). Instruction sheets explained the players had been given 650 pennies to play a game whose object was for each player to maximize winnings, since a portion of the money won would be retained at the end of the game. Players were told there would be one hundred trials and that they might ask technical questions to clarify the working of the game, but that there was to be no explicit communication between players.

The game was set up so that a barrier prevented players on either side of a table from seeing each other during the game. S informed E of his choice and was then told the other player's choice.

The Second Series

Some changes were made in the above procedure to form a second series of experiments. The subjects were freshmen and sophomores selected by the same method (19 pairs were used). The principal changes in procedure involved putting the players in separate rooms so that they had no idea of the other player's identity, changing the matrix slightly (see Figure V), so that less money could be given to the players ($1.50) and players could be told that any money won or lost during the game was theirs. They were told the game would consist of fifty iterations.

Theory of Games to Economics," unpublished B.A. thesis, Reed College, 1960; "An Empirical Description of the Prisoners' Dilemma Game," P-2091, The RAND Corporation (Santa Monica, 1960).

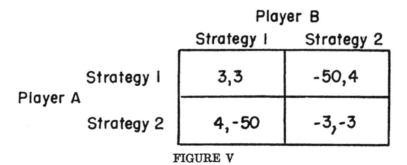

FIGURE V

The Third Series

The third series was done at M.I.T. using essentially the same procedure as the second series. Subjects were undergraduate males hired through the employment office (4 pairs were used). One change in procedure involved not specifying the number of trials the game would be played. Players were informed that the number of iterations would be determined by a random process with probability 1/100 that it would end *after* the 100th trial. Another change involved allowing players to write out a superstrategy after the 20th trial to prevent boredom. Players were given $5.00. This series of experiments permitted confirmation of past results and measured the variation in behavior between the two populations.

The Fourth Series

The fourth series of experiments was set up in the same way as the third with one change; now E matched S's choice, thus permitting derivation of the bottom curve (21 M.I.T. undergraduates were hired). Again players were permitted to write out a superstrategy. In both the third and fourth series, a second game was played, after completion of the first, where E answered strategy 2 to each choice of S. This second game provided some clue as to what an optimal teaching pattern would be as seen by the player. It also provided an approximation as to what behavior would be like in the case of a player who had seen through the game and decided to induce co-operation in an unusually slow opponent.

RESULTS AND DISCUSSION

The data can be summarized in a series of graphs. The top curve in Figures VI, VII, and VIII records the percentage of players choosing strategy 1. The curve is interpreted as the percentage of players actively attempting to induce co-operation, or at least attempting to get the other player to choose strategy 1. The lower

Players Co-operating in the Prisoners' Dilemma: First Series

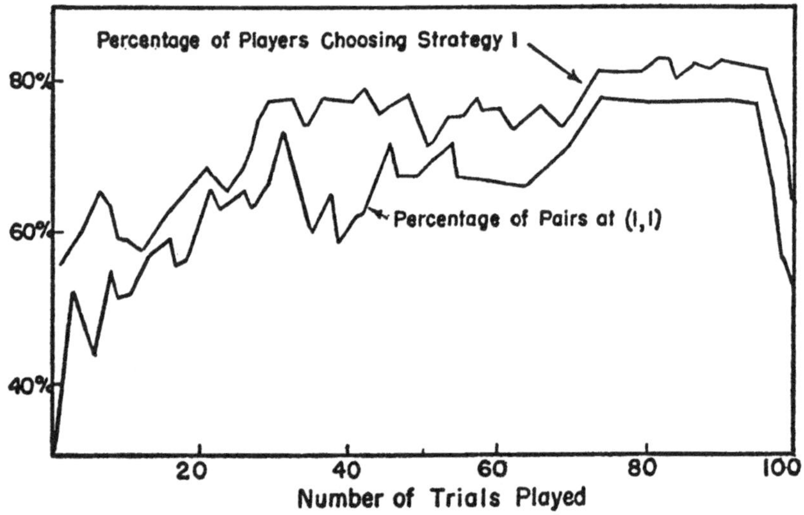

FIGURE VI

curve in these three figures portrays the percentage of pairs at (1,1) who have arrived at a co-operative union, at least temporarily. The closeness of the two curves in each of the three figures, particularly after the first moves, indicates that playing strategy 1 could not be accidental and that the only way a player could continue to play his co-operative strategy was in union with the other player. Thus, as the playing of strategy 1 cannot be conceived to be random, attention must focus on the dominant point of (1,1) rather than on a strategy choice of a single player, except insofar as the latter is used for communication. These curves provide evidence that the axioms of Luce and Raiffa are not good descriptions of behavior: players do collude. Furthermore, their theory is worthless normatively since players increase their earnings by not behaving according to these axioms.

The number of pairs at (1,1) is steady over time and thus can be used as a measure of the number of pairs who successfully formed a co-operative unit. Players found no small difficulty in actually forming this dyad since, even when it became evident to both players that they wanted to co-operate (especially in the first two series), succeeding in so doing was far from automatic or even assured. Players had to call upon tacit communication to help solve their problems of co-ordination at minimum cost.[7]

7. See T. Schelling, *The Strategy of Conflict* (Harvard University Press, 1960).

432   *QUARTERLY JOURNAL OF ECONOMICS*

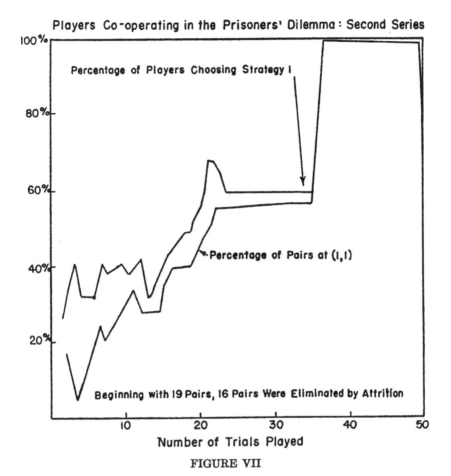

FIGURE VII

One way to quantify this argument involves comparing the curve of the number of players co-operating with an experimenter who simply matched their choices with one of the attempts at co-operation of two players. The fourth series was precisely the former situation. Thus, a comparison of the percentage of pairs at (1,1) in the first three series with the percentage of players choosing strategy 1 in the fourth series presents a first approximation of the difficulty of co-ordinating. A glance at Figure XII in which these four curves are presented reveals the curve of the fourth series rises more steeply than the other curves: co-ordination is more difficult than waiting for a single player to decide to be active.

Both the third and fourth series involved a second game in which the successful pairs of the third series and all players of the fourth series played a game in which the experimenter answered

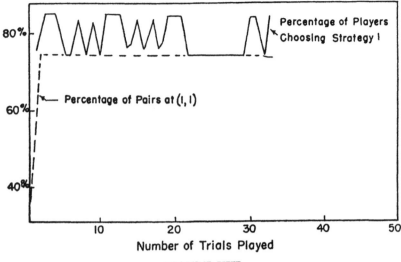

FIGURE VIII

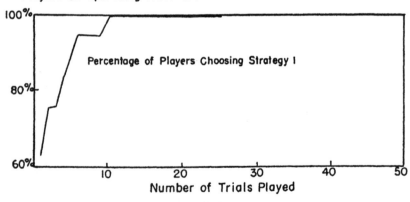

FIGURE IX

strategy 2 to every choice they made. Figure X represents the re-actions of players to a slow-learning partner. The curve of the number of strategy 1's chosen quickly falls to zero indicating that players would have little sympathy for slow-learning opponents.

In the first two series a definite number of trials was announced in advance. In pairs where co-operation was present, a notable amount of tension began to build up for the last few trials. The decision of whether to switch to strategy 2 on the last trials, and indeed, the trials directly preceding it, was made in different ways

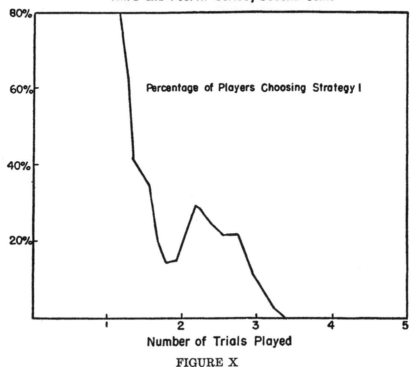

Reaction of Players to Slow-learning Opponents:
Third and Fourth Series, Second Game

FIGURE X

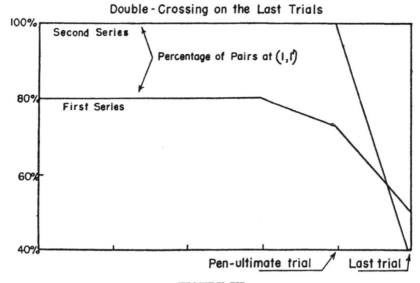

Double-Crossing on the Last Trials

FIGURE XI

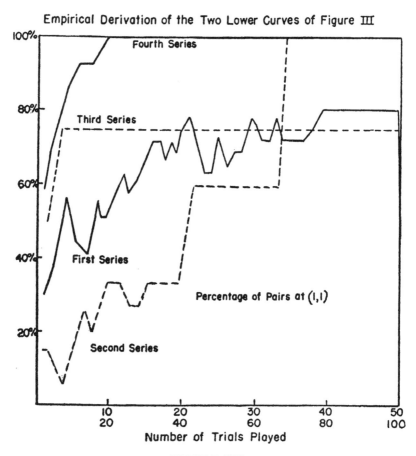

FIGURE XII

(see Figure XI). In the first series "double-crossing" (playing strategy 2) extended back as far as the penultimate trial since two players choose strategy 2 on the 99th trial (there is some evidence that this was due to an error in counting the number of trials and so was a mistake). In the second series double-crossing was restricted to the final trial. Since no fixed number of trials was stated for series three and four, the problem of the last trial was avoided.

CONCLUSION AND SUMMARY

This theory predicted that the percentage of players actively attempting co-operation would approach one hundred as the number of iterations increased, *ceteris paribus*, and that an objective

436   *QUARTERLY JOURNAL OF ECONOMICS*

function could be maximized by "exploiting" these behavior curves of the population from which players were drawn.

The lower two learning curves (Figure III) may be approximated by a graph of the percentage of players at (1,1) in the first three series and of players choosing strategy 1 in the fourth. These are approximations insofar as they represent small samples.

There are two notable differences between the theoretical curves and the behavioral ones of Figure XII. First the conjectured relation of the two curves was wrong ("passive E" lies above "two players"), indicating that the co-ordination problem is more difficult than expected. Co-ordinating takes a greater number of trials than are spent in letting a single player decide to be active. The second difference is that the curves are even more steep than anticipated. Thus, particularly in the last two series the chances are small that co-operation at (1,1) would not result.

HARVARD UNIVERSITY

[17]

PROBABILISTIC DESTRUCTION OF COMMON-POOL RESOURCES: EXPERIMENTAL EVIDENCE*

James M. Walker and Roy Gardner

Common-pool resources (CPRs) are defined to be natural or man-made resources in which: (*a*) yield is subtractable and (*b*) exclusion is non-trivial (but not necessarily impossible). Examples of CPRs include open-seas fisheries, unfenced grazing range, and groundwater basins. Scholars such as Gordon (1954) and Hardin (1968) argue that when individuals exploit CPRs, each is driven by an inexorable logic to withdraw more of the resource units (or invest less in maintenance of the resource) than is Pareto optimal. Rents are dissipated.[1]

Although the dissipation of rent from a CPR is a serious economic problem, even more urgent is the problem of the destruction of the resource. Many CPRs are fragile, and human exploitation can lead to destruction. A fishery is a simple example. If all the fish of a species are taken in a single period, the species becomes extinct and the CPR is destroyed. A more subtle example involving a geothermal CPR is given by Kerr (1991). The Geysers is a geothermal power source in northern California which has been exploited since 1960. Although grave uncertainties surround the underground structure of this resource, it is known to be fed by groundwater. This, when combined with geothermal heat, produces steam energy harnessed by electrical turbines at the surface. Due to expansion of electrical generating capacity, the safe yield of steam has been exceeded. The Geysers are rapidly drying up, and are almost certain to be destroyed by the end of the century. Similar considerations apply to global commons, such as the build-up of carbon dioxide in the earth's atmosphere. Trace levels of this gas do not affect life on earth. Current models of the atmosphere leave a wide zone of uncertainty as to what happens when carbon dioxide builds up in the atmosphere (Reilly *et al.*, 1987). At some level, as on the planet Venus, the carbon dioxide concentration destroys the biosphere.

A range of *safe yield* underlies each of these classes of CPRs. A natural regeneration process is present that implies a range of exploitation in which the probability of destruction is zero. When the safe yield is surpassed, the resource faces probabilistic destruction. Indeed, at high enough levels of economic activity, the resource is destroyed with certainty. The economic question is the

* Financial support from the National Science Foundation (grants nos. SES-8619498 and SES-4843901) and USDA Cooperative Agreement no. 43-3AEM1-80078 is gratefully acknowledged. We thank Sheryl Ball, Werner Guth, Steve Hackett, John Hey, Elizabeth Hoffman, Elinor Ostrom, and two anonymous referees for their comments. All data are stored on permanent NOVANET disk files. Send inquiries to Professor James M. Walker, Department of Economics, Ballantine 901, Indiana University, Bloomington, Indiana, U.S.A. 47405.
[1] See Gardner *et al.* (1990) for further discussion of the conceptual framework of a CPR dilemma.

trade-off between jeopardising the life of the resource and earning rents from it. It is the behavioural response of highly motivated decision makers to this economic dilemma that we focus on in this paper.

We frame the model and the laboratory CPR as non-cooperative games. These games have many Nash equilibria. We adopt as our refinement subgame perfection. When there are multiple subgame-perfect equilibria, we select among them using the principle of pay-off dominance (Harsanyi and Selten, 1988). We have two primary treatments, depending upon whether the safe zone consists of a single point or an interval. Our primary results are that: (1) if the safe zone consists of a single point, the resource is rapidly destroyed in accordance with subgame-perfect equilibrium; (2) if the safe zone is an interval, group behaviour in some instances tends to focus on the best available equilibrium, but in general this equilibrium cannot be sustained and the resource is destroyed. These results show how valuable agreement among appropriators of a CPR can be, not only in capturing rents but also in saving the CPR from destruction.

The paper is organised as follows. The next section models the one-period CPR and the repeated game with probabilistic destruction. Section II describes our experimental design and Section III our experimental results. The final section offers a conclusion and questions for further research.

I. MODEL OF A DESTRUCTIBLE CPR

A. *The CPR Constituent Game*

We shall first specify the class of constituent CPR games from which we draw our designs. Assume a fixed number n of appropriators with access to the CPR. Each appropriator i has an endowment of resources e which can be invested in the CPR or invested in a safe, outside activity. The payoff to an individual appropriator from investing in the CPR depends on aggregate group investment in the CPR, and on the appropriator investment as a percentage of the aggregate. The marginal payoff of the outside activity is w. Let x_i denote appropriator i's investment in the CPR, where $0 \leqslant x_i \leqslant e$. The group return to investment in the CPR is given by the production function $F(\Sigma x_i)$, where F is a concave function, with $F(0) = 0$, $F'(0) > w$, and $F'(ne) < 0$. Initially, investment in the CPR pays better than the opportunity cost of the forgone safe investment $[F'(0) > w]$, but if the appropriators invest all resources in the CPR the outcome is counterproductive $[F'(ne) < 0]$. Thus the yield from the CPR reaches a maximum when individuals invest some but not all of their endowments in the CPR.

Let $\mathbf{x} = (x_1, \ldots, x_n)$ be a vector of individual appropriators' investments in the CPR. The payoff to an appropriator, $u_i(\mathbf{x})$, is given by:

$$u_i(\mathbf{x}) = we \qquad\qquad\qquad\qquad \text{if } x_i = 0$$
$$w(e - x_i) + (x_i/\Sigma x_i)\, F(\Sigma x_i) \quad \text{if } x_i > 0. \qquad (1)$$

Equation (1) reflects the fact that if appropriators invest all their endowments in the outside alternative, they get a sure payoff (we), whereas if they invest some of their endowments in the CPR, they get a sure payoff $w(e-x_i)$ plus a payoff from the CPR, which depends on the total investment in that resource $F(\Sigma x_i)$ multiplied by their share in the group investment $(x_i/\Sigma x_i)$.

Let the payoffs (1) be the payoff functions in a symmetric, non-cooperative game. Since our experimental design is symmetric, there is a symmetric Nash equilibrium, with each player investing x_i^* in the CPR, where:

$$-w + (1/n)\, F'(nx_i^*) + F(nx_i^*)\left[(n-1)/n^2 x_i^*\right] = 0. \tag{2}$$

At the symmetric Nash equilibrium, group investment in the CPR is greater than optimal, but not all yield from the CPR is wasted.

There are several ways to interpret an equilibrium condition such as (2). One is in terms of disequilibrium, namely that any behaviour not satisfying (2) will not persist over time, but will disappear. A second interpretation is in terms of equilibrium, namely that once behaviour satisfies (2) that behaviour persists over time. Neither of these interpretations says anything about the dynamics of behavioural change. A third and much stronger dynamic interpretation of (2) is in terms of evolutionary stability. If behaviour is being selected according to replicator equations, (2) characterises the dynamically stable equilibrium of the associated dynamical system (Hofbauer and Sigmund, 1988).[2] A final interpretation is as a limited-access CPR (see, for example, Clark, 1980; Cornes and Sandler, 1986; Negri, 1989).[3]

Compare this equilibrium to the optimal solution. Summing across individual payoffs $u_i(x)$ for all appropriators i, one has the group payoff function $u(x)$,

$$u(x) = nwe - w\Sigma x_i + F(\Sigma x_i), \tag{3}$$

which is to be maximised subject to the constraints $0 \leqslant \Sigma x_i \leqslant ne$. Given the above productivity conditions on F, the group maximisation problem has a unique solution characterised by the condition:

$$-w + F'(\Sigma x_i) = 0. \tag{4}$$

According to (4), the marginal return from a CPR should equal the opportunity cost of the outside alternative for the last unit invested in the CPR. The group payoff from using the marginal revenue = marginal cost rule (4) represents the maximal yield that can be extracted from the resource in a single period.

B. *Finite Deterministic Repetition of the Constituent Game*

Denote the constituent game by X and let X be played a finite number of times T. Let t index the number of periods left before play ends, $t = 1, ..., T$. Let $\mathbf{x}_t = (x_{1t}, ..., x_{nt})$ be a vector of individual decisions at time t. An optimal return function defined recursively for player i, f_{it}, is given by:

$$f_{it}(\mathbf{x}_t) = \max_{x_{it}} u_{it}(\mathbf{x}_t) + f_{i,t-1}(\mathbf{x}_{t-1}) \tag{5}$$

---

[2] The proof of this result is available upon request.

[3] Consistent Conjectural Variation Equilibria may provide a useful method for a detailed analysis of individual subject behaviour in these experiments. See Mason *et al.* (1988) for a discussion of consistent conjectures equilibria for the CPR experiment. See Walker *et al.* (1991) for a discussion of several alternative theories that could be used to provide a solution to the core, constituent game.

where u_{it} is the contemporaneous return function for player i at time t as in (1), $f_{i,t-1}$ is the optimal return function for the next period, and $f_{i0} = 0$. The solution to (5) for all players i and all times t is a subgame-perfect equilibrium of X finitely repeated. If X has a unique equilibrium, then finitely repeated X has a unique subgame-perfect equilibrium (Selten, 1971). Thus (5) has a unique solution given by the solution of (2) in each period t.

C. Probabilistic Repetition of the Constituent Game

We model probabilistic destruction of the CPR as a 1-period hazard rate depending upon the current period's decisions. Formally, the decision environment is a finitely repeated game with an endogenous continuation probability $p_t(x_t)$. Define *LUB* as the lowest upper bound on exploitation with probability 1 destruction and *GLB* as the greatest lower bound with probability 0 destruction. We specify the *continuation* probability as follows:

$$p_t(x_t) = \begin{cases} 0 & \text{if } \Sigma x_{it} \geqslant LUB \\ p(\Sigma x_{it}) & \text{if } GLB < \Sigma x_{it} < LUB \\ 1 & \text{if } \Sigma x_{it} \leqslant GLB. \end{cases} \quad (6)$$

In the event $p_t(x_t) = 0$, the resource has been destroyed and play ends. The probability of destruction depends on aggregate exploitation through Σx_{it}, with $p_t(\mathbf{x}_t)$ a non-negative decreasing function of its argument. One has $0 \leqslant GLB < LUB$. *GLB* represents the safe yield and the interval $[0, GLB]$ the safe zone.[4]

In the presence of probabilistic continuation, the optimal return function is amended to:

$$f_{it}(\mathbf{x}_t) = \max_{x_{it}} u_{it}(\mathbf{x}_t) + p_t(\mathbf{x}_t) f_{i,t-1}(\mathbf{x}_{t-1}). \quad (7)$$

Since utility is linear, specification (7) implies risk neutrality on the part of all players. As before, a solution to the recursive equation (7) is a subgame-perfect equilibrium. It is important to note that even if the constituent game has a unique Nash equilibrium, (7) may have multiple solutions.

II. THE EXPERIMENTAL DESIGN

In our experimental investigation we have operationalised this CPR environment with eight appropriators $(n = 8)$ and quadratic production functions $F(\Sigma x_i)$, where:

$$F(\Sigma x_i) = a\Sigma x_i - b(\Sigma x_i)^2$$

with $F'(0) = a > w$ and $F'(ne) = a - 2bne < 0$.

For this quadratic specification, one has from (4) that the group optimal investment satisfies $\Sigma x_i = (a-w)/2b$. The CPR yields 0% on net when

---

[4] As a referee correctly points out, specification (6) is restrictive. It would be more general to make the probability of destruction depend on the entire history of the game. However, we view the ensuing complication, although interesting, as not the best starting point for our exploration.

Table 1

Parameters for the Constituent Game

Number of subjects	8
Individual token endowment	25
Production function (cents): market 2*	$23(\Sigma x_i) - 0.25(\Sigma x_i)^2$
Market 2 return/unit of output (cents)†	1
Market 1 return/unit of output (cents)	5

* Σx_i = the total number of tokens invested by the group in market 2. The production function shows the number of units of output produced in market 2 for each level of tokens invested in market 2.
† Subjects were paid in cash one-half of their NOVANET earnings.

investment is twice as large as optimal, $\Sigma x_i = (a-w)/b$. Finally, from (2), the symmetric Nash equilibrium group investment is given by:

$$\Sigma x_i = [n/(n+1)](a-w)/b.$$

This level of investment is between maximal net yield and zero net yield, approaching the latter as n gets large. One additional constraint that arises in a laboratory setting is that the x_i be integer-valued. This is accomplished by choosing the parameters a, b, d and w in such a way that the predictions associated with Σx_i are all integer-valued.

In particular, we use the parameters shown in Table 1. A group investment of 36 tokens yields the optimal level of investment. The symmetric constituent game has a unique Nash equilibrium, with each subject investing eight tokens in market 2. At the Nash equilibrium, subjects earn approximately 39·5% of maximum net yield from the CPR.

The experiments reported in this paper used subjects drawn from the undergraduate population at Indiana University. Students were volunteers recruited from Principles of Economics classes. Prior to recruitment, potential volunteers were given a brief explanation in which they were told only that they would be making decisions in an 'economic choice' environment and that the money they earned would be dependent upon their own investment decisions and those of the others in their experimental group. All experiments were conducted on the NOVANET computer system at IU. The computer facilitates the accounting procedures involved in the experiment, enhances across experimental/subject control, and allows for minimal experimenter involvement.

Subjects can be viewed as facing the constituent game to which a probabilistic structure has been attached. In the constituent game the decision task can be summarised as follows.

Subjects faced a series of decision periods in which they were endowed with a specified number of tokens, which they invested between two markets. Market 1 was described as an investment opportunity in which each token yielded a fixed (constant) rate of output and each unit of output yielded a fixed (constant) return. Market 2 (the CPR) was described as a market which yielded a rate of output per token dependent upon the total number of tokens invested by the entire group. The rate of output at each level of group investment was described in functional form as well as tabular form. Subjects were informed that they would receive a level of output from market 2 that was equivalent to the percentage of total group tokens they invested. Further, subjects knew that each unit of output from market 2 yielded a fixed (constant) rate of return.[5]

A. *Destruction Design I*

In Design I destruction experiments the decision task faced by our subjects is amended in the following manner:[6]

> The subjects were notified that the experiment would continue up to 20 rounds After each decision round a random drawing would occur which would determine if the experiment continued. For every token invested in market 2 by any participant, the probability of ending the experiment increased by one-half per cent. For example: if the group invested 50 tokens total in market 2, the probability of ending the experiment was 25%. The drawing at the end of each round worked as follows: a single card was drawn randomly from a deck of 100 cards numbered from 1 to 100. If the number on the card was equal to or below the probability of ending the experiment for that round (as determined by the group investment in that round) the experiment ended. Otherwise the experiment continued to the next round.

Thus the parameterisation was $GLB = 0$, $LUB = 200$, and the probability of continuation (6) was:

$$p_t(\mathbf{x}_t) = 1 - (\Sigma x_{it}/200). \tag{8}$$

The safe zone consisted of a single point, zero exploitation. The optimal solution can be found by solving (5) with a single player in control of all resources. Similarly, the subgame-perfect equilibrium can be found by solving (5) and exploiting symmetry. In Table 2 we present these solutions for the entire life of the resource, given that $T = 20$.[7] Three features of this symmetric subgame-perfect equilibrium path should be noted. In contrast to the optimal path, where only in the last four periods is there a positive probability of destruction, the subgame-perfect equilibrium path has a positive and growing probability of destruction throughout the experiment. At the outset, the one-period destruction probability is approximately 27% at the subgame equilibrium, and it rises to 32% by the end. With one-period hazard rates this high, it is unlikely (probability less than 0·05) that the resource will survive 10 periods. This increased probability of destruction accounts for the lower overall

---

[5] At the end of all experiments, subjects were paid privately (in cash) their individual earnings. All subjects in the destruction experiments had participated previously in an experiment using the constituent game environment with no destruction. Subjects in the destruction experiments were recruited randomly from this pool of experienced subject to ensure that no prior experimental group was brought back intact. Walker *et al.* (1990, 1991) provide a detailed account of behaviour in the constituent game environment. Complete instructions are available from the authors.

[6] The experimenter reviewed the announcement with the subjects and answered questions. Note that in the destruction experiments subjects were told explicitly that the experiments would last up to 20 periods. This information in the destruction experiments makes the optimisation task tractable.

[7] For periods 6–17, all values change monotonically except for optimal investment, which remains at 0.

Table 2
Dynamic Programming Paths, Design I

	Optimum path		Subgame-perfect equilibrium path	
Periods remaining	Aggregate investment	Optimal value per capita (cents)	Aggregate investment	Equilibrium value per capita (cents)
1	36·0	166	64·0	141
2	22·8	307	61·5	243
3	11·5	435	59·7	318
4	1·1	561	58·3	375
5	00·0	686	57·3	419
—	—	—	—	—
—	—	—	—	—
—	—	—	—	—
18	00·0	2,311	53·8	571
19	00·0	2,436	53·8	573
20	00·0	2,561	53·8	574

value of the resource to investors, slightly less than $6 each, or $46 aggregate (8 × 574 cents), as opposed to over $200 at the optimum. Finally, individual value stabilises at 574 for infinitely long experiments. Thus, $T = 20$ is long enough in theory to yield steady-state behaviour consistent with the optimal value function.

B. Destruction Design II

Our design I is unforgiving in the sense that any investment in the CPR leads to a positive probability of destruction. Our second design adds a safe zone for market 2 investment in order to investigate whether subjects might focus on a clear-cut safe investment opportunity. The announcement to subjects for design II is summarised as follows.

> The subjects were notified that the experiment would continue up to 20 rounds. After each decision round a random drawing would occur which would determine if the experiment continued. If the group invested 40 tokens or less in market 2, the experiment automatically proceeded to the next round. If the group invested more than 40 tokens in market 2, the probability of ending the experiment increased by one-half per cent for each token invested in market 2 by any participant. For example: if the group invested 50 tokens total in market 2, the probability of ending the experiment was 25%. The drawing at the end of each round worked as follows: a single card was drawn randomly from a deck of 100 cards numbered from 1 to 100. If the number on the card was equal to or below the probability of ending the experiment for that round (as determined by the group investment in that round) the experiment ended. Otherwise the experiment continued to the next round.

Thus the parameterisation was $GLB = 40$, $LUB = 200$, and the probability of continuation was given by (8) on the open interval (40,200). Design II gives subjects a large safe zone [o, 40] in which to exploit the resource.[8] Since the safe zone includes the one-period optimal solution, a coordinating rational agent would play 36 tokens each period to maximise rents.

Subgame-perfect Nash equilibria can be found by applying dynamic programming to (7). First, note that the Nash equilibrium path described for design I remains an equilibrium path for design II, since this path never enters the safe zone. There is, however, another equilibrium path in design II which is better in payoff space. This equilibrium path invests 64 tokens in market 2 with one period to go, but later switches to *GLB* at some critical time. That critical time is $t = 3$. Consider $f_{i2}(\mathbf{x_2})$. Suppose all players except player i are investing a total of 35 tokens. If i invests 5 tokens, then he gets a sure payoff of $u_{i2}(5) + 141$, leading to an overall two-period expected value of 306 cents. There is no threat of destruction in this case. Now suppose instead that player i makes the best response in the destruction zone to 35 tokens invested by the others. This turns out to be 17 tokens, leading to a 26% chance of destruction and an expected two-period payoff of 314 cents. Thus, with two periods to go, staying in the safe zone is not an equilibrium. Repeating the above calculations for $t = 3$, the safe investment yields an expected payoff of 408 cents over the last three periods, while the investment of 17 tokens (still the best response in the destruction zone) yields a payoff of only 390 cents. Thus, with three periods remaining, the future value of preserving the resource is sufficient to justify staying in the safe zone as a non-cooperative equilibrium. Since expected future value grows with time remaining, once this backward induction path enters the safe zone it stays there.[9] Indeed, this equilibrium path with an efficiency of 97% is nearly as good as the optimum path for design II. The optimal path and the best subgame-perfect equilibrium path are shown in Table 3. There is a

Table 3
Dynamic Programming Paths, Design II

Periods remaining	Optimum path		Subgame-perfect equilibrium path	
	Aggregate investment	Optimal value per capita (cents)	Aggregate investment	Equilibrium value per capita (cents)
1	36·0	166	64·0	141
2	36·0	331	61·5	243
3	36·0	496	40·0	408
4	36·0	662	40·0	573
5	36·0	827	40·0	738
—	—	—	—	—
—	—	—	—	—
18	36·0	2,978	40·0	2,883
19	36·0	3,144	40·0	3,048
20	36·0	3,310	40·0	3,213

[8] In the first three experimental runs this upper bound was set equal to 40. This slight change had no apparent effect on behaviour. We have therefore pooled all runs in the results reported here.
[9] Following Benoit and Krishna (1985), once we have a good and a bad subgame-perfect equilibrium, we can construct many others. These two equilibrium paths, however, seem to us the most likely to be observed in the laboratory.

dramatic difference in payoffs between the good equilibrium and the bad one; this environment gives a clear equilibrium focal point for behaviour. By investing 40 tokens in every period the group receives very close to optimal rents (99%) and runs no risk of ending the experiment.

III. EXPERIMENTAL RESULTS

Our experimental results are summarised by first examining aggregate investments. The aggregate results of all 12 experiments are presented in Table 4. All five design I experiments yielded investment efficiencies below 37%. The

Table 4

CPR Investments in Destruction Experiments

Experiment	Average tokens invested	Number of periods before destruction	Percentage of optimal income earned*
		Design I	
1	˙35˙25	4	19˙30
2	55˙00	4	22˙65
3	60˙33	3	17˙31
4	53˙00	6	36˙38
5†	65˙00	2	10˙80
		Design II	
1	42˙83	6	29˙59
2	59˙68	3	13˙39
3	63˙41	5	20˙91
4†	61˙34	6	25˙02
5	37˙94	17	83˙94
6	37˙93	15	74˙22
7	52˙50	2	9˙52

* Actual income earned/income using optimal path.
† Subjects experienced in a destruction experiment.

longest experimented lasted 6 periods. The average efficiency over all design I experiments was 21%, as predicted by subgame-perfect equilibrium. These results are striking. In a decision environment with a well-defined probability and significant opportunity costs of destruction, efficiency is very low and the resource is quickly destroyed. Individual and group investments in market 2 are well beyond optimum levels, with an average investment of 47˙1 tokens per period; 32% of all group outcomes lie in the interval [54–64] containing the subgame-perfect equilibrium path, 53% lie below 54 and 16% lie above 64.

In five of the seven design II experiments, destruction occurred early and efficiency was below 30%. Of these five experiments, the longest lasted 6 periods. In two design II experiments, destruction did not occur until late in the experiment (rounds 15 and 17) and efficiencies were high (74% and 84%). Overall average efficiency was 37% in design II, a significant increase over design I. Average investment in market 2 fell to 45˙9 tokens per period. It appears that in design II the large safe zone did serve as a focal point for many subjects. This is borne out by the data displayed in Table 5. A Kolmogorov–

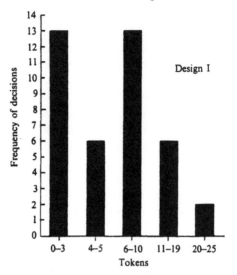

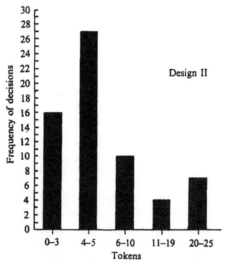

Fig. 1. Individual investments – market 2, period 1.

Table 5

Cumulative Investments in Market 2: Aggregate and Individual Data

Aggregate	$\Sigma x_i \leqslant 40$	41–53	54–64	> 64	
Design I	21%	32%	32%	16%	
Design II	39%	35%	19%	6%	
Individual	$x_i \leqslant 5$	$6 \leqslant x_i \leqslant 10$	$11 \leqslant x_i \leqslant 15$	$16 \leqslant x_i \leqslant 19$	$20 \leqslant x_i \leqslant 25$
Design I	54%	30%	10%	2%	4%
Design II	66%	22%	8%	2%	2%

Smirnov test shows a significant difference in the cumulative distribution of market 2 investments in the two designs. The percentage of periods where market 2 investment is less than or equal to 40 nearly doubles in design II. We can also see this effect in the individual data, although it is less pronounced.

At the individual level the data for the two experiments which survived the longest present a mixed picture. There were numerous periods in which: (*a*) a subset of players played well beyond the safe-strategy equilibrium; and (*b*) aggregate investment in market 2 was beyond the safe investment of 40 tokens. What is different about these two experiments is that in many periods a sufficient number of players made small enough investments in market 2 to offset the large investments by others. Further, in periods in which the groups invested beyond 40, a 'good' draw led to a continuation of the experiment. Subjects in these experiments made average market 2 investments of 38 tokens, below the safe focal point of 40 tokens, but in no period did the groups reach the safe equilibrium of every player investing 5 tokens in market 2.

These results are even more striking than those obtained in design I. In a decision environment with a well-defined probability of destruction, with a safe zone in which optimum rents could be obtained (and which included a safe subgame-perfect equilibrium path near the optimum): (1) in only two experiments did groups follow an investment pattern generally in the vicinity of the good subgame-perfect equilibrium (17 of 32 periods strictly in the safe zone); and (2) in the remaining five experiments groups followed an investment pattern dispersed around the bad subgame-perfect equilibrium.

Fig. 1 summarises first-period individual behaviour. The top panel displays observations from the design I experiments. Only 2 of 40 individuals play the safe strategy of investing 0 tokens in market 2. Further, the frequency of players investing 6 or more tokens in market 2 is high (21 of 40). In each of the 5 experiments, at least 2 players followed a strategy of investing 10 or more tokens. One might conjecture that, after an initial decision round with a significant probability of destruction, players would fall back to a safe strategy. In no experiment did all players fall back to cooperative strategies with very low levels of investments in market 2. Experiment 1 resulted in the most significant drop, with investments falling from an aggregate of 80 in period 1 to 32 in period 2. Even in this experiment, however, investments began to increase after period 2.

The first-period behaviour of design II is summarised in the lower panel of Fig. 1. Many players (43 of 64) did in fact play a strategy consistent with staying in the safe zone by investing 5 tokens or less in market 2. However, each experiment had at least two players investing beyond the safe strategy. The resulting outcome led in subsequent periods to an increase in market 2 investments by many players who initially followed the safe strategy.

IV. SUMMARY AND CONCLUSIONS

The results of these experiments are hardly cause for optimism with regard to CPR survival in environments where no institutions exist to foster cooperative behaviour. In our experimental setting, when there is a non-negligible probability of destruction, the CPR is in every case destroyed and, in most cases, rather quickly. The consequences of this destruction is a significant loss in rents. Even when there is a focal-point Nash equilibrium which is completely safe and yields near-optimal rents, subjects do not stabilise at this equilibrium.

The time-dependence problem our subjects face is far simpler than those faced in naturally occurring renewable resources. In fisheries, for instance, not only is there a clear and present danger of extinction, but also the one-period payoff functions fluctuate wildly. As discussed by Allen and McGlade (1987), these fluctuations are driven by both economic and biological forces. On the economic side, market prices vary. On the biological side, population dynamics are much more complex than assumed in standard bionomic models. In such models, extinction is a limit which is approached slowly, while in reality, many biological species have a population dynamic that is characterised by sudden extinction. Our design captures this feature of sudden extinction, without recourse to other non-stationarities. In the presence of naturally occurring non-stationarities, the task of learning the payoff functions, much less best responses, is formidable. There will usually be considerable uncertainty surrounding the safe zone (is there one, how large is it, etc.). As a result, there will be uncertainty about the best policy to improve the extremely low efficiencies. In the time it takes to learn in natural settings (void of institutions designed to foster cooperation) the resource may already be destroyed.

The behaviour in this laboratory CPR environment adds additional evidence to field data regarding the need for well-formulated and -tested institutional changes designed to balance appropriation with natural regeneration. Our laboratory setting offers one possible environment for investigating alternative institutions. One institutional change currently under discussion appears in Malik *et al.* (1991). In deliberations over re-authorisation of the U.S. Water Quality Act of 1983, one proposal involves the use of an environmental bond. Each period, appropriators post a bond of a determinate size, which they forfeit in the event that the CPR is destroyed (or some other well-defined measure of over-use). Otherwise, the bond is retained for another period. In our laboratory environment, one can show that posting a bond the size of the steady-state value in our design I is enough theoretically to induce appropriators to preserve the CPR. A somewhat smaller bond is sufficient to move appropriators to the safe zone in design II. Behaviourally, the mere fact of having to post a bond could serve to focus subjects on the safe zone, even if their behaviour is only limitedly rational. The laboratory investigation of such institutional reforms is one direction for research we plan for the future.

Indiana University

Indiana University and USDA-ERS

Date of receipt of final typescript: January 1992

REFERENCES

Allen, P. M. and McGlade, J. M. (1987). 'Modelling complex human systems: a fisheries example.' *European Journal of Operational Research*, vol. 30, no. 2, pp. 147–67.

Benoit, J. and Krishna, V. (1985). 'Finitely repeated games.' *Econometrica*, vol. 53, pp. 905–22.

Clark, C. (1980). 'Restricted access to common-property fishery resources: a game theoretic analysis.' In *Dynamic Optimization and Mathematical Economics* (ed. P. T. Liu), pp. 117–32. New York: Plenum Press.

Cornes, R. and Sandler, T. (1986). *The Theory of Externalities, Public Goods, and Club Goods*. Cambridge: Cambridge University Press.

Gardner, R., Ostrom, E. and Walker, J. (1990). 'The nature of common-pool resource problems.' *Rationality and Society*, vol. 2, no. 3, pp. 335–58.

Gordon, S. (1954). 'The economic theory of a common property resource: the fishery.' *Journal of Political Economy*, vol. 62, pp. 124–42.

Hardin, G. (1968). 'The tragedy of the commons.' *Science*, vol. 162, no. 1, pp. 243–8.

Harsanyi, J. C. and Selten, R. (1988). *A General Theory of Equilibrium Selection in Games*. Cambridge, MA: MIT Press.

Hofbauer, A. and Sigmund, K. (1988). *The Theory of Evolution and Dynamical Systems*. Cambridge: Cambridge University Press.

Kerr, R. A. (1991). 'Geothermal tragedy of the commons.' *Science*, vol. 258, pp. 134–5.

Malik, A., Larson, B. and Ribaudo, M. (1990). 'Nonpoint source pollution and economic incentive policies in the reauthorization of the Clean Water Act.' USDA, unpublished manuscript.

Mason, C., Sandler, T. and Cornes, R. (1988). 'Expectations, the commons, and optimal group size.' *Journal of Environmental Economics and Management*, vol. 15, pp. 99–110.

Negri, D. H. (1989). 'The common property aquifer as a differential game.' *Water Resources Research*, vol. 25, pp. 9–15.

Reilly, J. M., Edmonds, J. A., Gardner, R. H. and Brenkert, A. L. (1987). 'Uncertainty analysis of the IEA/ORAU CO_2 emissions model.' *The Energy Journal*, vol. 8, pp. 1–29.

Selten, R. (1971). 'A simple model of imperfect competition where 4 are few and 6 are many.' *International Journal of Game Theory*, vol. 2, pp. 141–201.

Walker, J., Gardner, R. and Ostrom, E. (1990). 'Rent dissipation in limited access common pool resource environments: experimental evidence.' *Journal of Environmental Economics and Management*, vol. 19, pp. 203–11.

Walker, J., Gardner, R. and Ostrom, E. (1991). 'Rent dissipation and balanced deviation disequilibrium in common pool resources: experimental evidence.' In *Game Equilibrium Models II: Methods, Morals, and Markets* (ed. R. Selten), Berlin: Springer Verlag, pp. 337–67.

[18]

COMMUNICATION IN COORDINATION GAMES*

RUSSELL COOPER
DOUGLAS V. DEJONG
ROBERT FORSYTHE
THOMAS W. ROSS

We present experimental evidence on nonbinding, preplay communication in bilateral coordination games. To evaluate the effect of "cheap talk," we consider two communication structures (one-way and two-way communication) and two types of coordination games (one with a cooperative strategy and a second in which one strategy is less "risky"). In games with a cooperative strategy, one-way communication increases play of the Pareto-dominant equilibrium relative to the no communication baseline; two-way communication does *not* always decrease the frequency of coordination failures. In the second type of game, two-way communication always leads to the Pareto-dominant Nash equilibrium, while one-way communication does not.

I. INTRODUCTION

In this paper we consider two types of experimental coordination games with nonbinding, preplay communication. The key characteristic of these simultaneous-move games is the existence of multiple, Pareto-ranked equilibria.

An example of a coordination game is displayed in Figure I. In this game both (1,1) and (2,2) are Nash equilibria, and the latter clearly Pareto dominates the former. Note too that strategy 3 supports the cooperative outcome but is a dominated strategy. Thus, one might view this game as a prisoner's dilemma game with an additional equilibrium. Due to the presence of this cooperative strategy, we refer to this game as a *cooperative coordination game* (CCG).

A second type of coordination game is illustrated in Figure II. This is a simple coordination game with two, Pareto-ranked equilibria and *no* cooperative, dominated strategy. To the extent that there is strategic uncertainty about the likely play of an opponent, strategy 1 is "safe" in that the player receives 800,

*Conversations with Thomas Palfrey about these issues have been quite helpful in formulating this experiment and thinking about our results. We also thank seminar participants at the University of Arizona, Boston University, Michigan State University, the University of Missouri, and the University of Pennsylvania and two anonymous referees. Financial support from the National Science Foundation, the Social Sciences and Humanities Research Council of Canada, and Arthur Young & Co. for this project is gratefully acknowledged. We thank Robert Pearson for providing programming assistance.

740   *QUARTERLY JOURNAL OF ECONOMICS*

Column Player's Strategy

Row Player's Strategy		1	2	3
	1	350,350	350,250	1000,0
	2	250,350	550,550	0,0
	3	0,1000	0,0	600,600

FIGURE I

independent of an opponent's play.[1] One important difference between the games is that the Figure II game does not have a cooperative, dominated strategy. Hence we refer to this as a *simple coordination game* (SCG).

These games represent, in an abstract fashion, the types of interactions prevalent in many recent macroeconomic models of coordination problems as well as models of networks, bank runs, team production problems, etc. For example, in Diamond [1982] the returns to an agent from undertaking a production opportunity is an increasing function of the number of others who have chosen to produce. Similarly, Bryant [1983] characterizes an economy in which the optimal choice of effort by one agent depends in a positive way on the effort level put forth by others. Cooper and John [1988] characterize the nature of the strategic complementarities in these and related examples. For many of these economies the Pareto-efficient equilibrium will be socially suboptimal due to the presence of externalities in payoffs, while for others, such as the economy described by Bryant, the Pareto-efficient equilibrium is also a Pareto-efficient allocation. The games considered in this paper, CCG and SCG, reflect these two theoretical possibilities.

Consideration of these games is also motivated by the simple game theoretic issue of selection in games with multiple equilibria in which the existing refinements are powerless. For example, Harsanyi and Selten [1988] emphasize coordination games in their theory of equilibrium selection.

---

1. This concept of a "safe" strategy is formalized by Harsanyi and Selten [1988] as a "risk dominant" strategy. Given the strategic uncertainty, the riskiness of strategy 2 might make strategy 1 focal. In fact, they use an example similar to our game (see Harsanyi and Selten, pps. 88–89) to discuss the possible conflict between risk dominance and payoff dominance and the role of preplay communication. We initially considered using the 2 × 2 game obtained by deleting strategy 3 in the game given in Figure I. Without preplay communication, coordination failures were not observed in that game so the game given in Figure II, which highlights strategic uncertainty, was used instead.

COMMUNICATION IN COORDINATION GAMES   741

Column Player's Strategy

		1	2
Row Player's Strategy	1	800,800	800,0
	2	0,800	1000,1000

FIGURE II

An important theme in these coordination games is the possibility that the Pareto-inferior Nash equilibrium is observed; i.e., coordination failures occur. Cooper, DeJong, Forsythe, and Ross [1990] provide experimental evidence on sequences of independent, one-shot coordination games, including CCG, without preplay communication. Except for the early rounds of play, a Nash equilibrium was observed, but the Pareto-dominant equilibrium was not always the experimental outcome. For example, the Pareto-inferior Nash equilibrium was observed for CCG.[2] Moreover, players seem initially to place some positive probability on their rivals being cooperative (i.e., playing strategy 3), even though this is a dominated strategy. As a consequence, altering the payoffs from a rival's play of a cooperative, dominated strategy can influence selection of a Nash equilibrium. In Cooper et al. [1990] we report that once strategy 3 is eliminated from CCG, the (2,2) outcome is observed. Thus, the source of the coordination failure in CCG is the presence of the cooperative strategy.

As reported in this paper, coordination failures always occur in game SCG in the absence of preplay communication. Since that game does not have a cooperative strategy, the source of the coordination failure is different than in CCG. Harsanyi and Selten [1988] suggest that the coordination failures reported here for SCG are associated with the "riskiness" of strategy 2.

One might conjecture that if players could communicate, prior to selecting an action, then the coordination failures would disappear as preplay communication would select a desired outcome. This corresponds to the view that play of a Nash equilibrium is the consequence of nonbinding, preplay communication through which players pick the best outcome from the set of self-enforcing agreements. From this perspective, communication focuses beliefs

---

2. Van Huyck, Battalio, and Beil [1990] provide independent evidence of coordination problems in a multi-agent, finitely repeated experimental coordination game.

on a particular equilibrium. If communication works to select an equilibrium, communication should overcome any coordination failures observed in experimental games without cheap talk.[3] A theoretical structure in which one can evaluate this role of preplay communication is provided in Section II.

In support of this conjecture Cooper, DeJong, Forsythe, and Ross [1989] present experimental evidence that preplay communication resolves coordination problems in a battle of the sexes game. Allowing one player to send a message to another prior to the choice of actions almost completely resolved coordination problems (ex post disequilibrium) observed in the experimental game without preplay communication. Consistent with theory, coordination problems were reduced but not eliminated when both players simultaneously sent a message prior to selecting their actions. Our interest here is whether or not the coordinating role of preplay communication extends to coordination games.

Our experimental design is described in Section III. It is similar to that used in Cooper et al. [1989], where players could engage in preplay communication. As in our previous work participants play a series of one-shot games in which they are anonymously matched with a sequence of opponents.

The results of the cheap talk treatments with one-way and two-way communication are described in Section IV.[4] For CCG, allowing preplay communication by a single player significantly increases the frequency of equilibrium outcomes. Further, play of the (2,2) Nash equilibrium is more frequent relative to the game without preplay communication. Nonetheless, a nontrivial number of coordination failures still arise. However, allowing both players to communicate simultaneously does not resolve the coordination problem: the (2,2) Nash equilibrium is not always observed more frequently than in the game without preplay communication.

---

3. Of course, this does not mean that the coordination failures explored in the theoretical literature in macroeconomics would necessarily be resolved by allowing such cheap talk. It is important to recognize that our results pertain to bilateral games in which communication is costless and highly structured. Preplay communication is likely to be quite expensive in large economies of the variety studied in macroeconomics.
4. Isaac and Walker [1986] and Palfrey and Rosenthal [1988b] also investigate the effects of cheap talk in experimental games. Isaac and Walker investigate the implications of preplay communication in the context of the voluntary contribution mechanism. They find that communication mattered and increased cooperative play. Palfrey and Rosenthal investigate the implications of allowing cheap talk in a contribution game with incomplete information about preferences. They report that communication improves on coordination of strategies.

Instead, there are frequent plays of the cooperative strategy as well as strategy 1.

For SCG, we find that one-way communication increases play of strategy 2 but leads to the (2,2) equilibrium only 53 percent of the time. However, the (2,2) equilibrium is observed almost 97 percent of the time with two-way communication.

Section V relates these findings to the model analyzed in Section II. Except for two-way communication in SCG, we reject that model since we fail to see play of the (2,2) Nash equilibrium as frequently as that theory predicts. This is in marked contrast to the results for the battle of the sexes game, reported in Cooper et al. [1989], where the effects of preplay communication were quite close to the theoretical predictions. We argue that the results for SCG are consistent with the theory of "risk dominance" and preplay communication proposed by Harsanyi and Selten [1988]: it requires both players to send messages that they intend to play strategy 2 before the players are willing to accept the "risk" of playing that strategy.

To better understand the results obtained in CCG, Section VI presents a game of incomplete information with egoists and altruists. Our consideration of altruism is motivated by a number of factors. First, there are frequent announcements and plays of the cooperative strategy in this coordination game without preplay communication. Second, Cooper et al. [1990] argue that the cooperative strategy is important in observed coordination failures. Third, since preplay communication has been shown to exacerbate attempts at cooperation in prisoner's dilemma games, the same effect might be important in understanding why coordination failures persist despite the introduction of preplay communication.[5] We find that in the game of incomplete information preplay communication might encourage attempts at cooperation which could then lead to either disequilibrium play or coordination failures. We argue that this model improves our understanding of the data generated in our cheap-talk experiments. We also present data from games in which we attempted to control for altruism.

Section VII offers some concluding comments and discusses extensions of our work. This includes a comparison of these results with those reported in Cooper et al. [1989] and some additional discussion of the role of altruism in our experimental work.

---

5. See, for example, the discussion in Dawes [1980].

II. Communication and Coordination

The coordination game with communication is a two-stage game between two players. In the first stage player(s) communicate by sending messages to one another. In the second stage actions are chosen. Since the payoffs are independent of the actual messages, this is a game of "cheap talk." Nonetheless, the messages may influence actual play by affecting the beliefs that agents hold about their opponents.

We restrict the messages in the first stage to lie in the set of strategies available to the agents. Two alternative communication structures are examined. First, only one player sends a nonbinding message of his intention to play a certain (pure) strategy. This structure is called one-way communication. Second, both players send messages to each other simultaneously. This is called two-way communication. After the round of communication, players simultaneously choose actions in the second stage of the game.

Here we explicitly analyze CCG; once reference to strategy 3 is eliminated, the analysis holds for SCG as well. The equilibria of the two-stage game can be quite complicated as they depend, in part, on the interpretation of the messages sent by the players. Let $\sigma^i(m_R, m_C)$ be the action chosen by player $i = R, C$ when the messages sent by the row and column player are given by (m_R, m_C).[6] For each pair of messages, $\sigma^i(\cdot)$ represents a mixed strategy over the three possible actions. The equilibrium of the game is given by $\sigma^{*i}(m_R, m_C)$ for $i = R, C$ coupled with a decision on what announcements to make in the first stage of the game, (m^*_R, m^*_C), such that the announcements and the actions, conditional on announcements, are best responses.

One equilibrium for this game is for the players to randomly send messages and for these messages to be ignored: $\sigma^{*i}(m_R, m_C)$ is independent of the messages sent for $i = R, C$. In this "babbling" equilibrium, messages are irrelevant. Hence, we know that any outcome of the one-stage game without communication is also an equilibrium for the game with communication. Cheap talk does not reduce the set of equilibria. However, recent work on nonbinding communication by Farrell [1985, 1987], Myerson [1987], and others has identified conditions under which it is possible for credible announcements to be made. These conditions involve restrictions on beliefs about the meaning of messages.

---

6. When communication is only one-way, then only one element of this vector is relevant. Here $i = R(C)$ refers to a row (column) player.

For *one-way communication* it is assumed (see Farrell [1985]) that if it would be optimal for the row player to honor his announcement if the column player believed the row player would honor it, then the announcement will be believed and honored. Thus, in CCG if the sender announces either strategy 1 or 2, this is the predicted equilibrium action for both players. Since strategy 3 is dominated, an announcement of 3 should be ignored, and play would then continue as if no announcement had been made.

If saying 2 leads to the play of 2, announcing and playing strategy 2 is a dominant strategy for the row player in the two-stage game with one-way communication. If this equilibrium occurs, announcements of 2, followed by the play of 2 by both players, avoid coordination failures.

Farrell [1987] proposes an equilibrium in which cheap talk matters in his analysis of the battle of the sexes game with *two-way communication*. We extend that logic to CCG with two-way communication. Farrell characterizes an equilibrium in which $\sigma^i(m_R,m_C)$ places all weight on m_i when $(m_R,m_C) \in \xi$, where ξ denotes the set of pure-strategy equilibria for the second stage of the game.[7] That is, if the players announce an equilibrium, they play it. For CCG announcements of (1,1) and (2,2) would translate into the play of the corresponding Nash equilibrium.

When the announcements do not constitute an equilibrium, Farrell assumes that play will evolve as if no announcements were made. That would occur in our model in the event that either player announces strategy 3 or when (1,2) or (2,1) is announced. Thus, $\sigma^i(m_R,m_C)$ is independent of (m_R,m_C) when $(m_R,m_C) \notin \xi$.

Associated with these $\sigma^i(\cdot)$ functions are implications for announcements in the first stage of the game. Since the observed experimental outcome of CCG without communication (see Cooper et al. [1990]) is the play of equilibrium (1,1), assume that disequilibrium announcements will lead to that same outcome. (As reported below, (1,1) is the observed outcome for SCG, so this assumption is reasonable for that game as well.) Thus, announcements of 2 dominate all other announcements in the first stage. As in the one-way communication game, this avoids all coordination failures since announcements of 2 by both players lead to the (2,2) equilibrium.

Thus, under either of these communication structures, one equilibrium for the game with communication is the announce-

---

7. For the game given in Figure I, $\xi = \{(1,1),(2,2)\}$.

ment of strategy 2 followed by its play. This equilibrium illustrates the value of preplay communication as a selection device.

It should be stressed, however, that there are a multitude of other equilibria in which communication matters. For example, one can simply permute the meaning of the announcements given in any of the equilibria above to arrive at other $\sigma^i(\cdot)$ functions that support the (2,2) equilibrium. Though we have concentrated on pure strategy equilibria, there will exist other equilibria in which the response to certain announcements are mixed strategies.[8]

III. EXPERIMENTAL DESIGN

The design of this experiment was similar to that in Cooper et al. [1989, 1990]. The study was conducted using eighteen cohorts of players, each consisting of eleven different players, recruited from undergraduate classes (sophomore and above) and MBA classes at the University of Iowa. Players were seated at separate computer terminals and given a copy of the instructions. Since these instructions were also read aloud, we assume that the information contained in them is common knowledge. These instructions can be found in Cooper et al. [1989].[9]

Each player participated in a sequence of one-shot games against different anonymous opponents within his cohort. One was designated the row player, and the other the column player. All pairing of players was done through the computer using the same procedure as in Cooper et al. [1989, 1990]. A player knew neither the identity of the player with whom he was currently paired nor the history of decisions made by any of the other players in the cohort.

As in Cooper et al. [1989, 1990], we induced payoffs in terms of utility using the Roth and Malouf [1979] procedure. In the matrix games each player's payoff was given in points that determined the probability of the player winning a monetary prize. At the end of each game we conducted a lottery where "winning" players received \$1 and "losing" players received \$0. This procedure is

---

8. For example, in the two-way communication structure, announcements other than (2,2) could map into the mixed strategy of the second stage game.

9. There are only two differences in instructions between the games reported here and those in Cooper et al. [1989]. First, we replaced the 2 × 2 battle of the sexes game with the two coordination games considered in this paper. Second, here we do not allow players the option of silence as in Cooper et al. [1989].

designed so that all players will maximize the expected number of points in each game regardless of their attitudes toward risk.

Each cohort participated in two separate sessions.[10] In Session I all players participated in ten symmetric one-shot dominant strategy games. During Session I each player played one game against every other player. Since there were an odd number of players, one sat out each period. Thus, Session I consisted of eleven periods. Also, players alternated between being row and column players during the periods in which they were active participants. Session I was conducted to provide players with experience with experimental procedures, to see how well the dominant strategy equilibrium prediction performed, and to provide some information about the rationality of their opponents.

In Session II all players participated in twenty additional one-shot games that differed from the game played in Session I. Each played against every other player twice: once as a row player and once as a column player. As in Session I one player sat out in each period, and players alternated between being row and column players during the periods in which they were participating. Thus, Session II consisted of 22 periods.[11]

The Session II games were all versions of the coordination game using the payoffs illustrated in Figures I and II. However, we varied the type of communication between the players. In the *no communication* games players simultaneously chose actions that determined their payoffs. For the *one-way communication* games the row player sent the column player a message announcing what the row player "plans to play" in the second stage. After all messages were received, the players simultaneously chose actions. In the *two-way communication* games both of the players simultaneously sent messages to each other. The exchange of messages was then followed by the simultaneous choice of actions. In the games with preplay communication, subjects were told: "You are not required to choose the action you announced in the first stage." Three replications were conducted for each communication treat-

10. Each cohort completed the two sessions in one to one and half hours. Payments ranged from $5 to $21.
11. Our objective was to have the pairings satisfy two conditions: (i) players were to alternate being row and column players and (ii) each player was to play every other player twice (in Session II). The ordering of the players and consequently the pair assignments were randomized at the beginning of each session. Finally, since these two conditions can only be satisfied with an odd number of players, one player sat out each period. Having that player draw the lottery ticket may also serve the purpose of convincing players of the credibility of the lottery procedure.

ment for a total of nine replications for each of the two coordination games.[12]

IV. RESULTS

In the Session I game with the dominant strategy, that strategy was played about 93 percent of the time over the eighteen cohorts. Thus, as reported in Cooper et al. [1989, 1990], the dominant strategy was almost always played.

In evaluating the Session II data for SCG and CCG, we tested for independence across periods, row and column players, and replications using announcements, actions in the no communication treatments, and actions conditional on announcements in the communication treatments. Unless otherwise stated, all data reported here are from the last eleven periods of each treatment pooled across row and column players.

A. Simple Coordination Game (SCG)

We conducted three replications for each of the three communication structures (no communication, one-way communication, and two-way communication) using the matrix given in Figure II. Our results are reported in Tables I–III for the last eleven periods of play by treatment.[13]

Table I provides information on announcements and actions taken in each of the three treatments and also presents the frequency of the possible action pairs by treatment. With no communication, coordination failures are observed: of the 330 total plays only 5 were of strategy 2. In contrast to the results reported in Cooper et al. [1990], these observations cannot be the conse-

---

12. One replication of CCG was previously reported as Game 3 in Cooper et al. [1990].

13. We used Fisher's exact test throughout this paper to test for the statistical significance of differences (see Kendall and Stuart [1979, pp. 584–86]). We tested for serial dependence in announcements, strategies played conditional on announcements and strategies played in the no communication treatment. These tests produced evidence of dependence using the data from all periods, but there was no evidence of dependence using the data from the last eleven periods of each replication. We failed to reject the hypothesis of no differences between row and column players, except for the obvious case of announcements in the one-way communication treatment. We also could not reject the hypothesis of no difference across replications in the two-way treatment. With one-way communication, however, one replication (replication 2) differed significantly from the other two in terms of announcements as well as strategies chosen given that the row player announced strategy 2. There were also significant differences in the strategies chosen given announcements of strategy 2 in the other two replications, but with a p-value of 0.047, this seems marginal. In what follows, we shall discuss these differences in replications in detail.

COMMUNICATION IN COORDINATION GAMES   749

TABLE I
SCG

	Strategy	
	1	2
Announcements		
No communication:	—	—
One-way:		
Rep. 1&3	19	91
Rep. 2	2	53
Total	21	144
Two-way:	0	330
Actions:		
No communication:	325	5
One-way:		
Rep. 1&3	88	132
Rep. 2	15	95
Total	103	227
Two-way:	15	315

	Action pair		
	(1,1)	(2,2)	(1,2), (2,1)
Treatment:			
No communication:	160	0	5
One-way:			
Rep. 1&3	25	47	38
Rep. 2	1	41	13
Total	26	88	51
Two-way:	0	150	15

quence of failed attempts at cooperation. Instead, we would argue,
following Harsanyi and Selten [1988], that play of strategy 1 is a
consequence of strategic uncertainty over the play of an opponent.
That is, unless one believes that the likelihood an opponent will
play strategy 2 is 8/10 or more, play of strategy 1 is optimal.

TABLE II
SCG
MAPPING OF ANNOUNCEMENTS TO ACTIONS
ONE-WAY COMMUNICATION

Announcement Row	Actions- Row, Column				
	1,1	2,2	1,2	2,1	Total
1	20	1	0	0	21
2	6	87	22	29	144
Total	26	88	22	29	165

TABLE III
SCG
MAPPING OF ANNOUNCEMENTS TO ACTIONS
TWO-WAY COMMUNICATION

Announcements Row, Col	Actions- Row, Column				Total
	1,1	2,2	1,2	2,1	
1,1	0	0	0	0	0
2,2	0	150	7	8	165
1,2	0	0	0	0	0
2,1	0	0	0	0	0
Total	0	150	7	8	165

Loosely speaking, a player must be convinced that his opponent will play 2 before it is best to do so.

The role of communication then is to provide a basis for the strong beliefs needed to overcome coordination failures. As indicated in Table I, these coordination problems are completely resolved by two-way communication: of the 330 plays, 315 of them are of strategy 2. In terms of announcements, strategy 2 was announced all 330 times. This is a dramatic improvement over the results without preplay communication and accords with the theoretical predictions of the Section II model.

Surprisingly, the results with one-way communication are different from either of the other two treatments. There are significantly more plays of strategy 2 in this treatment relative to no communication and significantly more plays of strategy 1 relative to the two-way treatment.

As indicated by Table I, the difference in the actions chosen in the communication treatments cannot solely be attributed to differences in announcements. In particular, 12.7 percent of the announcements were strategy 1 in one-way communication, and 0 percent in two-way. While this difference is statistically significant, it is not enough to account for the observed differences in play; strategy 2 was played 95 percent of the time in two-way communication but only 69 percent of the time in one-way communication. Instead, as we discuss below, these differences can be traced to how column players responded to the row player's announced intention to take action 2 when there was one-way communication.

In summary, we draw three conclusions from Table I.

FACT 1. In the game without communication play of the (1,1) equilibrium is observed.

COMMUNICATION IN COORDINATION GAMES   751

FACT 2. One-way communication increases the frequency of the (2,2) equilibrium, but a significant number of coordination failures were observed.

FACT 3. Two-way communication resolves coordination failures: strategy 2 is played almost all of the time.

The detailed results for the last eleven periods of play for the one-way communication treatment are presented in Table II. Note first that strategy 2 was announced 144 times or about 87 percent of the time.

As for the mapping between announcements and actions, 20 of the 21 times the row player announced 1, the (1,1) equilibrium was observed. Of the 144 times strategy 2 was announced in the last eleven periods, the (2,2) equilibrium was observed only 60 percent of the time, far less than predicted by the theory. In 28 instances the row player took action 1 after announcing action 2, while in 35 instances the column player chose to play action 1 after hearing the row player announce action 2. Coordination failures appear to be the consequence of receivers not best responding to announcements and, recognizing this, senders not following through on their announcements.

This can be seen directly by examining the first five periods of play in replications 1 and 3. On 39 occasions the row player announced his intention to take action 2. In eleven of these instances the column player chose action 1, while the row player deviated from his announcement only two times. In the ensuing periods the row players began to deviate from their announcement of action 2 with the same likelihood as the column players.

Additionally, the ability to achieve the (2,2) outcome in this game seems very sensitive to a small number of players choosing action 1, after saying or hearing an announcement of 2. Replication 2 illustrates this. In the first fourteen periods of play, there is only one instance where a row player announced action 2 and chose action 1 and the column player always took action 2 upon hearing an announcement of 2. In period 15 a column player chose action 1 after hearing an announcement of 2. This row player announced 2 but chose action 1 in two subsequent games and also later chose action 2 after hearing an announcement of 2. This player's choice of action 1 led a third player to begin choosing action 1 after they were paired. This provides an example of the potential instability of a (2,2) equilibrium, as a small perturbation away from the equilibrium can lead to further defections from announced actions.

FACT 4. Strategy 2 was announced 87 percent of the time in one-way communication, but this announcement was followed by play at the (2,2) equilibrium only 60 percent of the time. When strategy 1 was announced, the (1,1) equilibrium was observed.

As seen in Table III, two-way communication was much more successful in overcoming the coordination failures observed in the game without preplay communication. As indicated in this table, strategy 1 was never announced in the last eleven periods of play and was announced only 2.2 percent of the time in the overall game. Of these 165 observations in only fifteen cases did play not occur at (2,2): seven times the row player played 1, and eight times the column player played 1.

FACT 5. In two-way communication, strategy 2 was announced all the time, and the (2,2) equilibrium was observed 94 percent of the time.

B. Cooperative Coordination Game (CCG)

Table IV presents statistics on the frequency of play across the treatments, with particular attention to the combinations of strategies that constitute equilibria for CCG.[14] For the last eleven periods of play, the only rejection of independence in this game occurs in the frequency of announcements across the two-way communication treatment.[15] For that reason, the data for two-way communication are presented by replication.

From this table note first, as reported in Cooper et al. [1990], that coordination failures occur in CCG without preplay communication. That is, the (2,2) equilibrium occurs in only five of the 165 observations, while the (1,1) equilibrium is observed 103 times. In terms of the effects of preplay communication on the frequency of play of the (2,2) equilibrium, we find that

FACT 6. Equilibrium (2,2) was not always observed in one-way and two-way communication.

14. In Table IV (1&3) means either (1,3) or (3,1). This table and Table VII also includes an "egoist" treatment that will be explained and analyzed at the end of this section.
15. Again, using the tests described in footnote 13, we found evidence of serial dependence using the data from all periods, but there was no evidence of dependence using the data from the last eleven periods of each replication. We again fail to reject the hypothesis of no differences between row and column players, except for the obvious case of announcements in the one-way communication treatment. We also could not reject the hypothesis of no difference across replications except for announcements in the two-way treatment.

COMMUNICATION IN COORDINATION GAMES   753

TABLE IV
CCG
FREQUENCY OF EQUILIBRIUM PLAY

	N	(1,1)	(2,2)	(1&3)	(3,3)
Treatment					
None	165	103	5	6	
		(62.4%)	(3.0%)	(3.6%)	
One-way	165	25	111	12	3
		(15.2%)	(67.3%)	(7.3%)	(1.8%)
Two-way					
rep 1	55	35	3	7	1
		(63.6%)	(5.5%)	(12.7%)	(1.8%)
rep 2	55	19	6	12	1
		(34.5%)	(10.9%)	(21.8%)	(1.8%)
rep 3	55	6	39		
		(10.9%)	(70.9%)		
"Egoist"	55	4	44	2	
		(7.2%)	(80.0%)	(3.6%)	

In fact, there were frequent plays of (1,1), (3,1) (1,3), and (3,3) in both treatments.

The frequency of (2,2) play differed significantly across the replications in two-way communication. Replication 3 had the most plays of (2,2) followed by replication 2 and then replication 1.

The table is also useful for comparing the two communication treatments against the baseline of no communication. Compared with no communication, the frequency of (2,2) play is significantly higher in the one-way communication treatment. As for the two-way communication, in replication 1, the frequency of play of the (2,2) equilibrium does not differ from that observed in the game without communication. For replications 2 and 3 the frequency is significantly higher. Comparing one-way and two-way communication, the play of (2,2) is significantly less in replication 1 and 2 and no different in replication 3.

The data on announcements and the mapping from announcements to actions for the one-way treatment are reported in Table V. Announcements as well as players' responses to announcements can be determined from that table.

FACT 7. In the one-way treatment strategy 2 is not always announced.

As indicated in the table, the frequency of announcements of strategies 1, 2, and 3 were 7 percent, 72 percent, and 21 percent,

TABLE V
CCG
MAPPING OF ANNOUNCEMENTS TO ACTIONS
ONE-WAY COMMUNICATION

Announcement Row	Actions- Row, Column									Total
	2,2	3,3	1,1	1,3	3,1	2,3	3,2	1,2	2,1	
1		1	8		1			2		12
2	111								7	118
3		2	17	6	5		1	3	1	35
Total	111	3	25	6	6		1	5	8	165

respectively. One player in replication 1 always announced strategy 1 (five times) and accounted for about half of the announcements of 1. Three players, one in each replication, accounted for fourteen (40 percent) of the strategy 3 announcements.

As for the mapping between announcements and actions, when strategy 2 is announced by the row player, (2,2) is played 94 percent of the time. Announcements of 1 lead to the play of (1,1) 75 percent of the time. That is,

FACT 8. Announcements of 1 and 2 are generally followed by play of (1,1) and (2,2), respectively.

However, 21 percent of the announcements are strategy 3, and 86 percent of these announcements are followed by the play of (1,1), (1,3), (3,1), and (3,3).

We present the mappings of announcements to actions for the two-way communication treatment in Table VI.

FACT 9. Over one half of the announcements in the two-way communication treatment are different from 2.

In particular, 25 percent of the announcements are strategy 1, and 33 percent of the announcements are strategy 3.

FACT 10. Announcements of (2,2) are generally followed by the play of (2,2).

The results for (2,2) announcements are quite strong: of the 39 announcements of (2,2), play of this equilibrium is observed 38 times. Further, of the ten announcements of (1,1), this equilibrium is observed six times.

For the announcements of (3,3), (1,3), and (3,1), 93 percent were followed by the play of (1,1), (1,3), and (3,1). Play following

COMMUNICATION IN COORDINATION GAMES   755

TABLE VI
CCG
MAPPING OF ANNOUNCEMENTS TO ACTIONS
TWO-WAY COMMUNICATION

Announcements Row, Col	Actions- Row, Column									
	1,1	1,2	1,3	2,1	2,2	2,3	3,1	3,2	3,3	Total
2,2		1			38					39
3,3	11	1	2	1			3		1	19
1,1	6		1	1			2			10
1,3	19	2	1				1			23
3,1	11		1				2			14
2,3	6	2		5		1	3	2		19
3,2	2	2	1	5	5	1			1	17
1,2	3	2	1	1	1		1			9
2,1	2	1		8	4					15
Total	60	11	7	21	48	2	12	2	2	165

these announcements did not differ from the play in the no communication treatment. However, the play following announcements of (1,2), (2,1), (3,2), and (2,3) did differ significantly from play without communication.

For the two-way treatment our analysis also indicated that

TABLE VII
CCG
MAPPING OF ANNOUNCEMENTS TO ACTIONS
EGOIST

Announcements Row, Col	Actions- Row, Column									
	1,1	1,2	1,3	2,1	2,2	2,3	3,1	3,2	3,3	Total
2,2	1				29					30
3,3	3		1				1			5
1,1										
1,3										
3,1										
2,3				2	5					7
3,2		1		1	5					7
1,2				1	3					4
2,1					2					2
Total	4	1	1	4	44		1			55

both announcements and unconditional actions differed across replications. For this reason, Table VIII shows the announcements, actions, and certain action pairs by replication.

FACT 11. There are significantly more (fewer) announcements and plays of strategy 2 (1 and 3) in replication 3 than in replications 1 and 2.

From Table VIII note that strategy 3 was announced 44 times in replication 1 and 50 times in replication 2 but only 17 times in replication 3. In contrast, strategy 2 was announced 87 times in replication 3 but only 17 times in replication 1 and 34 times in replication 2. There are corresponding differences in play: strategy 2 is played 88 times in replication 3 but only 15 times in replication 1 and 29 times in replication 2.

V. MODEL EVALUATION

The model presented in Section II suggested that allowing preplay communication would overcome coordination problems so that the (2,2) equilibrium would be observed for both SCG and CCG. Further, that model had predictions about the mapping from announcements to actions. This section evaluates those predictions given the results reported above.

TABLE VIII
CCG
TWO-WAY COMMUNICATION
ANNOUNCEMENTS, ACTIONS, AND ACTION PAIRS

	Replications			
	1	2	3	"Egoist"
Announcements:				
1	49	26	6	6
2	17	34	87	80
3	44	50	17	24
Actions:				
1	86	66	19	15
2	15	29	88	93
3	9	15	3	2
Action pairs:				
(2,2)	3	6	39	44
(1,1)	35	19	6	4
(3,3), (1&3)	8	13	0	2

A. Simple Coordination Game (SCG)

The results, summarized in Facts 2 and 3, for the SCG seem qualitatively consistent with the predictions of the model of preplay communication. The results for two-way communication are quite strong: as predicted, strategy 2 is announced by both players, and it is generally played by both.

Though the results for one-way communication are not so strong, one-way communication clearly improves over the baseline in terms of the frequency of (2,2) outcomes. Further, consistent with the theory, when strategy 1 is announced, it is generally played by both players. However, in contrast to the theoretical model, when strategy 2 is announced, the outcome is not always (2,2), (see Fact 4).

One interpretation of the data which we cannot reject is that players are in the following equilibrium: play is at (1,1) following the announcement of 1 and at the mixed strategy equilibrium following the announcement of 2.[16] In the mixed strategy equilibrium of SCG, players choose 2 with probability 0.8 and obtain the same expected payoff as in the (1,1) equilibrium.

This equilibrium seems quite implausible, however, and instead we would conjecture that one-way communication is simply insufficient to convince the sender to take the risk that the receiver will play 2. Knowing this, the receiver may in fact play 1 as well. The tenuous nature of the (2,2) equilibrium with one-way communication was described in the previous section. This doubt about the action of a receiver is overcome by the two-way communication design since both players receive information about the likely play of their opponents. The fact that two-way communication overcomes risk dominance lends support to the prediction of Harsanyi and Selten [1988, pp. 89–90] that ". . . with preplay communication they may come to the conclusion that they can trust each other to choose [the payoff-dominant Nash Equilibrium]." While Harsanyi and Selten were not specific with regard to the communication structure, our results indicate that two-way communication is needed to support the Pareto-dominant Nash equilibrium.

B. Cooperative Coordination Game (CCG)

The results for CCG are not nearly as strong relative to the theory. The conflict between the model and the theory arises

---

16. We are grateful to a referee for pointing this out.

mainly in the nature of the announcements and not in the actions of the players given announcements.

For the one-way communication treatment, relative to the baseline of no communication, allowing a single player to make an announcement dramatically increases the frequency of play of the Pareto-dominant equilibrium. However, from Fact 6 we know that coordination problems were not completely resolved by one-way communication. Note from Facts 7 and 8 that the observed plays other than (2,2) were the consequence of messages other than 2, in particular announcements of 3. Thus, qualitatively the model's predictions are upheld though the results are not as strong as the theory suggests.

For two-way communication, as indicated by Fact 6, the (2,2) outcome was not observed in all replications. From Fact 9 this was mainly a consequence of messages other than (2,2), since from Fact 10 we know that announcements of (2,2) generally led to play of (2,2). Again, these messages generally included strategy 3.

The model can also be evaluated from the mapping between announcements and actions reported in Tables V and VI. Facts 8 and 10 provide strong support for the assertion that equilibrium announcements lead to equilibrium plays.

Overall, we find that coordination problems persist despite the introduction of cheap talk. The model does have the virtue of explaining part of the mapping between announcements and actions, particularly announcement of 2 (2,2) in the game with one-way (two-way) communication. The fact that the (2,2) outcome is not universally observed is the consequence of players making announcements other than strategy 2 in both communication treatments; announcements that often included strategy 3.

VI. ALTRUISM: THEORY AND EVIDENCE

The data from CCG are inconsistent with the predictions of the theoretical model in two important ways: (i) there are numerous announcements and plays of strategy 3 in the one-way communication treatment and (ii) the results for two-way communication are replication specific, particularly with regard to announcement and play of strategy 3. These anomalies point to the important role of strategy 3 in CCG. Since this is a dominated strategy, from the perspective of self-interested players, it is puzzling that it plays such an important role in CCG. However, there is now an abundance of evidence in experimental economics on the importance of cooperative play, particularly in prisoner's and social dilemma games.[17] Further, in Cooper et al. [1990] we found that play of the cooperative, dominated strategy in our coordination games was quite prevalent and that variations in payoffs from an opponent's play of that strategy influenced selection of a Nash equilibrium.

The point of this section is to evaluate the role of strategy 3 in CCG. We consider a model which allows for altruism and evaluate the possibility that the failure of preplay communication to lead to the (2,2) equilibrium in CCG is a consequence of cooperative play.[18] The cooperative strategy in CCG creates a tension between attempts at cooperation and reaching the Pareto-superior Nash equilibrium.

A. Theory

One leading explanation of cooperative play is that players believe they are involved in a finitely repeated game of incomplete information where there is some probability their opponent is a tit-for-tat player. Then, even if the game is played by purely self-interested players, there is an equilibrium where cooperation occurs for some periods (see Kreps, Milgrom, Roberts, and Wilson [1982]). That theory has no power in our experiment since players are involved in a series of one-shot games against anonymous opponents.

This then leads us to consider another explanation of observed cooperative play: the possibility that not all players are self-interested. We follow Palfrey and Rosenthal [1985, 1988a] and model altruism through an additional payoff a player receives from playing the cooperative strategy. We chose this model of altruism because it has some empirical support as discussed by Palfrey and Rosenthal. In addition, other, equally parsimonious, models of altruism were either clearly inconsistent with our data or led to

---

17. See, for example, Dawes [1980], Dawes and Thaler [1988], Isaac and Walker [1988], Palfrey and Rosenthal [1985, 1988], and Roth [1988] for a discussion of some of this evidence.

18. Once we introduce altruists, the terms, coordination failure, and Pareto-dominant equilibrium, need to be carefully defined. We shall refer to play of (1,1) as a coordination failure since it is the outcome of the interaction of two egoists who would be better off at the (2,2) equilibrium. We shall continue to term the (2,2) equilibrium, the Pareto-dominant equilibrium, which is appropriate *if* the interaction is between two egoists. As discussed later, there are new equilibria, (3,1) ((1,3)) if the row player is an altruist (egoist) and the column player an egoist (altruist) and (3,3) if both players are altruists.

predictions that were equivalent to those from our model.[19] It should be stressed that our goal here is modest: to suggest an alternative to the model of egoists that might account for some of the anomalies in our data.

Consider again the game presented in Figure I. The payoffs for egoists are given in the cells of the matrix. As in Palfrey and Rosenthal [1985, 1988a] suppose that a cooperative player receives, in addition to the payoffs in the cells of Figure I, a "warm glow" of δ from playing the cooperative strategy 3.[20] We assume that all players know that there are some cooperative individuals in the cohort with $550 \geq \delta \geq 400$ but that preferences are private information. Call players with $550 \geq \delta \geq 400$ altruists and those with $\delta = 0$ egoists, and let ρ denote the proportion of altruists in the population. These bounds on δ arise from the condition that strategy 3 be neither dominant nor dominated for altruists.[21] We assume that ρ is common knowledge.

19. As in Cooper et al. [1990], we also considered a model in which altruists' preferences were given by the minimum of the payoffs in a cell. Surprisingly, there were only pooling equilibria for that specification of altruism. In contrast to the warm-glow model described below, the proportion of altruists had to be relatively high in order to induce them to announce and play strategy 3. This condition was inconsistent with that needed to provide the correct incentives to egoists. Hence, the role of announcing strategy 3 as a signal of preferences could not arise in that model. The resulting pooling equilibrium would be rejected by our data. As in Cooper et al. [1989], we also considered a model in which the true payoff for some players was the sum of the payoffs in each cell of the matrix given in Figure I. This turns out to be equivalent to the warm-glow model for the parameters used here. A referee suggested to us a model of "reciprocal altruism" in which an altruist obtains an extra payoff from cooperation iff his opponent cooperates as well. This model has the same best-response pattern as the "min-model" mentioned above. This model did have separating equilibria if the extra payoff for altruists exceeded 1,187. This model shares with the model discussed in the paper an inability to explain announcements of 3 followed by plays of 1 in the one-way communication treatment.

20. See also Bergstrom, Blume, and Varian [1986] for a further discussion of warm-glow altruism. For altruists, view the payoffs in the modified Figure I that includes δ for playing strategy 3 as the actual utility levels for the individual players, and thus ignore the translation from points into dollars. In terms of our experiment we think of cooperative players as obtaining utility from playing 3 in addition to the points earned from the choice of this strategy. That is, suppose that the utility function for a cooperative player is $q[u(1) - u(0)] + u(0) + \psi C$, where $C = 1$ if the cooperative strategy is chosen and 0 otherwise. Here q is the number of points earned in the play of the game divided by 1,000 and ψ is the value of cooperating. One can then think of the δ associated with the play of the cooperative strategy as the "point equivalence" of this utility from cooperation.

21. Here we simplify matters by assuming that there are two types of agents: altruists with $550 \geq \delta \geq 400$ and egoists with $\delta = 0$. If $\delta \in (0,400)$, then 3 is still a dominated strategy, and this leads to behavior that is observationally equivalent to $\delta = 0$. If $\delta \geq 550$, then 3 is a dominant strategy. If altruists had $\delta \geq 550$, then the theoretical results reported in the Appendix would be altered in that (1) Proposition 1 would not hold as there would be no (2,2) equilibrium and (2) the value 4/13 in Propositions 3–6 would be replaced by 1/6. As we find no evidence of players always playing strategy 3, we restrict attention to $\delta < 550$. A less parsimonious model would specify a distribution of δ across players.

When $\rho > 0$, this is a game of incomplete information, as players do not know the preferences of their opponents. Preplay communication serves to signal types as well as influence the selection of an equilibrium.[22] To the extent that these two effects of communication conflict, cheap talk communication might not be as effective as in a game between egoists.

Appendix A contains an explicit model of this game of incomplete information. Here we summarize those results and use them to evaluate our data.

B. One-way Communication

For *one-way communication*, if $\rho > 4/13$, all players will announce 3 with the egoists playing 1 and the altruists choosing 3. Thus, cheap talk will provide no information. If $\rho \leq 4/13$, there exists a totally revealing equilibrium in which the egoists announce 2 and play it, while the altruists announce 3 and play it. In response to hearing 3, the egoists play 1, and the altruists play 3. Upon hearing 2, both egoists and altruists select strategy 2. Self-interested players choose not to announce 3 because the risk they will meet another egoist, and hence earn 350 from the (1,1) outcome, is too high when $\rho \leq 4/13$. Outcomes of (2,2), (3,3), (3,1), and (1,3) are consistent with this equilibrium. As Table V indicates that not all announcements were of strategy 3, we focus on this fully revealing equilibrium.

From Table IV 76.4 percent (126/165) of the observed outcomes coincide with those predicted by this model while only 111 are explained by a model with all egoists. However, of these fifteen additional observations, only seven are consistent with the theory in terms of the mapping from announcements to actions.

Furthermore, the model with all egoists predicted that the announcements of 3 (21 percent of the announcements) should lead to the (1,1) equilibrium. Instead, as noted earlier, 22.8 percent of those announcements were followed by the play of strategy 3. This play is consistent with a model with cooperative players, since altruists will play strategy 3 upon either saying or hearing strategy 3.

Still, there are 39 plays that are not predicted by the model; 25 of these are (1,1) which represents a coordination failure between egoists (since strategy 1 is a dominated strategy for altruists).

---

22. Ben-Porath and Dekel [1989] raise a similar point in their discussion of forward induction.

Table V illustrates the source of these plays of (1,1). Of the 35 announcements of strategy 3, seventeen of them led to play of (1,1). This is inconsistent with the predictions of a fully revealing equilibrium since altruists are the only players saying 3 and they should proceed to play it.

The model provides a means of estimating ρ from our data. Two estimates of the value of ρ are given in Table IX. For the one-way treatment the first estimate, ρ_1 is obtained from the frequency of the announcements of 2. The model in the Appendix gives the probability that a random player announces 2 as $(1-\rho)$. Based on the observed frequency of announcements of 2, we can then estimate ρ_1. The second estimate ρ_2 is calculated by taking the frequency of announcements of strategy 3 that are followed by the play of strategy 3 and dividing by the total possible announcements. In equilibrium these estimates should be the same. They differ because the play, in particular that following disequilibrium announcements, did not satisfy the predictions of the model. Still, we see that both estimates exceed zero, indicating the presence of altruists and both fall below the critical cutoff of 4/13.

C. Two-Way Communication

For *two-way communication,* the Appendix demonstrates that, if $\rho \leq 4/13$, a partially revealing equilibrium can be constructed in which altruists always announce strategy 3 while the egoists randomize between announcements of 2 and 3. Egoists who announce 3 and then play 1 are trying to profit by being matched with an altruist who always plays 3 when his opponent announces 3. Egoists who announce 2 play 2 regardless of the announcement of their opponent. So announcements of (3,2) or (2,3) lead to the play of (2,2). When ρ is low, the egoists will perceive a cost of announcing 3 and playing 1: there is a high probability that two egoists saying 3 will be matched and both play 1 leading to a payoff

TABLE IX
CCG
ESTIMATE OF ρ

| | One-way | Two-way by replication | | | |
		1	2	3	Egoist
ρ_1	0.29	0.26	0.21	0.05	0.09
ρ_2	0.09				
ρ_3		0.33	0.29	0.15	0.14

COMMUNICATION IN COORDINATION GAMES   763

of only 350. Thus, egoists will mix between announcing 2 and 3. Therefore, the model predicts that two-way communication may not yield the (2,2) outcome since the interaction between altruists and egoists can lead to considerable play of strategies 1 and 3.[23]

When the proportion of altruists is high enough, $\rho > 4/13$, a partially revealing equilibrium will not exist because the chance of being matched with another egoist and thus earning 350 from the play of (1,1) is sufficiently low that all egoists announce 3 and play 1. Here there is a pooling equilibrium in which all types announce strategy 3. As in the one-way communication treatment, we see no evidence of this announcement pattern and thus focus on the $\rho \leq 4/13$ case.

The observed play of (1,1), (2,2), (3,1), (1,3), and (3,3) reported in Table IV coincides with the predicted outcomes of this model. In fact, the new model accounts for 81 additional observations (49 percent) that are not predicted by the egoist model. However, only 22 of these additional observations follow from announcements of (3,3), (3,2), and (2,3) as predicted by the model with altruists. Many of the observed (1,1), (1,3), and (3,1) outcomes were preceded by announcement pairs in which at least one player announced strategy 1. In fact, if we interpret the announcements 1 and 3 as identical, then 49 additional observations are consistent with the predicted mapping between announcements and actions.

Further, from Table VIII note that there are numerous announcements of both strategies 2 and 3 as predicted by the theory. Since (2,2) announcements lead to (2,2) (recall Fact 8), the data are consistent with that feature of the model. Moreover, the observed play of (1,3), (3,1), and (3,3) stemming from announcements of (3,3) is consistent with our theory. The fact that 17/19 of the plays following announcements of (3,3) were combinations of strategies 1 and 3 is also explained by the model of altruism.

The explanation for Fact 11, the differences across replications in announcements and actions, can be attributed to differences in the proportion of altruists across cohorts. When ρ is high, the theory predicts more announcements of 3, both because there are more altruists and because there are more egoists pretending to be altruists.[24]

As was the case for one-way communication, we can estimate

23. The model also predicts that as ρ increases, the frequency of strategy 3 announced by egoists increases.
24. The model has an interesting feature that even a small value of ρ can create a considerable amount of announcements of 3 and plays of 1. As discussed by Haltiwanger and Waldman [1986], in games with strategic complementarities such as coordination games, altruists will have a large effect on the equilibrium outcome.

the value of ρ for this treatment by replication. The first estimate of ρ in Table IX, ρ_1, is again obtained from the frequency of the announcements of 2. According to the model, the probability that a randomly selected player will announce 2 is $1 - (13/4)\rho$. The second estimate ρ_3 comes from the observed play of strategy 1.[25] Except for ρ_3 in replication 1 these estimates of ρ fall below 4/13, the theoretical cutoff for the partially revealing equilibrium. Note though that these estimates all exceed zero, providing some support for the argument that not all players were self-interested. In replication 3 the low value of ρ implies more announcements and plays of 2 relative to the other replications in which the estimated value of ρ is higher. Overall, we would attribute the inability of cheap talk to lead to the (2,2) outcome, desired between egoists, to the presence of altruists in the cohorts in replications 1 and 2.

In our view, this model is a useful extension of that presented in Section II since it allows us to explain a greater proportion of the observed announcements and plays in our game. Since adding altruism gives us extra degrees of freedom to explain the results, we sought some independent evidence that altruism was important in the observed coordination failures with preplay communication. This evidence, reported next, is obtained by controlling, as much as possible, for altruism within a cohort.

D. Controlling for Altruism

To further evaluate the role of altruism in our results, we recruited players who had participated in a bargaining experiment reported in Forsythe, Horowitz, Savin, and Sefton [1988]. In that experiment two players were anonymously matched for a single period to play a dictator game. One (the dictator) was given either \$5 or \$10 and the option of giving \$X to the other player. Once the dictator decided on X, the participants were paid off, and the experiment ended. In the \$5 (\$10) game Forsythe et al. find that only 36 percent (21 percent) of the players set $X = 0$ and 22 percent (21 percent) gave their opponents \$2.50 (\$5) or more.

We recruited eleven players from this experiment who chose $X = 0$ and termed these players "egoists." The egoists participated in a two-way communication replication identical to that described

25. From the model in the Appendix the probability of observing the play of 1 is $(1 - \rho)\pi[\rho + (1 - \rho)\pi]$, where ρ is the proportion of altruists in the population and π is the probability that an egoist announces 3, which equals $9\rho/((1 - \rho)4)$. Note that the play of 1 can arise when an egoist saying 3 meets an altruist or another egoist saying 3.

above with one exception. At the start of the treatment the egoists were informed that the players in the experiment were chosen because they had not given anything away in the earlier experiment.[26]

The theory predicts that for low values of ρ, as in the egoist treatment, the outcome (2,2) should be observed most of the time and supported by announcements of strategy 2. Looking at Tables IV and VII, the egoist treatment seems to be close to this prediction. The (2,2) outcome was observed 80 percent of the time in this treatment. Strategy 2 was announced 55 percent of the time, and (2,2) announcements were followed by play of (2,2). Announcements and plays did not differ significantly between the egoist treatment and replication 3. In both, the (2,2) outcome was observed more than in the one-way treatment and the other two-way communication replications.[27]

VII. CONCLUSIONS

In previous work we have found that coordination failures can occur in coordination games. The point of this paper was to determine whether allowing preplay communication would overcome these problems.

Our results indicate that the lack of communication between individuals is not the source of the coordination problems reported in Cooper et al. [1990] for coordination games such as CCG. Allowing preplay communication does not uniformly lead to the play of the Pareto-dominant Nash equilibrium, nor is equilibrium

---

26. At the start of the egoist treatment, the following was read aloud: "Each of you previously participated in an experiment within the last year in which you were given a sum of money (either $5 or $10) and had the opportunity to give an amount of this to a person in another room. You each chose to keep the entire amount for yourself."

27. We also recruited eleven "altruists"; i.e., players who gave away at least 40 percent of their initial endowment in the dictator games. Overall, the altruist treatment was not significantly different from replication 2. Except for announcements, the treatment did not differ from replication 1 in the last five periods. See Lutzker [1960] for an attempt at separating egoists and altruists in a prisoner's dilemma game.

We only report details of the egoist treatment since our control of altruists was imperfect. In terms of our model of altruism, players recruited for the egoist experiment presumably had δ's which were zero or very low so that they were likely to view strategy 3 in the coordination game as dominated. However, the value of δ relative to 400 is more difficult to determine from the fact that they gave away money in the dictator game. Further, while players may act altruistically in a dictator game because of its asymmetric structure, they may not display the same preferences in other, perhaps more symmetric environments. As a consequence, we would argue that our control over payoffs in the altruist treatment was less successful than in the egoist treatment.

play always observed. Instead, one observes play of both the cooperative strategy and the strategy supporting the Pareto-inferior Nash equilibrium. This is inconsistent with the predictions of a model which assumes that egoists will use preplay communication to select the preferred Nash equilibrium.

To understand our observations for the coordination game with a cooperative strategy, we then considered an alternative model that allowed for the presence of some altruistic players in a given cohort. While the model accounted for only a few additional observations in the one-way communication treatment, for two-way communication the model with altruists explained a significantly greater number of the observed outcomes and also provided insights into the differences in outcomes across cohorts of players. Controlling for altruism enhanced the ability of preplay communication to resolve coordination problems.

For SCG the predictions of the theory are qualitatively supported. This is certainly the case for two-way communication when the (2,2) equilibrium is observed almost all of the time.

Two areas for future work emerge from this research. First, it is interesting to contrast the results from SCG with those reported in Cooper et al. [1989] for the battle of the sexes games. By definition there is no conflict in the simple coordination game, while conflicting interests are at the heart of the battle of the sexes games. Relative to this, note that one-way communication completely resolved coordination problems in the battle of the sexes game, while two-way communication was the better institution in SCG. In contrast to CCG the coordination problems in SCG were a consequence of the riskiness of the strategy supporting the Pareto-dominant equilibrium so that two-way communication was necessary to resolve strategic uncertainty. This suggests a general theme that may be worth pursuing: one-way communication is preferred in games of conflict, while two-way communication is needed to resolve coordination problems in games, such as SCG, in which strategic uncertainty leads to coordination failures.

Second, our work suggests, once again, the need for further theoretical and experimental consideration of cooperative play. There has been a considerable amount of cooperative play observed elsewhere in experimental games. Of this the work on finitely repeated prisoner's dilemma games has received the most attention and has been explained by reputation effects, such as those emphasized by Kreps et al. [1982]. Since the history-dependent strategies required to support cooperation are not feasible in our

COMMUNICATION IN COORDINATION GAMES   767

setting, we were forced to adopt a model with some altruists to explain our results. This leads naturally to a question of the relative importance of reputation effects and altruism in the games in which cooperative play has been observed.

APPENDIX

Here we formally consider equilibria of our games in which a proportion ρ of the players are altruists and the remainder are egoists. The payoffs for the egoists are given in Figure I while altruists receive an extra "warm glow" payoff of δ from playing strategy 3, where $550 \geq \delta \geq 400$. We assume that the proportion ρ is common knowledge but that players' preferences are not observable.

No Communication

For the game without communication there will exist a number of equilibria. Here we discuss two that are of special interest.

PROPOSITION 1. For all values of ρ there exists an equilibrium in which all players play 2.

Proof of Proposition 1. This is clearly an equilibrium since 2 is a best response to 2 for both egoists and altruists.

Q.E.D.

PROPOSITION 2. For all values of ρ there will exist an equilibrium in which egoists play 1 and altruists play 3.

Proof of Proposition 2. The expected payoff to an egoist from playing 1, $\rho 1,000 + (1 - \rho)350$, exceeds the payoff of $(1 - \rho)250$ from playing 2. For the altruists the expected payoff from playing 3 is $\rho 600 + \delta$ which is greater than the payoff from playing 2, $(1 - \rho)250$ as $\delta \geq 400$ by assumption. These are the only alternatives we need to check since strategy 1 is a dominated strategy for altruists and strategy 3 is a dominated strategy for egoists.

Q.E.D.

In addition to these pure strategy equilibria, there will also exist mixed strategy equilibria in the game without communication. For example, if $\rho < 1/6$, there will exist an equilibrium in which all the altruists play 3 and the egoists mix between 1 and 2.

When ρ exceeds 1/6, the return to playing 1 is sufficiently high that all egoists will play that strategy.

One-Way Communication

PROPOSITION 3. If $\rho > 4/13$, there is a nonrevealing equilibrium in which all players announce 3, egoists play 1, and altruists play 3. All other announcements lead to the play of 2.

Proof of Proposition 3. For the egoists the strategy of saying 3 and playing 1 yields $\rho 1{,}000 + (1 - \rho)350$. If they deviate and announce either 1 or 2, they will receive 550. When $\rho > 4/13$, $\rho 1{,}000 + (1 - \rho)350 > 550$. Egoists who hear 3 best respond by playing 1. This is a best response to an altruist's play of 3 and the play of 1 by another egoist.

For altruists an announcement of 3 yields $\delta + \rho 600$ in equilibrium which exceeds the 550 obtained by an alternative announcement. Altruists respond to the announcement of a 3 by playing 3 since this is the best response to either the play of 3 *or* the play of 1.

Q.E.D.

PROPOSITION 4. If $\rho \leq 4/13$, there will exist a totally revealing equilibrium in which altruists announce 3 and egoists announce 2. Egoists play 2 (1) in response to hearing 2 (3). Altruists play 2 (3) in response to hearing 2 (3).

Proof of Proposition 4. The proof given above indicates that when $\rho \leq 4/13$, egoists will prefer to announce 2 and play 2 rather than announcing 3 and playing 1. Egoists will respond to the announcement of 3 by playing 1 since, in equilibrium, the altruists announce and play 3. Further, the egoist will respond to the announcement of 2 by playing 2 since, in equilibrium, the announcer of 2 is playing 2.

For altruists, announcing 3 dominates announcing 2 by the argument given in the proof of Proposition 3. The altruist best responds to the announcement of 3 by playing 3 in response to the conjecture that the announcement of 3 was by another altruist. The altruist responds to the announcement of 2 by playing 2 since the egoist plans to play 2 after announcing it.

Q.E.D.

Two-Way Communication

Here we modify the notation introduced in Section II. Let $\sigma^i(m_R, m_C)$ be the mixed strategy of agent of type $i = A, E$ when the announcement is (m_R, m_C). The jth element in the vector $\sigma^i(m_R, m_C)$ is the probability that action j is chosen. Here we view the row player as the agent whose strategy we are describing. The notation $i = A$ refers to an altruist and $i = E$ refers to an egoist.

PROPOSITION 5. If $\rho \geq 4/13$, there will exist a nonrevealing equilibrium in which all players announce strategy 3. Further, $\sigma^A(3,3) = (0,0,1)$, $\sigma^E(3,3) = (1,0,0)$, and $\sigma^i(m_R, m_C) = (0,1,0)$ for $(m_R, m_C) \neq (3,3)$ for $i = A, E$.

Proof of Proposition 5. For egoists the returns to announcing 3 are $\rho1,000 + (1 - \rho)350$, and this exceeds 550, the gains from announcing anything else, as long as $\rho \geq 4/13$. Egoists best respond to an announcement of $(3,3)$ by playing 1 since this is their best response to the play of either 3 or 1.

The return for an altruist from saying 3 is $\rho600 + \delta$ which exceeds 550 if $\rho \geq 4/13$. Altruists respond to hearing $(3,3)$ by playing 3 since this is their best response to the play of either 3 or 1.

The play of $(2,2)$ by both types of players following any other announcement is a Nash equilibrium for the continuation game since both types of players respond to the play of 2 by selecting strategy 2.

Q.E.D.

PROPOSITION 6. If $\rho < 4/13$, there exists a sequential Nash equilibrium in which all altruists announce 3, a proportion π of the egoists announce 3, and the remainder of the egoists announce 2. Further, $\sigma^A(3,3) = (0,0,1)$, $\sigma^A(3,2) = (0,1,0)$, while $\sigma^E(3,3) = (1,0,0)$ and $\sigma^E(2,2) = \sigma^E(2,3) = (0,1,0)$. All other pairs of announcements lead to the play of $(2,2)$ regardless of the players types.

Proof of Proposition 6. For the egoists to be indifferent with respect to the announcement of 2 and 3, it must be the case that

(A1) $\qquad 550 = \rho1,000 + (1 - \rho)(\pi350 + (1 - \pi)550).$

The left side of this equality is the certain return to announcing 2. If the egoist announces 3 and plays 1, then with probability ρ the egoist meets an altruist and so earns 1,000; with probability

$(1 - \rho)\pi$ two egoists are matched, and each earn 350; while with probability $(1 - \rho)(1 - \pi)$ the egoist is matched with another egoist who says 2, and so both play 2. Note that here we use the fact that if an egoist says and hears 3, he will play 1. This is rational since the egoists best response to the play of either 1 or 3 is strategy 1. Note too that in the equilibrium, the egoist is assumed to play 2 in response to any other message. This is a consequence of the fact that playing 2 is a best response to the play of 2 by another player. For (A1) to be met with $\pi \leq 1$, it is necessary and sufficient that $\rho \leq 4/13$. From (A1), $\pi = \rho 9/((1 - \rho)4)$.

For the altruists the condition that announcing 3 be at least as good as announcing 2 is

$$(A2) \qquad \rho(600 + \delta) + (1 - \rho)(\pi\delta + (1 - \pi)550) \geq 550.$$

The right side is the return to announcing 3. With probability ρ the altruist is matched with another altruist, and both earn $600 + \delta$. With probability $(1 - \rho)\pi$ the altruist is matched with an egoist who says 3. In this case, the altruist plays 3 and earns δ. Finally, with probability $(1 - \rho)(1 - \pi)$ the altruist says 3 and hears 2, so that both players play 2 and the altruist earns 550. Thus, the actions assigned to the altruist for the various combinations of announcements are best responses. Using (A1), (A2) is met as long as $\delta > 400$ which has been assumed.

Q.E.D.

DEPARTMENT OF ECONOMICS, BOSTON UNIVERSITY
DEPARTMENT OF ACCOUNTING, UNIVERSITY OF IOWA
DEPARTMENT OF ECONOMICS, UNIVERSITY OF IOWA
DEPARTMENT OF ECONOMICS, CARLETON UNIVERSITY, CANADA

REFERENCES

Ben-Porath, Elhanan, and Edward Dekel, "Coordination and the Potential for Self-Sacrifice," mimeo, revised, May 1989.
Bergstrom, Theodore, Lawrence Blume, and Hal Varian, "On the Private Provision of Public Goods," *Journal of Public Economics*, XXIX (1986), 25–50.
Bryant, John, "A Simple Rational Expectations Keynes-Type Model," *Quarterly Journal of Economics*, XCVII (1983), 525–29.
Cooper, Russell, Doug DeJong, Robert Forsythe, and Thomas Ross, "Communication in the Battle of the Sexes Game," *Rand Journal of Economics*, XX (1989), 568–87.
Cooper, Russell, Doug DeJong, Robert Forsythe, and Thomas Ross, "Selection Criteria in Coordination Games: Some Experimental Results," *American Economic Review*, LXXX (1990), 218–33.
Cooper, Russell, and Andrew John, "Coordinating Coordination Failures in Keynesian Models," *Quarterly Journal of Economics*, CIII (1988), 441–63.
Dawes, Robyn M., "Social Dilemmas," *Annual Review of Psychology*, XXXI (1980), 169–93.

COMMUNICATION IN COORDINATION GAMES 771

____, and Richard H. Thaler, "Anomalies: Cooperation," *Journal of Economic Perspectives,* II (1988), 187–97.
Diamond, Peter, "Aggregate Demand Management in Search Equilibrium," *Journal of Political Economy,* XCI (1982), 881–94.
Farrell, Joseph, "Communication and Nash Equilibrium," working paper, GTE Laboratories, 1985.
____, "Cheap Talk, Coordination, and Entry," *Rand Journal of Economics,* XVIII (1987), 34–39.
Forsythe, Robert, Joel Horowitz, N. Eugene Savin, and Martin Sefton, "Replicability, Fairness and Pay in Experiments with Simple Bargaining Games," University of Iowa Working Paper 88-30, 1988.
Haltiwanger, John, and Michael Waldman, "The Role of Altruism in Economic Interaction," mimeo, UCLA, June 1986.
Harsanyi, John, and Reinhard Selten, *A General Theory of Equilibrium Selection in Games* (Cambridge, MA: MIT Press, 1988).
Isaac, Mark, and Mark Walker, "Communication and Free Riding Behavior: The Voluntary Contribution Mechanism," mimeo, University of Arizona, 1986.
____, and ____, "Group Size Effects in Public Goods Provision: The Voluntary Contribution Mechanism," *Quarterly Journal of Economics,* CIII (1988), 179–200.
Kendall, Maurice, and Alan Stuart, *The Advanced Theory of Statistics, Vol. 2* (New York, NY: Macmillan, 1979).
Kreps, David, Paul Milgrom, John Roberts, and Robert Wilson, "Rational Cooperation in the Finitely Repeated Prisoner's Dilemma," *Journal of Economic Theory,* XVII (1982), 245–52.
Lutzker, Daniel, "Internationalism as a Predictor of Cooperative Behavior," *Journal of Conflict Resolution,* IV (1960), 193–97.
Myerson, Roger, "Credible Negotiation Statements and Coherent Plans," Discussion Paper No. 691, Center for Mathematical Studies in Economics and Management Science, Northwestern University, 1987.
Palfrey, Thomas, and Howard Rosenthal, "Altruism and Participation in Social Dilemmas," Carnegie Mellon University, Working Paper #35-84-85, 1985.
____, and ____, "Private Incentives and Social Dilemmas: the Effect of Incomplete Information and Altruism," *Journal of Public Economics,* XXXV (1988a), 309–32.
____, and ____, "Testing for Effects of Cheap Talk in a Public Goods Game with Private Information," mimeo 1988b, *Games and Economic Behavior,* forthcoming.
Roth, Alvin E., "Laboratory Experimentation in Economics: A Methodological Overview," *Economic Journal,* XCVIII (1988), 974–1031.
____, and Michael W. K. Malouf, "Game-Theoretic Models and the Role of Bargaining," *Psychological Review,* LXXXVI (1979), 574–94.
Van Huyck, John, Raymond Battalio, and Richard Beil, "Tacit Coordination Games, Strategic Uncertainty and Coordination Failure," *American Economic Review,* LXXX (1990), 234–48.

[19]

AN EXPERIMENTAL STUDY OF THE CENTIPEDE GAME

By Richard D. McKelvey and Thomas R. Palfrey[1]

We report on an experiment in which individuals play a version of the centipede game. In this game, two players alternately get a chance to take the larger portion of a continually escalating pile of money. As soon as one person takes, the game ends with that player getting the larger portion of the pile, and the other player getting the smaller portion. If one views the experiment as a complete information game, all standard game theoretic equilibrium concepts predict the first mover should take the large pile on the first round. The experimental results show that this does not occur.

An alternative explanation for the data can be given if we reconsider the game as a game of incomplete information in which there is some uncertainty over the payoff functions of the players. In particular, if the subjects believe there is some small likelihood that the opponent is an altruist, then in the equilibrium of this incomplete information game, players adopt mixed strategies in the early rounds of the experiment, with the probability of taking increasing as the pile gets larger. We investigate how well a version of this model explains the data observed in the centipede experiments.

Keywords: Game theory, experiments, rationality, altruism.

1. OVERVIEW OF THE EXPERIMENT AND THE RESULTS

THIS PAPER REPORTS THE RESULTS of several experimental games for which the predictions of Nash equilibrium are widely acknowledged to be intuitively unsatisfactory. We explain the deviations from the standard predictions using an approach that combines recent developments in game theory with a parametric specification of the errors individuals might make. We construct a structural econometric model and estimate the extent to which the behavior is explainable by game-theoretic considerations.

In the games we investigate, the use of backward induction and/or the elimination of dominated strategies leads to a unique Nash prediction, but there are clear benefits to the players if, for some reason, some players fail to behave in this fashion. Thus, we have intentionally chosen an environment in which we expect Nash equilibrium to perform at its worst. The best known example of a game in this class is the finitely repeated prisoners' dilemma. We focus on an even simpler and, we believe more compelling, example of such a game, the closely related alternating-move game that has come to be known as the "centipede game" (see Binmore (1987)).

The centipede game is a finite move extensive form two person game in which each player alternately gets a turn to either terminate the game with a favorable payoff to itself, or continue the game, resulting in social gains for the pair. As

[1]Support for this research was provided in part by NSF Grants #IST-8513679 and #SES-878650 to the California Institute of Technology. We thank Mahmoud El-Gamal for valuable discussions concerning the econometric estimation, and we thank Richard Boylan, Mark Fey, Arthur Lupia, and David Schmidt for able research assistance. We thank the JPL-Caltech joint computing project for granting us time on the CRAY X-MP at the Jet Propulsion Laboratory. We also are grateful for comments and suggestions from many seminar participants, from an editor, and from two very thorough referees.

far as we are aware, the centipede game was first introduced by Rosenthal (1982), and has subsequently been studied by Binmore (1987), Kreps (1990), and Reny (1988). The original versions of the game consisted of a sequence of a hundred moves (hence the name "centipede") with linearly increasing payoffs. A concise version of the centipede game with exponentially increasing payoffs, called the "Share or Quit" game, is studied by Megiddo (1986), and a slightly modified version of this game is analyzed by Aumann (1988). It is this exponential version that we study here.

In Aumann's version of the centipede game, two piles of money are on the table. One pile is larger than the other. There are two players, each of whom alternately gets a turn in which it can choose either to take the larger of the two piles of money or to pass. When one player takes, the game ends, with the player whose turn it is getting the large pile and the other player getting the small pile. On the other hand, whenever a player passes, both piles are multiplied by some fixed amount, and the play proceeds to the next player. There are a finite number of moves to the game, and the number is known in advance to both players. In Aumann's version of the game, the pot starts at $10.50, which is divided into a large pile of $10.00 and a small pile of $.50. Each time a player passes, both piles are multiplied by 10. The game proceeds a total of six moves, i.e., three moves for each player.

It is easy to show that any Nash equilibrium to the centipede game involves the first player taking the large pile on the first move—in spite of the fact that in an eight move version of the game, both players could be multi-millionaires if they were to pass every round. Since all Nash equilibria make the same outcome prediction, clearly any of the usual refinements of Nash equilibrium also make the same prediction. We thus have a situation where there is an unambiguous prediction made by game theory.

Despite the unambiguous prediction, game theorists have not seemed too comfortable with the above analysis of the game, wondering whether it really reflects the way in which anyone would play such a game (Binmore (1987), Aumann (1988)). Yet, there has been no previous experimental study of this game.[2]

In the simple versions of the centipede game we study, the experimental outcomes are quite different from the Nash predictions. To give an idea how badly the Nash equilibrium (or iterated elimination of dominated strategies) predicts outcomes, we find only 37 of 662 games end with the first player taking the large pile on the first move, while 23 of the games end with both players passing at every move. The rest of the outcomes are scattered in between.

One class of explanations for how such apparently irrational behavior could arise is based on reputation effects and incomplete information.[3] This is the approach we adopt. The idea is that players believe there is some possibility

---

[2] There is related experimental work on the prisoner's dilemma game by Selten and Stoecker (1986) and on an ultimatum bargaining game with an increasing cake by Guth et al. (1991).

[3] See Kreps and Wilson (1982a), Kreps et al. (1982), Fudenberg and Maskin (1986), and Kreps (1990, pp. 536–543).

that their opponent has payoffs different from the ones we tried to induce in the laboratory. In our game, if a player places sufficient weight in its utility function on the payoff to the opponent, the rational strategy is to always pass. Such a player is labeled an *altruist*.[4] If it is believed that there is some likelihood that each player may be an altruist, then it can pay a selfish player to try to mimic the behavior of an altruist in an attempt to develop a reputation for passing. These incentives to mimic are very powerful, in the sense that a very small belief that altruists are in the subject pool can generate a lot of mimicking, even with a very short horizon.

The structure of the centipede game we run is sufficiently simple that we can solve for the equilibrium of a parameterized version of this reputational model. Using standard maximum likelihood techniques we can then fit this model. Using this assumption of only a single kind of deviation from the "selfish" payoffs normally assumed in induced-value theory[5] we are able to fit the data well, and obtain an estimate of the proportion of altruistic players on the order of 5 percent of the subject pool. In addition to estimating the proportion of altruists in the subject pool, we also estimate the beliefs of the players about this proportion. We find that subjects' beliefs are, on average, equal to the estimated "true" proportion of altruists, thus providing evidence in favor of a version of rational expectations. We also estimate a decision error rate to be on the order of 5%–10% for inexperienced subjects and roughly two-thirds that for experienced subjects, indicating two things: (i) a significant amount of learning is taking place, and (ii) even with inexperienced subjects, only a small fraction of their behavior is unaccounted for by a simple game-theoretic equilibrium model in which beliefs are accurate.

Our experiment can be compared to that of Camerer and Weigelt (1988) (see also Neral and Ochs (1989) and Jung et al. (1989)). In our experiment, we find that many features of the data can be explained if we assume that there is a belief that a certain percentage of the subjects in the population are altruists. This is equivalent to asserting that subjects did not believe that the utility functions we attempted to induce are the same as the utility functions that all subjects really use for making their decisions. I.e., subjects have their own personal beliefs about parameters of the experimental design that are at odds with those of the experimental design. This is similar to the point in Camerer and Weigelt, that one way to account for some features of behavior in their experiments was to introduce "homemade priors"—i.e., beliefs that there were more subjects who always act cooperatively (similar to our altruists) than were actually induced to be so in their experimental design. (They used a rule-of-thumb procedure to obtain a homemade prior point estimate of 17%.) Our analysis differs from Camerer and Weigelt partly in that we integrate it into a structural econometric model, which we then estimate using classical tech-

---

[4] We called them "irrationals" in an earlier version of the paper. The equilibrium implications of this kind of incomplete information and altruism has been explored in a different kind of experimental game by Palfrey and Rosenthal (1988). See also Cooper et al. (1990).

[5] See Smith (1976).

niques. This enables us to estimate the number of subjects that actually behave in such a fashion, and to address the question as to whether the beliefs of subjects are on average correct.

Our experiment can also be compared to the literature on repeated prisoner's dilemmas. This literature (see e.g., Selten and Stoecker (1986) for a review) finds that experienced subjects exhibit a pattern of "tacit cooperation" until shortly before the end of the game, when they start to adopt noncooperative behavior. Such behavior would be predicted by incomplete information models like that of Kreps et al. (1982). However, Selten and Stoecker also find that inexperienced subjects do not immediately adopt this pattern of play, but that it takes them some time to "learn to cooperate." Selten and Stoecker develop a learning theory model that is not based on optimizing behavior to account for such a learning phase. One could alternatively develop a model similar to the one used here, where in addition to incomplete information about the payoffs of others, all subjects have some chance of making errors, which decreases over time. If some other subjects might be making errors, then it could be in the interest of all subjects to take some time to learn to cooperate, since they can masquerade as slow learners. Thus, a natural analog of the model used here might offer an alternative explanation for the data in Selten and Stoecker.

2. EXPERIMENTAL DESIGN

Our budget is too constrained to use the payoffs proposed by Aumann. So we run a rather more modest version of the centipede game. In our laboratory games, we start with a total pot of $.50 divided into a large pile of $.40 and a small pile of $.10. Each time a player chooses to pass, both piles are multiplied by two. We consider both a two round (four move) and a three round (six move) version of the game. This leads to the extensive forms illustrated in Figures 1 and 2. In addition, we consider a version of the four move game in which all payoffs are quadrupled. This "high payoff" condition therefore produced a payoff structure equivalent to the last four moves of the six move game.

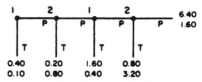

FIGURE 1.—The four move centipede game.

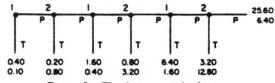

FIGURE 2.—The six move centipede game.

CENTIPEDE GAME 807

TABLE I
Experimental Design

Session #	Subject pool	# subjects	Games/ subject	Total # games	# moves	High Payoffs
1	PCC	20	10	100	4	No
2	PCC	18	9	81	4	No
3	CIT	20	10	100	4	No
4	CIT	20	10	100	4	Yes
5	CIT	20	10	100	6	No
6	PCC	18	9	81	6	No
7	PCC	20	10	100	6	No

In each experimental session we used a total of twenty subjects, none of whom had previously played a centipede game. The subjects were divided into two groups at the beginning of the session, which we called the Red and the Blue groups. In each game, the Red player was the first mover, and the Blue player was the second mover. Each subject then participated in ten games, one with each of the subjects in the other group.[6] The sessions were all conducted through computer terminals at the Caltech Laboratory for Experimental Economics and Political Science. Subjects did not communicate with other subjects except through the strategy choices they made. Before each game, each subject was matched with another subject, of the opposite color, with whom they had not been previously matched, and then the subjects who were matched with each other played the game in either Figure 1 and Figure 2 depending on the session.

All details described above were made common knowledge to the players, at least as much as is possible in a laboratory setting. In other words, the instructions were read to the subjects with everyone in the same room (see Appendix B for the exact instructions read to the subjects). Thus it was common knowledge that no subject was ever matched with any other subject more than once. In fact we used a rotating matching scheme which insures that no player i ever plays against a player who has previously played someone who has played someone that i has already played. (Further, for any positive integer n, the sentence which replaces the phrase "who has previously played someone who has played someone" in the previous sentence with n copies of the same phrase is also true.) In principle, this matching scheme should eliminate potential supergame or cooperative behavior, yet at the same time allow us to obtain multiple observations on each individual's behavior.

We conducted a total of seven sessions (see Table I). Our subjects were students from Pasadena Community College (PCC) and from the California Institute of Technology (CIT). No subject was used in more than one session. Sessions 1–3 involved the regular four move version of the game, session 4

[6]Only one of the three versions of the game was played in a given session. In sessions 2 and 6, not all subjects showed up, so there were only 18 subjects, with 9 in each group, and consequently each subject played only 9 games.

TABLE IIA

PROPORTION OF OBSERVATIONS AT EACH TERMINAL NODE

		Session	N	f_1	f_2	f_3	f_4	f_5	f_6	f_7
	1	(PCC)	100	.06	.26	.44	.20	.04		
Four	2	(PCC)	81	.10	.38	.40	.11	.01		
Move	3	(CIT)	100	.06	.43	.28	.14	.09		
	Total	1–3	281	.071	.356	.370	.153	.049		
High Payoff	4	(High-CIT)	100	.150	.370	.320	.110	.050		
	5	(CIT)	100	.02	.09	.39	.28	.20	.01	.01
Six	6	(PCC)	81	.00	.02	.04	.46	.35	.11	.02
Move	7	(PCC)	100	.00	.07	.14	.43	.23	.12	.01
	Total	5–7	281	.007	.064	.199	.384	.253	.078	.014

involved the high payoff four move game, and sessions 5–7 involved the six move version of the game. This gives us a total of 58 subjects and 281 plays of the four move game, and 58 subjects with 281 plays of the six move game, and 20 subjects with 100 plays of the high payoff game. Subjects were paid in cash the cumulative amount that they earned in the session plus a fixed amount for showing up ($3.00 for CIT students and $5.00 for PCC students).[7]

3. DESCRIPTIVE SUMMARY OF DATA

The complete data from the experiment is given in Appendix C. In Table II, we present some simple descriptive statistics summarizing the behavior of the subjects in our experiment. Table IIA gives the frequencies of each of the terminal outcomes. Thus f_i is the proportion of games ending at the ith terminal node. Table IIB gives the implied probabilities, p_i of taking at the ith decision node of the game. In other words, p_i is the proportion of games among those that reached decision node i, in which the subject who moves at node i chose TAKE. Thus, in a game with n decision nodes, $p_i = f_i / \sum_{j=i}^{n+1} f_j$.

All standard game theoretic solutions (Nash equilibrium, iterated elimination of dominated strategies, maximin, rationalizability, etc.) would predict $f_i = 1$ if $i = 1$, $f_i = 0$ otherwise. The requirement of rationality that subjects not adopt dominated strategies would predict that $f_{n+1} = 0$ and $p_n = 1$. As is evident from Table II, we can reject out of hand either of these hypotheses of rationality. In only 7% of the four move games, 1% of the six move games, and 15% of the high payoff games does the first mover choose TAKE on the first round. So the subjects clearly do not iteratively eliminate dominated strategies. Further, when a game reaches the last move, Table IIB shows that the player with the last move adopts the dominated strategy of choosing PASS roughly 25% of the time

---

[7]The stakes in these games were large by usual standards. Students earned from a low of $7.00 to a high of $75.00, in sessions that averaged less than 1 hour—average earnings were $20.50 ($13.40 in the four move, $30.77 in the six move, and $41.50 in the high payoff four move version).

CENTIPEDE GAME 809

TABLE IIB[a]

IMPLIED TAKE PROBABILITIES FOR THE CENTIPEDE GAME

	Session	p_1	p_2	p_3	p_4	p_5	p_6
	1 (PCC)	.06	.28	.65	.83		
		(100)	(94)	(68)	(24)		
Four	2 (PCC)	.10	.42	.76	.90		
Move		(81)	(73)	(42)	(10)		
	3 (CIT)	.06	.46	.55	.61		
		(100)	(94)	(51)	(23)		
	Total 1–3	.07	.38	.65	.75		
		(281)	(261)	(161)	(57)		
High	4 (CIT)	.15	.44	.67	.69		
Payoff		(100)	(85)	(48)	(16)		
	5 (CIT)	.02	.09	.44	.56	.91	.50
		(100)	(98)	(89)	(50)	(22)	(2)
Six	6 (PCC)	.00	.02	.04	.49	.72	.82
Move		(81)	(81)	(79)	(76)	(39)	(11)
	7 (PCC)	.00	.07	.15	.54	.64	.92
		(100)	(100)	(93)	(79)	(36)	(13)
	Total 5–7	.01	.06	.21	.53	.73	.85
		(281)	(279)	(261)	(205)	(97)	(26)

[a]The number in parentheses is the number of observations in the game at that node.

in the four move games, 15% in the six move games, and 31% in the high payoff games.[8]

The most obvious and consistent pattern in the data is that in all of the sessions, the probability of TAKE increases as we get closer to the last move (see Table IIB). The only exception to this pattern is in session 5 (CIT) in the last two moves, where the probabilities drop from .91 to .50. But the figure at the last move (.50) is based on only two observations. Thus any model to explain the data should capture this basic feature. In addition to this dominant feature, there are some less obvious patterns of the data, which we now discuss.

Table III indicates that there are some differences between the earlier and later plays of the game in a given treatment which are supportive of the proposition that as subjects gain more experience with the game, their behavior appears "more rational." Recall that with the matching scheme we use, there is no game-theoretic reason to expect players to play any differently in earlier games than in later games. Table IIIA shows the cumulative probabilities, $F_j = \sum_{i=1}^{j} f_i$ of stopping by the jth node. We see that the cumulative distribution in the first five games stochastically dominates the distribution in the last five games both in the four and six move experiments. This indicates that the games end earlier in later matches. Table IIIB shows that in both the four and six move sessions, in later games subjects chose TAKE with higher probability at all

[8]For sessions 1–3, 7 of the 14 cases in this category are attributable to 2 of the 29 subjects. In the high payoff condition, 4 of the 5 events are attributable to 1 subject.

R. D. MCKELVEY AND T. R. PALFREY

TABLE IIIA

CUMULATIVE OUTCOME FREQUENCIES

$$(F_j = \Sigma_{i=1}^{j} f_i)$$

Treatment	Game	N	F_1	F_2	F_3	F_4	F_5	F_6	F_7
Four	1–5	145	.062	.365	.724	.924	1.00		
Move	6–10	136	.081	.493	.875	.978	1.00		
Six	1–5	145	.000	.055	.227	.558	.889	.979	1.000
Move	6–10	136	.015	.089	.317	.758	.927	.993	1.000

TABLE IIIB

IMPLIED TAKE PROBABILITIES

COMPARISON OF EARLY VERSUS LATE PLAYS IN THE LOW PAYOFF CENTIPEDE GAMES

Treatment	Game	P_1	P_2	P_3	P_4	P_5	P_6
Four	1–5	.06	.32	.57	.75		
Move		(145)	(136)	(92)	(40)		
	6–10	.08	.49	.75	.82		
		(136)	(125)	(69)	(17)		
Four	1–5	.00	.06	.18	.43	.75	.81
Move		(145)	(145)	(137)	(112)	(64)	(16)
	6–10	.01	.07	.25	.65	.70	.90
		(136)	(134)	(124)	(93)	(33)	(10)

stages of the game (with the exception of node 5 of the six move games). Further, the number of subjects that adopt the dominated strategy of passing on the last move drops from 14 of 56, or 25%, to 4 of 27, or 15%.

A third pattern emerges in comparing the four move games to the six move games (in Table IIB). We see that at every move, there is a higher probability of taking in the four move game than in the corresponding move of the six move game (.07 vs .01 in the first move; .38 vs .06 in the second move, etc.). The same relation holds between the high payoff games and the six move games. However, if we compare the four move games to the *last* four moves of the six move games, there is more taking in the six move games (.75 vs .85 in the last move; .65 vs .73 in the next to last move, etc.). This same relationship holds between the high payoff games and the six move games even though the payoffs in the high payoff games are identical to the payoffs in the last four moves of the six move games.

There is at least one other interesting pattern in the data. Specifically, if we look at individual level data, there are several subjects who PASS at every opportunity they have.[9] We call such subjects *altruists*, because an obvious way to rationalize their behavior is to assume that they have a utility function that is

---

[9]Some of these subjects had as many as 24 opportunities to TAKE in the 10 games they played. See Appendix C.

monotonically increasing in the *sum* of the red and blue payoffs, rather than a selfish utility function that only depends on that players' own payoff. Overall, there were a total of 9 players who chose PASS at every opportunity. Roughly half (5) of these were red players and half (5) were in four move games. At the other extreme (i.e., the Nash equilibrium prediction), only 1 out of all 138 subjects chose TAKE at every opportunity. This indicates the strong possibility that players who will always choose PASS do exist in our subject pool, and also suggests that a theory which successfully accounts for the data will almost certainly have to admit the existence of at least a small fraction of such subjects.

Finally, there are interesting *non-patterns* in the data. Specifically, unlike the ten cases cited above, the preponderance of the subject behavior is inconsistent with the use of a single pure strategy throughout all games they played. For example, subject #8 in session #1 (a red player) chooses TAKE at the first chance in the second game it participates in, then PASS at both opportunities in the next game, PASS at both opportunities in the fourth game, TAKE at the first chance in the fifth game, and PASS at the first chance in the sixth game. Fairly common irregularities of this sort, which appear rather haphazard from a casual glance, would seem to require some degree of randomness to explain. While some of this behavior may indicate evidence of the use of mixed strategies, some such behavior is impossible to rationalize, even by resorting to the possibility of altruistic individuals or Bayesian updating across games. For example, subject #6 in session #1 (a blue player), chooses PASS at the last node of the first game, but takes at the first opportunity a few games later. Rationalization of this subject's behavior as altruistic in the first game is contradicted by the subject's behavior in the later game. Rational play cannot account for some sequences of plays we observe in the data, even with a model that admits the possibility of altruistic players.

4. THE MODEL

In what follows, we construct a structural econometric model based on the theory of games of incomplete information that is simultaneously consistent with the experimental design and the underlying theory. Standard maximum likelihood techniques can then be applied to estimate the underlying structural parameters.

The model we construct consists of an incomplete information game together with a specification of two sources of errors—errors in actions and errors in beliefs. The model is constructed to account for both the time-series nature of our data and for the dependence across observations, features of the data set that derive from a design in which every subject plays a sequence of games against different opponents. The model is able to account for the broad descriptive findings summarized in the previous section. By parameterizing the structure of the errors, we can also address issues of whether there is learning going on over time, whether there is heterogeneity in beliefs, and whether individuals' beliefs are on average correct.

We first describe the basic model, and then describe the two sources of errors.

4.1. *The Basic Model*

If, as appears to be the case, there are a substantial number of altruists in our subject pool, it seems reasonable to assume that the possible existence of such individuals is commonly known by all subjects. Our basic model is thus a game of two sided incomplete information where each individual can be one of two types (selfish or altruistic), and there is incomplete information about whether one's opponent is selfish or altruistic.

In our model, a *selfish* individual is defined as an individual who derives utility only from its own payoff, and acts to maximize this utility. In analogy to our definition of a selfish individual, a natural definition of an altruist would be as an individual who derives utility not only from its own payoff, but also from the payoff of the other player. For our purposes, to avoid having to make parametric assumptions about the form of the utility functions, it is more convenient to define an altruist in terms of the strategy choice rather than in terms of the utility function. Thus, we define an *altruist* as an individual who always chooses PASS. However, it is important to note that we could obtain an equivalent model by making parametric assumptions on the form of the utility functions. For example, if we were to assume that the utility to player i is a convex combination of its own payoff and that of its opponent, then any individual who places a weight of at least $\frac{2}{9}$ on the payoff of the opponent has a dominant strategy to choose PASS in every round of the experiment. Thus, defining altruists to be individuals who satisfy this condition would lead to equivalent behavior for the altruists.

The extensive form of the basic model for the case when the probability of a selfish individual equals q is shown in Figure 8 in Appendix A. Hence, the probability of an altruist is $1 - q$. This is a standard game of incomplete information. There is an initial move by nature in which the types of both players are drawn. If a player is altruistic, then the player has a trivial strategy choice (namely, it can PASS). If a player is selfish, then it can choose either PASS or TAKE.

4.1.1. *Equilibrium of the Basic Model*

The formal analysis of the equilibrium appears in Appendix A, but it is instructive to provide a brief overview of the equilibrium strategies, and to summarize how equilibrium strategies vary over the family of games indexed by q. We analytically derive in Appendix A the solution to the n-move game, for arbitrary values of q (the common knowledge belief that a randomly selected player is selfish) ranging from 0 to 1.

For any given q, a strategy for the first player in a six move game is a vector, (p_1, p_3, p_5), where p_i specifies the probability that Red chooses TAKE on move i conditional on Red being a selfish player. Similarly, a strategy for Blue is a vector (p_2, p_4, p_6) giving the probability that Blue chooses TAKE on the corresponding move conditional that Blue is selfish. Thus a strategy pair is a vector $p = (p_1, p_2, \ldots, p_6)$, where the odd components are moves by Red and the even components are moves by Blue. Similar notation is used for the four move game.

In Appendix A, we prove that for generic q there is a unique sequential equilibrium to the game, and we solve for this equilibrium as a function of q. Let us write $p(q)$ for the solution as a function of q. It is easy to verify the following properties of $p(q)$, which are true in both the four move and six move games.

Property 1: For any q, Blue chooses TAKE with probability 1 on its last move.

Property 2: If $1 - q > \frac{1}{7}$, both Red and Blue always choose PASS, except on the last move, when Blue chooses TAKE.

Property 3. If $1 - q \in (0, \frac{1}{7})$ the equilibrium involves mixed strategies.

Property 4: If $q = 1$, then both Red and Blue always choose TAKE.

From the solution, we can compute the implied probabilities of choosing TAKE at each move, accounting for the altruists as well as the selfish players. We can also compute the probability $s(q) = (s_1(q), \ldots, s_7(q))$ of observing each of the possible outcomes, T, PT, PPT, PPPT, PPPPT, PPPPPT, PPPPPP. Thus, $s_1(q) = q p_1(q)$, $s_2(q) = q^2 (1 - p_1(q)) p_2(q) + q(1 - q) p_2(q)$, etc. Figures 3 and 4 graph the probabilities of the outcomes as a function of the level of altruism, $1 - q$.

It is evident from the properties of the solution and from the outcome probabilities in Figures 3 and 4 that the equilibrium predictions are extremely sensitive to the beliefs that players have about the proportion of altruists in the population. The intuition of why this is so is well-summarized in the literature on signalling and reputation building (for example, Kreps and Wilson (1982a), Kreps et al. (1982)) and is exposited very nicely for a one-sided incomplete information version of the centipede game more recently in Kreps (1990). The guiding principle is easy to understand, even if one cannot follow the technical details of the Appendix. Because of the uncertainty in the game when it is not common knowledge that everyone is self-interested, it will generally be worthwhile for a selfish player to mimic altruistic behavior. This is not very different from the fact that in poker it may be a good idea to bluff some of the time in order to confuse your opponent about whether or not you have a good hand. In our games, for *any* amount of uncertainty of this sort, equilibrium will involve some degree of imitation. The form of the imitation in our setting is obvious: selfish players sometimes pass, to mimic an altruist. By imitating an altruist one might lure an opponent into passing at the next move, thereby raising one's final payoff in the game. The amount of imitation in equilibrium depends directly on the beliefs about the likelihood $(1 - q)$ of a randomly selected player being an altruist. The more likely players believe there are altruists in the population, the more imitation there is. In fact, if these beliefs are sufficiently high (at least $\frac{1}{7}$, in our versions of the centipede game), then selfish players will always imitate altruists, thereby completely reversing the predictions of game theory when it is

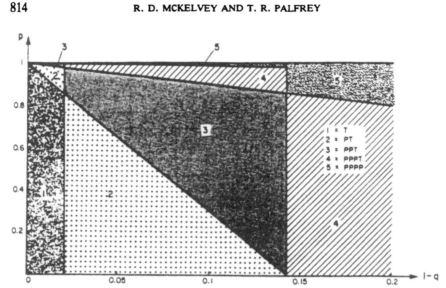

FIGURE 3.—Equilibrium outcome probabilities for basic four move game.

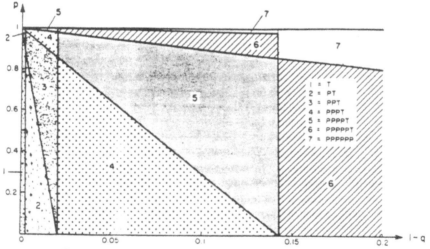

FIGURE 4.—Equilibrium outcome probabilities for basic six move game.

common knowledge that there are no altruists. Between 0 and $\frac{1}{7}$, the theory predicts the use of mixed strategies by selfish players.

4.1.2. *Limitations of the Basic Model*

The primary observation to make from the solution to the basic model is that this model can account for the main feature of the data noted in the previous section—namely that probabilities of taking increase as the game progresses.

For any level of altruism above $1/7^2$ in the four move game, and for any value above $1/7^3$ in the six move game, the solution satisfies the property that $p_i \geqslant p_j$ whenever $i > j$.

Despite the fact that the basic model accounts for the main pattern in the data, it is just as obvious that the basic model cannot account for the remaining features of the data. It is apparent from Figures 3 and 4 that for any value of q, there is at least one outcome with a 0 or close to 0 probability of occurrence. So the model will fit poorly data in which all of the possible outcomes occur. Nor can it account for any consistent patterns of learning in the data, for substantial variations across individuals, or for some of the irregularities described earlier.

To account for these features of the data, we introduce two additional elements to the model—the possibility of errors in actions, and the possibility of errors in beliefs.

4.2. *Errors in Actions—Noisy Play*

One explanation of the apparently bizarre irregularities that we noted in the previous section is that players may "experiment" with different strategies in order to see what happens. This may reflect the fact that, early on, a subject may not have settled down on any particular approach about how to play the game. Alternatively, subjects may simply "goof," either by pressing the wrong key, or by accidentally confusing which color player they are, or by failing to notice that is the last round, or some other random event. Lacking a good theory for how and why this experimentation or goofing takes place, a natural way to model it is simply as noise. So we refer to it as *noisy play*.

We model noisy play in the following way. In game t, at node s, if p^* is the equilibrium probability of TAKE that the player at that node attempts to implement, we assume that the player actually chooses TAKE with probability $(1 - \varepsilon_t)p^*$, and makes a random move (i.e. TAKE or PASS with probability .5) with probability ε_t. Therefore, we can view $\varepsilon_t/2$ as the probability that a player experiments, or, alternatively, goofs in the tth game played. We call ε_t the error rate in game t. We assume that both types (selfish and altruistic) of players make errors at this rate, independently at all nodes of game t, and that this is common knowledge among the players.

4.2.1. *Learning*

If the reasons for noisy play are along the lines just suggested, then it is natural to believe that the incidence of such noisy play will decline with experience. For one thing, as experience accumulates, the informational value of experimenting with alternative strategies declines, as subjects gather information about how other subjects are likely to behave. Perhaps more to the point, the informational value will decline over the course of the 10 games a subject plays simply because, as the horizon becomes nearer, there are fewer and fewer games where the information accumulated by experimentation can be capital-ized on. For different, but perhaps more obvious reasons, the likelihood that a subject will goof is likely to decline with experience. Such a decline is indicated in a wide range of experimental data in economics and psychology, spanning many different kinds of tasks and environments. We call this decline *learning*.

We assume a particular parametric form for the error rate as a function of t. Specifically, we assume that individuals follow an exponential learning curve. The initial error rate is denoted by ε and the learning parameter is δ. Therefore,

$$\varepsilon_t = \varepsilon e^{-\delta(t-1)}.$$

Notice that, while according to this specification the error rate may be different for different t, it is assumed to be the same for all individuals, and the same at all nodes of the game. More complicated specifications are possible, such as estimating different ε's for altruistic and selfish players, but we suspect that such parameter proliferation would be unlikely to shed much more light on the data. When solving for the equilibrium of the game, we assume that players are aware that they make errors and learn, and are aware that other players make errors and learn too.[10] Formally, when solving for the Bayesian equilibrium TAKE probabilities, we assume that ε and δ are common knowledge.

4.2.2. *Equilibrium with Errors in Actions*

For $\varepsilon > 0$, we do not have an analytical solution for the equilibrium. The solutions were numerically calculated using GAMBIT, a computer algorithm for calculating equilibrium strategies to incomplete information games, developed by McKelvey (1990). For comparison, the equilibrium outcome probabilities as a function of q, for $\varepsilon_t = .2$, are illustrated graphically in Figures 5 and 6.

4.3. *Errors in Beliefs—Heterogeneous Beliefs*

In addition to assuming that individuals can make errors in their strategies, we also assume that there can be errors in their beliefs. Thus, we assume that there is a *true probability* Q that individuals are selfish (yielding probability $1 - Q$ of altruists), but that each individual has a *belief*, q_i, of the likelihood of selfish players, which may be different from the true Q.[11] In particular, individuals' beliefs can differ from each other, giving rise to heterogeneous beliefs.

---

[10]An alternative specification would have it common knowledge that subjects believe others make errors, but believe they do not commit these "errors" themselves. Such a model is analytically more tractable and leads to similar conclusions, but seems less appealing on theoretical grounds.

[11]This is related to the idea proposed independently by Camerer and Weigelt (1988) and Palfrey and Rosenthal (1988), where they posit that subjects' beliefs about the distribution of types may differ from the induced-value distribution of types announced in the instructions.

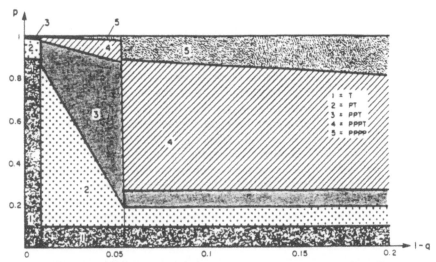

FIGURE 5.—Equilibrium outcome probabilities for four move game ($\varepsilon_t = .2$).

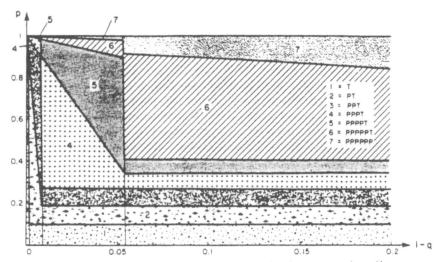

FIGURE 6.—Equilibrium outcome probabilities for six move game ($\varepsilon_t = .2$).

For individual i, denote by q_i the belief individual i holds that a randomly selected opponent is selfish. (We assume that each individual maintains its belief throughout all 10 games that it plays.) Because this converts the complete information centipede game into a Bayesian game, it is necessary to make some kind of assumption about the beliefs a player has about its opponent's beliefs, etc. etc. If there were no heterogeneity in beliefs, so that $q_i = q$ for all i, then one possibility is that a player's beliefs are correct—that is, q is common knowledge, and $q = Q$. We call this *rational expectations*. One can then solve for the Bayesian equilibrium of the game played in a session (which is unique), as a function of ε, δ, t, and q. An analytical solution is derived in Appendix A for the case of $\varepsilon = 0$.

To allow for heterogeneity, we make a parametric assumption that the beliefs of the individuals are independently drawn from a Beta distribution with parameters (α, β), where the mean of the distribution, q, is simply equal to $\alpha/(\alpha + \beta)$. There are several ways to specify higher order beliefs. One possibility is to assume it is common knowledge among the players that beliefs are independently drawn from a Beta distribution with parameters (α, β) and that the pair (α, β) is also common knowledge among the players. This version of higher order beliefs leads to serious computational problems when numerically solving for the equilibrium strategies. Instead, we use a simpler[12] version of the higher order beliefs, which might be called an *egocentric model*. Each player plays the game as if it were common knowledge that the opponent had the same belief. In other words, while we, the econometricians, assume there is heterogeneity in beliefs, we solve the game in which the players do have heterogeneous beliefs, but believe that everyone's beliefs are alike. This enables us to use the same basic techniques in solving for the Bayesian equilibrium strategies for players with different beliefs as one would use if there were homogeneous beliefs. We can then investigate a weaker form of rational expectations: is the average belief $(\alpha/(\alpha + \beta))$ equal to the true proportion (Q) of selfish players?

Given the assumptions made regarding the form of the heterogeneity in beliefs, the introduction of errors in beliefs does not change the computation of the equilibrium for a given individual. It only changes the aggregate behavior we will expect to see over a group of individuals. For example, at an error rate of $\varepsilon_t = .2$, and parameters α, β for the Beta distribution, we will expect to see aggregate behavior in period t of the six move games which is the average of the behavior generated by the solutions in Figure 6, when we integrate out q with respect to the Beta distribution $B(\alpha, \beta)$.

5. MAXIMUM LIKELIHOOD ESTIMATION

5.1. *Derivation of the Likelihood Function*

Consider the version of the game where a player draws belief q. For every t, and for every ε_t, and for each of that player's decision nodes, ν, the equilibrium solution derived in the previous section yields a probability that the decision at that node will be TAKE, conditional on the player at that decision node being selfish, and conditional on that player *not* making an error. Denote that probability $p_s(\varepsilon_t, q, \nu)$. Therefore, the probability that a selfish type of that player would TAKE at ν is equal to $P_s(\varepsilon_t, q, \nu) = (\varepsilon_t/2) + (1 - \varepsilon_t)p_s(\varepsilon_t, q, \nu)$, and the probability that an altruistic type of this player would take is $P_a(\varepsilon_t, q, \nu) = \varepsilon_t/2$. For each individual, we observe a collection of decisions that

---

[12] While it is simpler, it is no less arbitrary. It is a version of beliefs that does not assume "common priors" (Aumann (1987)), but is consistent with the standard formulation of games of incomplete information (Harsanyi (1967–68)).

are made at all nodes reached in all games played by that player. Let N_{ti} denote the set of decision nodes visited by player i in the tth game played by i, and let D_{ti} denote the corresponding set of decisions made by i at each of those nodes. Then, for any given $(\varepsilon, \delta, q, \nu)$ with $\nu \in N_{ti}$ we can compute $P_s(\varepsilon_t, q, \nu)$ from above, by setting $\varepsilon_t = \varepsilon e^{-\delta(t-1)}$. From this we compute $\pi_{ti}(D_{ti}; \varepsilon, \delta, q)$, the probability that a selfish i would have made decisions D_{ti} in game t, with beliefs q, and noise/learning parameters (ε, δ), and it equals the product of $P_s(\varepsilon, q, \nu)$ over all ν reached by in game t. Letting D_i denote the set of all decisions by player i, we define $\pi_i^s(D_i; \varepsilon, \delta, q)$ to be the product of the $\pi_{ti}(D_{ti}; \varepsilon, \delta, q)$ taken over all t. One can similarly derive $\pi_i^a(D_i; \varepsilon, \delta, q)$, the probability that an altruistic i would have made that same collection of decisions. Therefore, if Q is the true population parameter for the fraction of selfish players, then the likelihood of observing D_i, without conditioning on i's type is given by:

$$\pi_i(D_i; Q, \varepsilon, \delta, q) = Q\pi_i^s(D_i; \varepsilon, \delta, q) + (1-Q)\pi_i^a(D_i; \varepsilon, \delta, q).$$

Finally, if q is drawn from the Beta distribution with parameters (α, β), and density $B(q; \alpha, \beta)$, then the likelihood of observing D_i without conditioning on q is given by:

$$s_i(D_i; Q, \varepsilon, \delta, \alpha, \beta) = \int_0^1 \pi_i(D_i; Q, \varepsilon, \delta, q) B(q; \alpha, \beta) \, dq.$$

Therefore, the log of the likelihood function for a sample of observations, $D = (D_1, \ldots, D_I)$, is just

$$L(D; Q, \varepsilon, \delta, \alpha, \beta) = \sum_{i=1}^I \log\left[s_i(D_i; Q, \varepsilon, \delta, \alpha, \beta)\right].$$

For any sample of observations, D, we then find the set of parameter values that maximize L. This was done by a global grid search using the Cray X-MP at the Jet Propulsion Laboratory.

5.2. Treatments and Hypotheses

We are interested in testing four hypotheses about the parameters of the theoretical model.

(1) Errors in action: Is ε significantly different from 0?

(2) Heterogeneity (errors in beliefs): Is the variance of the estimated distribution of priors significantly different from 0?[13]

(3) Rational Expectations: Is the estimated value of Q equal to the mean of the estimated distribution of priors, $\alpha/(\alpha + \beta)$?

(4) Learning: Is the estimated value of δ positive and significantly different from 0?

---

[13] While homogeneity of beliefs is not strictly nested in the Beta distribution model (since the Beta family does not include degenerate distributions), the homogeneous model can be approximated by the Beta distribution model by constraining $(\alpha + \beta)$ to be greater than or equal to some large number.

The first two hypotheses address the question of whether the two components of error in our model (namely errors in action and errors in belief) are significantly different from 0. The second two hypotheses address issues of what properties the errors have, if they exist.

In our experimental design, there were three treatment variables:

(1) The length of the game (either four move or six move).

(2) The size of the two piles at the beginning of the game (either high payoff, ($1.60, $.40), or low payoff, ($.40, $.10)).

(3) The subject pool (either Caltech undergraduates (CIT) or Pasadena City College students (PCC)).

We also test whether any of these treatment variables were significant.

5.3. *Estimation Results*

Table IV reports the results from the estimations. Before reporting any statistical tests, we summarize several key features of the parameter estimates.

First, the mean of the distribution of beliefs about the proportion of altruists in the population in all the estimations was in the neighborhood of 5%. Figure 7 graphs the density function of the estimated Beta distribution for the pooled sample of all experimental treatments for the four and six move experiments, respectively. Second, if one looks at the rational expectations estimates (which constrain $\hat{\mu} = \hat{\alpha}/(\hat{\alpha} + \hat{\beta})$ to equal $\hat{Q}$), the constrained estimate of the Beta

TABLE IV

RESULTS FROM MAXIMUM LIKELIHOOD ESTIMATION[a]

	Treatment	$\hat{\alpha}$	$\hat{\beta}$	$\hat{\mu}$	$\hat{Q}$	$\hat{\epsilon}$	$\hat{\delta}$	$-\ln L$
Four Move	unconstrained	42	2.75	.939	.956	.18	.045	327.35
	$\mu = Q$	44	2.75	.941	.941	.18	.045	327.41
	$\delta = 0$	68	2.50	.965	.950	.21	.000	345.08
	$\sigma = 0$	—	—	.972	.850	.23	.020	371.04
Six Move	unconstrained	40	2.00	.952	.904	.06	.030	352.07
	$\mu = Q$	38	2.00	.950	.950	.06	.030	352.76
	$\delta = 0$	34	1.75	.951	.908	.05	.000	371.01
	$\sigma = 0$	—	—	.976	.850	.22	.030	442.96
PCC	unconstrained	42	2.75	.939	.974	.14	.030	464.14
	$\mu = Q$	40	2.75	.936	.936	.11	.040	464.57
	$\sigma = 0$	—	—	.952	.882	.18	.050	508.60
CIT	unconstrained	42	1.25	.971	.880	.22	.040	340.27
	$\mu = Q$	28	1.00	.966	.966	.22	.040	342.57
	$\sigma = 0$	—	—	.994	.750	.27	.010	424.83
	High Payoff	64	2.25	.966	.900	.22	.050	107.11
	All Four Move	48	2.25	.955	.938	.22	.050	435.73
	All Low	28	1.75	.941	.938	.14	.050	702.80
	All Sessions	40	2.00	.952	.930	.18	.050	813.38

[a]Rows marked $\mu = Q$ report parameter estimates under the rational expectations restriction that $\hat{\alpha}/(\hat{\alpha} + \hat{\beta}) = \hat{Q}$. Rows marked $\delta = 0$ are parameter estimates under the hypothesis of no learning. Rows marked $\sigma = 0$ are parameter estimates under the assumption of no heterogeneity.

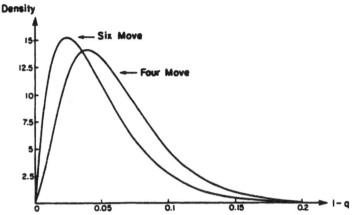

FIGURE 7.—Estimated distribution of beliefs for four and six move games.

distribution is nearly identical to the unconstrained estimate of the Beta distribution.

Furthermore, the rational expectations estimates of μ are nearly identical across all treatments. Therefore, if we are unable to reject rational expectations, then it would seem that these beliefs, as well as the true distribution of altruists are to a large extent independent of the treatments. The greatest difference across the treatments is in the estimates of the amount of noisy play. While the estimates of δ are quite stable across treatments, the estimates of ε are not. This is most apparent in the comparison of the four move and the six move estimates of ε. We discuss this below after reporting statistical tests. Finally, observe that in the $\sigma = 0$ estimates (no heterogeneity of beliefs), the estimate of μ is consistently much larger than the estimate of Q, and the recovered error rates are higher.

It might seem paradoxical that we estimate a level of altruism on the order of 5%, while the proportion of subjects who choose pass on the last move is on the order of 25% for the four move experiments and 15% for the six move experiments. One reason for the low estimate of the level of altruism is that in the theoretical model, part of this behavior is attributed to errors in action. But less obviously, it should be noted that because our equilibrium is a mixed strategy, there is a sample selection bias in the set of subjects who get to the last move: altruists are more likely to make it to this stage, since they pass on earlier moves whereas selfish subjects mix. Thus, even with no errors, we would expect to see a higher proportion of passing on the last move than the proportion of altruists in the subject pool.

5.4. *Statistical Tests*

Table V reports likelihood ratio χ^2 tests for comparisons of the various treatments, and for testing the theoretical hypotheses of rational expectations, learning, and heterogeneity.

TABLE V
LIKELIHOOD RATIO TESTS

	Hypothesis	Treatment	d.f.	−2 log likelihood ratio
Theoretical Hypotheses	Heterogeneity ($\sigma = 0$)	4-move	1	87.38*
		6-move	1	181.78*
	Rational expectations ($\mu = Q$)	4-move	1	.12
		6-move	1	1.38
	Learning ($\delta = 0$)	4-move	1	35.46*
		6-move	1	37.88*
Treatment Effects	4-move vs 6-move		5	51.16*
	4-high vs 4-low (Payoff Treatment)		5	2.54
	PCC vs CIT	All	5	17.94*
		4-move	5	9.63
		6-move	5	8.42

*Significant at 1% level.

Our first hypothesis—that $\varepsilon = 0$, can be dispensed with immediately. In both the four and six move experiments, setting $\varepsilon = 0$ yields a likelihood of zero. So this hypothesis can be rejected at any level of significance, and is not included in Table V.

To test for heterogeneity, we estimate a model in which a single belief parameter, q, is estimated instead of estimating the two parameter model, α and β (see Table IV, rows marked $\sigma = 0$). As noted earlier, homogeneity is approximately nested in our heterogeneity model. Therefore, we treat the homogeneous model as if it is nested in the heterogeneous model, and report a standard χ^2 test based on likelihood ratios. All statistical tests were highly significant (see Table V). Note that by setting Q and all q_i to one, then one obtains a pure random model where individuals PASS with probability $\varepsilon/2$. Hence for any probability of passing less than or equal to $\frac{1}{2}$, the pure random model is a special case of the homogeneous model. Thus the above findings mean we also reject the pure random model ($\varepsilon = 1$).

In the test for learning, the null hypothesis that $\delta = 0$ is clearly rejected for all treatments, at essentially any level of significance. We conclude that learning effects are clearly identified in the data. Subjects are experimenting less and/or making fewer errors as they gain experience. The magnitude of the parameter estimates of δ indicate that subjects make roughly two-thirds as many errors in the tenth game, compared to the first game.

The test for rational expectations is unrejectable in most cases. The one exception is for the CIT subject pool, where the difference is significant at the 5% level, but not the 1% level.

The payoff level treatment variable is not significant. This is reassuring, as it indicates that the results are relatively robust.

The other treatment effects, CIT/PCC and four move/six move, are both significant. One source of the statistical difference between the PCC and CIT

TABLE VI

CIT-PCC

ESTIMATES, BROKEN DOWN INTO FOUR MOVE AND SIX MOVE TREATMENTS

	$\hat{\alpha}$	$\hat{\beta}$	$\hat{\mu}$	$\hat{Q}$	$\hat{\varepsilon}$	$\hat{\delta}$	$-\ln L$
PCC 4	74.0	3.75	.95	.996	.210	.04	216.47
CIT 4	36.0	1.50	.96	.866	.220	.05	214.35
PCC 6	40.0	2.50	.94	.906	.060	.04	231.28
CIT 6	80.0	2.25	.97	.902	.060	.03	116.58

TABLE VII

CHI-SQUARED TESTS FOR DIFFERENCES IN ε AND δ ACROSS TREATMENTS
(UNDER ASSUMPTION THAT $\mu = Q$)

Parameter	Treatment	d.f.	$-2 \log L$ ratio
ε	4-move vs. 6-move	1	39.28[a]
	CIT vs. PCC	1	3.90
δ	4-move vs. 6-move	1	5.76
	CIT vs. PCC	1	.02

[a]Significant at $p = .01$ level.

estimates apparently derives from the fact that two-thirds of the CIT data were for four move games, while only half of the PCC data were for four move games. Consequently, we break down the statistical comparison between PCC and CIT into the four and six move game treatments (see Table VI). The subject pool effect is not significant in the six move treatment and is barely significant at the 10% level in the four move treatment (see Table V).

In order to pin down the source of the treatment effects we performed several tests. The first one was to test for differences in learning effects across treatments. This test is done by simultaneously reestimating the parameters for each of the different treatments, subject to the constraint that δ is the same for each treatment, and then conducting a likelihood ratio test. Second, we tested for differences in the noise parameter, ε. The χ^2 tests are reported in Table VII. The results reflect the estimates in Tables IV and V. The only significant (1% level) difference is the estimated initial error rate ε in the four move versus six move games. The CIT/PCC difference in ε is significant at the 5% level, but this is due to reasons given in the previous paragraph. The difference between δ in the six move game and four move game is significant at the 5% level.

5.5. Fit

In order to get a rough measure of how well our model fits the data, we use the unconstrained parameter estimates from Table IV to obtain predicted aggregate outcomes. Table VIII displays the predicted frequencies of each of the five possible outcomes of the four move game, and compares these frequencies to the observed frequencies. This comparison is done for each of the ten periods, t, $t = 1, \ldots, 10$, and for the time-aggregated data. Table IX displays

TABLE VIII

COMPARISON OF PREDICTED (FIRST) VS.
ACTUAL (SECOND) FREQUENCIES, FOUR MOVE
(CELLS 4 AND 5 COMBINED FOR COMPUTATION OF χ^2)

Period	n	ε	Predicted					Actual					χ^2
			$\hat{f}_1$	$\hat{f}_2$	$\hat{f}_3$	$\hat{f}_4$	$\hat{f}_5$	f_1	f_2	f_3	f_4	f_5	
1	58	.18	.106	.269	.291	.291	.042	.000	.276	.379	.241	.103	7.72
2	58	.17	.101	.292	.298	.271	.037	.103	.276	.345	.241	.034	.69
3	58	.16	.097	.314	.316	.241	.032	.034	.310	.379	.172	.103	3.11
4	58	.16	.096	.314	.316	.241	.032	.103	.276	.379	.172	.069	1.24
5	58	.15	.100	.329	.320	.223	.028	.069	.379	.310	.172	.069	1.04
6	58	.14	.095	.349	.335	.197	.024	.103	.310	.414	.172	.000	2.00
7	58	.14	.095	.349	.335	.197	.024	.069	.414	.448	.069	.000	9.39*
8	58	.13	.090	.369	.338	.181	.021	.069	.414	.345	.138	.034	.87
9	58	.13	.090	.369	.338	.182	.021	.103	.483	.310	.069	.034	5.10
10	40	.12	.095	.380	.348	.159	.017	.050	.450	.400	.050	.050	2.99
Total	562	—	.097	.333	.324	.218	.028	.071	.356	.370	.153	.050	

*Significant at .05 level.

similar numbers for the six move games. The last column of the table displays a χ^2 for each period, comparing the predicted to the actual values.[14]

It is evident from Tables VIII and IX that the fit to the four move games is better than that of the six move games. For the four move games, in only one of the periods (period 7), are the predicted and actual frequencies significantly different at the .05 level. In the six move games, there are six periods in which there are differences significant at the .05 level, and four of these differences are significant at the .01 level. The predicted frequencies for the four move games also pick up reasonably well the trends in the data between periods. Thus $\hat{f}_2$ and $\hat{f}_3$ increase over time, while $\hat{f}_4$ decreases, all in accordance with the actual data. In the six move data, on the other hand, the predicted frequencies show very small trends in comparison with those in the actual data. The tables can also be used to help identify where the model seems to be doing badly. In the four move games, the model overestimates f_1 and f_4 and underestimates f_2 and f_3. In the six move games, the model underestimates f_3.

The differences in fit between the four and six move games can be accounted for by the limitations of the model we fit. As noted earlier, the main difference between the estimates for the four and six move games is in the estimate of ε. In the four move games, we find a high value of ε = .18, while in the six move game we find a lower value of ε = .06. The reason for the differences in the estimates of ε between the four and six move games is fairly clear. In order to obtain a high value of the likelihood function in the six move games, the model is forced to estimate a low error rate, simply because there are almost no observations at the first terminal node.[15]

[14]The χ^2 statistic is not reported for the time-aggregated data, since the assumption of independence is violated.

[15]In fact, there were *no* such observations in the first 9 periods and only 2 in the last period.

TABLE IX

COMPARISON OF PREDICTED (FIRST) VS. ACTUAL (SECOND) FREQUENCIES, SIX MOVE
(CELLS 1 AND 2 COMBINED AND CELLS 6 AND 7 COMBINED FOR COMPUTATION OF χ^2)

Period	n	e	Predicted							Actual							χ^2
			$\hat{f}_1$	$\hat{f}_2$	$\hat{f}_3$	$\hat{f}_4$	$\hat{f}_5$	$\hat{f}_6$	$\hat{f}_7$	f_1	f_2	f_3	f_4	f_5	f_6	f_7	
1	58	.06	.035	.077	.096	.435	.275	.072	.010	.000	.103	.103	.310	.345	.103	.034	5.33
2	58	.06	.035	.077	.096	.435	.275	.072	.010	.000	.069	.172	.276	.379	.103	.000	10.41*
3	58	.06	.035	.077	.096	.435	.275	.072	.010	.000	.069	.103	.345	.345	.069	.069	5.32
4	58	.05	.030	.076	.113	.432	.273	.068	.009	.000	.034	.241	.414	.207	.103	.000	12.72*
5	58	.05	.030	.076	.113	.432	.273	.068	.009	.000	.000	.241	.310	.379	.069	.000	18.99**
6	58	.05	.030	.076	.113	.432	.273	.068	.009	.000	.069	.172	.552	.138	.069	.000	8.39
7	58	.05	.030	.076	.113	.432	.273	.068	.009	.000	.069	.276	.448	.172	.034	.000	17.98**
8	58	.05	.030	.076	.113	.432	.273	.068	.009	.000	.069	.276	.345	.241	.034	.034	15.68**
9	58	.05	.030	.076	.113	.432	.273	.068	.009	.000	.069	.172	.483	.207	.069	.000	3.86
10	40	.05	.030	.076	.113	.432	.273	.068	.009	.100	.100	.250	.350	.050	.150	.000	20.66**
Total	562	—	.031	.076	.108	.433	.274	.069	.009	.007	.064	.199	.384	.253	.078	.014	

*Significant at .05 level.
**Significant at .01 level.

The difference in the estimates of ε also accounts for the failure of the model to explain the trends in the six move data. The way that our model explains time trends is through the learning parameter, δ, which represents the rate at which the error rate, ε_t declines over time. As ε_t declines, the model implies that the game will end sooner, by predicting more frequent outcomes at the earlier terminal nodes. In the four move game, the initial error rate is $\varepsilon = .18$. With this high initial error rate, a decay of $\delta = .045$ is able to lead to substantial changes in predicted behavior. However, in the six move games, we estimate a significantly lower $\varepsilon = .06$. With this lower initial error rate, a similar rate of learning will lead to less dramatic changes in behavior.

Our model of errors assumes that in any given game, the error rate is a constant. In other words the likelihood of making an error is the same at each node regardless of whether the equilibrium recommends a pure or mixed strategy at that node. It might be reasonable to assume instead that individuals make more errors when they are indifferent between alternatives (i.e., when the equilibrium recommends a mixed strategy) than when they have preferences over alternatives (i.e., when the equilibrium recommends a pure strategy). In other words, the error rate may be a function of the utility differences between the choices. Such a model might be able to explain the behavior of the six move games with error rates on the same order of magnitude as those of the four move games. This in turn might lead to a better fit, and a better explanation of the trends in the six move games. We have not investigated such a model here because of computational difficulties.

One final point regards the comparisons between the take probabilities in the four move games and the six move games. As noted in Section 3, the aggregate data from the four move games exhibit higher take probabilities than the six move games at each of the decision nodes 1, 2, 3, and 4. But in contrast to this, when one compares the take probabilities of the last four moves of the six move game with the four move game (where the terminal payoffs are exactly comparable), this relationship is reversed; the six move data exhibit the higher take probabilities. Both of these features of the data are picked up in the estimates from our model. From Tables VIII and IX, the predicted take probabilities for the four move and six move games are $\hat{p}_4 = (.097, .368, .568, .886)$, and $\hat{p}_6 = (.031, .078, .120, .552, .778, .885)$, respectively.

6. CONCLUSIONS

We conclude that an incomplete information game that assumes the existence of a small proportion of altruists in the population can account for many of the salient features of our data. We estimate a level of altruism on the order of 5%. In the version of the model we estimate, we allow for errors in actions and errors in beliefs. Both sources of errors are found to be significant. Regarding errors in action, we find that there are significant levels of learning in the data, in the sense that subjects learn to make fewer errors over time. Subjects make roughly two thirds as many mistakes at the end of a session as they make in early play. Regarding errors in beliefs, we reject homogeneity of beliefs. However, we find that rational expectations, or on-average correct beliefs, cannot be rejected.

While we observe some subject pool differences, they are small in magnitude and barely significant. The payoff treatment had no significant effect. The only significant difference between the parameter estimates of the four and the six move games was that the estimated initial error rate was lower in the six move game. A model in which the error rate is a function of the expected utility difference between the available action choices might well account for the observed behavior in both the four and the six move games with similar estimates of the error rate. This might be a promising direction for future research.

Division of the Humanities and Social Sciences, California Institute of Technology, Pasadena, CA 91125, U.S.A.

Manuscript received May, 1990; final revision received February, 1992.

APPENDIX A

In this appendix, we prove that there is a unique sequential equilibrium to the n move centipede game with two sided incomplete information over the level of altruism (see Figure 8).

There are n nodes, numbered $i = 1, 2, \ldots, n$. Player 1 moves at the odd nodes, and Player 2 moves at the even nodes. We use the terminology "player i" to refer to the player who moves at node i. Let the payoff if player i takes at node i be (a_i, b_i) where a_i is payoff to player i and b_i is

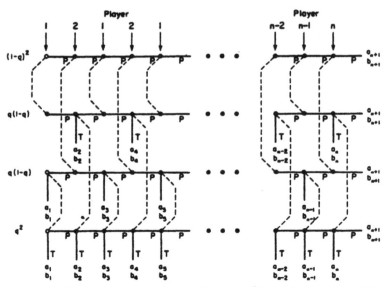

FIGURE 8.—Centipede game with incomplete information (dashed lines represent information sets and open circles are starting nodes, with probabilities indicated).

payoff to player $i - 1$ (or $i + 1$). Also, if $i = n + 1$, then (a_i, b_i) refers to the payoff if player n passes at the last node. Define

$$\eta_i = \frac{a_i - b_{i+1}}{a_{i+2} - b_{i+1}}.$$

We assume that $a_{i+2} > a_i > b_{i+1}$, and that η_i is the same for all i. We write $\eta = \eta_i$. (A similar solution can be derived when the η_i are different.)

Now a strategy for the game can be characterized by a pair of vectors $p = (p_1, \ldots, p_n)$ and $r = (r_1, \ldots, r_n)$, where for any node i, p_i is the probability that a selfish type takes at that node, and r_i is the conditional probability, as assessed by player i at node i, of the other player being selfish. Let q be the initial probability of selfishness. So $r_1 = q$.

LEMMA 1: *If $p \in \mathscr{R}^n$ and $r \in \mathscr{R}^n$ are a sequential equilibrium, then:*
(a) *for all i, $p_i = 0 \Rightarrow p_j = 0$ for all $j \leqslant i$;*
(b) $p_n = 1$. *Also, $p_i = 1 \Rightarrow i = n$ or $i = n - 1$.*

PROOF: (a) Assume $p_i = 0$. Clearly $p_{i-1} = 0$, because at node $i - 1$, the value to player $i - 1$ of passing is at least a_{i+1}, which is by assumption greater than a_{i-1}, the payoff from taking.
(b) By dominance, $p_n = 1$. Suppose $p_i = 1$ for $i < n - 1$. Then by Bayes rule $r_{i+1} = 0$, so $p_{i+1} = 0$ is the best response by player $i + 1$, since i's type has been revealed. But $p_{i+1} = 0 \Rightarrow p_i = 0$ by part (a), which is a contradiction.   Q.E.D.

Define $\underline{k}$ to be the first node at which $0 < p_i$, and $\overline{k}$ to be the first node for which $p_i = 1$. Clearly $\underline{k} \leqslant \overline{k}$. Then $\underline{k}$ and $\overline{k}$ partition the nodes into at most three sets, which we refer to as the *passing stage* ($i < \underline{k}$), the *mixing stage* ($\underline{k} \leqslant i < \overline{k}$), and the *taking stage* ($\overline{k} \leqslant i$). From Lemma 1 it follows that there are no pure strategies in the mixing stage. From Lemma 1(b), it follows that the taking stage is at least one and at most two moves.

LEMMA 2: *In any sequential equilibrium (p, r), for $1 \leqslant i \leqslant n - 1$,*
(a) $0 < p_i < 1 \Rightarrow r_i p_{i+1} = 1 - \eta$;
(b) $r_i p_{i+1} < 1 - \eta \Rightarrow p_i = 0$;
(c) $r_i p_{i+1} > 1 - \eta \Rightarrow p_i = 1$.

PROOF: (a) Assume $0 < p_i < 1$. Let v_i be the value to player i at node i given equilibrium play from node i on. Write $v_{n+1} = a_{n+1}$. Now if $i = n - 1$, then $v_{i+2} = v_{n+1} = a_{n+1} = a_{i+2}$. If $i < n - 1$, then by Lemma 1, $0 < p_i \Rightarrow 0 < p_{i+2}$, which implies $v_{i+2} = a_{i+2}$. Now in both cases $0 < p_i$ implies $v_i = a_i = r_i p_{i+1} b_{i+1} + (1 - r_i p_{i+1}) a_{i+2}$. Solving for $r_i p_{i+1}$, we get

$$r_i p_{i+1} = \frac{a_{i+2} - a_i}{a_{i+2} - b_{i+1}} = 1 - \eta.$$

(b) If $r_i p_{i+1} < 1 - \eta$, then at node i, $v_i \geqslant r_i p_{i+1} b_{i+1} + (1 - r_i p_{i+1}) a_{i+2} = a_{i+2} - r_i p_{i+1} (a_{i+2} - b_{i+1}) > a_{i+2} - (a_{i+2} - a_i) = a_i$. So $v_i > a_i \Rightarrow p_i = 0$.
(c) If $r_i p_{i+1} > 1 - \eta$, then $p_{i+1} > 0 \Rightarrow p_{i+2} > 0$ (by Lemma 1). Hence, $v_{i+2} = a_{i+2}$. By similar argument to (b), $v_i < a_i \Rightarrow p_i = 1$.   Q.E.D.

LEMMA 3: *For generic q, for any sequential equilibrium there are an even number of nodes in the mixing stage. I.e., $\overline{k} = \underline{k} + 2K$ for some integer $0 \leqslant K < n/2$. For any $k < K$,*
(a) $r_{\underline{k}+2k} = 1 - (1 - q)/\eta^k$;
(b) $r_{\overline{k}-1-2k} = 1 - \eta^{k+1}$.

PROOF: We first show (a) and (b), and then show $\overline{k} = \underline{k} + 2K$.
(a) For any node i, Bayes rule implies

(1) $$r_{i+2} = \frac{(1 - p_{i+1}) r_i}{(1 - p_{i+1}) r_i + (1 - r_i)} = \frac{r_i - p_{i+1} r_i}{1 - p_{i+1} r_i}.$$

By assumption $r_1 = q$. And since in the passing stage $p_i = 0$, it follows that $r_{\underline{k}} = q$. Now if both i and $i + 2$ are in the mixing stage, it follows from Lemma 1 that $i + 1$ is also, implying $0 < p_{i+1} < 1$. So by Lemma 3, $r_i p_{i+1} = 1 - \eta$. Hence, (1) becomes

(2) $$r_{i+2} = \frac{r_i - (1-\eta)}{1 - (1-\eta)} = 1 - \frac{(1-r_i)}{\eta}.$$

By induction, it follows that as long as $k < \frac{1}{2}(\bar{k} - \underline{k})$, then $\underline{k} + 2k < \bar{k}$ is in the mixing stage. So

$$r_{\underline{k}+2k} = 1 - \frac{1 - r_{\underline{k}}}{\eta^k} = 1 - \frac{1-q}{\eta^k}.$$

(b) As above, as long as both i and $i - 2$ are in the mixing stage, we get

$$r_i = 1 - \frac{(1 - r_{i-2})}{\eta}.$$

Solving for r_{i-2}, we get

$$r_{i-2} = 1 - \eta(1 - r_i).$$

Now from Lemma 2, it follows, since $p_{\bar{k}} = 1$,

$$r_{\bar{k}-1} = \frac{1-\eta}{p_{\bar{k}}} = 1 - \eta.$$

Hence, by induction, as long as $k < \frac{1}{2}(\bar{k} - \underline{k})$, we have

$$r_{\bar{k}-1-2k} = 1 - \eta^k(1 - r_{\bar{k}-1}) = 1 - \eta^{k+1}.$$

Finally, to show that there are an even number of nodes in the mixing stage, assume, to the contrary that there are an odd number. Then we can write $\bar{k} = \underline{k} + 2k + 1$ for some $k \geq 0$. Thus $\underline{k} = \bar{k} - 1 - 2k$. So by part (b) we have $r_{\underline{k}} = 1 - \eta^{k+1}$. But by (a) we have $r_{\underline{k}} = 1 - (1 - q) = q$, implying that $q = 1 - \eta^{k+1}$. For generic q, this is a contradiction, implying that $\bar{k} = \underline{k} + 2K$ for some $K \geq 0$. If $k \geq n/2$, then $\bar{k} \geq \underline{k} + n > n$, which contradicts Lemma 1(b). Hence $\bar{k} = \underline{k} + 2K$ for some $0 \leq K < n/2$. $\qquad Q.E.D.$

THEOREM 4: *For generic q, there is a unique sequential equilibrium (p, r) which is characterized as follows: Let I be the smallest integer greater than or equal to $n/2$. If $1 - q < \eta^I$, set $K = I - 1$, $\underline{k} = 1$, and $\bar{k} = 2I - 1$. If $1 - q > \eta^I$, let K be the largest integer with $1 - q < \eta^K$, $\bar{k} = n$, and $\underline{k} = \bar{k} - 2K$. The solution then satisfies*:
  (a) *if $i < \underline{k}$, then $r_{i+1} = q$ and $p_i = 0$;*
  (b) *if $i \geq \bar{k}$, then $r_{i+1} = 0$ and $p_i = 1$;*
  (c) *if $\underline{k} \leq i < \bar{k}$: (i) if $i = \underline{k}$, then $r_{i+1} = 1 - \eta^K$, and $p_i = (q + \eta^K - 1)/q\eta^K$; (ii) if $i = \underline{k} + 2k$, with $1 \leq k < K$, then $r_{i+1} = 1 - \eta^{K-k}$, and $p_i = (1 - \eta)/(1 - \eta^{K+1-k})$; (iii) if $i = \underline{k} + 2k + 1$, with $0 \leq k \leq K$, then $r_{i+1} = 1 - (1-q)/\eta^{k+1}$, and $p_i = \eta^k(1 - \eta)/(\eta^k - (1-q))$.*

PROOF: The formulae for r_i and p_i in parts (a), (b), and (c) follow by application of the previous lemmas together with Bayes rule. In particular in (a), $p_i = 0$ follows from the definition of $\underline{k}$, and $r_{i+1} = q$ follows from $p_j = 0$ for $j \leq i$ together with Bayes rule. In (b), $p_i = 1$ follows from the definition of $\bar{k}$, and $r_{i+1} = 0$ then follows by Bayes rule. In (c), all the formulae for r_{i+1} follow from Lemma 3. In (c) part (i), we set $\underline{k} = i + 1$ in (1) and solve for $p_{\underline{k}}$ to get

$$p_{\underline{k}} = \frac{r_{\underline{k}-1} - r_{\underline{k}+1}}{r_{\underline{k}-1} - r_{\underline{k}-1}r_{\underline{k}+1}}.$$

But $r_{\underline{k}-1} = q$ and $r_{\underline{k}+1} = 1 - \eta^K$. So

$$p_{\underline{k}} = \frac{q - 1 + \eta^K}{q\eta^K}.$$

In parts (ii) and (iii) of (c), we apply Lemma 2a to get that $p_i = (1 - \eta)/(r_{i-1})$. Substituting in for the values of r_{i-1} gives the required formulae.

Thus, it only remains to prove the assertions about $\bar{k}$ and $\underline{k}$. We first prove two preliminary inequalities. First, note, $\underline{k} > 1$ implies, by Lemma 2,

$$p_{\underline{k}-1} = 0 \Rightarrow r_{\underline{k}-1}p_{\underline{k}} \leqslant 1 - \eta$$

$$\Rightarrow q\left(\frac{q + \eta^K - 1}{q\eta^K}\right) \leqslant 1 - \eta$$

$$\Rightarrow q + \eta^K - 1 \leqslant \eta^K - \eta^{K+1}$$

$$\Rightarrow 1 - q \geqslant \eta^{K+1}.$$

Hence,

(3) $1 - q < \eta^{K+1} \Rightarrow \underline{k} = 1.$

Second, note $\bar{k} = n - 1$ implies, by Lemma 2,

$$p_{\bar{k}} = 1 \Rightarrow r_{\bar{k}}p_{\bar{k}+1} \geqslant 1 - \eta$$

$$\Rightarrow \frac{q + n^K - 1}{\eta^K} \geqslant 1 - \eta$$

$$\Rightarrow 1 - q \leqslant \eta^{K+1}$$

Hence,

(4) $1 - q > \eta^{K+1} \Rightarrow \bar{k} = n.$

Let

$$I = \left\lceil \frac{n}{2} \right\rceil.$$

There are two cases.

Case I: $1 - q < \eta^I$. From Lemma 3, we have

$$K < \frac{n}{2} \Rightarrow K \leqslant \left\lceil \frac{n}{2} \right\rceil - 1 = I \Rightarrow I \geqslant K + 1.$$

Thus we have $1 - q < \eta^I \leqslant \eta^{K+1}$. But from (3), this implies $\underline{k} = 1$. Now since $\bar{k} \geqslant n - 1$, it follows that $K = I - 1$, and $\bar{k} = \underline{k} + 2K = 2I - 1$.

Case II: $1 - q > \eta^I$. Now $p_{\underline{k}} > 0 \Rightarrow (q + \eta^K - 1)/q\eta^K > 0 \Rightarrow 1 - q < \eta^K$. Suppose $1 - q < \eta^{K+1}$. Then, from (1), we have $\underline{k} = 1$, and by the same argument as Case I, $K = I - 1 \Rightarrow 1 - q < \eta^{K+1} = \eta^I$, a contradiction. Hence we must have

$$\eta^{K+1} < 1 - q < \eta^K.$$

So K is the largest integer with $1 - q < \eta^K$. But now, from (4), it follows that $\bar{k} = n$.   Q.E.D.

In the centipede games described in the text, the piles grow at an exponential rate: There are real numbers $c > d > 1$ with $a_i = cb_i$ and $a_{i+1} = da_i$ for all i. So $\eta = (c - d)/(cd^2 - d)$. In our experiments $c = 4$, and $d = 2$, so $\eta = \frac{1}{7}$. The figures in the text correspond to the solution for the two and three round games ($n = 4$ and $n = 6$) for these parameters.

It is interesting to note that since the solution depends only on η, the above solution also applies if there are linearly increasing payoffs of the form $a_{i+1} = a_i + c$, and $b_{i+1} = b_i + c$ (with $c > 0$), as long as $a_i > b_{i+1} = b_i + c$. Hence picking a_i, b_i, and c so that

$$\frac{a_1 - b_2}{a_3 - b_2} = \frac{a_1 - b_1 - c}{a_i - b_i + c} = \frac{1}{7},$$

(e.g., $a_1 = 60$, $b_1 = 20$, $c = 30$) one can obtain a game with linearly increasing payoffs whose solution is exactly the same as the solution of the game with exponentially increasing payoffs treated in this paper.

APPENDIX B

Experiment Instructions

This is an experiment in group decision making, and you will be paid for your participation in cash, at the end of the experiment. Different subjects may earn different amounts. What you earn depends partly on your decisions, partly on the decisions of others, and partly on chance.

The entire experiment will take place through computer terminals, and all interaction between you will take place through the computers. It is important that you not talk or in any way try to communicate with other subjects during the experiments. If you disobey the rules, we will have to ask you to leave the experiment.

We will start with a brief instruction period. During the instruction period, you will be given a complete description of the experiment and will be shown how to use the computers. You must take a quiz after the instruction period. So it is important that you listen carefully. If you have any questions during the instruction period, raise your hand and your question will be answered so everyone can hear. If any difficulties arise after the experiment has begun, raise your hand, and an experimenter will come and assist you.

The subjects will be divided into two groups, containing 10 subjects each. The groups will be labeled the RED group and the BLUE group. To determine which color you are, will you each please select an envelope as the experimenter passes by you.

[EXPERIMENTER PASS OUT ENVELOPES]

If you chose BLUE, you will be BLUE for the entire experiment. If you chose RED, you will be RED for the entire experiment. Please remember your color, because the instructions are slightly different for the BLUE and the RED subjects.

In this experiment, you will be playing the following game, for real money.

First, you are matched with an opponent of the opposite color. There are two piles of money: a Large Pile and a Small Pile. At the beginning of the game the Large Pile has 40 cents and the Small Pile has 10 cents.

RED has the first move and can either "Pass" or "Take." If RED chooses "Take," RED gets the Large Pile of 40 cents, BLUE gets the small pile of 10 cents, and the game is over. If RED chooses "Pass," both piles double and it is BLUE's turn.

The Large Pile now contains 80 cents and the Small Pile 20 cents. BLUE can take or pass. If BLUE takes, BLUE ends up with the Large Pile of 80 cents and RED ends up with the Small Pile of 20 cents and the game is over. If BLUE passes, both piles double and it is RED's turn again.

This continues for a total of six turns, or three turns for each player. On each move, if a player takes, he or she gets the Large Pile, his or her opponent gets the Small Pile, and the game is over. If the player passes, both piles double again and it is the other player's turn.

The last move of the game is move six, and is BLUE's move (if the game even gets this far). The Large Pile now contains $12.80 and the Small Pile contains $3.20. If BLUE takes, BLUE gets the Large Pile of $12.80 and RED gets the Small Pile of $3.20. If BLUE passes, then the piles double again. RED then gets the Large Pile, containing $25.60, and BLUE gets the Small Pile, containing $6.40. This is summarized in the following table.

PAYOFF CHART FOR DECISION EXPERIMENT

		Move #				Large Pile	Small Pile	RED's Payoff	BLUE's Payoff
1	2	3	4	5	6				
T						.40	.10	.40	.10
P	T					.80	.20	.20	.80
P	P	T				1.60	.40	1.60	.40
P	P	P	T			3.20	.80	.80	3.20
P	P	P	P	T		6.40	1.60	6.40	1.60
P	P	P	P	P	T	12.80	3.20	3.20	12.80
P	P	P	P	P	P	25.60	6.40	25.60	6.40

[EXPERIMENTER HAND OUT PAYOFF TABLE]

Go over table to explain what is in each column and row.

The experiment consists of 10 games. In each game, you are matched with a different player of the opposite color from yours. Thus, if you are a BLUE player, in each game, you will be matched with a RED player. If you are a RED player, in each game you are matched with a BLUE player.

832   R. D. MCKELVEY AND T. R. PALFREY

Since there are ten subjects of each color, this means that you will be matched with each of the subjects of the other color *exactly* once. So if your label is RED, you will be matched with each of the BLUE subjects *exactly* once. If you are BLUE, you will be matched with each of the RED subjects *exactly* once.

We will now begin the computer instruction session. Will all the BLUE subjects please move to the terminals on the left side of the room, and all the RED subjects move to the terminals on the right side of the room.

[SUBJECTS MOVE TO CORRECT TERMINALS]

During the instruction session, we will teach you how to use the computer by going through a few practice games. During the instruction session, *do not hit any keys until you are told to do so*, and when you are told to enter information, *type exactly what you are told to type*. You are not paid for these practice games.

Please turn on your computer now by pushing the button labeled "MASTER" on the right hand side of the panel underneath the screen.

[WAIT FOR SUBJECTS TO TURN ON COMPUTERS]

When the computer prompts you for your name, type your full name. Then hit the ENTER key.

[WAIT FOR SUBJECTS TO ENTER NAMES]

When you are asked to enter your color, type R if your color is RED, and B if your color is BLUE. Then hit ENTER.

[WAIT FOR SUBJECTS TO ENTER COLORS]

You now see the experiment screen. Throughout the experiment, the bottom of the screen will tell you what is currently happening, and the top will tell you the history of what happened in the previous games. Since the experiment has not begun yet, the top part of the screen is currently empty. The bottom part of the screen tells you your subject number and your color. It also tells you the subject number of the player you are matched against in the first game. Is there anyone whose color is not correct?

[WAIT FOR RESPONSE]

Please record your color and subject number on the top left hand corner of your record sheet. Also record the number of the subject you are matched against in the first game.

Each game is represented by a row in the upper screen, and the player you will be matched with in each of the ten games appears in the column labeled "OPP" (which stands for "opponent") on the right side of the screen. It is important to note that you will never be paired with the same player twice.

We will now start the first practice game. Remember, do not hit any keys until you are told to do so.

[MASTER HIT KEY TO START FIRST GAME]

You now see on the bottom part of the screen that the first game has begun, and you are told who you are matched against. If you are a RED player, you are told that it is your move, and are given a description of the choices available to you. If you are a BLUE player, you are told that it is your opponent's move, and are told the choices available to your opponent.

Will all the RED players now choose PASS by typing in P on your terminals now.

[WAIT FOR SUBJECTS TO CHOOSE]

Since RED chose P, this is recorded on the top part of the screen with a P in the first RED column, and the cursor has moved on to the second column, which is BLUE, indicating that it is BLUE's move.

On the bottom part of the screen, the BLUE players are now told that it is their turn to choose, and are told the choices they can make. The RED players are told that it is their opponent's turn to choose, and are told the choices that their opponent can make. Notice, that there is now a Large Pile of $.80 and a Small Pile of $.20.

Will all the BLUE players now please choose TAKE by typing T at your terminal now.

[WAIT FOR SUBJECTS TO CHOOSE]

Since BLUE chose T, the first game has ended. On the bottom part of the screen, you are told that the game is over, and that the next game will begin shortly. On the top part of the screen, BLUE's move is recorded with a T in the second column. The payoffs from the first game for both yourself and your opponent are recorded on the right hand side of the screen in the columns labeled "Payoff." Your own payoff is in your color. That of your opponent is in the opponent's color.

Please record your own payoff on the record sheet that is provided.

[WAIT FOR SUBJECTS TO RECORD PAYOFFS]

You are not being paid for the practice session, but if this were the real experiment, then the payoff you have recorded would be money you have earned from the first game, and you would be paid this amount for that game at the end of the experiment. The total you earn over all ten real games is what you will be paid for your participation in the experiment.

We will now proceed to the second practice game.

[MASTER HIT KEY TO START SECOND GAME]

You now see that you have been matched with a new player of the opposite color, and that the second game has begun. Does everyone see this?

[WAIT FOR RESPONSE]

The rules for the second game are exactly like the first. The RED player gets the first move.

[DO RED-P, BLUE-P, RED-P]

Now notice that it is BLUE's move. It is the last move of the game. The Large Pile now contains $3.20, and the Small Pile contains $.80. If the BLUE player chooses TAKE, then the game ends. The BLUE player receives the Large Pile and the RED player receives the Small Pile. If the BLUE player chooses PASS, both piles double, and *then* the game ends. The RED player receives the Large Pile, which now contains $6.40, and the BLUE player receives the Small Pile, containing $1.60.

Will the BLUE player please choose PASS by typing P at your terminal now.

[WAIT FOR SUBJECTS TO CHOOSE]

The second practice game is now over. Please record your payoff on the second line of your record sheet.

[WAIT FOR PLAYERS TO RECORD PAYOFFS]
[MASTER HIT KEY TO START THIRD GAME]

We now go to the third practice game. Notice again that you have a new opponent. Will all the RED players please choose TAKE by typing T at your terminal now.

[WAIT FOR PLAYERS TO CHOOSE]

Since the RED player chose TAKE on the first move, the game is over, and we proceed on to the next game. Since RED chose TAKE on the first move, BLUE did not get any chance to move.

Please record your payoff for the third game on the third line of your record sheet.

[WAIT FOR PLAYERS TO RECORD PAYOFFS]

This concludes the practice session. In the actual experiment there will be ten games instead of three, and, of course, it will be up to you to make your own decisions. At the end of game ten, the experiment ends and we will pay each of you privately, in cash, the TOTAL amount you have accumulated during all ten games, plus your guaranteed five dollar participation fee. No other person will be told how much cash you earned in the experiment. You need not tell any other participants how much you earned.

Are there any questions before we pass out the quiz?

[EXPERIMENTER TAKE QUESTIONS]

O.K., then we will now have you take the quiz.

[PASS OUT QUIZ]
[COLLECT AND MARK QUIZZES]
[HAND QUIZZES BACK AND GO THRU CORRECT ANSWERS]

834   R. D. MCKELVEY AND T. R. PALFREY

We will now begin with the actual experiment. If there are any problems from this point on, raise your hand and an experimenter will come and assist you. When the computer asks for your name, please start as before by typing in your name. Wait for the computer to ask for your color, then respond with the correct color.

[START EXPERIMENT]
[CHECK THAT COLORS ARE OK BEFORE BEGINNING EXPERIMENT]

APPENDIX C

Experimental Data

The following tables give the data for our experiment. Each row represents a subject. The columns are

Col 1:   Session number
Col 2:   Subject number of Red Player
Col 2 + j: Outcome of game j. Letting k be the entry in this column, and n be the number of moves in the game ($n = 4$ for Exp. 1–4, $n = 6$ for Exp. 5–7), then

$$k = \begin{cases} \leqslant n \Rightarrow & \text{game ended with } T \text{ on move } k, \\ = n + 1 \Rightarrow & \text{game ended with } P \text{ on move } n. \end{cases}$$

The matching scheme was: In game j, Red subject i is matched with Blue subject $[(i + j - 1) \bmod m]$, where m is the number of subjects of each color in the session. Thus, with ten subjects of each color, in the first game, Red i is matched with Blue i. In the second game, Red i is matched with Blue $1 + i$, except Red 10, who is matched with Blue 1.

1	1	3	3	3	3	2	3	2	2	2	3
1	2	4	2	4	4	4	4	2	4	4	2
1	3	3	3	2	2	3	3	3	4	3	2
1	4	4	3	3	4	3	2	3	3	3	2
1	5	2	1	3	1	3	3	3	3	2	2
1	6	5	3	4	3	5	4	4	3	3	3
1	7	4	2	2	3	4	3	2	3	2	3
1	8	2	1	5	4	1	3	3	4	3	3
1	9	3	3	4	3	2	2	3	1	3	2
1	10	4	2	4	2	3	1	3	3	2	5

SESSION 1
(Four move, PCC)

2	1	4	4	3	3	2	4	2	2	2
2	2	2	1	4	1	3	2	2	2	1
2	3	3	3	2	2	1	1	1	1	1
2	4	3	3	3	3	3	2	3	2	3
2	5	3	4	2	3	2	3	3	2	3
2	6	3	3	3	2	3	3	2	3	2
2	7	2	4	3	4	5	2	3	2	2
2	8	3	2	3	3	2	3	2	3	2
2	9	2	4	2	3	4	2	3	2	2

SESSION 2
(Four move, PCC)

CENTIPEDE GAME

3	1	3	4	2	3	2	3	2	2	1	3
3	2	4	2	2	2	4	2	2	5	4	3
3	3	2	2	1	1	2	1	1	3	3	2
3	4	3	2	3	2	2	3	3	3	3	2
3	5	3	5	2	2	3	4	3	3	2	3
3	6	5	2	2	5	4	4	4	2	2	2
3	7	2	3	5	4	2	3	2	2	2	1
3	8	2	3	3	3	3	2	2	2	5	2
3	9	5	4	5	5	2	2	2	2	4	4
3	10	4	4	3	2	2	3	3	2	2	3

SESSION 3
(Four move, CIT)

4	1	2	4	5	4	2	4	4	2	4	4
4	2	3	3	2	2	2	1	1	1	3	2
4	3	4	2	3	2	3	2	3	3	2	3
4	4	2	3	2	3	2	3	3	2	2	2
4	5	3	3	3	2	5	4	2	2	2	1
4	6	3	3	2	5	4	2	2	2	2	2
4	7	3	3	5	4	2	1	3	2	1	1
4	8	3	5	4	2	3	3	2	2	2	3
4	9	3	3	3	3	3	2	2	3	3	2
4	10	3	2	1	1	1	1	1	1	1	1

SESSION 4
(Four move, High payoff, CIT)

5	1	5	5	7	4	4	2	4	2	4	3
5	2	3	3	3	3	3	4	2	3	2	2
5	3	5	4	4	3	4	3	3	3	3	5
5	4	3	3	3	3	3	3	3	3	3	3
5	5	5	4	4	3	5	4	4	5	5	1
5	6	4	3	4	3	4	3	3	3	3	3
5	7	3	3	3	3	3	3	5	4	4	2
5	8	5	5	4	4	3	3	3	3	2	1
5	9	5	5	5	5	5	4	4	2	4	4
5	10	5	4	5	5	4	5	2	4	4	6

SESSION 5
(Six move, CIT)

6	1	5	6	4	5	5	5	6	5	4
6	2	6	5	7	4	6	4	4	4	4
6	3	4	5	5	4	5	4	4	4	5
6	4	5	5	5	4	5	4	4	5	5
6	5	4	5	6	6	4	4	5	4	5
6	6	4	2	5	4	4	4	4	7	6
6	7	4	6	4	4	3	4	3	5	4
6	8	2	5	4	5	4	5	4	6	5
6	9	5	4	5	4	5	4	4	3	4

SESSION 6
(Six move, PCC)

7	1	4	4	4	3	3	4	3	3	3	3
7	2	2	5	4	2	5	4	3	5	3	4
7	3	5	3	2	5	5	4	5	5	4	4
7	4	4	2	5	4	6	6	5	4	4	4
7	5	2	5	5	4	5	6	4	4	4	4
7	6	7	6	6	6	5	4	4	4	4	6
7	7	6	4	4	6	4	4	4	4	6	6
7	8	4	5	5	4	4	5	5	4	5	4
7	9	4	3	5	5	5	4	4	5	4	4
7	10	6	4	2	4	3	2	3	3	4	3

SESSION 7
(Six move, PCC)

REFERENCES

AUMANN, R. (1988): "Preliminary Notes on Integrating Irrationality into Game Theory," Mimeo, International Conference on Economic Theories of Politics, Haifa.
—— (1987): "Correlated Equilibrium as an Expression of Bayesian Rationality," *Econometrica*, 55, 1–18.
BINMORE, K. (1987): "Modeling Rational Players," *Economics and Philosophy*, 3, 179–214.
CAMERER, C., AND K. WEIGELT (1988): "Experimental Tests of a Sequential Equilibrium Reputation Model," *Econometrica*, 56, 1–36.
COOPER, R., D. DEJONG, R. FORSYTHE, AND T. ROSS (1990): "Selection Criteria in Coordination Games," *American Economic Review*, 80, 218–233.
FUDENBERG, D., AND E. MASKIN (1986): "The Folk Theorem in Repeated Games with Discounting and Incomplete Information," *Econometrica*, 54, 533–554.
GUTH, W., P. OCKENFELS, AND M. WENDEL (1991): "Efficiency by Trust in Fairness?—Multiperiod Ultimatum Bargaining Experiments with an Increasing Cake," Technical Report, J. W. Goethe Universitat, Frankfurt.
HARSANYI, J. C. (1967–68): "Games of Incomplete Information Played by Bayesian Players," Parts (I, II, and III). *Management Science*, 14, 159–182, 320–334, 486–502.
JUNG, Y., J. KAGEL, AND D. LEVIN (1989): "On the Existence of Predatory Pricing in the Laboratory: An Experimental Study of Reputation and Entry Deterrence in the Chain-Store Game," Mimeo.
KREPS, D. M. (1990): *A Course in Microeconomic Theory*. New Jersey: Princeton University Press.
KREPS, D., P. MILGROM, J. ROBERTS, AND R. WILSON (1982): "Rational Cooperation in the Finitely Repeated Prisoner's Dilemma," *Journal of Economic Theory*, 27, 245–252.
KREPS, D. M., AND R. WILSON (1982a): "Reputation and Imperfect Information," *Journal of Economic Theory*, 27, 253–279.
—— (1982b): "Sequential Equilibria," *Econometrica*, 50, 863–894.
MCKELVEY, R. D. (1990): "GAMBIT: Interactive Extensive Form Game Program," Mimeo, California Institute of Technology.
MEGIDDO, N. (1986): "Remarks on Bounded Rationality," Technical Report, IBM Research Report RJ 54310, Computer Science.
NERAL, JOHN, AND JACK OCHS (1989): "The Sequential Equilibrium Theory of Reputation Building: A Further Test," mimeo, University of Pittsburgh.
PALFREY, T. R., AND H. ROSENTHAL (1988): "Private Incentives in Social Dilemmas: The Effects of Incomplete Information and Altruism," *Journal of Public Economics*, 35, 309–332.
RENY, P. (1988): "Rationality, Common Knowledge, and the Theory of Games," Technical Report, University of Western Ontario.
ROSENTHAL, R. (1982): "Games of Perfect Information, Predatory Pricing, and the Chain Store Paradox," *Journal of Economic Theory*, 25, 92–100.
SELTEN, R., AND R. STOECKER (1986): "End Behavior in Sequences of Finite Prisoner's Dilemma Supergames," *Journal of Economic Behavior and Organization*, 7, 47–70.
SMITH, V. (1976): "Experimental Economics: Induced Value Theory," *American Economic Review*, 66, 274–279.

[20]

Repeated Play, Cooperation and Coordination: An Experimental Study

THOMAS R. PALFREY

California Institute of Technology

and

HOWARD ROSENTHAL

Princeton University

First version received August 1992; final version accepted March 1994 (Eds.)

An experiment was conducted to test whether discounted repeated play leads to greater cooperation and coordination than one-shot play in a public good environment with incomplete information. The experiment was designed so that, theoretically, repeated play can sustain equilibria with substantially higher group earnings than result in the one-shot Bayesian Nash equilibrium. The design varied a number of environmental parameters, including the size of the group, and the statistical distribution of marginal rates of substitution between the public and private good. Marginal rates of substitution were private information but the statistical distribution was common knowledge. The results indicate that repetition leads to greater cooperation, and that the magnitude of these gains depends systematically both on the ability of players to monitor each other's strategy and on the environmental parameters.

1. INTRODUCTION

The theory of repeated games[1] has developed rapidly in the last ten years. A common theme of the work in this area is that repetition enables players to reach outcomes that would otherwise not be possible. Of particular interest is the fact that cooperative outcomes can be sustained as noncooperative equilibria of repeated games even though they fail to be equilibrium outcomes in the stage-game. Competitive players can do better with repetition than without repetition. On the other hand, one difficulty of most of this theory is that nearly everything can be supported as an equilibrium in the repeated game, not only the cooperative outcome. Thus, to say that cooperation is a clear prediction of the theory is too strong. Nevertheless, the suggestion that repetition of a stage game whose Nash equilibria are not Pareto optimal will usually lead to better outcomes is widely viewed as an implication of the theory.

As an empirical matter, this proposition invites testing. The literature in experimental economics and experimental psychology contains many studies of finitely repeated games.[2]

---

1. See Fudenberg and Tirole (1991, Ch. 5) for an extensive bibliography.
2. This dates back to work in the 50s and 60s on repeated bimatrix games, which is surveyed in Rapoport and Orwant (1962) and Gallo and McClintock (1965). Much of that research did not use financial incentives to induce the payoff matrices. There has been extensive work on finitely repeated games of cooperation in many settings, including public goods provision (Isaac and Walker (1991) and the articles they cite), oligopoly games (Friedman (1967, 1969), Alger (1987), Davis and Holt (1990), common pool resource usage (Walker, Ostrom, and Gardner (1990) and Ostrom and Walker (1991)) and other settings.

In contrast, to our surprise few laboratory experiments have been conducted which attempted to induce an infinite-horizon discounted supergame in a laboratory. In addition, there is a paucity of research on the corresponding one-shot games.

Most existing evidence about one-shot games of this sort comes either from the last round of play of a finitely repeated game with a known terminal period, or from experiments where subjects played the game only once.[3] The terminal period results (which generally indicate less cooperation in the terminal period[4]) are suspect because, in the context of a repeated game it is difficult to distinguish between the use of trigger strategies, as opposed to simply myopic one-shot play. The single play results (virtually all of it in the context of public goods provision)[5] are open to the criticism that subjects lacked sufficient task experience. In fact, task inexperience has been demonstrated to be an important factor in explaining cooperative play.[6]

An alternative, and we believe better, approach to studying one-shot games involves matching schemes so that each player's opponents change from game to game. This has been used in auction games[7] (Palfrey (1985)), bargaining games (Roth and Murnighan (1982)), and elsewhere in situations where collusion or supergame effects are thought to be potentially important (McKelvey and Palfrey (1992)). We have elsewhere used a version of this design technique to study one-shot public goods games (Palfrey and Rosenthal (1991a, b)), and it is becoming the standard methodology for studying one-shot games.

The experiment reported in this paper was designed explicitly to permit a careful comparison of one-shot games with the corresponding discounted, infinitely repeated games. Roughly half of our data is generated by a repeated design, in which a group of individuals play the same game repeatedly with a random stopping rule. The other half of the data is a one-shot design, where individuals play the same game many times, but group assignments are randomly and anonymously reassigned after each game is played. The experiment involved over two hundred subjects and thousands of stage games, which varied in their payoff matrices, information conditions, number of players, and monitoring technologies.

The basic stage games played were all variants of the well-known voluntary contribution public goods game where the production and contribution decisions are binary: a public good is produced if at least W of N players contribute a private good. The stage game also has an element of private information, in that players have different, privately known marginal rates of substitution between the private good and public good.

We use our data to investigate to what extent, and in what ways, repeated games can improve the degree to which the players coordinate and produce the public good. The stage game in fact presents two impediments to collective action as a result of the "threshold" nature of the public good technology. First, a player who believes the threshold is being met by others finds it in his interest to "free ride" and not contribute. Second, a

---

3. Since we began running the experiments reported here, there has been a flurry of independent experimental research aimed at comparing one-shot play and repeated play in prisoner dilemma games and related environments. This includes work by Prisbrey (1991), Cooper *et al.* (1991), Andreoni and Miller (1991), McCabe *et al.* (1991), and others. The only earlier work we are aware of that was explicitly designed for a one-shot vs. repeated game comparison is by Andreoni (1988), who uses random matching schemes to emulate one-shot voluntary contribution games.

4. See, for example, Selten and Stoecker (1988) for evidence about the terminal period of a finitely repeated prisoners' dilemma game, or Isaac, Walker and Thomas (1984) and subsequent work on finitely repeated voluntary contribution games.

5. Marwell and Ames (1979, 1980, 1981) and Schneider and Pommerhene (1981).

6. Isaac, Walker and Thomas (1984) and Andreoni (1988).

7. Most auction experiments have not used random matching schemes.

player who believes the threshold will not be met, even with his contribution, finds it in his interest not to contribute.

Players' strategic calculations weigh these two disincentives against the potential benefit from obtaining the public good. Since opportunities to coordinate in the one-shot game are absent, it is reasonable to expect that players will only use symmetric strategies represented by "cutpoints": if the value of the private good is below the cutpoint, contribute; otherwise, do not. The stable equilibria for such strategies, for the parameters we have chosen, are Pareto suboptimal and involve no contribution or relatively low rates of contribution.

When the games are repeated, Pareto-improving outcomes with higher levels of contribution can be sustained, even when the players continue to use symmetric cutpoint strategies. The expectation of future reciprocation diminishes the effect of the current incentive to free ride. An even higher degree of coordination could be achieved if the players could get together and sign a binding agreement that treated everyone symmetrically. They could agree to always meet the contribution threshold exactly. A random device would determine who would contribute for each repetition of the stage game. Such an agreement would lead to ex ante efficient behaviour. Decentralized (without contracting) versions of such agreements can always be sustained, for our parameters, in the repeated game. For example, we might observe rotation. In a 2 of 3 game, players "B" and "C" could contribute on the first round, "A" and "C" on the second, "A" and "B" on the third, "B" and "C" on the fourth, and so on. Alternatively, the players might separate, asymmetrically, into sets of "contributors" and "non-contributors." The above discussion suggests three distinct patterns of behaviour that might be observed under repeated play:

1. Symmetric cutpoints higher than the one-shot cutpoints.
2. Separation into roles of contributor and free-rider.
3. Rotation schemes.

The expected patterns of behaviour that would be exhibited under these three different solutions to the inefficiency problem are very different,[8] with the exception of unanimity games (where all of the private good is required for production of the public good). In this case, the three varieties collapse into a single repeated play equilibrium where all contribute.

What we observe in the repeated laboratory games is closest to the first two of these three patterns. On average, individuals contribute more under the repeated-game treatment than in the one-shot treatment. Although there is greater variance across individuals in their contribution rates in repeated games than in one-shot games, there is only very weak evidence indicating the second pattern. Indeed, only a few subjects were pure or almost pure free riders and no subject was a pure contributor. We do not observe any group rotation schemes that would support the third pattern. Only one individual rotated throughout an entire repeated game session. His behaviour was not reciprocated by the other members of his group; they used simple cutpoint strategies. While a few individuals at times may have attempted to encourage other players to rotate by systematically alternating their own contribution choices, these attempts invariably fail. Our results contrast sharply with results for analogous symmetric *two-person* games with complete information, where efficient alternation often emerges after only a few repetitions (Prisbrey (1991)).

---

8. Ostrom (1990) emphasizes the enormous variety of ways groups find to overcome these free rider/coordination problems in naturally occurring versions of the related "commons" problem. These include examples of rotation schemes that she documents, as well as other arrangements.

We suspect that, without communication, the coordination problem with more than two players is too complicated to overcome simply by repeated play. Even with communication, the coordination problem is by no means easy to overcome. In a one-shot game with preplay communication, Palfrey and Rosenthal (1991a) find no efficiency gain compared with no communication. In one-shot battle of the sexes games, Cooper *et al.* (1989) find increased efficiency with one-way communication, where the communicator effectively chooses the asymmetric equilibrium that favours her. Neither Palfrey and Rosenthal nor Cooper *et al.* have a repeated-game design, so alternation schemes are not possible.

Indeed, we find that the extent to which repeated play improves over one-shot play appears to be small. Not only do earnings fail to reach the ex ante efficient level that could be produced by rotation, they generally fail to reach the level that could be achieved by symmetric cutpoint strategies. In contrast, aggregate earnings in the one-shot play setting are almost perfectly predicted by the noncooperative solution (Palfrey and Rosenthal (1991a)). This contrast between our one-shot and repeated play results is not encouraging news for those who might wish to interpret as gospel the oft-spoken suggestion that repeated play with discount rates close to one leads to more cooperative behaviour. True enough, it does—but not by much.

Perhaps this is not surprising, given both the general difficulty of free-rider problems and the difficulty of the coordination problem in the experiment we conducted. After all, our experimental games had more than two players, incomplete information, and, in some cases, multiple symmetric equilibria in the one-shot game. The power of repeated play might be more forceful in simpler experimental environments. But we suspect that the power of repeated play is, if anything, even less forceful in the more complex natural settings that we are ultimately trying to understand. While repeated play makes possible cooperative gains, other ingredients are also needed for the lion's share of these gains to be reaped.

2. THE BASIC PUBLIC GOODS GAME

All the experiments are based on the *step level public goods game*. There are N players, each of whom has an endowment of a single indivisible unit of the private good. A simultaneous move game is played where each player has two pure actions to choose from: *contribute* and *not contribute*. If at least W players contribute, a public good is produced, each contributor receives a payoff of V, and each non-contributor receives a payoff of $V + c_i$ where c_i is the private value of player i's endowment. If less than W players contribute, each contributor receives a payoff of 0 and the non-contributors each receive a payoff of c_i. Table 1 gives the payoff matrix for a simple version of the game, where $W = 2$, $N = 2$.

The private endowment values are independent draws from an identical commonly known distribution, $F(c)$. Each subject observes his own private endowment value before moving, but does not observe the other players' private endowment values.

We conducted both one-shot and repeated-game versions for a variety of different parameters of N, W, and $F(\cdot)$. In the repeated-game versions, the value of c_i is redrawn before each play of the game. We also employ an additional treatment variable in the repeated games, which affects the ability of players to monitor the strategies of the other players. In one condition, players are informed of their opponents' moves and their opponents' private endowment values after each play of the game; in the other condition, players are only informed of their opponents' moves. The details of the experimental design are given in the next section.

TABLE 1

The step level public goods game when $W=2$, $N=2$

| | Player 2 | |
	contribute	not contribute
Player 1 contribute	1, 1	0, c_2
not contribute	c_1, 0	c_1, c_2

3. EXPERIMENTAL VERSION OF THE PUBLIC GOODS GAME

The subjects were 228 students recruited from the campuses of Carnegie-Mellon University, California Institute of Technology, and Pasadena Community College. Except where noted in Table 2, each session was run on networked personal computers. Subjects participated in a sequence of three sessions, one immediately following the other.[9] Component sessions in a triple session typically employed different treatments (for example, a change in the parameters). Table 2 provides the details. Each subject was paid privately in cash immediately following the final session. A triple session lasted between 45 minutes and 2 hours, including the preliminaries (instructions, questions and answers, quiz, and practice rounds). No subject participated in more than one triple session. Some Caltech subjects had prior experience with computerized double-auction market experiments.

All subjects were seated at terminals, separated by partitions, and assigned identification numbers. Instructions were read aloud to everyone at the same time.[10] Each session was divided into a sequence of periods (or rounds). In each period, the subjects were either divided into three-person or four-person groups. Each group then independently played the following game.

Each subject was endowed with a "token," with value of c_i payoff units (an artificial laboratory currency with a publicly known dollar-exchange rate). The computer screen displayed the individual's token value but not the token values of other group members. Thus, prior to play of a stage game, individual token values were always private information. Subjects were told that they could either "spend" their own token or "keep" it. If at least W subjects in a group chose "spend," then each member in the group earned V payoff units. In addition, non-spenders also earned their token values. If there were fewer than W spenders in the group, spenders earned 0 and non-spenders earned their token values. Token values were drawn independently from a uniform distribution using a random device on the computer in one-unit increments between 1 and a known maximum token value, C. This distribution was publicly announced and explained aloud to subjects during the instruction period.

To ensure that, insofar as possible, all aspects of the game except for the exact draws of token values and the personal identities of the other members in the group were common knowledge, we used the following procedure. First, the rules were publicly announced in great detail. Second, two practice games were played, to help the subjects familiarize themselves with the keyboard and the computer screen. Third, a quiz was given after the

9. Three of the nine-subject sessions were run as single sessions, rather than as triple sessions.
10. Palfrey and Rosenthal (1992) contains a copy of the instructions for one of the sessions.

TABLE 2A

Description of random group experiments

Date	Site	W	N	Range	Cents	C	Subjs.	Rounds	Reveal
7/13/88	CIT	1	3	90	0·5	1·5	12	30	No
2/15/89	CMU	1	3	90	0·3	1·5	12	20	No
2/16/89	CMU	1	3	90	0·3	1·5	12	20	No
7/31/89	CIT	1	3	90	0·3	1·5	12	20	No
8/8/89	CIT	1	3	90	0·3	1·5	12	18	Yes
1/22/87	CIT	2	3	90	1	1·5	9	20	No
12/3/87	CIT	2	3	90	1	1·5	9	20	No
12/20/87	CIT	2	3	90	1	1·5	9	20	No
2/15/89	CMU	2	3	90	0·3	1·5	12	20	No
2/16/89	CMU	2	3	90	0·3	1·5	12	20	No
7/31/89	CIT	2	3	90	0·3	1·5	12	20	No
8/8/89	CIT	2	3	90	0·3	1·5	12	20	Yes
4/27/89	CMU	2	3	90	0·7	2·25	12	20	No
5/2/89	CMU	2	3	90	0·7	2·25	12	20	No
8/3/89	CIT	3	3	204	0·1	0·995	12	25	No
9/4/91	CIT	3	3	204	0·1	0·995	12	20	No
7/21/88	CIT	3	3	90	0·5	1·5	12	30	No
2/15/89	CMU	3	3	90	0·3	1·5	12	20	No
2/16/89	CMU	3	3	90	0·3	1·5	12	20	No
7/26/89	CIT	2	4	204	0·1	2·22	12	17	No
7/31/89	CIT	2	4	90	0·3	2·25	12	20	No
8/8/89	CIT	2	4	90	0·3	2·25	12	20	Yes

practice rounds. Any incorrect answers by a subject were corrected in private, and all the correct answers were read aloud and explained.

After the quiz, the first stage game began. After every subject had made a spending decision, all subjects were told what the other members in their group did, their payoffs were calculated for them, and the session then proceeded to the next game (period). In the new game, subjects' new token values were again drawn randomly by the same procedure as the last game, independently from past draws. During the course of a session, subjects could press a key to obtain a history of previous games they had played.

Experimental treatments

There were two primary treatment variables: the parameters of the game, and whether the groups were randomly reassigned after each round or were fixed for the entire session. The sessions where groups were randomly reassigned after each play of the game approximate the case of "one-shot" play of the game. The sessions where groups were fixed approximate "repeated" play. The fixed-group treatment also incorporated a secondary treatment that varied the degree to which players could monitor the strategies of the other members of their group.

3.1. Parameters

The parameters varied were the threshold, W, the group size, N, and the maximum marginal rate of substitution of the private good for the public good, C/V. A total of six different parameter conditions were used. Table 2 summarizes the relevant design information.

TABLE 2B

Description of repeated group experiments

Date	W	N	Range	Cents	C	Subjs.	Rounds	Reveal
7/25/89	1	3	204	0·1	1·5	12	21	No
8/9/89	1	3	90	0·3	1·5	12	20	Yes
7/27/89	1	3	204	0·1	1·5	12	47	Yes
7/25/89	2	3	204	0·1	1·5	12	27	No
7/27/89	2	3	204	0·1	1·5	12	34	Yes
7/27/89	2	3	204	0·1	1·5	12	29	No
8/2/89	2	3	204	0·1	1·5	12	22	No
8/2/89	2	3	204	0·1	1·5	12	67	Yes
8/2/89	2	3	204	0·1	1·5	12	20	No
8/9/89	2	3	90	0·3	1·5	12	20	Yes
7/25/89	2	3	204	0·1	2·22	12	61	No
8/3/89	3	3	204	0·1	0·995	12	20	No
8/3/89	3	3	204	0·1	0·995	12	31	Yes
6/11/91	3	3	204	0·1	0·995	9	20	Yes
9/4/91	3	3	204	0·15	0·995	12	30	No
10/29/91	3	3	204	0·12	0·995	12	20	No
10/29/91	3	3	204	0·12	0·995	12	29	Yes
6/11/91	3	3	204	0·1	1·5	9	27	Yes
6/11/91	3	3	204	0·1	1·5	9	20	· Yes
9/4/91	3	3	204	0·15	1·5	12	20	No
10/29/91	3	3	204	0·12	1·5	12	34	No
8/9/89	2	4	90	0·3	2·25	12	20	No

Notes to Table 2:
Payoff unit This gives the upper end of the uniform (in integers) distribution of endowments in payoff units. This number and $\bar{C}$ can be used to calculate the payoff unit value of the public benefit, $B = $ payoff unit$/\bar{C}$.
Cents The number of cents paid per payoff unit earned in the experiment.
Subjects The number of subjects in the experiment.
Rounds The number of (non-practice) rounds for the given (W, N, C) parameters. In repeated groups after the first 20 rounds, a ten-sided die was tossed to see if the game continued. The stopping probability was 0·1.
Reveal "Yes" means all token values were revealed after each round. Subjects could match the individual token values and the decisions of the other members of their group. "No" means token values were not revealed.
Site All of the sessions in Table 2B were conducted at the California Institute of Technology (CIT) site. The sessions conducted on 9/4/91 used students enrolled at Pasadena Community College. Some of the 1989 CIT sessions included subjects who were enrolled in a special CIT summer programme for high school students.
Other The second session on 7/27/89 ended because of an unexpected computer crash following round 29. The second session on 8/2/89 had a computer crash in the eighth round, but was restarted and eventually lasted a total of 67 rounds. All three sessions on 8/9/89 were terminated immediately after round 20, without rolling a die.

3.2. *Random groups vs. fixed groups*

In the "repeated" condition, each subject was assigned to a group whose membership was the same in every game of that treatment and everyone was told this.

An "infinite horizon" was induced with a random stopping rule to determine when the repeated game would end. Each repeated game began with a sequence of 20 games. After the twentieth game, a ten-sided die was rolled, and the repeated game ended if a 4 was rolled. Otherwise, the session continued on to the 21st game. The rolling of the die followed every game thereafter, until a 4 was finally rolled.[11]

11. The longest repeated game lasted for 67 periods.

In the random-group condition (or "one-shot" condition), subjects were randomly reassigned to a new group after every game. They were never told the identity of current, future, or past group members. Each random treatment session lasted a fixed number of games, and subjects were informed of this before the first game was played.

3.3. The "Reveal" treatment: perfect vs. imperfect monitoring

In addition, there was a secondary treatment variable, called "Reveal." In some of the sessions, after a game was played, subjects were informed of the token values as well as the choices of everyone in their group. These sessions are referred to as "Reveal" sessions, and other sessions are called "No-Reveal" sessions. The motivation for the Reveal/No-Reveal manipulation is that theory suggests cooperation will be easier to sustain when the token values are revealed after each game, allowing subjects to more accurately monitor the other subjects' strategies. This monitoring permits a richer class of trigger strategies, which may be used to sustain higher contribution rates. In contrast, optimal rotation schemes can be supported even if token values are not revealed after each play of the stage game. This is discussed in more depth in the next section.

4. EQUILIBRIUM

4.1. Bayesian equilibrium in the one-shot game

The Bayesian equilibrium in a one-shot step level public goods game is characterized in Palfrey and Rosenthal (1991b). We summarize the main features below.

Without loss of generality, let $V = 1$. Assume F is differentiable and is strictly increasing between 0 and $C > 0$, with $F(0) = 0$, $F(C) = 1$ and density $f(c)$. A "cutpoint rule" for player i is a strategy with the property that there exists a critical cost, $\hat{c}_i$, such that i spends[12] if and only if $c_i \leq \hat{c}_i$.

In the one-shot game, it is easy to show that the optimal response for player i is always a cutpoint rule, given any strategy profile of the other players in the group. Therefore, we restrict attention to such strategies in our equilibrium analysis.

The basic features of the *symmetric* equilibria are as follows:

- In all equilibria $c^* \leq 1$ since contribution is a strictly dominated strategy when $c_i > 1$.
- If $W > 1$ then there always exists an equilibrium where all players adopt a cutpoint $c^* = 0$. That is, no-one ever spends. This is not the case if $W = 1$.
- If $W = N$, then there exists an equilibrium at $c^* = C$, if and only if $C \leq 1$.
- The interior equilibria are characterized as the set of all c^* between 0 and 1 that satisfy the equation:

$$c^* = Q(c^*, W, N, C) \tag{1}$$

where Q is the probability that a player is pivotal; this is the probability that exactly $W - 1$ out of the $N - 1$ players other than i contribute, given that they are using the cutpoint rule c^*, and given $F(\cdot)$. The exact formula for Q is:

$$Q(c^*, W, N, C) = \frac{(N-1)!}{(W-1)!(N-W)!} F(c^*)^{W-1}[1 - F(c^*)]^{N-W} \tag{2}$$

---

12. We use the terms "spend" and "contribute" interchangeably. In the actual experiment, we used the neutral "spend/keep" terminology.

The intuition is simple. The cutpoint is the point at which the opportunity cost of contributing equals the expected value of contributing. Since $V = 1$, this value is just the expected increase in the probability the public good will be produced.

- In all experiments F is uniformly distributed on $[0, C]$. For all experimental parameters with $W < N$, there is exactly one solution to (2) with $0 < c^* < 1$. This solution is "globally expectationally stable" (Palfrey and Rosenthal (1991*b*)), while the $c^* = 0$ equilibrium is unstable.
- If $W = N$, then $c^* = 0$ is the unique globally expectationally stable equilibrium for the experimental values of C.

Summarizing, for all parameter values of the games reported in this paper, there is a unique stable Bayes–Nash equilibrium to the one-shot game.

4.2. *Bayesian equilibria of the infinitely-repeated game with discounting*

Suppose the basic stage game is to be played an infinite number of times and players discount future payoffs with a common discount factor $\delta < 1$. (Recall that in the experiments the stage game is repeated 20 times, after which $\delta = 0 \cdot 9$ (termination probability of $0 \cdot 1$ in all subsequent periods). This was done to ensure that we had at least 20 rounds of observations for each repeated game. It is not difficult to show that any supergame equilibrium that can be supported with $\delta = 0 \cdot 9$ can be supported under the stopping rule we used.) As discussed in the introduction, it is natural to think of there being three distinct ways that repetition can lead to more efficient outcomes. These are: (A) repetition can support equilibrium cutpoints higher than the one-shot equilibrium cutpoints; (B) repetition can lead to a separation into some players who never contribute ("free riders") and others who frequently (or always) contribute ("activists"); (C) repetition can support time-varying cutpoint strategies in which players alternate between contribution and free riding (rotation schemes). In this section, we analyse one kind of supergame equilibrium that can arise for values of δ sufficiently close to 1, and characterize the critical value of δ needed to support these equilibria.[13]

A. *Optimal symmetric cutpoint strategies*

The Bayesian equilibrium in the one-shot game is inefficient. That is, there exist feasible outcomes with a higher expected surplus. The first-best solution has the W players with the lowest values of c_i contribute and the others not contribute, if and only if the sum of the W lowest values of c_i are less than or equal to N. Given the informational constraints, this is infeasible in the voluntary contribution game with the exception of the case when $W = N$ and $C \leqq 1$. A natural second-best solution to consider is a symmetric cutpoint rule that maximizes expected surplus.

For any given set of parameters, one can compute a value c^{**}, called the efficient group cutpoint, that represents the best symmetric cutpoint rule for the group as a whole. If everyone uses the cutpoint c^{**}, then, ex ante, each individual earns more than he would under any other rule that assigns a common cutpoint to all players. This rule will typically yield lower total expected payoffs to the group than the first-best solution, but higher payoffs than the best of the Bayes–Nash equilibria to the one-shot game.

---

13. A more complete characterization for all the different experimental parameters is given in Palfrey and Rosenthal (1992).

TABLE 3

Theoretical analysis results for the experimental parameters

	N	3	3	3	3	3	4
Parameters:	W	1	2	2	3	3	2
	C	1·5	1·5	2·25	1	1·5	2·25
Bayes one-shot symmetric cutpoints		0·47	0·38	0·0	0·0	0·0	0·30
Group optimal symmetric cutpoints		0·75	1·13	1·41	1·0	1·5	1·27
Earnings if endowments kept		0·75	0·75	1·13	0·5	0·75	1·13
Earnings for Bayes one-shot symmetric		1·35	0·86	1·13	0·5	0·75	1·19
Earnings for group optimal symmetric		1·44	1·17	1·20	1·0	1·0	1·48
Earnings for optimal rotation		1·5	1·25	1·75	1·0	1·0	2·13

The group optimal cutpoints can be calculated as follows. For any cutpoint $\hat{c}$, let

$$V(\hat{c}) = F(\hat{c})P_+(\hat{c}) - \int_0^{\hat{c}} cf(c)dc + (1 - F(\hat{c}))P_-(\hat{c})$$

denote the ex ante surplus to player i if everyone in the group (including i) uses $\hat{c}$ as a cutpoint rule, where

$$P_+(\hat{c}) = \sum_{j=W-1}^{N-1} Q(\hat{c}, j+1, N, C)$$

$$P_-(\hat{c}) = \sum_{j=W}^{N-1} Q(c^*, j+1, N, c)$$

are respectively, the probability the public good is provided if i contributes (P_+) and the probability the public good is provided if i does not contribute (P_-). Then a *group optimal cutpoint* is the cutpoint c^{**} that maximizes $V(\cdot)$[14]

The group optimal cutpoint can be supported as an equilibrium of the repeated game for all values of δ such that

$$P_+(c^{**}) - c^{**} + \frac{\delta}{1-\delta} V(c^{**}) \geq P_-(c^{**}) + \frac{\delta}{1-\delta} V_0$$

where V_0 is the value of the worst one-shot equilibrium payoff.[15] This inequality reduces to

$$\frac{\delta}{1-\delta} [V(c^{**}) - V_0] \geq c^{**} - Q(c^{**}, W, N, C).$$

It can be verified directly that this inequality holds for all of the experimental parameter values.

Often the optimal symmetric cutpoint lies strictly between 0 and C. This leads to a possible monitoring problem, if c_i is private information. When a player fails to contribute in a round, the other members of the group need to know his token value in order to ascertain whether the efficient cutpoint strategy has been violated, since punishment is appropriate only for "keepers" with token values below the cutpoint. This monitoring problem is eliminated in the "reveal treatment," since players are provided with the necessary information after each play of the game.

Table 3 summarizes the theoretical predictions for each parameter set. Finally, we next discuss briefly the other two ways repetition can improve efficiency, but do not go

14. In our experiment c^{**} is uniquely determined for all parameter values.
15. This gives an upper bound on the lowest value of δ that will support cooperation. This bound suffices for all of our experimental parameters.

into details because there is very little evidence for them in our experimental data. See Palfrey and Rosenthal (1992) for details.

B. Optimal asymmetric cutpoints

In the experiments where $1 < W < N$, there exist equilibria in the repeated game where the group divides into W players who always contribute and $N - W$ players who never contribute.[16] In general, these equilibria yield higher expected group payoffs than the optimal symmetric cutpoints, but there is considerable asymmetry in the expected payoffs to different members of the same group.

C. Optimal rotation schemes

In an optimal rotation scheme, in each round exactly W players contribute, regardless of their value of c_i, but the identity of the contributors rotates from round to round. For all of our experimental parameters, optimal rotation schemes are supportable in the repeated game. This is true *regardless* of whether the private c_i's are reported to all group members following the play in each round, since the strategies do not depend on c_i. These equilibria also generate approximately equal expected payoffs across group members and generate ex ante group payoffs higher than the optimal symmetric's cutpoint rules (except when $W = N$, in which case optimal symmetric cutpoint rules coincide with optimal rotation).

5. DATA ANALYSIS

We divide the data analysis into two parts. First we consider individual behaviour and organize the analysis of the data around the general observation that subjects in the experiment adopted cutpoint decision rules.[17] This leads to a natural comparison of the effects of the different treatment variables in terms of the differences in the distribution of measured cutpoint strategies. The second part of the analysis focuses on the central substantive issue we are investigating, namely the effect of repetition on efficiency. In that section we show that one-shot games generate efficiencies consistent with the Bayesian–Nash equilibrium predictions, and that repetition leads to higher efficiencies, but not as high as the theory of repeated games would suggest.

A. Individual behaviour

Dominance

In the one-shot games, if an individual contributes when $c_i > 1$, the player has taken a strictly dominated action. An initial hypothesis about rationality is that we should not observe such behaviour. In contrast, such strategies are not weakly dominated in the repeated games, and a natural hypothesis is that contribution rates when $c_i > 1$ will be

---

16. These roughly correspond to the asymmetric pure-strategy equilibria of a game of chicken, although for our experimental parameters, these are not one-shot equilibria.

17. Rotation schemes are inconsistent with cutpoint decision rules. Therefore, an immediate implication of the pervasive use of cutpoint rules is that rotation schemes were not observed. For this reason, we do not discuss rotation schemes in the remainder of this paper. Interested readers are referred to Palfrey and Rosenthal (1992), which documents the absence of rotation behaviour more thoroughly.

TABLE 4

Endowments at least equal to benefit: contributions and theory rounds (6–20)

Parameters:						
N	3	3	3	3	3	4
W	1	2	2	3	3	2
C	1·5	1·5	2·25	1	1·5	2·25
Repeated groups						
Actual spends	5	23	1	n.a.	53	0
Theoretical spends	0″	118***	30***	n.a.	222***	32***
Total observations	160	420	92	n.a.	222	101
One-shot groups						
Actual spends	3″	9†	4″	n.a.	9†††	5″
Theoretical spends	0	0	0	n.a.	0	0
Total observations	316	408	216	n.a.	188	309

Notes to Table 4:
The theoretical spends are calculated on the predictions of the symmetric cooperative cutpoint equilibrium for fixed groups and the actual token values used in the experiment. (For random groups, the non-cooperative prediction is always "keep" for endowments at least equal to the value of the benefit.)
*** The likelihood-ratio test that the actual spends were at a rate equal to the theoretical prediction was rejected at the 0·001 level or better.
″ The test was not performed because the theoretical level is 0.
† The likelihood-ratio test of the hypothesis that the probability of spending a token at least equal to the benefit was equal in the repeated and one-shot treatments was rejected at the 0·05 level.
††† The hypothesis is rejected at the 0·001 level.
″ The test was not carried out because the number of actual spends was small in both treatments.

greater in the repeated games than in the one-shot games.[18] Table 4 presents the contribution data[19] for $c_i > 1$.

In the one-shot games, a dominated action was taken in only 2% of the possible opportunities, demonstrating that subjects consistently avoid using dominated strategies in these one-shot contribution games. Also as predicted, dominated strategies are observed more often in the repeated games. Subjects contributed over 8% of the possible opportunities when $c_i > 1$, or more than four times as frequently compared to the one-shot games. This provides some weak evidence that repetition is having an effect on subject behaviour. However, this difference depended on the parametric treatment. Only in the treatments with $C = 1·5$ was there a significant effect of repetition[20] on contribution when $c_i > 1$. Table 4 also shows that, while the one-shot dominated actions were taken more often in repeated games, they were used much less than would be expected in the cooperative schemes. To illustrate how much less, Table 4 also displays, for each parameter set, the theoretical number of contributions when $c_i > 1$ which would have been observed in the group-optimal symmetric cutpoint equilibrium. This shows that subjects do not spend as often as predicted by the optimal repeated-game equilibrium when $c_i > 1$.

Cutpoint strategies

With the exception of rotation schemes, all of the theoretical models considered predict that subjects will use cutpoint strategies. For example, in the one-shot game, cutpoint

18. In fact, contribution when $c_i > 1$ would be regularly observed in either the group-optimal cutpoint equilibria or the efficient rotation equilibria.
19. Data are based on rounds 6 to 20. The first five rounds were excluded to control for inexperience and learning. Rounds 21 and higher in the repeated-game treatments were excluded to preserve comparability between the one-shot and repeated experiments. Inclusion of later rounds in the repeated-game sessions produces similar results. Table 7 gives an indication of the small magnitude of the differences depending on whether one uses all rounds or only rounds 6–20.
20. In the other moderate endowment treatment ($W = 1$, $N = 3$, $C = 1·5$), the group optimal symmetric cutpoint is less than one, so we predict no spends when $c_i > 1$ in the repeated game version in that treatment.

PALFREY & ROSENTHAL   REPEATED PLAY   557

TABLE 5

Percent correctly classified (rounds 6–20)

Parameters:	N	3	3	3	3	3	4
	W	1	2	2	3	3	2
	C	1·5	1·5	2·25	1	1·5	2·25
Fixed groups							
Average-session		82	84	88	81	76	87
Group		86	87	90	94	91	90
Subject		92	92	93	96	97	94
Std. Dev.-session		2	4	n.a.	18	8	n.a.
Group		5	8	6	8	9	4
Subject		8	11	7	8	6	7
Random groups							
Average-session		87	88	88	74	85	89
Subject		95	94	94	89	92	94
Std. Dev.-session		4	4	4	0·4	6	2
Subject		6	6	8	10	9	6

Notes to Table 5:
"Session" refers to the classification percentages that result when a common cutpoint is calculated for the 12 (or 9) subjects in a given session for the parameters. "Group" refers to a common cutpoint for all subjects in a distinct group. "Subject" refers to a cutpoint for each subject. Cutpoints were chosen to minimize classification errors. In computing the standard deviations, the unbiased estimator formula (division by NOBS-1) was used. The standard deviation for sessions was computed with sessions as the units of observation. Accordingly, "n.a." is shown for treatments with only a single session.

rules are always essentially unique best responses for any individual to any strategy profile of the other players. Therefore, regardless of a player's beliefs about what the other players are doing, some cutpoint strategy is an optimal decision rule.

The most striking feature of observed individual behaviour in these experiments is the pervasive evidence of cutpoint decision rules by subjects. Table 5 documents this.

That table reports the classification accuracy that results if one chooses, for each individual, the cutpoint that would minimize the total number of classification errors in spending. We also report classification accuracies under the restriction that all individuals in a session use the same cutpoint rule (the rows marked "session" in Table 5). For the repeated sessions we report classification accuracies under the weaker restriction that all members of the same group use the same cutpoint rule (the rows marked "group").

On average, we are able to assign a cutpoint to an individual and correctly classify nearly 95% of the spending decisions.[21] The low standard deviations of classification accuracy indicate that there are few individuals who are classified very poorly.

In the repeated-game treatment, we classify groups nearly as well as we do individuals, even though we buy back two or three degrees of freedom. This suggests that members of groups tend to adopt similar cutpoint strategies and indicates that there is little evidence that the coordination problem is solved by subjects adopting roles of "free rider" and "contributor." Except in the unanimity ($W=3$, $N=3$) games, there is also little deterioration in fit if we assign a common cutpoint to all subjects in the session. This shows that there is little variation across groups except in unanimity games.

For the unanimity games, classification accuracy falls substantially if a common cutpoint is assigned to all subjects in the session. This is an indication of strong group

21. More than 50% correct classification is guaranteed, even if subjects choose randomly. Monte Carlo results in Palfrey and Rosenthal (1991a) indicate overwhelming rejection of chance models for the levels of classification reported here.

effects for these games. Particularly with $C=1$, the data divides into groups that almost always produce the good and groups that almost never produce the good.

The classification analysis is similar in the one-shot treatments except that there is less deterioration in fit when the estimated cutpoints are constrained to be the same for all subjects in a session. An exception to this is the $W=3$, $N=3$, $C=1$ (one-shot) condition, where only 74% of spending decisions can be accounted for using a common cutpoint for each session.

In this case, in addition to the stable zero equilibrium, there is an unstable equilibrium where subjects all contribute. The 42% contribution rate suggests that some subjects made (unrewarded) efforts to obtain the high contribution equilibrium.[22] Our results suggest that repetition allows some, but not all groups, to arrive at this equilibrium. On the other hand, members of repeated groups that fail do not "waste" their tokens as frequently as participants in random group sessions.

The comparison of the constrained and unconstrained classification analysis provides a partial answer to the question of whether subjects adopt the same cutpoint rule. In the one shot games, this could only arise if different players have different beliefs about the others' behaviour. In the repeated games, this could be due to either different beliefs or they could be supergame equilibria. While there is apparently some variation in the specific cutpoint strategies individuals use, this variation is not large in magnitude. This is reflected in the standard deviation of the estimated cutpoints reported in Table 5. Related to this, there is little support for the hypothesis that in the repeated game subjects divide into activists, who always contribute, and free-riders, who never contribute in either the $W=1$ condition or the $W=2$ conditions.[23] In the $W=1$ and $W=2$ treatments, none of the subjects were activists in always contributing in rounds 6-20 and only two subjects were free-riders in that they never contributed. In fact only 12 of the 144 $W=1$ and $W=2$ subjects contributed two or fewer times in rounds 6-20. The two pure free riders did not succeed in "bluffing" the other members of their groups into high contribution rates. One free rider was in a 1 of 3 game, the other in a 2 of 4. The remaining subjects contributed at rates below that expected in either the symmetric group optimal cutpoint of the reduced $(N-1)$ game (1 of 2 or 2 of 3) and, a fortiori, what would be optimal for the entire group.[24]

Overall, cutpoints are well-predicted by Bayes-Nash equilibrium in the one-shot condition. For the parametric treatments in this paper average estimated cutpoints tend to be slightly greater than the Bayesian equilibrium prediction although the difference is not always statistically significant. (See Table 6.) There are a number of possible explanations for this, which are explored in Palfrey and Rosenthal (1991b).

In the repeated-game condition, average estimated cutpoints are higher than in the one-shot games. This is consistent with the hypothesis that repetition leads to greater cooperation. In Table 6 we present significance tests of the null hypothesis that the mean cutpoints are equal in the two conditions vs. the alternative that cutpoints are greater in the repeated condition than in the one-shot condition. Four of the six parameter sets show a statistically significant difference. Overall, the estimated cutpoints in the repeated

22. One subject, who had repeatedly spent his token, spontaneously remarked, while being paid, that he could not understand why the other subjects had been "so irrational."

23. In addition, we observed no obvious patterns indicating the use of trigger strategies or other punishment strategies, as are commonly invoked in the proofs of folk theorems (and in Section 3 of this paper). Absence of trigger strategies was also found by Sell and Wilson (1991), who investigate a different repeated game, also using a random horizon to induce discounting.

24. The only slight evidence that repetition led to asymmetry is that there was more variation in cutpoints across individuals for the repeated condition in three of the six parameter conditions.

PALFREY & ROSENTHAL   REPEATED PLAY   559

TABLE 6

Summary of repeated vs. fixed group comparisons

Parameters:	N	3	3	3	3	3	4
	W	1	2	2	3	3	2
	C	1·5	1·5	2·25	1	1·5	2·25
Equilibrium	c^*_{os}	0·47	0·37	0·00	0·00	0·00	0·30
Predictions:	c^*_{x}	0·75	1·13	0·94	1·00	1·50	1·27
	q^*_{os}	0·31	0·25	0·00	0·00	0·00	0·13
	q^*_{x}	0·50	0·75	0·62	1·00	1·00	0·57
Observations:	$\hat{c}_{os}$	0·50	0·55	0·34	0·42	0·34	0·60
	$\hat{c}_{x}$	0·48	0·68***	0·56**	0·73***	0·60**	0·60
	σ_{os}	0·23	0·22	0·21	0·24	0·29	0·27
	σ_{x}	0·25	0·29††	0·23	0·34†	0·54†††	0·26
	$\hat{q}_{os}$	0·28	0·35	0·18	0·42	0·25	0·22
	$\hat{q}_{x}$	0·34	0·44	0·28	0·77	0·41	0·24
	n_{os}	60	75	24	24	36	37
	n_{x}	36	84	12	69	42	12
	η_{os}	0·84	0·40	0·08	−0·18	−0·29	0·36
	η_{x}	0·82	0·52	0·37	0·59	−0·04	0·48 (ALL)
		0·84	0·60	0·37	0·72	0·43	0·48 (REVEAL)
		0·77	0·47	—	0·47	−0·39	— (NO REVEAL)

Notes to Table 6:
The subscripts *os* and ∞ refer to the one-shot treatment and the repeated-group treatment, respectively. The reported values of $\hat{c}$ are computed as the average of the cutpoints that are estimated for each individual. Each of these was estimated by finding the hypothetical cutpoint that minimized the classification errors of a subject's contribution decisions. The reported values of $\hat{q}$ are the averages that appear in Table 4. The reported values of σ are computed as the standard deviation of the individual estimated cutpoints. The reported values of n are the number of individuals who participated in that treatment. The reported values of η, the efficiency measure, is the total payoff to the subjects in excess of their endowments, normalized so that earnings equal to the endowments have $\eta = 0$ and earnings predicted by the optimal symmetric cutpoint have $\eta = 1$.
Significance tests See notes to Table 7 for parallel description and explanation.

condition are closer to the levels predicted by optimal symmetric cutpoints than the prediction of one-shot Bayes–Nash equilibrium.

Spending: does repetition lead to more contribution?

The findings about spending parallel the findings about cutpoints. For all six of our parameter sets, repetition leads to more contribution, as shown in Tables 6 and 7. Five of the six parameter sets show statistically significant differences over rounds 6 to 20. The data also shows that spending rates tend to be more dispersed with repeated play (Table 7), particularly for $W = N = 3$ sessions, where appropriate F-tests are highly significant.

In the repeated unanimity games with $C = 1·0$, the median contribution rate was 100%. Most groups in that treatment achieved nearly perfect cooperation. Some groups failed to coordinate; subjects in those groups typically had contribution rates near zero. On the other hand, the "no contribution" equilibrium was never observed. Although contributions tended to diminish over time in groups that had not coordinated, sporadic contributions continued. These sporadic contributions lowered efficiency, particularly in the eight groups that always or nearly always failed to obtain three contributions in a round.

For unanimity games with $C = 1·5$, most subjects contributed very little, but a few subjects had very high contribution rates. While some groups coordinated sporadically, no group sustained coordination throughout the experiment, and some groups did fully or nearly lock in on the 0% contribution equilibrium.

TABLE 7

Contribution rates

Parameters:		N	3	3	3	3	3	4
		W	1	2	2	3	3	2
		C	1·5	1·5	2·25	1	1·5	2·25
Rounds 6–20								
Average	repeated		0·34*	0·44***	0·28**	0·77***	0·41**	0·24
	one-shot		0·28‡	0·35‡‡‡	0·18‡	0·42‡‡‡	0·25‡‡‡	0·22
Std. Dev.	repeated		0·16	0·16	0·10	0·34†	0·37†††	0·15
	one-shot		0·13	0·14	0·11	0·21	0·16	0·11
All rounds								
Average	repeated		0·33	0·44***	0·23	0·76***	0·38**	0·26
	one-shot		0·29‡	0·35‡‡‡	0·18‡	0·43‡‡‡	0·25‡‡‡	0·24
Std. Dev.	repeated		0·15	0·14††	0·10	0·33††	0·31†††	0·12
	one-shot		0·14	0·10	0·09	0·19	0·15	0·10

Notes to Table 7:
Average: refers to the proportion of tokens that were contributed for all subjects in a given treatment. The standard deviations (*Std. Dev.*) are computed by calculating a spending rate (proportion of tokens contributed) for each subject in a treatment, and then computing the standard deviation of these individual spending rates.
Significance tests
The null hypothesis that the variance across subjects was equal in the two treatments vs. the alternative that the repeated variance was greater than the one-shot was tested by a standard *F*-test. The null hypothesis that the mean across subjects was equal in the two treatments vs. the alternative that the mean contribution rate was higher in repeated groups was tested by a standard *t*-test that allows for unequal variances. Using individual decisions rather than subjects as the units of observation, we also carried out the standard likelihood-ratio test of the null hypothesis that there was an equal contribution probability in the two populations. Because the effective number of observations was much higher in this test than in the *t*-test, *p*-values were lower for this test than for the *t*-test.
* One-tailed *t*-test (unequal variances) *p*-value ≤ 0.05.
** One-tailed *t*-test (unequal variances) *p*-value ≤ 0.01.
*** One-tailed *t*-test (unequal variances) *p*-value ≤ 0.001.
† *F*-test *p*-value ≤ 0.05.
†† *F*-test *p*-value ≤ 0.01.
††† *F*-test *p*-value ≤ 0.001.
‡ Likelihood-ratio test *p*-value ≤ 0.01.
‡‡‡ Likelihood-ratio test *p*-value < 0.001.

B. Efficiency: does repetition help?

In order to compare efficiencies across parametric treatments, we convert the actual earnings by subjects into an efficiency index. This is done by subtracting the endowments (token values) from earnings paid at the end of the session, and then dividing these net earnings by the net earnings that would have resulted (conditioning on the actual token value draws) if everyone had used the group-optimal symmetric cutpoint.[25] This results in a normalization that will equal 0 if no one ever contributes, and will equal 1 if everyone contributes using the group-optimal symmetric cutpoint strategy.

To test whether earnings are higher in the repeated-game sessions, we average all earnings within a parameter treatment. A comparison of the predictions of the different theoretical models is given in Table 3. The observed efficiencies, comparing one-shot games and repeated-games are reported in Table 6.

Except for the $W=1$, $N=3$ game, the results clearly show that repetition leads to efficiency gains. The differences are in the right direction for all of the other parametric

25. Table 3 shows the expected group earnings (net of endowment) for each parameter set in the one-shot equilibrium compared to the optimal symmetric cutpoint equilibrium.

treatments, and are significant at the 0·01 level. The repetition effect is especially strong in the $W=3$, $N=3$, $C=1·0$ game and in the $W=2$, $N=3$, $C=1·5$ game.

There is a plausible ex post rationale to explain why repetition failed to help in the $W=1$, $N=3$ game. This game is the most competitive, in the sense that the gains from cooperation are the least. This fact is reflected in the small difference between predicted *per capita* earnings in the one-shot Bayesian equilibrium (1·35) and *per capita* earnings with a group-optimal cutpoint (1·44). With so little separation between the predictions for the cooperative vs. non-cooperative outcomes, it is not surprising that we measured essentially no difference between the one-shot and repeated-play efficiencies in the $W=1$, $N=3$ game.

We also compare the efficiency in the Reveal and the No-Reveal treatments (Table 6). Revelation of token values after each play raised efficiency in all four parameter values where we conducted both treatments. Revelation makes its biggest impact in 3 of 3 games. This is a bit surprising since, as explained above, theory predicts that monitoring should not matter in these games.

A more detailed examination of the 3 of 3, $C=1·0$ games suggests that the magnitude of the reveal effect is not large. We conducted (see Table 1) six sessions with these parameters. In the two 8/3/89 sessions, earnings were actually slightly less in the reveal treatment. In the two 10/29/91 sessions, earnings were virtually identical in the two treatments. So the difference between Reveal and No-Reveal rests solely on the 6/11/91 session, in which all three groups coordinated fully from round three onward, having much higher earnings than the 9/4/91 session, when there was a very low degree of coordination. Thus it is possible that cohort effects may be magnifying the reveal effect. On the other hand, there is some support for the increased efficiency from token revelation in the data for the $W=N=3$, $C=1·5$ experiments. The two reveal sessions were on 6/11/91. Subjects in these sessions not only did better than the subjects in the No-Reveal setting of 9/4/91 but also bettered the 10/29/91 subjects who, as just reported above, achieved a high degree of coordination in the unanimity game with $C=1$.

Figure 1 plots the actual efficiencies of each one-shot session (horizontal axis) with the theoretically predicted efficiencies, calculated from the actual token values of the session. Two plots are superimposed in this figure, corresponding to the predictions of the one-shot Bayes–Nash equilibrium model (presented by a + sign) and the predictions of the optimal symmetric cutpoint model (represented by a ■ sign). If one of the theories were to fit the data perfectly, the plotted points would line up exactly on the diagonal of this figure.

The Bayesian one-shot predictions cluster quite closely about the diagonal. The Root Mean Square Error (RMSE) of the theoretical predictions is only 0·09. (See Table 8.) The average deviation of the theoretical prediction from actual earnings is only −0·02, showing that, over all the sessions, there is only a slight tendency to under predict earnings. In contrast, the optimal symmetric cutpoints, as expected, badly over predict efficiencies in the one-shot sessions. The average deviation is 0·261.

Figure 2 reports the repeated-game data in a similar way. With respect to fixed groups, the one-shot model no longer provides a good fit to the data. The RMSE more than doubles. Under-prediction is more substantial; the average deviation increases to −0·13 and is significant. As can be seen in Figure 2, the failure of the one-shot model here is partly the reflection of three sessions where the theoretical prediction is zero increase over the endowment but where the subjects actually gained nearly 0·5. These all represent $W=N=3$, $C=1$ experiments where all groups perfectly or nearly perfectly coordinated in Rounds 6 through 20. For the other parameters, the one-shot model is more accurate.

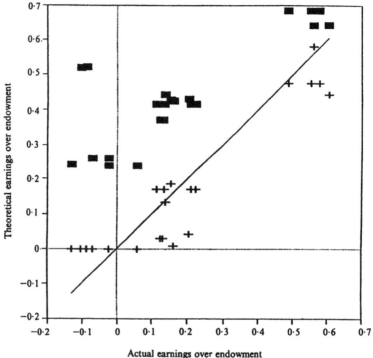

Key:
■ Optimum
+ One shot
— Predicted = Actual

Note: Each session appears twice, once for the optimal symmetric cutpoint predictions and once for the one shot symmetric cutpoint predictions. Computations reflect actual token values and are for rounds 6–20.

FIGURE 1

Session earnings, random groups

The optimal symmetric cutpoint model does not fit the repeated-game efficiency data better than the one-shot Bayesian equilibrium model. It continues to overpredict earnings, although by less with random groups, but the RMSE is in fact slightly higher than that for the one-shot model. These results again indicate that repeated play increases earnings, but only exploits a portion of the theoretically possible gains. Moreover, while, game theory is a highly accurate model of aggregate behaviour in one-shot games, no simple game-theoretic model adequately captures the repeated-game data.

Repeated play might produce results closer to the optimum predictions if the Reveal treatment were used in all settings. (But see the caveat in the discussion above.) When we regress actual earnings against those predicted with the optimal cutpoint, a constant, and a dummy variable for Reveal, we find that earnings are, significantly higher in the Reveal treatment (t-statistic $= 1 \cdot 879$, p-value $= 0 \cdot 03$). But, as can be seen visually in Figure 2, even if subjects do better in Reveal treatments, they still tend to earn less than would be available with the optimal symmetric cutpoint.

PALFREY & ROSENTHAL   REPEATED PLAY   563

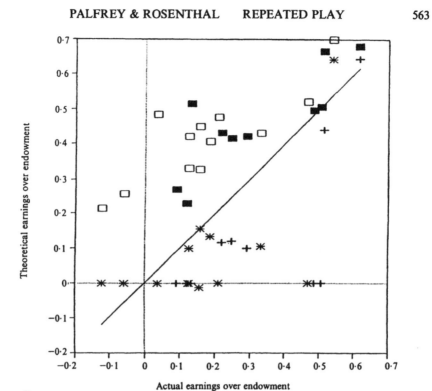

Key:
■ Optimum reveal
□ Optimum no-reveal
+ One shot reveal
✳ One shot no-reveal
— Predicted = Actual

Note: Each session appears twice, once for the optimal symmetric cutpoint predictions and once for the one shot symmetric cutpoint predictions. Computations reflect actual token values and are for rounds 6–20.

FIGURE 2

Session earnings, fixed groups

TABLE 8

Deviation of session earnings from theoretical predictions

	Random groups model		Fixed groups model	
	One shot	Optimal	One shot	Optimal
RMSE*	0·087	0·295	0·213	0·226
Ave. Dev.	−0·020	0·261	−0·129	0·194

Notes to Table 8:
* Root Mean Square Error.
All predictions calculated assuming subjects followed theoretical decision rules given their actual token values.

564 REVIEW OF ECONOMIC STUDIES

6. CONCLUSION

Most of the theoretical hypotheses were supported to some degree in the data. Game theory can account for many of the qualitative features of the data, particularly in the one-shot games. Subjects avoid dominated strategies and adhere to cutpoint decision rules that are, on average, very close to the ones predicted by Bayesian equilibrium. Repetition leads to more cooperative behaviour (more spending) and improves efficiency, and better monitoring has a similar effect.

On the other hand, subjects are unable to come close to fully exploiting the opportunities for coordination and cooperation in the repeated games. The only environment where full efficiency is often achieved is in the unanimity games which actually have a one-shot Bayesian equilibrium (albeit unstable) which yields full efficiency.

Thus, while the theory correctly predicts that repetition enhances efficiency, the observed magnitudes of improvement are much smaller than predicted. We conjecture one reason for this is that the theory lacks a good dynamic model of how players might reach an efficient equilibrium in a repeated game. This void in the theory is particularly evident when one considers rotation schemes, which are non-stationary and require a specific timing structure. In order for such schemes to ever come about, players in a group will have to go through some sort of "groping about" process in the early plays of the game, reminiscent of the process modelled by Crawford and Haller (1990). Apparently even relatively simple rotation schemes are very difficult to support, and unlikely to emerge spontaneously without explicit coordination devices, such as direct or mediated communication. We found essentially no evidence at all for implicit coordination of this sort.

Unanimity games are the only ones where a groping stage is not necessary. However, even in unanimity games, a sizeable minority of groups fail to coordinate, with success or failure largely determined in the early plays of the game. Again, this indicates a need to model the dynamic process of how players adjust their behaviour over the course of the repeated plays of the game. Yet a striking feature of the behaviour displayed in the experiments is the apparent use of heuristic cutpoints by the subjects. The high rates of classification success we obtained suggest that, after some initial rounds, individual behaviour is highly stable. At the same time, group behaviour is highly variable, particularly in the unanimity games with $C=1$ where groups bifurcated into fully cooperating groups and "failed" groups. From this perspective, the interesting dynamics may be packed into the initial experiences of groups.

Acknowledgements. The authors are thankful for the research support of the National Science Foundation through grants #SES-8718650 and #SES-9011828. The research assistance of Mark Fey, Jessica Goodfellow, and Jeff Prisbrey is gratefully acknowledged for their help in conducting the experiments. Sanjay Srivastava was instrumental in developing the computer network used for the experiments. We are grateful for detailed comments on earlier drafts by Roberta Herzberg and by Rosemarie Nagel. The exposition has benefitted from suggestions by three referees and an editor. Work on this paper began while Rosenthal was a Fellow at the International Centre for Economic Research and a Fellow at the Center for Advanced Study in the Behavioral Sciences. He is grateful for financial support provided by National Science Foundation #BNS-8700864 during his stay at CASBS.

REFERENCES

ANDREONI, J. (1988), "Why Free Ride?: Strategies and Learning in Public Goods Experiments", *Journal of Public Economics*, 37, 291–304.

ANDREONI, J. and MILLER, J. (1991), "Rational Cooperation in the Finitely Repeated Prisoners Dilemma: Experimental Evidence" (SSRI Workshop series No. 9102, University of Wisconsin).

ALGER, D. (1987), "Laboratory Tests of Equilibrium Predictions with Disequilibrium Data", *Review of Economic Studies*, 54, 105–145.

COOPER, R., DEJONG, D., FORSYTHE, R. and ROSS, T. (1989), "Communication in the Battle of the Sexes Game", *Rand Journal of Economics*, **20**, 568–587.

COOPER, R., DEJONG, D., FORSYTHE, R. and ROSS, T. (1991), "Cooperation without Reputation" (mimeo, Boston University).

CRAWFORD, V. and HALLER, H. (1990), "Learning How to Cooperate: Optimal Play in Repeated Coordination Games", *Econometrica*, **58**, 571–595.

DAVIS, D. D. and HOLT, C. A. (1990), "Capacity Asymmetries, Market Power, and Mergers in Laboratory Markets with Posted Prices" (Working Paper, Virginia Commonwealth University).

FRIEDMAN, J. W. (1967), "An Experimental Study of Cooperative Oligopoly", *Econometrica*, **35**, 379–397.

FRIEDMAN, J. W. (1969), "On Experimental Research in Oligopoly", *Review of Economic Studies*, **36**, 399–415.

FUDENBERG, D. and TIROLE, J. (1991) *Game Theory* (Cambridge, Mass.: MIT Press).

GALLO, Jr., P. S. and McCLINTOCK, C. G. (1965), "Cooperative and Competitive Behavior in Mixed-Motive Games", *Journal of Conflict Resolution*, **9**, 68–78.

ISAAC, R. M. and WALKER, J. M. (1991), "Costly Communication: An Experiment in a Nested Public Goods Problem", in T. R. Palfrey (ed.), *Laboratory Research in Political Economy* (Ann Arbor: University of Michigan Press).

ISAAC, R. M., WALKER, J. M. and THOMAS, S. H. (1984), "Divergent Evidence on Free Riding: An Experimental Examination of Possible Explanations", *Public Choice*, **43**, 113–149.

MARWELL, G. and AMES, R. E. (1979), "Experiments on the Provision of Public Goods I: Resources, Interest, Group Size, and the Free Rider Problem", *American Journal of Sociology*, **84**, 1335–1360.

MARWELL, G. and AMES, R. E. (1980), "Experiments on the Provision of Public Goods II: Provision Points, Stakes, Experience, and the Free Rider Problem", *American Journal of Sociology*, **85**, 926–937.

MARWELL, G. and AMES, R. E. (1981), "Economists Free Ride, Does Anyone Else?", *Journal of Public Economics*, **15**, 295–310.

McCABE, K., RASSENTI, S. and SMITH, V. (1991), "Cooperation and the Repeat Interactions of Anonymous Pairings" (mimeo).

McKELVEY, R. D. and PALFREY, T. R. (1992), "An Experimental Study of the Centipede Game", *Econometrica*, **60**, 803–836.

OSTROM, E. (1990) *Governing the Commons* (Cambridge: Cambridge University Press).

OSTROM, E. and WALKER, J. (1991), "Communication in a Commons: Cooperation Without External Enforcement", in T. R. Palfrey (ed.), *Laboratory Research in Political Economy* (Ann Arbor: University of Michigan Press).

PALFREY, T. R. (1985), "Buyer Behavior and the Welfare Effects of Bundling by a Multi-product Monopolist: A Laboratory Investigation", in V. Smith (ed.), *Research in Experimental Economics*, **3**, 73–104 (JAI Press).

PALFREY, T. R. and ROSENTHAL, H. (1991*a*), "Testing for Effects of Cheaptalk in a Public Goods Game with Private Information", *Games and Economic Behavior*, **3**, 183–220.

PALFREY, T. R. and ROSENTHAL, H. (1991*b*), "Testing Game-Theoretic Models of Free Riding: New Evidence on Probability Bias and Learning", in T. R. Palfrey (ed.), *Laboratory Research in Political Economy* (Ann Arbor: University of Michigan Press).

PALFREY, T. R. and ROSENTHAL, H. (1992), "Repeated Play, Cooperation, and Coordination: An Experimental Study" (Social Science Working Paper No. 785, California Institute of Technology: Pasadena, California).

PRISBREY, J. (1991), "An Experimental Analysis of Two-Person Reciprocity Games" (mimeo, California Institute of Technology).

RAPOPORT, A. and ORWANT, C. (1962), "Experimental Games: A Review", *Behavioral Science*, 1–37.

ROTH, A. E. and MURNIGHAN, J. K. (1982), "The Role of Information in Bargaining: An Experimental Study", *Econometrica*, **50**, 1123–1142.

SCHNEIDER, F. and POMMEREHNE, W. (1981), "Free Riding and Collective Action: An Experiment in Public Microeconomics", *Quarterly Journal of Economics*, **96**, 689–704.

SELL, J. and WILSON, R. (1991), "Trigger Strategies in Repeated-Play Public Goods Games: Forgiving, Non-Forgiving or Non-Existent?" (mimeo, Rice University).

SELTEN, R. and STOECKER, R. (1986), "End Behavior in Sequences in Finite Prisoner's Dilemma Supergames", *Journal of Economic Behavior and Organization*, **7**, 47–70.

WALKER, J., OSTROM, E. and GARDNER, R. (1990), "Rent Dissipation in a Limited Access Common-Pool Resource: Experimental Evidence", *Journal of Environmental Economics and Management*, **19**, 203–211.

[21]

The Role of Communication in Resolving Commons Dilemmas: Experimental Evidence with Heterogeneous Appropriators*

STEVEN HACKETT

School of Business and Economics, Humboldt State University, Arcata, CA 95521-8299

EDELLA SCHLAGER

School of Public Administration and Policy, University of Arizona, Tucson, Arizona 85721

AND

JAMES WALKER[†]

Department of Economics and Workshop in Political Theory and Policy Analysis, Ballantine 901, Indiana University, Bloomington, Indiana 47405

Received January 20, 1993; revised June 3, 1993

Communication has been shown to be an effective mechanism for promoting efficient resource use in homogeneous common-pool resource settings. Communication allows appropriators the opportunity to agree on an aggregate appropriation target and coordinate over the selection of input allocation rules. When appropriators are identical, these rules result in identical input allocations, which facilitates cooperation. We examine the robustness of communication as an efficiency-enhancing mechanism in settings where appropriators differ in input endowments. This heterogeneity creates a distributional conflict over access to common-pool resources. This conflict can cause self-governance to fail. We present findings from a series of experiments where heterogeneous endowments are assigned: (1) randomly, and appropriators have complete information, (2) through an auction, and appropriators have complete information, and (3) randomly, and appropriators have incomplete and asymmetric information. These findings are contrasted with rules from CPR field settings. © 1994 Academic Press, Inc.

I. INTRODUCTION

Common-pool resources (CPRs) are defined as natural or man-made resources in which (a) exclusion is nontrivial (but not necessarily impossible) and (b) yield is subtractable (Ostrom *et al.*, 1992). Individuals jointly using a CPR are assumed to face a social dilemma—often called the tragedy of the commons—in which individually rational resource users ignore the external harm they impose on other users, leading to outcomes that are not rational from the perspective of the group.

*We thank two anonymous referees for their constructive guidance. We also thank Ray Battalio, Elinor Ostrom, Jeff Banks, Tom Palfrey, and participants of the Fall 1992 meetings of the Economic Science Association for their useful comments. Financial support from National Science Foundation Grants SES-8820897, SES-8921884, and SBR-9222656 is gratefully acknowledged. The assistance of Dean Dudley in the Experimental Lab is also much appreciated. All data are stored on permanent NovaNET disk files.

†To whom correspondence should be sent.

100   HACKETT, SCHLAGER, AND WALKER

Policy proposals for resolving CPR dilemmas often follow one of two approaches
—privatizing the resource or centralizing its management within the state. As a
result, a single owner or regulator is deemed necessary if resource dilemmas are to
be resolved and resources used efficiently.

A growing body of field and experimental literature, however, provides considerable evidence that resource users confronted with CPR dilemmas may adopt
self-governing institutions that enable them to resolve their dilemmas. Further, the
ultimate success of resource users attempts to enhance CPR yield may differ based
on both the physical characteristics of the CPR and on the institutions governing
use. In particular, certain CPR settings may have production-based or
information-based characteristics that inherently lead to poorer performance.[1]
Moreover, within a particular CPR production setting, alternative governance
institutions can be expected to have differential effects on appropriator incentives
and CPR performance. The focus of this paper is endogenously determined
governance systems and their impact on resource use.

One critical factor that facilitates rule formation in field CPR settings is
face-to-face communication among resource users. Further, experimental research
on face-to-face communication has shown this mechanism to be a powerful tool for
enhancing efficiency. Accordingly, understanding the robustness of face-to-face
communication as a mechanism for facilitating cooperation is critical to understanding the evolution of self-governing institutions. As Dawes (1980) states, "The
salutary effects of communication on cooperation are ubiquitous" (p. 185).[2] On the
other hand, individuals who are permitted to communicate do not always achieve
optimal outcomes. The rule structure of permitted communication, as well as the
complexity of the social dilemma setting, affects the robustness of communication
in promoting cooperation.[3]

Most experimental research on communication has focused on collective action
problems in which individuals are homogeneous in decision attributes. It is
possible that the strong efficiency-enhancing properties of face-to-face communication are dependent upon homogeneities in decision attributes. In fact, the
literature provides several arguments that point to heterogeneity as a serious
deterrent to cooperation (Hardin, 1982; Johnson and Libecap, 1982; Libecap and

---

[1]The importance of the physical characteristics of the resource has been studied in a variety of
settings. For example, as pointed out by a reviewer of this paper, the particular form of the production
function for providing, maintaining, or using the resource can be critical in terms of both theoretic
predictions and behavior. See, for example, Dawes *et al.* (1986), Isaac *et al.* (1989), Harrison and
Hirshleifer (1989), and Bagnoli and McKee (1991). Further, the form of endogenously created
rule-governing institutions has also been shown to be dependent upon the physical characteristics of the
CPR. See, for example, Schlager (1990), Schlager *et al.* (1993), and Ostrom *et al.* (1994).

[2]Whether the social dilemma games are two-person or *n* person (Orbell *et al.*, 1988), single play
(Bornstein and Rapaport, 1988) or repeated play (Liebrand, 1984), time independent (Ostrom and
Walker, 1991; Isaac and Walker, 1991) or time dependent (Brechner 1977), individuals who use
face-to-face communication achieve superior outcomes compared to those who are not permitted to
communicate. These results from experiments utilizing face-to-face communication should not be
confused with the literature related to highly structured (non-face-to-face) "cheap talk" communication. See, for example, Palfrey and Rosenthal (1991). In this more formal/structured setting, Palfrey
and Rosenthal are unable to support the hypothesis that cheap talk improves efficiency in a public
goods provision problem.

[3]Several studies such as Orbell *et al.* (1988), Isaac and Plott (1981), Isaac *et al.* (1984), Isaac and
Walker (1985), and Ostrom *et al.* (1992) demonstrate the importance of the particular decision setting
in promoting the success of communication as an independent mechanism.

Wiggins, 1984; Isaac and Walker, 1988; Wiggins and Libecap, 1987; Ostrom, 1990; Kanbur, 1991; Hackett, 1992). For example, Kanbur (1991, pp. 21–22) argues,

... theory and evidence would seem to suggest that cooperative agreements are more likely to come about in groups that are homogeneous in the relevant economic dimension, and they are more likely to break down as heterogeneity along this dimension increases.

The task of agreeing to and sustaining agreements for efficient CPR appropriation is more difficult for heterogeneous appropriators because of the distributional conflict associated with alternative sharing rules.[4] In heterogeneous settings, different sharing rules may produce different distributions of earnings across appropriators. While all appropriators may be made better off by cooperating, some will benefit more than others, depending upon the sharing rule chosen. Consequently, appropriators may fail to cooperate on the adoption of a sharing rule because they cannot agree upon what would constitute a fair distribution of benefits produced by cooperating.[5]

Building on the experimental research of Walker *et al.* (1990), this paper examines a decision setting where individuals make input allocation decisions between a CPR and an outside alternative with a fixed marginal return.[6] Heterogeneity is introduced by varying the input endowments of experimental subjects. Heterogeneities in endowments imply that alternative rules adopted to reduce over-appropriation from the CPR will have differential effects on earnings across subjects. Two principal questions will be addressed: To what degree do heterogeneities hinder individuals' ability to coordinate their use of the CPR and what type of input allocation rules will be proposed and adopted?

Before turning to the laboratory study, in Section II we examine the case study literature and report on allocation rules observed in a diverse set of naturally occurring CPRs. This sample of field studies provides a benchmark for discussing the distributional implications of alternative rule types and creates a basis for understanding rules adopted in the laboratory. In Section III we present the decision setting for our experimental study. For comparison purposes, Section IV

[4]Sharing rules can be in the form of agreements regarding inputs or outputs. We use the term "input allocation" to refer to the decision to allocate inputs to the production process of appropriating from the CPR. We use the term appropriation to refer to the actual level of output resulting from this production process. Note that if users are homogeneous in technologies employed (as is the case in the experiments reported here), then identical input allocations imply identical appropriation. In the field, where technologies may differ, this may not be the case.

[5]These issues have recently been investigated in a theoretical context by Hackett (1992). His work suggests that heterogeneous resource endowments can lead to disagreement over the supply and implementation of rules that allocate access to CPRs. For example, consider the two allocation rules found in the field CPR cases we survey in Section II—equal appropriation and appropriation proportionate with capacity or historic use. The interests of large-endowment appropriators are served by proportionate allocations, while the interests of small-endowment appropriators are better served by equal-sized appropriation rights allocations. When self-governing CPR groups are heterogeneous, rule supply involves a trade-off between the cost of investing in the "social capital" necessary to reach consensus on an allocation rule and the added costs of monitoring and enforcing agreements opposed by some subset of appropriators.

[6]This decision setting focuses on a static non-time dependent characterization of a CPR problem. In the literature, this problem is commonly referred to as an "appropriation externality." We chose this particular setting to investigate the role of communication in heterogeneous settings due to its relative simplicity. Other studies, using subjects with homogenous attributes, have focused on CPR problems in the context of more complex physical settings, such as time dependence (Walker and Gardner, 1992; Gardner *et al.*, 1993).

102   HACKETT, SCHLAGER, AND WALKER

TABLE I
Description of Case Studies

CPR type	Location	Sharing rules	Documentation
Irrigation	Philippines	Proportional	Bacdayan (1980)
Irrigation	South and east Asia	Proportional	Bottrall (1978, 1981)
Irrigation	Philippines	Proportional	Coward (1979)
Irrigation	Philippines	Proportional	De los Reyes (1980)
Irrigation	Mexico	Proportional	Enge and Whiteford (1989)
Irrigation	Spain	Proportional	Glick (1970), Maas and Anderson (1978)
Irrigation	Sri Lanka	Proportional	Leach (1961)
Irrigation	Switzerland	Proportional	Netting (1981)
Irrigation	Iraq	Proportional	Spooner (1971, 1972, 1974)
Irrigation	India	Proportional	Wade (1988)
Irrigation	India	Equal appropriation	Seckler and Joshi (1982)
Irrigation	Africa	Equal appropriation	Gray (1963)
Groundwater aquifers	U.S.A.	Proportionate reduction	Blomquist (1992)
Grazing lands	England	Proportional	Slater (1907), Ault (1972)
Grazing lands	Switzerland	Proportional	Netting (1981)
Oil pools	U.S.A.	Proportionate reduction	McDonald (1971)
Fisheries	Australia	Equal appropriation	Sturgess *et al.* (1982)
Fisheries	Canada	Proportionate reduction and equal appropriation	Berkes and Pocock (1987)

summarizes results from Ostrom *et al.*, (1994) where individuals are homogeneous in input endowments. In Section V we discuss initial results from experiments where heterogeneities in endowments were assigned either randomly or through an auction mechanism. In Section VI we examine the robustness of our initial findings by exploring a situation with incomplete and asymmetric information regarding other appropriators' endowments. Section VII contains concluding comments.

II. CPR SHARING RULES FROM THE FIELD

Sharing rules used among heterogeneous appropriators in field settings may imply the regulation of inputs or outputs.[7] That is, these rules may restrict the allocation of inputs used to appropriate or they may restrict actual appropriation (withdrawal) levels. Table I presents summary characteristics from a sample of field settings where sharing rules were adopted.[8] This summary illustrates the

[7]Cases of self-governing CPR appropriator groups related to fisheries can be found in Berkes (1986), Cordell and McKean (1986), Ruddle and Akimichi (1984), Davis (1984), and Marchak *et al.* (1987). Groundwater cases in Southern California are described in Blomquist (1992). See Ostrom (1990) for other cases.

[8]The primary source for the case studies in Table I was Martin (1989). The cases in Table I do not represent an exhaustive survey of all case studies in Martin (1989). From a set of cases with well-documented allocation rules, this particular subset was chosen to illustrate the variety of rules found in the field. The distribution of rules illustrated in Table I, however, is supported in an extensive study by McKean (1992).

variety of rules adopted in the field and serves as a focus for comparing distributional characteristics of alternative rule types.

As Table I illustrates, *proportional rules* are commonly adopted among heterogeneous appropriators, with the basis for proportionality dependent upon a variety of factors. Appropriation rights are often proportionate to historic use levels, or to the quantity of land owned by resource users. For instance, groundwater pumpers in southern California reduced pumping in a manner proportionate to historic pumping levels to prevent the over-mining of groundwater basins (Blomquist, 1992).

Alternatively, the irrigators of Valencia, Spain, have been allocating irrigation water proportionate to land ownership since medieval times (Maas and Anderson, 1986).

> Proportionality was the organizing factor of the water distribution systems of medieval eastern Spain. Each irrigator received water in proportion to the amount of land he held. The water to which he was entitled, moreover, was not a fixed amount per unit of land, but rather a proportional one which varied with the volume of the river. All irrigators shared in times of abundance and were equally deprived in times of drought. (Glick, 1970, p. 207)

Appropriation of water in proportion to the amount of land held is also the organizing rule among irrigators located in the coastal lowlands in the province of Ilocos Norte, Philippines (Coward, 1979). If there is insufficient water to irrigate all of the land, the amount of land that can be irrigated is determined and the farmers "have their total farm size reduced proportionately" (Coward, 1979, p. 30). In addition to allocating water proportionally, the maintenance costs of operating the irrigation system are proportionally shared. That is, "the resources required to operate the system are requested from the water users in proportion to the shares they hold" (Coward, 1979, p. 31).

An alternative sharing rule, *equal appropriation*, involves a redistribution of resources which alters the status quo level of heterogeneities among appropriators. With an equal appropriation rule, a common appropriation ceiling is placed on all individuals. Appropriation heterogeneities are minimized, as all appropriators are permitted to withdraw only up to a certain amount. Such rules are often found in situations in which heterogeneities in appropriation capacities are minimal, such as the scallop fishers in the state of Victoria in Australia, where quotas were imposed to prevent the over-harvesting of scallops (Sturgess *et al.*, 1982).

There are, however, instances in which an equal appropriation rule has been used among appropriators with substantial heterogeneities. For example, equal appropriation rules are used on an irrigation system in India, in the village of Sukhomajri (Seckler and Joshi, 1982). The irrigation system for the village was created through an international development project. The project coordinators decided to allocate an equal amount of water to each landholder (Seckler and Joshi, 1982, p. 28). A water users association later took over the management of the irrigation system and changed the sharing rule to include landless villagers.

> Each *bona fide* family in the village—any group eating from a common hearth in Indian culture—is given a water coupon entitling them to the same quantity of water as any other family, irrespective of land ownership. The family can trade, give away, or sell the coupons as they wish, but with the approval of the Water Users Association. (Seckler and Joshi, 1982, p. 30)

Similarly, the Sonjo irrigators in the village of Kheri, located in northern Tanzania near the Kenya border, use an equal appropriation rule based on time.

104   HACKETT, SCHLAGER, AND WALKER

The source of their irrigation water is small streams and springs. "Primary rights for water are assigned to an individual for a full six hour period" (Gray, 1963, p. 58). Approximately 35 men in the village hold hereditary rights to the water. All other farmers must acquire water from these men.

> An individual of the privileged categories seldom requires all the water for the six hours to which he is entitled—even one with large landholdings–and frequently two hours is sufficient to soak his plots. The water that is left over may then be distributed to the men who are without any special rights. (Gray, 1963, pp. 59–60)

Men who do not have hereditary rights to water are often required to pay fees or pay other compensation for the water they acquire.

In some field settings more complex rules have been adopted that incorporate combinations of proportionate reductions and equal appropriation. For example, in 1982, the Ontario Ministry of Natural Resources and the Ontario Council of Commercial Fisheries created a new management plan that included individual transferable harvest quotas for Lake Erie (Berkes and Pocock, 1987). The plan was implemented in 1984 to address the over-harvesting of yellow perch, smelt, white bass, and walleye. Prior to implementation conflict emerged over how individual quotas should be allocated.

> Polls taken at the local association level indicated that the majority of fishermen at that time preferred an "equal split" formula within each licensing area, whereby all fishermen in an area would get the same quota. (Berkes and Pocock, 1987, p. 497)

The sharing formula eventually adopted, however, was based "on landings by license in the previous 10 years" (Berkes and Pocock, 1987, p. 497). In other words, the Ministry adopted a proportionate reduction from historic harvesting levels as an appropriation rule. A number of problems emerged, resulting in quota adjustments over subsequent years. For instance, in 1984, Port Stanley fishermen threatened to blockade the local harbor. Following this, the ministry granted an additional quota based on equal shares. In 1985, additional quotas were granted to fishermen in all of Lake Erie. In eastern Lake Erie, "license holders . . . voted on an allocation mechanism to distribute the extra quota, and a majority (44 to 33) opted for 'equal split'" (Berkes and Pocock, 1987, p. 498). The fishermen of western Lake Erie responded differently to the additional quotas by changing the sharing rule to reduce inequities in the quotas.

> The change established a formula with one-third equal share as a base and two-thirds on the basis of past performance. It was a compromise to satisfy the fishermen at the lower end of the quota scale, without reducing the quotas of those at the upper end. (Berkes and Pocock, 1987, p. 498)

An additional rule that appropriators could use, although one that we did not find in the case study literature, is an *equal absolute reduction rule*. For example, with regard to outputs, such a rule could require all appropriators to reduce their appropriation levels by an equal and absolute amount.

Clearly, as the above discussion of rules illustrates, different appropriation rules imply different costs for appropriators. Preferences across sharing rules will differ between large and small appropriators. Of the rules discussed thus far, large appropriators would prefer an equal absolute reduction rule the most. This is because they would be required to cut back their appropriation activities the least relative to the other rules. On the other hand, large appropriators would prefer an equal appropriation rule the least because they would be required to cut back their appropriation activities the most relative to the other rules. Small appropriators would have the opposite preference ordering.

Among heterogeneous appropriators there will generally be no rule that is universally preferred to all other rules. Consequently, appropriators are likely to disagree over the type of rule to adopt even though they may agree that they would be better off as a group if they reduced appropriation levels. It is such conflict over preferred sharing rules that may prevent heterogeneous appropriators from adopting a specific rule. Our experimental decision environment is designed to further explore the relationship between heterogeneity, self-governance, and sharing rules. In a controlled setting, we are able to more closely examine the evolution of successful agreements and measure the degree to which nonbinding agreements enhance efficiency. We now turn to a discussion of the decision environment examined in our laboratory investigation, and then to results.

III. THE EXPERIMENTAL CPR DECISION ENVIRONMENT

Theoretical Predictions

The single-play CPR game.   We first describe the class of single-play CPR games from which we draw our designs. Assume a fixed number n of appropriators with access to the CPR.[9] Each appropriator i has an endowment of inputs e_i which can be allocated to the CPR or allocated to an outside activity with a constant marginal return, w. The payoff to an individual appropriator from allocating inputs to the CPR depends on aggregate group allocations to the CPR and on the appropriator's allocation as a percentage of the aggregate. Let x_i denote appropriator i's allocation to the CPR, where $0 \le x_i \le e_i$. The group return to allocations to the CPR is given by the production function $F(\Sigma_{x_i})$, where F is a concave function, with $F(0) = 0$, $F'(0) > w$, and $F'(\Sigma_{e_i}) < 0$. Initially, allocating inputs to the CPR pays better than the opportunity cost $[F'(0) > w]$, but at some level of allocation (x_h) the outcome is counterproductive $[F'(x_h) < 0]$. Thus, the yield from the CPR reaches a *maximum net level* when individuals allocate some but not all of their endowments to the CPR.[10]

Let $x = (x_1, \ldots, x_n)$ be a vector of individual appropriators' input allocations to the CPR. The payoff to an appropriator, $u_i(x)$, is given by

$$
\begin{aligned}
&we_i, &&\text{if } x_i = 0 \\
&w(e_i - x_i) + (x_i/\Sigma_{x_i})F(\Sigma_{x_i}), &&\text{if } x_i > 0.
\end{aligned}
\tag{1}
$$

Equation (1) reflects the fact that if an appropriator allocates all of his endowment in the outside alternative, he gets a sure payoff (we_i), whereas if he allocates some of his endowment to the CPR, he gets a sure payoff $w(e_i - x_i)$, plus a payoff from the CPR. An appropriator's payoff from the CPR depends on the yield from total

---

[9]We rely significantly on the discussion in Ostrom *et al.* (1992) for our description of the game environment.

[10]One can interpret this environment as a limited access CPR (see, for example, Clark, 1980; Cornes and Sandler, 1986; Negri, 1989).

allocations, $F(\Sigma_{x_i})$, multiplied by his share of overall group allocations (x_i/Σ_{x_i}).[11] Previous studies have simplified the analysis of the CPR game by using designs that yield fully symmetric noncooperative equilibria. To see this, let the payoffs in (1) be the payoff functions in a symmetric, noncooperative game. Then each player allocates x_i^* in the CPR such that

$$-w + (1/n)F'(nx_i^*) + F(nx_i^*)((n-1)/x_i^* n^2) = 0. \qquad (2)$$

The focus of this paper, however, is on appropriator heterogeneity. In particular, the initial experimental design allows for two levels of input endowments. One subset of appropriators has large endowments, e_i^l, $i = 1, 2, \ldots, M$; the remaining appropriators have small endowments, e_j^s, $j = M + 1, M + 2, \ldots, N$, and $e_i^l > e_j^s$ (superscripts refer to endowment size). Parameters are chosen so that the Nash equilibrium is symmetric within appropriator type, but asymmetric across type; large appropriators allocate more inputs to the CPR than small appropriators.[12] This is accomplished by having the small players' endowment be a binding constraint in equilibrium. Allocations at the Nash equilibrium satisfy

$$-w + \left(x_i^*/(Z + Mx_i^*)\right)F'(Mx_i^*)$$
$$+ F(Mx_i^*)[Z + (M-1)x_i^*]/(Z + Mx_i^*)^2 = 0, \qquad (3a)$$

for $i = 1, 2, \ldots, M$, large-endowment players, and

$$x_j^* = e_j, \qquad (3b)$$

for $j = M + 1, M + 2, \ldots, N$, small-endowment players ($Z \equiv \Sigma_{x_j}^*$). Group allocations to the CPR at this asymmetric Nash equilibrium are greater than optimal, but not all rents from the CPR are dissipated (CPR *rents* per unit of input allocation are defined here to be the average revenue product of allocations to the CPR, less the average revenue product of allocations to an outside opportunity). To see this, compare this deficient equilibrium to the optimal solution. Summing across individual payoffs $u_i(x)$ for all appropriators i, one has the group payoff function $u(x)$,

$$u(x) = w\sum_{e_i} - w\sum_{x_i} + F\left(\sum_{x_i}\right), \qquad (4)$$

which is to be maximized subject to the constraints $0 \leq \Sigma_{x_i} \leq \Sigma_{e_i}$. Given the above

---

[11] If total input allocation is held constant, one token allocated to the CPR yields the same return regardless of the identity of the player making the investment. Thus heterogeneity is in endowments, not in appropriation skills.

[12] The Nash equilibrium can be made symmetric even with large- and small-endowment appropriators. In particular, a symmetric Nash equilibrium results as long as the small-endowment level is greater than or equal to that required for equilibrium play. In such a case small-endowment appropriators simply have a lower input allocation level in the outside market relative to large-endowment appropriators.

conditions on F, the group maximization problem has a unique solution characterized by the condition

$$-w + F'\left(\sum_{x_i}\right) = 0. \tag{5}$$

According to (5), the marginal return from a CPR should equal the opportunity cost of the outside alternative for the last input unit allocated to the CPR. While the asymmetric Nash equilibrium depends critically on the endowment parameter e_i, the group payoff maximizing level of allocation does not. There are many different rules that can distribute individual allocations to the CPR such that total rents from the CPR are maximized. Since endowments are heterogeneous, different rules (e.g., equal allocation to the CPR versus CPR allocations proportionate with endowment) imply different wealth distributions. Such inequities may lead to disagreement over the type of sharing rule, and ultimately a reduction in CPR rents.

Finite-repetition. Denote the CPR game by X and let X be played a finite number of times.[13] If the game has a unique equilibrium, then the finitely repeated game has a unique subgame perfect and subgame consistent equilibrium (Selten, 1971). Thus, Eq. (3) characterizes a finite sequence of equilibrium outcomes. This prediction is based on the assumption of a finite game of complete information. Our subjects know the game is finite. During recruitment, subjects are told they will participate in a 1- to 2-hour decision-making experiment. Further, subjects were explicitly informed of the endpoint of each treatment sequence prior to the beginning of that sequence. Although we do not have complete control over our subjects' understanding of their decision task, we make all information readily available to them.

Communication. Face-to-face communication represents an interesting empirical anomaly from the perspective of game theory. If the games implemented in our laboratory setting accurately induce the valuations corresponding to the payoff function of Eq. (1) and the experimental parameters of Table II, then finitely repeated, complete information, noncooperative game theory ascribes no strategic content to nonbinding communication.[14] Face-to-face communication (and resulting verbal commitments), however, may change subject's expectations of other players' responses. In particular, if subjects believe a cooperative play will induce

---

[13]Typically, the repeated game has many equilibria. Two equilibrium refinement principles are subgame perfection and subgame consistency. An equilibrium is subgame perfect if it prescribes equilibrium play on every subgame. An equilibrium is subgame consistent if it prescribes identical play on identical subgames.

[14]When the game X has a unique equilibrium x^*, neither finite repetition nor communication creates new equilibrium outcomes. Let c denote a communication strategy, in the communication phase C, available to any player. As long as saying one thing and doing another has no payoff consequences, then any strategy of the form (c, x^*) is an equilibrium of the one-shot game (C, X), and finitely repeated x^* is a subgame perfect equilibrium outcome of repeated communication $(C, X, C, X, \ldots, C, X)$. In this situation, subgame perfection is independent of communication.

TABLE II

Experimental Design Baseline: Parameters for a Given Decision Period

Subject type	Low endowment	High endowment
Number of subjects	4	4
Individual token endowment	8	24
Production function, Market 2[a]	$33(\Sigma_{x_k}) - 0.25(\Sigma_{x_k})^2$	$33(\Sigma_{x_k}) - 0.25(\Sigma_{x_k})^2$
Market 2 return/unit of output	$0.01	$0.01
Market 1 return/unit of output	$0.05	$0.05

Earnings per subject at group maximum evaluated at benchmark conventions

Equal allocation	$1.23	$1.70
Equal absolute reduction	$0.66	$2.26
Equal proportionate reduction	$0.94	$1.98
Earnings/subject at Nash equilibrium	$0.56	$1.33
Earnings/subject at zero net yield	$0.24	$0.72

[a]Σ_{x_k} = the total number of tokens allocated by the group in Market 2. The production function shows the number of units of output produced in Market 2 for each level of tokens allocated in Market 2. All payoffs include a per-period fee of $0.02 per token.

cooperation from others, then cooperating can be sustained as rational play in the framework of incomplete information regarding player types.[15]

In order for communication to enhance joint CPR payoffs, the appropriators must agree on (i) the target level of group allocations to the CPR, (ii) a rule for allocating the target input allocation across appropriators, and (iii) create the necessary "social capital" to attenuate cheating, since agreements are nonbinding. The existence of heterogeneity in endowments and in historic allocation levels has no effect on (i), but presumably elicits disagreement over (ii), which in turn may impair (iii). The research goal is to observe the effect of endowment heterogeneity on the success of communication as a rent-enhancing mechanism and on the form and success of sharing rules endogenously chosen by the subjects. Such rules can then be contrasted with those reported in Section II.

The Laboratory Setting and Design

Subjects and the experimental setting. The experiments reported in this paper used subjects drawn from the undergraduate population at Indiana University and the University of Arizona. Students were volunteers recruited from undergraduate economics, political science, and public administration classes. Prior to recruitment, potential volunteers were given a brief explanation in which they were told only that they would be making decisions in an "economic choice" environment and that the money they earned would be dependent upon their own allocation decisions and those of the others in their experimental group. All experiments were conducted on the NovaNET computer system. The computer facilitates the accounting procedures involved in the experiment, enhances subject control across experiments, and allows for minimal experimenter involvement.

---

[15]See McKelvey and Palfrey (1992) for a discussion of this argument for the case of the "centipede" game, in particular pages 804–805.

At the beginning of each experimental session, subjects were told that: (1) they would make a series of allocation decisions, (2) all individual allocation decisions were anonymous to the group, and (3) they would be paid their individual earnings (privately and in cash) at the end of the experiment. Subjects then proceeded at their own pace through a set of instructions summarized below.[16]

Subjects faced a series of decision rounds in which they were endowed with a specified number of tokens, which they allocated between two markets. Market 1 was described as an allocation opportunity which yielded a fixed (constant) rate of output per token, where each unit of output yielded a fixed constant monetary return. Market 2 (the CPR) was described as an allocation opportunity which yielded a rate of output per token dependent upon the total number of tokens allocated by the entire group. The rate of output at each level of group allocation to Market 2 was described in functional form as well as tabular form. Subjects were informed that they would receive a level of output from Market 2 that was equivalent to the percentage of total group tokens they allocated. Further, subjects knew that each unit of output from Market 2 yielded a fixed (constant) rate of monetary return.

Subjects knew with certainty the total number of decision makers in the group, their own token endowment, the total number of tokens in the group, the productivity characteristics of the CPR, and the number of decision rounds in the current treatment condition. Individual token endowments were publicly known. After each round, subjects were shown a display that recorded their profits in each market for that round, total group token allocations to Market 2, and a total of their cumulative profits for the experiment. During the experiment, subjects could request, through the computer, this information for all previous rounds for the current treatment condition. Subjects received no information regarding other subjects' individual allocation decisions.

Parameters and predictions. We operationalized this environment with eight appropriators ($n = 8$) and quadratic production functions $F(\Sigma_{x_i})$ for Market 2, where

$$F\left(\sum_{x_i}\right) = a\sum_{x_i} - b\left(\sum_{x_i}\right)^2, \qquad (6)$$

with $F'(0) = a > w$ and $F'(ne) = a - 2bne < 0$. For this quadratic specification, one has from (5) that the group-optimal token allocation satisfies $\Sigma_{x_i} = (a - w)/2b$. Further, the CPR yields 0% of optimal rents when token allocation is twice as large as optimal.

The Nash equilibrium for a finite game with complete information (based on an individual's payoff function as shown in Eq. (1)) for large and small appropriators is given by

$$\sum_{x_i} = (M/(M + 1))(a - w - bZ)/b, \qquad i = 1, 2, \ldots, M,$$

$$\sum_{x_j} = Z \equiv \sum_{e_j}, \qquad j = M + 1, M + 2, \ldots, N. \qquad (7)$$

---

[16]A copy of the instructions is available from the authors upon request. In the instructions, the term "token investment" was used instead of "token allocation."

These noncooperative allocations are between maximal net yield and zero net yield. The following constraints were placed on the choice of parameter values for a, b, c, d, e, and w in this study. First, to preserve equilibrium uniqueness, Nash equilibrium x_i and x_j must be integer valued, a constraint imposed by software design. Second, in order for heterogeneity in endowments to create a heterogeneous Nash equilibrium, the small players' endowments had to be sufficiently small to be a binding constraint in noncooperative play.

The specific parameters used for our experiments are shown in Table II. Each small player is endowed with 8 tokens per round, and each large player with 24. Further, each player is charged an endowment fee of $0.02 per token per period to lower the cost of the experiments. This fee is a sunk cost, thus having no effect on Nash equilibrium or optimal allocation levels.

These parameters lead to the following *benchmarks* that will be used for evaluating our experimental results. First, there exists a unique Nash equilibrium where total tokens allocated to Market 2 equals 96: (i) small endowment players each allocate all 8 of their tokens in Market 2 and (ii) large endowment players each allocate 16 tokens in Market 2 and 8 tokens in Market 1. At the Nash equilibrium subjects earn approximately 49% of the *maximum rents* from Market 2, the CPR. Computing earnings from both Market 1 and Market 2 at this equilibrium, small players receive a per-period payoff of $(8 \times \$0.09) - (8 \times (\$0.02) = \$0.56$. Large players receive a per-period payoff of $(8 \times \$0.05) + (16 \times \$0.09) - (24 \times \$0.02) = \$1.36$. In order to maximize group earnings, 56 tokens must be allocated to Market 2, yielding a group per period payoff of $11.78.

Various allocation rules can be used to achieve the group optimum of 56 tokens allocated to Market 2. Different allocation rules, however, generate meaningful differences in individual payoffs (displayed in Table II). Under the rule of *equal allocation*, each player allocates $56/8 = 7$ tokens at the group optimum. Each small player receives a net payoff of $1.23, while each large player receives a net payoff of $1.70. Using the noncooperative Nash allocation level as the reference point, *equal absolute reductions* in tokens allocated to Market 2 require each player to remove $40/8 = 5$ tokens from Market 2. Each small player allocates 3 tokens in Market 2, with a net payoff of $0.66. Each large player allocates 11 tokens in Market 2, with a net payoff of $2.26. (Note that small players are still better off with this convention relative to the Nash equilibrium.) Again using the Nash equilibrium as the reference point, an *equal proportionate reduction* in tokens allocated to Market 2 requires the group to cut token allocations to Market 2 by 42%. Each small player allocates 5 tokens in Market 2, with a net payoff of $0.94. Each large player allocates 9 tokens in Market 2, with a net payoff of $1.98.

Treatment sequences. Subjects participated in two (consecutive) 10-round sequences of the asymmetric game.[17] In the first 10 rounds subjects were not allowed to communicate. In the final 10 rounds the subjects were informed that prior to each decision round they would have the opportunity to discuss the allocation problem (10 minutes prior to the first decision round and 3 minutes prior to each

---

[17]After completing the instructions, subjects had the opportunity to participate in a series of five salient reward decision rounds with identical endowments of 20 tokens each. Otherwise the parameters were identical to those in Table I. These "trainer" rounds were implemented to give the subjects initial experiences with the logistics of the experiment.

subsequent round). No physical threats or side payments were allowed.[18] Thus, the structure of the experiment can be summarized as follows:

Sequence 1   Sequence 2
$X, X, \ldots, X$ $C - X, C - X, \ldots, C - X.$

Prior to each 10-round treatment sequence, four subjects were assigned the large token endowment (24 tokens each), while the remaining four subjects were assigned the small endowment (8 tokens each). Drawing from the literature on reward distribution, we used two different mechanisms for assigning the large- and small-endowment positions: random and auction. There is an emerging theoretical literature which suggests that these two methods of assigning advantageous positions will lead to different bargaining outcomes. Particularly prominent is the work of Guth (1988, 1992), who has developed an equity-theoretic model of bargaining behavior to explain such phenomena. The underlying notion in Guth's framework is that parties will respond to unequal positions with sharing rules that equalize net payoffs, when such rules are feasible. Thus, to equalize net payoffs in a setting where large token endowments are assigned with an auction, subjects with large endowments must be given the opportunity to allocate a greater number of tokens to the CPR to compensate them for the endowment purchase price.

Assignment of advantaged positions has been the focus of several experimental studies as well. Guth and Tietz (1985) study the effects of using a second price auction to assign strategically advantaged positions in the context of ultimatum bargaining.[19] The auction prices were private information. In the ultimatum bargaining game a proposer makes a once-and-for-all offer for dividing a fixed dollar sum, while another party can either accept the offer and the subsequent payoff, or reject the offer (in which case both parties receive $0). The subgame-perfect equilibrium with dollar payoff maximizers grants all but a penny to the proposer. Guth and Tietz found that participants paid more for the advantaged position and that share proposals were positively influenced by the auction prices. Hoffman and Spitzer (1982, 1985) similarly found that the strategically advantaged bargainer received larger shares when the bargaining positions were allocated based on superior performance in a game preceding the bargaining process.

While these laboratory findings suggest that assignment mechanisms in which the advantaged player somehow "earns" that position lead to bargaining outcomes closer to the (pecuniary) equilibrium predictions, the issue is not resolved for CPR problems. Given the nature of face-to-face negotiations in our CPR input allocation problem, there are many different input allocation rules that maximize CPR rents and are individually rational from the perspective of the noncooperative benchmark. The empirical question is how different mechanisms for assigning advantaged positions affect the choice of token allocation rules. Our use of these particular assignment mechanisms is not intended to replicate Guth and Tietz or Hoffman and Spitzer, but rather to study the effects of heterogeneity in two conditions which may be expected to imply the adoption of different allocation rules.

[18]Each person was identified with a badge. This facilitated player identification in our transcripts. If unanimous, players could forego discussion.

[19]In a second price auction the highest bid wins the auction, but the auction price equals the second highest bid.

112   HACKETT, SCHLAGER, AND WALKER

Our first method of assigning the token endowment positions was a random draw. Large endowments were assigned randomly prior to the 10 decision rounds without communication, and again prior to the 10 decision rounds with communication. The instructions for this randomization process are summarized below.

Subjects were informed that for each of the next 10 rounds one-half would be allocated 8 tokens, while the other half would be allocated 24 tokens. Tokens would be randomly allocated in such a way that each was equally likely to have 8 or 24 tokens.

The actual randomization process required one subject to "blindly" draw four slips of paper from a hat. The four subjects whose identification number was chosen (and noted publicly) received the endowment of 24 tokens. Token endowments are sufficiently unequal in our design that subjects cannot choose allocation rules that simultaneously equalize net payoffs and maximize total CPR rents. Thus Guth's prediction that parties will choose allocation rules to equalize net payoffs is not strictly feasible. There are different dimensions over which parties can equalize, however, and a prominent one in this CPR setting is to choose rules that allow each subject to allocate an equal number of tokens to the CPR.

A multiple unit ascending price auction was used as the alternative mechanism for assigning endowment positions. Prior to the 10 decision rounds with no communication and again prior to the 10 decision rounds with communication the subjects received a set of instructions summarized below.

For each of the next 10 rounds four subjects would be assigned 8 tokens, while the other four would each be assigned 24. Tokens would be assigned using an *auction* in which each subject bid for the right to have 24 tokens. The auction began with each subject raising their right hand. The auctioneer called out bids that increased every 5 seconds, in $0.25 intervals. When the auctioneer reached a bid that was the highest total amount a subject was willing to pay to have 24 tokens rather than 8 tokens each round, the subject should lower his or her hand. This meant the subject was out of the auction. When there were only four persons left with their hands raised the auction stopped. Each of the four persons remaining in the auction were allocated 24 tokens each round for the next 10 rounds, paying a one-time auction price equal to the last bid that was called by the auctioneer when the auction stopped. The four persons who dropped out of the bidding process were allocated 8 tokens each round.

This particular auction mechanism was chosen because of its demand-revealing characteristics. In particular, the price paid for the large-endowment position should theoretically correspond with the maximum value placed on this position by the subject with the fourth highest valuation. Thus, the four subjects who win the auction should be those who place the highest value on having the large endowment.

Recall that in this setting, Guth's (1988, 1992) model over bargaining outcomes predicts that individuals, when allowed to jointly choose an allocation rule, will fix token allocations such that individual payoffs *net of the auction price* are equalized. An implication of equalizing net payoffs is that the higher the auction price, the higher is the large endowment subjects' share of all tokens allocated to the CPR. Thus, while the overt objective is to design token allocation rules to equalize payoffs net of auction prices, a by-product of such rules will be a direct relationship between individual token endowments and individual token allocations to Market 2. We use the term "weak proportionality" to refer to this relationship.

TABLE III
Homogeneous Endowments: Rents as a Percentage of Optimum

	No-communication rounds		Communication rounds		
Exp. No.	1–5	6–10	11–15	16–20	21–25
		10-token endowments			
1	26	26	96	100	100
2	35	21	100	97	100
3	33	24	99	99	—
4	37	39	94	98	100
		25-token endowments			
1	35	−43	76	75	54
2	60	8	85	82	85
3	4	−8	61	68	68
4	−60	13	80	93	99
5	−24	−3	40	67	−15
6	36	−41	84	86	80

IV. EXPERIMENTS WITH HOMOGENEOUS ENDOWMENTS

The principal focus of this paper is the impact of endowment heterogeneities on the ability of individuals to coordinate their use of a CPR. To serve as a benchmark for purposes of comparison, we summarize results reported by Ostrom, Gardner, and Walker (1994), hereafter OGW, regarding behavior in CPR decision environments where subjects have identical token endowments. The decision setting in the OGW experiments is identical to our CPR game X, but with parameters chosen to yield a symmetric Nash equilibrium. Table III displays summary results on average rents as a percentage of optimum from two decision environments investigated by OGW.[20] In the low-endowment environment, each subject was endowed with 10 tokens per round. In the high-endowment environment, each subject's token endowment was increased to 25 tokens. In the first 10 periods of each of these experiments there was no opportunity for explicit communication. Following the 10th decision round, subjects were allowed the opportunity for face-to-face communication prior to each round.

These communication experiments provide strong evidence for the power of face-to-face communication. Players successfully used the opportunity to (a) calculate coordinated rent-increasing strategies, (b) devise verbal agreements to implement these strategies, and (c) deal with nonconforming players through verbal sanctions.[21]

In the low-endowment experiments, rents averaged over 98% of optimum following the introduction of the opportunity to communicate. This high degree of yield from the CPR is in contrast to an average of only 30% in pre-communication

---

[20]Our discussion of rents will be based on actual rents earned from Market 2 as a percentage of rents that would be earned if the group made the optimal investment in Market 2. Note that the outside opportunity cost of a token invested in Market 2 is the return in Market 1 ($0.05).

[21]Such sanctions could not be addressed to specific nonconformers since actual subject decisions were anonymous.

rounds. Defining a defection as a Market 2 investment larger than agreed upon, in the low-endowment environment, OGW identified only 19 defections from agreements out of 368 total decisions (a 5% defection rate).

The high-endowment (25 token) CPR game is a more challenging decision environment. While the equilibrium prediction for 10- and 25-token endowment games is identical, the disequilibrium implications of the 25-token game change considerably. Given OGW's parameterizations of the CPR game, with 25 tokens, as few as three subjects investing all of their tokens can essentially bring returns below that for Market 1 (full rent dissipation), while with 10 tokens it takes seven out of eight subjects to accomplish this much damage. In all six 25-token endowment experiments, rents increased dramatically over that achieved in the first 10 rounds, averaging 71% of optimum in contrast to -2% in pre-communication rounds. Experiments 1, 3, and 5, however, demonstrate the potential fragile nature of nonbinding agreements. In the high-endowment environment, OGW identified 100 defections from agreements out of 624 total decisions (a 16% defection rate).

Perhaps most importantly for our purposes, OGW's results reveal a notable behavioral regularity regarding rule choice. All agreements to cooperate featured rules specifying equal token allocations to the CPR. Homogeneity facilitated cooperation in that the equal allocation rule is simple and perceived to be fair in that subjects' payoffs are equalized. It is in this sense that heterogeneities can be important in the new experiments reported here. In the presence of endowment heterogeneities, sharing rules that equalize token allocations to the CPR will *not* generally yield equal earnings across subjects.

V. EXPERIMENTAL RESULTS

Overview

In this section we present an overview of the results from our four design cells: (1) no-communication random endowment assignment (NC-R), (2) communication random endowment assignment (C-R), (3) no-communication auction endowment assignment (NC-A), and (4) communication auction endowment assignment (C-A). The discussion focuses first on individual token allocations to Market 2, the CPR, followed by a summary of rent accrual as a percentage of optimum. This overview of results will be followed by a discussion of: (a) agreements to specific allocation rules and adherence to these agreements, and (b) auction prices.

Individual decisions. Figure 1 displays frequency distributions of individual Market 2 decisions for each of the design cells. Several summary points are of interest. First, note the similarity in decisions for both design conditions with no communication (the left-hand panels). Individual decisions are dispersed across the feasible token allocations with a modal allocation of eight tokens. Recall that low-token-endowment subjects had an endowment of eight tokens. The high frequency at eight can be attributed primarily to those subjects allocating their entire endowments in the CPR in numerous decision rounds (consistent with the Nash prediction).

Focusing on specific decision rounds, however, we do not observe a pattern of allocations (at the individual level) strictly consistent with the Nash prediction of 8

RESOLVING COMMONS DILEMMAS   115

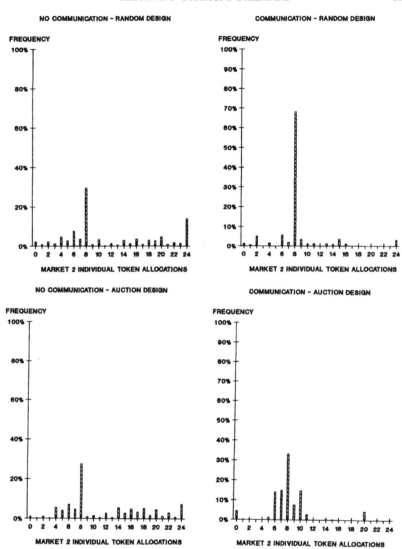

Fig. 1.   Individual token allocations for Market 2—frequencies across design conditions.

tokens for low-endowment subjects *and* 16 tokens for high-endowment subjects. To illustrate this result, consider the 10th round of experiment 1 of the NC-R design. The four large-endowment subjects allocated 18, 10, 15, and 24 tokens to Market 2, while the four small-endowment subjects allocated 8, 8, 8, and 6 tokens to Market 2. The results from this decision round are representative of decision rounds in other NC experiments in that a high percentage of low-endowment subjects allocate their entire endowment of 8 tokens to Market 2. The distribution

TABLE IV
Heterogeneous Experiments: Rents as a Percentage of Optimum

	No-communication rounds		Communication rounds	
Exp. No.	1–5	6–10	11–15	16–20
Random assignment of tokens				
1	31	38	98	100
2	56	25	80	81
3	53	42	98	97
4	62	57	97	98
Auction assignment of tokens				
1	61	54	91	90
2	31	29	98	98
3	58	68	98	98
4	34	30	97	100

of token allocations to Market 2 by high-endowment subjects, however, is quite varied, falling primarily in the range of 14 to 24 tokens.[22]

The opportunity to communicate led to a noticeable change in the pattern of Market 2 allocations. With the allocation rules agreed upon in communication rounds (discussed in more detail below), subjects concentrated their Market 2 allocations near the optimal allocation of 56 tokens aggregate. In the treatment condition C-R (upper right-hand graph), individual Market 2 allocations of 8 tokens represents the modal response (67%). In the C-A condition, however, we observe a spread of allocations clustered in the range of 6–10 tokens. An explanation for this behavior is provided in the subsection on allocation rules and defections presented below.

Rents. In the treatment conditions in which tokens were allocated randomly, rents could be dissipated through an excessive allocation of tokens to Market 2. In the auction treatment conditions, rents could be dissipated further by the competition for token endowments. For now, we focus on rent dissipation from over-allocation to Market 2, and turn to rent dissipation from the auctions in a later section. Table IV displays summary information regarding the level of rents generated across the four design conditions. For both treatment conditions with no communication, we observe a level of rent accrual relatively close to that predicted by the Nash equilibrium (48.9%). In condition NC-R, the overall mean rent is 45.3% of optimum and for NC-A the level is 45.8%. The opportunity to communicate leads to a noticeable shift toward optimality. In condition C-R, overall rents increase to an average of 93.6%, and for C-A the level is 96.1%.[23] Thus, even in an environment of extreme heterogeneity in subject endowments, communication

---

[22] Walker *et al.* (1990) also found little support for the Nash equilibrium prediction at the individual decision level.

[23] Comparing rents for NC-R vs C-R, NC-A vs C-A, and pooling within no-communication and communication conditions: (1) an hypothesis of no difference in means between no communication and communication is rejected ($\alpha = 0.05$ level, *t* test) and (2) an hypothesis that the samples are drawn from the same underlying distribution is rejected ($\alpha = 0.05$ level, Wilcoxon nonparametric test).

TABLE V
Summary Frequency of Allocation Rules: Allocations in Market 2

	Random		Auction	
	Proposed	Agreed	Proposed	Agreed
50% of endowment	1	0	1	0
Large, 66% endowment; Small, 33% endowment	1	0	0	0
Equal absolute reduction	0	0	1	0
Large = 6, small = 8	4	4	0	0
Large = 7, small = 8	1	1	0	0
Large = 7.5, small = 8[a]	7	7	0	0
Large = 8, small = 7	0	0	7	7
Large = 8, small = 8	19	18	9	4
Large = 8.5, small = 8[a]	0	0	2	2
Large = 9, small = 7	0	0	6	5
Large = 9, small = 8	2	1	0	0
Large = 10, small = 5	0	0	1	1
Large = 10, small = 6	0	0	10	10
Large = 10, small = 7	0	0	1	0
Large = 10, small = 8	0	0	9	9
Large = 11, small = 6	0	0	1	1
Large = 11, small = 7	0	0	1	0
Large = 11, small = 8	0	0	1	1
Large = 12, small = 8	1	1	0	0

[a]Subjects agreed to a rotation scheme of 7–8 or 8–9.

remains a powerful mechanism for promoting cooperation, resulting in rents very close to those observed in the homogeneous decision setting of OGW.

Allocation Rules and Defections

Allocation rules: Summary. Table V displays a summary of the allocation rules classified according to the two methods for assigning token endowments: random and auction. The frequencies with which each of the allocation rules were proposed or agreed upon are shown. Although there appears to be a rather diverse set of rules which were actually agreed to, a high percentage of these agreements can be summarized along a few simple principles. In all eight experiments, the endogenously agreed upon allocation rules were devised under conditions where subjects: (1) sought to maximize group returns, and (2) perceived an aggregate allocation of 64 tokens as the optimum.[24] In actuality, an allocation of 64 tokens yields rents that are 98% of optimum.[25]

---

[24]Evidence supporting this conclusion is found in transcripts of the communication rounds, available from the authors.

[25]Why 64? The summary table subjects received for payoff returns from Market 2 shows possible levels of Market 2 allocations (and resulting total, average, and marginal returns) for allocation levels beginning at 6 tokens and ending with 128—with intervals of 6 or 7 tokens. Sixty-four tokens is the level of allocation shown on the table to maximize group returns from Market 2. Thus, as observed in many experiments, subjects tended to ignore marginal returns and focus on a total return instead.

118   HACKETT, SCHLAGER, AND WALKER

The rules adopted for allocating tokens across group members varied between the random and the auction designs.[26] In the random design, recall that subjects could not simultaneously maximize group rents and equalize net payoffs. Subjects in this design agreed upon rules in 32 of 40 decision rounds. These rules can be principally organized around two distribution concepts: (1) equal allocations to the CPR, and (2) marginal reductions in payoff differentials by having small appropriators allocate marginally more tokens to the CPR than large appropriators. In particular, of the 32 agreements, 18 specified equal CPR allocations and 12 specified marginal reductions in payoff differentials.

In all experiments in the auction design, subjects adopted allocation rules that explicitly attempted to equalize net payoffs (net of auction price), while achieving close to optimal allocation in Market 2. Below we present a few representative comments which illustrate the nature of the discussion process:

"We have to decide which is the best number. ... I think the best number is 64. ... "

"Obviously we want to maximize our group return, right? ... that's at 64."

"We need to allow the people who bid for the 24 to make up their bid price."
In 36 of the 40 decision rounds, rules designed to equalize net payoffs resulted in subjects choosing allocation rules that allowed large appropriators to allocate more to Market 2 than the small appropriators. The most commonly agreed to allocation rule was a Market 2 allocation of 10 tokens by each large-endowment subject and 6 by each small-endowment subject. Under this rule large-endowment subjects had 62.5% of the total token allocation to Market 2, compared to their 75% share of total token endowment. Thus, this most commonly used rule is weakly proportionate with endowment shares.

Defections.   The occurrence of defections on agreed upon allocation schemes is relatively minor across the set of eight experiments. Agreements were reached in 72 of 80 decision rounds. In total, we observed 21 of 72 decision rounds—37 of 576 (6.4%) individual decisions—in which at least one subject was observed to have defected. These defection rates closely follow the rates observed by OGW in their low endowment design.

In all but three instances, the magnitude of the defectors' allocation to Market 2 was no more than 4 tokens above the agreement. Further, defection led to a breakdown of subjects' ability to adopt agreements in only one experiment. In experiment 2 of the C-R design, there was a round 1 defection of 16 tokens by one subject and 8 tokens by another. Following this defection, this group successfully reached agreement in only one of the nine remaining decision rounds. Thus, in 7 of 8 experiments, subjects were able to devise agreements, and maintain commitment to those agreements, over numerous decision rounds.

Auction Prices: NC-A and C-A Conditions

Price levels.   The auction we employed should yield reservation prices consistent with individuals' expectations of the value of having 24 tokens rather than 8. One

---

[26]Adopted allocation rules led to different patterns of investments across the random and auction designs. In the random design, small appropriators were more likely to invest larger numbers of tokens in Market 2 than in the auction design. The reverse holds for large appropriators. In both cases: (1) an hypothesis of no difference in means is rejected ($\alpha = 0.05$ level, t test) and (2) an hypothesis that the samples are drawn from the same underlying distribution is rejected ($\alpha = 0.05$ level, Wilcoxon nonparametric test).

TABLE VI
Auction Prices: Effects on Potential Earnings

No-communication rounds		Communication rounds	
Auction price ($)	Earnings as a % of optimum	Auction price ($)	Earnings as a % of optimum
5.25	52.6	8.00	66.3
7.75	26.5	7.25	73.7
9.50	42.8	9.75	65.1
8.25	26.4	7.00	75.0

possible source of these expectations is the value of the 16 additional tokens at the Nash equilibrium in the CPR game. The expected payoff for subjects with the small endowment is $0.56 per round, while that for large-endowment subjects is $1.36, a difference of $0.80 per round. Because auction winners were endowed with an additional 16 tokens in each of 10 rounds, this leads to a prediction of $8.00 as the auction price.

As displayed in Table VI, auction prices were similar across the eight auctions we conducted. The four NC-A auctions generated prices of: (1) $5.25, (2) $7.75, (3) $9.50, and (4) $8.25 for an average of $7.69. The four C-A auctions generated prices of: (1) $8.00, (2) $7.25, (3) $9.75, and (4) $7.00 for an average price of $8.00. Clearly, the auction prices are broadly consistent with Nash expectations. On the other hand, this does not rule out the possibility that they are consistent with other expectations. For example, in the C-A condition, one might conjecture that subjects may be forward looking in the sense that they anticipate group cooperation with an allocation to Market 2 of 64 tokens (the level of Market 2 allocations that they seem to perceive to maximize earnings). This conjecture yields a wide range of possible payoffs ($4.80 to $24.00) depending upon the distribution of tokens one anticipates for allocations to Market 2.[27]

Effects on net earnings. A fundamental behavioral question of this study concerns rent dissipation—with and without communication. At the individual level, the auction dissipated the added gains that could be earned from being a large appropriator. This occurred both in the communication condition, in which subjects explicitly tailored allocation rules to equalize payoffs net of auction prices, and in the no-communication condition, where such agreements were not possible. Consider the average net payoff for large appropriators relative to small appropriators. In all four replications under the C-A condition and three of four replications under the NC-A condition, large appropriators made less than small appropriators, but the difference averaged less than 10 cents per round. The exception was the first replication under the NC-A condition, in which large

---

[27]Alternatively, one might conjecture that observed auction prices are correlated more closely with the level of earnings subjects observed in prior treatment conditions. For instance, subjects might base their reservation price for bidding in the auction on average payoff per token calculated from prior experience. There is some support for this conjecture in our C-A design, but not in our C-R design.

120   HACKETT, SCHLAGER, AND WALKER

appropriators made an average of 51 cents per round more than small appropriators.[28]

At the group level, competition in the auction for tokens (larger endowments)
led to a significant loss in rents. This point is illustrated in Table VI. For each of
the eight auctions, Table VI displays the auction price (paid by each of four
bidders) and the effect on earnings relative to optimum. Specifically, for each
condition we report actual earnings (net of auction prices) as a percentage of
maximum possible earnings. These results point to significant losses in earnings
through competition for larger token endowments and through excessive token
allocations to the CPR. Thus, under the NC-A condition we observed rent
dissipation at two levels: (1) competition for endowments of tokens, and
(2) over-allocation to Market 2. Under the C-A condition rent dissipation occurred
primarily through competition for token endowments, since subjects used communication to overcome excessive allocations to Market 2.

VI. NEW DESIGN: COMMUNICATION IN A MORE "COMPLEX" SETTING

Theory and Experimental Design

One of the regularities observed in the experimental data is the extensive use of
allocation rules that either specified equal allocations to Market 2 (primarily the
C-R experiments) or were tailored to minimize net payoff differences (primarily
the C-A experiments). The results from the C-R experiments stand in contrast to
the predominant role of proportionate allocation rules observed in our field
sample, as described in Section II. One possible argument for this disparity is that
field settings are complex relative to the laboratory. One response to complexity
may be to experiment with a variety of rules, including proportionate rules. In our
initial experiments, there were only two types of appropriators. Moreover, an
individual's type and payoff function were common knowledge. This complete
information setting allows for rules to be a function of relative payoffs. These
conditions may not capture important complexities of many field settings. For
example, Wiggins and Libecap (1985) find substantial evidence that heterogeneity
and asymmetric information significantly increase the difficulties involved in using
communication to resolve CPR dilemmas in oil fields. This basic result is also
observed in the oil field unitization bargaining experiments of Wiggins *et al.*
(1991).

These issues led us to develop a set of *exploratory* experiments with a more
complex laboratory decision environment. These experiments depart from our
initial experiments in that: (1) they are operationalized with four endowment
classes—8, 12, 20, and 24 tokens—with two appropriators in each class, and
(2) information on each individual's token endowment is incomplete and asymmetric. To maintain anonymity regarding others' token endowments, tokens were
randomly assigned in private at the beginning of an experimental session. Thus,
individuals knew their own endowment, knew that the total tokens held by the

---

[28] In replications 1, 2, 3, and 4 of the NC-A condition, the average net payoff difference of large
relative to small was $0.51, −$0.05, −$0.10, and −$0.01 per round. For the C-A condition, the
differences were −$0.09, −$0.05, −$0.03, and −$0.04.

TABLE VII
New Design: Rents as a Percentage of Optimum

	No-communication rounds		Communication rounds	
Exp. No.	1–5	6–10	11–15	16–20
1	44	28	90	82
2	49	48	84	83
3	78	52	86	75

group was 128, but did not know the individual endowments of other subjects.[29] Subjects maintained their endowment type for the entire experiment. This procedure prevented subjects from deducing other endowment types from their own past experiences. As before, 10 rounds of the CPR game with no communication were followed by 10 rounds with communication.[30]

For experimental control, the CPR production function was not changed for this design. The idea was to hold the production function constant and observe the effect of a more complex environment in which more subject types exist and in which subjects may not be able to credibly communicate their endowment to others. Solving as in Eq. (7) above, the Nash equilibrium requires the 8-token and the 12-token players to allocate their full endowment in Market 2, while the 20-token and the 24-token players allocate 14.4. Since tokens in the experiment are not divisible, this Nash equilibrium is not unique; the two large-endowment types will mix between 14 and 15. Note, however, that this design maintains heterogeneity in CPR allocations at the Nash equilibrium, an important characteristic of our initial design.

Results

Three experiments using this design were conducted. Summary information on rents as a percentage of optimum is reported in Table VII. Means are calculated on data pooled from the first five and the last five decision rounds of a given treatment condition for each of the three experiments. The complexity of incomplete and asymmetric information on individual endowment holdings appears to have lowered the rent-enhancing properties of communication, although rents are increased relative to no-communication conditions. Compare rents in the communication condition of this more complex design (where tokens are assigned randomly) with rents generated in condition C-R of our initial design, as summarized in Table IV. In three of four experiments in the C-R condition, mean rents were higher than in any of the more complex experiments. Further, if data are aggregated by condition rather than by experiment, overall mean rents are 83.4% in the more complex design and 93.6% in the C-R condition.

Further evidence of the difficulties caused by this more complex environment is the frequency of failures to reach group-wide agreement on an allocation rule in

[29]A token allocation was written on each of eight slips of paper in a hat. Each subject blindly picked a slip of paper denoting their token allocation for each decision round of the experiment.

[30]As with earlier designs, experiments began with five preliminary rounds in which each subject was endowed with 20 tokens.

communication rounds. Of the 80 communication rounds in the *initial* experiments, only 8 ended without group-wide agreement on an allocation rule, and all of these occurred in experiment 2 of the C-R design (an overall 10% failure rate for agreements). Moreover, only 37 of the 576 individual allocation decisions in the rounds with agreements exceeded the agreement (a 6.4% defection rate on agreements). In contrast, in the 30 communication rounds in the new, more complex design, 9 ended without group-wide agreement on an allocation rule (a 30% failure rate).[31] Even when these groups reached agreement, the rate of defection was higher. Twenty-seven of the 210 individual allocation decisions in these rounds with agreements exceeded the agreement (a 12.9% defection rate). Thus the failure rate for agreements tripled, and the rate of defections on agreements approximately doubled.

This more complex setting elicited experimentation with a wider variety of rules than was observed in the initial designs. In the first experiment the only adopted allocation rule was equal CPR allocations—each subject allocates 8 tokens to Market 2. In the second experiment, during the first round of communication, subjects chose to implement a proportionate rule; subjects agreed to allocate one-half of their token endowment to Market 2. Substantial defections led to the breakdown of this agreement. In the remaining decision rounds, the subjects agreed to a more complex rotation scheme in which half of the subjects would allocate all tokens to Market 2, while the other half allocate no tokens to Market 2. In the third experiment, the initial agreement was equal allocation to Market 2. This rule was changed to a modified rotation scheme in which one subject allocated 12 tokens to Market 2, while the other subjects allocated between 6 and 8 tokens to Market 2. The rotation scheme lead to substantial confusion, however, and was later changed to a modified proportionate rule in which all subjects with more than 8 tokens allocated one-half of their endowment to Market 2. In a complex decision environment with extreme endowment heterogeneity and incomplete and asymmetric information, subjects appear to find it difficult to immediately identify the optimal group token allocation to Market 2 and to agree upon a mutually fair sharing scheme.

VII. CONCLUDING COMMENTS

Past experimental studies have demonstrated the efficacy of face-to-face communication as an institution to foster increases in efficiency in collective action situations. The results from this study demonstrate the robustness of this institution in situations of endowment heterogeneity. Heterogeneous appropriators, when allowed to engage in face-to-face communication, substantially increase the level of rents earned from the common pool resource. In addition, rent enhancement remains substantial (although reduced) under relatively severe conditions of four endowment types with incomplete and asymmetric information.

In seven of eight experiments of our first two design conditions, subjects chose and successfully maintained allocation rules which were consistent with approxi-

---

[31]Even this number is conservative because some of the "agreements" were very loose and informal, and only specified a range of token investment levels for each individual.

mate rent maximization. In our treatment design in which token endowments were assigned randomly, subjects most frequently adopted rules which called for equal allocations to the CPR. In our treatment design in which larger token endowments were purchased through an auction mechanism, subjects explicitly sought to adopt rules to achieve maximum rents and equalize payoffs net of auction prices.

In field CPR settings, we observe a substantial percentage of agreements in which appropriators agree to proportionate reductions in levels of appropriation. In the laboratory, proportionate rules begin to evolve, but only in particular circumstances. More specifically, in the laboratory, the evolution of allocation rules based on some aspect of proportionality appears to be: (1) a by-product of attempts to equalize payoffs net of the cost of obtaining large endowment positions, and (2) as a response to a limited information decision setting.

It is the results from our more complex, incomplete information design which point most directly to why one may observe institutions in the field which combine face-to-face communication with mechanisms that allow for the sanctioning of nonconforming behavior. Face-to-face communication is a powerful tool. It is handicapped significantly, however, in situations in which group members are unable to develop or sustain the social capital necessary for enduring commitments. Understanding further the origin and success of alternative rule mechanisms is important to understanding how individuals can develop self-governing institutions. It is a topic for our continued research.

REFERENCES

W. Ault, "Open-Field Farming in Medieval England: A Study of Village Bylaws," Harper & Row, New York (1972).

A. Bacdayan, Mountain irrigators in the Philippines, *in* "Irrigation and Agricultural Development in Asia" (W. Coward, Ed.), Cornell Univ. Press, Ithaca, NY (1980).

M. Bagnoli and M. McKee, Voluntary contribution games: Efficient private provision of public goods, *Econom. Inquiry* **29**, 351–366 (1991).

F. Berkes, Local-level management and the commons problem: A comparative study of Turkish coastal fisheries, *Marine Policy* **10**, 215–29 (1986).

F. Berkes and D. Pocock, Quota management and 'people problems': A case study of Canadian Lake Erie fisheries, *Transact. Amer. Fish. Soc.* **116**, 494–502 (1987).

W. Blomquist, "Dividing the Waters: Governing Groundwater in Southern California," ICS Press, San Francisco (1992).

G. Bornstein and A. Rapoport, Intergroup competition for the provision of step-level public goods: Effects of preplay communication, *European J. Social Psychol.* **18**, 125–142 (1988).

G. Bornstein, A. Rapoport, L. Kerpel, and T. Katz, Within and between-group communication in intergroup competition for public goods, *J. Exp. Social Psychol.* **25**, 422–436 (1989).

A. Bottrall, The management and operation of irrigation schemes in less developed countries, *Water Supply Management* **2**, 309–332 (1978).

A. Bottrall, "Comparative Study of the Management and Organization of Irrigation Projects," World Bank Working Paper 458, World Bank, Washington, DC (1981).

K. Brechner, An experimental analysis of social traps, *J. Exper. Social Psychol.* **13**, 552–564 (1977).

C. Clark, Restricted access to common-property fishery resources: A game-theoretic analysis, *in* "Dynamic Optimization and Mathematical Economics" (P-T. Liu, Ed.), Plenum, New York (1980).

J. Cordell and M. McKean, Sea tenure in Bahia, Brazil, *in* "Proceedings of the Conference on Common Property Resource Management," National Academy Press, Washington, DC (1986).

R. Cornes and T. Sandler, "The Theory of Externalities, Public Goods, and Club Goods," Cambridge Univ. Press, New York (1986).

E. Coward, Principles of social organization in an indigenous irrigation system, *Human Organiz.* **5**, 128–141 (1979).

124   HACKETT, SCHLAGER, AND WALKER

A Davis, Property rights and access management in the small boat fishery: A case study from southwest Nova Scotia, *in* "Atlantic Fisheries and Coastal Communities: Fisheries Decision-Making Case Studies" (C. Lamson and A. J. Hanson, Eds.), Dalhousie Ocean Studies Programme, Halifax, PNS (1984).

R. Dawes, Social dilemmas, *Annual Rev. Psychol.* **31**, 169–193 (1980).

R. Dawes, J. Orbell, R. Simmons, and A. van de Kragt, Organizing groups for collective action, *Amer. Polit. Sci. Rev.* **80**, 1171–1185 (1986).

R. De los Reyes, "47 Communal Gravity Systems: Organization Profiles," Institute of Philippine Culture, Ateneo de Manila University, Quezon City, Philippines (1980).

K. Enge and S. Whiteford, "The Keepers of the Water and the Earth: Mexican Rural Social Organization and Irrigation," University of Texas Press, Austin, TX (1989).

R. Gardner, E. Ostrom, and J. Walker, The nature of common-pool resource problems, *Rationality Soc.* **2**, 335–358 (1990).

R. Gardner, M. Moore, and J. Walker, "Groundwater Property Rights: Laboratory Evidence on the Performance of Entry Restrictions and Stock Quotas," Indiana University Working Paper 93-008, Bloomington, IN (1993).

T. Glick, "Irrigation and Society in Medieval Valencia," Harvard University, Cambridge, MA (1970).

R. Gray, "The Sonjo of Tanganika," Oxford Univ. Press, London/New York (1963).

W. Guth, On the behavioral approach to distributive justice—A theoretical and experimental investigation, *in* "Applied Behavioral Economics" (S. Maital, Ed.), Vol. 2, New York Univ. Press, New York (1988).

W. Guth, "Distributive Justice: A Behavioral Theory and Empirical Evidence," Ekonomiska Forskningsinstitutet Research Paper 6461, Stockholm (1992).

W. Guth and R. Teitz, Strategic power versus distributive justice: An experimental analysis of ultimatum bargaining games, *in* "Economic Psychology" (H. Brandstatter and E. Kirchler, Eds.), Rudolph Trauner Verlag, Linz, Germany (1985).

S. Hackett, Heterogeneity and the provision of governance for common-pool resources, *J. Theoret. Politics* **4**, 325–42 (1992).

G. Hardin, The tragedy of the commons, *Science* **162**, 1243–1248 (1968).

G. Hardin, "The Limits of Altruism: An Ecologist's View of Survival," Indiana Univ. Press, Bloomington, IN (1978).

R. Hardin, "Collective Action," The Johns Hopkins Univ. Press, Baltimore, MD (1982).

G. Harrison and J. Hirshleifer, An experimental evaluation of weakest link/best shot models of public goods, *J. Polit. Economy* **97**, 201–225 (1989).

E. Hoffman and M. Spitzer, The Coase Theorem: Some experimental tests, *J. Law Econom.* **25**, 73–98 (1982).

E. Hoffman and M. Spitzer, Entitlements, rights, and fairness: An experimental examination of subjects' concepts of distributive justice, *J. Legal Stud.* **14**, 259–297 (1985).

M. Isaac and C. Plott, The opportunity for conspiracy in restraint of trade, *J. Econom. Behav. Organiz.* **2**, 1–30 (1981).

M. Isaac, V. Ramey, and A. Williams, The effects of market organization on conspiracies in restraint of trade, *J. Econom. Behav. Organiz.* **5**, 191–222 (1984).

M. Isaac and J. Walker, Information and conspiracy in sealed bid auctions, *J. Econom. Behav. Organiz.* **6**, 139–159 (1985).

M. Isaac and J. Walker, Communication and free-riding behavior: The voluntary contribution mechanism, *Econom. Inquiry* **24**, 585–608 (1988).

M. Isaac, D. Schmidtz, and J. Walker, The assurance problem in a laboratory market, *Public Choice* **62**, 217–236 (1989).

R. Johnson and G. Libecap, Contracting problems and regulation: The case of the fishery, *Amer. Econom. Rev.* **72**, 1005–1022 (1982).

R. Kanbur, "Heterogeneity, Distribution and Cooperation in Common Property Resource Management," Background Paper for the World Development Report (1991).

E. Leach, "Pul Eliya," Cambridge Univ. Press, New York (1961).

G. Libecap and S. Wiggins, Contractual responses to the common pool: Prorationing of crude oil production, *Amer. Econom. Rev.* **74**, 87–98 (1984).

W. Liebrand, The effect of social motives, Communication and group size on behavior in an n-person multi-stage mixed-motive game, *European J. Social Psychol.* **14**, 239–264 (1984).

RESOLVING COMMONS DILEMMAS 125

A. Maas and R. Anderson, "...And the Desert Shall Rejoice: Conflict, Growth, and Justice in Arid Environments," MIT Univ. Press, Cambridge, MA (1986).

P. Marchak, N. Guppy, and J. McMullan, "Uncommon Property: The Fishing and Fish-Processing Industries in British Columbia," Methuen, Toronto (1987).

F. Martin, "Common Pool Resources and Collective Action: A Bibliography," Indiana University, Workshop in Political Theory and Policy Analysis, Bloomington, IN (1989).

S. McDonald, "Petroleum Conservation in the United States: An Economic Analysis," Johns Hopkins Univ. Press, Baltimore, MD (1971).

M. McKean, Success on the commons: A comparative examination of institutions for common property resource management, *J. Theoret. Politics* 4, 247–282 (1992).

R. McKelvey and T. Palfrey, An experimental study of the centipede game, *Econometrica* 60, 803–836 (1992).

D. Negri, The common property aquifer as a differential game, *Water Resour. Res.* 25, 9–15 (1989).

R. Netting, "Balancing on an Alp: Ecological Change and Continuity in a Swiss Mountain Community," Cambridge Univ. Press, New York (1981).

M. Olson, "The Logic of Collective Action," Harvard University Press, Cambridge, MA (1965).

J. Orbell, A. van de Kragt, and R. Dawes, Explaining discussion-induced cooperation, *J. Personality Social Psychol.* 54, 811–819 (1988).

E. Ostrom, "Governing the Commons," Cambridge Univ. Press, New York (1990).

E. Ostrom, J. Walker, and R. Gardner, Covenants with and without a sword: Self governance is possible, *Amer. Polit. Sci. Rev.* 86, 128–145 (1992).

E. Ostrom, R. Gardner, and J. Walker, "Rules, Games, and Common-Pool Resources," University of Michigan Press, Ann Arbor, MI, (1994).

K. Palanisami and K. Easter, Irrigation tanks of South India: Strategies and investment alternatives, *Indian J. Agr. Econom.* 39, 214–223 (1984).

T. Palfrey and H. Rosenthal, Testing for effects of cheap talk in a public goods game with private information, *Games Econom. Behav.* 3, 183–220 (1991).

K. Ruddle and T. Akimichi (Eds.), "Maritime Institutions in the Western Pacific," National Museum of Ethnology, Osaka, Japan (1984).

E. Schlager, "Model Specification and Policy Analysis: The Governance of Coastal Fisheries," Ph.D. Dissertation, Indiana University, Bloomington, IN (1990).

E. Schlager, W. Blomquist, and S. Tang, "All CPRs Are Not Created Equal: The Affect of Two Important Physical Characteristics on the Resolution of Commons Dilemmas," Working Paper, University of Arizona, Tucson, AZ (1993).

D. Seckler and D. Joshi, Sukhomajri: Water management in India, *Bull. Atomic Scientists* 25, 26–30 (1982).

R. Selten, A simple model of imperfect competition where 4 are few and 6 are many, *Internat. J. Game Theory* 2, 141–201 (1971).

G. Slater, "The English Peasantry and the Enclosure of Common Fields," Archibald Constable, London (1907).

B. Spooner, Continuity and change in rural Iran: The eastern deserts, *in* "Iran: Continuity and Variety" (P. Chelkowski, Ed.), New York University, Center for Near Eastern Studies and the Center for International Studies, New York (1971).

B. Spooner, The Iranian deserts, *in* "Population Growth: Anthropological Implications" (B. Spooner, Ed.), MIT Univ. Press, Cambridge, MA (1972).

B. Spooner, Irrigation and society: The Iranian plateau, *in* "Irrigation's Impact on Society" (T. Downing and M. Gibson, Eds.), University of Arizona Press, Tucson, AZ (1974).

N. Sturgess, N. Dow, and P. Belin, Management of the Victorian scallop fisheries: Retrospect and prospect, *in* "Policy and Practice in Fisheries Management" (N. Sturgess and T. Meany, Eds.), Australian Government Publishing Service, Canberra (1982).

R. Wade, "Village Republics: Economic Conditions for Collective Action in South India," Cambridge Univ. Press, New York (1988).

J. Walker, R. Gardner, and E. Ostrom, Rent dissipation in a limited-access common-pool resource: Experimental evidence, *J. Environ. Econom. Management* 19, 203–211 (1990).

J. Walker and R. Gardner, Rent dissipation and probabilistic destruction of common-pool resource environments: Experimental evidence, *Econom. J.* 102, 1149–1161 (1992).

126   HACKETT, SCHLAGER, AND WALKER

S. Wiggins and G. Libecap, Oil field unitization: Contractual failure in the presence of imperfect information, *Amer. Econom. Rev.* **75**, 368–384 (1985).

S. Wiggins and G. Libecap, Firm heterogeneities and cartelization efforts in domestic crude oil, *J. Law Econom. Organiz.* **3**, 1–25 (1987).

S. Wiggins, S. Hackett, and R. Battalio, Imperfect Information, Multilateral Bargaining, and Unitization: An Experimental Analysis, Photocopy, Indiana University (1991).

[22]

Mitigating the Tragedy of the Commons through Cooperation: An Experimental Evaluation[1]

Charles F. Mason and Owen R. Phillips

Department of Economics and Finance, University of Wyoming, Laramie, Wyoming 82071-3985

Received May 17, 1996; revised September 3, 1997

In a commons, each firm's costs rise with industry output. This externality can be mitigated if firms jointly restrict harvests, but higher prices result. Repeated interaction usually facilitates cooperation that lowers harvest rates. Increased cooperation suggests there should be more firms in the socially optimal market structure. Using experimental markets with two to five "firms," we observe the influence of industry size on harvest rates. Cooperation increases the socially optimal number of firms in markets when there are static externalities, but not for dynamic externalities. Finally, even when the initial stock is low, there is little tendency toward resource extinction. © 1997 Academic Press

1. INTRODUCTION

The tragedy of the commons is a frequently cited example of market failure. Each producer using the commons imposes an external cost on rivals. This externality can be both static and dynamic in nature. Static externalities reflect the traditional "crowding" problem (Brown [2]). Each firm's current production costs rise with industry output. Costs rise because the commons input becomes relatively scarce. There is a dynamic externality if current actions lead to higher future costs. Increases in current fish harvests, for one example, generally reduce the reproductive capacity of the cohort and so lower the size of future populations, making it more costly to locate and harvest fish in the future. Taking petroleum production as a second example, increases in current extraction rates tend to lower pressure in a deposit, making future extraction more costly. The social harm in both of these examples is that there is overexploitation of the resource, and the stock is too rapidly diminished.

A variety of solutions have been suggested to remedy the tragedy of the commons, including (i) imposing taxes on harvesters to reflect the external costs, (ii) limiting each firm's harvest, (iii) issuing a fixed number of harvest quotas and allowing firms to trade quotas, (iv) limiting the number of firms exploiting the

[1] This material is based upon work supported by the National Science Foundation under grant RII-86-10680 and the College of Business, University of Wyoming. Any opinions, findings, and conclusions or recommendations expressed in this paper are those of the authors and do not necessarily reflect the views of the funding agencies. We thank seminar participants at the Air Force Academy, Australian National University, Colorado School of Mines, University of Oregon, Weber State University, the Economics Science Association Conference in Austin Texas, and the Western Economics Association Meetings in San Diego. The constructive criticisms of Gerry Dwyer, George Evans, Tracy Lewis, Theo Offerman, Les Oxley, Jim Ziliak, and two anonymous referees greatly improved the paper. The usual caveat applies.

COOPERATION IN THE COMMONS?   149

resource, (v) creating private property rights for the resource, and (vi) providing an environment that facilitates self-organization to maximize social benefit (Ostrom [25]). The first three approaches will work only if the regulating agency has fairly complete information on costs and benefits, while the last three approaches have relatively small information requirements. Assigning property rights to a stationary common property resource, such as a grazing commons, can mitigate the externality, but this is impractical for fugitive resources such as oil pools or fisheries (Clark [7, p. 117]). Self-organization can be very successful if the costs of forming a coalition and reaching an agreement are relatively small (Ostrom, Gardner, and Walker [26]; Hackett, Schlager, and Walker [14]). There is disagreement, however, over the actual magnitudes of these transactions costs.[2] Partly because of the minimal information requirements, limiting the number of firms, generally to one, has been favorably regarded by economists for some time (Clark [7, pp. 35–44]; Scott [30]).

An important complication can arise if the common property resource does not have close substitutes. The resource could be distinguished from other potential substitutes because it possesses unique characteristics. That consumers regularly pay substantially higher prices for certain species of fish, such as halibut, is de facto evidence that consumers do not regard other species as close substitutes. Similarly, oyster connoisseurs may regard Gulf Coast oysters as having characteristics distinct from Pacific Coast oysters. It is also possible that transportation costs give producers some market power. For example, the delivery cost of crude oil is an important component of the full price paid by a refiner: West Coast refiners would rather receive their crude oil from Alaska than from the Middle East. These cases illustrate that efforts to limit production of a common property resource can generate market power, leading to pricing distortions. These anticompetitive effects must be weighed against the external cost distortions in determining the optimal number of harvesters.

Given a static externality and oligopoly, Cornes, Mason, and Sandler [8] analyzed the welfare effects of an increase in industry size. More firms plying the commons increase the cost externalities generated by crowding, but a larger number of firms also facilitates more intense competition, leading to lower output prices. It follows that the socially optimal industry size is generally larger than one, but is finite. In a continuous time model of a common property exhaustible resource with a crowding externality, Karp [17] showed that either the crowding effect will dominate or the price distortion effect will dominate for all industry sizes. In his model, the optimal number of firms is one if the crowding effect dominates and infinite if the price effect dominates. If agents interact repeatedly, it is well known that some degree of cooperation can result. Mason, Sandler, and Cornes [23] argued that this will

---

[2] Demsetz [10, p. 354] stated that the transactions costs associated with self-organization are "large." Johnson and Libecap [16] provided convincing anecdotal evidence that cost asymmetries greatly complicate the resolution of an externality. Ostrom, Gardner, and Walker [26] considered both costless and costly communication in their experiments; resolution of the commons externality is less successful in the latter treatment. The experimental design we use in this paper can be regarded as providing a limiting case where explicit communication is prohibitively costly. For example, cooperative ventures that seek to resolve commons dilemmas have often been attacked using antitrust statutes, with an evidentiary emphasis placed on communication (Johnson and Libecap [16]).

150   MASON AND PHILLIPS

increase the optimal industry size.[3] Whether cooperation actually results from repeated play in the presence of either a static or a dynamic externality is an empirical issue.

Existing empirical analyses of common property resources are generally case studies (e.g., Ostrom [25]). While providing useful information, it is hard to draw broad conclusions from these works. As far as we know there are no published cross-sectional studies, perhaps because the cost externality and levels of cooperation in selected market structures are not easily observed and measured. An obvious alternative is the use of laboratory markets to collect observations on the exploitation of a commons. While there is a literature on applying experimental techniques to gather data on behavior in a commons, limited attention has been paid to the role of industry size upon harvesting behavior. Further, these experimental studies have not put subjects in games that have repeated play for an indefinite number of periods, which is mathematically equivalent to an infinitely repeated game structure, nor have they directly considered the potential impact of current actions on future stocks of the resource.[4]

In this article we investigate how repeated interaction among harvesters allows more cooperative exploitation of a resource and lower harvest rates. To this end, we develop a model of firm behavior in a multiperiod version of the commons story. The optimal number of firms depends on the degree to which harvesters can cooperate, and on various demand and cost parameters. Then, we use a battery of experimental markets to evaluate harvest behavior in industries of various sizes. This lets us numerically determine the optimal number of firms in the industry. The experimental design analyzes the exploitation of a common property resource in markets with two, three, four, or five harvesters. We consider two sets of designs: one where the commons has only a static externality and one where there is a dynamic externality.

Our designs include parameters that make the optimal industry size three if harvests equal the Cournot equilibrium levels. We find that cooperation does mitigate the tragedy of the commons in the design with a static cost externality. In particular, individual harvests are significantly smaller than the Cournot levels in groups with two or three subjects, so that the empirically optimal industry size is four. On the other hand, there is little indication of cooperation when there is a dynamic externality. Here, the empirically optimal industry size equals the theoretical prediction of three.

We also inquire into the tendency for oligopoly to cause the extinction of a renewable resource. In this part of the study, we use 12 groups with 5 agents, and

<hr>

[3] This earlier paper used a conjectural variations approach, which can be regarded as a reduced form that characterizes dynamic incentives in terms of static rewards. Such an approach has fallen into disfavor among industrial organization economists, because it obscures some interesting dynamic elements. Our approach avoids these pitfalls.

[4] Ostrom, Gardner, and Walker [26] presented experiments with a fixed endpoint that is not communicated to subjects, which they regard as equivalent to a finite game. Hackett, Schlager, and Walker [14] included an announced finite end time. While cooperative behavior can emerge in a Nash equilibrium in finite games, it cannot be part of a subgame perfect equilibrium. By including a random termination rule in our experimental design, we sidestep this theoretical issue. Herr [15] considered the impact of industry size on welfare, though he considered only two industry sizes, one larger and one smaller than the optimal number his model predicts. Walker and Gardner's [31] design induced an equilibrium, where behavior changes over time, although they did not model any effect upon an underlying state variable such as the resource stock.

set the initial stock at a perilously low level. This stock 'is sufficiently small that extinction will inevitably result if players do not collectively limit their harvests until the resource has had a chance to recover. Such coordination should be more difficult as the number of firms rises, and so we focus on the largest group size in this part of the paper. While extinction does occur for some markets, in most cases, subjects implicitly agree to allow the stock to recover by limiting their harvests. Despite this cooperation early on, the steady state stock in these sessions is very close to the corresponding steady state stock for markets with five sellers, where the initial stock was set at a much higher level.

2. AN OLIGOPOLY MODEL OF THE COMMONS

The model that underlies our experiments is drawn from Mason and Polasky [21, 22]. In this model, there are a fixed number of firms exploiting a common property resource. Examples of such resources include grazing lands, oil pools, hunting grounds, forests, and fisheries. For purposes of expositional concreteness, we shall use the example of a fishery, with the understanding that much of our analysis is equally applicable to other common property resources. Each firm selects a harvest level every market period; harvests may be conditioned on the stock of fish in the commons at the start of the period.

Let S_t represent the stock size of the resource in period t. Initial stock size at the beginning of period one, S_1, is exogenously given. We define H_t as the total harvest in period t, and h_{it} and H_{it} as the period t harvest of firm i and the accumulation of all other firm harvests in period t, respectively. These three harvest levels have the relation $H_t = h_{it} + H_{it}$. Industry harvest cannot exceed the stock size at the beginning of any period t, so $H_t \leq S_t$. Because increased harvests raise marginal costs, equilibrium harvests commonly yield an industry harvest that is less than stock size. Therefore, we will assume that the stock constraint is not binding. The harvest is assumed to be perishable so that it cannot be stored from period to period; all harvested stock is thus sold in the period of harvest. The resource stock is linked intertemporally by the logistic growth function

$$S_{t+1} = S_t + gS_t[1 - (S_t/K)] - H_t, \tag{1}$$

where g is an exogenous parameter and K is the "carrying capacity" of the fishery. The interpretation of this stock equation is that in each period the stock grows by an amount that depends on the current stock and its relation to the carrying capacity of the system. On the other hand, the stock is depleted by an amount equal to current harvest. Hence the change in the stock equals the growth, less current harvest. Once the initial stock is specified, the entire system is endogenously determined.

The cost of harvesting the resource for a firm in period t depends upon its own level of harvest, the level of industry harvest in the period, and stock size (Brown [2]). We assume that harvest costs for each firm $i = 1, \ldots, N$ are additively separable,

$$C(h_{it}, H_t, S_t) = c_0 + [c_1(H_t) + c_2(S_t)]h_{it}, \tag{2}$$

where c_0 are fixed costs, c_1 is a nonnegative, nondecreasing function of industry harvest, and c_2 is a nonpositive, nonincreasing function of stock. The function c_1

reflects the static crowding externality, while c_2 reflects the dynamic externality. Thus, in the formulation with only a static cost externality, $c_2 = 0$ and $c_1' > 0$; in the formulation with a dynamic cost externality, $c_2' < 0$.

In each period, market price is determined by harvests according to the market inverse demand function $P(H_t)$. This is equivalent to assuming that firms sell their entire catch, which is a feature of Nash equilibrium (Mason and Polasky [21]). In addition, we assume that firms' harvests are strategic substitutes, i.e., that reaction functions are negatively sloped.

Letting δ represent the discount factor, common to all firms, firm i's present discounted value of profit in period t, V_{it}, satisfies the Bellman equation:

$$V_{it} = P(H_t)h_{it} - \left[c_0 + c_1(H) + c_2(S)\right]h_{it} + \delta V_{it+1}. \tag{3}$$

Each firm seeks to maximize this profit flow by choice of harvest strategy, taking the strategies of all other firms as given.

In a model with just static cost externalities, it is easy to observe cooperative incentives using trigger strategies. Suppose that all firms plan to harvest at the cooperative level h^c so long as no firm has defected in any previous period. If there has been an earlier defection, all players revert to the one-shot Nash (i.e., Cournot) harvest, h^n. Let $\pi_i(h^c)$ be the representative firm's static profits at the proposed cooperative harvest, let $\pi^d(h^c)$ represent the one time profits earned by optimally defecting given that all other firms are harvesting h^c, and let π^n be the Cournot/Nash profits. The strategy of harvesting h^c as long as all the rival firms do, but reverting to the Cournot harvest following a defection, can be supported as a subgame perfect equilibrium outcome path if and only if the one time increase in earnings from defection do not exceed the discounted flow of reduced profits resulting from punishment. This imposes a restriction on feasible values of h^c, referred to as an incentive constraint:

$$\pi(h^c) + \delta\pi^n/(1 - \delta) \le \pi_i(h^c)/(1 - \delta). \tag{4}$$

Because such trigger strategies can support smaller harvest levels for any given industry size, they tend to mitigate the cost externalities and enlarge the demand-side distortions. For this reason, successful cooperation makes the optimal industry size larger. Of course, the degree to which firms can successfully cooperate depends on the total number of firms in the market. A larger number of sellers offers the single firm smaller cooperative profits and larger defection profits. In light of Eq. (4), these effects on the relative returns make cooperation more difficult.

Analysis of behavior with dynamic cost externalities is more complex. This is because costs change from one period to the next when stock changes, so that the payoff functions change over time. In this context, firms will plausibly base their period $t + 1$ harvest on period $t + 1$ stock and period t industry harvest. Since all firms have the same payoff function, it is natural to restrict our attention to symmetric equilibria, where each firm uses the same harvest strategy, $h^e(S)$. The typical firm i seeks the solution to

$$\operatorname*{Max}_{h_{it}} P(H_t)h_{it} - \left[c_0 + c_1(H) + c_2(S)\right]h_{it} + \delta V_{it+1}$$

$$\text{s.t.} \quad S_{t+1} = S_t - (N - 1)h_t - h_{it} + gS_t(1 - S_t/K),$$

$$h_t = h^e(S).$$

Before proceeding to a discussion of cooperative strategies, we first briefly discuss the noncooperative equilibrium. Let the equilibrium noncooperative strategy be $h^n(S)$. In each period t, current harvests $h_t^* = h^n(S_t)$ will satisfy the nonlinear difference equation (Mason and Polasky [22])

$$
\begin{aligned}
[P'(Nh_t^*) - c(Nh_t^*)]h_t^* &+ P(Nh_t^*) - c_1(Nh_t^*) - c_2(S_t) \\
&- \delta c(S_{t+1})(\partial S_{t+1}/\partial h_t)h_{t+1}^* \\
&- \delta Ng(1 - 2S_{t+1}/K)[P'(Nh_{t+1}^*) - c(Nh_{t+1}^*)]h_{t+1}^* = 0. \qquad (5)
\end{aligned}
$$

The last term on the left-hand side of Eq. (5) represents the strategic effect from current actions. When a firm raises its current harvest, this lowers the next period's stock; in turn, this raises future costs, which forces each firm to lower its output next period. With this reduction in market output, prices increase and the crowding externality is lowered, both of which benefit the firm. This strategic effect gives each firm an incentive to raise its current harvests. With each firm behaving this way, all firms' current profits are reduced. As a result, there is an incentive for all firms to agree to lower harvests in each period. Thus, harvest functions more cooperative than $h^n(S)$ exist.

Consider such a cooperative harvest function, $h^c(S)$. A trigger strategy can then be described as follows: play $h^c(S)$ as long as no one has defected; if defection has occurred, play $h^n(S)$ everafter.[5] Using the cooperative harvest path and the implied resource stock path, one may derive the stream of present discounted profits for the typical firm under continued cooperation. The resultant cooperative value function depends on the current stock, $V^c(S)$. Similarly, one may calculate the noncooperative value function, $V^n(S)$. To demonstrate that this trigger strategy can form a subgame perfect equilibrium requires the confirmation that firms cannot gain from deviating from the actions specified, irrespective of the current state. Thus, we require that the two value functions satisfy

$$
\pi^d(h^c(S)) + \delta V^n(S) \le V^c(S) \qquad (6)
$$

for every possible stock level.[6] Because the resource stock changes over time, prior to convergence to the steady state, the three components in Eq. (6) also change over time; harvests that satisfy Eq. (6) in one period may not satisfy it in others. This renders tacit agreement on a cooperative path in the dynamic game much

---

[5] Alternatively, it is possible to construct a nonlinear Markov strategy that supports a cooperative-looking outcome, as in Dockner and Van Long [11]. While the outcomes of the two approaches can be similar, we use the dynamic variant on the trigger strategy to keep the exposition parallel to the static model.

[6] In addition, perennial play of the noncooperative harvest must be a Nash equilibrium. However, this is true by construction, since these noncooperative harvests are determined by closed loop equilibrium strategies (Mason and Polasky [22]). The trigger strategy we describe need not be optimal in the sense of delivering the highest discounted flow of profits. This is because the punishment phase is relatively mild; a strategy with a more intense punishment but of a shorter duration might establish more cooperative behavior. Even so, the essence of our remarks holds: it will be harder to maintain a given level of punishment in some states than in others, and ultimately this will make the task of implicitly agreeing on a cooperative path more difficult in the dynamic game than in a stationary game.

154   MASON AND PHILLIPS

more difficult than in a stationary repeated game. We therefore expect less cooperation when there is a dynamic externality.

The welfare consequences of varying the number of firms must properly take into account behavior along the path converging to a steady state, as well as behavior at the steady state (Karp [17]; Mason and Polasky [22]). Unfortunately, this greatly complicates the analytics. To make the empirical analysis tractable, we use steady state behavior as a proxy for the entire path. While this will introduce some approximation errors, it will not alter the final judgement as to the optimal number of firms if convergence to harvests near the steady state is fairly rapid. As we shall see, stocks tend to converge to their steady state levels quite rapidly in our experimental markets (see Figure 3).

Steady state is determined by two equations. One is the standard Nash condition, that no firm can unilaterally improve upon its profits given current costs (which of course are dependant upon current resource stock). The other is that there is no change in the stock of the resource, which requires the aggregate industry harvest to exactly offset the growth of the resource. Characterization of cooperative outcomes in the model with dynamic externalities is similar to the static case, in that each firm's actions must satisfy a variant of the incentive constraint identified above. Again, at this proposed equilibrium, industry harvest must just offset the resource growth. Inspection of Eq. (1) shows that more cooperative harvests will result in larger stocks and smaller growth rates. For both the static and dynamic cost externality cases, it is an empirical question as to whether increases in industry size are welfare-enhancing.

3. EXPERIMENTAL DESIGN

The purpose of our market experiments is to observe choice behavior when there is a static or dynamic cost externality and a fixed number of firms. Subjects take the role of a firm. Each experimental session involved a total number of subjects divisible by the number of firms in an industry, e.g., there may be 15 subjects for 3 markets with 5 firms in each market. Subjects were recruited from intermediate or more advance economics classes. They reported to a room with a personal computer (PC) at each seat. The PCs were linked to a mainframe VAX computer that networked the subjects. Each subject had a copy of the experimental instructions (available from the authors upon request). These were read aloud at the start of a session. They carefully described a payoff table, where payoffs depended on the number of firms in the industry. These payoff tables provided subjects with the calculated profits for each possible combination of "harvest" choices they and their rivals might collectively make. Individuals were randomly grouped and never knew the identity of other participants in their industry.

Subjects were told that tokens would be exchanged for cash at the end of the experiment, according to a prespecified exchange rate. We chose the exchange rate for each industry size so that monetary payoffs would be comparable.[7] Payments

---

[7] The exchange rates we used were 1000 tokens = $1 for the sessions with two subjects in each industry; 461.15 tokens = $1 for the sessions with three subjects in each industry; 212.31 tokens = $1 for the sessions with four subjects in each industry; and 173.55 tokens = $1 for the sessions with five subjects in each industry.

averaged around $15 in every session, and ranged from a low of about $7 to a high of about $22. Sessions typically lasted about $1\frac{1}{2}$ to 2 hours. To mimic a supergame with an infinite horizon, the computer program that managed the experiment invoked a random stopping rule. After 35 periods of play, the experiment terminated with probability equal to 0.2 at the end of each period. A description of this procedure was included in the instructions, so that it was common knowledge.

In those sessions where costs were dependent upon the current stock of the resource, the instructions contained a detailed description of the relation between current harvests and future stocks, and the link between stock and costs. A questionnaire (available upon request) was used to help students understand the way in which future costs were affected by current harvest levels. Every subject completed the questionnaire before the experiment began.

After the instructions were read, questions were taken and one practice period was held. In the practice period a monitor randomly chose a column value for all the subjects, who simultaneously chose a row value from a sample payoff table. This sample table was different from the table used in the experiment. Profits from the intersection of a row and the monitor's column were calculated and recorded by every subject. During the practice period we checked each subject to insure that they understood the payoff tables and how to keep a record of their choices and earnings.

In each period of the experiment, subjects made their choices simultaneously. The experiment was controlled by a master program which was run on the mainframe. This program collected all the subjects' choices, sorted them into the respective groups, and made the relevant calculations. The results from that choice period were then displayed on the subject monitors. Each subject was informed of the choices and payoffs for every subject in his or her group. This information allowed subjects to determine the aggregated total of all rival choices, but it also gave specific information on behavior of each rival. While we did not want to allow for face-to-face communication, this feature of our design allows individuals to implicitly communicate through their actions.[8] In the sessions with a dynamic cost externality, the computer also calculated the change in each group's stock of the common property resource as a result of group harvest and reported back the new stock level to each subject. Subjects wrote this information on a record sheet; they could always double check the computer's calculations from the payoff tables provided to them.

Our experimental sessions consisted of four industry sizes (two, three, four, or five agents acting as firms) and two cost structures (static cost externalities or dynamic cost externalities). In the discussion below, we continue with the notation set out earlier: h_{it} is firm i's period t harvest, H_{it} is the aggregated harvest of firm i's rivals in period t, H_t is industry harvest in period t, and S_t is the resource stock in period t. Also P_t is market price in period t and firm i's period t profits are π_{it}.

---

[8] For example, a subject could attempt to convince his or her rivals to reduce harvest by unilaterally doing so. Had we not provided information on each subject's actions, subjects could not know whether such a message was received by any rival, since an increase by some other subject could offset their reduction in harvest. Since it was common knowledge that every subject's choice was displayed on every monitor, a subject would know his or her actions had been observed by all.

156   MASON AND PHILLIPS

A. The Static Design

For the static cost structure, we write market demand as

$$P_t = 60 - (35/36)H_t. \qquad (7)$$

Each firm i's harvest costs are determined by industry harvest and its own harvest. In terms of the notation in Eq. (2) we set $c_1(H) = H/36$ and $c_0 = 75$, so that firm i's period t harvest costs are

$$C(h_{it}, H_t, S_t) = 75 + (H_t/36)h_{it}. \qquad (8)$$

Thus, the period t payoff to subject i is

$$\pi_{it} = (60 - (h_{it} + H_{it}))h_{it} - 75. \qquad (9)$$

We observe that these functional forms can be used to derive social welfare. Let us write net surplus for an industry whose period t industry harvest is H_t and where there are N firms operating as $SW(H_t; N)$. In light of Eq. (7), consumer surplus based on period t harvest H_t is $CS(H_t) = \frac{1}{2}(35/36)H_t^2$, and so we have

$$SW(H_t; N) = CS(H_t) + \sum_{i=1}^{N} \pi_{it}$$

$$= [60 - (37/72)H_t]H_t - 75N. \qquad (10)$$

In a payoff table, a subject's payoff is determined by the intersection of the column corresponding to the collective choice of all rivals and the row corresponding to the subject's own choice. A reduced-in-size copy of the table we used in the three-person static externality experiment is provided as an Appendix. To avoid the impression that the labels on available choices might influence behavior, we rescaled choice variables so that subjects picked values between 1 and 13. A choice of "1" corresponds to an output of 9, a choice of "2" corresponds to an output of 10, and so on. The combined choices of the two rivals lie between 2 and 26; these correspond to a range of outputs from 18 to 42.[9] The table is designed so that both the one-shot Nash and the fully cooperative levels are well removed from one another and the table corners; we did this to help overcome possible focal point effects. In our static two-agent design there were 12 subjects and 6 markets, in the three-agent game there were 15 subjects and 5 markets, in the four-agent experiment there were 12 subjects and 3 markets, and in the groups with 5 agents there were 15 subjects and 3 markets. As we mentioned above, all subjects in every market made quantity choices for at least 35 periods.

It can be readily verified that the Nash equilibrium of the one-shot game entails each player setting his or her harvest equal to $60/(N + 1)$, where N is the number of players in the experiment. With $N = 3$, this gives an output of 15 for each agent. This output corresponds to a choice of 7 in the appended table, so that the

---

[9] The reader may be concerned that the size of the payoff table makes the subjects' task so complicated as to render their decision problem impenetrable. However, Mason, Phillips, and Nowell [20] and Phillips and Mason [27] also used quite large payoff matrices, and their results suggest that subjects can make reasoned decisions even when faced with large payoff matrices.

Cournot equilibrium is found at the intersection of the 14th column and the 7th row. On the other hand, a fully cooperative regime would entail all agents selecting a harvest level of $30/N$, which is found at the intersection of the fourth column and the second row in the payoff table.[10] The parameters we selected above make three firms the socially optimal number of exploiters under Cournot behavior.[11]

B. The Dynamic Design

We introduce dynamic cost externalities into our experimental markets by allowing costs to be negatively related to the current resource stock, and having stock evolve over time by the logistic growth rule given in Eq. (1). This implies that current harvests affect future marginal costs, because they yield a reduction in future stocks. The specific functional relation for our experimental design, following the notation from Eq. (2), is $c_2(S) = 25 - S/12$ and $c_0 = 14.0625$. Thus, harvest costs are:

$$C(h_{it}, H_t, S_t) = 14.0625 + (25 - S_t/12)h_{it}. \tag{11}$$

The stock evolves according to the dynamic relation

$$S_{t+1} = S_t - H_t + 1.25S_t(1 - S_t/225). \tag{12}$$

In this specification, the "carrying capacity" of the system is 225 units. In the primary treatment group, the initial stock was specified as 120 units. In other treatments discussed below we set the initial stock at a much smaller level to investigate the likelihood that noncooperative harvests lead to extinction. We make demand in our dynamic design a simple linear form,

$$P_t = 60 - H_t, \tag{13}$$

so that the period t payoff to subject i is:

$$\pi_{it} = (60 - h_{it} - H_{it} - 25 + S_t/12)h_{it} - 14.0625. \tag{14}$$

As in the static case, it is straightforward to derive social welfare from these functional forms. However, the measure of social welfare must reflect the effect current actions have upon future costs. This shadow cost is $(\partial S_{t+1}/\partial H_t)c_2'(S_{t+1})$ (Mason and Polasky [22]); in light of Eqs. (11) and (12), this reduces to $H_{t+1}/12$. The measure of social welfare for the dynamic version of our model depends on both current and future harvests, as well as the number of firms in the industry:

$$SW(H_t, H_{t+1}; N) = [35 - \tfrac{1}{2}H_t + S_t/12]H_t - 14.0625N - H_{t+1}/12. \tag{15}$$

---

[10] The harvest choice that maximizes firm i's payoffs, given H_{it}, is easily seen to be $30 - H_{it}/2$. With N symmetric firms, $H_{it} = (N - 1)h_{it}$, and so one derives $2h_{it} = 60 - (N - 1)h_{it}$, or $h_{it} = 60/(N + 1)$. A fully cooperative regime entails industry activity equivalent to a monopoly. Here, if only one firm plies the commons, its optimal harvest is 30; if this is to be shared amongst the N cooperating firms, each gets $30/N$.

[11] The Cournot/Nash equilibrium industry harvests are 40, 45, 48, and 50 for industries with 2, 3, 4, and 5 firms, respectively. Using Eq. (10), the values of social welfare at these Nash equilibria are 1427.78, 1434.38, 1396, and 1340.28, respectively.

Finally, we observe that the steady state stock satisfies

$$1.25S_t(1 - S_t/225) = H_t.$$ (16)

This quadratic expression has two roots:

$$S^e = 225/2 \pm \tfrac{1}{2}[225^2 - 720H]^{1/2}.$$ (17)

The stable steady state is the positive root, call it S_+. The negative root, S_-, is the *unstable* steady state. That implies a minor reduction in stock below S_- would lead to extinction, unless harvests were dramatically reduced. Hence, extinction is a bona fide possibility in our design.

We incorporate the dynamic cost structure into our experiments by providing subjects with a "penalty" table that appears on their computer terminal at the start of each choice period. The penalty table informs the subject of the adjustment to his or her payoff that would occur as a result of each choice. This adjustment relates to the dynamic component of costs only; the static component is subsumed in the "gross" payoff table subjects have available to them.[12] In the dynamic version of our model, with the parameters specified, the optimal industry size is three firms.[13] In our dynamic two-agent design there were 14 subjects and 7 markets, in the three agent game there were 18 subjects and 6 markets, in the four-agent experiment there were 12 subjects and 3 markets, and in the groups with five agents there were 15 subjects and 3 markets. As in the static design, all subjects in every market made quantity choices for at least 35 periods.

For both the static and dynamic industry designs, we wish to test the hypothesis that subjects will be more cooperative than the one-shot Nash prediction; the optimal number of firms would then exceed three. Also, in the dynamic design we investigated the interaction of rivalry and dangerously low initial stocks of the resource. We observed the sensitivity of behavior to potential extinction of the stock. As we discussed above, there is a minimal level of the stock such that driving the current value below this cutoff can lead to extinction. The risk of extinction can be mitigated by cooperation, whereas it becomes more severe the more aggressive are players collectively. Hence, the possibility of extinction seems most likely for industries with five participants.

---

[12] Specifically, we identified the theoretical steady state stock with three firms, which is 180. We then we subtracted the implied unit cost of 10 (which equals $25 - 180/12$) off the demand intercept. The penalty table presented to our subjects is then based on a unit cost equal to $15 - S_t/12$ [$= (25 - S_t/12) - 10$]. In this design, we do not transform outputs into choices. Making such a transformation would add a layer of complexity to the instructions that does not appear in the static sessions. Whereas the dynamic cost design is considerably more complex than the static design anyway, we felt it was best to avoid this extra complication.

[13] The extra complication here is that the steady state harvest and stock must both be determined. To this end, one must solve a system of two equations in two unknowns. Write these steady state values as H^e and S^e, respectively. The steady state stock satisfies Eq. (17). The equation describing the steady state harvest is obtained from Eqs. (5), (11), and (13) by equating h_t^* and h_{t+1}^* to H^e/N. This yields, after rearrangement,

$$H^e = 420N/[12(N + 11) + \delta - N\delta(450 - 4S^e)/30].$$

Combining this with Eq. (17) in the text allows the determination of the steady state. Social welfare at these steady states can then be determined from Eq. (15). It is straightforward, though tedious, to obtain these values as 1224.4, 1233.1, 1223.7, and 1211.3, for $N = 2, 3, 4,$ and 5. For further discussion on the properties of the dynamic system and its steady state, see Mason and Polasky [22].

4. DESCRIPTION OF THE DATA

The results of our experimental sessions are summarized in Figs. 1–3. Because some sessions ended in period 35, when our random stopping rule was invoked, the time series is taken through 35 periods. Figure 1 shows average market choices, as a fraction of the Cournot level, for each of the four industry sizes in the static cost treatments. The schedules are labeled in terms of percent of their static Cournot choice, or %sc$i$, $i = 2, 3, 4, 5$, for the industry size. When the industry size is small, i.e., two or three firms, average choices are consistently below the Cournot level. In the sessions for market sizes of four or five, choices appear to fluctuate nearer the Cournot level. Thus, we generally observe movement toward less cooperation as the number of firms increases. Also, these four plots indicate that average choice behavior tends to become more stable over time, and differences become less dramatic, as shown by the averages after period 28.

Figure 2 displays average behavior in the dynamic treatments. Here we show average market choices as a percentage of the *steady state* Cournot harvest. The time series %dc$i$ in the figure shows for each industry size the proximity of the average choice to their dynamic Cournot (dc) outcome. Once again there is a tendency toward more aggressive behavior as the number of firms increases, although differences between these time series are not as distinct as in the static industries. These averages in the dynamic treatment suggest three observations. First, groups of two are slightly more cooperative than Cournot, while groups of three, four, and five are not. Second, we can see that behavior overall tends to be more aggressive in the dynamic cost externality treatment than in the static cost treatment. Third, after some point between periods 5 and 10, there is no further trend in the dynamic markets toward increased cooperation. We provide more careful econometric analysis of these observations in the next section.

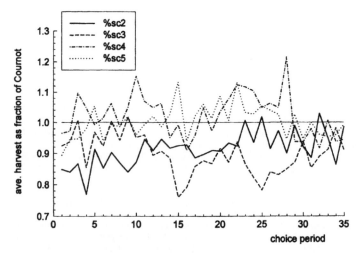

FIG. 1. Static externality markets.

160   MASON AND PHILLIPS

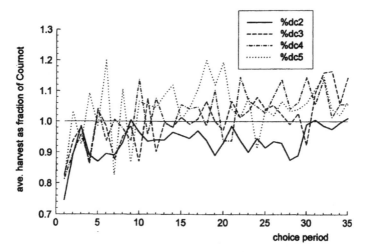

FIG. 2. Dynamic externality markets.

Figure 3 depicts the time path of the resource stock for each of the four industry sizes in the dynamic cost treatment. They are labeled *Si*, *i* = 2, 3, 4, 5, for the industry size. Two key points are apparent here. Our first observation is that stocks rise initially and quite rapidly. Second, stocks converge to a stable level early in the session. We note that the largest stable stock size exists in the duopoly market structure and average stable stock sizes diminish as the number of firms increases. The total difference, though, between the two-firm and five-firm industry cases is only about 10% of the two-firm stock level. There is little tendency for stocks to diminish over time, even in the larger size industries.

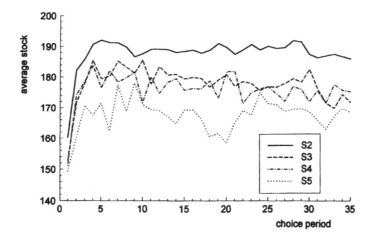

FIG. 3. Dynamic externality markets: The evolution of stocks.

COOPERATION IN THE COMMONS? 161

We anticipate that subject choices will be influenced by past choices and outcomes, because past events provide useful information upon which to base current choices. To investigate the dynamic linkage between past choices and current actions, we estimated autocorrelation functions for individual choices in each of the four industry sizes, in both the static cost externality and dynamic cost externality treatments. Correlations between current choice and choices lagged by $\tau = 1, \ldots, 9$ periods are provided in Table I. The information contained therein allows us to make a variety of observations. First, the estimated autocorrelations take smaller magnitudes as the number of lags gets large. For example, in our experimental markets with a static externality, estimated autocorrelations average 0.1267 over the first four lags and 0.1075 over the last four lags. In our experimental markets with a dynamic externality, estimated autocorrelations average 0.1805 over the first four lags and 0.1699 over the last four lags. This indicates that choices are convergent, though the process tends to be fairly slow. These relative magnitudes also suggest that subjects adapt their choices based on recent experience, which is indicative of learning. Second, despite the fact that the dynamic cost sessions entailed a more complex environment, there is little indication from the estimated autocorrelations that perturbations in behavior have a more persistent effect on behavior in the dynamic cost sessions. Third, the coefficient signs show that the impact of the past does not smoothly dampen over time. This means that choices are based on a process that is more complicated than a simple time series model, which in turn requires a more careful model of subject behavior. We now turn to the specification and estimation of such a model, and use these estimates to

TABLE I

Autocorrelation Functions for Individual Choices

	Group size			
Lag	2	3	4	5
	A. Static cost design			
1	−0.1062	−0.0764	0.3680	0.0777
2	0.0447	−0.0958	0.1720	0.2695
3	0.0733	0.1334	0.1845	−0.0763
4	0.0752	0.0321	0.1220	−0.1199
5	0.2652	0.0183	0.2546	−0.1871
6	−0.1660	0.0827	−0.0185	−0.0797
7	0.0683	−0.0646	0.0068	0.0869
8	0.0290	0.2363	0.0996	0.0861
9	0.0419	0.1920	0.1815	0.2804
	B. Dynamic cost design			
1	−0.0212	−0.2826	0.4035	0.0980
2	−0.1195	0.0199	0.2829	0.2418
3	0.0101	−0.0599	0.3279	0.1123
4	0.1982	−0.1418	0.3666	0.2015
5	0.0898	0.1860	0.5562	0.1963
6	0.0900	−0.3979	0.3932	0.0726
7	−0.0121	0.2028	0.3071	0.2184
8	0.1243	0.0891	0.1105	0.1893
9	−0.0819	0.0038	0.2054	0.2191

162   MASON AND PHILLIPS

draw inferences about the propensity of subjects to cooperate and implications for optimal industry size.

5. ECONOMETRIC ANALYSIS

We analyze the experimental data by treating each session as a pooled cross section/time series. In the sample, the number of equations (the cross-sectional element) is given by the number of participants. With this approach, the number of observations for each equation must be equal, and so is determined by the minimum number of rounds in any session, which is 35.

To model a subject's current harvest we use a partial adjustment model (Cason and Friedman [4]; Cheung and Friedman [5]; Sargent [29]). In this framework, changes in the subject's actions are proportional to his or her assessment of departures from the optimal action in the preceding period. In addition, recent models of learning in experimental games point to the possible role of profit feedback in influencing individuals' choices (Roth and Erev [28]). In this view, actions that yield an increase in payoffs should become more attractive, and hence more frequently be taken. For example, if an agent raises his or her period $\tau - 1$ choice by one unit above the period $\tau - 2$ choice, and then observes that period $\tau - 1$ payoffs exceed period $\tau - 2$ payoffs, the agent would be inclined to increase choice further in period τ. That is, agent i's period τ choice should be positively related to $\Delta \pi_{it-1}$, the difference between i's payoffs in periods $\tau - 1$ and $\tau - 2$. Changes in an agent's harvest may also depend on changes in the stock level for the dynamic treatment, since this will alter marginal costs.

To formalize these notions, we let h_{t-1}° be subject i's appraisal in period t of his or her optimal period $t - 1$ harvest. The direction of change in agent i's harvest from period $t - 2$ to $t - 1$ is measured by D_{it-1}, which takes the value 1 (respectively, -1) if $h_{it-1} - h_{it-2}$ is positive (negative); in the event $h_{it-1} = h_{it-2}$, $D_{it-1} = 0$. Change in stock is denoted by ΔS_t. Allowing for a disturbance term e_{it}, our partial adjustment model can then be written as

$$h_{it} = h_{it-1} + a_0(h_{t-1}^{\circ} - h_{it-1}) + cD_{it-1}\Delta\pi_{it-1} + e_{it} \qquad (18S)$$

in the static externality experiments and

$$h_{it} = h_{it-1} + a_0(h_{t-1}^{\circ} - h_{it-1}) + cD_{it-1}\Delta\pi_{it-1} + f\Delta S_t + e_{it} \qquad (18D)$$

in the dynamic externality experiments.[14] The parameter a_0 indexes the speed of adjustment. When $a_0 = 1$ choices adjust quickly to new information, while behavior is completely inertial when $a_0 = 0$. In general, smaller values of a_0 reflect more sluggish adjustment, with slower convergence of choices to a steady state.

The model is completed by describing the h_{t-1}°, the optimal harvest for period $t - 1$, as appraised by agent i in period t. This will generally be a function of H_{it-1}, the sum total of all the rivals' harvests. To keep the analytics tractable, we take this

---

[14] While it is conceivable that agents might base their harvest on current stocks in a model without dynamic externalities, Mason and Polasky [22] demonstrated that such behavior is not generally part of a closed loop equilibrium. Correspondingly, we do not include stock as a regressor in the formulation for the static markets.

to be a linear function, and assume $h^\circ_{i-1} = a_1 + a_2 H_{it-1}$.[15] Combining this with Eqs. (18S) and (18D) and rearranging, we obtain the regression equations

$$h_{it} = a + b_0 h_{it-1} + b_1 H_{it-1} + c D_{it-1} \Delta \pi_{it-1} + e_{it} \qquad (19S)$$

in the static externality experiments and

$$h_{it} = a + b_0 h_{it-1} + b_1 H_{it-1} + c D_{it-1} \Delta \pi_{it-1} + f \Delta S_t + e_{it} \qquad (19D)$$

in the dynamic externality experiments. These formulae should be read as reduced forms, where we have used the parameter definitions $a = a_0 a_1$, $b_0 = 1 - a_0$, and $b_1 = a_0 a_2$. While information on the underlying parameters a_0, a_1, and a_2 might conceivably be of interest, the parameters a, b_0, and b_1 are more directly relevant to our discussion, as they form the basis for our estimation of equilibrium industry harvests below. By construction, we expect b_0 to be between 0 and 1, with larger values corresponding to more sluggish adjustment.

In addition to the feedback effects from changes in payoffs, learning is likely to have an effect on the pattern of the disturbance term. McKelvey and Palfrey [24] model this impact through a decaying exponential component of the error. To this end, we allow the variance of the error term to change over time. Specifically, we assume var$(e_{it}) = f(t)\sigma^2$; the McKelvey and Palfrey form of learning would entail $f'(t) < 0$. In addition we assume the disturbance term has mean zero, with no correlation between subjects or across time, $E e_{it} e_{js} = 0$ if $i \neq j$ or $t \neq s$. With the lagged structure in (19), we forfeit the first two observations, leaving 33 observations for each equation.

In light of the assumed time dependency of the variance term, a generalized least squares approach will yield more efficient estimators than ordinary least squares. Correspondingly, we use a feasible generalized least squares approach. We first conduct OLS to obtain residuals and use these residuals to form estimates of the variance in each period. The estimated covariance structure is then used to perform weighted least squares. As a by-product of this approach, we are able to identify any trends in the variance over time. We identify the linear trend in the natural log of these variances; a negative trend would indicate an exponential decay in variance over time. As a final point, we note that a version of Eqs. (19) applies to all members in a given group, so that the right side for each individual consists of *lagged* endogenous variables. Although estimation of simultaneous equation systems using OLS generally yields inconsistent results, this is not the case when the right-side variables are predetermined.[16]

---

[15] An alternative is to use a weighted average of past choices by subject i's rivals. While Cason and Friedman [4] found some support for this more elaborate model, Mason and Phillips [19] provided evidence that the simpler one-lag specification provides a satisfactory characterization of agents' beliefs.

[16] Of course, the disturbances are likely to be contemporaneously correlated, so that OLS will generally yield biased and inconsistent estimates of the covariance structure. An approach that takes this covariance into account is straightforward to apply. We conducted such an approach; the results were indistinguishable from the results reported in this paper. Because this approach is far more cumbersome to exposit, we opted to describe the simpler version. Finally, we note that the inclusion of a lagged dependent variable renders the traditional Durbin–Watson test invalid. In place of the Durbin–Watson statistic, we therefore report Durbin's h-statistic. Under the null hypothesis of no serial correlation, this statistic is asymptotically distributed as a standard normal variate, and so significance of the h-statistic is gauged through a simple t-test (Fomby, Hill, and Johnson [12, p. 244]).

164   MASON AND PHILLIPS

Our estimation results are summarized in Tables II and III. In Table II, the estimates of the parameters a, b_0, b_1, and c from Eq. (19S) are represented by α, β_0, β_1, and γ, respectively. In Table 3, the estimates of a, b_0, b_1, c, and f from Eq. (19D) are represented by α, β_0, β_1, γ, and ϕ, respectively. We also indicate the number of subjects and the total number of observations used in the estimation procedure, next to the size of the industry in the specific session.

From these estimates we construct a maximum likelihood estimate of the steady state industry choice. To do this, we assume each player chooses h^e for three consecutive periods and neglects the disturbance term (Fomby, Hill, and Johnson [12]). In this case $\Delta \pi_{it-1} = 0$ and $H_{it-1} = (N-1)h^e$. Using these facts and inserting α and β_0 into Eq. (19S), the estimated equilibrium industry harvest for the static design is

$$H^e = N\alpha / [1 - \beta_0 + (N-1)\beta_1].$$ (20)

TABLE II

Behavior with Static Costs

	Parameter	Estimate	Standard error
Two-firm industry	α	9.267	0.822
(12 subjects, 396 observations)	β_0	0.2917	0.0427
	β_1	0.1247	0.0400
	γ	0.0038	0.0015
	H^e	31.756	0.396
R^2: 0.9563			
Decay rate in residuals: 0.0229			
Durbin's h-statistic: 0.9022			
Three-firm industry	α	6.036	0.7368
(15 subjects, 495 observations)	β_0	0.3533	0.0401
	β_1	0.0897	0.0255
	γ	0.0002	0.0018
	H^e	38.748	0.9013
R^2: 0.5403			
Decay rate in residuals: 0.0070			
Durbin's h-statistic: -0.7243			
Four-firm industry	α	7.103	0.9668
(12 subjects, 396 observations)	β_0	0.3426	0.0457
	β_1	0.0254	0.0240
	γ	0.0032	0.0016
	H^e	48.895	0.8640
R^2: 0.6527			
Decay rate in residuals: 0.0162			
Durbin's h-statistic: 0.4239			
Five-firm industry	α	5.808	0.8987
(15 subjects, 495 observations)	β_0	0.4960	0.0357
	β_1	-0.0232	0.0197
	γ	0.0023	0.0197
	H^e	48.655	0.7161
R^2: 0.6736			
Decay rate in residuals: 0.0120			
Durbin's h-statistic: -1.076			

TABLE III

Behavior with Dynamic Costs

	Parameter	Standard Estimate	error
Two-firm industry	α	20.382	1.915
(14 subjects, 476 observations)	β_0	0.0697	0.0591
	β_1	-0.1196	0.0640
	γ	0.0040	0.0023
	ϕ	-0.0515	0.0313
	H^e	38.825	1.166
Equilibrium stock: 187.784			
R^2: 0.6103			
Decay rate in residuals: 0.0069			
Durbin's h-statistic: 0.2737			
Three-firm industry	α	13.882	1.112
(18 subjects, 612 observations)	β_0	0.0344	0.0433
	β_1	0.0231	0.0301
	γ	0.0037	0.0019
	ϕ	0.0047	0.0150
	H^e	44.936	1.083
Equilibrium stock: 179.595			
R^2: 0.2595			
Decay rate in residuals: 0.0065			
Durbin's h-statistic: 0.4492			
Four-firm industry	α	12.053	2.176
(12 subjects, 408 observations)	β_0	0.2528	0.0592
	β_1	-0.0852	0.0471
	γ	0.0003	0.0024
	ϕ	0.0265	0.0336
	H^e	48.073	4.873
Equilibrium stock: 175.770			
R^2: 0.4034			
Decay rate in residuals: 0.0095			
Durbin's h-statistic: 0.2808			
Five-firm industry	α	6.993	1.572
(15 subjects, 510 observations)	β_0	0.3184	0.0474
	β_1	-0.0852	0.0323
	γ	-0.0773	0.0023
	ϕ	-0.0076	0.0245
	H^e	49.956	6.848
Equilibrium stock: 173.033			
R^2: 0.3500			
Decay rate in residuals: 0.0070			
Durbin's h-statistic: -1.513			

To derive the steady state industry choice in the dynamic design, we follow the same procedure with the added condition that $\Delta S_t = 0$ in a steady state. The same formula given in Eq. (20) results. These procedures yield consistent estimates of equilibrium industry behavior in each design. We note that it is straightforward to use the covariance information on the estimates from Eq. (19S) in the static treatment or Eq. (19D) in the dynamic treatment to consistently estimate the variance of H^e.[17] Finally, the exponential decay rates in the variances are included in Tables II and III. An exponential decay in variance occurred for every industry size in both the static and dynamic externality treatments.[18]

There are three salient features of the results in Table II. First, the estimated adjustment parameter β_0 is significantly less than 1 in all cases. This indicates that individuals do adjust their actions over time, with play converging to a steady state. Second, this steady state is significantly more cooperative than Cournot in the two- and three-firm industries (industry choices of 40 and 45, respectively). However, equilibrium behavior does not significantly differ from the Cournot level in the four- and five-firm industries (48 and 50, respectively). Third, evidence of learning is conveyed by the presence of exponential decay in variance over time for every industry size. Finally, the lagged change in profits has a positive and significant effect on current choice for the regressions with two and four agents in a market, consistent with the Roth and Erev [28] learning model.

The results in Table III indicate that play in the dynamic treatments is indistinguishable from Cournot for each group size. Also, relative to the static design, play in the dynamic markets is significantly less cooperative in those industries with two or three firms. The lack of cooperation may be attributable to the inherent difficulty in tacitly agreeing on a cooperative path, because the unit cost function and hence payoffs are changing over time as stock changes. For these estimates there again is evidence of learning, in that the variance of the residual term decays over time for every market size. However there is less indication that the payoff–reinforcement learning model is at force here. While the coefficient on lagged change in payoffs is positive and marginally significant for the three-agent dynamic cost sessions, it is negative and significant for the five-player session, and insignificant for the two- and four-player sessions. As in the regressions for the static cost treatment, the adjustment parameter is significantly smaller than 1 for all sessions. These parameter estimates are smaller than the corresponding estimates in the static treatment, suggesting more rapid convergence of play in the dynamic cost treatment.

The estimated values of steady state industry harvest can be used to determine the optimal industry size. To do this, we insert the estimated steady state harvests into Eqs. (10) and (15) to procure estimates of social welfare for each industry size in the two treatments. The implied asymptotic standard errors are obtained by applying the method described in footnote 17. The total surplus estimates are

---

[17] The consistency follows immediately from Slutsky's theorem. To obtain the asymptotic variance of a continuous function $f(\theta)$ of a maximum likelihood estimator of a vector of parameters, θ, calculate the quadratic form $g(\theta)'V(\theta)g(\theta)$, where $g(\theta) = \partial f(\theta)/\partial\theta$ and $V(\theta)$ is the associated maximum likelihood estimator of the covariance matrix for θ (Fomby, Hill, and Johnson [12, Corollary 4.2.2]).

[18] There is a concern that the variance in the disturbance term may not be homoscedastic, even after accounting for temporal effects. In particular, one may wonder if there are individual-specific variances. To test for the presence of heteroscedasticity in the weighted regression (i.e., after accounting for temporal effects) one regresses the square of the residuals upon the explanatory variables. The presence of a significant relationship, as measured by the R-squared, is taken as evidence of heteroscedasticity. Fomby, Hill and Johnson [12] contains an excellent discussion of these issues. On conducting such a robustness check, we obtained R-squared values of 0.0450, 0.1121, 0.0738, and 0.0572 for the static sessions, and 0.0480, 0.0640, 0.0436, and 0.0468 for the dynamic sessions. In no case was the R-squared very large, and so we conclude that there is little indication of heteroscedasticity in the weighted regression model. Put differently, any heteroscedasticity in the original regression model is well accounted for by a model that allows the variance to differ across time.

COOPERATION IN THE COMMONS?   167

TABLE IV

Implied Estimates of Social Welfare

Industry size	Estimated SW	Std. err. of est.
A. Static costs[a]		
Two-firm industry	1237.14	10.824
Three-firm industry	1328.33	18.183
Four-firm industry	1405.14	8.420
Five-firm industry	1327.77	7.156
B. Dynamic costs[b]		
Two-firm industry	1181.39	13.687
Three-firm industry	1191.48	6.930
Four-firm industry	1170.94	7.266
Five-firm industry	1146.52	4.244

[a] t-statistics for (i) $SW_4 - SW_3 = 3.833$ and (ii) $SW_4 - SW_5 = 7.002$.
[b] t-statistics for (i) $SW_3 - SW_2 = 0.658$ and (ii) $SW_3 - SW_4 = 2.045$.

presented in Table IV. In addition, we provide asymptotic t-tests on the difference between the estimated value of equilibrium social welfare at the apparent optimal industry size and the value at industry sizes with one more or one less firm. There are two key points here. First, the optimal number of firms in the static cost treatment is four, and this is larger than the optimal number of firms in the Cournot model. Equilibrium social welfare is significantly larger with four agents than with three or five agents in the static sessions. Second, equilibrium social welfare is largest at an industry size of three firms in the dynamic sessions. While the increase in social welfare going from two to three firms is not significant, there is a significant reduction in social welfare associated with the addition of a fourth firm. With dynamic cost externalities there is little indication that cooperation can mitigate the tragedy of the commons.

6. ON EXTINCTION

An additional issue we wish to explore in the context of dynamic externalities is that of extinction. There has been considerable public concern that harvesters of a commons may take the resource to extinction, as exemplified by the creation of the International Whaling Commission and passage of the Marine Mammal Protection Act of 1972. These concerns are also evident in publications by watchdog groups like the Worldwatch Institute. Looking back on this period, Brown, Kane, and Ayres [3] wrote "[d]uring the heyday of unrestricted commercial fishing in the latter half of the nineteenth century, many sea mammals were hunted nearly to extinction."

The public debate sparked a flurry of interest by resource economists in the early 1970s (Bachmura [1], Clark [6], Gould [13], and Lewis [18]). Lewis showed that it can be an equilibrium for firms to extinguish a renewable resource if each firm's optimal harvest rate is bounded away from zero for arbitrarily small stock levels. Similarly, for extinction to be socially optimal, marginal net benefits must be positive at industry equilibrium harvests as the stock level tends to zero. More recent literature has argued that harvesting to extinction is unlikely, because as populations shrink it becomes prohibitively costly to further exploit them (see

DasGupta [9] for a survey). This line of reasoning pays specific attention to the role of stock in affecting harvesting costs, and is best associated with our dynamic externality analysis.[19]

Walker and Gardner [31] addressed the likelihood of resource extinction in an experimental setting. In their paper, extinction is regarded as a stochastic event with a probability linked to current harvests; they have no dynamic externalities. Their model applies to a commons that have the potential of going extinct in a single time period. For many common property resources this may be an unlikely event. An alternative interpretation, and one that is consistent with our design, is that extinction may occur probabilistically within a given period if the current stock is sufficiently depleted. If group k's stock is close to S_-, the negative root from Eq. (17), then Eq. (18D) implies there is a positive probability that group k's harvest will exceed the growth for period t by enough that period $t + l$ stock falls below S_-. In such an event the potential for extinction becomes much greater. Hence our design regards movement toward extinction as a cumulative phenomenon, rather than a dramatic—almost instantaneous—event. Our subjects have the opportunity to adapt their behavior over time as extinction becomes progressively more or less likely.[20] For stock levels near the critical value S_-, reductions in harvests are likely to salvage the resource—not just for that period, but for the near future as well. Extinction should therefore occur less frequently.

We believe that the most likely context for resource extinction in our design is when there are five players and the initial stock is set very small. To investigate the likelihood of extinction, we ran four additional sessions in the five-player dynamic cost externality design. Fifteen subjects participated in each of these sessions, so that there were three industries in each session, for a total of twelve industries. The initial stock was 36 units in these sessions, which is smaller than the unstable steady state. For these subject groups, if the stock became negative, it was reset to 36. This allowed us to observe if such groups repeatedly would drive their stock to extinction or if instead they learned from past extinction events to behave more efficiently. Such a phenomenon could occur with agents that harvest naturally occurring common property resources, such as fisheries, and can move from one resource pool to the next.

Four of the twelve groups drove the resource to extinction at least once. In fact, each of these four groups drove the resource to extinction three or more times.

---

[19] In the context of our experiments $P' = -1$, $c = -S/12$, $P = 60 - H$, $\delta \leq 1$, $c_2 = 25 - S/12$, and $\partial S_{t+1}/\partial h_t = -1$. As we note below, we shall experimentally investigate this possibility with $N = 5$. Exploiting symmetry, industry harvests are five times the individual firm's harvest. Recall that the strategic effect would induce each firm to expand its harvest. Also, firms cannot anticipate harvesting more next period than the steady state harvest, which is roughly 10 in this context, the first term in the second line of Eq. (5) is no smaller than -1. It follows that the firm's equilibrium harvest must satisfy

$$-h^* + 60 - 5h^* - 25 + S/12 - 1 \leq 0 \quad \text{or} \quad h^* \geq 34/6 + S/72.$$

In the limit, then, each firm harvests no less than five units, and so Lewis' condition is met. Thus, if stocks become low, it can be an equilibrium for agents to extinguish the resource. On the other hand, since the optimal industry size is three, marginal net social benefits are negative at any stock for a five-firm industry. Thus, the necessary condition for extinction to be socially efficient fails here.

[20] In one of Walker and Gardner's [31] designs, the equilibrium entails rising harvest over time, so that the probability of extinction also rises over time. Thus, their model induces agents to increase their harvests as extinction becomes more likely. In contrast, our model induces agents to reduce harvests as extinction becomes more likely.

Two of these groups learned to restrict their initial harvests, so that the resource ultimately recovered. The remaining two groups were consistently unable to limit their harvests, and they repeatedly drove the resource to extinction. In the remaining eight groups, harvests were sufficiently small in the first few periods that the stock grew rapidly, i.e., the industry itself moved away from extinction of the resource. These observations were collected under conditions most likely to cause the resource stock to fall to zero. Nevertheless, two-thirds of the industries did not drive the resource to extinction. We conclude that the threat of extinction of a resource need not be an important phenomenon when there is a dynamic stock externality.

For these 12 industries, Table V reports the results from dynamic regression model discussed in Section 5. The key point to be gleaned from this set of estimates is that steady state choices in these experimental markets are not significantly different from those in the initial five-firm dynamic cost experiments, as reported in Table IV. While subjects tended to limit their initial harvests, so as to allow the resource to recover, their ultimate behavior was no different from behavior in the initial five-firm dynamic cost experiments.

7. CONCLUSIONS

Our goal in this paper has been to identify the effect, if any, that cooperative tendencies have upon the interplay between the cost externality and pricing behavior when firms exploit a limited access commons. In our static cost externality treatment, cooperation is apparent in industries with two and three firms, and so there is the possibility that welfare is enhanced by increasing the number of firms and realizing lower prices. In our experimental markets, increasing industry size from two to four agents generated significant welfare gains. This is important in limited access commons since the remedies that are often proscribed—restricting access or imposing large license costs—need not be consistent with welfare maximization. Indeed, it is a fair concern here that limiting access may be welfare-reducing, because it may engender collusion and increase any price distortions more rapidly than reducing cost-side externalities.

TABLE V

Extinction Regressions, Five-Person Experiments

Parameter		Estimate	Standard error
Initial stock = 36	α	6.368	0.6053
(60 subjects, 1980 observations)	β_0	0.3409	0.0264
	β_1	-0.0006	0.0136
	γ	0.0003	0.0015
	ϕ	-0.0055	0.0098
	H^e	48.132	2.659

Equilibrium stock: 175.687
R^2: 0.2189
Decay rate in residuals: 0.0017
Durbin's h-statistic: 0.7778

170   MASON AND PHILLIPS

On the other hand, we also found very little tendency for players to cooperate in common property industries subject to dynamic cost externalities, a structure that is arguably more important for resources that tend to be found in the same location over long periods of time. In this setting, increasing the number of firms from two to three did raise welfare, but further increases were welfare-reducing. For this class of resources the results in Cornes, Mason, and Sandler [8] seem applicable: the potential harm from sharply limiting entry may be less significant.

In the dynamic cost externality sessions, we also investigated the tendency for agents to dissipate the resource stock over time. When subjects started to reduce stocks in these treatments, unit costs increased. In response, subjects reduced their harvests sufficiently that the stock rebounded. The implication is that, at least in the context of our stylized markets, we find little evidence that extinction is a likely result when costs are linked to stocks.

Recent experimental evidence points to the possibility that agents can negotiate arrangements that greatly reduce the externalities associated with exploitation of a commons when they are able to engage in costless face-to-face communication. This has important policy implications, in that direct governmental intervention limiting the number of harvesters may be unnecessary when private parties can negotiate a socially desirable outcome. If these negotiations are not low cost, either because of the inherent difficulties in forming a coalition and reaching an agreement or because of the potential that such agreements may be regarded as a violation of antitrust statues, it is still possible that the parties will be able to reach a tacit agreement. While our results suggest this outcome is relatively unlikely if the number of agents is large, such tacit agreements could take place in tightly held oligopolies.

COOPERATION IN THE COMMONS?

APPENDIX

The Other Persons' Summed Choice

Your Choice	2	3	4	5	6	7	8	9	10	11	12	13	14	15	16	17	18	19	20	21	22	23	24	25	26
1	222	213	204	195	186	177	168	159	150	141	132	123	114	105	96	87	78	69	60	51	42	33	24	15	6
2	245	235	225	215	205	195	185	175	165	155	145	135	125	115	105	95	85	75	65	55	45	35	25	15	5
3	266	255	244	233	222	211	200	189	178	167	156	145	134	123	112	101	90	79	68	57	46	35	24	13	2
4	285	273	261	249	237	225	213	201	189	177	165	153	141	129	117	105	93	81	69	57	45	33	21	9	-3
5	302	289	276	263	250	237	224	211	198	185	172	159	146	133	120	107	94	81	68	55	42	29	16	3	-10
6	317	303	289	275	261	247	233	219	205	191	177	163	149	135	121	107	93	79	65	51	37	23	9	-5	-19
7	330	315	300	285	270	255	240	225	210	195	180	165	150	135	120	105	90	75	60	45	30	15	0	-15	-10
8	341	325	309	293	277	261	245	229	213	197	181	165	149	133	117	101	85	69	53	37	21	5	-11	-27	-13
9	350	333	316	299	282	265	248	231	214	197	180	163	146	129	112	95	78	61	44	27	10	-7	-24	-41	-58
10	357	339	321	303	285	267	249	231	213	195	177	159	141	123	105	87	69	51	33	15	-3	-21	-39	-57	-75
11	362	343	324	305	286	267	248	229	210	191	172	153	134	115	96	77	58	39	20	1	-18	-37	-56	-75	-94
12	365	345	325	305	285	265	245	225	205	185	165	145	125	105	85	65	45	25	5	-15	-35	-55	-75	-95	-115
13	366	345	324	303	282	261	240	219	198	177	156	135	114	93	72	51	30	9	-12	-33	-54	-75	-96	-117	-138

REFERENCES

1. F. T. Bachmura, The economics of vanishing species, *Natural Resources J.* **11**, 674–692 (1971).
2. G. Brown, An optimal program for managing common property resources with congestion externalities, *J. Polit. Economy* **88**, 163–174 (1974).
3. L. R. Brown, H. Kane, and E. Ayres, "Vital Signs 1993," Norton, New York (1993).
4. T. N. Cason and D. Friedman, Learning in markets with random supply and demand, Working paper, University of California-Santa Cruz, 1995.
5. Y.-W. Cheung and D. Friedman, Individual learning in normal form games: Some laboratory results, Working paper, University of California-Santa Cruz, 1995.
6. C. W. Clark, Profit maximization and the extinction of animal species, *J. Polit. Economy* **8**, 950–961 (1973).
7. C. W. Clark, "Mathematical Bioeconomics: The Optimal Management of Renewable Resources," Wiley, New York (1990).
8. R. C. Cornes, C. F. Mason, and T. Sandler, The commons and the optimal number of firms, *Quart. J. Econom.* **100**, 641–646 (1986).
9. P. DasGupta, "The Control of Resources," Harvard University Press, Cambridge, MA (1980).
10. H. Demsetz, Towards a theory of property rights, *Amer. Econom. Rev.* 347–359 (1967).
11. E. J. Dockner and N. Van Long, International pollution control: cooperative vs. noncooperative strategies, *J. Environ. Econom. Management* **25**, 13–27 (1993).
12. T. Fomby, R. C. Hill, and S. Johnson, "Advanced Econometric Methods," Springer-Verlag, New York (1988).
13. J. R. Gould, Extinction of a fishery by commercial exploitation: a note, *J. Polit. Economy* **90**, 1031–1039 (1972).
14. S. Hackett, E. Schlager, and J. Walker, The role of communication in resolving commons dilemmas: experimental evidence with heterogeneous appropriators, *J. Environ. Econom. Management* **27**, 99–126 (1994).
15. A. Herr, An experimental study of pure group size effects in the commons, Working paper, University of Indiana, 1995.
16. R. Johnson and G. Libecap, Contracting problems and regulation: the case of the fishery, *Amer. Econom. Rev.* **72**, 1005–1022 (1982).
17. L. Karp, Social welfare in a common property oligopoly, *Internat. Econom. Rev.* **33**, 353–372 (1992).
18. T. R. Lewis, The exhaustion and depletion of natural resources, *Econometrica* **47**, 1569–1571 (1979).
19. C. Mason and O. Phillips, Dynamic learning in a two-person experimental game, Working paper, University of Wyoming, 1996.
20. C. F. Mason, O. R. Phillips, and C. Nowell, Duopoly behavior in asymmetric markets: an experimental evaluation, *Rev. Econom. Statist.* **74**, 662–670 (1992).
21. C. F. Mason and A. S. Polasky, Entry deterrence in the commons, *Internat. Econom. Rev.* **35**, 510–530 (1994).
22. C. F. Mason and A. S. Polasky, The optimal number of firms in the commons: a dynamic approach, *Canad. J. Econom.*, in press (1997).
23. C. F. Mason, T. Sandler, and R. Cornes, Expectations, the commons, and optimal group size, *J. Environ. Econom. Management* **15**, 99–110 (1988).
24. R. D. McKelvey and T. Palfrey, An experimental study of the centipede game, *Econometrica* **60**, 803–836 (1992).
25. E. Ostrom, "Governing the Commons: The Evolution of Institutions for Collective Action," Cambridge University Press, Cambridge (1990).
26. E. Ostrom, R. Gardner, and J. Walker, "Rules, Games, and Common Pool Resources," University of Michigan Press, Ann Arbor (1994).
27. O. R. Phillips and C. F. Mason, Mutual forbearance in a conglomerate game, *Rand J. Econom.* **23**, 395–414 (1992).
28. A. E. Roth and I. Erev, Learning in extensive form games: experimental data and simple dynamic models in the intermediate term, *Games Econom. Behav.* (Special Issue: Nobel Symposium) **8**, 164–212 (1995).
29. T. J. Sargent, "Bounded Rationality in Macroeconomics," Oxford University Press, Oxford (1993).
30. A. D. Scott, The fishery: the objectives of sole ownership, *J. Polit. Economy* **63**, 116–124 (1955).
31. J. M. Walker and R. Gardner, Probabilistic destruction of common-pool resource: experimental evidence, *Econom. J.* **102**, 1149–1161 (1992).

[23]

KYUNG HWAN BAIK, TODD L. CHERRY,
STEPHAN KROLL and JASON F. SHOGREN

ENDOGENOUS TIMING IN A GAMING TOURNAMENT

ABSTRACT. This paper examines the theoretical background and actual behavior in a gaming tournament with endogenous timing where a person has more incentive, structure, and time to form a strategy. The baseline treatment suggests that subgame perfection is a reasonable predictor of behavior — subjects made 170 of 208 theoretically predicted choices of best actions, with the majority of mistakes made in timing choices by the players who did not survive the cut to the second round. Four sensitivity treatments established that the design feature that lead to more predictable behavior was time to think — 745 of 960 correctly predicted decisions with more time versus 595 of 960 with less time. A random effects Probit model suggests that the key design feature that closed the gap between predicted and observed behavior was not necessarily the non-linear payoffs created by the tournament design, but rather that the key was providing people with more time to think about their strategy.

KEY WORDS: Contests, Gaming tournament, Timing

1. INTRODUCTION

Contests between unevenly matched contenders – favorites and underdogs – involve the strategic commitment of effort (Dixit 1987). A favorite is the player whose odds of victory exceeds one-half at the Nash equilibrium; an underdog's odds are less than one-half. Baik and Shogren (1992) show that when the favorite and underdog can choose who commits effort first, the subgame perfect equilibrium is when the underdog leads and the favorite follows. Both players find it profitable when underdog moves first because he reveals his relative lack of strength, thereby allowing the favorite to respond efficiently. Since the underdog expects the favorite to react in proportion to his effort, he reduces his effort too. Therefore, endogenous timing of moves reduces the resources wasted in the contest relative to a clash in which timing is fixed. The endogenous timing framework has been applied to several explicit contests including defense (Hirshleifer 1995), environmental disputes (Baik and

2   K.H. BAIK, T.L. CHERRY, S. KROLL AND J.F. SHOGREN

Shogren 1994; Hurley and Shogren 1997), rent seeking (Leininger 1993; Baik 1994; Nitzan 1994), R&D with spillovers (De Bondt and Henrique 1995; De Bondt 1997), commercial policy (Syropoulus 1994), and has found some empirical support from track-and-field data from the 1992 Barcelona Olympics (Boyd and Boyd 1995).

Subgame perfection and backward induction are the key concepts to the underdog-leads/favorite-follows equilibrium in an endogenous timing contest. Subgame perfection was formulated to restrict players to credible strategies, thereby ruling out incredible threats on- and off-the-equilibrium path. Subgame perfection requires each player to (1) look forward and think about every possible subgame that could be reached in the game tree of the contest, (2) guess what actions players would take in each subgame, and (3) work backwards, using those guesses, to decide what action to take once and for all at the beginning of the contest (Camerer 1997). Each player looks ahead and reasons backward to reduce the number of likely equilibria in the contest. The subgame perfect equilibrium is a set of strategies, one for each player, such that in any subgame the strategies form a Nash equilibrium (Selten 1965; Fudenberg and Tirole 1991). Equilibria that are not subgame perfect are argued to be less likely to occur, and thus should be ruled out as possible outcomes.

While subgame perfection is the most commonly used solution concept for multi-stage games of complete information, the concept has had mixed success as a predictor of observed behavior in laboratory gaming experiments. Although some researchers have found a reasonable correspondence between predicted and observed behavior (e.g., Harrison and Hirshleifer 1989), most have not (e.g., Camerer et al. 1993; McKelvey and Palfrey 1992; Ochs and Roth 1989; Roth 1995). And even if a person can be trained to use backward induction to think about strategy, looking ahead and reasoning back is unnatural to people who do not see the value in thinking about events that do not seem likely to occur (i.e., ruling out off-the-equilibrium path behavior). In fact, lab results testing the endogenous timing model do not support the subgame perfect equilibrium (see Shogren and Hurley 1997). Underdogs did not always lead – only 35-58 percent of the time, and favorites did not always follow – only 55-77 percent. Underdogs who did lead usually overinvested in effort, and favorites who followed often underinvested. Total rent dissipation was also greater than predicted.

The poor correspondence between predicted and observed behavior in gaming experiments motivated Camerer (1997) to argue for a 'behavioral game theory'.[1] He proposes that game theorists would benefit by taking a perspective that balances over-rational equilibrium analysis and under-rational adaptive analysis driven by pattern recognition from empirical data. Camerer's approach has three steps: begin with a situation in which game theory has a prediction; if actual behavior differs, think of explanations of the unpredicted behavior; and then extend the theory to incorporate these explanations. He suggests three methods to extend game theory–nonexpected utility theory (e.g., prospect theory), learning (e.g., updating beliefs), and pregame theory (e.g., mental models of what people are actually thinking about, see Neale and Bazerman 1991). A maintained belief in behavioral game theory would suggest that the endogenous timing model might need to be overhauled with new behavioral restrictions that will serve to close the potential gap between theory and observation.

This paper takes another perspective on how to close the potential gap between theory and observation in an endogenous timing model – the inclusion of an institutional context that rewards competition over seemingly trivial differences in measurable performance. Economic models often maintain that absolute payoffs motivate individual behavior, even if a trivial difference exists between measurable performance and the associated payoffs from optimal and suboptimal behavior. A person is presumed to be purposeful as he finds it worthwhile to capture the extra unit of satisfaction, however small, but evidence from the lab suggests that people are not so exact in their ability or willingness to discern and react to trivial differences in payoffs. The smaller the gap between optimal and suboptimal payoffs the more likely a person is to misbehave (e.g., Harrison 1989). Trivial payoff differences do not really punish deviations from optimal behavior, regardless of whether utility is assumed to be ordinal or cardinal. Thus, a researcher must choose either to reformulate the model to include behavioral extras in the utility function (e.g., altruism, envy, spite, errors), or to impose an institutional context that provides sufficiently high rewards for trivial differences

4   K.H. BAIK, T.L. CHERRY, S. KROLL AND J.F. SHOGREN

in measurable performance such that self-interest is rewarded, even encouraged.

Following Shogren (1997), this paper takes the second path. We consider whether tournament incentives can close the gap between predicted and actual behavior in the endogenous timing game. In the wild, tournaments have emerged as the exchange institution that pushes high-ability people to exert the extra effort needed to win when the difference between winning and losing is measured in fractions of seconds/points or parts per billion. Tournaments with non-linear payoffs that increase at an increasing rate are designed to reward a trivial numerical deviation between optimal and suboptimal behavior by a substantial difference in payoffs (e.g., Lazear and Rosen 1981; Drago et al. 1996; Frank and Cook 1996). Many sports, such as track-and-field, tennis, and golf, use a non-linearly increasing reward system where the winner's payoff is often twice that of the runner-up (see Ehrenberg and Bognanno 1990); performance pay in top management positions use a similar reward structure (e.g., Jensen and Murphy 1990). A tournament incentive scheme with non-linearly increasing payoffs mimics a hierarchy of exchange institutions that reward rational self-interest by providing a reason to look ahead and reason back despite our predilection to ignore unlikely events.

Specifically, we explore the correspondence between predictions and actual behavior about subgame perfection in Baik and Shogren's contest (1992) with endogenous timing. Our gaming tournament examines how three key design features affect behavior in non-linear payoffs, structure to the decision frame, and more time to think about strategy. Though our results suggest that tournament-style incentives can improve the correspondence between theory and behavior, surprisingly more time to think is the driving force that closes the gap. This result contrasts findings in two prior gaming tournaments, in which rational self-interest organized behavior best even though the time to form a strategy was limited to less than an hour. This suggests that the short time frame typically provided in the lab for people to think strategically might be insufficient. They might not have sufficient time to think through all the potential interactions and decisions of others.

2. SUBGAME PERFECTION IN A CONTEST WITH ENDOGENOUS TIMING

Consider a contest where two risk-neutral players, A and B, compete to win a fixed reward, G. Let x_A and x_B represent the observable and irreversible effort expended by players A and B to influence their probabilities of winning the contest, $p_A = p_A(x_A, x_B, \alpha)$ and $p_B = 1 - p_A$, where α is a parameter of relative ability. Player i selects a level of effort, x_i, to maximize his expected payoff, $E\pi_i = p_i(x_A, x_B, \alpha)G - x_i$. Define the favorite as the player whose odds of victory exceed one-half at the Nash equilibrium; the underdog implies the opposite (Dixit 1987).

The endogenous-timing game has the following structure. First, the players announce simultaneously and independently when they will expend their effort – the first period or the second period. If both players chose to move at the same time, i.e., both chose first period or both chose second period, they play a simultaneous-move game. If one player picks the first period and the other picks the second, they play a Stackelberg leader game. Then, knowing who will move when, the players choose their effort levels in the period they selected in the announcement stage. Given asymmetric ability and a logit-form contest-success function, the subgame perfect equilibrium is when the underdog expends his effort before the favorite does (Baik and Shogren 1992).

The logit-form probability-of-winning function in our gaming experiment is $p_A(x_A, x_B, \alpha) = x_A/(x_A + \alpha x_B)$. Let $\alpha = 2$, which implies that player A is the underdog and B is the favorite. Figure 1 illustrates the players' expected payoffs, given $G = 1440$. In our experimental design we use five effort levels for each player. Player A chooses from rows R1 through R5, while player B chooses from columns C1 through C5: R1 = C1 = 0, R2 = C2 = 180, R3 = C3 = 270, R4 = C4 = 320, R5 = C5 = 720. Player A's payoff is the first number in each cell, and player B's is the second. For example, if A selects R2 and B selects C2, A's and B's expected payoffs are 700 and 1180 tokens.

Three main subgames exist in Figure 1, each with its own Nash equilibrium. Firstly, the Nash equilibrium in the simultaneous-move subgame is (R4, C4) = (560, 1040): neither player has an unilateral incentive to deviate from his strategy, given the strategy of the

6   K.H. BAIK, T.L. CHERRY, S. KROLL AND J.F. SHOGREN

PLAYER B

		C1	C2	C3	C4	C5
P	R1	400 / 400	1660 / 400	1570 / 400	1520 / 400	1120 / 400
L A	R2	400 / 1660	1180 / 700	1210 / 580	1204 / 536	960 / 380
Y E R	R3	400 / 1570	1043 / 747	1090 / 610	1093 / 557	893 / 357
A	R4	400 / 1520	982 / 758	1034 / 616	1040 / 560	858 / 342
	R1	400 / 1120	700 / 640	747 / 503	758 / 442	640 / 160

Figure 1. The 5 × 5 Payoff Table

other player. Secondly, the Nash equilibrium in the favorite-leads subgame is (R1, C5) = (400, 1120). Thirdly, the Nash equilibrium in the underdog-leads subgame is (R2, C3) = (580, 1210). Recall that subgame perfection requires that each strategy is a Nash equilibrium in each subgame including the entire game. Since both players' expected payoffs in the underdog-leads subgame exceed those in the other two subgames (favorite: 1210 > 1120 > 1040, underdog: 580 > 560 > 400), the subgame perfect equilibrium is when the underdog moves first and selects R2 and the favorite follows and selects C3.

3. BASELINE TREATMENT: DESIGN

Economic rationality usually presumes that the absolute payoffs in Figure 1 should motivate behavior. Even if a trivial difference exists between measurable performance and the associated payoffs from optimal and suboptimal behavior, a person still tries to capture the extra unit of satisfaction, no matter how large or small. This presumption of absolute payoffs underlies the standard gaming experiment that uses multiple trials, say 20-30 trials run over two hours, to give people a chance to learn from repetition (see for example Shogren and Baik's, 1991, 1992, lab evaluation of Nash equilibria in a contest model). Each player would face a different opponent for each trial, one trial would be selected at random to determine take-home pay, and each token in the 5x5 matrix would be worth, say $0.01 each. Therefore, the expected payoff in the subgame perfect equilibrium (R2, C3) would be 580 tokens – $11.60 for the underdog, and 1210 tokens – $24.20 for the favorite.

But people who confront a new or unfamiliar task in an experimental setting often deviate from predicted behavior in the lab because their decisions feel rushed, their reasoning unstructured, their payoffs flat (Plott 1996). Evidence from the lab suggests that people are not so exact in their ability or willingness to discern and react to trivial differences in payoffs (Harrison 1989). In Figure 1, this is the case – deviating from subgame perfection to the simultaneous-move Nash equilibrium only results in 20 and 170 less tokens for the underdog and favorite, or a loss of $0.02 and $0.16 per trial (at 2 cents per token divided over 20 trials). People have weak incentive to go through the trouble of determining the optimal strategy for such a small gain. Given trivial differences in outcomes, choices seem myopic and random as people probe for profitable behavior. Although experience can make behavior more purposeful, it is no guarantee that actual choices will conform to predictions (Kagel 1995).

Given this backdrop, we designed our baseline treatment with three key features to induce behavior more in line with predictions: players had up to two days to think about their gaming strategy, each player specified a strategy on how they would play, and each player filled out his strategy sheet using an explicit backward induction decision framework. A player was eliminated if he was not one of the highest ranked players after a round was complete (Shogren 1997).

The baseline treatment was designed as follows. First, players were randomly assigned as either an A- or B-player. Each player independently filled out a 'Strategy Sheet', or a set of best actions, based on the 5×5 Payoff Table. Players knew their strategy would be played against the strategies of all opposing-type players, and would determine how far he or she would advance in the tournament and his or her take-home-pay. The players also knew that they would

8   K.H. BAIK, T.L. CHERRY, S. KROLL AND J.F. SHOGREN

receive the set of best actions selected by all of the opposing-type players in the previous round; this created a common information set.

Name
_____

Your task is to define a complete strategy as to how you will play the 5 × 5 Payoff Table. Your strategy has two parts.

Part 1. Part 1 has three choices. Please answer all questions. An incomplete strategy will be removed from the tournament. When defining your strategy, be sure to consider how an A-type player is likely to respond. Remember that each A-type player will be defining his or her own strategy by taking into account your likely response.

CHOICE L. Leader—If I lead and pick my column first before the A-type player selects his or her row, I will pick column _____?

CHOICE F. Follower—If the A-type player leads and I follow, then if the A-type player selects:
   row R1 I will select column _____?
   row R2 I will select column _____?
   row R3 I will select column _____?
   row R4 I will select column _____?
   row R5 I will select column _____?

CHOICE S. Simultaneous Moves—If both the A-type player and I select our respective row and column at the same time, then I will select column _____?

Part 2. In part 2 you must decide whether you would prefer to lead or follow (circle one).
   (a). Lead   (b). Follow

Return this Strategy Sheet to:
   Professor Jason Shogren
   School of Forestry and Environmental Studies
   Yale University
   New Haven, CT 06511
   (203) 432-5135

Figure 2. Strategy sheet – B – Round 1

A Strategy Sheet had two parts – best action and timing – presented in a backward inductive structure (see Figure 2). The high-point elimination tournament had five rounds. Round 1 was the 'qualifying round' that accommodated all who wanted to play. In Round 2, the field was cut to the top sixteen players – eight A- and B-

ENDOGENOUS TIMING IN A GAMING TOURNAMENT   9

players. In Rounds 3 and 4, the field was cut to eight and four players. Round 5 was the final round, matching the top A- and B-player. 'Top players' were the A- or B-players with the greatest average scores at the end of a round. In Round 1, if a player's average score was one of the top 8 A- or B-players, he or she advanced; if not, he or she was eliminated. If there was a tie between two or more players, a random draw determined who advanced. If the player advanced, he or she submitted a new strategy that could be the same as in Round 1 or could differ. This strategy was matched with the strategies of the top 8 opposing-type players, and his average score was calculated. If his average score was one of the top 4 A- or B-players, she advanced; if not, he or she was eliminated. This continued for Rounds 3 & 4 until the final A- and B-player remained.

A player's payoff was determined by how far he or she advanced in the tournament. The value of a token increased at an increasing rate by round – \$0.005 in round 1; \$0.02 in round 2; \$0.04 in Round 3; \$0.08 in Round 4; and \$0.15 in Round 5. For example, if an A player advanced to Round 3, but no further, and his or her average score was 700 tokens for Round 3, his or her payoff was \$28 (700 tokens @ \$0.04). If he or she advanced to Round 5, and if his or her score was 700 tokens, his or her payoff was \$105 (700 tokens @ \$0.15).

Twenty-six students from the Yale School of Forestry and Environmental Studies participated in this experiment. All subjects were inexperienced with gaming experiments that tested endogenous timing and subgame perfection. In Round 1, each player was given a set of instructions, a 5 × 5 Payoff Table, and a Strategy Sheet.[2] They were given two days on the honor system to think independently about their strategy and turn in their Strategy Sheet to the monitor. The monitor calculated the average scores, and informed those that advanced to the next round – giving them a new Strategy Sheet and the set of Strategy Sheets of all the opposing-type players who advanced. Eliminated players were paid the value of their average tokens for that round. This process was identical for Rounds 2 through 5. Note that in the later rounds, the majority of subjects turned in their strategy sheet within one day.

TABLE 1. Summary of underdog (A) strategy selections, average tokens and prize money

Player	Round	Lead	Follow a	b	c	d	e	Sim.	Tim.	Avg. Tok.	Effic. (%)	Prize $
A3	5	c	c	c	c	c	c	c	c	580	100	$84
	4	c	c	c	c	c	c	c	c	580	100	
	3	c	c	c	c	c	c	c	c	580	100	
	2	c	c	c	c	c	c	c	c	577.5	99.6	
	1	c	c	c	c	c	c	c	c	583.7	100.6	
A30	4	c	c	c	c	c	c	c	c	580	100	$44.8
	3	c	c	c	c	c	c	c	c	580	100	
	2	c	c	c	c	c	c	c	c	577.5	99.6	
	1	w	c	c	c	c	c	c	w	532.4	91.8	
A23	3	c	c	c	c	c	c	c	c	580	100	$22.4
	2	c	c	c	c	c	c	c	c	577.5	99.6	
	1	w	c	c	c	c	c	c	w	532.4	91.8	
A22	3	c	c	c	c	c	c	c	c	580	100	$22.4
	2	c	c	c	c	c	c	c	c	577.5	99.6	
	1	c	c	c	c	c	c	c	w	532.4	91.8	
A16	2	c	c	c	c	c	c	c	c	577.5	99.6	$11.55
	1	c	c	c	c	c	c	c	c	583.7	100.6	
A1	2	c	c	c	c	c	c	c	w	540	93.1	$10.8
	1	c	c	c	c	c	c	c	c	583.7	100.6	
A2	2	c	c	c	c	c	c	c	w	540	93.1	$10.8
	1	c	c	c	c	c	c	c	w	532.4	91.8	
A29	2	w	c	c	c	c	c	c	w	540	93.1	$10.8
	1	w	c	c	c	c	c	c	w	532.4	91.8	
A7	1	c	c	c	c	c	c	w	w	514.7	88.7	$2.57
A5	1	c	c	w	w	w	w	w	w	449.9	77.6	$2.25
A4	1	w	c	c	c	c	c	c	w	532.4	91.8	$2.66

c—theoretically predicted response on strategy sheet; w— unpredicted response.

ENDOGENOUS TIMING IN A GAMING TOURNAMENT   11

TABLE 2. Summary of underdog (A) strategy selections, average tokens and prize money

Player	Round	Lead	Follow a	b	c	d	e	Sim.	Tim.	Avg. Tok.	Effic. (%)	Prize $
B19	5	c	c	c	c	c	c	c	c	1210	100	$156
	4	c	c	c	c	c	c	c	c	1210	100	
	3	c	c	c	c	c	c	c	c	1210	100	
	2	c	c	c	c	c	c	c	c	1146	94.7	
	1	c	c	c	c	c	c	w	c	1103	91.2	
B25	4	c	c	c	c	c	c	c	c	1210	100	$83.2
	3	c	c	c	c	c	c	c	c	1210	100	
	2	c	c	c	c	c	c	c	c	1146	94.7	
	1	w	c	c	c	c	c	c	c	1106	91.4	
B4	3	c	c	c	c	c	c	c	c	1210	100	$41.6
	2	c	c	c	c	c	c	c	c	1146	94.7	
	1	c	c	c	c	c	c	w	c	1103	91.2	
B12	3	w	c	c	c	c	c	c	c	1210	100	$41.6
	2	w	c	c	c	c	c	c	c	1146	94.7	
	1	w	c	c	c	c	c	w	c	1103	91.2	
B3	2	c	c	c	c	c	c	c	c	1146	94.7	$22.93
	1	c	c	c	c	c	c	c	c	1106	91.4	
B8	2	c	c	c	c	c	c	c	c	1146	94.7	$22.93
	1	c	c	c	c	c	c	c	c	1106	91.4	
B23	2	c	c	c	c	c	c	c	c	1146	94.7	$22.93
	1	c	c	c	c	c	c	c	c	1106	91.4	
B24	2	c	c	c	c	c	c	c	w	1070	88.4	$21.4
	1	c	c	c	c	c	c	c	c	1106	91.4	
B22	1	w	c	w	c	c	w	w	c	1095	90.5	$5.47
B26	1	c	c	c	c	c	c	c	w	1055	87.2	$5.27
B2	1	c	c	c	c	c	c	c	w	1055	87.2	$5.27
B14	1	w	c	w	c	c	c	c	w	1014	83.8	$5.07
B17	1	c	c	w	c	w	w	c	w	1055	87.2	$5.27
B6	1	w	c	c	c	c	c	c	w	1014	83.8	$5.07
B20	1	c	c	c	c	c	c	c	w	1053	87.0	$5.26

c—theoretically predicted response on strategy sheet; w— unpredicted response.

12   K.H. BAIK, T.L. CHERRY, S. KROLL AND J.F. SHOGREN

4. BASELINE TREATMENT: RESULTS

Tables 1 and 2 summarize the theoretically predicted and incorrect choices of best actions and timing for the underdogs (A) and favorites (B). Since the tournament structure eliminates players choosing the worst strategies and the remaining players learned about the strategies their opponents had chosen before, an obvious bias exists in favor of subgame perfection in the later rounds. Therefore, the most important indicator of rational behavior is the choices made in Round 1. The results in Round 1 support subgame perfection. The twenty-six subjects made 170 of 208 predicted choices (82 percent); those who did make mistakes mostly erred in choices of timing – 8 of 11 underdogs elected to follow, while 6 of 15 favorites chose to lead. About seventy percent (26 of 38) of the incorrect choices were made by the ten players who did not survive the cut from the first to the second round. The eight favorites who did survive the cut made only four deviations from subgame perfection in 64 total choices (8 choices per person), while the eight underdogs made eight deviations in 64 total choices. By Round 2, the remaining sixteen subjects made 122 of 128 theoretically predicted choices (95 percent), again most errors were in the underdogs' timing choices. After another eight players were eliminated, the remaining subjects in Rounds 3, 4, and 5 (eight, four, and two) made 111 theoretically predicted choices out of 112 choices (better than 99 percent). Tables 1 and 2 also show that mean efficiency, defined by the percent of the potential rewards (A-580, B-1210) actually captured, equaled 90.7 percent in Round 1, increasing to 100 percent in Rounds 3-5 for all remaining players.

These results differ from the standard multiple-trial design reported in Shogren and Hurley (1997). Given the low opportunity cost of deviating from the subgame perfection equilibrium, underdogs led in only 35 to 58 percent of all trials, while the favorites followed in 55 to 77 percent of all trials. The mean efficiency was also low – about 70 percent. The baseline treatment out-performed the standard treatments because players specified a complete strategy, had more time to think about that strategy, and had a monetary incentive to use that time wisely. They took the first round seriously instead of using it to explore how different choices affected payoffs, as often happens in standard multiple-trial designs. And the players who survived to Round 2 only received the set of strategies of the opposing-type players who also made the cut, thereby reinforcing rationality in the later rounds.

5. SENSITIVITY TESTS: DESIGN

We now explore which of the three key design features affected gaming behavior the most: non-linear payoffs, time to think, or backward induction. We ran four sensitivity tests off the baseline treatment that varied the three design features (Friedman and Sunder 1994):

- *Payoff structure (L vs. NL)*: In two treatments, each token was worth $0.04, independent of which rank a subject achieved (L). In the two other treatments, a player's payoff was determined by the amount of tokens and the rank, as in the first experiment (NL). The best A-player and the best B-player faced an exchange rate of $0.15 per token, the second-best a rate of $0.08, third- and fourth-best $0.04, fifth- through eighth-best $0.02, ninth- and tenth-best $0.005. For example, if an A-player had an average score of 617 that gave his or her rank four among the A-players, his payoff was $24.68 (617 tokens at $0.04).[3]
- *Time to think (T vs. NT)*: In two treatments, the subjects were given 20 hours on the honor system[4] to think independently about their strategy, and turn in their Strategy Sheets to the monitor (T). In the other two treatments, all subjects were gathered in a room and had 20 minutes in each round to think about their strategies (NT).
- *Strategy sheets (F vs. O)*: In the baseline treatment, we imposed an explicit form of backward induction on the players. One might object that this protocol does not test whether a player is dynamically rational, rather it simply tests his cognitive capacity. We addressed this question by using two types of Strategy Sheets: subjects received either the baseline Strategy Sheet – one sheet with all four parts ordered as one would backward induct (O); or four sheets in random order with each part of the strategy on a separate page (F), thereby allowing the subject to choose how to form his or her strategy.

TABLE 3. Sensitivity treatments

Treatment	Design feature		
	Time	Structure	Payoffs
1	20 minutes	Four sheets	Non-linear
2	20 hours	Four sheets	Linear
3	20 minutes	One sheet	Linear
4	20 hours	One sheet	Non-linear

Table 3 shows the configuration of the four treatments: #1: [NL, NT, F]; #2: [L, T, F]; #3: [L, NT, O]; and #4: [NL, T, O]

Eighty students from the University of Wyoming participated in the sensitivity treatments. All were inexperienced with gaming experiments that tested endogenous timing and subgame perfection. Each treatment had ten A-players and ten B-players. Players were first randomly assigned as either an A- or B-player. In Round 1, each player was given a set of instructions, a 5×5 Payoff Table, and a strategy set. In Rounds 2 and 3, each player was given a clean copy of the strategy sheet. After Round 1 and 2, players were shown the ranking and amount of tokens of all players of their type; they were not shown the strategies of the other players. The average token earned was calculated for each player after each round to determine his or her rank in the A- or B-group. No players were eliminated.

6. SENSITIVITY TESTS: RESULTS

Tables 4 and 5 summarize the actual correct choices by sensitivity treatment and by design parameter. Using a chi-square test, we examine the behavioral differences between the round 1 results from the baseline (Yale) and sensitivity treatments (Wyoming) to determine if some basic difference existed between the subject pools. We cannot reject the null hypothesis that the proportion of correct answers is independent of the setting (i.e., Yale or Wyoming) with a chi-square statistic of 1.66 (critical values are 3.84 for 5% and 6.63 for 1%).

The key result is that time-to-think was the most important design parameter; more time led to more rational behavior, whereas non-

TABLE 4. Number of correct choices by sensitivity treatment

Treatment	Round 1			Rounds 1–3		
	correct choice	total responses	percent correct	correct response	total responses	percent correct
1	80	160	50%	269	480	56%
2	122	160	76%	373	480	78%
3	108	160	68%	296	480	61%
4	122	160	76%	372	480	78%
Total	432	640	68%	1310	1920	68%

TABLE 5. Comparisons of correct choices under different design features

Comparison	Round 1			Rounds 1–3		
	correct response	total responses	percent correct	correct response	total responses	percent correct
Time						
More	244	320	76%	745	960	78%
Less	188	320	59%	595	960	59%
Payoffs						
Linear	230	320	72%	669	960	70%
Non-Linear	202	320	63%	641	960	67%
Structure						
Four sheets	202	320	63%	642	960	67%
One Sheet	230	320	72%	668	960	70%

linear payoffs and backward induction did not. Behavior matches predictions better when people have more time to think about their strategy. Table 5 shows that in round 1 people with more time made more correct choices than those with less time, 76% (244 of 320) versus 59% (188 of 320). This pattern held over all 3 rounds: 78% (745 of 960) versus 59% (595 of 960).

Given the success of previous gaming tournaments, we find it surprising that the non-linear payoff structure did not seem to improve performance (see Table 5): Round 1–72% (230 of 320) versus

16   K.H. BAIK, T.L. CHERRY, S. KROLL AND J.F. SHOGREN

TABLE 6. Random effects probit results: sensitivity treatments

Variable	Round 1			Rounds 1–3		
	Coefficient	Slope	t-ratio (slope)	Coefficient	Slope	t-ratio (slope)
α	0.71E-05	0.25E-05	0.00	0.15	0.05	1.03
β_{TIME}	0.52*	0.18*	3.27	0.60*	0.21*	3.89
β_{PAYOFF}	0.24	0.08	1.48	0.04	0.01	0.24
$\beta_{ONE\text{-}SHEET}$	0.27	0.09	1.57	0.16	0.05	0.95
rho	0.16**			0.21*		
Log-lkhd	−378.84*			−1090.90*		
N	640			1920		

* ** significant at the 1% and 5% levels

63% (202 of 320) correctly predicted decisions with linear and non-linear payoffs; and in all 3 rounds–70% (669 of 960) versus 67% (641 of 960). More structured reasoning also did not induce more rational behavior: Round 1–63% (202 of 320) versus 72% (230 of 320) correctly predicted decisions with unstructured and structured; and in all 3 rounds–67% (642 of 960) versus 70% (668 of 960).

To test the statistical robustness of these observations, we estimate the following random effects Probit model for our data (Butler and Moffitt 1982):

$$y_{it} = \alpha + \beta_{TIME}\ TIME_{it} + \beta_{PAYOFF}\ PAYOFF_{it}$$
$$+ \beta_{ONE\text{-}SHEET}\ ONE\text{-}SHEET_{it} + u_t + v_{it},$$

where the dependent variable, y_{it}, denotes a correct response on the strategy sheet for person $i\,(i = 1, \ldots, N)$ in trial $t\,(t = 1, \ldots, T)$ ($y_{it} = 1$ if correct; 0 otherwise); α is the constant term; $TIME_{it}$ represents whether person i had more time-to-think in trial t ($TIME = 1$ if 20 hours; 0 if 20 minutes); $PAYOFF_{it}$ represents whether person i had a non-linear payoff schedule ($PAYOFF_{it} = 1$ if non-linear; 0 if linear); $ONE\text{-}SHEET_{it}$ denotes whether person i had one strategy sheet where the questions were in backward order ($ONE\text{-}SHEET_{it} = 1$ if one-sheet; 0 if four sheets); u_{it} represents a random individual effect; and v_{it} represents the contemporaneous error term.

Table 6 presents the estimated coefficients and slopes from the random effects Probit model.[5] Surprisingly, only more time-to-think, TIME, was statistically significant (1% level). For all rounds, time-to-think increased the probability of a correct answer by 21 percentage points.[6] Forcing people to backward induce did not improve performance as ONE-SHEET$_{it}$ was insignificant. The non-linear payoff scheme did not seem to induce more correct responses–PAYOFF$_{it}$ was not statistically significant, though close to the 10% level ($p = 0.11$). This is in contrast to the observed behavior in two prior gaming tournaments. In a bargaining tournament, predicted rational self-interested behavior dominated the data even though time was limited to 10-minute bargaining sessions (Shogren 1997). In a hour-long centipede tournament, predicted backward inducting behavior increased in the practice rounds even though no money was exchanged. Simply introducing the idea that the players would eventually compete in a rank-order tournament was enough to trigger the predicted self-interested behavior (Shogren and Hurley 1997). More time-to-think is important in this gaming tournament, perhaps because the normal form 5×5 payoff table took longer to comprehend than a standard bargaining lottery schedules or a typical centipede game tree. Additional work exploring the interaction between how the game is framed and the time to think about it seems a most useful future research direction.

7. CONCLUDING COMMENTS

This paper examined predicted and actual subgame perfection behavior in a gaming tournament with more or less time, structure, and incentive to form a strategy. Our goal was to construct an institutional context in the lab that increased the odds that we would observe gaming behavior agreed with predictions. We focused on a tournament institution that rewards competition over seemingly trivial differences in calculable accomplishments. We structured the payoffs to mimic a tournament where fewer deviations lead to increasingly higher rewards, we used a strategy sheet that explicitly leads them to use backward induction, and we gave some people two days to think about their strategy. The results suggest that it is possible to construct a lab environment so that subgame perfection

Experiments in Environmental Economics I

18   K.H. BAIK, T.L. CHERRY, S. KROLL AND J.F. SHOGREN

can be a reasonable predictor of behavior in an endogenous timing contest. Unexpectedly, it was not the non-linear tournament payoffs but the extra time-to-think that was the key design feature driving actual behavior toward that predicted by subgame perfection. Giving people enough time to think about an interesting puzzle seemed to be motivation enough; the potential big payoff was icing on the cake.

We think that more appreciation of the significance of time-to-think might impact future gaming experiments. Most lab games expect people to form strategies and make decisions within a short time frame, often less than 5 minutes per round. In this short-time environment, repetition of task is supposed to prevail on people to learn the rational strategy. Often this ploy works; but just as often repetition can quickly contaminate or distort an equilibrium. When one or two players make irrational choices and these players are randomly matched with other rational players, the rational ones must alter their strategies to account for potential incredible threats in later rounds. It will be helpful to explore further whether a design with fewer rounds with ample time to work through the ins-and-outs of alternative strategies would generate more predictable behavior relative to more rounds with limited time. Additional research examining the interaction of time and payoff structure to improve the correspondence between the theory and behavior in other games would be most useful.

ACKNOWLEDGMENTS

Thanks to Sean Fox, Jack Hirshleifer, Terry Hurley, and the reviewers for their comments. Shogren acknowledges the financial support of the EPAT-MUCIA-USAID project and the John Bugas Fund, University of Wyoming; and he thanks the Yale School of Forestry and Environmental Studies for their hospitality.

NOTES

1. Camerer (1997) considers three areas in which violations are present – social allocations, choice and judgments, and strategic situations. *Social allocation* issues occur because the basic assumption of self-interest fails under many experimental settings. Most efforts sidestep the issue by simply assuming that

ENDOGENOUS TIMING IN A GAMING TOURNAMENT   19

one's utility function can include the utility of others. *Choice and judgment* issues arise when people do not perceive the game clearly and consistently. Two
violations are at issue – behavior changes when the description of the game
changes even though outcomes do not change, and overconfidence about
one's own relative skill. *Strategic situations* issues emerge because the strategic reasoning principles widely used in game theory may be irrelevant to the
average Joe (e.g., irrelevance of labels and timing, iterated dominance, and
backward induction).

2. The complete set of instructions are available from the authors on request.
3. On a practical note, the four sensitivity treatments cost the same, independent
   of the payoff format.
4. To help subjects adhere to the honor system, the monitors gave subjects different times to pick up and hand in their strategy sheets and avoided recruiting
   subjects that obviously knew each other.
5. An LR test determined that an effects model is preferred over the basic model.
   Results were consistent across fixed and random effects specifications.
6. The slope coefficient presents the probability of a correct answer given the
   other independent variables are evaluated at the mean.

REFERENCES

Baik, K.H. (1994), Effort levels in contests with two asymmetric players,
   Southern Economics Journal 61: 367–379.
Baik, K.H. and Shogren, J. (1992), Strategic behavior in contests: Comment,
   American Economic Review 82: 359–362.
Boyd, D. and Boyd, L. (1995), Strategic behavior in contests: Evidence from the
   1992 Barcelona-Olympic-games, *Applied Economics* 27: 1037–1043.
Butler, J. and Moffitt, R. (1982), A computationally efficient quadrature procedure
   for the one factor multinomial probit model, *Econometrica* 50: 761–764.
Camerer, C. (1997), Progress in behavioral game theory, *Journal of Economic
   Perspectives* 11: 167–188.
Camerer, C., Johnson, E., Rymon, T. and Sen, S. (1993), Cognition and framing
   in sequential bargaining for gains and losses, in: *Contributions to Game Theory*,
   K. Binmore, A. Kirman, and P. Tani (eds.), Cambridge, MIT Press, pp. 27–47.
De Bondt, R. (1997), Spillovers and innovation actions, *International Journal of
   Industrial Organization* 15: 1–28.
De Bondt, R. and Henrique, I. (1995), Strategic investments with asymmetric
   spillovers, *Canadian Journal of Economics* 28: 656–674.
Dixit, A. (1987), Strategic behavior in contests, *American Economic Review* 77:
   891–898.
Drago, R., Garvey, G. and Turnbull, G. (1996), A collective tournament, *Eco-
   nomics Letters* 50: 223–227.
Ehrenberg, R. and Bognanno, M. (1990), Do tournaments have incentive effects?,
   Journal of Political Economy 98: 1307–1324.

20   K.H. BAIK, T.L. CHERRY, S. KROLL AND J.F. SHOGREN

Frank, R. and Cook, P. (1996), *The Winner-Take-All Society. Why the Few at the Top Get so Much More than the Rest of Us*, New York, Penguin USA.

Friedman, D. and Sunder, S. (1994), *Experimental Economics: A Primer*, Cambridge, Cambridge University Press.

Fudenberg, D. and Tirole, J. (1991), *Game Theory*, Cambridge, MIT Press.

Harrison, G. (1989), Theory and misbehavior in first-price auctions, *American Economic Review* 79: 749–762.

Harrison, G. and Hirshleifer, J. (1989), An experimental evaluation of weakest link/best shot models of public goods, *Journal of Political Economy* 97: 201–225.

Hirshleifer, J. (1995), Theorizing about conflict, in: *Handbook of Defense Economics*, K. Hartley and T. Sandler (eds.) Amsterdam, North-Holland.

Hurley, T. and Shogren, J. (1997), Environmental conflicts and the SLAPP, *Journal of Environmental Economics and Management* 33: 253–273.

Jensen, M. and Murphy, K. J. (1990), Performance pay and top-management incentives, *Journal of Political Economy* 98: 225–264.

Kagel, J. (1995), Auctions: A survey of experimental research, in: *Handbook of Experimental Economics*, J. Kagel and A. Roth (eds.), Princeton, NJ, Princeton University Press, pp. 501–585.

Lazear, E. and Rosen, S. (1981), Rank-order tournaments as optimal labor contracts, *Journal of Political Economy* 89: 841–864.

Leininger, W. (1993), More efficient rent-seeking–A Münchhausen solution, *Public Choice* 75: 43–62.

McKelvey, R. and Palfrey, T. (1992), An experimental study of the centipede game, *Econometrica* 60: 803–836.

Neale, M. and Bazerman, M. (1991), *Cognition and Rationality in Negotiation*, New York, Free Press.

Nitzan, S. (1994), More on more efficient rent seeking, *Public Choice* 79: 355–356.

Ochs, J. and Roth, A. (1989), An experimental study of sequential bargaining, *American Economic Review* 79: 355–384.

Roth, A. (1995), Bargaining experiments, in: *Handbook of Experimental Economics*, J. Kagel and A. Roth (eds.), Princeton, NJ, Princeton University Press, pp. 253–348.

Plott, C. (1996), Rational individual behavior in markets and social choice processes, in: *The Rational Foundations of Economic Behavior*, K. Arrow, E. Colombatto, M. Perlman, and C. Schmidt (eds.), London and New York, MacMillan and St. Martin Press.

Selten, R. (1965), Spieltheoretische Behandlung eines Oligopolmodells mit Nachfrageträgheit, *Zeitschrift für die gesamte Staatswissenschaft* 12: 301–324.

Shogren, J. (1997), Self-interest and equity in a bargaining tournament with non-linear payoffs, *Journal of Economic Behavior and Organization* 32: 383–394.

Shogren, J. and Baik, K. H. (1991), Reexamining rent seeking in the laboratory, *Public Choice* 69: 69–79.

Shogren, J. and Baik, K. H. (1992), Favorites and underdogs: Strategic behavior in an experimental contest, *Public Choice* 74: 191–205.

Shogren, J. and Hurley, T. (1997), Tournament incentives in environmental policy, in: *Sustainability and Global Environmental Policy*, A. Dragun and K. Jacobsson (eds.), Cheltenham, UK, Edward Elgar Publishing Ltd, pp. 213–232.

Syropoulus, A. (1994), Endogenous timing in games of commercial-policy, *Canadian Journal of Economics* 27: 847–864.

Addresses for correspondence: T.L. Cherry, S. Kroll, J.F. Shogren, Department of Economics and Finance, University of Wyoming, Laramie, WY 82071-3985, USA

Phone: (307) 766-2178; Fax: (307) 766-5090
J.F. Shogren, E-mail: jramses@uwyo.edu

K.H. Baik, Department of Economics, Sung Kyun Kwan University, Seoul 110-745, Korea

Name Index

For Product Safety Concerns and Information please contact
our EU representative GPSR@taylorandfrancis.com Taylor & Francis
Verlag GmbH, Kaufingerstraße 24, 80331 München, Germany

T - #0100 - 230425 - C0 - 244/160/30 - PB - 9781138717336 - Gloss Lamination